PONNIY

Ponniyin Selvan

Book 5: The Zenith of Sacrifice

Kalki R Krishnamurthy

Translated from the Tamil by
Pavithra Srinivasan(Chapters 1-16)
Varsha Venugopal (Chapter 17 onwards)

Title : Ponniyin Selvan
Author's Name : Kalki R Krishmurthy
Translation Copyright ©Varsha Venugopal
Published by Zero Degree Publishing

Zero Degree Publishing
No.55(7), R Block,
6th Avenue, Anna Nagar
Chennai - 600040

Website: www.zerodegreepublishing.com
E Mail id: zerodegreepublishing@gmail.com
Phone : 89250 61999

Zero Degree Publishing First Edition: July 2022
ISBN : 978-81-949734-2-3
TITLE NO ZDP : 47

Rs. 1150/-

Cover Art : Art Muneeswaran
Layout : Vidhya Velayudham
Printed in India.

Publishers' Note

Writers are the cultural identity, the memory of the aeon, the conscience and the voice of the society. By the sheer magic of their art, they surpass the barriers of language, land and culture. Any country should pride itself on possessing writers – national assets – whose works in translation have the potential to catapult them into international renown.

The Latin American Boom during the 1960s and '70s was a launchpad era that thrust names such as Julio Cortázar, Gabriel García Márquez, Carlos Fuentes, Jorge Luis Borges and Mario Vargas Llosa into the Anglophone literary world where they enjoyed a plausive reception.

Publication of translated nineteenth-century Russian literature fetched Tolstoy and Chekhov iconic status. Due to the availability of and the demand for their works in translation, Haruki Murakami of Japan and Orhan Pamuk of Turkey have become bestselling writers to watch in the present day and age.

What we understand from all of this is that translation and publication are fruitful endeavors that engage national writers and their oeuvres with the world at large and vice versa.

Zero Degree Publishing aims to introduce to the world some of the finest specimens of modern Indian literature, to begin with, we take great pride in introducing Tamil literature in English translation because, as Henry Gratton Doyle said, "It is better to have read a great work of another culture in translation than never to have read it at all."

– *Gayathri Ramasubramanian & Ramjee Narasiman*

Publishers

We dedicate this book to Pavithra Srinivasan, translator par excellence and a dear friend, whom we lost suddenly in 2021. It was Pavithra who crafted the definitive translation of Ponniyin Selvan, and her warmth, talent, and enthusiasm will be greatly missed.

- Publishers

Dedication

To Kalki R Krishnamurthy—who opened my eyes to the wonderful world of history, and guided my first hesitating steps towards the incredible world of historical fiction. From you I learnt my past; through you, I look to my future.

- Pavithra Srinivasan

Contents

1

Voices, Three

In the ancient Naagaippattinam Choodamani Viharam did Ponniyin Selvar linger with a good deal of patience, even as eagerness thrummed through every nerve in his body for an audience with his parents. The urge to convince them of his innocence about coveting the throne of Ilankai, to disabuse their minds against such utterly and completely baseless allegations—not to mention the deep-seated desire to absolve himself of the cardinal sin of having disobeyed his father's express commands—surged through him every moment, burgeoning with every day. Soon, he thought, soon …

… but only in the event of consent from his sister, he decided. Only upon her approval and sanction could a Thanjai journey be even mildly contemplated.

A resolution that, though entirely satisfactory, meant an indefinite stay here—resulting, consequently, in almost unendurable boredom. Some hours he managed to spend by participating in the resident *bikshus'* rituals and worship, their *araadhanais* and *poojais*; still others in gazing, appreciatively, at the admirable murals upon the *viharam*'s walls. A good many hours were devoted too, it must be admitted, to elaborate conversations with the monks in general and the Acharya *bikshu* in particular—a pastime which afforded the prince a deal of satisfaction and enjoyment ...

... for the former had delighted in a sojourn of many years amongst the many countries that littered the vastness beyond the eastern seas, traversing the numerous kingdoms between and betwixt China and the Isles of Saavakam—and was thus in the enviable position of being able to speak most knowledgeably about the various cities, customs, lifestyles, history and peoples therein.

A great many island-*rajyams* scattered to the south of China, in those days, formed a conglomerate under the massive Srivijaya *samrajyam*; in addition, such countries and cities as Arumana Naadu; Kaambojam; Maanakkavaaram; Thalaithakkolam; Maapappaalam; Mayirudingam; Ilankaasokham; Thaamaralingam and Ilaamuri Dhesam were either part and parcel of, boasted alliance or claimed friendship with this colossal empire. And towering amongst them all, a colossus in wealth, prosperity and fame was the magnificent city of Kadaaram, an entity in its own right.

Needless to say, not a moment passed without Ponniyin Selvar asking—nay, pestering—the Acharya *bikshu* to share all he knew about these fascinating kingdoms. The monk obliged without hesitation, relating, with a wealth of detail, their ecology, bounties both natural and commercial; their trade and economy; the gold and precious stones that flooded the markets and equally, rice and luscious sugarcanes in a way that fairly challenged prosperous Chozha Nadu. Their affluence, he described, was no less than

Thamizhagam's, passing on to a fairly involved history of the intimate trade relations between both countries—relations, he stressed, that had lasted for generations. He spoke of the many temples and breathtakingly beautiful sculptures of those lands, painstakingly and lovingly created by the craftsman, sculptors and artisans who had journeyed thither from Pallava Nadu; he mentioned the illustrious music, dance and art-forms that held sway there, chiefly courtesy Thamizhagam's own talented artists. He expounded on the all-pervading presence of such Indian epics as Ramayanam and Mahabharatham, and pointed out that deities such as Vinayakar, Subramaniar, Siva Peruman, Parvathi, Thirumaal together with a host of others co-existed, even flourished with the Buddhist faith, the twain so intertwined in the hearts of the population that they, no longer able or even willing to distinguish and differentiate between them, worshipped all without prejudice. In addition, Agasthya Muni, venerated as the father of Thamizh, had achieved special status among these peoples and was deified accordingly, with several shrines to his credit.

All these Arulmozhi Varmar learnt, listening with a gratifying deference, asking for, receiving and then confirming, more than once, details such as the best routes for travel both by land and sea, and the perils en route, not to mention conveniences and facilities. "Would there occur, perchance, another opportunity for your sojourn amongst these kingdoms, *Swami*?" he asked, once.

"By the grace of Buddha Bhagavan, mayhap, my prince—but why dost thou ask?'

"That I may accompany you, of course."

"I am but a *sanyaasi*, a monk who has renounced the world while thou—thou art the blessed son of a Chakravarthy who rules all the world; how then, may the two of us embark on a journey together? Why, the mere circumstance of having to care for thee in this *viharam* for a protracted period is a weight almost too great to bear, for my heart thuds with terror of what may befall any moment—"

"Allow me to relieve you of this onerous responsibility, *Swami*; I shall leave this very moment—"

"Thy highness must kindly disregard my hasty words, for I have expressed myself most deplorably, harbouring one sentiment while phrasing the exact opposite. Thy care is an arduous burden but one I shoulder willingly as I consider it a great good fortune—for such has been the goodwill and kind patronage shown to the Buddhist faith by thy illustrious father the Chakravarthy and thy gracious sister, Ilaiya Piratti. Our repayment of this debt under the circumstances, my prince, would barely fulfill a thousandth of what is thy due … indeed, far less, for is thine own benevolence any less? Thy generosity in renovating Anuradhapuram's dilapidated *sthupams* and derelict *viharams*—ah, could one banish such compassion from memory? It was as recompense towards such magnanimity that the *bikshus* came to thee with the bejewelled crown of Ilankai, but thou—why did thou refuse, my prince? Had thou but accepted and ascended the throne of Ilankai as an independent king, why, thou—thou wouldst have been able to journey to these south-eastern *rajyams* at the head of your own naval fleet consisting of hundreds of ships, and an endless retinue to boot! In which case," the *bikshu* pointed out, "there would have been no need whatsoever to consider a journey in this monk's wake …"

"*Gurudevare*," began the prince, with an air of intensity. "Have you ever read the *grantham* Mahavamsam?" The change of tack was sudden. "The legendary chronicle of Ilankai royalty?"

"Pray, what sort of question is this, *Ayya*? Could I have ascended to the dignities of the head of the Choodamani Viharam without having done so?"

"I beg your pardon. Indeed, questioning you thus is akin to demanding if you are literate. In which case, you must be aware, of course, of who in that glorious lineage committed exactly what sort of outrageous atrocity, mustn't you? The son who imprisoned his father—the father who murdered his son—the mother who poisoned her offspring—the child who tortured his mother by burning her alive—and as though relations between parents and heirs were not thus, the exploits of various *chithappas*, uncles, *sitrannais*, *periyannais*, brothers and sisters scattered through the pages … ah, words couldn't possibly do justice to their barbaric behaviour! Aren't these the events the Mahavamsam chronicles—the horrendous crimes perpetrated by the Ilankai royals, *Gurudevare*?"

"Indeed, yes and likewise does it record the retribution they endured—rightly—for their heinous work. Pray do not fail to recollect that this, in essence is the purpose of such chronicles; the Mahavamsam makes an example of royals; it details such horrors and exhorts the populace to abjure such crimes and embrace the path of *dharma*. It is a sacred book; a holy work; a beacon of light illuminating the path of righteousness; an extraordinary composition without compare in the whole world!" The Acharya *bikshu*'s voice rang out, with a sort of breathless emotion.

"I wasn't seeking to cast slurs upon the Mahavamsam, *Swami*—merely, it was my intention to point out the horrendous consequences of unhealthy desires; the way want corrupts and twists men into creatures more despicable than demons. And to have refused a throne sullied by such monstrous sins; caked with the grime of heinous crimes … was that so very wrong of me?"

"The reasons thou so clearly elucidate were the very ones that spurred the Ilankai's *bikshus*' offer of the throne; they wished to change the entire lineage and conceive a new one, with thee as the progenitor—and yes, thou wert wrong indeed to disregard it; disregard a heaven-sent opportunity to ascend to the dignities of

Eezham—to spread and defend, like Ashokavardhanar, the holy tenets of Buddhism …"

"Manifestly unfair, *Gurudevare*, to compare the legendary Ashokavardhanar who ruled almost all of Bharathakandam with me, a mere boy desperately seeking asylum in this *viharam*—a boy unworthy, in fact, of even becoming your disciple, let alone protecting the sacred Buddhist faith …"

"Thou shalt not speak thus, my prince, for thou art but unaware of the phenomenal power, the *maha sakthi* that resides deep within thee. If thou shalt but acknowledge and accept Buddhism with all thy heart, thou shalt attain and achieve great heights not unlike Ashokavardhanar himself—"

"From my earliest years Vinayakar, Murugan, Parvathi, Parameswaran, Nandhi, Bhringi and Chandikeswarar have resided and reigned in the sanctum sanctorum of my heart; surely I shall have to drive them all out summarily, before establishing Buddha Bhagavan in their place? Forgive this servant, *Gurudevare*, for it wasn't with the intention of embracing Buddhism that I volunteered to accompany you on your travels, but only with the overwhelming desire to cross the seas and see those distant lands with mine own eyes … but now that I think again—"

"The error is mine, rather, my prince, for I clearly misinterpreted thy words. And yet, thou art not without a connection to the faith for in a previous birth, it was Buddha Bhagavan who was incarnated as Sibi Chakravarthy, the very personification of benevolence who hacked away his own flesh for a dove. As scions of that venerated emperor, your ancestors claim the title Sembian—a fact that I most straitly adjure thee, not to forget."

"I don't, *Swami*, not at all and even if I ever indulged in the attempt, the blood that runs hotly in my veins doesn't. Sibi and

Manuneedhi Chozhar on the one hand mingle in my flesh and very bones, exhorting me to *Throw myself into the service of others; to surrender all I have; to sacrifice my body, heart and soul for the good of my brothers!* cajoling, pleading—while, on the other hand Karikal Valavar, Vijayalaya Chozhar and Paranthaka Chakravarthy blend in my very blood, commanding me to *Take up your sword; muster all the four armies; march in all four directions; venture upon the sea; expand the empire's dominions and establish glorious Chozha supremacy such as the world has never seen!* Badgering, persuading endlessly—and then, as if these were not enough, I'm bombarded by a third veritable pantheon of ancestors consisting of *sivanadiyaar* Kochenganaan, Thondai Mandalam's staunch Adithya Chozhar and Saint Kandaradhithar hold sway in my heart, beseeching me to *Devote myself to sacred renovation; raise colossal Siva shrines; construct temples with gopurams that rival the magnificent Mount Meru and pierce the very skies!* Counselling ceaselessly and I—I flail and flounder helplessly in a morass of conflicting commands, surrounded as I am by a multitude of venerable forefathers; so aggravating do I find this constant harassment that I've sometimes actually considered embracing the Buddhist faith and donning the robes of a monk," declared Ponniyin Selvar. "Kindly indulge me, *Swami*, by educating me about the sacred tenets of Buddhism and the Bhagavan himself, won't you?"

Acharya *bikshu*'s countenance brightened immeasurably, at this encouraging speech. "Could there possibly be anything thou dost not know, about both those revered subjects, my prince?"

"There—those murals, yonder—describe those if you will. That one where a prince is shown attempting to leave in the dead of the night; what is its significance? The lady asleep beside him; who is she? And the child slumbering in the cradle?" The questions fairly tripped off the prince's tongue. "And that *rajakumarar*'s face ... why is it practically wreathed in worry?"

"In His youth, *Ayya*, Buddha Bhagavan was a prince such as thy gracious self, born into royalty, and had wed a ravishing maiden past price, called Yashodharai; a boy had lately been born as well. Prince Siddharthar's father, the king, was ready to bequeath the kingdom to his son—his son who, however, yearned for nothing more than to discover a means to relieve mankind of its endless miseries and worldly tribulations; a yearning for the fulfillment of which He was prepared to sacrifice His beloved wife, precious child and illustrious kingdom. And that, my prince, is the mural that depicts His departure from His palace at midnight … surely thou art familiar with this legend?"

"Indeed, yes, I've listened to more than one retelling—but none of them made an impression upon me the way this painting has done; I'm hard put to stop myself from shaking awake Yashodharai and uttering a warning: Make haste and halt Siddharthar, for he's abandoning you! Be that as it may, pray continue: what of the next mural?"

The monk duly obliged, describing in great detail the rest of that gallery's works—for deep down, in his devout heart of hearts, there could not but exist the vain hope that Arulmozhi Varmar might, after all, embrace Buddhism; how wondrous would that be? And so he went on, detailing with considerable fervour Siddharthar's saga, ending, finally, with a profoundly moving description of the last mural: one which depicted Siddharthar receiving, after an arduous penance, glorious enlightenment under the Bodhi tree.

"*Gurudevare*, would it—" the prince began, at the end of this recital. "Would it displease you if I were to proffer an opinion contradicting yours?"

"As someone who has subdued and conquered all five senses, not to mention acquired complete and utter control over my mind—thou art free to speak thy mind."

"I don't believe Siddharthar attained holy enlightenment as he performed penance under the Bodhi tree."

Acharya *bikshu*, that elevated soul supposedly the subjugator of all paltry faculties, not to mention the conqueror of a superior mind revealed, at this comment, a rather pinched countenance.

"A branch of the Maha Bodhi *virutcham*, my prince, was transported with all due care to Ilankai during the times of Ashokavardhanar; a branch that has put forth roots, flourished and survived for more than a thousand years without the slightest sign of withering or deterioration. Why, thou may have glimpsed that sacred tree thyself, in Anuradhapuram ...why then, the disbelief?"

"I didn't mean to imply the non-existence of the Bodhi tree; neither did I intend to insinuate that Siddharthar didn't perform holy penance underneath—what I do challenge, is the contention that that was where He received enlightenment ... for it is my humble conclusion that He did so the moment He left behind, at midnight, His cherished wife, beloved son and rightful kingdom to discover a way to liberate the miserable masses of humanity. Never, in all my life, not in all the histories have I ever heard of such a miraculous act for see you, Ramar sacrificed his kingdom to fulfill his father's royal command; Bharathar, his young brother accomplished the same out of devotion to his elder sibling; Maharaja Harichandrar renounced his *rajyam* in a bid to keep his word; even the legendary Sibi Chakravarthy hacked away his flesh only because he'd offered asylum to a dove. But Siddharthar? Siddharthar pledged nothing to no one; offered neither His word nor swore a sacred oath; neither fulfilled anything nor cared to—He left of his own volition, sacrificed all at nobody's prompting, to discover a way of wiping away humanity's sorrow. Could anything, any wondrous achievement, any momentous feat accomplished after He received enlightenment possibly hope to compare? Therefore, would it be erroneous of me to surmise that Buddha Bhagavan attained glorious illumination the moment he stepped outside the confines of the royal palace?"

Ponniyin Selvar's heartfelt words fell upon the avidly listening Acharya *bikshu*'s ears like the proverbial drops of divine ambrosia. "*Ayya*," he began, equilibrium restored. "There is a great deal to thy explanation; indeed there is—be that as it may, since it was under the Bodhi tree that the Bhagavan realized the means of humanity's liberation, it was then that He began to preach to the masses."

"In much detail have I heard Buddha's sermons, *Swami*—but it's always seemed to me that His actions spoke more truly than His speech; that His life expounded more lessons than His word. Forgive me, but I find myself wishing to follow in His footsteps. I mentioned just a while ago about my forefathers' exhortations, their three different voices screaming three different messages in my tortured heart, subjecting me to endless anguish, didn't I? I wish, now, to rid myself of their torment; relieve myself of their responsibility," the prince paused. "I beseech you to accept me as your disciple."

"Much virtue must I have accumulated, my prince, to receive a student such as thee but I fear that I am neither deserving nor courageous enough to embark on so onerous a task. Thou may, however, submit a petition for the same when the Buddhist Mahasangam convenes in Ilankai."

"I entertain no doubts about your worthiness but you mentioned something about courage, which I couldn't quite understand."

"Indeed, yes; I lack the fortitude. For see thou; a rumour has been spreading around Naagaippattinam for the past two days—I am unaware of even who might have begun it—that thou art in this *viharam* and that we, the *bikshus* in residence, have been most industriously engaged in the attempt to convert thee into a Buddhist monk. Thus whispers the local population and the general mood seems to be that of rage; reports are even bruited abroad of a full-fledged attack upon these walls, led by the people, in a bid to discover the truth!"

"Ah, what heights of absurdity? What does it matter to the townspeople if I should embrace Buddhism—what concern is it of theirs; what right have they to be roused to such wrath if I don saffron and embark on the route to renunciation; if I enter the *sanyaasa asramam*? It isn't even as though I'm bound in matrimony, and am committing the cardinal sin of abandoning my wife and children, am I?"

"Their rage is not directed at thee, *Ayya*; rather at us, the monks whom they believe to be deceiving thee into converting to Buddhism. If a mere rumour should incite such fury, imagine the consequences should it turn out to be true? Why, the people would simply rise up and raze down this *viharam*; annihilate us without a trace. We have been leading a fairly blameless existence here thus far, thanks to thy gracious father's benevolent rule.

"Bodhiyan thirunizhar punitha! Nir paravuthum
Methagu Nandhipuri Mannar Sundara
Chozhar vanmaiyum vanappum
Thinmaiyum ulagir siranthu vaazhgenave!"

Thus do we pray every day, that Buddha Bhagavan preserve the Lord of Nandhipuri, Sundara Chozhar in strength, beauty and keep him in excellent health for long—and I have no desire whatsoever to destroy this peaceful state of affairs," explained the *bikshu*. "Hence my comment about lacking courage."

No sooner had he concluded than a clamour arose at the entrance of the *viharam*; the concerted din of many, many human voices as they rose and blended in a veritable roar.

"It appears that the good people have foregathered to prove the truth of my claim," the *bikshu* offered, once he had listened to the cacophony for a while. "I know not how I am to resolve such a situation; I can do naught but appeal to Buddha Bhagavan, who alone must show the way!"

And indeed, the chants and shouts of men and women, thousands upon thousands of them resounded about Choodamani Viharam, rising like a tsunami with every passing moment.

Hidden Meanings and Explanations

Chithappas; Sitrannais; Periyannais...

Father's younger brother; Step-mother or aunt, younger and older.

2

Along Came Murugaiyan!

Acharya *bikshu* and Arulmozhi Varmar listened, for a while, to the rising, thunderous roar of heaving humanity not unlike the deafening crash of surging seas, outside the Choodamani Viharam …

… an experience which left the prince prey to a great deal of anguish; was it not on his account that this venerable monastery and its *bikshus* were subject to such extraordinary distress? "I'm grieved, *Swami*, that you should have been forced to endure such vexation because of me," he voiced his unhappiness.

"Were our tribulations to multiply a hundred-fold on thy account, Highness, it would still matter not the slightest," assured the monk. "Hardly sufficient recompense, would it be, towards the endless aid rendered by thee and thy illustrious family?"

"It isn't just that," the prince attempted to elaborate. "I've never approved of this sort of—of clandestine behaviour; why must the people be bamboozled into thinking that I'm not here when in fact, I am? And why implicate you in this duplicitous dealing, this lie which goes against all the dictates of *sathyam*, of truth? My physical recovery is complete, thanks to your conscientious care; I wish, now, to leave the confines of this *viharam* and reveal myself to the people—and to inform them, in addition that it was you who offered me gracious asylum in the first place, and dragged me back from the abyss of death," he explained. "For, see you, this revered Choodamani Viharam must not—*shall not* suffer the slightest indignity on my account!"

"Nothing has occurred here that is in contravention to the dictates of the truth, *Ayya*. That thy foes are straining every last nerve to discover thy whereabouts has been proven by the rumours they have been spreading industriously around Naagaippattinam, for the past two days … in which case, how could it be otherwise than beneficial, pray, to keep your presence here a secret? It is, in fact, a decision well in keeping with established tradition that requires royals to lie hidden, invisible to the public, for brief periods. Did not the legendary Pandava brothers wander incognito for a whole year? And could it then be possibly claimed that the righteous Dharmaputhrar acted in contravention of *sathyam*?"

"I could never hope to win an argument against your illustrious self, *Gurudevare*, aware as I am of your superiority in knowledge and debate—but I should like to enlarge and emphasize on a point you just made about the Pandavas: they were forced to conceal themselves on account of the *sool*, the vow they made in fulfillment of the rigorous conditions of their banishment—but no such vow, I might point out, constrains me. As for the foes you mention—heavens, what foes could they possibly be? Why must anyone nurse the slightest enmity towards me, as I nurse not the slightest ambition towards the throne? And even if there be some, I shall reveal my true sentiments and make them my friends, thereby removing all your anxieties … and if the people should gain some satisfaction at my being alive, well, then all the better! Surely that would be no great loss?"

"Thy speech is naught but the truth, my prince and in thy place, there can be no doubt that I would have done the same—except for one, very considerable obstacle: our pledge to your blessed sister, Kundhavai Devi. Thou hast declared more than once that the Chozha dynasty has never before borne a *maatharasi* of such extraordinary foresight and wisdom as Pazhaiyarai Ilaiya Piratti … but it is my humble opinion that no clan has had that great good fortune—and if such a lady desired us to keep you here until she indicated otherwise, would it be wise to act in opposition? Especially if she had good reason, as I firmly believe? A great deal of feverish talk abounds, on the one hand, of a host of Chozha lords and chieftains engaging in heinous conspiracies against Sundara Chozha Chakravarthy's family and on the other, of Pandiya rebels weaving complex, secret plots to exact revenge. That we, the inmates of this Buddhist monastery might be hand-in-glove with these parties is a suspicion that has sparked, I gather, in the hearts of the people, a righteous fury that has provoked them into crowding at the *viharam*'s entrance. Now, think, I beg thee: would it be advisable to reveal thyself at such a sensitive juncture, fanning the flames of wrath into an inferno?" The *bikshu* pointed out. "Far better, would it not, that we endure some slight inconvenience in our attempts to safeguard thy person? Certainly, we have not the slightest intention of shirking our duty—"

Even as Acharya *bikshu* came to the end of this peroration, a junior monk hastened into the chamber with an air of barely suppressed agitation. "The situation is out of hand, *Swami*," the words tripped off his tongue. "Thousands have surrounded us, screaming that they ***wish to see the prince this very instant***! Not all our protestations that he is not here have convinced them; they insist on shouting that only a thorough search of the *viharam* mounted by themselves will satisfy them—and unless we find a way to assure them, I'm afraid we'll find the monastery overrun by an unruly mob!"

"But—what sort assurances could we possibly offer them, pray?" The Chief *bikshu* asked, bewildered. "Only Buddha Bhagavan possesses the power, I admit, of effecting a change in their sentiments."

"If *Gurudevar* would graciously condescend to indulge me, I believe I have a notion," the prince interrupted, at this point. "Since your disciples have issued the people a vehement denial of my presence, it would quite spectacularly defeat the purpose—not to mention turning your monks' declaration into a lie—were I to suddenly put in an appearance, the mob's ire might well turn into full-blown mania—"

"Indeed it will and thus, our fate to endure," prophesied the *bikshu*.

"Far better, wouldn't it be, to simply fulfill your disciples' declaration? Put theory into practice?"

"A feat that would be impossible even to one of thy stature, my prince. What the monks said is set; what is done is done. How, then, could their words be proven true?"

"There might be a way, after all. Couldn't I make my exit from this *viharam* the moment people enter?"

"Ah—! And must we thrust thee away, thus? Ought we to descend to such depraved depths merely to save our pitiful skins?"

"Pray disabuse your mind of such sentiments, *Gurudevare*; this is neither depravity nor irredeemable sin. Half a *kaadham* from here, in Anaimangalam lies the Chozha palace; I shall travel there the same way I did a few days ago, to meet my sister—by canal," explained the prince. "And once it is convenient to do so ... why, I could return!"

This solution, presented in a well-thought out fashion, seemed rather to the Acharya *bikshu*'s taste. "Why, yes, indeed," he mused thoughtfully. "Such a scheme would make it unnecessary for thee, of course, to reveal thyself at once, while also fulfilling thy gracious sister's objective ... but stay; what if people were to crowd around the *viharam*'s exit to the canal as well? And glimpse thee in the boat?"

"A strategy might be employed in such a scenario as well, *Gurudevare*," the junior monk interrupted the conversation again."We could simply ask one of those at the entrance to enter the *viharam* and make a search himself."

"That ought to be enough, surely?" The Acharya queried. "Once he is satisfied, he would return outside and inform the rest, would he not?"

"And if he should be detained within for a while," the young monk continued. "It would be night soon and thus convenient for the prince to leave. It behooves me to draw your attention to something else: the signs of an approaching storm are unmistakable; waves the size of mountains rising and falling are visible even from here, and the sea's turbulence is increasing by the moment ..." the monk paused. "Perhaps this, then, is the grace of Buddha Bhagavan, after all? Perhaps He, in all His compassion has ordained that this storm shall destroy our distress and cast away all cause for anxiety?"

"Pray do not entertain such sentiments," the elder *bikshu* gently admonished. "Must the sea surge and a storm seethe merely to deliver us from discomfort?"

"It occurs to me too, that your disciple's scheme might be put to the test, *Swami*," the prince suggested. "Should one man amongst the many outside be permitted to enter, I might speak with him and change his mind."

"A thought that has occurred to me as well—for, two days ago, a boatman and his wife from Kodikkarai arrived at the *viharam*'s entrance an enquired about the prince. They were adamant in believing that he was here; indeed, the woman went so far as to scream and shout her fury—"

"Ah, did she? And who was this boatman?" The prince demanded. "What was his name, do you know?"

"Certainly; Murugaiyan, he called himself and mentioned that he was Kodikkarai Thyaga Vidangar's son—"

"And a man I am well-acquainted with; he would do naught against my wishes … but why wasn't he brought to me?"

"We believed that his wife would be incapable of guarding our secret. She and her husband are, in fact, to be found amongst the crowds …"

"The fruit has slipped into the milk, as the saying goes," exulted the prince. "Pray make sure to bring in Murugaiyan stealthily. He wouldn't cross a line of my drawing—and once night falls, he could row me to Anaimangalam himself."

"I believe it serves us ill to bestow trust in anyone these days, Highness," put in the elder bikshu. "Furthermore, I have reason to believe that it was this same boatman and his wife behind the rumours flying around Naagai the past two days—"

"Even if that were true, it matters not; someone ought to be brought into the *viharam*, after all and as well him as any other. While it's true that he dances to his wife's tunes, he certainly wouldn't disregard my wishes for hers. If possible, make sure he's the one brought in!"

The Acharya having assented to this plan, the junior monk departed. A few moments of reflection, however, and the elder *bikshu* spoke up again. "Forgive me, but I find that my mind is not at rest. I shall step outside and gauge the sentiments of the gathering outside for myself," he said, as he prepared to leave. "Neither this venerable, ancient Choodamani Viharam nor thy gracious self shall suffer damnation or danger for my lapses!"

ꕥ

Hidden Meanings and Explanations

"... The Pandavas were forced to conceal themselves on account of the sool, the vow they made in fulfillment of the rigorous conditions of their banishment ..."

Arulmozhi Varmar is referring, here, to a particularly heart-wrenching episode of the Mahabharatham, where the five Pandava brothers, the eldest of whom is Yudhishtrar (also called Dharmaputhrar as he was believed to be the son of Yamadharma Raja, the God of Death—and incidentally, renowned for his sense of justice) lose several games of dice against their cousins, the Kauravas. The terms of the loss were:

1. To leave the kingdom and go into forest exile for twelve years.

2. To spend the thirteenth year incognito, and if they were exposed, to go into another exile lasting thirteen more years.

The tale of how the Pandavas spent their exile is an exciting and intriguing one, full of incredible twists and turns ... and to be enjoyed best in its entirety, on its own.

3

THE SEA SEETHES!

The sight that met Acharya *bikshu's* startled eyes outside the *viharam* was one calculated to terrorize even the most stalwart of hearts … for a heaving throng of several thousands was jostling, cheek by jowl, at the gates.

That this was a volatile crowd could not have been more obvious, judging by their forbidding expressions and frenzied shouts—a volatile crowd teetering on the edge of reason and poised for a descent into madness; it would not take much for the simmering passion to explode into a raging inferno. Many held menacing swords, spears, staffs and other such instruments of destruction while some brandished equally deadly crowbars; perhaps, if the *bikshus* did not fall in line, they simply intended to demolish the monastery right down to the last brick?

Not without rationale either, this wrath; hostilities between Chozha and Eezha kingdoms were of long standing—dating from the reign of Paranthaka Chakravarthy, in fact—and countless, the warriors sacrificed to this martial cause. It is entirely natural, is it not, to transfer hatred for one thing, towards others connected to it; to tar with the same brush all things related? Chozha citizens had borne much in the performance of their duty but there is a limit to patience, after all; mounting public outrage against Ilankai and all its attendant concerns could not but be aimed at the Buddhist faith as well, holding such sway over the island. All the common public needed was one flimsy reason; one paltry matchstick of an excuse to set alight the burning fuel of fury drenching every surviving monastery in Thamizhagam and the monks residing therein.

To Acharya *bikshu*, watching the unstable mob at the gates, it seemed that such a fatal circumstance had been established; that this indeed was the moment and this, the excuse. Someone, some evildoer, he was sure, had spread baseless rumours and incited the average citizen to such unbearable anger that it was doubtful if the *viharam* would survive—ah, a grievous peril from which only Buddha Bhagavan could save them! The Lord grant His holy grace!

At sight of the revered monk, however, the crowd's emotions, already roused to a fever-pitch, seemed to boil over; their shouts a din that almost shattered eardrums. "Return Ponniyin Selvar to us—else we'll raze the monastery down to the ground!" The screams and yells from thousands of acrimonious throats rivalled the resounding roar of the ocean … but even amidst the clamouring human voices, Acharya *bikshu* could not help but notice that the sea's sonorous crashing had steadily been rising too. The junior monk had been right: a vicious, wicked storm was approaching the shore with incredible, unbelievable speed and would make landfall, likely, with devastating consequences … but now, a fresh concern assailed his already beleaguered heart: even should the *viharam* escape the wrecking fury of the people, would it survive the calamitous destruction of a cyclone?

By this time, though, the younger *bikshu* had taken a hand in the proceedings, gesturing to the churning, heaving throng to assume some semblance of composure and thus, some measure of quiet.

"Peace, good people, peace," he entreated. "I have with me our revered Chief and thus, I must beg your gracious selves to calm down—for you can hardly enter this *viharam* all at the same time, can you? Choose one or even two amongst yourselves, if you will; they may enter and initiate a comprehensive search … the conclusions of which you must accept as final. These terms find satisfaction, I hope; now, which of you shall come with me, into the precincts?"

"Me!"—"I shall!"—"Take me!"—shrieked an hundred voices, upon which the junior *bikshu* raised a hand, once again, for quiet.

"Screeching all at once is hardly likely to benefit either of us; choose a representative—why, I shall offer what assistance I can in this regard: is there anyone here who has glimpsed Ponniyin Selvar within the last month? If there be, point him out and I shall take him with me," offered the monk. "It will come in useful to identify the prince, as well."

"*We* will!" Raakkammal, having planted herself at the forefront of the mob all this while and shrieking at the full pitch of her excellent lungs, promptly stepped forward.

"We have seen him!"

The junior monk turned to the boatman. "*Appane*, is she speaking the truth?"

"Not entirely, *Swami*," came Murugaiyan's incurably truthful answer. "She hasn't seen the prince within the last few weeks—but I have, in Ilankai, and even fell at his feet and begged forgiveness for the grievous harm I caused, all unwittingly. As for his gracious pardon, granted so mercifully with such a kind smile upon his lips … I remember everything as if it happened yesterday," he explained soulfully. "Without a doubt, I would recognize him."

"If this indeed be the case, you are the man for this task. As for your wife's impetuous speech—likely, since you have seen Arulmozhi Varmar, she felt that she could claim to have done so as well. Even now, she is sure to accept your verdict, once you have made a search of the *viharam* yourself—doubtless, she is aware of the strict condition about women not being allowed into monasteries housing *bikshus* observing strict penances. In which case … come, will you?" And, not content with verbal instructions, he descended the front steps, took Murugaiyan by the hand, guided him back up the stairs and turned around to address the public. "This boatman appears to have met the prince fairly recently and I am escorting him within. Murugaiyan shall institute a comprehensive search in the premises and inform you of his findings. This is acceptable to you all, I presume?"

Said public, however, did not seem quite so enthused about this eminently sensible plan; their "We accept!"—"Yes!" were mere mumbles and those, few and far in-between while some turned to each other and enquired "Is this some kind of trick, do you think?" in low, secretive murmurs that rivalled the sea's discontented rumbles.

These signs of unease were not lost on the junior *bikshu*, who was quick to call upon an ally at this sensitive juncture. "Good people," he bellowed. "Here is my revered Acharya, to whom you may address any query. Meanwhile, I shall take this man inside and show him around to his satisfaction," he dragged Murugaiyan within.

The crowd, thus discarded summarily at the entrance, now gazed upon the elderly monk, the very personification of dignity, his mien proclaiming majesty and countenance glowing with inner tranquility … their tongues collectively tied, for not a one dared put forth an insolent question, cowed as they were with not a little deference, tinged with devotion.

For his part, Acharya *bikshu* bent his thoughtful gaze upon the unsettled crowd before him … and then, towards the equally unsettled sea behind them.

"I am aware, good people, of your reason for gathering here this day—as also the great love you bear for the Chakravarthy's blessed son Arulmozhi Varmar, known popularly as Ponniyin Selvar. Like you, this servant too cherishes enormous affection for the prince. Ah, well do I remember the day terrifying reports arrived that he was lost at sea—for I stood on these very steps, tears streaming down my face like a waterfall! Indeed, no one bearing the slightest affinity for the Buddhist faith could fail to admire and respect him; such has been his stellar service towards Buddhism and its *bikshus*. Having affirmed that, my people, could we possibly be a party to any heinous scheme to harm such a one, a benevolent prince who ordered the renovation of ruined *viharams* and ravaged *sthupams* destroyed during the times of famed Buddhist kings in the venerated *kshethram* and holy pilgrimage city of Anuradhapuram? We prayed constantly, know you, that he might be unharmed; that news of the sea claiming him would prove false—for we, good people, have more cause than you, to cherish the highest regard for him …"

"Therein lies the reason for our fear," barged in someone amidst the gathering. "We're terrified lest your amazing regard and enormous affection for him should lead you into shaving his head, wrapping a saffron robe around his person and turning him into a monk!" he snapped smartly.

Galeer!—burst a mocking cackle of ill-concealed glee from those surrounding him at this badinage.

Appreciative the crowd might have been at the unknown's witticism—but it was productive of quite a different reaction in

Acharya *bikshu* ... who seemed to have been seized by a storm of intense emotion. Here indeed, his heart pointed out, was the perfect opportunity to settle the peoples' suspicions. Bolstered by this conviction and without pausing to think, he revealed his heartfelt sentiments unreservedly, framing them almost like a vow:

"Never shall I entreat Ponniyin Selvar and the Chakravarthy's beloved son, Arulmozhi Varmar, to embrace Buddhism—nay, not even should he offer to do so, himself! Never, ever shall I subject myself, nor be a party to the travesty of divesting his head of hair, discarding his formal attire and investing him with saffron robes, or otherwise engaging in converting one who is your beloved, has captivated all your hearts and is destined to one day rule the world! Thus do I solemnly swear, upon the holy Buddha's lotus feet! *Buddham kachaami*! *Dharmam kachaami*! *Sangam kachaami*!"

These passionate words, delivered in a stentorian voice reverberating like a majestic crash of thunder, certainly had their effect. The transformation that swept through a visibly moved crowd was undeniable; their hearts had clearly melted, while tears trembled on the lashes of many. For a brief space, a deep and respectful silence prevailed.

"It is entirely natural, I should say, for you to cherish such love and affection for the prince who is the apple of Chozha Nadu's eye and is dear to all," continued Acharya *bikshu*. "Your concerns regarding Ponniyin Selvar now being set at rest, pray, *pray* divert your minds and hearts towards your own homes and hearths! It would not be an exaggeration, good people, if I were to say that a cyclone of proportions unseen and unheard of, thus far, is fast approaching us; there! Look behind you!"

They did—to stare, transfixed, at a fantastic sight that had been unseen and unheard of in all the days of their lives, in truth; a phenomenal sight—nay, petrifying!

The sea was surging, surging; its mammoth waves curling and rising, rising, rising so high that they seemed to touch the roiling, frothing black clouds scudding across the sky at breakneck speed … but the wall of water did not seem to be stopping or even slowing down; far from restricting itself to self-appointed, natural confines, it appeared, to the watching public that it would soon be upon them—in which case, it was doubtful if they, and even the Choodamani Viharam itself would survive.

Even as the crowd watched, stunned almost to the point of paralysis, Acharya *bikshu* renewed his entreaty. "Over there—cast a glance upon Naagai, your home!"

At a little distance north of the monastery sprawled the city, its dimensions considerable, stretching far and wide. In close proximity to the sea were situated such distinguished buildings as warehouses and toll-booths while beyond spread the residential quarters, expanding to the east, west, north and south for at least half a *kaadham* …

… residential quarters into whose streets the sea had now begun to encroach, having already submerged the customs-houses.

Anchored boats and canoes had been amongst the first casualties, of course, dancing high in the sky, bobbing as they were at the crests of wave-mountains. Their sails had long since fallen prey to ferocious winds; tattered shreds the only remnants, still fluttering valiantly in the gaining gale.

"Many tales have we heard of the sea claiming the legendary Kaverippattinam, long ago," called out Acharya *bikshu*. "May Buddha Bhagavan save our Naagaippattinam from a similar, wretched fate—but make haste, make haste; return to your homes; save your children, your family and your worldly goods as much as you can!" His voice was husky with emotion, by the time he finished.

The words of warning had barely left his lips before the motley mob began to recede and surge towards the city, rather emulating the sea itself as the frontrunners took to their heels and the rest followed in their wake. At first, they managed to retain some semblance of discipline, moving as a cohesive unit but form and shape soon deserted them as all scattered in four directions, running hell-for-leather until the area which had, until recently, been thronging with people, was suddenly, completely empty …

… empty except for boatman Murugaiyan's wife Raakkammal, who simply planted herself where she was, arms and legs akimbo. "My husband!" She screeched, again and again. "My husband!"

"He will come to no harm, *Thaaye*," the *bikshu* attempted to re-assure her. "Save yourself, rather; he will return, safe—"

"No, no—how can I leave without my husband?" Raakkammal shrieked more than ever. "I'm coming into the monastery—"

"No, *Amma*, you cannot; are you not aware that women are forbidden from entering *viharams* wherein *bikshus* dwell?" The monk pointed out.

By now, one of the men who had stayed back while the massive crowd unexpectedly scampered hell-for-leather, stepped up to the distraught woman, whispered something into her ears, grabbed her hand and dragged her away forcefully—to which cavalier treatment Raakkammal, wonder of wonders, submitted, albeit unwillingly, and began to follow in his wake.

Ah, who might this unknown be—and what is his connection with her? Wondered Acharya *bikshu* before re-entering the *viharam* and approaching Ponniyin Selvar's seat to find Murugaiyan, now sans all astonishment, harking reverently to the prince.

"You must return tonight, Muruga, and row me to Anaimangalam," Arulmozhi Varmar instructed.

"To wait all those hours is now unnecessary, my prince," the *bikshu* interrupted. "The crowd outside has dispersed; thou may depart this very moment." Upon which he proceeded to retail all that had occurred.

"If this be the case, *Swami*, why must I leave?" the prince objected. "Since everyone's gone, anyway—"

"—but there is no guarantee that they might not return," interjected Acharya *bikshu*. "Besides, didst thou not mention just a while ago that thou wouldst make good our pledge? It behooves thee now to most graciously do so," adjured the monk.

In truth, the *bikshu*'s exhortations concealed another, far deeper unease; a very real panic, in fact, that the surging sea would claim Choodamani Viharam for its own. Hence his haste in bundling away the prince for Anaimangalam which lay to the east, further away from the sea and therefore a reasonably safe haven; the waters were unlikely to reach the small town and even if they should, would be unlikely to submerge the Chozha palace.

The prince accepting the older man's word, the command was given to bring around the boat.

Meanwhile, Acharya *bikshu* took the opportunity to address a gathering of his fellow monks. "We follow the divine and most compassionate Buddha Bhagavan. The people of Naagai are now subject to a grievous adversity; I saw the sea surge into the city at an ominous speed. Roofs are flying off homes even now, unable to resist the gale; trees are splintering as we speak. Hordes of citizens, including the infirm, and the young are desperate to escape, without the means to do so. Therefore," his eyes swiveled around his audience. "Go amongst them; scatter in all four directions and lend a helping hand to whoever you see; offer what assistance you can. Aid the very old and the very young first; rescue as many as you can from the vengeful wrath of Samudhra Rajan! And I," he concluded. "As one stricken in years, shall stay here and conduct the evening worship."

The *bikshus* duly dispersed.

In due course, the boat drifted up the canal to the *viharam* entrance; the prince paid his respects to his preceptor, took his leave and climbed into the craft. Acharya *bikshu* stood gazing at it as the little boat floated further and further away, and finally vanished.

A rare, unearthly halo appeared to glow about his wise features, clothing him in an aura of spiritual radiance.

4

The Submersion of Nandi

Even as they progressed along the canal, the prince could not help but notice that the water level was steadily, yet inexorably rising with every passing moment—and Murugaiyan, deft oarsman though he was, still found his dexterity taxed to the hilt, trying to maintain control of the craft.

Meanwhile, the cause of this upheaval was not behindhand in gaining strength with every second; *sada-sada-sada*!— trees on both banks crashed to the ground, upended by gale-force winds that swept across the landscape.

By now, the boat was in the vicinity of the *mandapam* that had providently provided a meeting-place for Arulmozhi Varmar and Kundhavai; the prince craned his neck to catch a glimpse … only to realize, with a start, that the Nandhi was almost completely submerged; a sure sign of how high the water had risen.

"Stop the boat, Murugaiya!" He shouted out—a command which, though instantly obeyed, led to rather uneasy consequences as the boatman could barely still the heaving, rocking craft, desperately though he might try.

The prince leapt off the boat and onto the *mandapam*; then, he grabbed hold of an uprooted tree nearby, and clambered upon its roof. Gaining a foothold of sorts, he stared around.

The sight that met his eyes was not promising.

The entire region east of the canal had vanished under a veritable *jalapralayam*, a massive deluge; half the coconut grove had already fallen prey to vicious winds … and when Arulmozhi Varmar peered through a gap, it was to see the surging sea already at the grove's edge.

He stared towards the north now, in the direction of Choodamani Viharam—to discover the ocean having encroached the entire area in front and right up to the stairs at the entrance.

Something flashed through Ponniyin Selvar's mind, then—a flash of insight that shed illumination, like a shard of lightning—and sent a chill coursing through his veins, prickling his skin. "Murugaiya," he called out again. "Turn the boat—return to the monastery!"

Thyaga Vidangar's son, bound by boundless and unswerving devotion to the prince, not to mention a nearly lifelong habit of near-dumbness, obeyed his command without a word of protest. Despite the time taken returning to the *viharam* being considerably shorter than what it had been setting out, each moment still seemed an impassable aeon, to the agitated royal—not entirely without reason, for by the time they reached their destination the seething, heaving sea had practically surrounded the precincts; the waters rising, rising without pause …

… an appalling development for, unlike the magnificent monasteries of Eezham that rivalled the very mountains in majesty and stature, the Choodamani Viharam of those days was no colossal structure and was, indeed, of such underwhelming proportions that, should the sea surge inland further, the topmost spire, the *sikaram* would go under.

Such being the situation, Ponniyin Selvar gauged his chances, spied a *mandapam* not as yet consigned to a watery grave and leapt onto its roof. Abandoning any attempt to descend to the lower levels, he dashed here and there, spurred by an agitation that could find no other release—but even here, on the so-called upper levels, he discovered that he had to cleave through chest-level water … and yet, the object of his frenzied search was nowhere to be found. More and more did his disappointment grow, until he reached the sanctum where resided, in state, Gauthama the Buddha's statue, at whose chest the ocean lapped.

Arulmozhi Varmar paused here, and stared around. There being no sign of his quarry, a sudden impulse prompted him to plunge into water, peer around, and—

"Aha!" The exclamation of mingled relief, astonishment and exhilaration was enough to proclaim that his search was at an end; the one who was sought had finally been found …

… found, well below the churning waters, underneath the Holy Buddha where Acharya *bikshu* huddled, his hands curled around the Bhagavan's lotus feet in a crushing embrace.

Ponniyin Selvar plunged into the seething deluge the next instant, dived to the floor, broke the monk's iron-hold around the statue with not inconsiderable force and pulled him into his arms—a feat that required no great exertion underwater but proved quite otherwise above for the *bikshu*, though spare, was well-muscled with height to match; the effort of shouldering his dead weight to safety left the prince breathless.

"Murugaiya," he called out, almost at the end of his tether. "Murugaiya!"

"Here I am," answered that worthy, rowing close to his lord.

Arulmozhi Varmar stepped towards the boat, Acharya *bikshu* still in his arms, his legs stumbling with exhaustion.

5

A Calf Bereft of its Mother

Adjusting the considerable weight of Acharya *bikshu* in his arms, the prince leapt nimbly into the boat—which rocked violently as though ghouls had taken control, almost tipping over at one point but righting itself just in time, courtesy Murugaiyan's considerably dexterous skill.

"Row hard, now!" The prince gasped out instructions. "Row straight to Anaimangalam—*row*!" The last words may have erupted in a veritable scream … but Murugaiyan heard nothing as, by now, the cyclone had reached its terrifying zenith; Arulmozhi Varmar's shouts were snatched from his lips and tossed away, lost to the thunderous fury of shrieking gales and surging seas. His features indicated his sentiments, however and the boatman, astute enough to understand his lord's wishes without verbal assistance, plied the craft with renewed fervour in the direction of the Chozha palace.

Not an easy task; monumentally more difficult this time around as he had to navigate the rapidly drowning *sikarams* and Buddha statues of Choodamani Viharam, each of which posed a solid obstacle—but Murugaiyan was no novice; a veteran used to pitting his courage and expertise against raging cyclones and tearing gales on heaving seas and churning oceans … and rowed the little boat with such consummate ease and supreme capability that earned Arulmozhi Varmar's admiration. A yearning to relieve at least some of his burden, despite the boatman's efficient execution seized him—only to be discarded summarily, as this would mean releasing the monk.

As though to prove the validity of his concern, Acharya *bikshu* suddenly, frantically attempted to free himself of Ponniyin Selvar's firm grasp.

The boat was skirting the statue of Buddha at that moment. The water was already to the Bhagavan's eyes; there seemed to be no doubt that soon, the sea would claim Him completely.

Sensing, perhaps, his intention, Arulmozhi Varmar tightened his hold on his preceptor, whose features reflected considerable astonishment … astonishment that the prince's slender hands—hands, part of a body that had been ravaged so grievously by the brutal ague too—could possess such raw strength. Was this, perhaps, what it meant when a steely heart could invigorate and energize the physical body?

The craft floated past the figurine, now rapidly sinking; the *bikshu*'s eyes locked on to it, tears flooding down his lean cheeks without pause. "What hast thou done, my prince?"

The words, uttered in a voice hoarse with emotion, were too low to be heard—but Arulmozhi Varmar divined them anyway, skilled as he was in reading lips. "Surely, *Swami*," he spoke, bending close to the monk's ear. "I ought to be the one asking thus?"

"This *viharam* has stood here for more than five hundred years, Highness, even during the lifetime of the blessed saint Dharmapadha; not even the Pallava emperors, ferocious followers of the Veera Saivite faith destroyed it—but alas, *alas* that I should see this ancient monastery devastated before my very eyes! A building such as this, constructed out of mere brick, could never survive the ocean's vicious assault; when the waters finally recede only a few ruined walls will stand," lamented Acharya *bikshu*. "Why, then, must I still live?"

"Ruined *viharams* can always be renovated; why, should it be the gracious Buddha Bhagavan's will, I might undertake that sacred task myself," assured the prince. "But I can't do the same if you departed this world, can I?"

More debate was not possible at that moment or indeed, for a time, not with the fierce winds and ferocious seas launching a full-fledged rampage across the region—not to mention the appalling sights that met their horrified eyes and rendered them completely speechless.

Large vessels, their sails shredded beyond recognition and smaller boats and canoes, out on innocent fishing expeditions were now careering towards land—many, on a direct collision course with stalwart buildings, devilishly dancing trees and sandy shores—flung mercilessly by wind and water, smashing to smithereens.

Flimsy roofs, unable to withstand the vicious gale, simply flew off homes and flung themselves into the flood. Some floated, upon which people manage to clamber, hanging on with a great deal of difficulty. "***Oh***!" Their screams and cries of distress rent the air.

Trees, massive in height and girth were torn up from the earth by the whirlwinds, some crashing upon the deluge; like the roofs, these too proved an unexpected oasis amidst the desert of hopelessness, as some clutched branches and roots in a slender bid to save themselves.

Goats and cows swept by on the waters, blaring in mind-numbing terror.

All these ghastly sights and more Arulmozhi Varmar and the *bikshu* watched, their hearts well-nigh bleeding with compassion and sympathy, exacerbated all the more by the mortifying awareness that neither could do the slightest to assist the sufferers.

Murugaiyan, however, bent his concentration upon his task, his eyes never swerving for one moment either this side or that as he navigated the boat.

Choodamani Viharam was situated almost on the shores of Naagai, from where the canal struck out south for some distance, before turning south-west for roughly half a *kaadham*, then twisting, heading due south again ... and it was at this second, rather opportune bend that the Anaimangalam Chozha palace was established.

By the time they arrived at the Nandhi *mandapam*—once more, on this eventful journey—not only had the famed bull submerged completely, but the structure itself was in imminent danger of going under, for the waters now lapped at the edges of the roof. Most of the tall, slender coconut trees in the groves thickly clustering the area had fallen to the gale; the few that still valiantly remained upright swung madly in the wind like mindless ghosts whipping about in a supernatural frenzy, their tresses flying everywhere. Some, indeed, sacrificed several long stalks at regular intervals, them being ripped and flung far away. But stay, what was this? What was this creature, on top of the Nandhi *mandapam*?

A calf. Young and vulnerable, reft from its mother, God knew how, and now stranded on top of the sinking structure! It had managed to scramble on to the roof, somehow, and was now staring around here, there, everywhere, its large eyes wide with fear and incomprehension. Its body shivered often, and uncontrollably, and its unsteady legs trembled."*Amma*!" came its thin, terrified cry now and then, falling faintly upon the ears of those in the boat.

Ayyo, the poor thing, a quick tendril of sympathy wrung the prince's heart. *I wonder what will be this motherless calf's fate*?

Even as the words darted through his brain, a large coconut tree crashed upon the rear of the *mandapam*; had it fallen even a little forward, the calf would have been done for.

A mammoth wave reared up suddenly over the structure, prompted by the upended tree—and the little animal, already on its last, trembling legs now faltered, unable to withstand the sudden assault and tumbled off the top of the *mandapam* into the water. Buffeted and battered mercilessly by the heaving floods, it floundered helplessly.

Even while monitoring its travails, the prince had continued to maintain his iron grip on Acharya *bikshu*—but so carried away was he by the calf's sudden fall that he uttered an exclamation—"*Ah*!"—and slackened his grasp for one moment, just one moment …

… a lapse that was all that was needed for the monk to plunge into the water.

Alarmed at these developments, Murugaiyan dropped his oars instantly and grabbed Arulmozhi Varmar, who glared at him with considerable exasperation, growled out a "*Let go*!" and promptly shook his hands. By this time, Acharya *bikshu* had struck out towards the hapless creature—which, completely and naturally consumed by a powerful will to live, was managing to keep its head above the churning water—and caught hold of its little front legs in a death grip. He cleaved back towards the boat, dragging the calf in his wake, whereupon the prince lent a hand; the duo collectively heaved their refugee into the craft, after which Ponniyin Selvar provided his mentor with the same assistance.

The calf that had somehow managed to stand on its feet all this time, was suddenly swamped by a wave of exhaustion; rocked by a surging wave, tottering legs gave away and it crumpled—thankfully, into the boat. The monk sat down at once, took its head upon his lap and began to caress the terrified animal.

"And you were willing to sacrifice your life just a while ago, clutching Buddha Bhagavan's feet in Choodamani Viharam," the prince remarked. "Had you succeeded, could you have been able to save this speechless creature, here and now?"

"Indeed, thou stopped me from committing a grievous crime, *Ayya*, for which I give thee thanks. The act of saving this calf has afforded me great satisfaction; I would not grieve much even if Choodamani Viharam should be ruined beyond reprieve."

"Such gratification at having rescued just one calf?" The prince marvelled. "But—what of the countless lives caught in this cyclone? Thousands of men, women and children, the old and infirm suffer—while dumb creatures such as goats, cows, horses and birds simply lose their lives," he lamented. "How could we possibly attempt restitution for these grievous fatalities?"

"*Ayya*, we can only do our pitiful best and no more, for it lies not in us to prevent natural calamities. Is it within our puny power, I ask thee, to close a lid over a screaming whirlwind? Shield the entire earth from a massive downpour? Or provoke one? Or even raise a wall against a mammoth tsunami? Ah, to witness the awe-inspiring sight of a volcano spewing forth liquid fire, or the earth shattering in an earthquake … *I* have, in the eastern kingdoms beyond the seas; now, how may we redress these horrifying misfortunes? Only offer aid to those suffering before our very eyes—"

"But why do they occur in the first place, *Gurudevare*? Why do appalling gales and awful earthquakes rage? Why do agues and plagues ravage the populace? Whose responsibility is it when man and beast suffer so wretchedly? I understand that we can do nothing to prevent such disasters, but couldn't God? Why doesn't He prevent such terrible catastrophes from wreaking havoc? Why watch His creatures undergo such dreadful adversity and not succour them?"

"Saints and sages from time immemorial have tried to glean answers for the very questions you now pose, Ponniyin Selva—but such explanations as they have wrought, have not always satisfied everyone. It is for this reason that Buddha Bhagavan speaks not of God; indeed, delves not even into the slightest research on that subject. His sermons simply revolved upon these basic tenets: *Offer aid to all; relieve every living creature's distress; it is in these acts that you will find true anandham, bliss and from such an elevated state attain nirvana—release from the snares of happiness and sorrow*!"

The boat, meanwhile, had duly followed the canal's course to the west and was now well on its way towards Anaimangalam.

For his part, Ponniyin Selvar was lost in reverie, mulling over Acharya *bikshu*'s exposition of Buddhist doctrines and comparing it with those handed down by his ancestors. *Assist fellowmen* was a credo insisted upon by Saivite and Vaishnavite traditions as well; wasn't there even the venerable Sanskrit adage: *Paropakaaram, idham sareeram; To serve others, is the very purpose of this body's existence*? And yet, there was also his forefathers' unswerving insistence on belief in God, and the sacred duty of devotion to Him; their fashioning the Creator as Rudhran or Samhara Murthy, the Lord of Destruction and Maha Vishnu, the Lord of Compassion; their constitution, flowery description and worship of the Goddess, the Jaganmatha and simultaneously conceiving her as kind, merciful Uma Devi, the very personification of love, and the hideously gruesome Durga Parameswari, the embodiment of righteous wrath! Now, which amongst these ideologies was right? Could a deity venerated as Mother to the very earth possibly manifest as the ghastly, macabre Ranabhadhra Kali? But why not, pray? A mother very often embraces and kisses her child with affection; yet slaps him in anger at others. The infant may not understand his mother's shifting moods … but surely that didn't mean that she didn't love him?

Twilight had fallen, by the time the boat approached the Chozha palace; to the passengers, it was obvious that the edifice had escaped the sea's ravages. Murugaiyan maneuvered his craft expertly, into the ornate quay in the vicinity.

Nature too, it seemed, had rather resolved upon exercising compassion upon the ragged travelers for despite the furious storm and raging seas, a ferocious downpour had held off—at least, until then—with only a gentle drizzle in appearance. It was only after the boat docked did the rain gods finally release their fury, and a deluge began to fall in earnest.

The security guard stationed at Anaimangalam palace stood at the entrance with a burning torch, engaged in earnest conversation with those from the surrounding areas, who claimed shelter for the night from the harsh elements.

The moment he caught sight of a craft upon the quay, however, he raised aloft the *theevarthi*, to glimpse …

… the beloved countenance of Ponniyin Selvar …

… which caused him to forget everything and run at full tilt towards the jetty.

Prince and *bikshu* had descended from the boat and onto the landing-stage by this time, and managed to help the calf clamber up the steps as well.

The guard hastened forward and bent in a bid to prostrate himself at the feet of Arulmozhi Varmar, who clutched him in an equally hasty bid to stop him. The torch, knocked out of the sentry's hand in the minor scuffle, thudded into the canal and burned incandescently for a brief moment before being extinguished.

"I was worried about the Choodamani Viharam myself, Highness," he blubbered. "And here you are, safe and sound—praise be!"

"Why … did you know, then? That I was there?"

"Certainly, *Ayya*—when Ilaiya Piratti and the Kodumbalur princess arrived. Her royal highness commanded me, in fact, not to reveal your presence to anyone."

"A command you must continue to obey. Now, who are the people at the entrance?"

"Asylum-seekers from seaside villages; the sea surged into their homes and they've gathered here, begging for the night's shelter … but you arrived just in the nick of time; I shall drive them out—"

"No, not at all; allot them space to stay and sleep; ascertain food supplies and make arrangements for meals—but do not breathe a word about me to a soul. A stroke of luck too that your torch fell into the canal and went out; now, take us to the *mael maadam* by an alternate route!"

Their entrance into the palace coincided with the exact moment nature finally decided to raise its performance a notch; ***Cho!***—the searing storm achieved a crescendo as a veritable deluge sheered across the terrain, falling in a torrent.

6

Murugaiyan Weeps!

Our honoured readers would have divined, by now, that the heart-stopping incidents of the previous episodes in Naagai, occurred almost in conjunction with the day the tree crashed behind Mandhakini's palanquin in the vicinity of Thanjai, and the hour the boat drifted away, most inopportunely, from the gale-battered shores of the Veera Narayana Lake.

Pandemonium, and not Pazhaiyarai's Sundara Chozhar reigned supreme, the night of the cyclone in Naagaippattinam and its environs. It was everyone for themselves as each sought to do anything to save their own lives; mercy and compassion, it must be admitted, were at a premium—despite which depressing circumstance, the monks of Choodamani Viharam still managed to lend what assistance they could, to the afflicted.

That same night saw Ponniyin Selvar and Acharya *bikshu* awake long into the wee hours in the Chozha palace of Anaimangalam, their anxious discussion circling mostly around the ravages of the storm; the raging of the seas and inevitably, the endless suffering and losses sustained by the wretched populace.

At an opportune moment, the prince bid forth the palace's administrative official-in-charge, the *maniyakkaaran*, and made enquiries of the current condition and stock available in the granaries and the treasure-vaults. In addition to a surplus of food-grains, there were also, it was learnt, twelve copper pots overflowing with gold coins, generously allocated by devout Sembian Maadevi towards the sacred stone renovation of the Neelaayathaatchi *Amma*n's shrine, in Thirunaagai Kaaronam.

"There are resources enough, here, *Gurudevare*, to satisfy even your benevolent heart and fulfill the holy tenets of Buddha Bhagavan. Pray, spend every last grain in assuaging the gnawing hunger of the poor; distribute every last coin towards building homes for those who have lost theirs," Ponniyin Selvar offered.

"But—how may I?" objected the *bikshu*. "It would be one thing to use the food; the gold, however, was provisioned for the express purpose of temple restoration by Periya Piratti … would it not be unconscionable to spend it upon other considerations? Would not that gracious lady be grieved?"

"As to that, Acharya, allow me to make to my elder grandmother my worthy excuses … but now, the money on hand must and shall succour the suffering populace in its time of need—for in the future, I shall raise hundreds of *sivaalayams* in a manner that shall fill to the brim even her pious heart with happiness. Towering *gopurams* shall I erect; *sthupams* piercing the very sky shall I raise, and neither shall bend the knee before any paltry tsunami. A massive temple shall I establish in Thanjai, the celestial proportions and majestic height of which shall cause it to be titled Dhakshina Meru, by awed spectators! Anguish not, *Ayya,* should Choodamani Viharam have been annihilated to mud and brick this day—for I shall construct, right by its side, a monastery of immoveable, unshakable stone that shall not budge even an inch under the most dreaded deluge!" The prince finished, in a voice well-nigh throbbing with passion.

"That thou should offer such enthusiastic pledges to the future is a source of immense gratification to me, Ponniyin Selva," the *bikshu* smiled.

"It does seem as though divine will has ordained the continuation of my existence in this world for a while, that I may accomplish marvelous feats—else, why would He deliver me from quite so many hazards? It was evident even today, I believe … for witness the sudden appearance of Murugaiyan on the scene at exactly the right moment! Without him, we'd have still been in the Viharam, happily ignorant of the fact that the sea might surround us so quickly."

"Thou speak the truth; who might have expected that a catastrophe that had not occurred in five hundred years might have done so now, within the space of a bare *muhurtham* on a humdrum afternoon? Buddha Bhagavan, the very personification of the ocean of compassion, rescued you from the surging sea and through you, this paltry human as well. I consent, here and now to your admirable arrangement: spending coin from the royal treasury might enflame Periya Pazhuvettarayar but distributing gold from Periya Piratti's renovation fund certainly would not vex that gracious lady; I acquiesce with all my heart. But surely—surely it would behoove us all if thou were to initiate such a benevolent and auspicious task? For, this poor ascetic can hardly undertake such an onerous responsibility—"

"Standing at the forefront of relief efforts could not but defeat the purpose of my concealment, *Gurudevare,* and expose me to the full blast of public scrutiny—an eventuality we discussed and decided against. Well do I remember your sage counsel about the

Pandavas and their exile, incognito, not to mention the wisdom of Thamizhagam's own Poyyaamozhi Pulavar in his illustrious Thamizh Marai:

"Vaimai enappaduvathu yaadhenin, yaadhonrum
Theemai ilaatha solal!"

[*To speak the truth, is to speak such that no hurt or harm is caused.*]

and,

"Poimmaiyum vaimai idatha, purai theerntha
Nanmai payakkum enin!"

[*Falsehood may also be uttered in the place of Truth, should it result in great good.*]

"My sister, a byword for wisdom and forethought, believes that revealing my presence at this time would fling Chozha Nadu into a morass of chaos and confusion; in truth, my concealment harms nothing and no one and so, you must be the one to assume the responsibility of dispensing money and meals to the pitiful masses afflicted by this horrendous cyclone."

"I find that my sentiments, however, have undergone a change, Ponniyin Selva; for some unusual reason, I believe that the time has arrived for thee to reveal thyself, and to succour the people," the monk amended. "I shall go further and say that I consider this to be Buddha Bhagavan's sacred will …"

… at which point conversation ceased, perforce, as both became aware of a rather unnerving sound: someone sobbing without restraint. Acharya *bikshu* and Arulmozhi Varmar turned around, startled—to see Murugaiyan slumped in a corner, covering his face with his hands and sobbing unabashedly.

Moved by such naked emotion, the prince went to the man, took him by the hands and brought him back to his seat. "Good God, what is it?" he demanded. "Why do you weep so?"

"My wife," Murugaiyan moaned. "My wife …" He stuttered and then, seemingly incapable of saying anything more, relapsed once more into sobs.

"Indeed, indeed, your wife, we're afraid, completely slipped our memories; considering the ferocity of the gale and rain this night, it's entirely natural that you should be concerned about her fate. Nevertheless, there's nothing we can do at midnight; we'll mount a search upon sunrise," the prince reassured.

"I'm not worried about her—her safety, *Ayya*," the boatman hiccupped, gratified. "No danger would've threatened her; she's encountered and survived storms and floods more vicious than this one …"

"Then why the tears, pray?"

After a pause, Murugaiyan began, stammering and stumbling through the following recital. "I am full of remorse for all the doubts I had about her. She was the one, you see, who persuaded me to leave Kodikkarai, for she suspected that you might be hid away in Choodamani Viharam. It was on her insistence that I even came here; I was terrified that she intended you some harm, but now—" He gulped. "*Now,* I see how wrong I was! You praised this petty boatman a while ago, Lord; that God had made me the instrument of your escape—but I say, here and now, that it was my wife who prodded me into doing so … and when I remember how ill I've thought of her, I couldn't help but weep so!"

Arulmozhi Varmar, listening to this artless account, felt the faint, alarming stirrings of quite a different suspicion. Aloud, however, "*Appane*, your wife is a chaste woman, an *utthami* and it was certainly wrong of you to have doubted her," he said. "But how on earth did she guess my presence here?"

"She knew that my *athai* and my younger sister Poonguzhali rowed to Naagai, and drew her own conclusions."

"Your aunt?" The prince straightened, now in the grip of some excitement. "Who?"

"The mute one—she saved you more than once from peril in Ilankai, *Ayya*."

"Ah—! And where are they now, your *athai* and Poonguzhali? What of their fate? You did mention that they arrived here—"

"They did, yes ..." Murugaiyan paused, gripped by emotion. "But their journey was—was forced to a stop!" And then his voice became wholly suspended by tears as he began to sob again, in earnest.

It was a considerable while before Ponniyin Selvar, setting aside his own burgeoning anxiety, could soothe him into some semblance of tranquility and finally draw out details; details of the abduction of *Oomai Rani* by a band of uncouth ruffians. His wrath knew no bounds as the boatman poured this piece of news into his ears—but when he heard that Raakkammal had tried not only to prevent the abductors from carrying out their fell intentions, but had also been soundly thrashed and lashed to a tree into the bargain, his doubts ceased to exist; they were, if anything, replaced now with respect and a grudging admiration. "Did you listen to that, *Gurudevare*?" He demanded, turning to the older man. "If there's a living deity in this world that I revere with all my heart, it's the Lady of Ilankai, the very queen of those isles; Mandhakini Devi—and those who harm a hair on her head shall find absolutely no mercy in me. It matters not a jot that the Pazhuvettarayars issued commands for my imprisonment—but if they've dared threaten *Oomai Rani*, I shan't spare them—and won't rest until I've razed their clan to the ground! Even should it be my own parents who've intended her harm, I shan't and won't forgive them ... I'm leaving for Thanjavur tomorrow; I shall disguise myself as a merchant and travel with Murugaiyan as my guide, for I can't rest until I discover the Queen of Eezham's fate! It now lies with you, Acharya, to aid those afflicted by the storm and if you won't deign to do so under your own aegis, then kindly establish the *Eezhathu Nachiyaar Arachaalai*—and dispense food and money under its auspices," rattled off the prince. "I'm not sure if you knew, but she's a proponent of Buddhism; indeed, her usual abode, when in Bodha Theevu—which the people call Boodha Theevu now—is the Buddhist monastery …"

Acharya *bikshu* agreed to this instantaneous change of plans without a word of protest.

By the next day, the cyclone's fury had burnt itself out and the seething oceans had subdued … but the aftermath of these destructive forces were beyond all description. Half the homes of Naagai were now crumbling ruins, having lost their roofs; the walls barely standing. And in one of the streets housing such pitiful structures now walked Arulmozhi Varmar, in merchant-garb, a bundle slung over his shoulder while Murugaiyan followed dutifully, lugging an even bigger sack, both taking in the devastation wrought by nature's unstoppable ferocity spread all around them.

From behind one of the wrecked walls of a dilapidated house, a pair of eyes tracked their progress avidly—eyes that belonged to none other than Raakkammal. She held herself in patience until the prince and the boatman were almost abreast of her …

… before erupting abruptly from her hiding-place, and flinging herself at the feet of Arulmozhi Varmar.

In vain did Murugaiyan try to desperately draw her attention, going so far as to place a finger on his lips, and hushing her in a fair imitation of a whirlwind himself—all to no avail.

"Oh, Blessed Son of the Chakravarthy!—Warrior among warriors! —Ponniyin Selva!—The darling of Chozha Nadu!—The virtue of all our penances!—Were you saved indeed, from drowning in the Choodamani Viharam? Have you returned to us now, safe and sound? Ah, fortunate indeed are my eyes to savour such a sight!" She screeched at the full pitch of her excellent lungs.

The collective attention of everyone hurrying hither and thither along the streets, engaged on their own business until that moment was arrested instantly upon that raucous cry—

—and converged upon the prince.

7

Ecstasy of the People

Raakkammal's shrieks first startled Murugaiyan, and then almost stunned him into paralysis—after which his senses rallied somewhat; he glared at his obstreperous wife even while gesturing furiously at her. "Good God, Woman, what're you babbling about? Have you lost your wits? Are you mad—"

"No; *you* are! And your father, and his father before him! Don't tell me you didn't recognize this man? Didn't know at a glance the warrior who won Eezham and vanquished King Mahindan to the hills? Didn't realize the identity of the Chakravarthy's blessed son; the apple of every Chozha citizen's eye; Ponni's favoured child, saved by Mother Kaveri herself?" Raakkammal's bosom heaved with mingled outrage and indignation. "If that be the case, why're you starting out on a journey with him? And where?"

"I'm afraid you've mistaken me for someone else, Woman," the prince interjected at this point. "I'm a merchant from Ilankai; I was the one who engaged this man for my guide … is he your husband? Take him with you if you wish—but pray don't screech heedlessly!"

By now, a crowd had begun to gather around the dueling duo and their uncomfortable third wheel; a crowd that swelled and grew before their very eyes with each passing moment—and every pair of eyes was now raking the prince up and down, subjecting him to a keen scrutiny.

Arulmozhi Varmar's tempered speech, however, only seemed to ratchet up Raakkammal's distempered freak. "*Ayyo*, good God, what on earth's this?" She shrieked now to the high heavens. "Could it be that Ponniyin Selvar has been afflicted with the dreaded *sithabramai*? Did the sea claim your consciousness—or did those wretched *bikshus* addle your brain with some sort of evil *mandhiram*? Have they brainwashed you into believing yourself to be another? Or … heavens above—could it possibly be?" Her eyes widened. "Are you dead now and your sacred body in possession of an expert in switching souls? Does he inhabit your—no, no, it couldn't be—think, *Komagane*, think well and think hard; bend your thoughts towards the truth: you are no measly merchant but Sundara Chozha Chakravarthy's precious son; born to unite the whole world under your divine rule. And if you should doubt me, look at your palms; those blessed, blessed palms—for upon them, you'll discover the lines of a conch and discus!"

Prince Arulmozhi Varmar instantly closed said palms into fists. "Will you not be quiet, Woman?" He admonished her through gritted teeth, turning around to Murugaiyan simultaneously. "What sort of nonsense is this? Can't you possibly stop this shrieking?"

That worthy, obedient to Ponniyin Selvar's prodding, promptly sidled to his wife. "For heaven's sake, Raakkamma, let be, will you?" He muttered into her ear, exasperated. "Quiet—quiet! The prince wishes to travel to Thanjavur in the guise of a merchant, so no one shall recognize him!"

Her response to this revelation was a positive bellow. "*Adappaavi*, you idiot! Why couldn't you have mentioned this sooner? You were insistent that he wouldn't be in the *viharam*—your wits had gone begging then, and clearly haven't returned! *Ayyayyo*, what have I done? What a terrible, unforgivable sin is mine! My passion has pushed me into blurting out your presence; forced me into betraying you and ah—! Those wretched Pazhuvettarayars are even now seeking the slightest excuse to seize and fling you into prison! And I—I, knowing all this, have yet exposed you thus … but fear not; fear not, my prince for those dreaded Pazhuvoor lords shan't harm a hair on your precious head—for there are lakhs upon lakhs of people like myself and my husband who shall stand by your side, shoulder to shoulder, ready, willing and able to protect you!" She turned to glare around the considerable throng now pressing upon them on all sides, every inch of her proclaiming righteous rage. "You agree with me, don't you? None here is in the Pazhuvettarayars' employ, is he? If you should be, step out! Step out now—but you'll have to kill me first; only over my dead body shall you get to him!" Her yells reverberated across the street as she squared her shoulders.

The populace, avidly drinking in this masterly performance, was swift to take its cue. "Long live Ponniyin Selvar!" rose an enthusiastic shout, followed by "Long live the Warrior among Warriors Who Conquered Eezham!" The chants, not unnaturally, echoed far beyond the present confines and before long, more crowds surged through, melding with the first and one member of said congregation happened to be the Head of Naagai's Enperaayam Guild.

This worthy now pushed through the jostling public to the forefront. "We had heard that you dwelt in the Choodamani Viharam, *Komagane*, but did not dare believe that rumour—for rumour we considered it. But now, the truth has been revealed. Yesterday's cyclone may have wreaked untold devastation upon this city … but it brought you forth, safe and sound, did it not? *Now* we can forgive this dreaded storm and its callous calamities with all our hearts for you are amongst us—and to have you set foot here is Naagai's blessing indeed!"

If nothing, this expression of bureaucracy served to convince the prince that there was no more purpose to concealment.

"I thank you for your kindness, *Ayya*—indeed, I'm exhilarated beyond measure by the love of this gracious city's citizens," he spoke, in calm tones. " … but pray bid me farewell, for I must reach Thanjavur with all possible speed, for which was I donned such a disguise in the first place."

But to even a mere mention of this hasty departure the crowd would not consent. "No, never—not for a moment!" A lone voice rose in a stentorian shout. "His Highness cannot leave until he has partaken of our humble hospitality for at least a day!" Thousands and thousands of voices promptly took up the refrain, adding their entreaties: the prince ought not to leave without a day's rest and a taste of what generosity in them lay.

It was now the turn of the Enperaayam Guild's Head, to snatch up the reins of persuasion. "Witness the overwhelming love and affection my people cherish for your gracious self, my prince? You must, *must* postpone your departure for a few hours at least and accept our modest gestures of goodwill," he cajoled … but as the prince stood still, his face carefully expressionless, changed his tactics. "Ah, are we not to be as fortunate as those Buddhist *bikshus*? Only yesterday the good people of Naagai almost demolished the Choodamani Viharam to the last brick, labouring under the painful suspicion that the monks had hidden you away—a creditable intention put paid to by the storm which, however, shouldered the right noble cause; the monastery is now in ruins!"

"Good God, *Ayya*," the prince was finally goaded to retort. "Pray don't accuse them of heinous crimes; it was at my request that they harboured my pitiful self as I lay ravaged with fever and fighting for my very life. Had it not been for them, straining every nerve to release me from the bonds of Yaman's dreaded soul-rope, dragging me back from the jaws of certain death …! My heart is wrung at the news of the *viharam*'s destruction; I consider it my bounden duty to renovate it!"

"Ah, and to think we knew nothing of all this! But now that we do, and aware as we are of your sentiments, we shall take it upon ourselves to restore the monastery to its original, pristine state—but you shall accept our entreaty and deign to be our guest!" the Head re-iterated.

"Indeed—indeed!" Tens of thousands of voices echoed his request in tones that well-nigh touched the heavens.

"And any delay incurred may well be made up," the Head hastened to sweeten the deal. "You have embarked on this journey by foot, your highness—but all roads in the Chozha *rajyam* are choked, I am sure, with the storm's excesses; the rivers are in full spate and the good God alone knows when you shall arrive at your destination. Now we, if you please, shall arrange for an elephant … and even escort you as far as Thanjavur!" he finished, not unnaturally pleased with this display of benevolence.

The crowds were swelling, swelling with every moment, during this magniloquent speech.

For his part, Arulmozhi Varmar found himself slipping into a reverie. There was no doubt now that circumstances were irrevocably altered; the fat, in fact, was in the fire owing to the incurable stupidity of Raakkammal who had shouted out his secret to the whole world—wait, had it truly been an act of idiocy, or had the woman an ulterior motive? Whatever her rationale, matters were now at such a pass that it would be impossible to ignore the love of these people, or refuse their undeniable overtures of hospitality. Not only would such a callous gesture cause grievous hurt but the very purpose of his journey might be overset. No, he would have to tarry awhile, at least until the afternoon, and soothe the many ruffled feathers; also offer what consolation he could for those afflicted by the severe storm. But, ah! How wise, how astute of Ilaiya Piratti to have pointed out that nothing but upheaval and pandemonium would be the result of revealing his identity? How right, how absolutely had she been! *In truth, there's no equal for her sheer brilliance*, he thought exultantly. *All this nonsensical squabbling about heirs to the Thanjai throne—surely it ought to be Kundhavai Devi with the sceptre and crown, holding sway over Chozha dominions?*

Even as he mused on this improbable event, he noticed the already surging throng rapidly burgeoning to uncontrollable proportions—their enthusiasm and exhilaration increasing at a proportionate rate. Gone were the alarms and excursions about the storm; consigned to the past were its recent havoc and devastation; forgotten was even the deadly loss of life. From somewhere arrived score upon score of elephants, horses, palanquins, sacred banners, standards, musical instruments such as *perigais*, *ekkaalams* and many more; the entire population seemed to have collectively banished every last, horrifying memory of the ignominious cyclone.

It behooved him, the prince decided, to depart only after at least half a day. "Believe me when I say that I have no desire whatsoever to trample upon the desires of so many, *Ayya,*" he addressed the Head of the Enperaayam Guild. "I shall stay here until the afternoon and leave in the evening," He paused. "To this scheme at least, I have your leave, I hope?"

The congregation's ecstasy knew no bounds when news spread of the prince's acquiescence to their insistent request—and promptly found relief in indulging in every possible expression. Musical instruments began to blare while here and there, on the very streets, jousts with staffs and impromptu displays of swordsman began in earnest, accompanied by joyous bursts of song and *kuravai koothu*—uninhibited exhibitions that made progress towards the Chozha palace fraught with difficulties, but which the prince and his party managed, after a fashion, and despite the many impediments.

Not that Ponniyin Selvar was allowed respite even after reaching his destination, for news of his emergence had spread like lightning through the surrounding villages and people were converging upon Naagai in droves, while expressing their heartfelt desire to seek a royal audience.

Arulmozhi Varmar was not backwards either in obliging them, stepping outside often and anon to enquire after their well-being and the extent of cyclone-induced losses with a sincerity and empathy that could not but afford intense gratification. He even promised, once he reached Thanjavur, to make adequate reparation for the damages incurred … a promise, he noticed, that did not earn as much gratification, however. Random remarks about *whether the Pazhuvettarayars' authority will be quelled*, could not but fall on his ears—and what was worse, in his opinion, were comments about the Chakravarthy's state of health and the succession—conversations that were conducted in subdued tones, almost whispers and yet, he observed grimly, calculated to reach him.

Meanwhile, the various officials and chiefs of the city's Aimperunkuzhu and Enperaayam Guilds had assembled forthwith; preparations commenced towards a sumptuous banquet in the prince's honour, not to mention a feast with delicious trimmings for the delectation of those seeking an audience. Every grain that had survived the cyclone's ravages was gathered while as for vegetables—what problem in procuring them, when countless were the plantain and coconut trees felled by the storm, thus affording a rich crop? Surely an hundred thousand could be fed upon their luscious bounty?

And finally, even these extravaganzas were at an end; every meal finished and every morsel eaten. The hour of the prince's departure approached; he walked to the front of the palace's impressive *mael maadam* with folded hands betokening farewell.

Below, the streets were galvanized for action, complete with all the accoutrements for a truly magnificent procession: a splendidly decorated elephant for the royal passenger's exclusive use stood ready; stallions and *rishabams* pranced before and behind; standard and emblem-bearers stood at rigid attention holding aloft the insignias that proclaimed their office while musicians awaited, ready to strike their instruments at a moment's notice. As for the people … ah! They jostled for space, a vast multitude heaving, churning and roaring as far as the eye could see, not unlike the ocean just a day before.

To all outward appearances and untrained eyes, Prince Arulmozhi Varmar seemed in excellent spirits, his mien proclaiming delight and his countenance, a charming smile. Inside, however, his heart was a seething maelstrom, wrought with a desperate anxiety to learn the fate of *Oomai Rani*, who claimed his love and affection a ten, nay a thousand-fold more than his own mother. A mild hope that he might pick Raakkammal's brain vanished, when he realized that she had disappeared into the melee that exploded upon his emergence, leaving Murugaiyan to scramble through the crowd, somehow, in the wake of the prince. And no, he had no inkling of his wife's whereabouts either.

Then, there was the other source of apprehension gnawing his conscience: the Pazhuvettarayars' unconscionable allegation—levied far before—that he had attempted to seize the throne in direct contradiction of the Chakravarthy's wishes; what if the populace's enthusiastic espousal served to bolster their outrageous claims? *If only I could somehow loosen this city's stranglehold of love*, he was driven to musing. *If only I could escape this terrifying whirlpool of the peoples' thunderous approval!*

It was at this juncture that something occurred—something entirely unexpected.

Even as he continued to pose on the upper balconies, palms still folded, counting down the moments for departure, the office-bearers of the Aimperunkuzhu and Enperaayam Guilds respectively arrived, and ranged themselves at the palace entrance,

Suddenly, as though rehearsed well in advance, hundreds of *perigai*, *murasu* and *ekkaalam* instruments now drowned out even the rumbling seas, rising to a concerted crescendo for a handful of moments—before ceasing abruptly, leaving behind a hushed multitude, agog with barely contained anticipation. Correctly interpreting the sign, the senior-most of the gathered officials stepped forward, ascended with immense dignity to the *nila medai*, the moon terrace at the front and addressed the prince right regally:

"A petition, Ponniyin Selva; a most humble, respectful plea to thee, from the people of Naagai and every village in its environs!

"Greatly concerned are we, about the Chakravarthy's health—and our anxiety rendered even more acute by a report that has reached us: that the Pazhuvettarayars and several other lords of the realm have convened and agreed upon Madhuranthaka Thevar as successor to the Emperor—Madhuranthaka Thevar, who has never yet entered the battlefield. Should he truly ascend the throne, it would be the Pazhuvoor lords who rule, and the other chieftains' word, the law. As for Prince Aditha Karikalar, he has not set foot within Chozha Nadu for the past three years; many are the reasons mentioned for his prolonged absence—one among them being that he cares not for the throne, and does not wish to rule. If this indeed be the case, who is the next rightful heir? Thy gracious self, Highness; the illustrious virtue borne of Chozha Nadu's penances; the favoured child, saved by River Kaveri and the Warrior of warriors who conquered Eezham! Good people," he turned towards the crowd thronging at the entrance. "Do you concur, all of you? Have my words your approval?"

The roar that erupted and thundered through the air fairly set all eight directions trembling. "***Yes, yes, indeed, yes**! **We agree**!*" screamed a thousand, ten thousand voices in unison, followed by an hundred thousand shrieks of "Long live Ponniyin Selvar!" that blended and merged into one confused, indistinguishable howl that reverberated to the very heavens…

… a howl that ceased, as though mesmerized by a powerfully hypnotic *mandhiram*, the moment the prince's lips began to move in reply.

"I am cast into transports at your overwhelming love for me, *Ayya*, but your way of displaying it is far from seemly. It appears to have slipped your collective memories that my beloved father, Sundara Chozha Chakravarthy is a *jeeviyavanthar* who still resides upon this earth; thus, you must unite with me, all of you, in seeking his continued good health and long life; *Chakravarthy needuzhi vaazhga*! must be the refrain on your lips! Where, pray, is the need to discuss the succession while he still lives?"

But the foremost of the city fathers, it seemed, had a fitting rebuttal to this eminently reasonable speech:

"To choose an heir to the throne while a king is still upon it has been a long-held tradition from time immemorial, Ponniyin Selva; did not the Hero Who won Madurai and He Who Sheathed the Roof of Thillai Ambalam, Maha Paranthaka Chakravarthy resolve upon his successor even while he lived? And was that not how thy own father ascended to his dignities?"

"Indeed, he did—therefore, it is he who possesses the right to choose who may come after him, surely? Inappropriate, you would agree that you and I should squabble over what concerns us not?"

"Certainly we are in agreement that the right to appoint an heir rests with the Emperor—a right and privilege that may be exercised to the full, were he indeed in possession of the freedom to do so.

However," the official spread out his hands expansively. "have not the Pazhuvettarayars fairly imprisoned him in the Thanjai fort? In fact, begging thy pardon for so saying, but—a good many of us doubt that the Chakravarthy is even alive. We should much prefer to follow thy illustrious self, and ascertain the truth for ourselves. And if, by great fortune, should we find the Chakravarthy in the enjoyment of good health, we shall submit to him our plea; a petition that desires thy gracious highness to ascend to the throne after him. And then … well, it shall be as his royal majesty pleases!"

A good many of us doubt that the Chakravarthy is even alive …

Arulmozhi Varmar's heart seized at these ominous words. Days and months, even up to this very hour had he spent indulging in optimism—but the official's speech thrust his spirit into almost unbearable turmoil. He found himself prey to the most lowering depression; an alarm, nay almost panic that spread its dreaded tendrils through him. A sudden delusion held him in a vicious grip; a delusion that the Emperor's life was in grave peril while he, his son was elsewhere, too far away to lend the slightest assistance—and then there was *Oomai Rani*, cruelly abducted by rank ruffians … no, no, not for another moment could he tarry; no more! No more! Thanjai beckoned insistently; he had to leave right away.

An almost unbearable agitation now had him in its unrelenting clasp and in an instant, he had made his decision.

Argument with these worthy citizens would be pointless and lead to nothing but an unnecessary delay; if he accepted their stipulation and embarked on his journey … why, doubtless time and distance would provide enough and more opportunities for new strategies, surely?

"Far be it from me to stand in your way, *Ayya*," he assented with every semblance of graciousness. "Everything you said, thus far, about the Chakravarthy, has invested in me a desire to seek an audience with him at once and you, good people, may accompany me with my good will. As for the succession," he paused, for effect. "You and I shall be ruled by his desire!"

Prince Arulmozhi Varmar departed Naagai upon his elephant in a very little while. With him, towards Thanjai, travelled thousands in a massive procession—a procession that continued to swell and grow, with every step.

8

PAZHUVETTARAYAR IN A BARGE

Our esteemed readers might recall that it was on the day of the storm that Periya Pazhuvettarayar left Kadambur for Thanjai. He travelled upon the regular road until the Kollidam, branching to the west upon its banks. Rather than barge through every meandering Chozha village on an endless journey, he much preferred to head towards Thiruvaiyaaru and there, ford the river.

Contrary to his usual custom of progressing with an impressive retinue consisting of hundreds, the Pazhuvoor lord set off with a skeleton crew of ten; the fewer people knew of this unforeseen expedition the better, he felt.

By the time he reached the quay on the northern banks at Thiruvaiyaaru, however, that huge river was in full, glorious spate, the waters brimming on both sides in almost the proportions of a deluge; there were promising signs of a ferocious gale whipping up, as well. Impossible to even consider ferrying the horses on the modest barge that awaited him; far better to leave them here to be of use on the return journey—and so, it was only the Pazhuvoor lord who eventually clambered on to the boat, with his reduced entourage.

Mid-river, though, the storm escalated into a full-fledged cyclone; despite the oarsmen's considerable dexterity and consummate skill, the barge was pulled in diametrically opposite directions: the river's headstrong current to the east, and the stubborn gale winds to the west. The boatmen, for their part, tried desperately to steer south … and the craft, caught between three equally relentless forces, began to corkscrew viciously, caught in a roiling, seething maelstrom …

… a maelstrom that rivalled the one currently savaging Pazhuvettarayar's stalwart heart.

That his wits commonly went begging in Nandhini's mesmerizing presence was nothing new. Every word she uttered carried immeasurable weight; every sentiment expressed found an unerring echo in his quivering heart. Her slightest wish—even if it was to engage in an act he found distasteful in the extreme and had done so, for years—was a strict command to be carried out and what was more, now seemed immensely agreeable as well. Even if his conscience should harbour the slightest objection, his lips, he found, were always quick to acquiesce, saying *Yes; of course; by all means*! before he knew it—and well, once his word was given, he was loathe to break it.

Now, too such was the case; bidden to bring Madhuranthaka Thevar from Thanjai, he had set out in obedience to Nandhini without a moment's hesitation, a vast number of suspicions rearing their inopportune heads to torment his quailing heart only *after* he had commenced his journey.

Oh, not for a moment did he cast doubts on Nandhini's chastity—not that, never! But the knowledge that he had left her behind, alone and in the midst of three well-proportioned young men arose often, driving darts of exquisite agony into his soul.

And after all, reasons plenty, hadn't he, to harbour the most loathsome hatred towards Kandamaaran, Vandhiyathevan and Aditha Karikalan? Take the Kadambur prince, for instance: appearing as he had before Pazhuvettarayar and Nandhini at midnight in the treasure vault and referring to his wife as *your daughter*—! The excruciating pain of that unthinking remark has been branded upon his heart as though with molten iron … and it was the resulting, seething wrath that had prompted him into ordering the cavern-guard to carry out a secret assassination. Later, he had regretted this unseemly impulse and somehow Kandamaaran had survived the attack, though how his would-be assassin had died remained a mystery. That he could gather no details about his death rankled—as also the fact that the Kadambur prince had spent his convalescence in the Pazhuvoor palace for an appreciable amount of time, nursed most lovingly to health by the Ilaiya Rani.

Vandhiyathevan too—and he had disliked that youngster on sight; impudent, uncouth, insolent jabber-jaw that he was! Pazhuvettarayar's dislike had sharpened into outright hostility when he learnt that the boy had had the audacity to deliver some sort of warning to the Chakravarthy himself—privately, no less—and then managed to escape Thanjavur with no one being the wiser. Nor had he forgotten Chinna Pazhuvettarayar's sly hint that Nandhini's hand was evident in said escape—why, what a farrago of nonsense! He had not credited a word of that ridiculous allegation, especially after it had been revealed that the Vaanar lad was, in fact, the confidential envoy of Kundhavai Piratti and Prince Arulmozhi Varmar … which precluded any connection with Nandhini. And yet—and yet! His iron heart withered under a blast-wave of white-hot jealousy, each time he thought of that strapping young man in connection with the Ilaiya Rani.

And then, there was, finally, Aditha Karikalar.

Word had reached Periya Pazhuvettarayar that Chozha Nadu's crown prince had yearned, once, to wed a priest's daughter—a priest's daughter who was Nandhini, in truth. They had met, now, this strange pair; a meeting contrived too, with considerable perseverance by his own wife; why? Of one thing, though, he was sure: Aditha Karikalan might be the greatest lout in history, without an ounce of deference towards his elders and betters … but he was still a Chozha lout, born into one of Thamizhagam's greatest dynasties—one whose scions lusted not after the wives of other men, not to mention that Karikalan's conduct was unsullied when it came to women. But … what of Nandhini herself? Could he be certain that her conduct was similarly without blemish? And he, Pazhuvettarayar, to have taken her commands to heart and actually come this far; was that well done of him? What he knew of her antecedents was laughably negligible, while his own brother Kalanthaka Kantan had issued warning after covert warning on more than one occasion. They would not—would not turn out to be valid, would they? Nandhini would not betray him, would she? Ah, the endless tales he had heard of vicious, vengeful women who stopped at nothing to exact their revenge—did they truly exist? And could it be—was the Ilaiya Rani one of them?

The very idea was enough to enflame into a raging inferno the smouldering embers of hatred … while also fanning into red-heat, the ever-burning blaze of lust that threatened to annihilate his soul.

He shook his head and cleared his throat in a desperate attempt to extinguish the exquisite torment of both emotions, and it was only the painful awareness of the presence of ten others that stopped his powerful palms from striking his forehead in an agony of mortification. Despite himself, however, deep, shuddering sighs erupted from him, and he clutched the edges of the barge with his thick fingers as though in a death grip.

"I shall know all—all, within the next two days," he pledged to himself, through gritted teeth. "And never—not ever shall I repeat my mistakes!"

Hidden Meanings and Explanations

" ... scions who lusted not after the wives of other men ..."

The beautiful, chaste phrase Kalki uses to describe this sin is "***piranil vizhaiyum throgam***," an unforgivable crime denouncing which Thiruvalluvar has dedicated an entire set of verses under the title "***Piranil Vizhaiyaamai***."

9

The Banks Break!

Not that the rest of the barge's passengers were aware, in any way, of Pazhuvettarayar's inner turmoil, choosing, instead and rather conveniently, to believe that his unease rose chiefly from the circumstance of their craft being tossed about wildly by the cyclone …

… which led to another, alarming conclusion: if the Pazhuvoor lord, famed as much for his strength of mind as his stalwart courage should fall prey to so much apprehension, what of their own, considerably punier selves? If *he* could be so anxious, what of them? His retinue now, seized by a panic about the boat capsizing any moment, began frantically seeking ways to save their skins, somehow.

In the end, however, it seemed that they would not be destined for such dire straits for the barge, heaving and swinging amidst the storm-tossed waves for what seemed like hours, approached the opposite bank barely half a *kaadham* east of the proposed quay. *No cause for worry, then*, was the general consensus, as the passengers heaved a deep sigh of relief—

—a relief that was short-lived, when one of the trees swaying in the dance of ghouls upon the bank, chose this moment to splinter. The wind promptly picked up the hapless trunk and gleefully dropped it into the river, almost on top of the barge.

Despite the oarsmens' every effort—and they pushed themselves to the very limits—the boat stubbornly stayed where it was ... and the inevitable happened.

Thadaar!—the tree almost exploded into the barge, which immediately gave up the ghost and capsized ... flinging its occupants headfirst into the raging river.

Having been in momentary expectation of exactly this terrifying scenario and therefore, mulling over possible means of escape, Pazhuvettarayar's entourage rather kept their heads when actually confronted with their worst fears, despite being considerably in over it. The proximity to the shore meant that several struck out strongly towards land; some clambered on to trees; still others managed to clutch at anything without grabbing distance while still managing to keep afloat.

All except for the Pazhuvoor lord himself who, having been lost in reverie, had not anticipated this disaster in the slightest and was caught completely unawares, plunging into the frothing floods and carried away a tremendous distance before he was even aware of it. By the time he struggled to the surface, having gulped a good deal of water, inhaled some, gotten more in his ears, thrashing and flailing clumsy arms and legs, gasping for breath, both barge and passengers had vanished from sight. It was also around this time that he realized something else: the ferocious current was dragging, dragging him inexorably towards the middle of the massive river.

At once, the *kizhavar*'s valiant old soul thrilled to this new challenge—for was he not a veteran of an hundred battlefields? Had he not found himself in a thousand perilous situations; fought the most terrifying odds? Had he not, often and anon, snatched victory from the very jaws of defeat? A new exhilaration coursed through his veins; indomitable courage and unassailable fortitude raced through his body as he prepared to face his foe; very well, he would grapple with this formidable enemy, pit his strength against nature, and seize his victory!

Battle fairly enjoined, he glanced about and spotted a piece of driftwood. Catching it in a death grip, he began to strike out roughly in the direction of the bank, fighting the mighty current and the raging storm simultaneously. At times, when both threatened to overwhelm him, he ceased to struggle and simply floated; at others, desperately attempted to clamber onto the shore—before being betrayed by banks made a morass by slippery mud, courtesy the relentless downpour. Thwarted of his intentions and thrown back into the river, Pazhuvettarayar was reduced to clutching at the log he had just discarded.

More than a *jaamam* after nightfall, after enduring an ordeal that seemed to drag on interminably, struggling endlessly against a force that seemed intent on suffocating him, his legs finally touched solid ground at one point, pushed into a dense cluster of coarse, unruly *naanal* reeds upon the river bed. Grabbing hold of the flexible growth, the old man stumbled and staggered towards shore.

Finally on firm land, he cast his eyes around. *Kanaanthakaaram*, a deep, profound darkness hung like an impenetrable cloak on all sides. The area seemed deserted, with no sign of habitation nearabouts; certainly no village—not even a settlement. He must have been dragged at least one-and-a-half-*kaadhams* east from the Thiruvaiyaaru ferry, he estimated; *indeed, indeed! I have likely come ashore somewhere in the vicinity of Kudandhai and must make my way to the city this very night*, he strategized.

But nature, that stern mistress, was not yet done.

It was then that the cyclone reached its terrifying zenith; gales shrieked through the region like a hundred thousand ghosts howling their wrath, nearly shattering ear-drums; trees splintered, their crashes rending the air; thunder roared and rumbled with a deafening din that seemed to herald the annihilation of the very cosmos. And then … fell the rain, in a veritable deluge.

Surely there ought to be a ruined mandapam or a dilapidated temple hereabouts

… a riverbank that was almost flooded, thanks to the deluge up to the very brim, even overflowing upon land; the unending rain that still fell in a solid sheet, not to mention the stifling blanket of darkness that lay over everything—all of which meant that the valiant *kizhavar*, plodding slowly along, noticed not the swelling stream that intercut his path, right on the banks. He was forced to do so, however, hesitating when the flow appeared to reach his knees and stopping, startled, when he found himself thigh-deep in water … after which there was no more time to reflect as quite suddenly, he found himself headfirst in the flood …

… for the mighty Kollidam had finally broken its banks and the flood, coursing south at that point, grabbed him, tumbling and toppling on its merry way and as the gradient beyond shore was quite deep, seemed to plunge him deep, deep, almost to *athalapaathaalam*, the very depths of the netherworld.

Even righting himself in the seething river after the barge capsized had presented no complications—but not this time; this time, he rolled and plunged, rolled, rolled, rolled and plunged ever more to the deep. Down, down, down he went; his eyes bereft of sight and his ears, hearing. Nothing he could do helped him right himself and cleave back to the surface. Worse, air had begun to run out; he was suffocating. A giant, ruthless demon had him in his crushing grip, pushing, pushing, tumbling and flipping him over and over while dragging him inescapably towards the netherworld …

… a cruel demon none other than the vicious force that had demolished the Kollidam's banks and was even now rushing at breakneck speed through the crack, rapidly widening it into a chasm; a terrifying demon from whose clutches it seemed escape was impossible—*how indeed, when my flailing feet cannot feel the floor—my scrabbling hands can find no purchase—my heaving lungs struggle to breathe—my mangled throat is crushed by a vice—my ears throb as though shattered …Durga Parameswari—Devi! Will I ever escape intact from this appalling calamity? Nandhini, you wretch—it is because of you that I am trapped thus—look at what you have done—ah, no, ayyo, you are to be pitied, for I left you to fend for yourself amidst those rogues—chee! Of all the idiotic—what on earth did I ever gain by surrendering so completely to your beauty? What was my pleasure for being so moved by your pathetic plight and offering marriage? What did I ever end up with except endless anguish and finally, a torturous loss of peace? And now—now finally, to die alone thus, suffocating, struggling to breathe while grappling desperately with Kollidam's vicious waters well nigh crushing me through the banks! An ignoble death, unmourned, unmarked, for not even the honour of a hero-stone shall be mine, nor a memorial, upon my buried body—this valiant body bearing sixty-four phenomenal battle scars—this body, which shall likely never be recovered! God in heaven, I am about to be plunged into some muddy morass fathoms deep in the river bed—no one shall even know my eventual fate! That, or this wretched flood shall tumble my carcass onto some murky bank, to be the feast of wild dogs and jackals—!*

These and a thousand more such random, scattered thoughts flashed through Pazhuvettarayar's frenzied brain—before stuttering to a stop for at this point, mercifully, consciousness deserted him.

Thadaar!—the sensation of something battering his head returned him, once more, to the land of the living. His sturdy hands appeared to be gripping something solid—stone, or hard earth—and some force seemed to be thrusting him stubbornly to the surface. Nothing loath to make use of such heaven-sent help, he gathered whatever scrap of strength was left in his body, anchored his hands—and propelled himself upwards …

… to find himself, the next instant, on firm, stone floor.

With considerable difficulty, he tried to pry open eyelids that had practically gummed shut—and was almost blinded by the unexpected radiance that flooded his sight. But ah, what was this—what glorious vision; what celestial presence—for it was Goddess Durga Parameswari's sacred countenance itself, blessing his eyes! *Ah, Devi, Devi, what heavenly grace is Yours—what compassion, what mercy—for You have rescued me from an ignominious life upon earth, and received me straight into Your divine presence, haven't You—*

—wait.

No, no, this was not heaven; not the Goddess's celestial abode—but Her earthly home, upon this very world. The resplendence before him was Her figurine—and he was 'lying, right now, in the *ardha mandapam* adjacent to the *garbagriham*, the sanctum sanctorum. *Minuk, minuk*, flickered a small lamp beside the deity and he realized that it was this light that had almost blinded him, just moments ago. Outside, the rain was still driving down at full strength; the gale still whipping about ferociously—but neither water nor wind had managed to put out this little flash of fire in the heart of Devi's shrine … ah, was this, perhaps an omen? A sign that Durga Parameswari's heavenly compassion was still his? That She yet smiled upon him? For what was this, if not proof that no matter the devastating disasters, no matter the grievous perils, the radiance that was his life could never, ever dim? *Ah, Jaganmatha, Mother to the entire World, praise be to Thee, and Thy grace and compassion!—all my prayers to Thee were not in vain, indeed!*

The *kizhavar* raised himself in a bid to stand. His body trembled almost uncontrollably; understandable, surely, considering the hours upon hours he had spent thrashing through the merciless floodwaters? Stripping his sodden clothes, he yanked off the screen that usually hung in *sannithis* such as this one for rituals; toweled himself dry and then wrapped the rough cloth around his waist.

Glancing around, he saw that the small space was cluttered with ritually broken coconut shells, fruits, *pongal* and other offerings; the priest and other worshippers had likely dropped everything and taken off, then and there. Why, though? What had driven them away? Wind and rain? Or the Kollidam's broken banks? Whatever the reason had resulted in his great good fortune, for, not content with saving him from terrible floods, his patron Goddess awaited him with delicious *prasaadham*, intent on alleviating hunger pangs, as well.

There seemed no choice but to spend the night here and in truth, a better place could hardly be found. Although, he mused, the deluge was likely raging around the little shrine this very minute—a situation that might well spell danger, for the foundations were probably being eroded now and the entire structure might soon be swept away. Still, an unlikely eventuality this very night—but there was no leaving the shrine even if it came to pass, for neither his body nor spirit possessed the strength to do so.

Pazhuvettarayar stepped towards the sanctum, devotion limning every line of his body. He gathered the offerings strewn about and made an excellent meal; what food remained he carefully covered up. Then, sleep pressing on his heavy eyelids, he lay on the floor before the Goddess in a manner of prostration.

Within moments, the Pazhuvoor lord was fathoms deep again—this time, in slumber.

10

Insight, in Sight!

First the torturous floodwaters; then the breaking banks—the resultant, tremendous struggle against two such indomitable natural forces had taken their considerable toll; even Periya Pazhuvettarayar, indefatigable warrior that he was, had his limits and once stretched out on the hard stone floor, slept like a log, plunged into a black void into which neither thought, emotion, nor lacerated sensibilities had any power to obtrude. Eventually, however, even such debilitating exhaustion as his receded and once his body received some rest, said thoughts and emotions began to make themselves felt, albeit lightly.

Once, the Goddess Durga Parameswari emerged from Her stone image, took four steps forward and bent close to him. "*Adei,* Pazhuvettaraya," issued forth blessed words even as divine eyes, alight with celestial fire, bored into him. "You and your clan have served me faithfully for generations; thus, my words of caution: the woman you have in your palace now, by name Nandhini—is nothing but a demon in the guise of a woman; a weapon with no other intention but to annihilate the Pazhuvoor and Chozha dynasties; a conspirator who seeks the right moment to exact her vengeance. Before you embark upon anything else, detach yourself from her wretched clutches; discard all emotion for her—above all, dethrone her from your heart and your palace … else, prepare to endure endless anguish, for dishonour and disgrace shall be yours and your clan's, for eternity!" The next instant, She had vanished into her sanctum.

Pazhuvettarayar startled awake in a pool of perspiration, his body shuddering almost uncontrollably. It seemed almost inconceivable to him that the scene he had witnessed was just a dream but it could not have been anything else, could it?

Dawn had broken well over the heavens. The storm's fury had abated somewhat; the rain had ceased too—except for an incessant roaring—***Cho!***—that seemed to reverberate around the region. Stepping gingerly to the edge of the *mandapam*, he peered carefully over to gauge the situation.

The sight that met his eyes was not one calculated to inspire his jaded heart with enthusiasm.

What had begun as an insignificant break in the banks had now widened into a yawning, terrifying chasm; *gubu—gubu—gubu*—poured, what seemed almost half the river's flood through this new and promising course; certainly, the east and south appeared to be nothing but a heaving, endless sheet of water. To the west raged, roared, tumbled, swirled, leapt and bounded the deluge a little beyond the temple; further away, however, stretched a dense jungle of squat trees and coarse shrubs through the length and breadth of the region. This, then, must be the forest immediately abutting the village of Thiruppurambiyam, Pazhuvettarayar conjectured. And within that straggling foliage, somewhere, must be the memorial that still held the hero-stone erected in honour of the Ganga king Prithvipathi.

Memories surfaced, thick and fast, of the ferocious, phenomenal war that had scarred the area around this very memorial an hundred years ago—memories that highlighted his ancestors' incredible feats of valour and extraordinary acts of courage, in service to the Chozhas—service, honourable, conscientious service that had distinguished him and his clan—an illustrious, ancient clan whose sterling reputation might yet be tarnished by Nandhini, perhaps? Could there—could there possibly be an iota of truth in Durga Parameswari's sage warning?

Whatever the reality, it behooved him now to step with extreme care, not to mention rootling into and realizing Nandhini's heart, her *andharangam*—all of which could be accomplished only if he managed to extricate himself from his present difficulties, surely? Thiruppurambiyam might allow him to obtain some aid; some others might have escaped the floods and found their way there as well, which meant safety in numbers … but how on earth was he to ford this raging flood and actually reach the village, in the first place?

He stared at the waters as they poured through the chasm, swirling and whirling around the temple. *Heavens, these roaring currents are powerful enough to tumble and sweep away even crazed mammoths! How on earth am I to even attempt a crossing? There is no doubt that the floods are gouging out the foundations of the shrine this very moment; my last asylum might crash to the ground at any time—if it still stands, it is only by the divine grace of the blessed Goddess. Still I must, must find a way to escape; waiting until the floods subside is hardly viable—who knows how many days that might take?*

Thankfully, all was not lost; there appeared yet another way … in the form of a sprawling, gargantuan neem tree right across the shrine, still valiantly upright, somehow, through the vagaries of the severe storm—but the same floods bounding across the landscape, the self-same currents scouring the temple's foundations were even now subjecting the tree's roots to the same, unrelenting treatment; the chances of it falling long before the shrine—and if it did, in the direction of the jungle in the west, thereby acting as a bridge—were quite high. Even if such a possibility did not actually come to fruition and the tree swept away, it would still be washed ashore at some point. All he needed to do was clamber on when it fell … and he would be free of this temple oasis, and in a position to escape.

Until then, though, this would have to remain his refuge, with its serendipitous store of *prasaadham* which would last, thanks to the grace of the Goddess, at least a day more. Nothing else could he do, could he, until one of two things happened: the fall of the tree, or recession of the floods?

No, no need for haste, no reason to hurry; there must still be tasks to complete, some great work to be accomplish on earth—else, Devi Jaganmatha, Mother to the whole World might not have spared him; might not have saved him from an ignominious, watery grave. Probable, therefore, that She might yet guide him towards a course of action?

The day passed; the storm wreaking its havoc, *athaahatham* across every step of the land as it finally swept towards the west.

Even *thoovaanam*, that gentle drizzle soft as flower petals, had tapered away, releasing the landscape from its wet spell—but Pazhuvettarayar found himself imprisoned still, in Durga Devi's shrine for, though the Kollidam's floods seemed to have subsided somewhat, the chasm from the broken banks appeared to have only widened. Neither the surging of waters around the temple, nor the deepening of the bed had seen any secession; the currents were bad and the depths worse, if anything. How was he to gauge it? Or plunge through the twisting and tumbling floods? Dare he even consider the possibility?

In the end, it was dusk when the eventuality Pazhuvettarayar had been anticipating finally occurred: the Neem tree across the temple crashed to the ground … thankfully, towards the west and spanning the waters raging through the broken banks; he prepared to clamber over it and thus ford the waters. Some little hesitation about the complexities of picking his way through dense jungle sans a path did obtrude—but not for more than a few moments; go he would. Not before tendering his thanks towards the celestial power that had been his saving grace from a calamity of disastrous proportions, however; he duly turned in the direction of Durga Parameswari, approached the sanctum, folded his palms and fell in prostration …

… when an unearthly voice assaulted his ears.

His body prickled with goose-bumps in startled reaction. *Good God, is it the Goddess Herself, perhaps? Durgaiyamman, speaking to a mere mortal? Wait, no, no—it comes not from within the shrine but without—a little distance from here, in fact,* he divined, with some relief.

"Mandhiravaadhi?" Called out the disembodied voice. "Mandhiravaadhi!" After a pause, it continued. "Ravidasa—Ravidasa!"

Strange that it seemed rather familiar.

Pazhuvettarayar straightened majestically, rose to his full height, stalked towards a pillar and from behind it, peered in the direction of the shout—and caught sight of a figure beyond the broken banks, near the head of the upended tree. That raucous cry for *Mandhiravaadhi*! Bizarre, half-formed suspicions—suspicions fostered by his brother long ago, but to which he had never really given any credence—now reared their unsightly heads; *ah, am I about to unravel mysteries hitherto hidden, by the great grace of the Goddess*? The idea took hold in him and he stayed rooted to the spot.

The vague shape on the opposite banks had now climbed onto the tree and was beginning to ford the floods, he noticed.

Then, Periya Pazhuvettarayar did something rather extraordinary; something he never had done before: he retreated into the *mandapam*, lay down on the floor—and pretended to be asleep.

Such was his eagerness to catch a glimpse of this mysterious entity, this *mandhiravaadhi* named Ravidasan—for he suspected that this might be the same man who had visited Nandhini in his palace, at times. Of what unusual sort was his connection with his wife? And who might be the stranger who was seeking him now, at such an outlandish time? Why?

If I could have these questions answered, I might be able to divine Nandhini's motives; understand once and for all, if she is truly betraying me, he mused. *And if I should ever get Ravidasan in my clutches* … he ground his teeth. *I shall not release him until I learn the truth*!

The newcomer tiptoed to him as he lay still, in pretended sleep. "Ravidasa," he called again. "Ravidasa?"

Aha, that voice—a voice he had heard, before—surely it belonged to the Thevaralan who had delivered a flurry of predictions even as he danced about in a frenzy during the Velanaattam in Kadambur, that fateful night? *Ought I to wrap my hands around his scrawny neck and choke the truth out of him? No—no, I shall wait; far more important to use this man to bait Ravidasan, surely*?

"Fathoms deep in slumber before sunset, Mandhiravaadhi?" Cackled the voice, again. "Or are you dead and gone for good?" The man stepped forward and touching Pazhuvettarayar's slack body, flipped him over in a bid to glimpse his face. To this rather cavalier treatment the *kizhavar* submitted, lying like a marionette with its strings cut, careful not to betray himself.

In the fading light, as twilight melded into night and the last moments of dusk blended into the beginnings of darkness, as shadows crept long over the landscape, the Thevaralan (yes, it was indeed him) saw Periya Pazhuvettarayar. Unable, or rather unwilling to believe the evidence of his own vision, he knuckled his eyes well and truly before staring hard, once more, at the figure at his feet. And then—

"Ooh—ooh! Oh—oh! Ah—ah!" Erupted from his throat a series of weak shrieks that yet reverberated with overwhelming panic, mind-numbing terror, supreme astonishment and frank disbelief …

… and he took to his heels, dread yapping at his shadow.

Such was his incredible speed that by the time Pazhuvettarayar opened his eyes and sat up, he had cleared in two bounds the *mandapam* with the *balipeedam* up front, and was even now scampering across the Neem tree bridge, his feet slipping and sliding in his haste to get away—get away—*get away*—leaping and sprinting to the opposite bank and was soon lost to sight amidst an impenetrable jungle of trees and shrubs.

Pazhuvettarayar watched, bemused and unblinking, his panicked retreat but the moment he vanished from view, a vague, half-formed regret seized him; regret that he had not seized him when he had the chance.

Impulse prompted him into action; he jumped up and followed in the Thevaralan's wake—but what he possessed in courage and intrepidity he, unfortunately lacked in strength and stamina; where his prey had almost effortlessly sailed across the rugged trunk, Pazhuvettarayar could only stumble over, making his slow, staggering way, holding onto branches here and there.

Once on the other side, he noticed a trail snaking through the jungle floor—a trail whose muddy surface, when he trained his eyes upon it, revealed fresh tracks. This, then, must have been the Thevaralan's path; he strode down it, swiftly.

Despite these being the days of the waxing moon, illumination was faint as clouds still scudded thickly across the dark sky. The forest resounded with garbled, indefinable sounds. Countless creatures to whom this tropical landscape was home and which had suffered through the tribulations of storm and rain were screeching and crying out their happiness, now that their trials were ended.

The track ran for a while… and then tapered away. Not for Pazhuvettarayar, however, who plunged through whatever path he espied through gaps offered by recalcitrant scrubland—for he was determined to run the Thevaralan and his quarry, Ravidasan the Mandhiravaadhi to earth—and find them he would, even if it took all night.

After nearly a *jaamam* of endless traipsing through barely discernable forest paths, thrusting through copses and bumbling amidst shrubbery, his reward came—in the form of faint illumination, at some distance. Judging by the way it kept moving, it seemed likely that the source of light was a torch, held aloft by someone picking their way across the area.

Keeping his eye on his target, Pazhuvettarayar strode swiftly forwards, drawing close with every moment.

Eventually, the torch flared bright as though to illumine a dilapidated, decrepit *mandapam* holding a lonely vigil within the dense jungle—and then blinked out. One glimpse at the structure, and Pazhuvettarayar realized that it was none other than Prithvipathi's memorial, in Thiruppurambiyam. Creeping towards the crumbling edifice, he sidled up to one wall, plastered his ear to the surface—and listened.

Indeed; his expectations were not in vain… for he could hear conversation—and not even the whispered tones of conspirators but the voices of two men who cared not to lower their voices.

"Do you have any idea how long I've been hunting for you, Mandhiravaadhi?" The Thevaralan demanded hotly. "I was worried that you hadn't been able to get away—or that Yaman had spirited you away as well!"

Ravidasan cackled, the notes rumbling around the *mandapam*.

"Why would Death stalk me, when He approaches Sundara Chozhan and his two sons? Tomorrow," he practically smacked his lips with relish. "Tomorrow, their lives shall come to a sudden end!"

Lightning flashed, at that moment—a jagged shard of blinding radiance that bathed earth and sky.

11

The Mandapam Tumbles

Blinding though the flash of lightning, it allowed a fleeting moment of illumination—enough for Pazhuvettarayar to determine the identities of the two schemers within the *mandapam*. One of them, Ravidasan, his memory obligingly reminded, he had glimpsed more than once in his very palace; the one who had a score of magic trick and spells up his sleeve, Nandhini had mentioned and incidentally, also the one his brother Kalanthaka Kantan had cautioned against. The other was the Thevaralan, he of the dervish dance in Kadambur—but had that truly been the first time he had set eyes on the man? What was his real name, anyway? But wait ... could it—could it quite possibly be? Was he—was he Parameswaran, the employee he had dismissed from royal service aeons ago? Be that as it may, it behooved him to listen carefully to their conversation.

"This has been your constant refrain for ages, now," the Thevaralan's tone held more than a hint of complaint. "*The hour is nigh*, you grandstand; *Yaman will fling his noose any moment*—but all He does is make off with a whole host of people except Sundara Chozhan, languishing in sickbed for three years … not to mention terrified of going next or nigh his blessed sons! Remember how the two of us strained every last nerve in Eezham?"

"Never you fret, *Appane*; Yama Dharmarajan is possessed of more foresight and wisdom than either of us—for, see you, He has tarried thus long only to ensure that all three departed this world the same day … and that day will be tomorrow. Thanks be that you've arrived in the nick of time; ah, none more worthy to be His sacred envoy, a true harbinger of Death! But why do you shiver so? Almost drowned in the Kollidam's deluge, did you? You've managed to find a boat, I hope?"

"Yes, but it was the devil's own work to keep it moored in place against the vicious winds and ferocious floods, I tell you. Not to mention hunting high and low for you … you asked why I was trembling, didn't you? I saw the dread Lord of Death just now, that's why. Face to face, before my very eyes—no, I glimpsed Yaman's older brother! That explains a fit of the jitters, if you must know the truth."

"What on earth are you blubbering about, Parameswara? Yaman—and his elder brother indeed! And why must you fear them? It ought to be the other way around, surely?"

Pazhuvettarayar could not help but feel, it must be admitted, a sharp pinprick of unease at Ravidasan's mention of his cohort's name; had he been right in his suspicions, then? It certainly seemed like it. And the Lord of Death's dread sibling in question could be none other than his own self, he reasoned. Heart and hands quivered with the desperate need to just step out, wrap his fingers around the man's throat and choke the life out of him—but though it went much against the grain, he preserved himself in patience; more than his thirst for blood was his hunger to listen to their conversation …

… for they had made no mention of Nandhini, yet.

Besides, what lay behind the *mandhiravadhi*'s sinister declaration about Yaman visiting all of Sundara Chozhan's family, tomorrow? Had it just been a random remark borne of malice? An astrological prediction wrestled out of royal horoscopes? Or did he truly possess a miraculous host of tricks and spells as Nandhini had claimed? And what if his outrageous announcements turned out to be true, by some heinous twist of cruel fate?

The treacherous path to my ambitions would be instantly smoothed, spoke a tiny voice, in his mind. *No more would there be a need to engage in a convoluted apportioning of the samrajyam … still, Parameswaran, here; what is his part in this contorted piece of theatre? But then, there was the terrible oath he swore twenty years ago. that he would annihilate the entire Chozha clan … wait, he is speaking again and—aha, about me, to boot! I may as well listen.*

"I did arrive here this morning according to your instructions, but you were nowhere to be found," the Thevaralan recounted, peevishly. "I searched everywhere I could, worried that you'd perhaps been hurt in the cyclone and hiding to escape the wind and rain. I spied a tiny shrine by the Kollidam where the banks had broken; it seemed to me that someone was fast asleep within. I wondered if it might be you and crept in to confirm … but who do you think I saw? Periya Pazhuvettarayan himself, large as life and twice as natural—!"

"***Ha—ha—ha***!" The *mandhiravaadhi* released a veritable bellow of laughter that set birds roosting in the forests shrieking ***kreech—kreech***! while owls rumbled in muted tones. "Was it Pazhuvettarayan indeed?" He demanded. "Or his apparition?"

"Not that, no, for I touched to flip him over that I could gaze into his face—and there was no mistaking those features. Ravidasa, could it be that Yaman has *two* elder siblings? One with the same twisted grimace of a face, grisly whiskers and gory scars?"

"Without a doubt you saw Pazhuvettarayan and none other. Last evening he boarded a barge to cross the Kollidam—and was left floundering in the floods when the craft capsized near the banks. His retinue made landfall, though and are hunting for him even now—however, judging by what I overheard when the posse returned from a trip to the chasm, they believe him to have drowned. You likely did see the man … or was it, perhaps, his corpse?"

"Surely it's impossible to see the pupils of dead eyes? But this one's were shut tight when I turned him over. He seemed only to be in a deep sleep."

"And you? What on earth did *you* do, fool? Leave him to have his beauty sleep out?" Ravidasa raged. "Why couldn't you have at least dropped a boulder on his blasted head?"

"Hence proven that you know nothing about that one's skull. Flinging a rock upon it would splinter the rock, not the head."

"Fair enough; why not drag him into the floods roaring through Kollidam's broken banks?"

"Haven't I been screaming at you that I was shaken at the very sight of him as though I'd glimpsed Yaman's *annan*—why, my heart went thudding *thik—thik—thik*! against my ribs even back when I danced in his presence, at Kadambur. If he'd recognized me—"

"And you're still shivering about that now—why?"

"I suppose I always shall a little, as long as he's alive … ah, I ought to have shoved him into the seething river when I had the chance, as you said; now I'm worried that—"

"You needn't; in a way, as well that he lives for when Sundara Chozhan and his sons are dead and gone for good, the lords and chieftains will splinter into two factions and fight to the death:

Pazhuvettarayars and Sambuvaraiyars on one side; Kodumbalur Velaan and Thirukkovilur Malayaman on the other … and an excellent advantage that would prove to our sacred cause, for while they're intent on slaughtering each another, we shall marshal our own forces—"

"There's this adage that comes to mind: *A moustache on an aunt, makes her an uncle,*" the Thevaralan remarked, reminiscently. "That's how unsound your theory is, for anything more unlikely I've yet to hear. Everything you retailed now, all your fanciful outcomes about kings and lords killing themselves is a certainty only upon the deaths of Sundara Chozhan and his sons on the morrow; where's the guarantee that *that* will ever happen? And if you only knew that—"

"Know what? What do you speak of?"

"Arulmozhi Varman is alive—in Nagapattinam! The people around those parts have all risen up and are clamouring to the skies to crown him Chakravarthy of Chozha Nadu. Heard that piece of news?"

"I hadn't but as it so happens, I didn't need to," Ravidasan laughed again—a merry, full-throated peal that reverberated around the *mandapam*. "Because, you see—I knew. Who on earth did you think exposed him? None other than our Revadasa Kramavithan's very own daughter, Raakkammal—and the wife of boatman Murugaiyan!"

"Well, what a wonderful reveal, to be sure—but what's the point of it? Why go to all the trouble of bringing him to the limelight when he's going to be surrounded by hordes of heaving masses every moment of the day?" the Thevaralan remonstrated. "Especially when we couldn't harm a hair on his head in Ilankai where he wandered about with just two or three companions—"

"I did say that that actually boded well, now that the Lord of Death shall seize their souls on the same day …"

"… and you haven't mentioned yet how He would sneak upon a prince amidst lakhs of people, Ravidasa."

"But sneak He would, *Appane*; sneak, sidle and slink up to him, sit upon the tip of the mahout's goad—and snatch the prince's life at absolutely the right moment! The good, loyal people of Chozha Nadu shall lead their precious *ilango* in a stately procession towards Thanjai but ah, alas! A misfortune of some sort shall befall the ill-starred mahout, and our own Revadasa Kramavithan shall take his place. As to what happens next," Ravidasan spoke with relish. "Surely your imagination can conjure the rest?"

The awed silence that followed illustrated the effect of his dramatic pronouncement. "I'll admit that there's no equal to your wits," the Thevaralan spoke, slowly. "And we can be sure, in addition, that our cohort shall fulfill his mission. Now, what of Sundara Chozhan? And the arrangements towards his fate?"

"I've secreted Soman Saambavan in Pazhuvettarayan's treasure vault—oh, not empty-handed; with a spear, of course. There's a subterranean passage within that runs straight to Chozhan's palace; I've even pointed out his very bedchamber—even a man blinded in both eyes could simply take aim at the spot, launch the lance and assassinate the target. Naturally," Ravidasan explained with some pride. "I've warned our man not to ruin everything by rushing in, but wait until tomorrow."

"Why, though? Wouldn't it be better to finish the job when the opportunity presents itself?"

"You little nincompoop. Wouldn't news of Sundara Chozhan's murder put his sons on their guard? Not that the death of that doddering *kizhavan* ravaged by ill-health is going to make much of a difference, but—be that as it may, what news from your side? How are they all at the Kadambur palace; what's the status—for surely, the mission there tomorrow night is the most important of all?"

"Oh, Kadambur is overflowing with joyous spirit, make no mistake; every moment overwhelmed with dramatic romances and matrimonial alliances ..." the Thevaralan paused. "You know, I don't like your placing such trust in Pazhuvoor Ilaiya Rani—"

"The Pazhuvoor Rani? Scorch your tongue, man and address her by her rightful title, Pandi Maadevi—forgotten, have you, that Veera Pandiyar made her his *pattamakishi* a bare two days before his death? Slipped your mind, has it that she too swore a bloody vengeance towards his murder? Didn't she accept, from the hands of the Pandiya scion, the clan's celestial sword at this very place a week ago?"

"Indeed, yes, of course—but if you'd only seen your blessed Pandi Maadevi sailing gaily across the Veera Narayana Lake on a lighthearted picnic last evening—"

"Why, how could she have been otherwise, pray? Nandhini has no equal, I tell you, when it comes to concealing her true emotions and presenting a completely different face to the world. How else could she have managed to survive three whole years in Pazhuvettarayan's palace? Or aided and abetted us and our cause, from within? Wait, you mentioned a while ago that you spied that old war-dog in the Durgaiyamman shrine, didn't you? Now, I heard that his barge had capsized in the Kollidam—but why on earth did he depart Kadambur in the first place?"

"I'm not very sure, but I was told that he'd undertaken to escort Madhuranthaka Thevan to the Sambuvaraiyars; from what I learnt, he left yesterday morning. Once the gates closed after him, the princes embarked on a hunting expedition while the princesses set off on a merry *jalakreedai*, to disport themselves in the lake waters. And if you'd only been privileged to see the delightful tableau both parties presented as they returned together, the very picture of debauched pleasure ... well, you wouldn't be quite this assured, is all I can say."

"You needn't entertain the slightest anxiety; surely the consummate ease with which she bundled Pazhuvettarayan to Thanjai ought to reveal Pandi Maadevi's true state of mind?"

"As to that, who, when it comes to female caprice, can consider himself an expert?" The Thevaralan countered. "How may one divine her rationale for packing off the Pazhuvoor *kizhavan*—searing vengeance? Or sweet, deliciously secret romance?"

"Have a care to your words, you blithering idiot! Those ridiculous starts are all done; it's been many a day since Nandhini consigned them to the past. Towards Karikalan she now harbours nothing but the deadliest hatred ..."

"I wasn't referring to him—" the Thevaralan protested a trifle uneasily. "—but Vandhiyathevan. Forgotten, have you, that she's spared his life twice or thrice?"

Ravidasan's amused cackles were even louder, third time around; in fact, he could barely seem to contain himself. "Indeed, the reason for that Vaanar boy's survival shall be revealed soon—mind, you're not going to be the only one bowled over with astonishment when it finally does happen; many, many more shall drown in a veritable sea of amazement—and Sundara Chozhan's precious, precious daughter Kundhavai is certain to be foremost among them. Well, and why wouldn't she be?" he elaborated with relish. "Especially when she realizes that the *sukumaaran* to whom she's lost her heart turns out to be her darling *thamaiyan*'s bloody assassin?"

"Good God Ravidasa, what on earth are you—is this true indeed? Vandhiyathevan the one to fulfill our sacred mission—has he finally thrown in his lot with us, then?"

"Neither the time nor the place to pelt me with such questions. Frankly, what does it matter whose hand completes the task as long as it does so with a Pandiya sword emblazoned with the blessed fish insignia—and the blame falls on Vandhiyathevan? Now," Ravidasan demanded. "*Now* what do you say about our queen's ingenuity, eh?"

"Ask me when it's all gone perfectly according to plan."

"Regardless, there's no doubt that Karikalan's spirit shall depart this earthly abode tomorrow night. Nandhini shall fulfill her responsibility to the cause—and so must we."

"Which would be?"

"Waiting, at the appointed hour, with all possible readiness in the secret passage leading out of the Kadambur palace. That's the path Nandhini will take once the mission is accomplished; we will be her escort to refuge in the Kolli Hills overnight, from where we shall watch Chozha Nadu dissolve into the most appalling, excruciating chaos. And if it could be managed—"

"What? If what could be managed?"

"Every last grain in Pazhuvettarayan's treasury ought to be transported out through the secret passage. Ironic, wouldn't it be, if Chozha wealth was going to be the means of Chozha Nadu's complete annihilation? If Chozha gold were to fund enemy hordes?" And consumed by unholy mirth, Ravidasan chuckled again.

"All very well, but I'd preserve my patience before erecting such monumental castles in the air," Parameswaran, He of the dervish-dancing Thevaralan fame, interjected caustically. "We've to ford the Kollidam first and then get to Kadambur; all the time in the world to contemplate burgling the Pazhuvoor treasury, if everything goes to plan at the Sambuvaraiyar palace. Well? What say you? Shall we attempt a crossing right now?"

"No, not at all; time enough to climb into a boat after daybreak. The winds would have died down by then, hopefully; likewise, the floodwaters."

"Then—do we bed down in the memorial for the night?"

Ravidasan sank into thought for a few moments—at which inopportune point a raucous concerto arose in the distance, courtesy an ill-assorted pack of jackals. The *mandhiravadhi's* sturdy frame juddered almost despite himself.

"Why—" the Thevaralan noticed his discomfiture with some surprise. "You, shivering and shaking at the sound of a few measly creatures!"

"*Appane*, your tone wouldn't drip with such disdain had you been the one snared in a terrifying nightmare, buried up to your neck in a soul-sucking quagmire while an hundred jackals stalked around, baying for your blood! Neither a lion's thunderous roar nor a crazed elephant's deafening trumpet has the power to unman me … but my insides quake at a jackal's howl! Come, come away—we'll leave right now! I've no intention of spending what's left of the dark hours in this God-forsaken cemetery; we'll seek our beds in a shrine or *chathiram* in the vicinity of some village nearabouts … failing those, there's always the Durgaiyamman temple you mentioned, on the banks of the Kollidam. And if that doddering old man should still be there, as well make short work by shoving him into the floods. A vast favour in fact, I should say; were he to survive until the day after tomorrow, unbearable sorrow would be his fate!"

Needless to say, almost every word of this extremely illuminating conversation had fallen on Periya Pazhuvettarayar's pricked ears … dripping steadily into them as though drops of scorching, burning lead. His stalwart heart seethed, stormed and churned as though the womb of a massive, searing volcano; the knowledge that the lady with whom he had fallen in love—at whose feet he had laid his heart—was a vicious woman hell-bent on vengeance upon the Chozhas for the death of Veera Pandiyan—that she had systematically, ferociously and willingly deceived him for three whole years … ah, the torment, the unbearable anguish, the sheer, agonizing humiliation!

Six generations. Six generations of Pazhuvoor lords had served the Chozhas with faith and honour; six generations had clasped their suzerains' hands in perfect amity and goodwill, their relationship strengthening beyond just fealty and progressing to family; their bonds of brotherhood bolstered by ever richer bonds of blood. Why, who were Sundara Chozhan and his sons but his own folk? Was the Emperor's grandmother not a member of the hoary Pazhuvoor clan? His own numerous resentments were of very recent date, weren't they? Yes, Aditha Karikalan had been a brat, an unprincipled lout with the manners to match and Malayaman had been unfortunate enough to earn his ill-will … but heavens, was that reason enough to engage in heinous conspiracies? *Have I truly descended to such despicable depths as to plot, scheme and engineer their horrible destruction? Given way to such hatred and loathing that I allowed the Chozhas' most lethal foes into my own palace, turning a blind eye as they looted and burgled my own treasury to fund Chozha annihilation?*

In the wake of such searing realizations reared another horrifying train of thought: aha, could these *chandaalars* be right? Were three truly devastating deaths about to occur simultaneously in three different locations on the morrow?

No—no, no, no, no—not as long as there is breath in this body; not as long as I live shall I allow this calamity—I must and shall stop them; sixty naazhigais still remain until the fatal hour—much could be accomplished before then. I must speed overnight to Kudanthai; send messages to Thanjai and Naagai; return to Kadambur hotfoot—return before these murderous maniacs—

—wait.

Why let them set foot in Sambuvaraiyar's stronghold, in the first place? Why not just strangle them here and now? Why not forestall disaster? True enough that I have no weapon, but why must I, when I possess arms steely as Vajrayudham? But stay; I may be unarmed but there is no reason they are; sharp blades might lie snug in their waistbands—small but nevertheless, lethal—not that I shall be standing by, waiting until they raise them; I shall wrap my fingers around their throats and choke the lives out of their bodies even before the thought crosses their minds, but … would it be right to end them here, thus?

Still, everything that I could possibly hope to learn from them I have, by the glorious grace of my patron Goddess Durga Parameswari who capsized my barge and made it possible to unearth terrifying secrets. Surely it is my sworn duty to protect the Chakravarthy and his kumaarars, his sons from the grievous peril that stares them in the face—especially Karikalan in Kadambur? Any ill that befalls him would reflect appallingly on me and mine; the Pazhuvoor clan's reputation would be marred beyond reprieve for eternity. Six generations of unswerving loyalty and unwavering devotion would be as dust with this one calamity—nothing, nothing could bring more dishonour if the Crown Prince of Chozha Nadu were to be assassinated by the demon in damsel's guise that I have been fool enough to harbour in my own palace!

Aha!

His mind lapsed, once more, into the recent rut of burning mortification, self-recrimination and a sort of wondering disillusionment. *Could such a ravishingly beautiful countenance possibly be suffused with vicious aalahaala poison? Could burning vengeance possibly lie concealed behind a charming smile that illumined all the three worlds? Could there—could there be an iota of truth in the words of these rampant rogues?*

In a rather bizarre way, said rogues' outrageous speeches which had roused such raging fury in his roiling heart … had also lit a rather surprising spark of satisfaction: Nandhini may have been a devious conspirator bent on Chozha destruction; a two-faced witch deceiving him with monstrous lies about eternal love—but not because of her infatuation with Karikalan, Kandamaaran or Vandhiyathevan! No, she had not betrayed her lord because she cared about those lecherous louts, those misbegotten *moudekans*, those curs! Her motives were pure, in a way: she had encouraged, flirted and spoken in such caressing style merely to use them towards her own, secretive ends …

… and the knowledge could not but soothe the hurt deep, deep down in his aching soul; the pain of horrifying treachery; the agony of spurned passion in his heart of hearts. Some little gratification this small revelation afforded. *Rescuing Karikalan from assassination is my inescapable duty not only to save my clan from irreparable ill-repute and my own self from irredeemable dishonour—but also to prevent Nandhini from descending into gory sin beyond reprieve. Why, I might even be able to turn her away from such a heinous mission; it could be that she is bent on such destruction because she is tangled in a web of these murderous maniacs' making—perhaps she has no choice, caught in their wretched toils … why not procure her freedom once and for all, by throttling these scoundrels?*

Such enervating thoughts were naturally productive of some uplifting of spirits; almost despite himself, the valiant *kizhavar* cleared his throat—a growl not unlike a lion's majestic roar that reached the conspirators … and startled them out of their wits.

"Who is it?" Parameswaran the Thevaralan barked. "Who's there?"

Aware that not only was there no more chance of concealment but also no purpose, Periya Pazhuvettarayar stepped out and revealed himself.

As the two Pandiya Abathudhavis stared, stupefied, at the tall, imposing figure suddenly looming from the shadowy gloom of a dark and stormy night, their nemesis—certainly, it could be nothing else—broke into loud, devilishly macabre cackles. "The elder brother of Yaman," it announced.

The accompanying laugh seemed to thunder about the entire forest, setting it trembling with dread.

The moment they realized the unnerving identity of the newcomer, Ravidasan and the Thevaralan sprang up, ready to take to their heels—not that Pazhuvettarayar would allow it, not for a moment; he caught them both easily, stretching out impossibly long arms—the *mandhiravadhi*'s neck with his right and the Thevaralan's shoulder with his left—and the two, in the grasp of limbs strong as Vajrayudham, found themselves struggling mightily, in absolute vain.

Herculean strength notwithstanding, Pazhuvettarayar, well aware that he could not hold onto both forever, flipped the Thevaralan in a way that made him flop to the floor head-first; placed a muscled leg firmly upon his back and leaning on it, began to strangle Ravidasan with two hefty hands.

Not that the Thevaralan stayed underfoot, happy to be trampled; with considerable difficulty, he eased out the dagger at his waist and pushed it upwards in a bid to stab his assailant's leg. Pazhuvettarayar, not unaware of his paltry attempts, promptly swung his other foot in a sharp kick at Parameswaran's wrist; the knife flew, clanging to the ground a good distance away.

The Thevaralan's hand flopped down at this attack, seemingly lifeless—but not before the squirming man realized that the foot keeping him clamped to the ground had slipped just a tad. Quick to seize his opportunity, he twisted and writhed until he was free, jumped up instantly and began to rain blows on Pazhuvettarayar with his uninjured arm—blows that felt, frankly, like he was pummeling a stone wall. The old man seemed to feel nothing; in fact, it was Parameswaran who felt his fist grow sore and worried that it might soon share the fate of his other, useless limb.

Ravidasan, meanwhile, had been straining every last nerve to unclamp the fingers around his throat, to no avail; the old man's iron grip relaxed not a whit. The *mandhiravaadhi* was rapidly approaching a state of collapse: his eyes began to start out of his head;

his tongue, thick and unwieldy, slurred the words. "Thevarala—quick—quick—climb—climb onto the temple spire and—and—push down the *mandapam*!"

His cohort instantly dashed away and leapt upon the upper level of the crumbling memorial to where a section of the *mandapam* appeared to have fractured, poised to crash down at the slightest excuse—a circumstance both had noticed and filed away for the future … a future that appeared to have arrived now, without warning, as the Thevaralan recognized Ravidasan's quavering hint. Positioning himself, he gathered what strength was left in him—and pushed against the precariously perched stones …

… which thundered to the ground with a deafening rumble, taking a nearby tree in tow.

Pazhuvettarayar, who comprehended what was happening, freed one hand from Ravidasan's neck and held it out in a vain bid to arrest the fall of the structure.

The *mandhiravaadhi* was swift to make use of this opportunity, twisting out of the old man's choke-hold, and leaping away in one swift bound.

Tree and trickily-balanced *mandapam* both crashed upon Pazhuvettarayar who crumpled to the ground, unconscious.

12

Disappearance of the Dhoomaketu

When Pazhuvettarayar finally regained consciousness after an interminable time—it was to a scene of unbelievable carnage and chaos.

Janajanajana—! clanged broadswords, thrumming as metal bruised metal; *Boom*—! thundered *perigais* elsewhere, to the rhythm of glory; *Maharajadhi Raja Pandiyar Vaazhga*! roared thousands upon thousands of voices; *Death to Pandiya foes*! screamed still more; *Run*, shrieked others—*Run, for the Ganga king has fallen*!; *Wait—stop*! rose shouts and cries in a vain bid to halt the deserters.

Abruptly, a hush descended upon the bloody battlefield. Pazhuvettarayar stared about … and witnessed that stalwart king Vijayalaya Chozhar, entering the lists despite the lack of legs—carried by a mighty man built along gigantic proportions. The veteran on his shoulder wielded two giant broadswords even as his mouth opened in a roar: "Stop, Chozha men; halt, Pallava warriors! Whether at six or at hundred, Death comes to us all—stay, stay here—gather at my side—follow my lead—together, we shall hack our foes into pieces!" That stentorian voice and its heartening message was not without effect: men—Chozha and Pallava alike—who had taken to their heels, running helter-skelter in every which direction slowed; the disappointment, despair and sheer, mind-numbing panic that had dulled senses and weakened limbs slowly receded, to be replaced by grit, valour and a newfound exhilaration at the sight and sound of their king. Soldiers who had stumbled in retreat now swung around, regrouped and began to advance.

Pazhuvettarayar turned, once more, to stare at the remarkable catalyst to this marvelous transformation. Then, his eyes swiveled despite himself to the man who hefted him—ah, wait, wait—who was this but—oh, wonder of wonders; it was none other than himself! He—the other Pazhuvettarayar—balanced Vijayalaya Chozhar with one hand and with sword held in the other, plunged through a sea of enemies ... and wherever the dynamic duo went, Pandiya heads simply rolled off shoulders and onto the bloody, torn-up ground.

Battle had turned indeed: now, it was the Pandiya *sainyam* that turned tail in retreat while the Chozhas and Pallavas harried after in pursuit; all eight directions reverberated as *jaya perigais* thundered in triumphant, magnificent victory. Ahead of even the Pallava Chakravarthy sat Vijayalaya Chozhar, occupying pride of place while the Pazhuvoor lord stood by his side. "Great warrior among warriors," the suzerain addressed the vassal. "Today, your indomitable courage turned humiliating defeat into honourable victory; Chozha Nadu is now an independent kingdom, divested of the bonds of serfdom; you, your valiant son Aditha Chozhan and all your descendents shall henceforth rule over your own *rajyam* as free rulers bound to none!"

The Chozha king turned at once to his faithful ally. "*Athaan*," he addressed Pazhuvettarayar by the affectionate term for a cousin, his aunt's son. "Yours is the hand that won us our land; you shall be the Chozha *Senathipathi* and *Dhanaadhikaari*—and so shall your sons, for as long as they claim fealty to me and mine," he declared—and the Pazhuvoor lord's face, lined and scored by battle-scars, brightened with pride.

But then …

… then, the ancestor's radiant countenance clouded over; its contentment marred by sheer, unadulterated fury as they rested on that of his descendent. "You despicable cur," he spat. "Rogue—scoundrel—treacherous, misbegotten rat! An ax-handle born to betray your own blood! You—you have …" His eyes bored into the younger's like gimlets. "Ruined and reduced to dust our clan's reputation, honour and goodwill, hard-earned over six generations! Descended to such depraved depths as to forsake your friends, your lord and master! Abandoned much-vaunted principles to throw your home open to sworn Chozha foes! Committed the unforgivable crime of distributing your own treasure to vengeful villains! Are you not the sole reason for the Chozhas' imminent, utter annihilation? Have you not heaped disgrace and dishonour upon us all for eternity? Will not this humiliation smear our lineage for as long as the earth endures? This infamy shall never pass—never—never—never!" The older man cursed, tears coursing down his weathered cheeks.

Several other Pazhuvettarayars from various generations followed in swift succession, each recounting their own deeds of valour and loyalty; each denouncing his treachery and perfidy; all showering a litany of curses: "*Chandaalaa*! You paltry excuse for a lord—you *kuladhrogi—rajadhrogi*! Have you no shame for having ruined the reputation and honour reaped by each one us; the goodwill and glory towards which we gave our lives? Where have your wits gone begging?"

His ancestors vanished in a mist of opprobrium; a whole host of Kodumbalur Velirs and Thirukkovilur Malayamans took their place: "*Chee*, you pitiful waste of a man! Those endless boasts about you and your clan being the solid foundation upon which rested the entirety of the Chozhas—what of them all, now? Surely you are now the Yaman that stalks and not the Guardian that serves? Ah, you traitor," they mocked. "What of your stateliness and prestige now? What of your famed honour?"

And then … then came the worst of all for in the wake of his staunchest enemies followed the people of Chozha Nadu, hordes of men and women who gathered stones and mud in their hands—and began to fling them upon him. But then …

… then arrived Sundara Chozha Chakravarthy.

He weaved through the unruly crowds, stumbling on unsteady legs, glaring at the Velirs, Malayamans and others as he passed them. "*Chee*, what detestable acts are these? How could you fling rubbish on this warrior among warriors, upon Pazhuvettarayar himself? How dare you abuse him as a traitor?" He drew up his weakened body, suddenly appearing a figure of majesty. "I care not if I and mine are destroyed because of his so-called betrayal, but none of you have cause to heap such baseless allegations upon him. Now, *Dhanaadhikaari*," he turned to the bowed Pazhuvoor lord. "You shall accompany me to the palace!" Both subjects and king then promptly vanished in a smoke of vague contrition and comprehension, leaving behind …

… Kalanthaka Kantar. "Did you see hear the Emperor, *Anna*?" He demanded, stepping forward. "Such faith, such belief in our clan's devotion—how could we betray him? How could we—how could you harbour in your own palace a vile, vicious woman, a witch, a ghoul bent on destroying his dynasty?" He too, disappeared in a cloud of disapproval, ushering in …

… Vandhiyathevan, Kandamaaran and a crowd of youngsters of their own ilk, who were swift to surround Periya Pazhuvettarayar. "Well, *kizhava*? Your grisly moustache might have grayed but your lechery and lust haven't, have they?" They cackled. "Romance has ruined you, hasn't it? Ah, those sixty-four wounds that decorate your body; what say they, now? Are they battle-scars that proclaim your unmatched valour—or wriggling worms that declare your pay for ultimate betrayal?" Too much, too much, the mocking snorts and taunting snickers; he moved to whip out his trusty broadsword to take their sneering heads off their shoulders … but alas! No blade hung at his waist.

It was now Kundhavai Piratti's turn to make an appearance. The dainty princess waved a dignified hand, silencing the sniggering youths at once. "*Paatta*," she addressed the old man. "Ignore their ridiculous remarks. Drive out the deadly cobra masquerading as a damsel in your palace, and all will be well," she counseled sweetly.

They disappeared as one—and it was now the turn of generations of Pazhuvoor women to appear: tens, hundreds, thousands of them! Six generations of womenfolk surrounded him on all sides. "*Ayyayo*!" They shrieked in heartrending anguish as one. "Must this be your fate? Must all the glory earned by our valiant clan be reduced to nothing? Must our lineage crumble under the weight of your heinous sin? Did we not send all our husbands, elder brothers, younger brothers and even our very own sons, borne for ten months to the battlefield for Chozha Nadu? Did not our brave men shed blood, sacrifice their lives for the Pazhuvoor clan? Did they not win magnificent glory and add splendid luster to our name? And now you—" they wailed. "Haven't you ground everything to the dust in a bare moment?"

"Retreat to the *anthappuram*, good women," the words seemed almost strangled but Pazhuvettarayar managed to utter them with considerable difficulty. "No blame shall attach to us on my account …"

Said women simply turned and pointed as one—and from that direction approached the Lord of Death, Yama Dharmarajan Himself upon his mammoth mount of a buffalo, a spear in one hand and the rope of souls in another. "My thanks to you, Pazhuvettaraya," he rumbled as he passed the old man with supreme nonchalance. "Have you not performed a wondrous service in assisting me to seize the souls of Sundara Chozhan and his two sons at the same time? I owe you gratitude—"

"No—I have not!" Pazhuvettarayar screamed at the top of his lungs. "Stop—halt—I did not help—I will stop you—Yama—stop—***stop***!"

He rushed forward to bar the celestial being—but could not. Something, some power seemed to be dragging him back; some terrible weight appeared to be shoving him to the depths. He could not move—could not take a step—could not budge an inch from where he stood.

"Ah, we were right!" The Pazhuvoor women screamed and lamented. "See—witness your plight!" They wailed again, some sobbing and weeping while still others shook and groaned in terrible, wrenching grief.

Too much—too much—these cries and shrieks were too much—they blasted through the air and tore at his ears and plunged into his heart—too much! Unable to bear a moment more of this torturous anguish, Pazhuvettarayar tried to speak … but the women's wails drowned out his feeble expostulations. The tormented voices rose, rose and rose; no, he could not take any more of this—Pazhuvettarayar tried to clap his hands over his ears … but could not. His arms simply would not move. They lay where they were, still and lifeless.

Gathering what strength he had left, Pazhuvettarayar drew a deep breath, finally shook his hands free—and found his eyelids snapping open. Simultaneously, consciousness returned and with it the heartening realization that all the scenes, shouts and horrifying tableaus from a while ago had merely been borne of dreadful hallucinations. The lament remained, though, still ringing appallingly in his ears; a howling, shrieking lament that would not cease. But wait, these were not the anguished screams of women but …

… the terrifying yowls of jackals!

Abruptly, fragments of the conversation that had fallen on his ears as he was slipping into unconsciousness swam to the surface of his murky mind.

The kizhavan is finally dead, said one voice.

You'd better make sure of it. Pazhuvettarayan's hold on life is remarkable; even Yaman is terrified of approaching him … trailed away the second.

Death might, but deadly jackals won't; they'll take care of what little life remains. By dawn, there'll be nothing left but a heap of bones picked clean, the first asserted.

At a good time, sighed the second. *When you shoved the splintered mandapam, I mean. Else, it would be me enduring this fate and the kizhavan would have strangled me—*

Try and move the stones, will you? May as well check if we can—

Moments later, *No—not an inch; there's no budging this pile,* came the mandhiravaadhi's relieved voice. *Well, would you look at that? We've actually managed to build one a herostone out of another's memorial!* And he broke into appreciative cackles.

That's enough of your mirth, cut in the first voice, exasperated. *Come! Any more delays and the boat's going to fly off its moorings in this wind; there'll be no crossing the Kollidam, mind!*

Their speech now fresh in his memory, Pazhuvettarayar took stock of his surroundings and his own perilous state—making the daunting discovery that a part of the structure had indeed fallen on him … and it was this massive weight pinning him to the ground—

—but wait.

How was it that he could still breathe?

Well, thank heavens for small mercies as the tree had crashed on to him first and then the *mandapam* on top; the trunk had, in effect, saved his life. Had the memorial tumbled on him directly, his chest and skull would have been crushed instantly.

With relieved gratification arrived surprised comprehension at his body's sheer endurance and incredible stamina—both of which had ensured his survival in the face of such a debilitating, suffocating weight. Certainly, his grasp on life was exceptional, but would it continue to be so? Was it in him to hold on for the foreseeable future?

Indeed, there was no question or choice; it would have to be. He must and should endure. Endure, and ensure that he stopped the ruin that stared the Chozhas in the face. Stop their annihilation, else the other eventuality—eternal damnation to him and his clan—was a certainty. And that certainty—one that would earn for him his ancestors' blistering curses and righteous wrath at his ignominious failure—was one that ought not to ever transcend from possibility to reality. All of which meant that this tree and the *mandapam* atop must be removed at any and every cost. Panic could not but course through his beleaguered veins at the very idea. *Ayyo, how long have I have been trapped underneath? There is no way to gauge the passage of time; what if every event I have been anxious about has already occurred?*

Meanwhile, the jackals' yowls sounded closer and closer; why, he could practically hear their raspy breath above his head! Ah, was he of so little account—was he such a weak, paltry thing that even petty animals began to nose around him for a snack? Ha, he would see about that—he would make sure they knew better—he would take a hand in the proceedings with relish—!

In the event, Pazhuvettarayar took more than a hand; he took both. Gathering every last scrap of strength he possessed, he sucked in as much of a breath as he could—and pushed. Pushed the tree on his shoulders and thereby, the stones above. Such was the humongous pressure he exerted that the heavy trunk actually began to rise, inch by agonizing inch—and with it, massive chunks of stone which moved and soon, slid off. ***Hoongh—hoongh***! whooshed his heavy, stertorous breathing which produced one excellent side-effect: they sent the sniffing jackals scurrying hotfoot.

Finally, finally, after a *naazhigai* that seemed like an endless *yugam*, an aeon, tree and stone that had well-nigh shackled him to the ground finally shifted enough to release him … and Pazhuvettarayar simply lay there for a while, inert from the exhaustion, heaving great, deep breaths, savouring the sweet, sweet taste of freedom.

His eyes travelled upwards. The *mandapam*'s collapse and the wholesale tree-fall in the wretched cyclone meant that his view was more or less unobstructed—and the sky spread above in a vast expanse, clear of dark, roiling storm clouds. Now stars twinkled merrily, as though some divine hand had strewn fistfuls of diamonds across the heavens, only now and then concealed behind wispy, ethereal clouds hardly worth the name, scudding by swiftly, soundlessly within moments.

Suddenly, something caught his eye—a rather unusual star in the northern sky—why, why … this was the comet, wasn't it? Was it the *dhoomakethu* indeed, that celestial object with an impossibly long tail—now, just a small pinprick of light? Now, trailed by a small puff of what seemed like a mere foot of unsubstantial smoke? A comet that had, even ten days ago, nearly consumed a vast section of the sky, now diminished to such miniscule proportions—why? What on earth could it mean? What possible explanation could there be? Puzzled, he removed his sight from the sky and swiveled his gaze here, there, everywhere on the ground …

… and realized that the jackals were still there.

Ten, twenty, fifty of the snarling, slavering predators, sniffing and snorting, their cruel eyes glowing like burning embers in the forest's dreadful darkness—waiting, no doubt for the *kizhavan* to breathe his last … ah, well. At least they had the decency to show Pazhuvettarayar some deference, at any rate.

Abruptly sky, earth and the entire forested region were bathed in a brilliant flash of light—light that nearly blinded the Pazhuvoor lord, who blinked rapidly. That certainly was not lightning; what else could it be? His eyes, now regaining vision scanned the heavens … to see a dazzling streak blazing across the expanse at an angle; so dazzling that he had to close his eyes again for a fraction—but which, when he re-opened them, had diminished and kept diminishing rapidly with every passing moment until—there! It was gone—vanished—disappeared as though it had never existed, and pitch blackness clothed the area, once more.

What on earth could this phenomenon possibly be, Pazhuvettarayar wondered, peering into the sky once more, gazing at where the vastly reduced comet had shimmered before—only to make an astonishing discovery.

The *dhoomakethu* was no longer there.

Aha, so it has fallen! What now? He gabbled to himself. *What is the significance of this?* Nothing but disaster and devastation on a cosmic level. A sign, a divine portent that calamity awaited royals; that someone, some member of the ruling family was about to die a horrible death. That, at least, was the long-held, powerful belief among people, although there were those that argued that this was merely fanciful superstition. Well, its truth or otherwise would be established on the morrow … wait, tomorrow? Or today? This very day for ah, over there—dawn was breaking over the eastern skies; sunrise was imminent … *and by tonight, three assassinations were likely to occur in three different locations; assassinations that only I have knowledge of—and therefore only I have the power to prevent. And if I did—if I did, why, then I would have defeated the ill-effects, the cosmic catastrophe that is the consequence of a dhoomakethu's dreaded fall! But if I don't …*

… no, he could not even consider such an appalling possibility.

But I must, he swore to himself. *I must and shall stop their executions—I shall preserve three Chozha lives at all costs—and first amongst those is Aditha Karikalan's—the most important, the most significant, for any danger to him will be my own downfall. I must cross the Kollidam right now and return to Kadambur but before I do, it is as important to send swift warnings from Kudanthai to Thanjai and Naagai and after … well, all shall be as fate wills. So much I can do, but only so much and no more.*

Having resolved upon his duty, Pazhuvettarayar rose—or rather, attempted to rise for every inch of his battered body, every pore, was a mass of pain. Where the tree had crashed, his entire chest flared with almost unbearable agony. One leg felt as though it had been fractured while bruises littered his entire frame.

Not that the valiant *kizhavar* cared in the slightest. He gritted his strong teeth, paused a moment and with one deep breath and great effort, straightened to his full height. Then, he stared around. Thankfully, the prowling jackals had given him up as a lost cause and retreated—or, even more likely, had been terrified into the gloomy forest by the blinding radiance of the falling *dhoomakethu.*

Estimating the approximate direction in which Kudanthai lay, he began to walk steadily, placing one aching foot in front of the other in a determined gait.

His path was littered liberally with trees uprooted courtesy the storm and regions inundated by the Kollidam's broken banks—

but Pazhuvettarayar cared not a jot for either ruined landscape or bloated rivers; heart's endless turmoil effectively drowned out by the body's hundred ills. Still, time hastened entirely too quickly for his liking and it was eventually almost two *jaamams* after daybreak when he finally neared his destination. Making an incursion into the magnificent city's *madhya pradhesam*, its heart out of the question; his very state would prompt people to surge around him in moments and pelt a thousand questions—questions he would be hard put to answer and which would, moreover, preclude the accomplishment of his mammoth missions with the speed and consummate skill they demanded.

No, he would have to pause in some sparsely inhabited section before the city borders, catch hold of someone to send palm-leaves to Thanjai and Naagai—and then employ a vehicle of some sort to carry him to Kadambur. Then, he remembered something—

—the astrologer in the vicinity of the Durgaiyamman shrine.

Why, yes ... not only was his residence in an isolated region with next to no homes nearby, but the man himself was a dignified personality, possessed of an amiable nature and excellent character. In addition to these sterling qualities was the fact that he was the confidante of the royal family and the Mudhanmandhiri ... what of it, though? Anyone would be eager to render assistance in a circumstance such as this; more so, if they happened to be on warm terms with the royals. Also ... ah! As good a time as any to confirm if the astrologer was, in truth, an expert in his field—and if *jothidam* itself was as accurate a science as it claimed to be.

Accordingly, Pazhuvettarayar approached the *Amman* shrine and the astrologer's home gingerly, his tired eyes first taking in the giant tree upended by the storm and then—an ornate chariot harnessed with two horses.

He paused at the sight, the strangeness accentuated by the bizarre structure of said chariot, whose upper section literally consisted of a boat. Vessels like these, he knew, were often employed during emergencies involving travel during floods; if, while crossing bloated rivers, the waters rose without warning the boat could simply be detached; the horses would be released from harness that they might swim to shore while the boat might carry the passengers to safety.

As accommodating as they were, chariots like these were rather rare in Chozha Nadu; whose was this one? Possibly a property of either the palace or the chief minister—and its occupants were likely within the *jothidar*'s home this very moment, seeking predictions. Now, who could they be? *Dare I ask the charioteer—no, no, as well send him into a spiral of panic; I shall simply barge in and see for myself. Whoever it is, I could beg and plead to borrow the chariot for Kadambur, couldn't I?*

He was almost at the astrologer's door … when, from within floated out voices; feminine voices—and Pazhuvettarayar reared back, startled. Why—why, it almost sounded like …

… Ilaiya Piratti Kundhavai.

What on earth was *she* doing here? And why choose *this* of all times, to put in an appearance?

An instant later, he revised his rather precipitate reflections; it might not be unwelcome at all, her sudden visit—in fact, this could be an excellent turn of events; the fruit slipping into the milk, as the saying went. Informing her of all that had transpired would be lifting a crushing weight off his chest; dropping just a hint of the unimaginable peril that encroached upon her father and younger brother would be more than enough for that wise young woman, intelligent beyond her years, to take the required precautionary measures. *And then I could leave for Kadambur with a light heart; surely there lies the most important of all my duties?*

His entrance upon the *jothidar*'s threshold resembled that of another's bold and brassy one a few months in at least one respect:

the same guard stepped forward once more and barred his way—being singularly unable to recognize the battered old man in all his dirt and bruises. Hence the stentorian bellow of "***Stop***!" that would have frozen a lesser man in his tracks …

…which Pazhuvettarayar was not. With a ***hoongh***! that might have put a massive bull to the blush, he grabbed the man by the scruff of his neck, and gave a hearty push. Such was its force that the disciple somersaulted into the street and sprawled on his back.

Meanwhile, ground shuddering as though under the gargantuan feet of a mammoth, the Pazhuvoor lord stalked forth and entered the astrologer's dwelling.

13

Kundhavai Seeks a Boon

Kundhavai Piratti and Vanathi were indeed the *jothidar*'s guests when Pazhuvettarayar effected an unexpected entrance into the modest residence.

If Eezham Rani's disappearance that dawn had destroyed what remained of the princess's already fragile tranquility, Poonguzhali's mysterious and simultaneous vanishing had escalated her almost unbearable unease. A visit to the Mudhanmandhiri had revealed the receipt of a communiqué concerning Arulmozhi: the severe storm in Naagai had revealed his presence and the good citizens, overjoyed with the unforeseen disclosure, were now surging alongside him towards Thanjai in uproarious procession.

It was virtually her undoing, this report; her agitation now knew no bounds. Disaster was afoot, she felt certain; nothing good could come out of exposure at this juncture. It behooved her to waylay Ponniyin Selvan somewhere on his journey and relay all that had transpired in Thanjai. Other reasons too were there, for her decision: should he attempt a grand entrance into the capital surrounded by screaming hordes, the Pazhuvettarayars would throw in all their considerable might to bar him. News had reached her, meanwhile, of Boodhi Vikrama Kesari having marched as far as Kodumbalur, a massive southern army in tow—and the chances of both armies clashing in the vicinity of Thanjai were too great to ignore. Her father's heart was sure to be torn by an anguish that might imperil his very life … and who knew what other, devastating consequences were in the offing? Chozha souls were already writhing under the lash of the catastrophic cyclone, the embers of their discontent seething, smouldering, seeking an excuse, some paltry reason to explode into a roaring inferno—an inferno of civil war that would ruin the entire *rajyam*; a war that once began, could hardly be called to a simple halt. Rather than let matters unravel to such an irreparable extent, wouldn't it answer more to the purpose to prevent such an appalling eventuality from even occurring, in the first place? Else every effort thus far, every excruciating attempt to steer the course of events would have been in vain—yes, she'd have to halt Arulmozhi's journey and hold him in Pazhaiyarai for a while at least; bid Periya Pazhuvettarayar from Kadambur, if possible; convince him that her younger brother had neither desire nor intention to rule; receive the older man's consent and then—only then could she escort her *Thambi* to Thanjai.

Having resolved matters thus to herself she set off—Vanathi following substance like shadow—not even informing her beloved father of her hasty departure but only taking her mother and Aniruddhar into her confidence.

Before Pazhaiyarai, however, there was somewhere else she wished to go; someone else she hoped to visit once more: the Kudanthai astrologer. After all, it is but natural to seek cosmic assistance, some celestial solace about the future during times of extraordinary distress, isn't it?

Asking that the chariot be parked by the *Amman* shrine as was her wont, she entered the humble dwelling and had only just begun to recount her considerable trials—when, from outside came the raucous cacophony of some commotion, and then she heard something that made her skin prickle with goose-bumps …

… a ***hoongh***!

An unmistakable harbinger of the *Dhanaadhikaari* himself; none but Periya Pazhuvettarayar possessed such a majestic snort—Pazhuvettarayar, who seemed to be thrusting aside the disciple outside in a bid to enter.

How on earth did he get here? Why—especially at this, of all times—ah, was he too here for predictions? And if that was the purpose of his visit, I could divine his state of mind by listening to his conversation with the astrologer, she theorized. *Certainly it would be a convenience to comprehend Periya Pazhuvettarayar's thought processes at a moment that portended calamity for the rajyam and the royal family wholesale. Here indeed, is an excellent, heaven-sent opportunity … in which case, catching sight of me and Vanathi might prove problematic. What might be his sentiments? What would he think; what conclusions would he draw—why, doubtless, all the wrong ones. My best course of action at this point would be to conceal myself from his sight …*

… which Kundhavai promptly did, having telegraphed her intentions to the astonished astrologer, grabbing Vanathi by the hands and hastily vanishing into the adjacent chamber.

The door had barely closed behind them when Pazhuvettarayar entered with a heavy tread.

The *jothidar* scrambled to his feet, wide-eyed, hands folded with deference—while his esteemed guest leveled a hard stare at him, staring round and about almost simultaneously. Judging by the way his face fell, surprise and dismay flitting across his grim features, he found not what he sought. Only for an instant, though: the warrior was too much a veteran of worldly affairs to reveal his emotions; he schooled his countenance into an emotionless mask the next instant. "Do you know me, *jothidar*?" he barked at his hapless host. "It is I, *Dhanaadhikaari* Periya Pazhuvettarayan in the flesh—ha, why do you gawp so? Surely I have not changed beyond recognition … now, I have great need of you—I require your assistance for an extremely important task. But first, get me some food; I am famished beyond belief. I shall explain everything as I eat," he finished.

"*Ayya*, what—what possible aid could this poor servant render the likes of you?" Most uncharacteristically, the astrologer stuttered and stammered. "Blessed must have been my forefathers to have you seek out this petty hut! Alas that I find myself unable to present you with the sumptuous feast your exalted status deserves but everything in this humble abode is yours for the taking, believe me. Ah, to see you stand, thus—pray, *pray* take a seat—forgive me, forgive me, great lord, for not having extended the hospitality that is your due right away; it is just that I was taken aback at your sudden arrival—ah, this pathetic servant's pitiful dwelling does not even possess a seat worthy of your distinguished self—I must beg your gracious indulgence to sit upon these *peedams*," he flustered about, gesturing to the simple wooden planks Kundhavai and Vanathi had occupied bare moments earlier.

For one long moment, Pazhuvettarayar gazed intently at the aforesaid seats and the fragrant flowers strewn around them. "No, *jothidar*, I shall not; I have neither the time nor inclination to sit down to a leisurely meal—rather pack in a leaf what you can spare in the way of food; I must send a message this very moment to my brother Kalanthaka Kantan in Thanjai; if you could procure an *olai* and quill, I shall … wait, no! I cannot spare the time to write elaborate missives either—" he turned to the astrologer. "Could you travel to the capital at once with my signet ring? Or, stay—your disciple at the entrance seems a hefty, well-muscled fellow—could you dispatch him with all possible haste?"

"These and whatever your other commands I shall fulfill, my lord—both I and my disciple if that pleases you—but *Dhanaathipathi*, I insist, nay, I beg and plead your illustrious self to tarry awhile in this poor servant's hut, and partake of my humble hospitality before you leave—!"

"Your sentiments do you credit, *jothidar* but pray, why demean yourself often and anon with these pathetic epithets—especially when word is that kings and princesses step gladly into this humble hut, as you phrase it … in fact, if there is one among the motley crew who has not sought your predictions, it is I—a grievous error, a lapse of judgment I see now, for if I had … perhaps none of the dreadful calamities, the devastating catastrophes that stare us in the face might have never been—"

"Your words worry me greatly, *Ayya*; what calamities? What catastrophes? True indeed that I was startled at the sight you presented—were you tormented by the cyclone and floods? I heard reports that the Kollidam had broken its banks; was that the reason for—good God, *Dhanaathipathi*, the Ilaiya Rani—does she fare well?"

A wild bark of terrifying laughter escaped Pazhuvettarayar at the astrologer's welter of questions. "Nothing has befallen the young queen of Pazhuvoor; nothing at all! She has neither been drenched by the downpour nor drowned in the floods; safe and snug she lies in the Kadambur palace as far as I know—but whether that wretched *chandaali* shall remain thus by this time tomorrow, I cannot say … could *you*, *jothidar*? Would they be true, the reports I have heard about the numerous royal horoscopes you hoard? Nandhini—that evil witch, that *mohini*, the ghoul I was fool enough to lose my head over and wed in my dotage—you do not, by any chance, possess her *jaathakam* too, do you?"

"Good God, *Dhanaathipathi*, what appalling words are these? Do you—can you possibly be testing me?" The astrologer's voice shook perceptibly as his anxiety ratcheted several notches. "I am afraid I do not possess the Ilaiya Rani's horoscope—although it may not be outside the realm of possibility to draw one, if you would graciously provide me with her date and time of birth," he offered, timidly.

"Unnecessary; I can perform that measly task myself—for I have assumed control over her life-span and longevity by determining her death at my own hands. Tell me, rather, of your predictions for others: what is the Chakravarthy's future likely to be? What of his life—ah, you shake your head; you will not reveal a thing for you believe me to be putting you on trial. Or perhaps the entirety of your area of expertise is a sham and *jothidam*, the sphere of charlatans; who knows? Horoscopes aside, however … did you know that the *dhoomakethu* fell from sky to earth this morning, having haunted the heavens for months? And if you did, could you possibly reveal the significance of such a cosmic event? Is it an ominous portent? A foretelling of grievous disaster? Does it augur misfortune for the Chakravarthy and his children? Should you refuse to answer these questions, your science is nothing but a carefully packaged sheaf of lies!"

"Pray, *pray* do not arrive at such hasty conclusions, *Dhanaathipathi*. I must beg leave here to inform you that tradition—custom that has been handed down generations of astrologers—dictates that predictions ought not to be made when it comes to royal affairs. To answer your question about the comet—no, I did not actually see it fall, although I did register a blinding flash of light and was astonished enough to step out and investigate. The *dhoomakethu*, whose tail had been shrinking for a while, was nowhere to be seen. Word is that the appearance and disappearance of such a celestial object portends affliction and adversity to the royal family—but such a prediction belongs not to the realm of astrology but rather, long-held popular belief. Not that I subscribe to such, believe me, for I learnt that even as of this morning, the Chakravarthy enjoyed good health."

"That, indeed, is an excellent stroke of luck; one that I hope holds good tonight for if he survives until tomorrow, there shall be no further cause for anxiety. And—what know you of Ponniyin Selvan?"

"Only that he has reached as far as Thiruvaarur, very late last night, *Ayya*—that he was being surrounded by a heaving mass of thousand, ten thousand, a lakh even—dragging him to Thanjai against his will—"

"Ah, how fortunate if those surging crowds actually manage to accomplish their mission and carry him to safety … but could they? Could millions, thronging their lord on all sides possibly halt the progress of Yaman? Tell me, *jothidar*—tell me, you who profess to predict the future—speak! Or if you will not, *I* shall: great danger awaits the Chakravarthy and his two sons this very day—grave peril, grievous ill for Yama Dharman stalks them, approaching closer, closer with every step: the Emperor's Death crouches in the subterranean treasury vault of the Pazhuvoor palace; Arulmozhi's Death hides upon the tip of his mahout's goad—and the onerous responsibility of halting them and saving both father and son is yours! Your disciple may journey to Thanjai with my signet ring while you hurry to Thiruvaarur with a warning for Ponniyin Selvan. Now, will you do this? Will you go? Will you start at once and stop Death in its terrible tracks?"

His auditor found himself floundering in a veritable sea of confusion. A faint suspicion about Pazhuvettarayar's mental health reared its head; could the man possibly be suffering from *sithabramai*? No, that did not seem likely, since words followed thought and thought, fairly sane reasoning. In the awe-inspiring grip of wrath and turmoil he might be, but every utterance appeared to ring with conviction; resonate with truth. Well, doubtless, every syllable had fallen on the ears of Ilaiya Piratti next door; her opinion ought to be divined but first ... this *kizhavan* ought to be packed off, right away. "With Durga Parameswari's bountiful grace, I shall contrive to fulfill your commands to the best of my ability," he promised.

His speech was accompanied by the mellifluous tinkling of feminine anklets.

"Aha, there sound Her celestial *silambu* ornaments; it would seem that the Goddess has indeed signified assent by tapping her feet. I can depart for Kadambur now with a light heart and relieved mind. Give me leave—"

"But you mentioned that you were famished; if you could only accept my humble fare—"

"No, no, not at all; every vestige of my hunger and thirst have flown and I too must fly, fly to Sambuvaraiyar's palace ... that chariot by the temple; whose is it? I shall commandeer the vehicle and return it when I am at the Kollidam—once I have detached the boat, of course—"

"*Ayya*, that chariot—" the astrologer fumbled and faltered. "That *radham*—oh pray, *pray* do not seize it—I must beg of you, for my sake—I crave mercy upon this pitiful self—"

"This overwhelming display of emotion—! Unnecessary, *jothidar*, for I covet this chariot for only one reason: to save the crown prince of Chozha Nadu—an intention and act that I am sure will have the blessings of the divine Durga Parameswari ... which she will signify by sounding Her anklets again and by this shall I know Her will—hark!"

Indeed, even as he spoke, Ilaiya Piratti Kundhavai opened the door to the chamber adjacent, stepped out, and walked with dainty steps forward, her *silambu* ornaments tinkling gently, melodiously, with every step.

Her entrance seemed not to faze Periya Pazhuvettarayar, who was neither surprised nor startled in the slightest at her sudden appearance. "Ah, my suspicions were not without foundation then," he remarked. "I guessed you might be in the next room, *Thaaye*, but alas, lacked the courage to see you—to raise my eyes to your gaze—which is why I spoke in tones loud enough to breach walls." He paused. "You heard everything I told the astrologer, did you not?"

"I must beg forgiveness, *Ayya*," Kundhavai answered, contrite. "Pardon my transgressions—your sudden arrival here plunged me into confusion; I wasn't even sure of your identity—which is why I was forced to eavesdrop upon your conversation. I ask pardon again—"

"Nothing you have done requires such, *Thaaye*; rather, it is I who must crave forgiveness—in fact, I wonder if I am even worthy of so doing. Perhaps I shall be, if I manage to reach Kadambur by tonight and save the crown prince from his fate. For see you ..." he paused, almost overcome. "Three years were this *kizhavan*'s eyes firmly closed, confined to darkness by black lust, by despicable *mohaanthakaaram*; you moved heaven and earth to return my vision—dropped endless hints to restore sight ... not that any stratagem worked in the slightest. You were not the only one; my brother Kalanthaka Kantan worked tirelessly as well to open my eyes but his efforts were to no avail either. But last night—last night, Durga Parameswari achieved what you could not; Her divine grace made it possible for me to overhear the heinous conversation of two Pandiya plotters—and the truth finally dawned; that I had harboured, nay nourished, cherished, lavished love, loyalty and affection on a dreaded *chandaali*, a wretched conspirator, a wicked witch, a venomous cobra in my own palace. She moulded me into a betrayer of clan and king; a *kuladhrogi*, a *rajadroghi*—plundered Chozha treasury and distributed its wealth to Pandiya assassins! Until I wrap my fingers around that vile wench myself—squeeze the life out of her lying throat by tonight, the flames that scorch my heart shall not burn out—!"

Even as the words spluttered from rigid lips through gritted teeth, Kundhavai did something entirely unexpected: she bent …

… and prostrated full length at his feet.

Pazhuvettarayar paused mid-rant, thought and word frozen in stunned astonishment when she rose, deference limning every line of her body. "I crave your indulgence *Ayya*, in granting me a boon," she begged.

"Your highness appears to be testing me," the old man faltered, before regaining his characteristic control. "No—no, do not—for I have realized—ah, more than anyone the severity of my crimes; the terrifying consequences of my unthinking actions. My only priority now is to seek redemption; find a way to set things right … but before that, three members of the Chozha family must be saved from unimaginable peril this very day; your father and brothers ought to be rescued without a scratch on them. Aid me towards that end; wait just this one day and I shall come to you myself tomorrow, and ask, *What is my punishment? How may I cleanse my sins*?" He finished, voice throbbing with an abundance of feeling.

"Questions that I shan't answer and redemption I won't give—for I don't believe that I am worthy of granting either. You stand to me in the position of my grandfather and remain one who claims my father's reverence. No, *Ayya*, you must believe me when I say that I seek from you a boon, in all sincerity—"

"Ask what you will, then, with no more roundaboutation, for none of us have the luxury of time."

"Promise me that you will grant it."

"No recompense can redress the treachery I have perpetrated against you and yours—but by all means, I shall fulfill your wish, whatever it be. Come now, quick!"

"Then, this is the boon I seek." Kundhavai turned her level gaze upon him. "Give me your word that you shan't harm a hair on Ilaiya Rani Nandhini's head."

"*Amma* ..." Pazhuvettarayar stared back at her. "What on earth are you playing at? Is this indeed the moment to engage in childish games? I may have indeed lost my head in my dotage—but surely that is no reason to scramble what little wits I retain and turn me into a complete, blubbering idiot? How could I possibly ensure that the rest of those nefarious plotters come by their just desserts if I do not first levy upon Nandhini the punishment she deserves? No, I must and shall kill her with my own bare hands—after I have revealed to her my heart's turmoil and bludgeoned into hers that she never did manage to pull the wool completely over this *kizhavan*'s rheumy eyes and after—after ... I shall slay her with my broadsword, for anything less than such an execution would be beneath me; I would have failed to uphold honour and discharge my rightful duty. And then ... then I shall meditate upon what might be my own, rightful punishment. Therefore, go, my dear. Go; do what you can; strain every nerve to save your father and your brothers from the annihilation that awaits them today. Go—!"

"I will, *Ayya*—but surely my bounden duty extends to my sister as well? For Ilaiya Rani Nandhini is my blood ... and any harm you do her too, is betrayal to the Chozhas!"

For long moments Pazhuvettarayar stared at her, seemingly drowning in a sea of boundless astonishment. "Am I still sunk fathoms deep in dreams, perhaps?" His lips murmured, almost despite himself.

"No, you aren't; what you see and hear now is the clear, untarnished truth. Pray, *pray* bend your thoughts towards the past; recall incidents long gone," Kundhavai was insistent. "Think back to the day when my young brother Arulmozhi toppled into the Kaveri; do you remember a *maatharasi* saving him from a watery grave? She is the Ilaiya Rani's mother. Hark back to the day you escorted the young queen to the palace immediately after your wedding; do you remember my father falling unconscious? His reaction was rooted in the belief that he had seen Nandhini's mother, for he'd believed her to be dead all these years; hence his shock—"

Pazhuvettarayar did recall the incidents mentioned … along with certain others as well; incidents that seemed connected—such as one midnight when he had stood Nandhini before Sundara Chozha Chakravarthy, who had screamed in fear at the very sight of her … and toward which unnerving occurrence his beloved wife had supplied very creative explanations.

"I sense that you do not sport with me, *Thaaye*," he admitted, slowly. "Indeed, fate, it seems to me, is the one orchestrating this strangest of games for—for if the Ilaiya Rani is your *thamakkai*, then she is sister to Aditha Karikalan as well … wait, are you the only one aware of this truth? Who else knows about this? What about the Chakravarthy?"

"Until two days ago, my father believed that my *periyannai* was dead; he even mistook her for a ghost and flung a lamp at her head when she appeared unexpectedly. It was only much later could he be brought to comprehend reality …"

"That was not what I meant, *Amma*; does Aditha Karikalan know that the Ilaiya Rani is his sister?"

"He should, by now, for I dispatched a Vaanar warrior—one he'd sent me before with an *olai*—with the information."

"Aha, you refer to Vallavarayan Vandhiyathevan, I suppose?"

"Your supposition would be correct, *Ayya*."

"I am not so sure that he discharged his mission—and even if he had, unlikely that Karikalan believed him, for even I don't, to tell the truth. I doubt that the Ilaiya Rani knows this either. Not that it makes a difference whether she does or does not; the conspirators will simply find another means to carry out their fell intentions—this very night. But *Amma* …" Pazhuvettarayar sighed. "What you have revealed to me just now makes my responsibility even more terrifying; my duty more horrendous—for it now lies upon me to prevent Ilaiya Rani from commit that heinous sin, *sahodhara hathi*, murdering her own brother. I shall leave for Kadambur right away, in your chariot, of course. As for ensuring that the Chakravarthy and Ponniyin Selvan come to no harm …" he gazed intently at her. "That rests with you."

"You need entertain not the slightest apprehension, *Ayya*; I'm leaving for Thanjai this very moment—having decided to arrange for conveyance from Pazhaiyarai. Have no fear about Ponniyin Selvan either, for his date and time of birth shall act as powerful talismans and protect him."

"I trust you will disregard these so-called astrological predictions, my girl; do not throw caution to the winds, I beg of you, when it comes to your family's safety! Astrologers rarely reveal the truth even if they are aware of it and often spout vague nothing-sayings that could predict more than one outcome—and then, when the worst happens, promptly declare *Did I not say so*? Even if you must trust astrology …" he levelled a pointed stare at the *jothidar*. "Do not trust astrologers!" And with this last, damning Parthian shot, Pazhuvettarayar left like a rumbling whirlwind …

… allowing, bare moments later, for the entrance of Azhwarkkadiyaar. "An excellent sentiment with which I concur wholeheartedly," announced that worthy.

14

Vanathi's Vow

"Heavens!" Kundhavai marveled at this unlooked-for entrance of an unforeseen guest. "Where on earth have you sprung from, Thirumalai? Whatever for?"

"All a result of this duplicitous astrologer's deceitful predictions, *Ammani*. Would you believe it? I asked him only this morning, *Will my mission be a success*? He swore that it would—but how could that possibly be, when I couldn't budge even a step from here? Which explains my agreement with Pazhuvettarayar's finely expressed and strongly worded sentiment: is it that our *jothidar* is a fraud, or is *jothidam* itself the domain of charlatans? Hence my return—and hearing the Pazhuvoor lord's voice within confirmed my suspicions that it was likely the man at fault and not the science," Azhwarkkadiyaan explained. "But I didn't expect to see your highness here, in truth."

"It would've been beyond bizarre if you had. Be that as it may, what was the purpose of your visit? What mission was yours that required a prediction of success?" Kundhavai snapped out the questions. "You may share details, I hope? Surely they're not a secret?"

"There can exist no secret that cannot be revealed to you, surely? Merely that the Mudhanmandhiri dispatched me to Naagai last night upon the Chakravarthy's orders—to escort the prince home, of course. I was bidden to deliver an *olai* to Sembian Maadevi as well, on my way … when did you start from Thanjai, *Devi*?"

"A little after daybreak. Why do you ask?"

"Only to discover if Kodumbalur forces had surrounded the fort."

"Wait—***what***?"

"Indeed—why, didn't you know? Two reports awaited the Chief Minister when he returned home at the conclusion of his audience with the emperor: one, of course, was that the prince had embarked on his journey from Naagai, surging towards Thanjai amidst a sea of subjects …"

"A report I too, comprehended this morning; it was to stop him in his tracks that I set out, in the first place … but what was the second?"

Azhwarkkadiyaan's eyes swiveled from her to her companion. "*Amma*," he began, pointing a finger at Vanathi. "Was there a reason for bringing along the Kodumbalur princess?"

"Only habit, of course; she wished to accompany me, as always, and as always, I obliged. Is there a reason for your question?"

"There is." Thirumalai paused, as though to gather his thoughts. "But her presence makes it awkward for me to communicate the second piece of news—"

"An awkwardness you needn't feel; know you not that she is my most intimate confidante? She may be privy to anything I am," Kundhavai insisted.

"Nevertheless, it does concern the princess, here. The report received by the Mudhanmandhiri last night informed that the Senathipathi of the Southern Forces, Boodhi Vikrama Kesari was approaching Thanjai with all possible speed at the head of a massive armed force—in addition, there was an *olai* from the man in question himself, alleging that the Pazhuvettarayars had imprisoned the Emperor within the capital and the *ilango* in some other, unspecified, secret location. There was also a demand that the elder Pazhuvoor lord resign from his post as *Dhanaadhikari* and Chief of Thanjai Security, besides relinquishing the prince to safety—else, as of this evening the Chozha capital would be under siege … *Ammani*, were you truly not aware that Kodumbalur forces had already begun to march upon Thanjai from the south and the west?"

"No, not at all; the Mudhanmandhiri mentioned not a word of any of this—"

"If he had, likely you wouldn't have departed the fort nor the Kodumbalur princess removed hastily from the premises, which, I suspect, may have been his primary intention—"

"Why, though? What harm could her presence have caused?"

"Possible imprisonment by Chinna Pazhuvettarayar …"

"*Dare* he?" Kundhavai breathed. "Do you speak the truth, indeed?"

"Certainly, *Devi*. Furthermore, if only you were privy to the additional communiqués dispatched by the Chief of Southern Forces—"

"More of them? What else—what more?"

"Prince Arulmozhi Varmar and Kodumbalur princess Vanathi ought to be united in matrimony at once; since it appears to be Aditha

Karikalar's irrefutable intention to refuse the throne, Ponniyin Selvar ought to be announced the heir and his ascension recognized with a *yuvarajya pattabhishekam*. He's announced that *Should these stipulations not be followed to the letter, I shall raze down the Fort of Thanjai within three days*! Indicated, also, is the fact that any and every one of his decisions, whatever they might be, has the full and unconditional support of Chozha citizens."

"*Akka*," Vanathi, who had been listening to this peroration, wide-eyed, interjected. "Has my *periyappa* suddenly and inexplicably run mad?" Her tone throbbed with barely concealed wrath.

"I don't see any reason for annoyance, Vanathi—all he's done is divulge the hopes harboured by many for a long time … especially now that the Pazhuvettarayars have begun negotiations for Madhuranthaka Thevar to ascend the throne. I'm not surprised that the Kodumbalur king and Thirukkovilur Malayaman are revealing their heart's desire; allowing their ambitions into the open—"

"Indeed; the latter has likely already marched towards Kadambur with a phenomenal force of his own, *Thaaye*—at least, so I inferred from his conversation, corroborated by the report received by the Mudhanmandhiri—"

"But they couldn't possibly be aware of what I know now; I must, *must* speak to them and stop this internecine war from exploding—how, though, I don't quite know—"

"I'm afraid the situation has already gotten considerably out of hand; a war along the scale of the massive Mahabharatham shall and will occur at any moment—"

"Ah, you're right to equate it to the Kurukshethram, Thirumalai, for this conflict—if it ensues—will involve cousins, every ally a relation and shall escalate into a full-fledged war raining death and destruction on all! Hark, Vanathi: my grandfather's father, Paranthaka Chakravarthy, chose for himself a bride from the

Pazhuvoor clan; his daughter and my young grandmother married into the Kodumbalur family. My grandfather Arinjayar in turn took to wife a princess from the same clan while my father wedded a consort from the House of Thirukkovilur. You see, now, how all three of these ancient lineages have forged intimate bonds with ours over generations; have merged their blood, bone and flesh such that one can no longer be distinguished from the other? But now, these very kings and princes, who once clasped hand and heart in amity, now gird their loins for battle—ah, what am I to say of a fate that has brought them to this—this terrible, appalling war that will likely ruin the *rajyam*?"

"I couldn't care less about their friendship and fealty *Akka*; they might batter each other till the end of the world—but why must *periyappa* drag my name into this mess?" Vanathi raged. "I wish I could go to him this very instant and pick a quarrel—"

"An exercise in futility, I'm afraid, *Kanne*; he's likely to listen to neither your remonstrations nor our combined pleas; they never do, these *kizhavars* like your *periyappa*, to us mere girls … no, any hope of preventing this war from ever occurring in the first place rests with my *Thambi* Arulmozhi Varman—Thirumalai, having started on your journey, why return? And what news of my brother's current whereabouts?"

"Word is that he intended to leave Thiruvaarur last night, but had to postpone his departure owing to the completely flooded landscape—incidentally, the reason for why I couldn't proceed beyond Pazhaiyarai, as well, for the Kudumurutti, having broken banks into the bargain, is in full spate—"

"A deluge that must subside at some point and when it does, surely Arulmozhi's route must take him past here? We've no choice but to cool our heels, until then. My only anxiety is that nothing, no dreadful calamity must occur at Thanjai, meanwhile … Thirumalai," Kundhavai straightened. "I wonder if you couldn't possibly return to the capital with my message to the Kodumbalur king? That he oughtn't to besiege the fort until Arulmozhi arrives?"

"*Akka* …" Vanathi took a step forward. "May I accompany him?"

"But—to what purpose, Dearest?"

"Quarrel with my *periyappa*."

"What about? And do you believe, in truth, that he'd call a halt to hostilities at one word from you?"

"He might or mightn't; he might hack everyone he pleases and go on a rampage all the way to hell for all I care … but he mustn't and shouldn't drag my name into all this—*that* I shall insist on."

"Drag your name into everything? Whatever about?"

"Surely you haven't…" Vanathi lowered her head, suddenly overcome by bashfulness. "You haven't forgotten what this Veera Vaishnavite mentioned just moments ago?"

"Why, whatever did anyone say about—Thirumalai, what on earth did you mention regarding this young woman?" Kundhavai seemed all at sea.

"I believe she's referring to the report I communicated about the Senathipathi demanding the wedding of this maiden here to Ponniyin Selvar."

"But …" Kundhavai turned bewildered eyes upon her companion. "What possible objection could you possibly have to this scheme? You do wish to wed him, surely?"

"Why debate on whether I wish it or not? What does it matter? All I object to is my father elaborating and enlarging on marriage and coronation while making me the point of contention; implicating me in his plans—why, it's almost as though he's instigating a war to push me onto the Chozha throne—"

"Why, it's almost as though the Kodumbalur princess hates, loathes and detests the throne," rang out a female voice at this moment, and everyone whipped around to see the speaker—

—who happened to be Poonguzhali.

"Heavens, Girl," Kundhavai's gaze travelled up and down her form in astonishment. "How on earth did you turn up here? And there we were, hunting high and low for you and the Eezham Rani this morning … wait, where's your aunt?" She demanded.

"Forgive me *Devi*, for she dragged me through the Pazhuvoor palace's subterranean vault against my will and bundled me out of the fort. I imagine the very idea of my lingering there for even the space of a day was loathsome to her—as it was to me, I must admit. If the very notion of the *simmaasanam* could disgust the Kodumbalur princess—" Poonguzhali threw a sideling glance at that young woman. "Surely the very idea of palace-life would be repulsive to the rest of us?"

"Your answer has no relevance whatsoever to my question," Kundhavai's brows wrinkled. "Frankly, your mental state seems rather questionable—"

"Her state, mental or otherwise, has never been better, *Akka*; her only motive is to demean me," Vanathi flashed. "She's accusing me of nursing designs towards the Chozha throne—and that I wish to wed Ponniyin Selvar to become a Maharani and for no other reason! I see it all; her mind and her meaning—"

"*Paambin kaal paambariyum*, as the saying goes," Poonguzhali replied silkily, looking as though butter would not melt in her mouth. "I suppose a snake knows it own kind—"

"Stop—cease your squabbles this moment, girls; opportune words at an appropriate moment seems a skill lacking in both of you. Now," Kundhavai turned to the boat-girl. "Poonguzhali, where's your aunt?"

"In the Pazhuvoor palace's treasure vault."

"Why?"

"An assassin cowers in those subterranean caverns with a spear and—aha, *what* the two of us put him through at dawn," Poonguzhali spoke with some relish. "To think of him running helter-skelter through the cavern, out of his mind with sheer, mind-numbing terror—convinced that we were two ghouls out for his blood—" and she broke into merry peals of appreciative laughter.

Forget questionable mental states, this girl's certainly afflicted by sithabramai, Kundhavai mused, as she stared at her. "And? What next? Who was he? Why hide in the treasury? And how did you know all this?"

"I'm afraid I don't, *Devi*—but my aunt, devoid of either speech or hearing, possesses an amazing ability to comprehend secrets completely unknown to the rest of us. Somehow she realized, when none of us did, that the man was concealed in the subterranean cavern's shadows to assassinate someone in the palace. Do you remember when she attempted to break the hands of the ten-headed Raavanan?" Poonguzhali asked. "Could you guess her motive?"

"I couldn't but if you know, pray reveal it at once!"

"I know you decided that she was a *pichi*, a mad woman, when you glimpsed her trying to destroy the sculpture," Poonguzhali's eyes bored into those of the princess. "But my aunt's no lunatic—for, between Raavanan's hands exists the entrance to the secret passage leading straight to Pazhuvettarayar's treasure vault."

"Aha!" Kundhavai marveled. "Is that so, indeed?"

"And the answer, as well, to the puzzle of how the Eezham Rani entered the palace," Azhwarkkadiyaan quipped.

"All these years—and none of us even suspected the existence of a secret passage such as this," Ilaiya Piratti murmured. "Be that as it may, why didn't you return and inform us of all this? Why leave your aunt all alone?"

"Her stubbornness, I suppose. She insisted that she'd take care of the hiding excuse for man … and practically drove me out."

"What? But why—wait, was there something else? Another task far more important that she wished you to complete?"

"Yes, *Ammani*."

"And what would that be, my girl?"

"My aunt's marvelous extra sensory perception must have revealed to her, somehow, that Ponniyin Selvar too was in grave peril—and she sent me to wherever he was."

"Ah, so you were on your way to him … but if that be the case, why halt here?"

"No, I …" Poonguzhali paused. "I may as well confess the truth, I suppose: no longer do I care to embroil myself in these endless royal coils, *Devi*, nor interfere in palace affairs. I was on my way to Kodikkarai when this Veera Vaishnavite caught sight of me and insisted that I accompany him here—which I wouldn't have, had I suspected your presence."

"Well, really …" Kundhavai paused. "But why this sudden hatred towards palaces—indeed, towards us, my girl? What did anyone ever do to you that you harbour such hatred?"

"Nothing, *Ammani*; nothing has occurred and no one is responsible—and I cherish not the slightest resentment towards anyone. I suppose I detest royal life the same way some detest thrones …" Another sidelong glance at Vanathi and this time, Poonguzhali's short bark of laughter did not attempt to conceal her scorn. "That's it, really."

And that really seemed to be it … for Vanathi, forced, thus far, to speechless indignation, her face suffused with an agony of frustration stalked forward. "*Akka*!" She called out, wrath limning every inch of her body and finding release in an explosion of words. "She means to insult me all over again—but hark: I swear upon your blessed, divine feet—swear on the celestial *Akasavaani*, Spirit of the Skies and *Bhoomadevi*, Mother of all Earth—I swear to you here and now: should Ponniyin Selvar escape this horrendous, grievous peril; should he condescend, with all his pure heart, to take this pitiful hand of mine in marriage; should I be the recipient indeed of such amazing, astonishing good fortune—I shall never, not ever, take my seat upon the Thanjai throne!" Her bosom heaved with emotion. "*Sathyam — sathyam —* ***sathyam***!"

15

The Roof Drifts

The Kodumbalur princess's ringing declaration died away, leaving behind an awed silence tinged with horror.

No one, not a single soul having expected such an avowal, it was a moment before her audience came to itself—and predictably, it was Ilaiya Piratti who regained equilibrium first.

"Good God my girl, what sort of a vow is this?" She cried out, her voice fairly vibrating with indignation, dismay and a note that could only be described as a blend of frustration and boundless compassion. "Why? ***Why*** would you descend to such lunacy—nay, stupidity? What a nonsensical thing to say—what a ridiculous pledge to swear—how could you spout such absolute drivel—as though in the grip of outrageous madness—"

"No, *Akka*; I'm neither a lunatic nor in the grip of madness—my mind is clear and my senses have never been more ordered,"

Vanathi stated, fairly calmly. "I've only announced in public what I'd thought over and resolved upon these many days, in private."

Before the beleaguered Kundhavai could think to offer a fitting reply, something else snagged her attention and made her wince: a crack of laughter from Poonguzhali, ill-timed, inopportune—and with a note of undeniable delirium. *Heavens, she seems to have well and truly lost her wits,* thought the princess as the boat-girl first broke into maniacal cackles … and then covered her face with her hands, shaking with sobs. Then, abruptly, as though in crowning frenzy to protracted hysteria, she ceased to weep and began to sing in low, broken tones:

"Why anguish, my soul,
When tumbling seas lie smooth?"

Kundhavai turned to stare at Azhwarkkadiyaar, her fine eyes burning with exasperation and barely concealed chagrin. "At this rate, these two maidens are going to confuse my already chaotic mind and push me over the precipice of insanity," she complained. "Why on earth would you halt your journey to the prince and turn back with this girl in tow?"

"As you say, I did set out to meet Ponniyin Selvar but couldn't, what with the entire landscape under water—at which point I caught sight of this young woman in the same plight, stranded on land. Upon her suggestion that she might row the both of us to our destination if I could procure a boat, I retraced my steps to the *jothidar*. Imagine my delight when I spied your boat-chariot by the temple! I was sure that I could borrow it with your permission—a ruse that's come to naught, now that Pazhuvettarayar's made off with it!" that worthy finished, half mournfully.

"Well, any suggestions?" Kundhavai asked, finally. "You too were listening to Pazhuvettarayar, weren't you?"

"Indeed, *Thaaye*—and having done so, every moment wasted here seems like an aeon … for, judging by this young woman's words, horrendous peril seems to be approaching the Chakravarthy with every instant—a peril of which not even the Mudhanmandhiri is aware. Therefore, it's of the utmost importance that you leave for Thanjavur with the Kodumbalur princess for if this young lady's father truly has laid siege to the capital, none but your illustrious self can cleave through—not to mention the fact that Vanathi Devi's presence would prove a significant advantage. Meantime, I shall bring this boat-girl back to her senses, procure a boat somewhere, somehow, and find my way to Ponniyin Selvar," Thirumalai promised. "In fact, I've already dispatched the astrologer's disciple on an errand to find a craft—"

Vanathi, on whose ears these assured words had fallen, now stumbled up, staring at the spy, eyes eerily, impossibly wide. "No! —no!" She shrieked suddenly, at the top of her lungs. "I must—shall go to Ponniyin Selvar! And if I die, it shall be at his feet!"

Kreech! —erupted an unearthly, inhuman screech from Poonguzhali at these frenzied words. "I can't accompany you, Vaishnavite!" She screamed in turn. "My lovers call me to Kodikkarai—my lovers, who spew flames and fire at midnight, call for me—I showed them to the Vaanar warrior too, the one who carried an *olai* from the princess—I must go!" Her voice rose to a crescendo. "*I must go to them*!"

"*Amma*!" The Kudanthai astrologer, who had refrained from participating in the conversation and stayed a silent, albeit startled spectator, suddenly seemed to find his voice as well. "*Amma*—quiet, please—***silence, all of you***!"

Speech ceased for a long moment at his peremptory command; human commotion receded … only to give way to another, inhuman one—a sound, nay a roar—a resounding, reverberating roar that prickled the skin with goose-bumps—a vast, resonating

Boom! that seemed to echo around the earth, like the deafening din of an ocean at the height of a treacherous cyclone.

"Ah, that you should seek out this wretched sinner's hut at this of all times, gracious ladies!" The astrologer's face was bleached with terror. "That I, who predict the fortunes of the entire kingdom should have not seen fit to warn you away from here—" he lamented.

"But, *Ayya*—" Kundhavai interjected. "What on earth—what's this new danger that's set you in a quake?"

"*Thaaye*, my disciple cautioned me this morning that the floodwaters were in such spate as to break the Arisilaaru's north banks—a calamity that would ensure all of that river's waters gushing into the Kaveri—a disaster that would see Ponni flood her banks … and which would drown this paltry dwelling completely, for it stands very close to the course—come, come away—come out!" The *jothidar*'s anguished screams preceded his own precipitous exit through the door. "Outside—*now*!"

His guests pelted to the entrance in his petrified wake, only to see him point a trembling finger to the southwest, his features twisted into a grimace of pure panic. "There!"

There, indeed … appeared an unbelievable phenomenon. Strange. Unearthly. Bewitching, even—but utterly terrifying …

… for, what seemed a green wall approximately the height of half a coconut tree—a wall, slightly curved, that stretched on both sides as far as the eye could see—was barreling towards them with a roar …

… a roaring, rumbling wall, the onlookers comprehended in an instant, that was none other than the Kaveri's terrifying flood, having finally broken banks, hurtling towards them at an incredible speed.

"Come, *Amma*—come now, right this moment!" The *jothidar* shrieked, almost stamping his feet in anguish. "Run—run to the

Amman temple—our only hope is to climb onto the *mandapam*—there is no other way—Thirumalai, an excellent scheme, that—to send my disciple for a boat," he panted. "Now, come—***run***!" And he suited action to word.

The rest were not loathe to following his example, especially Poonguzhali, whose mania seemed to have evaporated, miraculously at the looming devastation. "There's no need to fear, *Devi*," she called out, her voice vibrant with its customary courage. "I've seen and conquered floods far more terrifying than this one!" She raced at breakneck pace towards the structure, clambering onto it well ahead of the others.

The floodwaters was now almost upon them, curling around the temple and lapping at the knees of those who still stood on the ground. While the *jothidar* and Azhwarkkadiyaan managed to emulate Poonguzhali and pulled themselves on top of the *mandapam*, stumbling and staggering, the two princesses still remained below.

Not for lack of trying, though and Kundhavai, made of sterner stuff, reached up, to find her hands in the iron grip of the boat-girl, who was quick to heave her up.

Finally, Vanathi alone still swayed on land, rocked by the floods—having tried twice to clamber onto the structure and slipped, both times.

Not in the least inclined to leave her to own devices, the two women atop their temporary sanctuary attempted to haul her up bodily; Ilaiya Piratti grabbing an arm and Poonguzhali, the other.

The Kodumbalur princess, consumed until then with survival, suddenly raised her head—to see one of her hands firmly in the boat-girl's clasp.

Abruptly, something inside her snapped; she shook her hand, still in the offending grip vigorously and hung free of Poonguzhali …

… only to be simultaneously bereft of Kundhavai's grasp too.

In an instant she was in freefall, down, down …

… ***thop***! She crashed—only into the water of course but which now came to her neck. Neither feet nor hands could find purchase in the swirling floods and she found herself borne, much against her will, further and further away by the powerful current.

"***Ah***!" Those left on the *mandapam* shrieked despite themselves as they watched the disaster unfold, almost in a matter of moments.

Even as they continued to gape, aghast, the floods carried a flailing Vanathi to the astrologer's home within a few scant seconds—and deposited her on the roof, over which she clambered, gratefully. *Thank heavens I'm out of danger*, scudded the thought through her mind.

The sentiments of the others were identical as they saw where the waters threw her and her mad scramble to safety. *All danger is at an end*, was the general, relieved consensus. *Now, she can be rescued when the boat arrives*, ran their reflections. "Hold fast!" They creamed as one. "Hold on to the roof; *don't let go*!"

No question of disregarding their directives, of course, Vanathi thought as she hung on grimly, with all the tenacity of one newly forced into survival …

… only to feel, in a while, the whole roof swaying slightly. *Heavens*, she wondered, alarmed. *Are the walls crumbling*?

Indeed they had; the astrologer's home was almost no more—except for the roof …

… which began to drift upon the waters, now completely untethered from its moorings …

… and on top lay Vanathi, still holding on for dear life.

Even as her makeshift raft sailed gaily away, she turned to look back towards those still atop the *mandapam*. "*Akka*, I'm going to him—

I'm going to Ponniyin Selvar!" She screamed. "Mother Kaveri is taking me to her son!"

The wind snatched the words from her lips and flung them far and wide; she hoped with all her fluttering heart that they had fallen on the others' ears.

Poonguzhali's ears, especially.

Meanwhile, upon the floodwaters drifted, drifted the *jothidar*'s roof endlessly …

… and so did Vanathi.

16

... AND POONGUZHALI LEAPS!

Veteran travelers through Chozha Nadu would have doubtless observed a phenomenon peculiar to the landscape: its bountiful rivers—sources of great natural wealth that produced grain and rice in such prodigious quantities as to give birth to the phrase *Chozha valanaadu sorudaithu*—were nearly always on a gradient higher than the banks on both sides, which facilitated the waters flowing from the larger river into the numerous canals that then fed the farms flourishing around the *rajyam*.

Matters being thus, forcing floods to follow the river's pre-ordained course would be an act of herculean proportions, would it not? For, the banks on either side ought to be of a height that would constrain said floods—else the waters, instead of hurtling along the bed would breach the embankments and, like unruly rainwater pouring everywhere, were likely to submerge the entire area, thus rendering it a quagmire useful to neither man nor beast.

Aware of their rivers' natural propensity for recklessness, Chozha monarchs of yore expended considerable effort and ingenuity in raising the banks of the Kaver and her branches, big and small; it cannot be unknown to our readers that Karikal Peruvalathan pressed prisoners from the Eezham wars into Chozha service by bidding them build gigantic banks along the Ponni.

Further, it was with the intention of raising water-levels in her distributaries that the Chozhas constructed the magnificent Kallanai a *kaadham* east of Srirangam; an engineering marvel that considerably increased the elevation and allowed the roaring waters to surge ever more, into the smaller rivers branching from the bigger.

Thus it was that Chozha Nadu, even centuries past, had boasted water resources unparalleled and unequalled; its rivers seemingly perennial and the resultant prosperity exceptional, through a combination of the eternal natural and continual artifice; integrating the complicated wild with constant construction and thereby, receiving the blended bounty of both.

But just as nature proved utterly benevolent in some respects, so too did she assume an overpoweringly dangerous aura in others—an aura that manifested often as severe cyclones and worrisome whirlwinds on the eastern Chozha coast; storms that battered the shore as they swirled north, sometimes, to where massive rivers such the Krishna and the Godavari joined the sea or into the Kalinga Kingdom, annihilating the area with pouring deluges or roaring gales as their temperament saw fit, causing devastation on an unimaginable scale … or at other times, tearing viciously into Chozha Nadu itself, blasting through the landscape at breakneck pace. A frequent occurrence in the *rajyam*'s natural history, this, when ferocious gales roared between Kodikkarai and the Kollidam's mouth, sometimes whipping up the raging oceans to such a fever pitch that they rose up in terrifying tsunamis, ravaging the coast and submerging entire towns. After all, the existence—and later, horrifying destruction—of Kaveripattinam, also known as Poompuhar, a city claimed by the ravenous sea is an event corroborated, as we well know, by historical sources.

Rivers in full spate broke their banks, their higher elevation in comparison to the low-lying lands resulting in a water-logged, completely flooded landscape; villages and settlements often found themselves underwater and the local population forced, desperately to seek shelter—and it was here that the numerous shrines liberally dotting the region offered welcome refuge.

History reveals that Adithya Chozhan, son and heir to Vijayalaya Chozhan, raised hundred and eight temples all along the *mahanadhi* Kaveri's course from her source in the Sahya Hills to her eventual destination where she inevitably united with the sea; temples which served a spiritual purpose during ordinary times but which he might have intended to afford asylum during extraordinary times, such as horrendous floods—after all, people could climb onto the spires and *mandapams* and find some temporary solace, could they not?

In addition to the submersion of areas, there was another, fairly common consequence of such massive floods: an entire shift in the waterways. Many are the ancient tales and histories that recount rivers such as the Arisilaaru and Kudamurutti changing courses and deviating directions more than once in their lengthy lifespan.

Now, to return to our own saga: the vicious whirlwind that churned the seas as Parthibendran's vessel navigated a wretched journey from Ilankai to Chozha Nadu, successfully maneuvered Arulmozhi Varmar into the sea in an attempt to rescue Vandhiyathevan and then, mission accomplished, barreled along the coast into Kalinga Nadu where it finally, and thankfully, made a rather brief bow and vanished for good.

The one that swirled into existence when Ponniyin Selvar was residing incognito in the Choodamani Viharam, however, decided that it would make a bigger mark upon the world than its paltry sibling and effected a brutal entrance into Chozha Nadu itself. It blasted its ferocious way due west across the trembling landscape, devastating both banks of the Kaveri within the space of a single night, flexing its phenomenal strength in a display of divine play that wrecked havoc all next day in the Kongu country before it finally blew itself out … but not before ensuring a terrifying downpour as a last, parting shot—a downpour that swiftly strengthened into a deluge further west, resulting in a colossal surge of water that swelled the Kaveri, Kollidam and all their distributaries the day after. Many promptly broke their banks and almost all of Chozha Nadu sank under the combined onslaught of river, rain and roaring floods.

Not Chozha citizens however who, well aware of their kingdom's propensity for natural disasters were not fazed in the least. Neither alarm nor petrified panic did they betray at nature's debilitating vagaries but followed procedures devised for exactly such circumstances. First in the survival scenario, of course, was to reach higher ground which included the tops of temples; the floods would recede as swiftly as they surged; those who had lost homes would be equally swift to rebuild instead of collapsing in a heap and lamenting *Ayyo, we've lost shelter*! … for that was not the Chozha way.

They were sturdy, these people of yore; sturdy of body and steady of heart; brimming with spirit and self-esteem but absolutely devoid of vices such as apathy and crippling anxiety—else, how could they have accomplished the magnificent feats and splendid achievements the world marvels at, even today?

Intense anxiety was the first sensation to flood the senses of those safe upon the *mandapam* when Vanathi failed to claim the same refuge—anxiety which transformed into equally intense relief when they glimpsed her clambering onto the astrologer's roof by some bizarre, miraculous twist—relief that, in Ilaiya Piratti's case almost swelled into enthusiasm. After all, hadn't she always been an advocate for pushing Vanathi into borderline perilous situations to keenly observe her conduct? A maiden about to wed a warrior among warriors and take up position as his consort ought to be a woman of rare courage and daring, surely? A queen in waiting ought to be trained and whipped into shape as empress, surely? Towards this end had Kundhavai Devi laboured, employing her considerable wits and acumen into devising tricks and stratagems designed to encourage and empower the Kodumbalur princess—stratagems that she felt, with some complacence, had begun to produce results.

We saw, didn't we, that Vanathi had rather renounced her fainting spells of late? Now indeed occurred a circumstance, seemingly divinely ordained and with none of Kundhavai's elaborate machinations to test her fortitude and fearlessness, holding, as she was, precariously onto a flimsy roof amidst a roaring, seething deluge. Would she manage to retain her wits and not give way to blind, numbing panic? Would she remain brave and hold onto her senses until the astrologer's disciple arrived with a rescue boat? Yes, of course she would; all the training and endless coaching ought, surely to come to her aid at this most crucial of moments? Act her guide to equilibrium?

Thus far she'd arrived in her cogitations when Azhwarkkadiyaar caught her attention. "Wait," he muttered. "What on earth—*Thaaye*, it seems to me that the roof's moving!"

"And it seems to me that your eyes are at fault; it's the water that flows, creating an illusion of—" But even as she said the words, the same suspicion darted through her mind, revealing itself in her face.

"Observe carefully, *Amma*," Thirumalai reiterated.

"*Ayyo*, what fresh disaster is this?" Ilaiya Piratti murmured, appalled.

Azhwarkkadiyaar turned to the astrologer. "Do you think your disciple will arrive with the boat any time soon?"

"Oh, enough—enough of waiting and trusting the *jothidar* and his faithful follower—Thirumalai, save Vanathi if you can; else, I shall have to brave the floods myself," Kundhavai announced, voice throbbing with emotion. "If anything should befall her, I shan't live another moment!"

"Not that I need counsel you but it's during such extraordinary times of unimaginable peril that one must needs maintain a level of calm, *Thaaye*. I'm willing and able to sacrifice my life in an instant for the Kodumbalur princess but consider, I beg of you, if such an act is likely to improve, in any way, the current situation. In the absence of the boat I might, of course, swim towards and even clamber onto the roof—but will that insubstantial structure support the both of us? Or sink completely and fling us to the mercy of the raging floods? One must expend some little thought upon—"

He paused, mid-speech, at Poonguzhali's sudden crack of laughter; spy and sovereign princess turned as one, to gaze at her. "By the time our valiant Veera Vaishnavite finishes expending what little thought he has, the Kodumbalur lady's life would've come to a summary end," she gurgled irrepressibly.

"An occurrence that would doubtless send our dear boat-girl into transports of delight," Azhwarkkadiyaar snapped—a riposte which had the effect of transforming that young woman's mirth into seething wrath in an instant; Poonguzhali's charming countenance burnt with almost uncontrollable fury.

"Not, however, that such a calamity would ever come to pass," As though he hadn't noticed her reaction, Thirumalai continued soothingly. "For He Who Receives the Whole World under His Wing while He Reclines upon a Banyan-leaf shall extend His divine protection towards Vanathi as well; the Gracious Lord Who guards the cosmos in the guise of the *macha*, *koorma* and *varaha* incarnations shall, without a doubt, save the Kodumbalur princess too—ah, there comes the astrologer's disciple—and with a boat, to boot!" And indeed, a boat could be seen in the direction he pointed, braving the currents to approach the *mandapam*, moment by agonizingly slow moment.

Meanwhile, the rickety roof that was still Vanathi's sole refuge was drifting, drifting away in slow increments but even so, it would take a considerable amount of time for the rescue vessel to reach them—time the Kodumbalur princess did not have, as she floated farther and farther from them … and was in danger of being lost to sight.

Comprehending—as the disciple probably did not—that it was imperative he reach Vanathi at once, the group atop the *mandapam* shouted at him to row faster. They waved, screeched, yelled, which the recipient of these complicated communiqués interpreted in his own way and began to ply his oars swiftly towards *them*.

"Grant me permission, *Devi*," Poonguzhali turned to the distrait Kundhavai. "I'll swim to the boat, head him off towards the Kodumbalur princess and take her in."

Ilaiya Piratti stared at her, torn. Not far from her memory was the picture of Vanathi plunging into the water precisely because Poonguzhali had offered a hand—and the young woman seemed to sense the reason for her hesitation. "Believe me when I say that it's my duty to rescue her," she said, earnestly. "After all, my carelessness led to the princess's fall, didn't it?"

"Believe me when I say that it isn't you I disbelieve but Vanathi," Kundhavai sighed.

"Ah, she might refuse to climb into a boat I'm in, you say? Well, in that case," Poonguzhali dived into the waters neatly, even as she spoke. "I shall heave her in—and jump out!" And she cleaved through the current, striking out towards the boat.

"I used to entertain the highest of hopes of your *saasthram*, *Ayya*," Kundhavai turned to address the *jothidar*. "Today, however, is the day I renounce my convictions."

"Mine, on the other hand, have achieved completion only this very day, *Devi*. The Kodumbalur princess's horoscope indicated extreme peril today and I must admit I harboured the gravest of fears that it might have arrived in the person of Pazhuvettarayar—and was surprised when it took another form. She will, however, survive this danger—ah, the astonishing lines in her palms—her awe-inspiring destiny—have no doubt that everything, every last word of my prophecies in her regard shall come true!" The astrologer announced in ringing tones.

"Here's a pretty tale indeed," Kundhavai remonstrated. "There's no way any of your predictions could be fulfilled now, could they? Not even should Vanathi escape the horrendous fate that stares her in the face—surely you heard that young woman's vow just a while ago, in your own home?"

"Whatever the vow—whenever sworn—and whosoever's the pledge, my prophecy must and shall be fulfilled; should they fail, I take my vow here and now: I shall fling my precious palm-leaves and manuscripts into the Kaveri and renounce my vocation!" The *jothidar* roared at the full pitch of his emotions.

"I'm afraid Mother Kaveri hasn't been patient enough to wait until you did the deed," Azhwarkkadiyaar intercepted at this moment, wryly. "She's confiscated them herself!"

The astrologer stared around, aghast at the truth of these words. "For all that, however," he muttered, *sotto voce*, with more than a hint of defiance. "My predictions cannot but come true!"

❧

Hidden Meanings and Explanations

" ... macha, koorma and varaha incarnations ..."

Azhwarkkadiyaar is referring, here, to the first, second and third of Thirumaal's ten incarnations—also known as the *Dasavathaaram*—where He assumed the forms of a fish, tortoise, and a boar, to save humankind.

17

THE ELEPHANT SENT HIM FLYING!

We ask our esteemed readers to recall that the day before the events of the previous chapter, we had left Arulmozhi Varmar in the capable hands of the people of Naagaippatinam, who hosted him with great pomp and ceremony. When the celebrations finally wound down, the prince mounted a grandly decorated elephant and bid them farewell. Loath to say goodbye, a swarm of people flocked around him declaring, "We will come to Thanjavur, too!"

It was nightfall by the time the prince and his impulsive party arrived at the first stop of their journey, Thiruvarur. The townspeople had received word of the prince's imminent arrival, so the weary travellers were accorded a royal welcome and their every need tended to diligently. Buoyant crowds gathered in the streets all the way from ancient Gunavaasal up to Kudavaasal, hoping for a glimpse of their dear prince. The town's four *raja veethis* were packed with such dense throngs that there was hardly enough space for a handful of seeds to fall. Pretty *thoranams* were strung across the entrance of houses in honour of the prince and the Chozha palace at Thiruvarur had been lavishly bedecked by its staff to befit its august visitor. A sumptuous feast of grand proportions had been arranged for the prince as well his motley companions.

In fact, an angry cyclone had torn through the town just the night before; but news of the prince's arrival had lifted dampened spirits, giving way instead to a cloudburst of joy that engulfed the whole town. The streets thrummed with activity. Cheerful tunes filled the air, deftly played on a variety of musical instruments; there was song and dance everywhere, from lively *kuravai koothus* to delightful *bommai aattams*; some even flaunted their impressive martial arts skills, amazing onlookers with their spirited displays of *kathi vilayattu* and *kazhi vilayattu*.

Next to the Nataraja *peruman* who dances in rapture at Thillai Ambalam, it was the Thyagaraja *peruman* of Thiruvarur whom the Chozha people of Thanjavur held in great reverence. They had made generous endowments to the temple as a mark of their piety. Arulmozhi Varmar was the only member of his family who had never been to Thiruvarur, so it was only to be expected that the temple trustees compelled him to pay a visit to the shrine. The prince duly obliged their request, but his mind was preoccupied with other matters, brooding on the mire of difficulties that lay ahead. That was a pity, for the distractions kept him from fully appreciating the deity who looked especially resplendent in the magnificent *thirukolam* that his devotees had lovingly adorned Him with.

After the priests performed the ceremonial *aaradhanai* and *archanai* for the deity, they offered the prince *prasadam* which he accepted. As he was leaving, the prince turned to the temple attendants. "How did the deity come to be known as Thyagarajar, the King of Sacrifice?" he asked, curious.

Thrilled at the prince's interest, the attendants earnestly launched into a breathless series of captivating tales that illustrated the gracious selflessness of Siva *peruman*, the greatest among the trinity of gods. They explained how the Lord of lords, who wielded the power to make or unmake the three worlds with an offhand thought, had endured several trials and tribulations for the good of His people. Seeking peace and prosperity for all beings, He had retreated from the world to go into austere meditation at a desolate burial ground; He then graciously relinquished this demanding endeavour at the entreaties of the *devas*, consenting for their sake to wed Uma, daughter of the mountain king. In His aspect as the Supreme Mendicant, the temple caretakers said, the Lord humbly assumes the form of Bhikshadanamurthy, who wanders the universe in search of alms. They warmly described His cosmic dance of bliss at Thillai Ambalam and recounted the astonishing story of the hapless Pandiya king who, in a moment of ill-judgement, dared to strike the Lord Himself for idling on the job as a menial *coolie* – a role He had readily taken on in the place of an ardent devotee who was too old for labour.

It was this divine altruism and boundless compassion that was characterized by the Thyagaraja *peruman* at Thiruvarur. The temple attendants reminded Arulmozhi Varmar that his ancestors had lived in this very town in the olden days - it was here, in fact, that Manu Needhi Chozhar had famously sacrificed his dear son to deliver justice to a cow who had lost her calf.

Arulmozhi Varmar found himself entranced. Until this moment, his thoughts had been full of the Buddha, whose tales of sacrifice and mercy had struck a chord with him. Now, deeply moved by the stories describing the benevolence of Lord Siva, he meditated at length on the Lord's astonishing capacity for selfless love. Another touching legend had reached him from beyond the seas as well, of an *avatara purushan* who had appeared in a far-off country to the west. This beloved son of God had allowed himself to be cruelly nailed onto a cross, choosing martyrdom for the good of the people. As Arulmozhi Varmar contemplated these tales, the thought arose that it was sacrifice that propelled man to divinity. So convinced was he of this epiphany that he felt nothing but misery at the thought of the adulatory multitude who wished to see him crowned the King of Thanjavur. Their fierce devotion felt like a force of nature that had him trapped in an unyielding prison of love and affection. Determined to free himself of its restraints, the prince began to actively plan his escape.

Meanwhile, the temple rituals had come to an end and the prince was led to a splendid feast. The people of Thiruvarur pulled out all the stops to amuse him, presenting an impressive line-up of fabulous shows. The prince, however, was not particularly interested in the revelries; he patiently sat through it all, gamely putting on a show of great enthusiasm.

It was midnight by the time the prince finally arrived at the Chozha palace in Thiruvarur. He was met with grave news - heavy rains had ruthlessly lashed the regions to the west of Thanjavur, dangerously swelling the rivers Kaveri and Kollidam as well as their tributaries. The waters had overflowed their banks in gushing torrents, causing a deluge of catastrophic magnitude. It had inundated large swathes of land, transforming the surrounding terrain into impassable wetlands. The prince was informed that he could not travel under these conditions. Advisors pointed out that extending the stop at Thiruvarur would be the prudent option; the prince could safely proceed once the floodwaters had retreated.

Arulmozhi Varmar received the news in dismay, bristling at the suggestion to delay his journey. He was burning with a barely-concealed impatience to reach Thanjavur - did they think it could be doused by mere floods? To be fair, his advisors did have a point. Travelling in these circumstances will certainly be impossible with a large retinue in tow. However... yes, if he were to go by himself atop an elephant, why, there's no reason to put off the journey! Surely there is no river en route to Thanjavur that is too deep for an elephant to cross! In any case, the prince was unconcerned about that particular problem. He had never been afraid of water, after all. The river Ponni bore him a love more faithful perhaps than his own mother's; and he would be in the care of mother Kaveri herself, who had saved his life once before when he was a child. What did he have to fear from water?

No, his immediate problem was the sea of people who besieged him. Ponniyin Selvar suddenly thought of Ramar, who had slipped away from the people of Ayodhya in the still of the night. Perhaps he could follow suit and quietly resume his journey in the dark when the people were sure to be asleep! The sensible thing to do, the prince decided, would be to keep the mahout informed so that the elephant could be ready when the time came to leave.

His mind made up, the prince immediately ordered a palace attendant to bring the mahout to him. The attendant obediently went up to the palace entrance and looked all around. He returned shortly by himself, reporting that while the elephant was tied up in the courtyard, the mahout was nowhere to be found.

"He is probably on the streets, enjoying the song, dance and *kaliyattam*. Bring him to me when he returns. Better yet, send somebody to fetch him right away," commanded the prince.

"As you wish, my prince," replied the attendant with deference. "A man is waiting at the palace entrance for an audience with you," he added after a pause. "He says that he is the *padagotti* Murugaiyan and claims to bear a message of urgent importance. He is being rather adamant about seeing you," he finished apologetically.

The prince felt a pang of pity for Murugaiyan. He had forgotten about him in the midst of all the excitement. Perhaps Murugaiyan could help him steal away to Thanjavur... The prince instructed the attendant to send him in at once. To the prince's consternation, Murugaiyan flung himself at his feet as soon as he appeared and proceeded to sob with childlike abandon. It was only after considerable effort that the prince managed to console the poor man, enough at least for him to unburden himself of his peculiar story.

It transpired that Murugaiyan had been separated from his wife in the clamour at Naagaippattinam, and had promptly set about searching for her when he reached Thiruvarur. He had tramped through the milling crowds for one whole *jaamam* when he spotted his wife at the corner of a nondescript road branching off from a *raja veethi*. To his amazement, she wasn't alone; she was escorted by the prince's mahout! The two scurried away down the dark alley, oblivious to Murugaiyan who tailed them at a discreet distance. Presently, they paused at the entrance of a house from which an unknown man emerged. It was evident that he had been expecting them, for he immediately joined the company and the three of them set off together in a tearing hurry.

Murugaiyan was devastated. All sorts of ugly suspicions assailed him and he began to imagine the most terrible things about his wife's chastity. Burning with rage, he determined to learn the truth behind the whole affair; instead of confronting the three then and there, he decided to stay on their trail. The odd group led him down a remote path past the town limits through the ridges of fields and across irrigation channels, finally stopping at a dismal graveyard. Murugaiyan's skin crawled with apprehension but he managed to pluck up the courage to move closer and conceal himself behind a tree.

As Murugaiyan watched unnoticed, the stranger scooped up handfuls of the grey ash scattered over the graveyard and smeared them all over his body. Having completed this macabre ritual, he proceeded to chant ominous incantations in a harsh tone. When he finished, he fixed his glittering eyes on the mahout. "Your life will be in grave danger tomorrow," he proclaimed with an imperious air. "Be on your guard."

The mahout visibly blanched. Trembling, he stammered, "What sort of danger? How will it come? Tell me more! How am I to survive it without knowing more?"

The *mandhiravadhi* looked at him with deep pity. "The elephant will suddenly go into a state of musth. It will fling you aside as you approach and go on a murderous rampage. The people will blame you for the elephant's mania. They will snatch away your *angusam* and kill you," he predicted, sympathy lacing his voice.

"*Ayyayo*! How will I escape this fate?" howled the mahout in terror.

"Best you keep away from the elephant tomorrow," advised the *mandhiravadhi* firmly.

"And be subject to royal punishment for insubordination?" wailed the mahout.

The *mandhiravadhi* took a couple of seconds to muse upon this dilemma. "Come to my house. I have an enchanted amulet that will protect you. You must wear it when you report to work tomorrow," he said. "Also, you must leave your *angusam* behind when you go," he added, almost like an afterthought.

"As you say, *ayya*," replied the mahout, relief flooding his voice. A sudden thought seemed to occur to him. "And the prince? Will he be in danger?" asked the mahout with concern.

"How do I know?" the *mandhiravadhi* replied bluntly. "I can answer that question only if the prince himself puts it to me."

Murugaiyan lost his nerve. He fled the graveyard, racing towards the palace as if his life depended on it. The message he had been desperate to deliver to the prince was the *mandhiravadhi's* dreadful prediction that the elephant would go wild the next day. As

Murugaiyan finished narrating his queer tale, he broke down and dissolved into a fresh bout of abject sobs.

"*Appane*, why do you cry?" asked Ponniyin Selvar gently. "You have rendered me a great service by delivering the warning on time. I will take care of things from here," he said in a reassuring tone.

"*Ayya*, my wife's involvement in this matter terrifies me. I simply don't know what to make of Rakkammal anymore. All my old suspicions are flooding back... I am at my wit's end!" confessed Murugaiyan tearfully.

"Put your mind at ease, Murugaiyan. I will bring her around," promised the prince. "For now, it is important that you retrace your steps to locate the mahout and bring him to me," he finished. The gravity of the errand was not lost on Murugaiyan, who set out with resolve.

Having dispatched the *padagotti* on his new mission, Ponniyin Selvar sunk into deep thought. What did Murugaiyan's strange experience presage? The prince carefully analyzed the facts at hand from all possible angles. He cast his mind back to Ilaiya Piratti's misgivings about the Pazhuvettarayars' endgame. She had also urged him, he remembered, to be on high alert for the Pandiya insurgents who were reportedly hatching a deadly plot against the kingdom. Perhaps Murugaiyan had unwittingly stumbled onto a conspiracy against the prince. Or perhaps the whole thing was just a piece of petty mischief. Either way, something had to be done about it. The prince pondered on the situation until he saw the solution. Matters under control, he gave in to the delicious drowsiness that washed over him and fell into a tranquil sleep.

Rising at first light the next morning, the prince prepared himself for travel. He saw the elephant tied outside the palace entrance and approached it cautiously. The pachyderm raised its trunk in a show of affection and caressed him gently. The prince recalled the *mandhiravadhi's* prophecy as reported by Murugaiyan – the elephant will go into musth, he had said. The animal, however, seemed to give no indication of aberrant behaviour; it seemed quite unlikely that it would run amok.

The prince turned his attention away from the elephant. "Where is the mahout?" he asked. The question resonated through the courtyard, provoking a flurry of activity. A chorus of voices arose in response, each echoing the prince's query - *where is the mahout*, people cried as word spread of the prince's summons. The place was packed, even at this early hour. The prince's self-appointed travel guides were clustered at the palace entrance - they had assembled at the crack of dawn, ready at a moment's notice to resume their expedition under their exalted companion. The prince noticed Murugaiyan flailing about in the teeming crowds, bravely trying to make his way through the crushing mass of people. It was only after Ponniyin Selvar beckoned to him that the throng parted, allowing him to approach the prince. Murugaiyan came bearing news – hours of intense search had failed him in tracking down the mahout, but he had been able to locate his wife. She had professed herself dumbfounded by Murugaiyan's version of events; she had vehemently denied having gone to the graveyard at all and summarily ended the argument by accusing him of rank lunacy.

"She is the least of my worries, Murugaiyya," said the prince once he had heard the report. "Now untie the chain around the elephant's foot," he instructed. As Murugaiyan set to obeying the command, a shout rang out – "Why, here is the mahout! He has arrived at last!" Joyous cries followed the announcement – "Here he is, here he is!" True enough, the mahout was sprinting towards the palace, *angusam* in hand. The crowd hastily gave way, the people on each side falling over each other in an attempt to create a path for him.

Ponniyin Selvar heaved a sigh of relief. He turned towards the mahout who was hurrying towards him. Poor man! The night before had plainly taken a toll on him. He seemed to have come unhinged with fear; he had lost all composure and his face was aflush with nervous excitement.

Clutching his *angusam* tightly, the mahout drew close to the elephant and lightly touched its trunk with his free hand. In the blink of an eye, the elephant wound its mighty trunk around his torso and lifted him overhead in one swift movement, as if he weighed nothing more than a sack of feathers. The animal let loose an ear-shattering trumpet and the stunned audience felt the blood freeze in their veins. The elephant sent the mahout flying a great distance away; his *angusam* landed even further.

"The elephant has gone mad!" screamed someone, breaking the deathly silence. Soon the cry was on everyone's lips as they ran helter-skelter and the crowd exploded in all four directions, scattering like beads from a split necklace.

18

THE DOUBLE-CROSSED MAHOUT

A contemporary scholar conjectures that opportunity is just another name for God. The theory is that God dons the garb of chance when He – or She – is not interested in drawing attention to the divine play at work. Humanity's history is bestrewn with the remarkable stories of renowned warriors and achievers whose rise to glory was enabled by the manifestation of golden opportunities. Some say that it was heavenly grace that delivered such providence to these luminaries; others attribute the good fortune to their *jadagam,* speculating that it was an auspicious time of birth that championed their success; still others give the credit to *karma*, rationalizing their lucky breaks as a reward from Brahma Himself for their good deeds in a past life.

We humbly ask our valued readers to pause and indulge us in an exercise of imagination. How would the course of history have changed if the Mahatma Gandhi had not received an opportunity to work in South Africa? Could he have accomplished the feats he is lauded for today, adored by the people as the father of our nation and an *avatara purushan* in his own right?

Indeed, it is a well-known fact that it was opportunity that served as the catalyst in shaping the lives of illustrious personages like Chandragupta Vikramadithan, Julius Caesar, Napoleon Bonaparte, the Duke of Wellington and George Washington, to name just a few. If this leads you, dear reader, to conclude that God plays favourites among his children – banish the thought! It is our belief that the hand of God has played a part in the triumphs of many apart from those whose lives have made it to the annals of history; He constantly seeks to lift humanity through countless opportunities that He continues to provide us with even today.

And therein lies the rub. You see, man's success isn't guaranteed when an opportunity falls into his lap; he must rise to the occasion and prove himself worthy of victory by displaying the ingenuity and will to make good use of the chance he is given. Oblivious to their good fortune, millions let rare occasions go unused, never knowing that they have missed the opportunity of a lifetime. They live simple, ordinary lives and depart this world without making their mark. There are some, however, who are smart enough to recognize such a chance when it is handed to them. They are the ones who ride the tide of history, emblazoning their names on the mind of humanity before they go in glory to meet their maker.

What other explanation can there be for the striking disparity between the lives led by people born on an identical day and time?

Arulmozhi Varmar was at such a momentous juncture. A golden opportunity stared him in the face as the crowd broke into pandemonium following the elephant's dreadful attack on the mahout. If the prince had let this chance slip through his hands that day, it is possible that we would be narrating a different story today;

the very name of Raja Raja Chozhar might have been relegated to little more than to a footnote in Thamizh Naadu's glorious history. Luckily for us, Arulmozhi Varmar was gifted with the acuity as well as the capability to recognize providence and leverage it to its full potential. As the mayhem erupted around him, he recalled Murugaiyan's account from the night before. The mahout *must* have been a hostile imposter – why else would the elephant have thrown him down?! This startling revelation unleashed a veritable barrage of questions - Who was the stranger? Why had he come? What had he planned to do? If the prince had given in to the moment and dallied upon these puzzles, he would have lost that precious window of opportunity which presented itself; his plan of resuming the journey to Thanjavur free of his entourage was of the highest priority, and he wouldn't get a better opening than this.

Arulmozhi Varmar seized his chance. He drew Murugaiyan to his side and whispered instructions in his ear. The *padagotti* lent him his shoulders and the prince leapt onto the elephant's back, toppling the *ambari* which rolled away into the chaos below. The prince spoke softly to the elephant, which seemed to understand exactly what he was saying. The animal took one step forward and then another; it picked up pace as it cut through the frantic throngs. Trumpeting lustily, it began to run.

As if on cue, Murugaiyan started up a shout. "*Ayyo*!" he yelled. "The elephant has gone berserk! Flee, flee for your lives!"

Fright escalated into pure panic. People lost no time in making themselves scarce, darting in any direction that led them away from the elephant. Some slipped into the small lanes and streets adjoining the courtyard, diving headlong into unlocked houses to hide away from the bedlam. What else could they be expected to do with a mad elephant on the loose? Even the most intrepid warrior will be unapologetically practical when taking stock of such a situation; when all's said and done, no man has the power to meet an elephant's strength, even with a weapon on hand. The crowd had all sorts in attendance that day - men and women, young and old, all unarmed. Little wonder then that they beat a hasty retreat in the face of such mammoth danger.

In the meanwhile, the prince had already crossed Thiruvarur and was guiding the elephant down a path that headed northwest. He meant to make his way to Pazhayaarai in the hope that his sister would be there, for he intended to consult with her before proceeding to Thanjavur. Besides, his army of admirers may yet catch up with him if he took the predictable route to Thanjavur; he had a much better chance of travelling unnoticed if he went off the beaten track. The change in course could be defended easily enough if the need arose – after all, a rampaging elephant can hardly be expected to follow a sensible route. It took the prince just a fraction of a second to think through these possibilities; as soon as he settled upon a plan of action, he urged his obliging mount towards the northwest. The elephant lumbered along at a brisk pace. Together, prince and pachyderm traversed vast fields, cutting across ridges and irrigation channels that lay in their way. Sometimes they encountered wide tracts of land that lay dolefully submerged under the floodwaters, but the elephant regally took it all in its stride, effortlessly forging ahead without a care in the world. A rush of euphoria surged through the prince as an inexplicable excitement gripped him; his heart swelled with pure joy. He felt exhilarated, like a bird that had broken free of its gilded cage and was now soaring through the blue skies. Every instinct in his being told him that he was embarking upon a pivotal journey, one that would set in motion a chain of far-reaching events. The prince's eyes sparkled with anticipation.

Back at the courtyard, Murugaiyan was embroiled in an adventure of his own. As the elephant carried away Ponniyin Selvar, he raised a great hue and cry. "The elephant has gone mad," he hollered as he ran towards the spot where he thought the mahout must have fallen. A short distance from the Chozha palace where the prince had been hosted lay the magnificent Kamalalayam, a colossal temple tank that was renowned throughout the kingdom. Murugaiyan made his way to its banks, looking high and low for the mahout. The place was awash with people who had sought refuge from the charging elephant; some had even plunged into the water in a frantic bid for safety. One man among them seemed to be particularly distressed. He floundered about desperately as he swam towards the shore and scrambled onto the bank. Murugaiyan looked at him closely. Why, this was the *mandhiravadhi* who had accompanied Raakkammal and the mahout the earlier night! He had to have been born under a tremendously lucky star; it must take a singularly sturdy lifeline to survive an elephant attack, after all. For there was no doubt that he was the very same man who had, just a short while ago, bolted towards the elephant brandishing an *angusam* in his hand. It was not clear what had happened to the *angusam*; perhaps it had fallen into the tank too. Murugaiyan approached the man. "Here you are, mahout!" he exclaimed. "What a stroke of fortune to survive an ambush by an angry elephant! Where is your *angusam*?"

Kramavithan – who also went by the name Revadasan – gave a start and looked Murugaiyan over from head to toe. "What did you say?" he asked, surprised. "Who on earth are you? I took a bath in the tank and have only just come ashore."

"Oho, is that a fact? I'm to believe that you aren't the mahout we all saw a short while ago, is it? That you weren't thrown down by the elephant?" demanded Murugaiyan. "Well, in that case, where is the mahout?" he asked triumphantly.

Kramavithan's eyes widened in disbelief. "How am I to know? Why the devil are you asking me?" he replied in frank amazement.

"Come now, *mandhiravadhi*, drop the act. Don't bother trying to pull a fast one on me," replied Murugaiyan sternly. "Wasn't it you who took the mahout to the graveyard last night and warned him that the prince's elephant would go berserk? I wonder," he continued thoughtfully, "why you failed to heed your own warning and put yourself in danger! Well that's your problem, not mine. Tell me, where is the mahout? And where is my wife, Raakkammal?"

Kramavithan's face froze in a mask of pure astonishment and yes, some fear, too. "Mahout? Raakkammal? Have you gone insane?" he cried out as he looked around furtively.

"Yes! I've gone stark raving mad, just like the elephant!" retorted Murugaiyan. "Come now, out with it – where is the mahout? Confess, or else..." he commanded authoritatively.

Revathasan fixed his eyes upon Murugaiyan and suddenly smiled. "You call me a magician, but you appear to be a greater wizard than I. You know everything, don't you? I see that there really is no point in hiding anything from you," he remarked. "I had come running to the palace courtyard to protect the prince from danger. I wanted to warn him not to mount the elephant since I knew that it would go into musth. No good deed goes unpunished, it seems – look at the state I am in now!" he rued. "Look, your wife and the mahout are in a house over there. I will take you there myself if you want to see them," he said, adopting a soothing tone. "I trust the prince is unharmed by the incident? He hasn't been hurt, has he?" he asked earnestly.

"The prince is well. In fact, it was he who ordered me to fetch you as well as the mahout."

"You must make sure that the prince rewards me well.. after all, I did save his life!... Ah! There!" exclaimed the *mandhiravadhi* in wonder, abruptly falling into silence.

Murugaiyan followed his gaze. The *mandhiravadhi* was staring intently at an *arali* shrub growing on the banks of the Kamalalayam. Tangled among its leaves was an object resembling the tip of a spear, partially hidden under the foliage. "Ah! *Angusam*!" cried the *mandhiravadhi* and broke into a run towards the bush. Murugaiyan raced him to the finish and dove into the shrub; he gripped the handle of the *angusam* and lifted it gingerly.

When Murugaiyan turned around, the *mandhiravadhi* was nowhere to be seen. "*Adada*! I have been tricked!" he groaned. Murugaiyan ran hither and thither in search of his quarry but his efforts were in vain. The *mandhiravadhi* Kramavithan had melted into the crowds gathered upon the Kamalalayam's banks, vanishing from sight like a phantom.

Murugaiyan noticed that the people were starting to make their way back to the Chozha palace. However, there was no time to analyse the situation; Murugaiyan had work to do yet.

Murugaiyan threw his mind back to the events that had unfolded the previous night. He concentrated on recollecting the route that had led him to the *mandhiravadhi*'s house. Having found his bearings, Murugaiyan set off in the direction where he thought it lay. As he walked through the *raja veethi*, he traversed clusters of animated groups in which the excited townspeople were chattering away with one another. A few had seen the mad elephant's rampage first-hand. "It looked like there was somebody atop the elephant!" they reported, baffling their audience. Some rejected their account. "Impossible! It began to run amok as soon as it hurled that mahout, didn't it? Who could have mounted such an enraged elephant in that horrifying moment?" they argued. The crowds tirelessly dissected the incident from all possible angles, jabbering among themselves as they marched back to the Chozha palace. They were anxious to see for themselves that their beloved prince, the apple of their eyes, was unhurt from the whole affair.

Murugaiyan continued down a path that led him away from the moving crowds. He stopped at the mouth of a lane. The street lay silent and deserted, since almost everyone was on the *raja veethi* leading to the palace. Murugaiyan advanced down the lane, keeping his eyes peeled as he walked. The place looked different in the daylight; he found it unexpectedly difficult to single out the house he had seen the earlier night. Among all the houses bordering the street, one in particular was bolted from the outside. Murugaiyan paused. He thought he could hear sounds of moaning coming from within. The building next door was a dilapidated, abandoned structure. Murugaiyan entered the idle property and clambered onto its roof; he then made a great leap to jump into the *muttram*, the open courtyard, of the bolted house. He spotted the mahout, just as he had expected. The mahout was beside himself with rage. Not only was he bound to a pillar, but his hands and feet were also strapped for good measure. He was making a desperate effort to untie himself by gnawing through the ropes holding him in place. He paused writhing now and then to roar in anger and despair. As soon as he noticed Murugaiyan, his face lit up. The mahout recognized Murugaiyan from seeing him in Naagaippattinam and knew that the *padagotti* had the prince's ear. He cried out to him frantically, "Murugaiyya! Untie me, untie me! Those *chandaalas*, those horrid fiends, they have tricked me! The prince... he's not in any danger, is he?"

Murugaiyan gave the mahout a short, precise account of the morning's events, untying the knots as he spoke. In turn, he asked the mahout what had happened to him. The mahout replied in hesitant stutters. It emerged that the mahout had been offered an enchanted amulet that was to protect him in the event that the elephant did go mad. He was brought to this house upon that pretext; the *mandhiravadhi* had then chanted strange spells, burning liberal amounts of *saambraani* as he did so. The smoke, the mahout said, had made him feel lightheaded and drowsy. He supposed that he had fallen asleep, for he woke up to the awful discovery that he had been quite firmly tied to the pillar.

The pair fled the house and hastened to the Chozha palace. When they reached, they saw that a vast multitude had assembled in the royal courtyard. Anxiety was in the air; worried murmurs rippled through the ranks and distress was etched upon people's faces. The prince was missing and no one had any reliable news about what had happened to him. A few pointed out that they had seen someone mount the elephant as it broke away. Perhaps, they ventured, that had been the prince.

It was well-known throughout the Chozha empire that the prince wielded near-magical expertise when it came to taming elephants. Why, he could even communicate with them! Some warmed up to the idea that it was indeed Ponniyin Selvar who had been spotted atop the elephant; they conjectured that he had mounted the animal in an effort to soothe its madness and protect the people from its temper.

It was at this very moment that Murugaiyan and the mahout arrived at the palace. When the troubled crowd heard the mahout's story, they were aghast. This man who had held the mahout captive in order to impersonate him – the very fellow they had seen run towards the elephant, *angusam* in hand – why, he must have been sent by the enemies of the Chozha clan!

"Perhaps he was here at the behest of the Pazhuvettarayars," speculated a few, a hypothesis that the livid throng was quick to believe. The people grew increasingly wrathful towards the Pazhuvettarayars and many departed for Thanjavur without a second thought. A lone faction made inquiries into the path taken by the elephant while the rest doggedly set forth upon the road leading to Thanjavur, their impulsive journey fuelled by rage.

Hidden Meanings and Explanations

Raja veethi - The main street, literally translates to the kingsroad

Jaamam - A measure of time equalling 3 hours. Also measured as 7 ½ *naazhigai*, with each *naazhigai* measuring 24 minutes.

Saambraani - Frankincense

19

THIRUNALLAM

As she floated at the whim of the floodwaters that had broken away from the river Kaveri, Vanathi held onto the thatched roof of the *josiyar*'s hut – and her own life - with all the might she could muster. The waters dragged her further and further in an easterly direction. Sometimes they flowed at a sluggish pace; at others, the current seemed to awaken with renewed strength and its monstrous force yanked her along like a doll. At times, the thatched roof was helplessly ensnared in eddies that made it spiral clumsily in dizzying circles.

Occasionally, the flood flowed along elevated lands where the waters lost some measure of their depth. These instances offered Vanathi a vantage point from which she could see the breathtaking extent of the flood. It seemed to have unleashed a merciless love for the land, for its waters embraced as much of it as they could. The splendid *mandapams* that graced the banks of the Kaveri lay submerged; even the formidable trees dotting the landscape had been engulfed by the deluge. Vanathi had but a moment to take in these sights; she scarcely had any time to consider approaching dry land before the currents insistently towed her away to deeper waters.

Truth be told, Vanathi didn't really have the heart to make her way ashore. An inscrutable certainty had taken hold of her, leaving her convinced that these feisty Ponni waters would deliver her to Ponniyin Selvar if only she held on. Her mind kept going back to the Pazhuvettarayar's veiled warning about the perils that lay in wait for the prince. She felt in her bones that the river Kaveri herself was carrying her to the prince so that she could shield him from harm.

Vanathi suddenly gripped the thatched roof even harder in exasperation, her knuckles turning white. *Aha*! How arrogant that Poonguzhali is, to take the liberties she does with the prince! She even has the temerity to involve herself in his affairs! To be fair, her boldness was perhaps not unjustified. At the end of the day, doesn't the prince owe his very life to Poonguzhali?... No, that was quite unacceptable. Why, Vanathi herself had heard the Kudanthai *jothidar*'s words, hadn't she? It is the design of Fate that creates mischief for the prince, bound as She is by the horoscope plotted at the time of his birth; these knaveries pose no real threat to his life! What can mere seas, storms or floods do to a person who was born to rule the world? Naturally, it falls to someone or the other to be the pawn that helps him dodge the pitfalls that surface along the way. Poonguzhali should, in fact, count herself fortunate that she had the opportunity to render such honourable service! How could she imagine that it grants her the licence to behave as she does with the prince? Despite Vanathi's profound vexation, dear readers, we regret to admit that deep down, she yearned for a similar threat to present itself to the prince so that she could rise to the occasion too.

Ever so often, when the thatch swirled around in the occasional whirlpool, Vanathi thought that she could spot a boat in the distance. It seemed to carry a man and a woman, though it wasn't clear who they were. The woman was clearly in charge; she was deftly navigating the boat through the capricious waters. Vanathi wondered if it was Poonguzhali. Was she coming to save Vanathi? Could Ilaiya Piratti have sent her to offer aid? That would be the last straw! It was bad enough that the prince owed a debt of gratitude to her. Vanathi couldn't bear the thought of such an obligation foisted upon herself as well. No, she must never permit that indignity to be put on her!

At times, it looked as if the boat was approaching closer to her; at others, the rapids swept away the thatch so swiftly that it left the boat far behind. It was at such a moment when the boat was out of sight that the thatch unexpectedly changed direction and drifted towards the south. The unrelenting waters tugged it along southwards for quite a distance; the thatch hurtled past the southern banks of the Kaveri river and continued upon its course until it reached a vast plain inundated by the torrents, looking for all the world like a great new sea that had materialized upon the land. Vanathi strained her eyes until she caught sight of the horizon. *Aha!* The landmass appeared to be a riverbank.... Yes, this was indeed the bank of the Arisalaaru river! The gushing floodwaters that had cleaved away from the Kaveri had drowned the lands along its calamitous course, only to now merge with the Arisalaaru and drain into this very river basin. The southern bank was situated upon a higher gradient which brought the unruly torrent under some control. The freshets coalesced with the river in an orderly fashion, politely submitting to the Arisalaaru's course without breaking its perimeter. The picturesque riverside scenery with its lush, green canopy of trees seemed familiar to Vanathi. Wisps of faint memories rose unbidden, reminding Vanathi of what felt like the long-forgotten scent of an earlier life. No, no, that was quite far-fetched - this place had to be an old haunt, one that she had frequented in this very lifetime. It suddenly dawned on Vanathi that she must be nearing the idyllic temple town of Thirunallam, where stood an important shrine that venerated Lord Siva. Sembian Madevi, daughter of the esteemed Mazhavaraiyar, dearly wished to serve the deity by rebuilding the sanctuary in handsome granite in remembrance of her beloved husband, the noble Kandaradhitha Chozhar. Thirunallam was also home to the exquisite *vasantha maaligai* - the spring palace - of the Chozha royals. Once, Vanathi recalled, she had accompanied Ilaiya Piratti on a visit to this elegant palace on the invitation of Sembian Madevi. She remembered being enchanted by the sights and sounds of the palatial edifice and its beautiful grounds; the gardens had thrummed with sweet birdsong and Vanathi had been captivated by the melodious tweets and trills that saturated the air. *Aha!* Vanathi caught her breath as she revisited the past. It was at Thirunallam that a stirring incident had taken place, leaving behind an indelible impression; it was a memory, she felt, that would never release her from its grasp.

20

Fledglings

When Vanathi had first arrived in Pazhaiyarai, the bountiful waters merrily leaping and rolling over the lands of Chozha Naadu fairly drowned her in a sea of wonder. Her own Kodumbalur laid claim to no river; instead, it was bestowed with a smattering of lakes that transgressed their banks when the rains came and moodily turned dry as twigs in the summers. Kodumbalur did not have reservoirs like these. Chozha Naadu's delightfully lively rivers heaved with abundant waters that jubilantly chased their course; rivulets gurgled as they twined around one another, meshing into capricious whorls and eddies that rippled through the cascading streams. Viridescent ponds seemed to laugh with joy as a profusion of lotuses and red water lilies lushly carpeted their waters, virtually hiding them from the sun. Their mesmerizing beauty would transfix Vanathi, who spent many pleasant hours gazing at the view. The lotuses vaunted their broad, beautiful leaves which resembled verdant umbrellas sheltering the little fishes that darted about in the pond. Vanathi delighted in watching silver droplets of water glide across their waxy surface like tiny pearls. Shiny black beetles wooed lotuses and water lilies alike, nimbly flitting about the flowers in bewildering loops as they hummed their hypnotic songs. The spectacle would transport Vanathi to realms of ecstasy where she would lose all track of time.

When Sembian Madevi had welcomed Kundhavai and Vanathi to Thirunallam - found on the maps of today as the village Konerirajapuram - it was at the stately spring palace where they had spent their sojourn. Sembian Madevi and Kundhavai would often be engrossed in erudite talks exploring the history of the Saivite *kuravar* clan, whose sublime *pathigams* dripped with the nectar of bhakti like sweet honey from a comb. Vanathi was not particularly interested in these conversations herself. Instead, she found herself drawn to the sylvan gardens skirting the palace, where cool ponds exulted in their treasure trove of fragrant lotuses that shivered in bunches upon their waters as black beetles courted them with their giddy dance. She loved to watch the waters of the river that babbled by the palace, bewitching her with its swirling, roiling waters; delicate, scarlet *kadamba* flowers bobbed prettily upon its surface, vibrant companions to the sprightly waters. Where could she find such enchanting scenes in Kodumbalur?

One day, the daughter of the noble Mazhavaraiyar Sembian Madevi and Ilaiya Piratti Kundhavai were absorbed in their conversation. As Vanathi approached, Ilaiya Piratti called out to her. "Vanathi, why don't you visit the gardens? I will join you there shortly," she suggested.

Vanathi didn't need to be told twice. Her eyes sparkled as she joyfully ran to the gardens with a skip and a hop. She lingered in the park, wandering the expansive grounds to her heart's content. She strolled towards her favourite stamping ground, the banks of the lotus pond. A dense thicket of trees encircled the pond, so tall and imposing that they fairly shut out the sky. Yet, there was one venerable specimen that was taller than its formidable companions; it towered among the rest like a splendid giant, its many spreading branches bestowing it with an impressive girth to boot. It was an old *iluppai* tree, heavy with sweet-smelling blossoms. The ground could hardly be seen under a carpet of fallen *iluppai* flowers, whose heady scent was carried throughout the gardens by the cool breeze. Choosing a gnarled root that looked quite comfortable to sit upon, Vanathi nestled against the tree's sturdy trunk. It was a lovely spot to rest in. From here, Vanathi could enjoy a panoramic view of the beautiful estate as the melodious cries of birds fell on her ears like honey on the tongue. Her heart swelled with inexpressible joy, the likes of which she had never known before. Vanathi was convinced that it would burst, unable to contain the waves of happiness that surged through her. She had never dreamed that life could contain such unearthly bliss.

Vanathi rapturously drank in the view. The lattice of tree branches that stretched out in front of her had gaps large enough to accommodate a view of the river merrily flowing in the distance. It was such a charming scene that Vanathi found her eyes drawn to the riverside every once in a while. It was at one such moment that she caught sight of a young man swimming in the river. He was unfamiliar to her, but the lustre of his glowing complexion was apparent even at this distance; he glided smoothly through the waters with confident, powerful strokes that subdued the reddish-brown currents. Vanathi could glimpse a part of his lean, muscular physique as he swam. Fascinated, she gazed at him unawares. Her cheeks flushed hot with mortification as soon as she realized what she was doing. *Chee, chee! Come now, Vanathi*, she thought to herself sternly, *you can't go around making sheep's eyes at some youngster... why, this insolence hardly becomes you!* As far as Vanathi was concerned, modesty and reserve formed an essential part of her identity as a lady of refinement and she held dear her reputation for innocence and naiveté. Deeply abashed by her brief fall from grace, Vanathi determinedly turned away to look upon other, chaster views, but her traitorous eyes betrayed all attempts at discipline to rove once again to the riverside. She grew increasingly vexed with herself. Perhaps the only way to salvage this disgrace was to get up and leave forthwith. It was at this precise moment that a gripping event made itself known to her, distracting her from self-chastisement.

Vanathi suddenly became aware of the mewling cries of fledglings, not too far away from where she was sitting. So piteous did they sound, that she got up to investigate without a second thought; what she saw stopped her heart in terror and pity at once. Perched upon the forks of a branch was a bird's nest, from which tiny fledglings were shrieking frantically, craning their necks out in panic. To Vanathi's delicate sensibilities, the cries of distress sounded heartbreakingly emotive, carrying within them layered tones of petrified terror and abject pleas for help. Mortal danger was nearing them in the form of a wild cat, which was slowly but surely stealing towards the nest.

"Ayyo!" A scream of pure fear escaped Vanathi's lips. A concerned voice instantly rose in response. "What happened?" it shouted, accompanied by the sound of hurried footsteps. Vanathi turned to see someone running anxiously towards her to help. It was the same youth whom she had seen swimming in the river just moments ago; he had evidently heard her cries and quickly climbed ashore in alarm.

Suddenly, two large birds appeared on the scene. They circled the nest in agitation, screeching loudly and wildly flapping their wings. They were the parents of the fledglings, Vanathi realized. Judging from their long beaks, they were woodpeckers. One of them continued to hover around the nest while the other flew towards the wild cat with belligerence, wielding its sharp beak menacingly.

It was, in truth, part bravado - it posed no real threat to the cat, which could quite easily make a tasty morsel of the bird if it drew close enough. But the bold woodpecker tried its best to beat back the predator - after all, the very lives of its chicks were at stake. Vanathi, who had lost both her parents when she was quite young, felt deeply moved by the sight.

The cat stood still, biding its time. It suddenly extended a velvety paw towards the fledgling nest; sharp claws dug into the nearest corner, eliciting a scream of horror from Vanathi. The young man arrived at this very juncture, demanding to know what the matter was. Painfully shy, Vanathi found herself tongue-tied in his presence. She merely pointed to the bird's nest in response to his worried questions.

The young man had, until now, thought that it was the girl who was in grievous danger. When he followed Vanathi's pointing finger, he understood the situation. He turned back to her and smiled. Vanathi's heart skipped a beat. She lost herself in his warm gaze and friendly smile; why, she even momentarily forgot about the fledglings.

The young man, however, didn't hang around. He bolted towards the tree and positioned himself directly under the forked branch that cradled the bird's nest. The youth proceeded to reproach the wild cat in no uncertain terms, letting it know exactly what he thought of its behaviour, with dark threats thrown into the bargain. The cat swivelled towards him angrily, hissing and spitting as it registered its vehement protest against his interference in the matter. "What a mischievous cat this seems to be!" exclaimed the young man as he picked up a small rock and aimed it skillfully at his mark. The stone struck the branch with considerable force, flustering the animal. Quick as lightning, it jumped lithely onto another tree and from there, onto another branch; it soon disappeared into the thick foliage.

One crisis had been averted, but another sprung up in its place. The wild cat had pawed at the fledgling nest before it hastily retreated, had it not? The animal's villainy had left the nest rather unsteady; the stone's impact upon the branch made it even shakier. If the nest had been knocked down, it would have spelt a poor end for the fledglings and their recent triumph over death would have been short-lived. As it happened, the nest was not unseated though it did sway dangerously; a moment later, it slid a few inches down the fork in the branch. Mercifully, a corner of the nest remained wedged onto the branch, saving it from tumbling down. The lives of the tiny fledglings hung in the balance. The woodpeckers circled the nest in a panicked frenzy, shrieking in terror and helplessness all the while. The nest dangled so precariously that it seemed like a gust of wind could blow it down to the ground; it would be impossible for the chicks to survive a fall from such a height.

The young man took a beat to assess the situation. At first, he seemed to consider climbing the tree to save the nest; he evidently found the solution lacking, for he discarded the idea for a better one the very next moment. He turned to Vanathi. "*Penne*! Come here," he said. "I will be back in just a minute - if the nest falls before I return, catch it safely in the folds of your *saree*." Having dispensed his instructions, he broke into a run.

The lad reappeared quickly just as he had promised, except that this time, he was seated on an elephant. Vanathi thought she understood what he planned to do and retreated to the steps of the lotus pond to watch.

The elephant lumbered towards the tree, stopping at its base. Perched atop the tusker, the youth could reach out to the nest quite easily. He carefully took it in his hands, making sure to be gentle with the chicks; he then placed it back into the crevice of the forked branch as it was before. The woodpeckers screeched raucously, louder than Vanathi thought possible. Only this time, they were squawks of pure joy.

A good deed done, the lad turned around expectantly. He then looked all about him. "*Penne*! Where have you disappeared to?" he cried. Vanathi felt enormously bashful all of a sudden and turned quiet as a mouse. The young man dismounted the elephant, puzzled. He surveyed the gardens once again.

A thought struck Vanathi, one so comical that she chortled despite herself. Drawn to her peals of laughter, the young man appeared on the steps of the lotus pond. "*Penne!* Why are you laughing? What on earth is so funny?" he demanded.

Vanathi's heart leapt at his warm, rich voice and she caught her breath. Painfully shy, she averted her eyes and looked around awkwardly to avoid meeting his gaze.

"Come now miss, do tell. Why did you laugh? Won't you share the joke with me?" pressed the youth. Vanathi composed herself with some effort. "Oh, it's nothing, really," she replied lightly. "Only, it occurred to me what a fine warrior you must be, deploying an elephant to fight a cat!" The young man burst into laughter. "Why, miss, was that really a cat?" he quipped. "I feared that you were under attack from a tiger, going by your screams a short while ago!"

Diffidence gave way to boldness and Vanathi straightened her back imperiously. "Aha! Is that what you thought? A strange presumption, to be sure. Why would I be afraid of a tiger in the heartlands of Chozha Naadu, whose very banner carries one as its emblem?" she retorted. "Are you a Pandiyan?"

The lad looked delighted at Vanathi's riposte. His face brightened and a broad grin spread over his features. "I'm no foreigner, miss. I am a son of this very soil. I've been to battle for it, you know - atop an elephant, of course. And who are *you*? Which town are you from?" he asked interestedly. "What a chatterbox you seem to be!"

Piqued, Vanathi drew herself up to her full height. "Have a care for your words, mahout!" she replied indignantly. "What is it to you who I am?"

"Alright, then, I'll hold my tongue - it looks like you're high society, too good for the likes of me!" said the young man. A tone of petulance had crept into his voice. "I'll take your leave now, while I have some dignity left!" he declared and walked up the steps in a huff.

Vanathi felt a warm, familiar tingle spread across her cheeks as her heart beat a bit faster. "Mahout, mahout!" she called out impishly, dimples playing at the corners of her mouth. "Won't you take me for a ride upon your elephant?"

The lad stopped and turned to look at her thoughtfully. "I don't see why not," he admitted. "What do you propose to give me as payment?" he enquired politely.

"Payment?" Vanathi echoed, rather pompously one might add. "I will petition my uncle to grant you a post in the Kodumbalur palace. Or perhaps you would find being the general of the elephant regiment more to your liking? That can be done as well," she offered regally.

"Oho. You are the princess of Kodumbalur, then," replied the youth, his eyebrows knitting together. The smile slid off his face and the merry twinkle in his eyes dulled. It was clear that their pleasant banter had come to an end.

"Is it such a bad thing to be? Do you hold the princess of Kodumbalur in such low esteem?" remarked Vanathi, crestfallen. "I suppose you won't take me for a ride upon your elephant, now?" she asked, hurt.

"Well, the elephant stables at the Kodumbalur palace must have enough elephants and mahouts to spare. What good will I do there?" he replied. He briskly ascended the steps of the lotus pond.

For a minute there, Vanathi felt sure that he would turn around. But the young man proceeded to his elephant without a glance. He simply mounted the animal as Vanathi watched and left wordlessly.

The incident lingered with Vanathi. She thought often of the mahout, her heart swelling with an indefinable joy as she pictured his sinewy frame and cheerful face; even his mellow voice resounded sweetly in her ears. She chuckled in spite of herself as she recalled how the young hero had come to the rescue of the small fledglings, grandly mounted upon an elephant; she then felt embarrassed a moment later for reasons she couldn't explain. Then she remembered his distasteful expression upon discovering that she was a princess of Kodumbalur, and fresh anger arose within her as she brooded upon his inconceivable arrogance. In short, the mahout dominated her thoughts, whether in fondness or fury. Vanathi piled torture upon her already muddled state of mind by wondering at the propriety of it all.

The court was abuzz with the talk that Ponniyin Selvar was to make an appearance at Thirunallam to pay a visit to his *thamakkai*, Ilaiya Piratti. All the damsels of the palace - Vanathi included - were eager to catch a glimpse of the prince, the darling of Chozha Naadu; after all, such chances don't crop up often. Rumour had it that the prince had already arrived, but he was yet to be spotted on the premises of the *anthapuram*. Many young ladies expended great efforts to create serendipitous occasions that might land them in the prince's presence; but Vanathi, sweet, self-effacing and reticent, couldn't bring herself to engineer such artifices. Is it surprising that lady luck smiled upon her? For Vanathi, purely by chance, caught sight of Ponniyin Selvar atop an elephant as she was standing on the palace balcony one day. Her eyes widened in disbelief. There, seated upon the elephant, was the young man she had naively taken to be a mahout! The lad whom Vanathi had teased and brazenly ordered about was none other than the illustrious Arulmozhi Varmar himself, the young prince celebrated by the entire empire! Vanathi was dumbstruck. Presently, she turned to the maidens accompanying her; she asked them - more than once, to be sure - whether the gentleman really was Ponniyin Selvar. Fact firmly confirmed, she flushed with shame and humiliation. Mere words cannot describe her chagrin at what she now perceived to be an unbearable ignominy.

Vanathi relived the entire incident in excruciating detail. She recalled with painful precision how she had proudly offered the prince - one born to rule the world, no less - a position in the Kodumbalur palace as the head of its elephant stables. On one hand, the memory sent her into convulsions of laughter at the absurdity of the proffer; on the other, it sunk her into the gloomy depths of mortification, driving her to bitter tears of despair at her folly. She grew increasingly convinced that the prince's countenance had abruptly changed because of her impertinence - 'Mahout!' she had addressed him, with great authority to boot! Vanathi was quite certain that the encounter had left an uncharitable impression on the prince, who doubtless now found her deeply wanting in the very qualities she held so much store by - docility, restraint, propriety and modesty, all crucial hallmarks of a woman of breeding. Despondency weighed on her as she reflected upon her irreparable reputation with the prince. She contemplated giving up all claims to her life; she thought often of surrendering to the cold depths of a river or a pond. More than once, she tried confessing her sin to Ilaiya Piratti Kundhavai. Regrettably, her courage failed each time and the words froze upon her tongue. Vanathi realized that the prince hadn't reported the incident to Kundhavai Devi; Ilaiya Piratti would have doubtless broached the matter with her if he had. The prince's benevolence in refraining from airing her indiscretions offered her a semblance of solace amidst the bleak misery. Vanathi determined to beg the prince's forgiveness in person as soon as she could, for, she felt, that was the least she could do before seeking comfort in the afterlife. Alas, she lacked the courage for this course of reparation as well.

When Vanathi returned to Pazhaiyarai, she discovered that she had been robbed of its charms - the thought of chancing upon the prince was too dreadful to consider, and she had a harrowing time trying to stay out of his path. She beat a hasty retreat when she sensed his presence in the vicinity, disappearing into hideaways where she thought he was unlikely to appear. As far as Vanathi was concerned, it was easier to look death in the eye than to face the prince. Vanathi's companions found her inordinate timidity puzzling; Ilaiya Piratti, unaware of what had transpired at Thirunallam, was mystified by her behaviour as well. Unable to find a rationale, they chalked up Vanathi's strange antics to her diffident nature.

To her utter dismay, Vanathi soon discovered that Ponniyin Selvar had another valid reason to detest her. She realized that her uncle intended to wed her to the prince in what was plainly an opportunistic alliance for he, along with the rest of the world, believed that Arulmozhi Varmar would ascend to power after his father and reign over the vast Chozha empire. It was patently obvious that Boodhi Vikrama Kesari had shipped her off to Pazhaiyarai as part of this grand design - that was what the palace maidens suggested to each other at any rate, arching their brows meaningfully at each other and making snide remarks. They were quite open about their views at times. "Be honest, now - this is why you elude the prince, is it not? Your schemes are more transparent than you think, you know!" they would tease her, a tad more unkindly than not. Vanathi's ears would burn with shame at these words. She couldn't help but think that their hurtful taunts perhaps carried a kernel of bitter truth; she cast her mind back to that day at Thirunallam, when the prince's face fell upon learning her identity as the princess of Kodumbalur.

Vanathi's heart churned unpleasantly as she grappled with the swarm of emotions that assailed her. She hadn't yet come to grips with her feelings when she learned that Ponniyin Selvar was to take up arms to join the Chozha forces fighting the war in Eezham. Elaborate arrangements were made to give the prince an auspicious send-off. The palace women were to assemble in order to wish him a safe return, bearing auspicious *mangala deepams* - brightly lit lamps - as they bade him well. Naturally, Vanathi had to be there; she could hardly ask to be released from such a significant ceremony. In truth, she too yearned to see the prince before he left for war. She resolved to beg his forgiveness through her expressive eyes and countenance if words failed her once again. As it happened, her elegant plan went awry. As the prince approached Vanathi and locked eyes with her, she fell into a swoon and the *deepam* tumbled from her hands. The rest, of course, is history - our learned readers no doubt remember the incidents that came to pass following this moment.

It was these events and others that swam before Vanathi's eyes as she floated towards Thirunallam on the Kundanthai *jothidar's* rickety thatch. As she reviewed the past, Vanathi realized that Ponniyin Selvar must bear some compassion for her in a corner of his heart; he had certainly made efforts to make his solicitude known to her, both directly and with the help of his sister, Ilaiya Piratti - she could see that now. Still, Vanathi mused, there remained a spanner in the works, a hindrance that stunted the prince's affection. It was clear to her that Ponniyin Selvar harboured deep misgivings about the virtue of any affinity that may lie between them, sensing opportunism in the place of candour - he must resent having to endure the contrivances of those who wished to gain from his hypothetical ascent to the throne. Vanathi had to admit that one couldn't fault him for that; it was quite a reasonable assumption given that her own uncle had been quite explicit about his vested interests in the matter on multiple occasions. Come to think of it, Ilaiya Piratti herself was an accessory to this plan, was she not? Everybody knew that. Even that young boat girl Poonguzhali made fun of Vanathi on this count, did she not? Hardly surprising then, that the entire affair had left a sour taste in the prince's mouth, spoiling his fondness for her.

But surely, the prince must change his view if he learns of the vow that Vanathi had made a short while ago! His affection for her would turn wholesome, would it not? Vanathi wondered if he would come to know of her decision. Perhaps she should tell him herself? *Adi, silly Vanathi - you are at a loss for words in his presence, don't you remember? Irony of ironies! You talked his ear off at Thirunallam with your inane prattle, convincing him that you're an insufferable vayaadi. Then you turned quiet as a statue in later encounters, refusing to speak or even glance at him! Poor, wretched, desolate Vanathi! Don't let yourself down the next time you gain an audience with the prince; speak up and let him know what lies in your heart! Tell him, 'Even if you do ascend the Chozha throne, I myself will not. This is a vow I intend to hold steadfast! Even if you were to remain a mahout, all I desire is a place beside you upon your elephant - that would be a sweeter paradise than heaven!"*

Now that is a fine speech. If that doesn't do the trick, nothing will. There only remains the small matter of actually saying it to the prince. Would such an opportune moment arise? Where is this flood taking me, anyway? Will I spend my last moments floating upon these beastly waters thus? No, that is quite ludicrous… There, there is the shore! That structure must be the maguda kalasam cresting the Thirunallam spring palace! It seems like only yesterday that the prince came riding upon an elephant to save those fledglings. He spoke to me so sweetly that day!

What, now? Something approaches in the distance… an elephant! With a mahout on top of it, no less! Look how easily the animal navigates the floods, treating the force of their swift currents with scorn; it looks like a large hill moving through the waters! It has already reached the shore and is now moving towards the west bank. Who can its mahout be? He cuts such a striking figure, sitting with such regal composure upon the elephant... perhaps… chi! You must have feathers for brains to think such an odd thought! Why, for the love of all that is good, would the prince be here of all places - all by himself, besides, with just an elephant for company?

I can't possibly suspect every mahout I see to be the prince just because I mistook him to be one, can I? That's utterly daft. But how does that matter in any case? Even if the gentleman is nothing more than a mahout, he is in a position to help me, is he not? It is possible, even, that he will take me along on the elephant once he learns who I am and deliver me to Ponniyin Selvar!

Having perceived this unexpected ray of hope, Vanathi cried out with all her might. "Mahout, mahout!" she called, loud as she could. The elephant, however, showed no signs of stopping; the mahout didn't even glance in her direction! It was not certain whether the mahout was unable to hear her cries for help or whether he wilfully turned a deaf ear to her plight. The elephant picked up pace and stamped around a bend in the river bank, disappearing from Vanathi's sight.

Vanathi had little time to nurse her disappointment, for a terrifying realization dawned upon her. The rickety thatch began to spin in the floodwaters at a dangerously rapid speed. Yes, yes, it wasn't just her imagination - the floodwaters had gained momentum, flowing at a violently fast rate. The riverbank was fast approaching, as were the thick, gnarled roots of the enormous trees that grew upon its sides. There was no doubt about it - the thatch was on a perilous course, one that would leave it splintered by the sturdy roots upon impact. If that disaster came to pass, the thatch would certainly sink; and then what would Vanathi do? Could she survive the collision and swim ashore? Or would the fiendish eddies smash her upon the roots as well, spelling her doom?

Ayyo! A new peril seems to have surfaced to add to my misery - what is it that lies amidst the roots? Vanathi gave a start of fear as she realized that it was an enormous crocodile, opening its massive jaws as wide as it could. It was almost too frightening to look at. Was that truly a crocodile and not just some repulsive doll? Maybe it was a hallucination, Vanathi hoped.

Here, the shore has come already... and there are the tree roots, waiting to decimate this derelict thatch!

Vanathi shut her eyes and prayed fervently. "*Thaaye*, Durga Parameshwari! Divine mother! This orphan girl knows no other refuge but You. Please take me unto Your lotus feet!"

ꕥ

Hidden Meanings and Explanations

Pathigam- Here, hymns in praise of the divine

Mangala deepam - An auspicious send off for the young prince, wherein the young damsels of the palace gather to carry brightly lit lamps.

21

Lives hang in the balance

There are some circumstances in which, it is said, a mere second can feel as long as a *yugam*, an entire epoch; it was precisely in such a situation that Vanathi found herself. As she squeezed her eyes shut and desperately invoked the grace of Durga Parameshwari, the thatch continued upon its treacherous course to doom, ruthlessly swept away by the swirling eddies. The anticipated collision took place in a matter of moments; but to Vanathi, who was paralyzed with fear, it felt like she hurtled along for aeons before the impact finally came. Her eyes flew open when her body sustained a large, unexpected shock - Vanathi discovered that while the thatch had disintegrated when it smashed against the roots, she herself had escaped its fate by virtue of a misshapen bough that had stopped the waters from carrying her away - as luck would have it, the upper half of her frame was well and truly caught in its bend, sparing her the collision. Even in her dazed state, Vanathi discerned the serendipity of her condition and gripped onto the branch as tightly as she could. The floodwaters seemed unwilling to part ways with her. Her feet were caught in the hideously powerful undertow of the eddies, which seemed to be doing its damnedest to pull her back into the waters. So forceful was the current, that Vanathi feared it would tear her legs clean off her body. Her *saree* was also caught in the flow; it tugged insistently at her, threatening to drag her down into the floodwaters.

Then, a miracle happened - a wave of remarkable courage and resolve swelled in Vanathi out of nowhere. She grit her teeth as she strained every muscle in her arms to pull herself up onto the bough, vaulting on top of the branch through sheer force of will. She spied a wide, sturdy bough overhead, one that forked into two branches; deeming it stout enough to bear her weight, she chose a comfortable spot along its length and plopped down firmly. Relatively safe for the moment, Vanathi set about wringing out the folds of her *saree*, which was understandably soaked through.

All of a sudden, she heard the sounds of vigorous thrashing coming from the waters below. With a start, she remembered the crocodile that she had seen just before she shut her eyes.

Vanathi bent down with caution and closely surveyed the waters roiling below her. The crocodile's thick, armoured tail immediately caught her eye, for the reptile was whipping it violently from side to side. The rest of its body was obscured by the wreckage of the thatched roof that had been rent asunder. The crocodile seemed to be caught under the debris; it was using its powerful tail to twist and turn its body in a frenzied attempt to wiggle out from under the fragments. Little by little, the massive beast emerged from under the ruins until it was completely free. Gloating over its success, the crocodile lay there with its mighty jaws wide open, drawing attention to its cavernous mouth. Vanathi couldn't help but feel that the gesture was directed towards her. 'Come on, then,' the creature seemed to be telling her. 'We both know how this will end - you have to fall in my mouth sooner or later!'

Still exhilarated from her recent brush with death, Vanathi scoffed at the crocodile. "So you have designs of swallowing me, do you? Oh crocodile, no sleight of hand or tail will find purchase with me! There's no point in baring your sharp teeth at me, either. Don't depend upon me to sate your hunger - find another prey to fill your stomach!" she declared.

Her words clearly had an effect on the reptile; it fixed its cold, frightening eyes upon her in an unblinking stare, seemingly sizing the hunt at hand.

"Oho!" cried Vanathi. "You're still tempted at the thought of eating me, I see!" She looked all around her to get the full measure of this new predicament. Unfortunately, her situation did look rather bleak. The only branches that hung down low enough to offer her a safe descent were those hanging over the swirling waters; there was no such path that led to the bank. She couldn't climb down the trunk either, for the crocodile lurked in the tangled roots at the base of the tree, eager to make a meal of her. There was no question of jumping into the river from the low-hanging branches - the swirling, churning waters were waiting to whisk her away to the netherworlds. Vanathi couldn't even look at the waters for too long, for the whirling eddies made her head spin in circles. "The branches overhanging the bank are higher, but that may not be a big problem. It should be possible to jump down to the ground one way or another," she decided, getting up to walk across to the other side.

Vanathi made a few attempts to get up and stand, but her legs began to shake like a leaf every time she tried; they had grown numb from being in the water for such a long time. "Chee! What has come over you, legs?" said Vanathi crossly. She sat down once again with a resigned air - there was nothing she could do but wait. This was now a battle of wills between Vanathi and the hungry crocodile. Who had greater reserves of patience? Time would tell.

The shrill blast of an elephant's trumpet pierced the air, startling Vanathi. The pachyderm that she had seen cross the river a short while ago to head west, seemed to be returning. Vanathi also noticed a boat approaching along the edge of the river, carrying two passengers. Yes, there was no doubt about it - one of them was the *jothidar's* acolyte while the other, Vanathi realized with a pang of consternation, was Poonguzhali! Was it her fate to be rescued by her after all?

The boat reached the foaming waters near the base of the tree. It was easy enough for Poonguzhali to spot Vanathi perched upon a broad branch. "Hello, princess!" she called out with a short laugh. "You've chosen a good spot to hide in, I see. Now, make haste and climb down! Do you see that elephant in the distance? Do you know who rides it?"

The truth suddenly dawned on Vanathi, but she needed to hear it said. "Who?" she asked in turn.

"The very soul you floated away in search of - the prince!" replied Poonguzhali.

Delighted, Vanathi gazed with wonder at the person approaching on the elephant. it was only when he drew nearer that she registered the inelegance of her situation. She couldn't possibly let the prince see her plonked awkwardly atop a tree! Deciding that it was better to climb down to the boat as Poonguzhali had advised, she peered down to assess the descent.

She saw that the boat had started to drift away, unable to brave the rapid currents of the floodwaters. Vanathi drew in a sharp breath as Poonguzhali leapt down, choosing to stay rather than go with the vessel. *Ayyo*! What had that girl done? Did she not notice the giant crocodile lying in wait nearby? A million panicked thoughts ran through Vanathi's mind in the blink of an eye and urgent, garbled words came spilling out of her mouth as she shouted at Poonguzhali in alarm.

Poonguzhali could only make out a single word amidst all the gibberish directed at her - '*crocodile*!' Unnerved, she turned around slowly. Yes, there it was, quite close to her - an enormous crocodile, opening its snaggle-toothed jaws as wide as it could! As Poonguzhali turned to look at the beast, it emphatically thumped its scaly tail upon the water in ominous acknowledgement of her presence.

There was no doubt that Poonguzhali was exceptionally brave - after all, she had admirably held her own against all sorts of dangers. But what advantage can bravery bring when confronting a ten-foot long crocodile hungrily opening its yawning jaws? A tiny misstep would mean certain death! If Poonguzhali wasted another second in making herself scarce, she might just find herself in the creature's eager mouth. But how was she to escape? The only recourse available to her was to get back onto the boat!

Arriving quickly at this conclusion, Poonguzhali dove into the water. The boat, meanwhile, had floated farther away; unable to keep the craft in place, the *jothidar*'s disciple had decided to put down anchor at a spot further ahead along the edge of the bank. He had not noticed the mortal danger that Poonguzhali was facing.

Poonguzhali began to swim towards the boat. She found that the savagery of Kaveri's waters were fiercer than even the vast sea and its towering waves; the strong undertow of the maelstrom pulled her downwards as she fought to swim against the currents. She also noticed that the crocodile had begun to hunt her - it was on the move and close behind, ready to catch her as its prey. Poonguzhali fought a rising panic as she realized that her *thalappu* - the train of her *saree* - had snagged itself on a bent branch, making the matter dicier.

Vanathi was watching the entire scene unfold from the safety of her perch. All she could think of was Poonguzhali's bitterly cruel speech earlier in the day; she recalled how the words had left her cut to the quick, provoking the solemn oath from her lips. She also remembered how she had scorned Poonguzhali's helping hand, only to plummet into the floodwaters that had swallowed up the *jothidar*'s home. These sour thoughts surfaced and disappeared in an instant; for Vanathi was also quick to remember that it was this very boat girl who had saved Ponniyin Selvar from the sea and delivered him safely to the Choodamani Viharam. Surely, she, along with all of Chozha Naadu, owed her a debt of overwhelming gratitude for this act of succour! There, there comes the prince upon the elephant. God forbid that he finds this boat girl in the grip of a crocodile - won't he fall into a state of agony and torment? What would he think of Vanathi? In fact, it could be said that Vanathi was partly responsible for the danger the girl faced - after all, wasn't it to save her that the boat girl had come here all this way?

All these thoughts raced through Vanathi's mind in one-hundredth the time that it took you, dear reader, to read about them. Not for nothing do they say that thoughts fly faster than the wind; among all the fleet-footed entities in this world of ours, thoughts are indeed the swiftest.

The brief but intense bout of soul searching helped Vanathi decide quite firmly where her duties lay. Without a second thought, she swiftly climbed down to a low-hanging branch and lay face down, straining to stretch her arms as far as she could to grab hold of Poonguzhali's hair. Poonguzhali looked up; she made no effort to free herself but stretched her own arm towards Vanathi in turn. The young women locked hands, each holding onto the other as tightly as they could. As Vanathi began to tug Poonguzhali to safety, the spirited boat girl gripped a bough with her free hand to pull herself up out of the water; she smoothly hoisted herself up onto Vanathi's branch. Alas, the girls had little time to cheer - their combined load was too much for the limb to bear and the bough stooped dangerously, dipping towards the floodwaters. Thinking fast, Poonguzhali tried to clamber higher up to lighten the load, but her foot slipped, failing to find its grip. The very next moment, Poonguzhali found herself dangling above the seething waters, saved only by Vanathi whose hands clasped one of her own as tightly as they could.

The crocodile had been engrossed in a crisis of its own, navigating the thick, tangled roots that stood between it and its prey. When the reptile finally emerged into the open, it saw Poonguzhali swaying unsteadily from the branch. The beast opened its terrible jaws wide in anticipation. Poonguzhali's very life hung in the balance, dependent on Vanathi's tenacious grip.

Vanathi's slender, frail arms burned with pain. She thought that they would be wrenched from their sockets, unable to bear the heaviness of Poonguzhali's unbelievably strong body - her athletic physique felt like one hewn from solid diamond. Vanathi's heart jumped into her throat. She was frightened to death at the thought of Poonguzhali slipping away from her grasp into the crocodile's jaws below. If that tragedy came to pass, Vanathi could never look the prince in the eye - frankly, it would be far better to share Poonguzhali's fate than to face the prince. Yes, Vanathi decided firmly, that was what she would do if she failed the boat girl.

The elephant was closer, now. The prince approaches on his mount. Will these feeble hands find the strength to hold onto Poonguzhali until he comes to the rescue?

The pachyderm reached the river bank at long last. It stopped beneath the tree and announced its arrival with a deafening trumpet that thundered through the environs. The crocodile heard the roaring blare and looked back, distracted from its prey. Only the good Lord knows what ran through the creature's mind, for it immediately recoiled and made a hasty retreat into the jumbled thicket of roots, hiding itself away from sight.

Vanathi, still prone upon the branch, looked down at the elephant. She saw the person sitting atop the animal - yes, that was the prince! That was Ponniyin Selvar himself!

"Mahout, mahout! Do save us piteous maids like you did those hapless chicks that day!" whispered Vanathi softly to herself.

Impossible; it was simply impossible to hold onto this boat girl any longer. A minute more and her arms would surely tear away from her shoulders. *Appappa! This girl has such a lovely name - Poonguzhali, evoking the soft, fragrant petals of a flower - and her body, rugged and heavy, carries none of its daintiness! It feels like it has been chiselled from pure steel!*

"Oh mahout, mahout, won't you come to our rescue soon?" implored Vanathi.

Poonguzhali screeched at the top of her voice.

Vanathi heard the scream and despaired, devastated at the thought that the crocodile had seized Poonguzhali. A nameless fear gripped her heart with its icy fingers and Vanathi shut her eyes, petrified.

The intolerable load that weighed down her arms grew heavier and more insistent. Judging it to be the crocodile trying to drag Poonguzhali away, Vanathi held on even tighter, eyes shut all the while; she tugged desperately at Poonguzhali, attempting to haul her up to safety.

"Let go, Vanathi... *let go*!" The prince's sweet voice fell on her ears like nectar on the tongue. Not knowing what she was doing anymore, Vanathi blindly followed the instructions and simply let go. The weight that had threatened to rip away her arms lightened and then ceased altogether.

When Vanathi opened her eyes, she saw that the elephant had wrapped its mighty trunk around Poonguzhali's waist. As Vanathi released her hold, the courteous tusker carefully lifted the boat girl and set her down lightly upon the bank. Poonguzhali had closed her eyes, too - she must have screamed when she felt the elephant winding its trunk around her.

Vanathi recalled how she too had shrieked just like that in one instance - in fact, if she remembered correctly, she had screamed at the top of her lungs before dropping to the ground in a faint. That wasn't too long ago and yet, here she was today, boldly facing much greater perils with creditable equanimity and aplomb. Vanathi couldn't help but feel amazed by the change she saw in herself. What a pity that Ilaiya Piratti wasn't here to bear witness to her courage and praise her, as she doubtless would! No matter; she will learn of this incident one way or the other and Vanathi would get her due. To more immediate affairs - what of her fate? Was Vanathi to be left sitting on the tree while the prince whisked Poonguzhali away?

Well, Vanathi thought, that would not be entirely unjustified. It was her own folly that had landed her in this pickle, after all.

Quite to the contrary, the elephant extended its trunk once again. This time, it reached out for Vanathi, who closed her eyes in reflex. The very next moment, she felt the elephant enfold her gently in its trunk; she was lifted from her perch and set down softly upon the bank. When she opened her eyes, she found herself standing next to Poonguzhali.

Vanathi glowed with a sudden rush of affection and warmth towards the boat girl; before she knew what she was doing, she had clasped Poonguzhali in a tight embrace.

Poonguzhali's eyes welled up with tears. "Princess, you have saved my life today; I owe you my very breath," she said, in a voice choked with emotion. "I had set off on the boat intending to redeem you from the floodwaters. Instead, it was you who kept me from falling into the crocodile's mouth. I shall be beholden to you as long as I live."

"Poonguzhali, was it really me who saved your life?" replied Vanathi. "It was that mahout who saved the both of us, wasn't it? It is to him that your gratitude is due!"

"My life is of minor concern to me; however, I cannot draw my last breath before discharging an obligation to my aunt. She has charged me with delivering a pressing message to her beloved son," disclosed Poonguzhali in a solemn tone.

Vanathi looked up at the man seated upon the elephant. A sudden, puckish joy seized her. "Mahout, mahout," she called out in a voice ringing with mischief. "Will you give us both a ride upon your elephant?" she asked, as she broke into silvery peals of laughter.

22

Happiness and Misery

The prince alighted from the elephant, shaking with mirth at Vanathi's words. "Aha! Mounting an elephant is a tricky business you know, as dicey as sitting on a throne. Not only is it difficult to climb onto one, but it is also devilishly hard to keep your seat. As for dismounting an elephant - now that is the most onerous task of them all!" declared Ponniyin Selvar, his eyes twinkling. "Still," he mused, "I suppose one has to experience such hardships once in a while."

"And yet, there are some who weather such trials for the most trivial of reasons," said Vanathi innocently. "Why, some even come charging upon an elephant to rescue helpless chicks!"

"So you do remember that incident, Vanathi! I assumed that you had forgotten all about it since you never brought it up," replied the prince with a grin.

"Heroes who travel the world for noble quests may forget such trifles, not poor maids who spend their lives confined to palaces. What else can we do but reminisce about our little adventures, sparse as they are? Of course I remember how you came atop an elephant that day; I also remember the scowl that appeared on your face upon discovering that I belonged to Kodumbalur stock!" said Vanathi.

"I had reason to behave as I did that day, Vanathi," replied the prince with a plea in his voice.

"I am well aware, *ayya.* I also know that the reason holds true even today," said Vanathi quickly. "You are the cherished son of the emperor who reigns over the world; the very Ponniyin Selvar that a thriving Chozha Naadu prizes as a treasured gem. As for me, I was born and brought up in arid lands. I am merely the daughter of a minor duke; an orphan, in fact, of one who fell in the war!"

"Oh Vanathi, you're being unjust. Surely I am undeserving of those words!" cried the prince. "No matter, we'll leave this be; there's no time to waste, for I must leave for Thanjai without delay. Now tell me," he asked curiously, "however did *you* come to be here? And why were you all by yourself? I gather that you came floating upon a thatched roof, is that right? Also, where did this damsel appear from? How did she get caught in such a terrifying peril?"

"Oh, joy!" an indignant voice erupted from between them. "I am *so* pleased that you deigned to spare a thought for me. I've only been standing right here all this while!" It was a rather miffed Poonguzhali who had clearly been waiting for her chance to speak. "May I take a minute to have a word with you in private?" she asked the prince with great civility. "I will deliver the message I bear for you and make myself scarce!"

It was a rather curious thing, but coming face-to-face with the prince seemed to have struck a vein of familiarity and droll wit in both the maidens.

"Samudhra Kumari! Did you really think I had forgotten you?" smiled the prince. "Why, you were the one who turned a deaf ear to my cries, if you recall - you hurriedly jumped into your boat and vanished without a word! Who would have thought that you would soon be swinging languidly between a bough above and a crocodile below? Heavens, that sight shall stay with me as long as I live and breathe!" laughed the prince. "Nor will I ever forget Vanathi's exquisite agony as she struggled to pull you up! But tell me, how did the pair of you find yourselves here? And why? Come now, won't someone acquaint me with the facts?"

"Ponniyin Selva! Your esteemed *thamakkaiyar* and I sought to meet you on the path to Thanjai. We hoped to dissuade you from your journey, for Ilaiya Piratti fears that your arrival in Thanjavur will incite a cataclysmic war. She wishes to confer with you."

"Where is Ilaiya Piratti now?"

"Kudanthai."

"How did you come to be here by yourself without her?"

"Ilaiya Piratti and I paid a visit to the Kudanthai *jothidar* along the way. While we were there, the river Kaveri went into spate - her gushing waters broke through the banks with such great force that they swept away the *jothidar*'s home. My prince, it is said that mother Kaveri offered you succour as a child. I myself am quite familiar with the love you bear for the Ponni river. All the same, I am forced to wonder if she has an element of cruelty in her. It chills me to the bone to think of the destruction she has wrought upon our cities, people and animals."

"Vanathi, don't vilify mother Kaveri so! That queen among women nurses a boundless love for Chozha Naadu. When the passion overwhelms her, the waters reflect her deep ardour and overflow their boundaries, breaking through the banks. It is nothing but ignorance that prompts some to find fault with such a mother. Why, some even denounce the Sea King for transgressing the boundaries of the coastline; but Poonguzhali, I'm sure, will never place such blame at his feet!"

"Forgive me, my prince. I shall not find fault with mother Kaveri, either. The river breached its banks in a rush of affection, as you put it, while your noble sister and I were at the Kudanthai *jothidar's* home. Your revered *thamakkaiyar* and the rest of our group acted swiftly and climbed atop a temple *mandapam*; I failed to emulate their prudence, so the torrents swept me away. Fortunately, the *jothidar's* thatched roof served me as a passable float and I came drifting upon the floodwaters to this place."

"I suppose Poonguzhali climbed into her boat to save you. A fine plan, indeed! Except, Gajendran here ended up having to rescue the both of you from danger instead. What an intelligent animal this elephant is! It held you damsels ever so gently, treating you like fragile garlands; it even took great care to set you down lightly upon the ground. And yet, it was this very elephant who brutally grabbed a mahout this morning as he ran towards it with an *angusam* in hand - it hoisted him overhead and mercilessly swung him in circles before sending him hurtling through the air. He fell such a great distance away that it is quite unlikely that he survived."

"*Ayyo*! How strange! I wanted to ask you about that, myself…"

"What did you want to ask?"

"If you had faced any danger from the mahout or the *angusam*..."

"It is true that there was the threat of danger. How the deuce did you come to know of it, though? Was it foreshadowed by our visionary the *jothidar*? Hasn't Ilaiya Piratti relinquished her dottiness for fortune-telling yet?"

"It wasn't the *jothidar* who told us; we wouldn't have believed him even if he had. It was Periya Pazhuvettarayar who sounded the alert."

"What on earth... Who did you say?!"

"Yes, my prince. It was none other than the Dhanaadhikaari Periya Pazhuvettarayar who sounded the alert. He arrived all of a sudden at the *jothidar*'s hut while we were there, bringing news of great peril that lay in wait for you. He even told us about the *angusam*, warning of the poison in its tip!"

"A miracle, indeed! I wonder how he came to know of the affair. Has he turned soothsayer too? Or maybe, just maybe.... Could he be the mastermind behind the entire plot as the rumours say?"

"No, my prince, these machinations are not his doing. We learned that the Dhanaadhikaari had uncovered this intrigue whilst spying upon a covert exchange between the Pandiya conspirators..."

"Is that so? Did he have anything else to report from his surveillance?"

"My blood runs cold to merely think of it, let alone say the words out loud. He informed us that the vile connivers have hatched a plot to dispatch you, your illustrious father and the noble elder prince Aditha Karikalar to Yama's abode, all in the course of a single day. After delivering his report, Periya Pazhuvettarayar made haste for Kadambur in a bid to protect prince Aditha Karikalar; before he left, he prevailed upon Ilaiya Piratti to warn you and the Chakravarthy of what lies ahead..."

"His words of caution have become reality in my case, so the warning must hold true for the others as well," said the prince thoughtfully. "Samudhra Kumari! Did you say that you have a message for me?"

"Yes, my prince. The *Oomai Rani* of Eezham has charged me with delivering you to Thanjai forthwith..."

"Ah!" he exclaimed. "I have quite neglected to ask you about that matter; in fact, it was for the Eezham Rani that I had left for Thanjai in such a tearing hurry. I was told that she had been bound and dragged to Thanjavur forcibly - is that true?"

"Yes, *ayya,* the report is true. However, the Mudhanmandhiri Aniruddha Bhramaraayar had only done so with good intentions…"

"That was Aniruddhar's doing, is it? He must have taken her for an audience with my father. Did the Chief Minister's plan succeed? Did the Eezham Rani and the Chakravarthy meet?"

"Yes, they did."

"Then my dearest wish has been fulfilled," said Ponniyin Selvar in delight. "No news can bring me greater joy! As long as my aunt is with him, my father's life is in no danger. The Eezham Rani is blessed with exceptional foresight - surely you are sensible to her remarkable abilities, Poonguzhali!"

"Yes, I am. No harm can approach the Chakravarthy as long as the Eezham Rani is beside him. But…" Poonguzhali bit her lip as she trailed off.

"But? What makes you hesitate, Poonguzhali?"

"I am reluctant to say this, my lord; words fail me. The Eezham Rani perceives that her time is coming to an end. She dearly wishes to see you before she closes her eyes forever!" said Poonguzhali softly.

"What did you say?" the prince asked, aghast. "Your tidings brought me such happiness to begin with - now your terrible summons feels like a thunderbolt! I must tarry no further. Vanathi, please deliver my apologies to Ilaiya Piratti!" said prince Arulmozhi Varmar, his face set with resolve.

ꕥ

Hidden Meanings and Explanations

Thamakkai/Thamakkaiyaar, Thamayan/Thamayanar - Elder sister and elder brother, respectively

23

The Armies Approach

The splendid city of Thanjai had been in a hustle and bustle of feverish activity all day. The metropolis rumbled as her people went about their chores, giving rise to a din as loud as the billowing ocean waves that broke upon its shores at night. For a rumour had started to travel along the grapevine, one that consigned to oblivion the furious tempest as well as the destruction and fatality that it had left behind in its wake. Word was that the warrior who had conquered Eezham, the prince who reigned over the heart and soul of the Chozha people, the Ponniyin Selvar himself had emerged in the open as a consequence of the storm that had ravaged Naagaippatinam; it was said that he was on his way to Thanjai, accompanied by a dense throng that intended to see him crowned as the Chakravarthy. At first, the news made the rounds as nothing more than mere whispers of gossip and speculation; that it was a fact was shortly confirmed by people who had seen the prince with their own eyes in Naagaippatinam. The report kindled a veritable storm of emotions in the hearts of the good people of Thanjavur, not unlike the squall that had shaken the city not two days ago.

The townspeople decided that all of Thanjavur would accord the prince a royal welcome of baronial pomp, the likes of which had never been seen or heard of in the town's history. Large crowds descended upon the public squares and people chattered away with each other in excitement. The streets surrounding the fort walls were bedecked in as grand a fashion as possible; from *melams* and *thalams* to *thaarai* and *thappattai,* an astonishing variety of percussion instruments and horns were gathered for the celebration, the minstrels ready to play them at a moment's notice. Those skilled in song and dance eagerly prepared themselves for the occasion, intent on displaying the full extent of their creative prowess. Many, especially the younger ones, flexed their ingenuity in planning costumes and accessories - they wanted to present themselves at their dazzling best, adorned with all the finery at their disposal. A few enterprising ones planted themselves at the four-way junction that led to Thanjai city, for they intended to win the honour of being among the very first to welcome the prince. Alas, others were quick to deduce their strategy; they found themselves greatly amused by the fawning enthusiasm and hooted with laughter as they took good-natured digs at the self-appointed welcome party.

It wasn't just the suburbs that were galvanised into a storm of activity. Inside the fort too were a number of telltale signs suggesting that important events were expected to transpire. That morning, the fort opened its gates according to its customary schedule. Hawkers tramped through carrying their wares of vegetables, curd and buttermilk; workers hurried to their posts in the fort; a few carried petitions soliciting relief for the destruction wrought by the aberrant bout of rain and storm. Once the Velakkara Regiment had passed through the fort gates, however, they abruptly slammed shut without warning. The clanging sounds of enormous metal latches securing the gates resounded through the environs; locks were heard emphatically bolting the fort door. Those who sought to enter the fort thereafter were stopped by its guards and summarily denied admission. It was unusual for the fort to bar its gates thus while the morning was yet young; the townspeople couldn't help but wonder as to why this was the case. Even as the crowd was aflutter with speculation, another oddity took place - the drawbridge that offered passage across the moat was also drawn up, ensuring that no one could even approach the fort gates.

Those close to the North Gate, which served as the main passage into the fort, made enquiries into the states of the West and South Gates. They discovered that those had been battened down and their drawbridges raised as well, just like the North Gate. The finding left them greatly amazed. How strange! they remarked to one another. There is no war expected, is there? It doesn't look like enemy troops are on the move; the foes who command such battalions are, for the moment, not active in the territories bordering the north, south, east or west. In any case, even if the Rettai Mandalam armies endeavour to launch a strike from the North, how could they hope to cross the Kollidam, Kaveri and other rivers at this time? Those great rivers are currently in spate, aren't they? Such was the puzzled talk among the people who dwelt in the suburbs encompassing the Thanjai fort.

"Could these arrangements be an attempt to prevent Ponniyin Selvar from entering the fort?" wondered some. "That must be it," agreed others. This speculation grew wings and rapidly spread through the populace which was growing increasingly mercurial.

"Who do these Pazhuvettarayars think they are, to deny entrance to the prince who is descended from the very lineage of Vijayalaya Chozhar himself?" cried out an indignant few. "If this truly is their design, why, we will be left with no choice but to bring down these very fort walls!" they declared, bracing themselves for extreme measures.

The origins of the phantasm we call rumour and its inexplicably swift method of dispersion will forever remain an impossible mystery. For another terrifying report began to spread among the people - it was whispered that the Sundara Chozha Chakravarthy had finally succumbed to the imminent death that had darkened his doorstep for a long time.

"I heard that the Chakravarthy is no more. Is that true?" they asked each other at first. Some remembered that they had seen a falling star earlier that morning; it had blazed brightly against the sky for a single moment, throwing glorious beams of light on all sides before it winked out over the horizon. The people decided that this was incontrovertible proof of the Sundara Chozhar's demise. "If true, what will happen next?" they fretted, quite naturally beset with worry. Will trouble arise regarding the royal succession? Will the chieftains split into opposing factions and go to battle? Will the noble Chozha *samrajyam* crumble under the weight of these political faultlines? Will hostile armies once again make an incursion into this majestic empire that had luxuriantly thrived over the past century virtually unopposed?

A loud cry cut through the din all of a sudden - "There, the armies approach!" it exclaimed. Many ran to see the truth of the statement for themselves, some even climbing tall buildings for a better vantage point. The sight that met their eyes was as frightful as it was astonishing.

In those days, there existed three wide roads that led to Thanjai from the west and the south-west. One was a path that led to Rameswaram through Kodumbalur; another ran through Madurai to lead towards the southern Pandiya kingdom; yet another long, wide road meandered through Uraiyur, leading to the city of Karur and the Chera kingdom.

That afternoon, all the three roads carried snaking columns of soldiers smartly marching shoulder-to-shoulder. The eye could see only the regiments that led the company from the front; there seemed to be no end to the array of troops following their lead. The men-at-arms stomped forward with great purpose as the battalion spilled over the horizon, row after unending row.

Fortunately, the great flag that fluttered at the forefront of the armies bore the noble ensign of a tiger; no one who saw it could bear a doubt that these forces were hostile. These were the armies of the Chozha *samrajyam*! But why were they marching onward? To what end?

As the contingent neared, it became clear that the flags bearing the crest of a tiger also carried the regalia of various nobilities, indicating that the approaching army was, in fact, a band of allies. There came the vast regiments of the Paranthaka Chozhar that pledged fealty to the Kodumbalur clan; the great forces of the Therintha Kaikolaar of the southern Pandiya kingdom; and finally, the formidable corps of Arinjaya Chozhar that had been deployed in the Eezham wars. The townspeople of Thanjai soon discovered that the General of the southern armies, Boodhi Vikrama Kesari himself was on the march with the allied troops. From this piece of news, it became quite easy to guess at why the forces were advancing. It was no secret that Boodhi Vikrama Kesari, the Periya Velar of Kodumbalur, desired to see Ponniyin Selvar wed to Vanathi, beloved daughter of the Siriya Velar of Kodumbalur who was martyred in the Eezham wars. It was also quite well known that the Periya Velar wished for Ponniyin Selvar to ascend the Chozha throne. So it seemed rather befitting that the General was advancing upon Thanjai with a large army at his command while prince Arulmozhi Varmar approached the city from the east followed by a retinue of the public.

The townspeople knew that the Pazhuvettarayars and their chieftain allies sought to establish Madhuranthakan as the crown prince. They quickly surmised that the Kodumbalur Boodhi Vikrama Kesari had gathered his considerable southern forces in order to display the strength of his will to see their dear Arulmozhi Varmar seated upon the throne.

A wave of pure elation rippled through the people at this realization and what it implied. They decided that they would give a warm welcome to these vast armies that rolled over the horizon like a great swell in the ocean. They would strive to show them cordial hospitality; why, they would give them a delicious feast!

The Thanjai of days gone by was dotted with traveller's inns run by the industrial collectives of the time - the Kodumbalur Manikramathar, the Thiruppurambiyam Valanjiyar, the Uraiyur Dharma Vanigar and the Nana Desadisai Aayirathu Ainutruvar, to name a few. It was here that preparations for the feast were underway in full swing; the genial hosts expected to feed thousands at these inns and set to work that very afternoon.

With word of a grand banquet in the air, the townspeople grew even more jubilant than before. They briskly saw to their tasks as they scuttled hither and yon, stopping only to hold the occasional conversation in tiny, animated groups. Caution was thrown to the winds as the people spoke their minds unguardedly with each other; practically all of them supported the cause of Arulmozhi Varmar, after all. The regiments finally reached Thanjai and the troops proceeded to set up camp, pitching tents here and there. The townspeople paid a cordial visit to the army camp, quickly becoming great friends with the soldiers.

The armies advancing from all the three roads had reached Thanjai before the sun sank beneath the horizon and darkness fell. As for the fourth direction, there the Vadavaaru river flowed along the Thanjai fort; since it was in spate, there was no possible way for an army to reach Thanjai from that side. But, the company decided, there was no real need to use that route.

We have already seen in our story, haven't we, the principal North Gate of the Thanjai fort? You may recall that it was this very gate through which Vandhiyathevan gained entry into the fort for the first time, as he cleverly followed Nandhini Devi. The Senathipathi Boodhi Vikrama Kesari's own camp had been set up such that it afforded an unencumbered view of this main gate, keeping it firmly within his sight.

One *jaamam* after nightfall cloaked the city, the Senathipathi conducted a reconnaissance of the fort perimeter before returning to his camp. By the time he got back, however, a few hundreds had already gathered awaiting his presence. Among them were the heads of the Velir and Kaikolaar armies as well as the brave captains of the Chozha troops that had tasted success at Eezham; the leaders of the Pandiya Mandalam and Kongu Naadu had assembled as well. The illustrious crowd also counted the heads of formidable business organisations, with the notable inclusion of those who led the powerful Nana Desadisai Aayirathu Ainutruvar - these influential men conducted maritime trade with the distant kingdoms that lay across the seas, amassing such fabulous wealth that they assembled private troops to protect ships that carried precious cargo; in fact, they even commanded their own fleet of warships that accompanied their trade vessels on voyages. Further, the Imperum Kuzhuvinar of Thanjavur as well as the chiefs of the Enper Aayathin were also present at the meet. Such was the constellation of luminaries who had gathered at the General's tent.

Hidden Meanings and Explanations

Melam, thaalam, thaarai, thappattai - Percussion and wind instruments of Thamizh Naadu.

Velakkarai Padai, Velakkara Regiment - The personal bodyguards of the Chozha Emperor. It is said that these elite warriors took an oath before the Goddess to chop off their own heads if they failed in their duty to protect the king.

24

Political counsel

Once the preliminary cordialities had been accorded to his visitors, the Kodumbalur Periya Velar came straight to the heart of the matter.

"Each and every one that I had sent a message to has gathered here it seems," began the Senathipathi with satisfaction. "Only old Malayaman of Thirukovilur has not joined us today; I am certain, however, that there must be a good reason for his absence. We have all assembled to discuss a subject that is deemed by many to be a dangerous one. The entire world is aware of the unshakeable loyalty we bear for the Chozha family as well as the Sundara Chozha Chakravarthy - the strength of our fealty has been proven many times over in countless incidents. Nevertheless, our enemies will no doubt denounce this assembly as one against the wishes of the Chakravarthy; they may even accuse us of gathering our forces with the intention of waging war against him. Yet, we are unable to meet with the Chakravarthy; we are deprived of even a minute's worth of private audience with which to understand his personal wishes. The reasons behind this state of affairs is common knowledge, I believe. We are told that the Chakravarthy is detained at Thanjai fort in consideration of his health. It occurs to me however, that the truth is quite different - it appears as if the Pazhuvettarayars are holding him prisoner. I confess that I am unsure of your views on the matter… "

The Senathipathi paused. A chorus of voices erupted in response, declaring their consensus - "Yes! That must be the truth! They have imprisoned the Chakravarthy!"

"Judging from your vociferous concurrence, it is clear that we all stand united by the same thought. Since the time of Vijayalaya Chozhar, countless soldiers have bled and given up their very lives on the battlefield in service to the empire - it is their noble sacrifice that nourished the Chozha *samrajyam,* enabling it to grow into the magnificent empire that it is today. It is a point of great pride for all of us to count ourselves as subjects of Chozha Naadu. It is to protect such a noble heritage and empire that we have come together today. Let us be clear - this gathering is by no means a conspiracy against the Chakravarthy. His enemies have kept him prisoner for three years, claiming that he suffers from ill health. Recall that the illustrious Vijayalaya Chozhar - that exalted warrior who bore ninety six battle wounds upon his body - erupted as a force upon the Thiruppurambiyam battlefield in his eightieth year, deftly wielding a sword in each hand; it is said that the path he blazed through the warfield was littered with bloody piles comprising the heads of his enemies. It is this remarkable lineage of warriors that the Sundara Chozhar belongs to. Are we to believe that a descendant of such stock declines to even emerge from his room on account of ill health? It occurs to me that the turncoats who plot against Sundara Chozhar and hold him prisoner employ the vile, eldritch arts of black magic to subject him to psychological attacks - they keep him under a mist of confusion, dazed and disoriented. If the Chakravarthy were in full command of his senses, would he entertain the thought of Madhuranthakan as the crown prince - a mere boy who has not even clapped his eyes upon a battlefield? Would he even consider the ghost of that suggestion, he whose own sons are two mighty warriors equal to Bhima and Arjuna of yore?"

The crowd rustled uneasily. "How do we know whether that is indeed the Chakravarthy's intention?" asked many.

"True," agreed the Senathipathi. "We have no direct confirmation of this fact. It is entirely possible that it is a piece of mischief fabricated by the Pazhuvettarayars. Consider, however, that even the Mudhanmandhiri Aniruddha Brahmaraayar believes this intelligence to be true..."

"Perhaps Aniruddhar has struck an alliance with them, who knows?" pointed out someone from the crowd.

"That is possible, of course. We have all gathered here today precisely to reveal the truth behind this whole affair. You are all aware, I trust, of the hearsay spreading in this great city of Thanjai today; I myself do not have an ounce of belief in the rumour. I have full faith that we will soon gain an audience with the Chakravarthy. When we meet with him, we must ask him what his wishes are regarding the succession. If the Chakravarthy declares his intent to anoint Madhuranthakan the crown prince, will you all agree?"

A huge cry of dissent arose from the crowd. "We won't, we won't!" they exclaimed.

"I wouldn't agree either. For I believe that if the Chakravarthy is truly clear-minded, he would never make such an announcement. After all, the matter of succession had already been decided upon in the time of Paranthaka Chakravarthy - it was the King's dying wish for the descendants of Sundara Chozhar to ascend the Thanjai throne. I myself was present when he made this decree; I heard it with my own ears. I'm certain that there are many in this crowd who were also present that day. The late, great Kandaradhithar endeavoured to raise his son free of the desire to rule the kingdom. It is also well-known that his *dharmapathini* the Periya Pirattiyar - the very embodiment of Siva *bhakthi* - the noble Sembian Maadevi herself is determined to prevent Madhuranthakan from being made the crown prince. We must trust that there is an important reason for her objection.

With matters as they are, why should Sundara Chozhar wish to instate Madhuranthakan as the crown prince? I shall provide further proof of the acute confusion I suspect him to be under. After dispatching Veera Pandiyan and decimating the Pandiya armies, my brother gathered whatever forces he could to chasten the Eezham king who had extended his support to the Pandiyas. Alas, we failed to back him with the necessary troops, arms and ammunition, leaving him martyred upon the battlefield. The Ponniyin Selvar and myself made haste to wipe away this terrible blemish that had stained Chozha Naadu, dimming the glory of its famed courage. Together, we annihilated the armies of Eezham and captured Anuradhapuram. We forced Magindhan to flee into hiding in the recesses of Malai Naadu. All of you are aware, I trust, that in all this we received no support at all from the Dhanaadhikaari Pazhuvettarayar. It was the great industrial leaders that you see amongst you today who came to our aid by sending us sorely-needed rations of food. Even so, our soldiers had to face a number of trials. How then did we surmount these grave obstacles to lay waste to Magindhan's armies? The credit goes to the incomparable Ponniyin Selvar, first among the greatest warriors of the Chozha clan - he kept our spirits high with his rousing leadership even when the going was tough. What do you think was the prize that the Chakravarthy bestowed upon such a valiant warrior, his own son? He accused the prince of sedition and issued an order to bring him in chains! Would someone in his right mind make such a command?"

"Senathipathi!" called out someone from the gathering. "Once again, you speak of orders dictated by the Chakravarthy. Where is the proof that it was indeed the Chakravarthy who issued them?"

"There is no proof. We have convened so that we can put our questions directly to him and learn the truth of the matter. Consider deeply - if such a directive turns out to have been given without the Chakravarthy's consent, how fearsome must be the danger that the Chozha *samrajyam* faces! Think, I urge you, of the consequences. The men who were sent to imprison the prince refused to follow their orders. The prince acceded to his father's wishes and boarded the vessel of Parthibendra Pallavan of his own accord. The voyage reportedly met with a terrible storm; there followed a rumour that the prince had drowned at sea. I did not believe it when I heard it. I was of the firm belief that the Sea King had not dragged Ponniyin Selvar to his cold depths. Others who travelled on the ship survived; how, then, could the prince alone have drowned? I suspected a conspiracy to restrain the prince when he came ashore; I surmised that Ponniyin Selvar had gained knowledge of the plot and made his escape. I firmly believed that he was unharmed and somewhere safe - a number of you professed to share my belief, too. Our faith has not gone in vain. We have received reports that the prince appeared in public on the day that the storm wrecked Naagaippattinam; even as we speak, the Chozha people accompany him to Thanjai in a cloud of triumph and joy. We have all assembled here with the intention of extending our support to his cause. However, those vile connivers have been up to their old tricks… "

"What, what?" asked many, worry suffusing their tones.

"I received the report just a few minutes before I reached our gathering. As the prince prepared to depart from Thiruvarur this morning, his elephant went wild and attacked the mahout. The animal reportedly went into a rage and ran amok. My information says that the prince disappeared in the mayhem."

"*Ayyayo*! This is horrifying news!" some cried in alarm. "Do the gods support those devious conspirators?" rued others in despair and worry.

The Senathipathi raised his hands and gestured for them to calm down.

"I was shaken when I heard the news. It took me considerable effort to gather my composure and come here to our conference. The prince Arulmozhi Varmar is as ingenious a man as he is a redoubtable warrior on the field; he will not fall prey to webs of deceit woven by traitors. I fully expect to receive good tidings about him soon. Meanwhile, the question remains - what must we do at this critical juncture? What should be our course of action? I am eager to know your opinions on the matter!"

The Senathipathi ended his address to the assembly, which proceeded to pour forth a medley of suggestions. They were all more or less in consensus regarding the key issues; it was the smaller, inconsequential decisions that they were unable to agree upon. The delegates said that arrangements must be made on priority to win an audience with the Chakravarthy; they thought it imperative to speak directly with him so that they make known their refusal to accept Madhuranthakan on the Chozha throne. Others insisted on further stipulations. "Either the Chakravarthy must dismiss the Pazhuvettarayars from their position of dictatorship," they declared, "or the Chakravarthy must depart Thanjavur for Pazhaiyarai."

"Aditha Karikalar has already been honoured with the *yuva raja pattabhishekam*; he is the rightful heir to the throne," pointed out some. "If he refuses the throne of his own will, the right of succession devolves to Arulmozhi Varmar. We must speak our minds clearly to the Chakravarthy, leaving no room for doubt. We must secure his approval, too. If we are denied the opportunity to meet with the Chakravarthy, if the fort gates do not yield to us - why, we will be left with no resort but to lay siege to the fort!"

A few were doubtful of this course of action. "Until we receive news of the prince, it is best to wait," they suggested, adding, "We must send a messenger to Aditha Karikalar and bring him here, as well."

"What is the use of waiting? Sundara Chozhar's battalions are on the march, under the command of the Pazhuvettarayars. They advance from Mazha Naadu on the other bank of the Kollidam. At present, those armies cannot reach here for their route is blocked by the Kollidam and other rivers that are in great spate. This is the moment to attack the fort and redeem the Chakravarthy from the Pazhuvettarayars' prison!" insisted the dissenters.

As the spirited debates picked up pace, one of the soldiers guarding the tent entered hurriedly. He whispered something into the Senathipathi's ear. The General looked at the crowd. "I will be back shortly," he said politely. "Please continue the discussions." He left the tent without another word.

Hidden Meanings and Explanations

Yuva raja pattabhishekam - The coronation of a prince as the heir to the throne

25

At the Mouth of the Fort

Boodhi Vikrama Kesari emerged from the deliberations underway in his tent and leapt onto his horse. He sped towards the North Gate of the Thanjai fort. As he spurred his horse onward, he spied an elephant approaching the North Gate, carrying a mahout and two women. The mahout held a horn in his hand; this he brought to his mouth and sounded heartily, generating a tremendous, ear-ringing blare. In a piercing voice that resounded throughout the vicinity, the mahout shrieked -

"The cherished daughter of Paranthakan Siriya Velar who was martyred in the Eezham war, the adopted daughter of the Periya Velar, the Senathipathi Boodhi Vikrama Kesari, the dear, beloved companion of Ilaiya Piratti of Pazhaiyarai, Vanathi Devi comes. Make way, make way!"

When the mahout reached the banks of the moat that encircled the fort gates, he lifted the horn to his lips and blew the instrument once again. Before its echoes could subside, he shouted once again, his tone shrill and high -

"The Kodumbalur princess Vanathi Devi comes bearing a message from Ilaiya Piratti to the Chakravarthy. She also brings an important message from Periya Pazhuvettarayar to Chinna Pazhuvettarayar! Open the fort gates! Make way! Make way this instant for the Kodumbalur princess and her dear friend, the lady Poonguzhali! Open the fort gates!"

The mahout's words left the Boodhi Vikrama Kesari utterly amazed; mere words cannot describe the astonishment he felt at that moment. Curiously enough, the mahout's voice sounded familiar, like one that he had heard on another occasion in another time. Who was he, anyway? Though, to be honest, his identity hardly mattered. Surely, the most important task at hand was to ascertain if it was truly Vanathi atop the elephant - she needed to be stopped from entering the fort! If that did turn out to be Vanathi, perhaps it was for the best, after all. It was better for the child to stay by his side until these grave issues reached a resolution. With these thoughts in mind, the Senathipathi urged his horse forward and drew closer to the elephant. One of the many soldiers who rode with him brought forth a flaming torch; its light fell on the people seated on the elephant, revealing that the two women were indeed Vanathi, the daughter of the Siriya Velar, and Poonguzhali just like the mahout had announced.

"Child, Vanathi!" began the Senathipathi. His words were promptly cut short by the mahout, who had enthusiastically sounded the horn yet again. *How to stop this wretched fellow from blowing that infernal horn of his?*

Fortunately, the women on the elephant had noticed the figure on horseback by this time; they peered down to determine who it was.

Vanathi instantly said something to the mahout and dissuaded him from blowing his horn a fourth time. "*Periyappa*, is that you?" she cried out. "Then the rumours must be true!"

"Yes, child. It is me," replied the Senathipathi. "But what is this peculiar turn of events? Were you really the one elected to deliver their messages? Couldn't Ilaiya Piratti have found someone else to carry out the task, especially with matters as dire as they are?" he asked, disbelief ringing in his tone.

"Yes, *periyappa*! It is precisely because of this situation that she has tasked me with delivering these messages. We received word of your army's siege upon Thanjai fort. If anyone else had been dispatched, your armies may have barred the way. Even if you allowed the messenger to proceed, the authorities inside the fort may have refused to admit him," pointed out Vanathi. "I was sent in the belief that it would make matters easier. Poonguzhali was sent to accompany me…"

"Yes, yes," said Periya Velar impatiently. "This boat girl is quite the crafty one, I am aware. But tell me - what important message do you bring, that it needs to be delivered in the dead of the night?"

"A very important one, *periyappa*. I bring tidings of Ponniyin Selvar for the Chakravarthy," replied Vanathi placidly.

"Aha! Tidings of Ponniyin Selvar!" repeated the Periya Velar in wonder, his face brightening with undisguised eagerness. "Do you know anything of him?"

"Why, yes I do," answered Vanathi. "Quite a lot, in fact. He is the greatest among warriors, the boldest of the brave; he is one unaffected by the force of the Kaveri and will not drown even if falls into the heaving waters of the sea; none who approaches him seeking help will be turned away; none who lent him aid in times of need and danger will be left forgotten; he is devoted to his parents, obedient to their wishes; he stores great respect by his *thamakkaiyar*, his elder sister; he is quite disinterested in politics…"

"That is enough, already!" The Senathipathi cut into Vanathi's speech rather impatiently. "That was not what I asked you for! Is the prince well? Do you know where he is at the moment?"

"He is well, *periyappa*. I do know where he is." Vanathi paused for a fraction of a second. "I cannot, however, reveal the details to you."

"What!" exclaimed the Periya Velar in frank amazement. "You cannot tell me? Not even me? Is it really you that speaks these words, Vanathi?"

"Yes, *periyappa*, it is. I have given my word that I will not speak to anyone of the place that the prince is at."

Fury surged through the Senathipathi; its searing heat coursed through his veins and a great anger boiled up within him. "Girl! When I sent you to Ilaiya Piratti, I was under the impression that you would be raised well. And now here you stand, adamantine and headstrong! Enough, enough! That's quite enough of the time you have spent in Pazhaiyarai. Get down! I will make sure that you are sent to Kodumbalur before I attend to other matters at hand!" thundered the Periya Velar, ire evident in his tones.

"*Periyappa*! I do not desire to set foot on Thanjavur soil, either. That's why I am sitting on top of an elephant," answered Vanathi, undaunted. "It was just this morning that this animal picked up one fellow and hurled him a great distance away; so, please do not come nearer. Once I have delivered the messages in my keeping, I will come to you myself. I will not object if you send me away to Kodumbalur then. Please, do not bar my way now!" she said.

The Boodhi Vikrama Kesari mused upon her words. "Alright, child. I will not stop you from going forward. But tell me - what will you do if the fort gates do not relent?" he asked.

"*Periyappa*! You have come here with such a great army at your command. What are they for? If the fort gates do not yield, mobilize your forces to break them open!"

Boodhi Vikarama Kesari swelled with pride upon her words. "Child!" he spoke exultantly. "Your words mark you as a true sovereign descended from the Kodumbalur lineage! If the need arises, that is exactly what I shall do. But that won't be necessary, I think. After all, who is Chinna Pazhuvettarayar to deny you admittance into the fort, one who comes bearing a message from Ilaiya Piratti to the Chakravarthy? He would never dare do a thing like that. However, do deliver a message from me to Chinna Pazhuvettarayan. Tell him - if the smallest of harm befalls you while you are within the fort walls, I will uproot his entire clan and lay it to waste! Tell him too that my compatriots and I have gathered here to meet with the Chakravarthy and learn of his wishes directly from him; if the necessary arrangements aren't made by the time morning passes into noon on the morrow, we will launch an attack upon the fort. Please deliver this message to him!" said Periya Velar, his voice edged with resolve.

"So be it, *periyappa*!" replied Vanathi. Seizing the moment, the mahout exuberantly blew his horn once again. "Make way for the Kodumbalur princess!" he shouted. "Open the fort gates!"

26

Vanathi Makes Her Entrance

Inside the fort, Chinna Pazhivettarayar found himself thrown into speechless confusion. He was lesser to none in matters of valour and courage; but so accustomed had he become to consulting his *thamayanar* before taking action, that the crises demanding his attention left him quite flustered. He struggled desperately like a bird that had lost its wings.

Since dawn that terrible day, a series of frightful news had come to his ears one after the other.

One account said that it had been more than two days since Periya Pazhuvettarayar had left for Thanjai from the Sambuvaraiyar's palace at Kadambur. A sudden, chaotic storm had descended on the day of his departure; it had whipped the waters of the Kollidam into heavy turbulence, capsizing many boats that were journeying on the river.

Another report followed on the heels of this troubling information. A man appeared, claiming to have been part of the retinue that had travelled on Periya Pazhuvettarayar's boat; he said that the vessel had drowned in the stormy waters and that he himself only managed to come ashore battling the odds.

Soon, a spy came bearing the news that the prince Arulmozhi Varmar had emerged from the Choodamani Viharam at Naagappattinam, where he had been biding his time all along. The prince was on his way to Thanjai accompanied by a sea of people; he had spent the night at Thiruvarur. The spy said that he had journeyed through the night to deliver this piece of intelligence, arduously navigating vast tracts of waterlogged land.

Shortly after, a man arrived with a message from the Sambuvaraiyar. He reported that Thirukovilur Malayaman was assembling a great army and that prince Aditha Karikalar's fury was mounting by the day; the Sambuvaraiyar had bade him deliver the message along with a request for Periya Pazhuvettarayar to return to Kadambur at the earliest.

Periya Pazhuvettaryar hadn't yet reached Thanjai, even. How was he to depart for Kadambur at once? A sense of dread gnawed at Chinna Pazhuvettarayar's heart; he feared that the tempestuous floodwaters of the Kollidam had managed to sweep away the formidable old man whom even Yama, the Lord of Death, hesitated to approach.

To top it all off, a horrifying piece of news was delivered to him by his agents in the south as a matter of dire urgency; their report came as a thunderbolt out of a clear blue sky. It said that troops of soldiers were on the march upon all the three roads that led to Thanjai, a fearsome multitude of them; the approaching armies commanded a vast number of warriors who pressed forward in seemingly endless numbers as they advanced from the south. He was also informed that the Kodumbalur Boodhi Vikrama Kesari himself marched with the company.

It was upon hearing this very report that Chinna Pazhuvettarayar had issued the command to shut the fort gates. He also enforced a prohibition on movement through the fort, preventing anyone from entering or exiting the premises. The Velakkara Regiment that had reported for duty was charged with guarding the Chakravarthy's chambers from all sides; Chinna Pazhuvettarayar deployed his own troops to defend the fort. Chinna Pazhuvettarayar fully intended to apprise the Chakravarthy of these developments; only, he wished to consult the Mudhanmandhiri Aniruddhar first. It was true that he placed little stock in Aniruddhar. However, it was undeniable that his presence inside the fort afforded Chinna Pazhuvettarayar a strategic advantage given that the *Mudhanmanthiri* now could not take any action without his knowledge. It would be prudent, felt Chinna Pazhuvettarayar, to give an ear to his advice and feign acquiescence - this way, he would be spared the blame for any blunders that may crop up in this precarious situation. Taking Aniruddhar along for an audience with the Chakravarthy would also save him the trouble of delivering the news independently.

Chinna Pazhuvettarayar was of the belief that the advancing troops were part of an artful plot hatched by prince Arulmozhi Varmar and Boodhi Vikrama Kesari, who wished to strike a marriage alliance with the former; after all, both parties were approaching Thanjai with their men from two different directions in what seemed suspiciously like a pincer manoeuvre - what other aim could such a strategy have but to capture the Thanjavur fort? If Chinna Pazhuvettarayar were to brief the Chakravarthy of these developments single-handedly, it would be difficult to convince the emperor of the truth in his words. On the other hand, the Chakravarthy would be left with no choice but to believe the report if the Mudhanmandhiri Aniruddhar was part of the discussion as well.

The Mudhanmandhiri Aniruddhar was feeling a bit unsettled, as well. Truth be told, he was not entirely in favour of Ilaiya Piratti

Kundhavai's departure from Thanjai that morning. His unease was further aggravated by the disappearance of the Eezham Rani and Poonguzhali. Where could they have gone? How did they travel? Why did they leave? The questions yielded no satisfactory answer even after much deep thought. The news that Boodhi Vikrama Kesari was on the march with his armies had also left him considerably agitated.

Even so, he had advised Chinna Pazhuvettarayar to defer relaying the new developments to the Chakravarthy.

"I am told that the Chakravarthy is particularly weighed down by his mind today. It was the Queen's maid-in-waiting who brought me the information. His delicate state may not be able to bear the news of Boodhi Vikrama Kesari; the shock may cause a blood vessel in his brain to burst, endangering his life. Already, a rumour circulates in Thanjai city that the Chakravarthy has perished. Please consider the chaos that will follow if that tragedy comes to pass in reality; such disorder would certainly be a convenient outcome for your rivals. It is best to exercise patience before we take a decision regarding this matter. Let us first learn of Boodhi Vikrama Kesari's true intention; I am sure that we will have also received news of Periya Pazhuvettarayar and Ponniyin Selvar by then as well. Until that time, be patient," advised the Mudhanmandhiri Aniruddhar. Kalanthaka Kantar too felt that this was the sensible course to pursue.

"In that case, I leave the task of briefing the Chakravarthy at the appropriate time in your hands; I will take on the responsibility of defending the fort," replied Chinna Pazhuvettarayar before taking his leave from the Mudhanmandhiri.

Chinna Pazhuvettarayar then surveyed the perimeter of the fort, closely inspecting every inch of the boundary walls. Based on his findings, he drew up the plans to secure the fort as thoroughly as possible. It was necessary to strengthen the fort so that it could endure a multi-day siege; preparing the garrison to launch active defence and counter campaigns was equally important too, in the event that the Kodumbalur armies attempted to annex the fort by breaking down the gates or scaling the walls. Chinna Pazhuvettarayar realized that he had to deploy his most dependable warriors in strategic positions throughout the fort. The boundary walls also required immediate repair and fortification where they were vulnerable.

Chinna Pazhuvettarayar efficiently set about making the necessary arrangements. Even as he was engrossed in this monumental task, his mind was working furiously to solve another strategic problem - how could he ensure that he received intelligence about new developments that may take place outside the fort?

The Thanjai fort was equipped with just two subterranean passages. One began from Periya Pazhuvettarayar's palace and led outside the fort. However, this path would be futile for anyone's use for a few days as the exit was currently besieged by the floodwaters of the Vadavar river; if the passage gates were to be opened, the treasury would be inundated.

The other underground tunnel originated at the palace of the Mudhanmandhiri Aniruddhar. No one could use that path without Chinna Pazhuvettarayar's knowledge - he had stationed guards at its exit point near the fort walls. It was Chinna Pazhuvettarayar's intention to use this very passage to dispatch his most loyal men to surveil the situation outside the fort; they would be sent after the second *jaamam* of the night had passed. Arrangements also had to be made to consign men to Kadambur and Pazhaiyarai so that they could bring back news of Periya Pazhuvettarayar and Ponniyin Selvar.

As Kalanthaka Kantar made his military and intelligence preparations, a soldier appeared in some haste reporting that two women had appeared at the North Gate; they were seated upon an elephant and their mahout was calling for the fort gates to open for them. When Chinna Pazhuvettarayar learned that one of the women was none other than Vanathi, he was struck with great astonishment. What cheek to demand admittance into the fort at a time when her *periyappa* was bringing down a siege upon the stronghold, surrounding it with his armies? His first thought was to deny the call; a formulation of curt refusal sprang to his lips - 'The gates will certainly not open.' When he reached the North Gate in person, however, he discovered that he had undergone a change of heart.

"To allow fear to decline entry to a small girl - for shame! That would be nothing short of a disgrace to my valour!" he thought. Chinna Pazhuvettarayar's change of heart was also driven by a keen curiosity - he wanted to know why the girl was so insistent on entering the fort.

Chinna Pazhuvettarayar climbed to the topmost step at the entrance of the fort gate and looked down. The report was true - apart from the mahout, there were only two women seated on the elephant and one of them was indeed Vanathi. Kodumbalur Periya Velar was engaged in a conversation with her; a portion of their exchange fell upon his ears. He heard and saw Periya Velar advise Vanathi against entering the fort; he also witnessed Vanathi's obstinate refusal to heed his words. That seemed to cause the Senathipathi considerable vexation, prompting Chinna Pazhuvettarayar to grow more amenable towards opening the fort gates for Vanathi after all.

He saw Periya Velar stand aside as the elephant took a few steps forward towards the edge of the moat. The mahout blew his horn once again and delivered his herald as he had before - "Open the fort gates for the Kodumbalur princess! Make way immediately for Vanathi Devi, who brings messages from Periya Pazhuvettarayar to Chinna Pazhuvettarayar and from Ilaiya Piratti to the Chakravarthy!"

The words wiped away whatever little hesitation remained in Chinna Pazhuvettarayar's heart. It was strange indeed that Periya Pazhuvettarayar would choose to send him a message through Vanathi; there could well be some trick in this whole affair. And if deception lurked at its heart, why, Chinna Pazhuvettarayar would sniff it out in an instant! Could that chit of a girl even dream of pulling a fast one on him? We'll see about that!

A horn at the top step of the fort blared in response to the mahout's call. A flaming torch appeared, throwing light on a row of spears whose tips glittered threateningly as they caught the beams. Sharp-pointed arrows were nocked against taut bow strings, ready to be let loose at a single command. In the centre of this formidable show of defence stood the figure of a man. "The gates will open for the Kodumbalur princess!" it called out in a booming voice. "If anyone apart from the elephant and its riders tries to pass through, they will be dispatched to Yama's abode upon the instant!"

The announcement prompted Boodhi Vikrama Kesari and his retinue to move further away.

The fort gates creaked open and the drawbridge was lowered. The elephant walked across the bridge, which creaked and shook dangerously in protest. Vanathi felt a prickling of fear, but her apprehensions were unfounded. The elephant reached the side of the moat safely and entered through the open fort gates. As soon as the animal was inside, the drawbridge was raised once again and the gates clanged shut.

Chinna Pazhuvettayar, also riding an elephant, approached the one that Vanathi was seated upon. "Welcome, princess," greeted Chinna Pazhuvettarayar, his stentorian voice booming through the environs. "It gives me great pleasure that you have accepted to come here as my guest despite the remonstrances of your *periyappa*. Have no fear, for no harm will befall you on these premises."

"*Ayya*! I am not the least bit frightened at the prospect," replied Vanathi. "As long as I fulfill my charge to deliver the messages I bear, I am not worried even at the thought of being clapped in chains and imprisoned in the dungeons!"

27

Stop right there!

The subject of dungeons brought back a flood of memories to Chinna Pazhuvettarayar; he quite forgot the etiquettes of conversation. "Yes, you have been to the dungeons once already!" he exclaimed. "You went with Ilaiya Piratti, didn't you - both of you sought to learn about the spy who escaped with his findings!"

"No, *Ayya*! You are quite mistaken. We went to the dungeons that day not in search of a spy but a messenger dispatched by the crown prince Aditha Karikalar."

"No doubt that was what you thought when you went," replied Chinna Pazhuvettarayar wryly. "How do you know whether he is a spy or a messenger? You are just a young girl who knows nothing. No point in debating the subject with you, is there? Tell me," he asked smugly, "did you learn anything at all about him from that little jaunt?"

"No. The person we had gone to meet had made off without your knowledge - the command of Pazhuvoor Ilaiya Rani Nandhini Devi had beaten us to the chase," replied Vanathi, steady and self-composed. "Such a pity! Though, what could you have done, after all?"

Chinna Pazhuvettarayar bit his lips angrily in frustration. The excessive leeway that his *thamaiyanar* had allowed Ilaiya Rani despite his words of caution had become a subject for mockery even at the hands of juveniles like this young girl! Chinna Pazhuvettarayar concealed the burning humiliation he felt with some effort. "You played your part too by setting free that eccentric fellow!" he pointed out lightly.

"*Ayya*! The eccentric fellow you speak of is none other than Senthan Amudhan, one engaged in the holy service of *pushpa sevai*. If perchance you learn the magnitude of the boon received by Chozha Naadu in return for his freedom, you will no doubt be struck amazed!"

"Girl! Nothing can surprise me anymore. I have become quite inured to the feeling given the strange list of benefactors that this Chozha *rajyam* already finds itself indebted to! Why, you yourself have come here to offer aid to Chozha Naadu, haven't you?"

"Yes, *Ayya*. If it were not an important matter, would your *thamaiyanar* have sent word to you? Through a naive girl like me besides, one unaware of worldly affairs?"

"My *thamaiyanar* grows more intelligent by the day, it seems; that is quite clear from the fact that he has sent you with his missive," remarked Chinna Pazhuvettarayar drily. "Quickly, now - what is the message you bear?" he asked.

"I was asked to inform you that it is a mistake to remain complacent about the Pandiya Naadu conspirators," replied Vanathi quietly. "A cabal of Veera Pandiyan's *abathudhavis* schemes some variety of a truly terrible plot; they intend to sate their revenge upon the Chozha clan on this very day. Periya Pazhuvettarayar has sent a dire warning exhorting you to protect the Chakravarthy with all your might."

Silence reigned momentarily before Kalanthaka Kantar burst into laughter. "Is this the important message that he sends?" he asked, voice dripping with ill-concealed sarcasm. "And here I was, thinking that he had sent word through you of your *periyappa* and his forces! Well then - if your *periyappa* acquiesces to remain outside in charge of the Kodumbalur armies at the gates, I shall remain inside to ensure that no harm befalls the Chakravarthy. Neither you nor Ilaiya Piratti herself need worry on this account!"

"*Ayya,* Periya Pazhuvettarayar anticipated such apathy and sent another message as well," replied Vanathi. "He said that you had cautioned him about a certain *manthiravadhi* who paid frequent visits to Pazhuvoor Ilaiya Rani's palace. He regretted that he did not pay heed to your warnings, which had stoked great anger in him instead. Here are his own words that I am charged with delivering to you -

Thambi! I have committed a grave mistake. The manthiravadhi Ravidasan is none other than the Pandiya conspirator; he is the one who leads Veera Pandiyan's abathudhavis. He has taken an oath to wreak irredeemable devastation upon the Chozha clan; he aims to bring nothing less than annihilation and despair. One among his men will attempt an assault upon the Chakravarthy this very day; do not remain complacent! You must proceed with great care.

"There!" Vanathi exclaimed. "My duty is done!"

Kalanthaka Kantar froze at Vanathi's words. Truly, such a message could not have originated from anyone but the *periyavar* himself!

"If what you say is true, why did he not come here at once? Why send you in his stead?" he asked, alarmed.

"He didn't. This message was given to Ilaiya Piratti; she was the one who bade me deliver it to you. As for Periya Pazhuvettarayar, he has returned to Kadambur to protect Aditha Karikalar for danger lies in wait for him as well today."

"Where did he return from? Where did he meet you?" asked Kalanthaka Kantar.

"At Kudanthai, in the *jothidar's* house. If you still have misgivings, then hear this as well - when your illustrious elder brother was crossing the Kollidam river, a violent storm upended his boat. He survived the calamity and reached ashore. As he recuperated at the *pallippadai*, he overheard the exchanges between the conspirators," said Vanathi. "*Ayya*! Must we continue our conversation thus in the open? May we go inside the palace?" she asked with some apprehension.

"*Penne*!" said Chinna Pazhuvettarayar, a smirk playing upon his lips. "Even if your words are true, rest assured that none can enter the fort past the guards, however cunning a conspirator he may be. Why," he continued kindly, "I allowed you entry only on account of your being a maiden."

"Why would the conspirators attempt to enter the fort? What if they are already inside?"

"Impossible," declared Chinna Pazhuvettarayar.

"Fine, then. That is your responsibility in any case. My duty… "

"Has been fulfilled, yes," cut in Kalanthaka Kantar impatiently. "And now you will turn back."

"No, *Ayya*," replied Vanathi politely. "I have discharged but one half of my obligation. Only when I deliver Ilaiya Piratti's message to the Chakravarthy can I consider my charge complete."

"You may deliver that message to me as well."

"I am afraid that is quite impossible. It is Ilaiya Piratti's express command that the message must be delivered to the Chakravarthy in person. Here, I bring Ilaiya Piratti's own signet ring."

"Ah!" exclaimed Chinna Pazhuvettarayar, exasperated. "These confounded signet rings turn up in the oddest of hands! What proof do you have that it was given to you freely by Ilaiya Piratti? Your own *periyappa* lays siege to the fort as we speak. How am I to place my trust in you?" he demanded.

"What do you have to fear from a defenceless maiden like me?" asked Vanathi.

"Girl!" bristled Chinna Pazhuvettarayar. "None in the noble lineage of the Pazhuvoor clan know the meaning of the word fear."

"In that case, please grant me leave to enter the palace. You can come along, too," offered Vanathi.

"I'm told that the Chakravarthy is feeling worse for the wear today," demurred Chinna Pazhuvettarayar. "His mind battles greater distress than usual."

"I have come bearing news that will alleviate his anguish. *Ayya*!" exclaimed Vanathi suddenly. "If you knew the details of the message I bear, you will deeply regret delaying my errand so."

Astonishment dawned on Chinna Pazhuvettarayar's face. "*Penne*! Could it be… do you bring word of the younger prince Ponniyin Selvar?"

"Yes, Thalapathy."

"Aha!" cried Chinna Pazhuvettarayar. "Is the prince well? Where is he headed now? Could it be that the conspirators plotted to harm him too? "

"Yes. There was a moment when his very life was in danger from the Pandiya conspirators. By the grace of God, he was unharmed. He is well and safe," said Vanathi. "This news should bring you happiness, surely?"

"A fine question! Would anyone grieve to hear of the prince's wellbeing instead of rejoicing? Come, come," said Chinna Pazhuvettarayar in changed tones, urging his elephant forward as he spoke. "I am loath to while away the time chatting with you thus. Come inside the palace and deliver whatever message you bear directly to the Chakravarthy."

In truth, he was eager to learn about the prince. He had never considered Arulmozhi Varmar a rival to his son-in-law in the matter of succession; he knew too well that the Chakravarthy had no such intention himself. Arulmozhi Varmar himself was not the sort to disobey his father's words. Chinna Pazhuvettarayar's only worry was Kundhavai. Would that she held back from meddling in the affair and creating mischief! Could she have hatched some wily scheme in this regard? Perhaps she has won over Arulmozhi Varmar to her side; it is possible that the message she sends her father carries wicked drivel to further her cause. No matter; if this Kodumbalur girl really does bear tidings of the prince for the Chakravarthy - why, the emperor is sure to share the message with him! It would be easy then, to determine the necessary course of action based on its contents. Perhaps he could utilise this audience with the Chakravarthy to his own end too - it would serve as a good opportunity to apprise him of Boodhi Vikrama Kesari's cunning ploy of gathering forces against the Thanjai fort.

The elephants stopped at the palace entrance. Chinna Pazhuvettarayar smoothly alighted from his mount in a single fluid motion. The other elephant bent down and rested its knees upon the ground like a great mountain taking a bow, upon which the women and the mahout disembarked as well. Chinna Pazhuvettarayar called over the soldier guarding the palace entrance and spoke to him; the man then opened the palace entrance gates for the visitors.

As the group proceeded to the palace, Kalanthaka Kantar's heart pricked with restlessness and anxiety. He found himself unable to brush off the terrible message that Vanathi had delivered claiming it to be his *thamaiyanar's* words. His peace of mind had been greatly disturbed by the chilling information it contained about the *manthiravadhi* Ravidasan. He had already known, of course, about the *abathudhavis* of Veera Pandiyan; but he hadn't dreamed that they had enjoyed unfettered access to the Thanjai fort itself!

Chinna Pazhuvettarayar had been under the impression that Pazhuvoor Ilaiya Rani's association with the *manthiravadhi* was chiefly to help her entice the Periya Pazhuvattarayar and bring him under her spell. He had thought that she planned to create a rift between the brothers. The news brought by this girl made it evident that the truth was far more terrifying than he had imagined. Even so, reasoned Chinna Pazhuvettarayar, what could *manthiravadhis* and conspirators accomplish in this stronghold? Not even a fly was admitted into the Chakravarthy's chambers without his consent and the Chakravarthy himself never emerged from his quarters. Perhaps it was better, after all, to focus on fortifying the security details outside the palace. Many had gained entrance into the fort citing the storm and floods; some had even claimed to have an audience with the Mudhanmandhiri. It was unknown whether these outsiders had vacated the fort premises. Shutting the fort gates this morning had been for the best after all - any conniver with evil designs on his mind could be now rooted out with an iron hand.

Such were Chinna Pazhuvettarayar's thoughts as he proceeded to the palace. When he reached its doors, he beckoned to his men who were detailed nearby; these warriors were ever-present at their stations, prepared to fight at a moment's notice. Chinna Pazhuvettarayar directed the soldiers to conduct a thorough search of the fort, authorising them to apprehend anyone of a dubious nature. He also ordered them to send to him the head of the Velakkara Regiment; he intended this elite unit to forego their sleep for the night in order to vigilantly guard the palace and its immediate surroundings. In the midst of this planning, Chinna Pazhuvettarayar suddenly paused. What had become of the girls? He turned around to see that they had crossed the moon courtyard facing the palace and were nearing the first doorway. But… who was this third figure that follows them? His turban marks him out to be the mahout. Aha! Why is that fellow entering the palace? What business could he possibly have inside? What sort of task would require him to have an audience with the Chakravarthy?!

A ghastly thought struck Chinna Pazhuvettarayar, stopping his heart; hot fury bubbled up within him. Could this be a vile ruse? Could that man be the conspirator he was on the lookout for? Perhaps the wretch had tricked these gullible women and infiltrated the fort in the guise of a mahout! Had he himself been duped, too? How could he stand by and watch enter the palace a Veera Pandiya *abathudhavi* seeking to assassinate the Chakravarthy? Had matters come to such a sorry pass that Kalanthaka Kantar stands to ruin his own legacy with such a dishonourable stain? Or perhaps… could this sly stratagem be Boodhi Vikrama Kesari's doing? Whatever be the case, it shall be straightened out this instant!

Kalanthaka Kantar swiftly crossed the courtyard in four angry strides, drawing close to the mahout. "*Adei*! Stop right there!" he roared in a livid rage. "Why must you enter the palace? What business could a mahout possibly have inside?" he thundered, roughly grabbing hold of the man's arm in a vise-like grip.

The girls turned back at the sound of his fury. Their faces showed a curious mixture of fear, surprise and interest; enigmatic smiles tugged at their lips. "*Ayya*, that… he…" Vanathi started to say something and stopped, hesitant.

But Chinna Pazhuvettaryar had flown into a blind rage; he didn't deign to give her a single glance nor was he the least bit interested in what she had to say. The mahout seemed quite taken aback; it was becoming clearer every second by the man's clumsy fumbling that his suspicion was not unfounded. Another terrible thought came to Chinna Pazhuvettarayar - could this be that Vaanar scamp who led him down the garden path on an earlier occasion before slipping away? Had he come to trick him once again?

Chinna Pazhuvettarayar tightened his grip in anger. "Ada! Tell me the truth, spit it out! Are you truly a mahout? Or are you that odious spy who escaped me once before?" he growled, menace edging his voice. "You won't get away this time!" Chinna Pazhuvettayar roughly swivelled the man to bring him face-to-face.

The gentle glow of the flickering lamps that shone on the front *mandapam* of the palace illuminated the mahout's face, throwing light upon his majestic features.

"Thalapathy! I truly am a mahout as well, among other things. I have never sought to escape your presence. I have come to surrender myself to you," said the mahout.

Kalanthaka Kantar gazed at that face; he listened in silence to the voice that fell upon his ears. He thought that all the seven heavens had fallen on his head at once; he stood rooted to the spot in pure stupefaction. The thought of releasing his grip did not cross his mind, dazed as it was. His fist slackened of its own accord, letting go of prince Arulmozhi Varmar.

Hidden Meanings and Explanations

Pallippadai - A temple constructed upon a cemetery of a king

28

Cheers abound!

Only the good Lord knows what enchantment lay in Arulmozhi Varmar's golden face. His features showed not the slightest hint of anger or distaste; instead he looked quite guilty at being found out, like that Kannan of yore caught red-handed stealing butter. The prince's face held no contempt; there were no traces indicating that he meant to castigate Chinna Pazhuvettarayar for daring to confront him in such a harsh manner.

And yet, Chinna Pazhuvettarayar - that lionheart whose very name was a byword for valour and indomitable will - felt his arms and legs tremble when he looked upon that face; beads of sweat appeared on his blanched face and his lips went dry. Hardly aware of what he was doing, Chinna Pazhuvettarayar brought his hands together in a respectful greeting. "Ponniyin Selva! The warrior who conquered Eezham! Chozha Naadu's treasured son!" he said reverentially. "Why the disguise? Why the pretence? What crime have I committed to be punished in this manner? I beg you, deign to show grace to this accursed wretch and pardon my sin; all I ask is but a single word of forgiveness! Ah, I have turned blind even though I have both my eyes!" cried out Chinna Pazhuvettarayar in chagrin, voice trembling with deep emotion.

The prince stopped him as he opened his mouth to speak again. "Thalapathy! How could you come to believe that what you did was a crime? How can a mere youth like me - a naive young man - be in a position to forgive you?"

"It would not be reprisal enough to chop off this vile hand that dared to hold you thus; and this blighted tongue that insolently addressed you as *Ada*... it would not be enough even if it was torn out of my mouth!" agonised Chinna Pazhuvettarayar in chagrined tones.

"Your words sound bitterly harsh to my ears; pray, stop!" cried out Ponniyin Selvar. "All you did was fulfill the duty you are charged with - where is the crime in that? If anything, the mistake is mine; I was the one who snuck through in the guise of a mahout... "

"True," replied Chinna Pazhuvettaryar in awe. "I never dreamed that such a thing would come to pass. Why should someone like you, my dear prince, resort to an act like this? Oh, what a sorry welcome I have given you, a peerless warrior of Chozha Naadu! If I had but known, why! I would have waited for you at the very front gates and accorded a welcome befitting your royal person; I would have arranged for all the due ceremonies in their full grandeur - the beats of the victory drums heralding your arrival would have reverberated for miles in all the eight directions!" exclaimed Chinna Pazhuvettarayar.

"I came in disguise precisely because you would do that," replied the prince with a smile. "Times are strange and such pomp ill befit them. But you know that, of course - didn't the Kodumbalur princess deliver the warning she bears of the conspirators' nefarious schemes? Her words have the ring of truth," he said.

"My prince!" cried Pazhuvettayar, suddenly aggrieved. "Do you perchance count me as one among those vile fiends?"

"Heavens, no!" exclaimed the prince. "My heart feels full upon seeing the capable arrangements you have set in place to protect my esteemed father, the Chakravarthy. I shall first seek his audience and then…"

"*Ayya*!" interrupted Chinna Pazhuvettarayar as another terrible thought occurred to him. "Did you think, perhaps, that I would prevent you from seeing your noble father?" he cried. "Why," he exclaimed with an edge of wrath, "if some scoundrel has poisoned your ears with the thought that I am capable of being such a base wretch…"

"I simply wouldn't have believed it, Thalapathy," finished the prince kindly.

"Then why come in this guise at all?" he asked in wonder.

"Think, Thalapathy - could I have entered the fort any other way? The southern armies encircle the fort perimeter, leaving no place unguarded. The Periya Velar himself has come here as well. You must know the reason for his presence…"

"My prince! I was justified, wasn't I, in closing the fort gates?" pleaded Chinna Pazhuvettarayar. "Surely that was no crime?"

"Entirely justified - that was the right thing to do. Periya Velar's mind has grown muddled. I had to come in disguise fearing that he would stop me from entering the fort; that is why I even brought his daughter along. Thankfully, I escaped his gaze. But *your* sharp eyes caught me out!"

"Ah, my ignoble eyes were blinded, my prince. Else, would I have not recognised you the minute I saw you?" rued Chinna

Pazhuvettarayar. "Please grace me with your forgiveness, my prince, this rogue that dared to address you boldly as mahout!"

"Please don't say such things, Thalapathy. I have never considered you any different from my own father. You had dispatched men to bring me here in chains... "

"Good God!" cried Chinna Pazhuvettarayar in shock. "Did you think that it was I who sent men to imprison you, my dear prince? It was your illustrious father the Chakravarthy who issued the order, for he yearned to look upon you..."

"Did you think I was unaware of that, Thalapathy? When the men came for me in Ilankai, my companions advised me that it was not the Chakravarthy who had issued such a command but the Pazhuvettarayars..."

"Ah!" cut in Chinna Pazhuvettarayar in anger. "Without a doubt, that notion must have come from our rivals!"

"I told them," continued the prince, "that I consider any order issued by the Pazhuvettarayars to be inviolable, like I do my own father's. I have journeyed to this fort braving wild seas, violent storms, torrential rains and vast floods. I thought, at first, to learn of your wishes as soon as I passed through the gates at the palace entrance; I do not wish to meet my father without your command..."

"My prince!" cried Chinna Pazhuvettarayar. "Do you still test me? Who am I to command you to meet your father? If you so desire, I will accompany you to the Chakravarthy's chambers; if you would like me to stay back, why - I will remain here in this very spot until further word from you! The prince's wish is my command," said Chinna Pazhuvettaryar with deference.

"As matters stand, Thalapathy, it seems like you must remain here - we have continued our conversation in the open for far too long," said the prince, his lips twitching. "Look there!"

Chinna Pazhuvettarayar turned to look in the direction that the prince was pointing. The garrison men whom he had left standing a little distance away had moved closer. It wasn't just them, either - the soldiers who were detailed to guard the palace entrance had also appeared. Further away, Chinna Pazhuvettarayar saw the Velakkara Regiment; some had broken their ranks and were fast approaching the party.

Those who had drawn closer gazed at Ponniyin Selvar with fervour. When Chinna Pazhuvettarayar turned back, he saw that the prince's face shone as it bathed in the light of the lamps.

One of the warriors raised a cry, "Long live the prince!" Another shouted joyously, "Long live Ponniyin Selvar!" A third joined in, "Long live the brave warrior that beat back Magindhan and conquered Eezham!"

Hearing their cries, the men of the Velakkara Regiment hurried over. A chorus of voices shouted in delight, "Long live Ponniyin Selvar!" The rousing cheers and cries of celebration resounded throughout the vicinity. The shouts were rather feeble at first, since the men were standing at the palace doorway; and yes, because Chinna Pazhuvettarayar was present, too. The cheers sounded like the soft rustling made by the leaves of a peepal sapling as the wind brushes past their branches. We shall see in later chapters how this whisper grows into a thunderous rallying cry, one louder even than the din of a thousand waves rolling upon the face of the great sea.

"Thalapathy! We have erred in remaining so long in the open. You understand now, don't you, why I felt the need to remain anonymous until I had entered the palace?" asked the prince.

"Quite well. I shall becalm these men and come to you. Please, my prince, go inside at once," said Kalanthaka Kantar.

29

The Perilous Fallouts of Suspicion

Once he saw that Ponniyin Selvar had entered the palace, Kalanthaka Kantar strode towards the Velakkara Regiment gathered at the palace entrance.

“What is all this hue and cry?” he boomed. “Don’t you know that the Chakravarthy rests in the palace chambers? Don’t you know that the fort is, at this very moment, under siege from enemy forces?” he asked sternly.

“*Ayya*!” It was the head of the Velakkara Regiment who spoke. “Are the armies surrounding our fort truly hostile forces? How did the Kodumbalur Velar come to be our enemy?”

Searing anger surged within Chinna Pazhuvettarayar at this impertinence; it took some effort to suppress it. “That question needs to be put to him,” he replied curtly. “If he isn’t our enemy, why would he advance upon us with his armies and surround the fort?"

"We hear that he intends to make sure that Ponniyin Selvar is anointed the crown prince," said the leader of the Velakkara Regiment.

Chinna Pazhuvettarayar looked hard at all the soldiers of the regiment. "Would you all agree to such a plan?" he asked. The head of the Velakkara Regiment turned back to look at his men. "Speak your mind!" he said. The warriors immediately raised a cry of enthusiasm. "Yes, we agree! Long live Ponniyin Selvar! Long live the prince who conquered Eezham!" they cheered, with cries much louder and more emphatic than before.

An unpleasant red flush made its way across Chinna Pazhuvettarayar's face; his moustache twitched in annoyance. He bit down upon the sharp words that were forming on his tongue. "Should the decision of anointing a crown prince defer to the Periya Velar's wishes in the matter? Or yours, perhaps?" he remarked acidly. "Is there no room for the Chakravarthy's wishes?"

"Thalapathy!" exclaimed a soldier suddenly. "Is the Chakravarthy well? Is that an established fact?" he asked.

"What sort of a question is this?" snapped Kalanthaka Kantar.

"There are all sorts of rumours in town regarding the Chakravarthy," explained the leader of the Velakkara Regiment. "Why, even we have not seen him today. We're worried about his health."

"Haven't we already spoken of this?" replied Chinna Pazhuvettaryar in frustration. "Didn't I explain the reason why you cannot see the Chakravarthy? His mental anguish weighs heavy on him today. He did not wish to admit anyone into his presence; in fact, he even declined to come to the *sabhamandapam*!"

"What is the reason for his anguish? Why should he refuse us an audience?" pressed the chief of the Velakkara Regiment. "Surely there's no harm in telling us the answers to the questions?"

"Very well," said Chinna Pazhuvettarayar through clenched teeth. "I will tell you. The Chakravarthy's despondency has worsened because he had no tidings of the younger prince from Eezham. Now, with the prince himself here..."

"We want to see the prince!" cried out a soldier, suddenly reminded of his desire. "We want to see him well lit," he added as an afterthought.

"Yes!" shouted the others in joy. "We want to see him! Long live the prince that conquered Eezham!" they cried as one.

"The prince must present himself to the Chakravarthy, first. Later - if he so desires - he will present himself to all of you," replied Chinna Pazhuvettarayar tightly.

"Would he? Or perhaps... perchance, would he be sent to the dungeons?" demanded one of the men.

On any other day and time, such impudence from the Velakkara Regiment would have provoked Chinna Pazhuvettarayars' forces to fall upon them in fury, instigating a veritable war; the matter would have blown into disastrous chaos. Today, however, Kalanthaka Kantar's men kept their peace, perhaps as a consequence of having seen the stately face of the prince just a short while ago.

Chinna Pazhuvettarayar's hand strayed towards the sword at his belt. For an instant, he thought to behead the warrior who had put that audacious question to him; all it would take was a single blow from his blade. He composed himself the next second and broke into humourless laughter.

"All of you heard him, did you not? He asks if the prince will be sent to the dungeons! A fine question!" thundered Chinna Pazhuvettarayar.

"It is not within my authority to either anoint the prince or to send him to the dungeons. Whatever happens will happen at the behest of the Chakravarthy. If the prince is to be consigned to the dungeons, he will be led through this very path - you may have your fill of him then!" he said, his eyes flashing dangerously. He turned swiftly on his heels and strode to the entrance, looking superbly unconcerned by the cries that had started up again.

Chinna Pazhuvettarayar saw Poonguzhali standing near the palace doorway. "*Penne*! Why do you remain here? Were you stopped from entering the palace?" he asked.

"No one stopped me. I remain here of my own accord, *Ayya*," replied Poonguzhali.

"Why?"

"Father and son are to meet each other after a long parting. What business have I at such a reunion?"

"You, at least, retain faith that the Chakravarthy lives! I must count my blessings, I suppose."

"It is not mere faith I hold; I saw the Chakravarthy alive and well with my own eyes before returning to this place."

"Do you see those men there, the soldiers of the Velakkara Regiment? Pray tell them what you saw; they seem to be quite suspicious about the matter!" grumbled Chinna Pazhuvettarayar.

"Their suspicions are unfounded at this particular moment. But who can say that it will remain so in the next?" replied Poonguzhali, catching Chinna Pazhuvettarayar off-guard.

"Girl!" he exclaimed in vexation. "Are you bent on infuriating me like the rest? Have all of you gone mad?"

"Thalapathy! Many do think that I am mad. I think so myself, sometimes. But it is because of this madwoman's advice that the prince is at this fort today, unharmed; it is also why he is able to meet the Chakravarthy while he yet lives..."

"Aha!" cried Chinna Pazhuvettarayar. "You seem to think that the Chakravarthy's life is on a countdown of sorts! Do you spout such nonsense out of belief in superstitious fools and moronic *jothidars*? Or do you know something that I don't?"

"Are the fools and *jothidars* you speak of the only ones who think that the Chakravarthy's time is up? Why, it was just a short while ago that you heard your *thamaiyanar's* message!" replied Poonguzhali.

"How am I to be certain that it is true?" demanded Kalanthaka Kantar.

"Why would the Kodumbalur Ilavarasi lie to you?"

"Who knows? Perhaps she wishes to sit on the throne like the others and become Queen..."

"Thalapathy! I too believed that to be true once upon a time," replied Poonguzhali earnestly. "Then I heard the princess take a certain oath this morning; I couldn't help but change my mind about her intentions," she said, a strange wistfulness lacing her tones.

"*Penne*!" smirked Chinna Pazhuvettarayar. "Do you perchance share that desire?"

"Thalapathy! I must be mad as you say; why else would I stand here talking to the likes of you?" retorted Poonguzhali, her eyes ablaze. She abruptly turned to leave.

A sudden change came over Kalanthaka Kantar. "Girl, pray soothe your anger!" he called out. "Tell me what you had to say and then leave!"

Poonguzhali turned to look at Chinna Pazhuvettarayar. "Yes, it needs to be said; otherwise we will both deeply regret the omission in the future," she said soberly. "*Ayya*! Should mortal danger touch the Chakravarthy, town and country will lay the blame solely at your feet. The people will come to loathe you; why, so will your own soldiers!"

A shadow darkened Chinna Pazhuvettarayar's features; his face shrunk and hardened. "If such an event comes to pass, I won't wait for such blame. My life will depart from this body before those words of censure reach my ears," he said grimly. "When the Velakkara Regiment took their sacred oath in the temple of the Goddess Durga Parameswari, it was I who led them all - I was the first to speak those noble words. I will not hesitate to die to fulfill that vow!" he declared, reminding Poonguzhali of the terrible oath he had sworn.

"What is the point of such a gesture? The Chozha *samrajyam* will mourn the loss of an irreplaceable warrior even as they grieve over the Chakravarthy," responded Poonguzhali quietly. "Wouldn't prudence serve you better than a resignation to death?" she asked.

"Girl!" cried Chinna Pazhuvettarayar, stung. "Do you accuse me of carelessness? Look, look at all these able warriors who surround the palace, guarding it without blinking their very eyes! Why do you think they're so alert? Why, even the Mudhanmandhiri himself cannot enter the palace without my knowledge. Do you know that?"

"I am aware, Thalapathy! Though, tell me - can danger not approach from within?" asked Poonguzhali.

"What rubbish!" scoffed Chinna Pazhuvettarayar. "Do you think that the palace women are capable of slipping poison to the Chakravarthy to kill him? Or perhaps… do you harbour suspicion about the Kodumbalur maiden who just entered the palace?" he asked, suddenly solemn.

"Heavens!" cried out Poonguzhali, horrified at the suggestion. "None who doubt that poor, naive damsel will meet a peaceful end! She is not capable of such deviousness. *Ayya*! Is there not an underground passage that runs beneath the palace?" she asked.

Chinna Pazhuvettarayar looked dumbfounded. "What do you know of that tunnel? How did you come by that knowledge? That path is unknown to the world save three or four people! Why, none who come by that information can leave this palace alive!" he cried out in trepidation.

"I learned of it just this very morning. I also spied a Pandiya conspirator hiding there with a sharp spear in hand," said Poonguzhali.

Chinna Pazhuvettarayar's heart stopped in pure fear. "God save us!" he whispered. "That is frightful news! That passage… do you know where it ends?" he asked Poonguzhali in panicked tones.

"It runs through the treasury," replied Poonguzhali.

"Aha!" exclaimed Chinna Pazhuvettarayar as a horrible realisation dawned on him. "Your report may well be true. This must be the handiwork of that demoness in the guise of a woman, that she-devil who has ensnared my *thamaiyan*! *Ayyo*! How much I endeavoured to warn him about her!" he lamented. "*Penne*! Are your words the truth? Did you see him with your own eyes? How did you learn of that passage?" he asked in urgent tones.

"My *athai* took me there this morning…"

"Who is she, your *athai*?"

"The woman who was brought here from Kodikkarai in the palanquin that you sent at the behest of the Mudhanmandhiri, *Ayya*!" replied Poonguzhali quickly. "While we stand here discussing the crisis at hand…"

"You're right, of course," agreed Chinna Pazhuvettarayar, his voice taking on a steely edge. "I will repair at once to the Periya Pazhuvoor palace to make the necessary arrangements. In the meanwhile, you..."

"I will stay right here in this corner and keep watch," finished Poonguzhali.

"Aha!" cried Chinna Pazhuvettarayar suddenly. "How am I to trust you? How do I know that you are not part of that villainous cabal of conspirators? Perhaps you're trying to trick me to send me away from here!"

"Thalapathy, come with me. Bring a torch and accompany me to the passage! We will both learn the truth for ourselves. I will tell you everything else I know of the matter on the way..." said Poonguzhali.

Chinna Pazhuvettarayar went to the doorway. He called out to a few loyal men and spoke to them; Poonguzhali deduced that the warriors were bid to go in haste to the Pazhuvoor palace. When the Thalapathy returned, he held a flaming torch in his hand that he had taken from one of the soldiers.

"Girl! Lead the way. Let me see for myself the truth of your words," said Kalanthaka Kantar.

The Chinna Pazhuvettar was unable to trust Poonguzhali wholeheartedly yet; a niggling suspicion remained gnawing at his heart. Was it possible that this girl intended to dupe him with her lies? Was she fishing for information about the underground passage, contriving events so that he led her straight to it himself? Could this be a ploy to lead the Kodumbalur forces through the tunnel into the fort? He would not be tricked in such a facile manner. If her intent was discovered to be as he suspected, she would be handed a fitting penalty. *Did she think that I could be deceived like Periya Pazhuvettarayar? Let her lead the way. Her claim to knowledge about the underground passage must first be put to test. Then one can investigate her claim about the conspirators concealed there. If perchance that news was indeed true… dear Lord! What grave danger that would spell! Fortunately, it shouldn't be too hard to thwart such a plot. Any conspirators in the passage will be cornered and caught like foxes hiding in their holes… and then of course, they will be put to death.* Such were the thoughts of Chinna Pazhuvettarayar as he followed Poonguzhali, whose swift stride left him astonished.

Poonguzhali's agitation had reached its peak, reflecting in her rapid pace.

She was no stranger to eccentricity and drama - after all, her life seemed to be full of such incidents of late. But she had never encountered an affair as peculiar as the one that had transpired that morning.

While the dawn was still young, her *athai* had woken her up from sleep with a gentle touch. Above the women's quarters where she slept was a latticed window on the first floor. When Poonguzhali awoke, she spied a hard, cruel face staring out from behind the bars; it vanished from sight almost immediately. Mandhakini rose silently and took Poonguzhali with her to the closed *sirpa mandapam*. There, there again was the frightful face that she had seen in the window! She caught sight of it near a sculpture of Raavana, the Ilankai king of antiquity. The ghastly visage materialised between the statue's many heads and the Kailayam mountain in its hands; it disappeared once again in the blink of an eye.

The two women drew nearer to the sculpture and examined it closely. Poonguzhali noticed an entrance to an underground tunnel hidden between the statue's heads. The pair entered the passage, with Mandhakini taking the lead and Poonguzhali following behind. Thick darkness enveloped them in the tunnel, blacker than pitch. Poonguzhali could not see a thing. She blindly stumbled along the path as she held onto her *athai's* hand. The pair eventually climbed a few steps that lay along the route, stepping into what seemed to be a *mandapam*. Light was absent here, too - gloomy darkness reigned with no relief, forcing the women to feel their way through the *mandapam* to avoid bumping into the pillars and walls. Shortly, weak beams of light streamed in through what must have been small windows. Poonguzhali realized that it had become late morning already; she also deduced that both of them were, in fact, wandering about in the treasury. There was little hope that they would be able to catch the man her *athai* Mandhakini came in pursuit of - the stygian *nilavarai* offered countless recesses in which to lurk and hide; only the good Lord knew where he lay concealed. Why, he could sneak up behind the pair and stab them to death; there was no one to challenge or deter him here.

As these thoughts ran through Poonguzhali's mind, Mandhakini screeched all of a sudden. Her voice sounded quite peculiar; if Poonguzhali hadn't known better, she would have been hard put to say whether the harsh scream belonged to a human or an animal. A howl of terror rose in response, one that was quite clearly a man's; the sound of hurried, frantic footsteps followed, revealing a shadowy figure on the run.

Poonguzhali realized that it had to be the man in the window and suppressed a giggle; he had evidently taken to his heels in fright thinking her *athai's* unusual voice to be that of a ghost or a demon. Mandhakini screamed once again, sending the man fleeing in pure fear; he ran straight into a wooden door that he proceeded to thump upon frantically with his fists. When it finally opened, Poonguzhali saw a girl standing in the doorway. The man spoke to her; she seemed to hesitate at his words, prompting him to issue dark threats. She turned back and the man remained at the doorway, peering inside with some impatience. The girl returned in a short while with a lamp in her hand. She entered the dark *nilavarai* with the man. Mandhakini swiftly pulled Poonguzhali behind a wide pillar, hiding away from their line of sight. The flickering lamplight allowed both women to see the man's features quite clearly.

The man and the girl with the lamp went deeper into the *nilavarai*. "Ghosts, he says. Demons, he says," exclaimed the girl. "You've just had a good scare! Why is it that a coward like you has been entrusted with this task?" she asked with some contempt. Poonguzhali found that she could hear her loud and clear; the task she referred to, however, was unclear.

When the strange pair had disappeared into the recesses of the *nilavarai*, Mandhakini caught hold of Poonguzhali's hand once again and dragged her through the open door. They followed a narrow footpath, finally emerging into a large garden. There, in a solitary corner, Mandhakini told Poonguzhali all that she wanted to say through signs and gestures. "My end is near," she signed. "I wish dearly to look upon the prince for one last time before I close my eyes forever. You must deliver this message to him and bring him back with you."

We are familiar with the depth of the love that Poonguzhali bore for her aunt, aren't we? Having heard such terrible words, she had no heart to leave aunt's side; but she couldn't bring herself to disobey her, either. She came to a decision upon realizing that this would afford her the opportunity to see Ponniyin Selvar once again. Taking leave from her aunt, Poonguzhali scaled the boundary wall that ran around the garden and jumped over to the other side; she then proceeded to surmount the walls of the fort in Thanjai city. It was there that she met Azhwarkkadiyaan. She learned that he too was on his way to Ponniyin Selvar at the behest of the Mudhanmandhiri. It was but natural to go together; the Veera Vaishnavite made her journey easier than she had thought it would be.

That day, luck was on her side. The pair caught sight of Ilaiya Piratti's chariot at the entrance of the Kudhanthai *jothidar's* home. They entered hoping that Kundhavai Devi may have word of the prince; instead, they unexpectedly learned the chilling news about the Pandiya conspirators from Periya Pazhuvettarayar himself. Poonguzhali too shared her belief that the man lurking in the treasury was one of their rank. She despaired at the thought that Ponniyin Selvar may face danger from these fiends. It was Vanathi's entirely unexpected oath that had come as a soothing balm to her troubled heart. It was when she had set out to save Princess Vanathi that Poonguzhali had run into the prince.

It had given her immense satisfaction when the prince heeded her suggestion regarding the travel to Thanjavur. Poonguzhali was aware the prince had often travelled in Ilankai posing as a mahout in order to conceal his true identity. She hadn't forgotten her encounter with him there - Ponniyin Selvar had broken away from the Senathipathi and the soldiers, rushing towards the seashore on his elephant with Poonguzhali seated behind him. It was this memory that kindled an idea in Poonguzhali. It would not be possible to access the fort if the prince went alone, she pointed out; but if he were to take Vanathi and Poonguzhali with him upon his elephant, he may gain entry with people thinking him to be a mere mahout.

"Samudhra Kumari!" the prince had cried out in delight. "That is an excellent suggestion! You have all the capabilities to serve as the Mudhanmandhiri of a great empire!" Poonguzhali's heart swelled with joy as she thought of his words of praise time and again.

But what was the point of carrying out her plan with such flawlessness thus far? Poonguzhali had expected, upon her return, to find Mandhakini *athai* at the Chakravarthy's side in his chambers; it had come as a rude shock to discover that she wasn't there. It was quite impossible to make enquiries about her with anyone else in the palace or the fort. Poonguzhali's heart was gripped with fright when she remembered the message her *athai* had communicated to her in sign. "My end is near," she had said. Poonguzhali was in the throes of despair.

"What was the point of all my cleverness and hard work in bringing the prince here?" she thought. "*Athai* is nowhere to be found." Her heart beat faster as she considered the dreadful possibilities. It occurred to Poonguzhali that her aunt could be in the *nilavarai*. Perhaps… could that vile conspirator have ended her life in the darkness? Poonguzhali couldn't even bear to imagine such a thing; the very thought broke her heart.

She realized that she had to hasten to the *nilavarai* through the underground passage to discover the truth for herself. However, the palace was in chaos - the prince's arrival had sparked much celebration and joyful ruckus. The palace women flitted about in excitement; they appeared in droves to peek into the Chakravarthy's chambers and left as quickly as they came. If anyone were to see Poonguzhali go to the *sirpa mandapam* all by herself, what would they think of her? In fact, that may not be the prudent course of action if the conspirator still lurked there. Even Poonguzhali, bold as she was, felt fearful of entering that dark *nilavarai.* She decided that it was best to apprise Chinna Pazhuvettarayar and take him along to inspect the treasury.

Time was of the essence; it had taken longer than she had thought to argue her case with Kalanthaka Kantar and change his mind about the urgency of the crisis. It was with this thought in mind that Poonguzhali now walked as fast as she could. A sixth sense whispered darkly to her that a disaster would take place soon; she prayed with all her heart that it should befall her and spare her aunt.

When they entered the *sirpa mandapam*, she spied a black shadow falling upon the upper storey of the palace; it seemed like a murky figure was moving quickly along the wainscoting. Was it real? Or was Poonguzhali imagining things? She stopped to scrutinise the matter.

"*Penne*! Why do you stop? Are you afraid, perhaps, that your lies will soon be found out?" asked Chinna Pazhuvettarayar sharply.

The words stung Poonguzhali who strode ahead of him and walked faster than before.

When they reached the sculpture of Raavana, Poonguzhali pointed out to Chinna Pazhuvettarayar the entrance that lay concealed between the statue's heads and the Kailayam mountain.

"Very well," said the Thalapathy. "Enter and lead on." A strange reluctance came over Poonguzhali; her entire body trembled and shook. All of a sudden, an unearthly screech pierced the air. Poonguzhali immediately recognized it to be the voice of her *athai* Mandhakini; the scream seemed to be coming from the Chakravarthy's chambers inside the palace. Her hesitation vanished. Paying little heed to Chinna Pazhuvettarayar, Poonguzhali raced towards the source of the sound. The frightful howls continued without ceasing, terrifying in their intensity.

When she reached the Chakravarthy's chambers, Poonguzhali saw a scene that would forever remain etched upon her heart like a painting.

The Chakravarthy was lying down on his bed, his hands tightly grasping those of his beloved son Arulmozhi. Mandhakini faced the two of them, wailing desperately. Malayaman's daughter and her soon-to-be daughter-in-law Vanathi were standing by the side of the bed. They were all staring in bewilderment at Mandhakini, who was shrieking wildly as one in the throes of a frenzy.

No one noticed the sharp spear that came whistling from the upper *mandapam*.

Poonguzhali sprung to the side of her aunt.

30

She Becomes a Goddess!

Poonguzhali moved as swiftly as she could, but there was never any hope of competing with the speed of a spear that had been hurled down with force. By the time Poonguzhali had reached her aunt, its cruel tip had pierced through her rib.

Mandhakini fell to the floor with one last dreadful howl.

Heart-rending wails of shock and pity arose from those in the room. Like Poonguzhali, they tried to run towards that queen among women who had crumpled to the ground.

From the upper storey of the palace came the sounds of someone running in haste; clay pots came raining down from all directions as they were thrown with force from above. One of them fell upon the bright lamp that was burning by the side of the Chakravarthy; its light winked out and darkness shrouded the room.

For a brief time, havoc prevailed in the chamber and the long corridors that ran around it. Footsteps thudded all around them as men ran hurriedly to and fro. Chinna Pazhuvettarayar's voice tore through the darkness. "A lamp!" he roared. "A lamp!" Suddenly, a woman shouted in terror. "*Aha*! *Ayyo*!" she screamed. It sounded like the voice of the Maharani. Chills went up every spine and their bodies trembled.

Even in the midst of all this commotion, Poonguzhali maintained her focus; she ran to her aunt Mańdhakini and gently took her upon her lap.

She heard a voice weeping, heartbroken and weighed down with unbearable grief.

Chinna Pazhuvettarayar's voice suddenly sounded sharply near the doorway. "Who goes there? Who the devil is it? Stop!" he cried. Poonguzhali had an inkling of who the fleeing stranger might have been.

At that very instant, two servants entered the room bearing flickering lamps. The scene that they illuminated was one profoundly astonishing; no one had seen such a miracle in all their lives.

The Emperor Sundara Chozhar, whose legs had lost their strength - the ailing Chakravarthy who had been unable to take a single step these past three years - he had climbed down from his bed to walk to Mandhakini. He was sitting beside her with the prince at his side.

The spear had violently pierced through one of Mandhakini's ribs to come out the other side. Thick red blood dripped from its tip onto the floor.

Malayaman's daughter Vanama Devi stood beside the bed that the Chakravarthy had been lying down upon. Next to her was a pillow that the Emperor had used to support his head; it had been stabbed by a sharp blade that was still sticking out from it.

When the lamps were brought in, the Maharani looked at the bed. Her eyes widened with pure wonder when she saw the Chakravarthy was sitting down upon the floor instead. Ponniyin Selvar gently raised Mandhakini's head and placed it upon the Chakravarthy's lap.

Tears streamed down Prince Arulmozhi Varmar's face.

The Chakravarthy wept without restraint in loud, convulsive sobs.

It took Poonguzhali a second to take in all these sights; the very next moment she had deduced the events that had taken place in the darkness.

The man who had hurled the spear from the upper storey had realized that his attempt had been thwarted by the *Oomai Rani*; he had then proceeded to throw down any old junk that was at his hands with the aim of putting out the lamplight. When darkness fell, he had jumped down into the chamber; under the impression that the Chakravarthy was lying upon the bed, he had stabbed the pillow with his dagger before making his escape.

The Maharani had known that the Chakravarthy was in danger - she had run towards the bed in alarm when the man shoved her roughly aside, prompting the shrieks of fright that they had heard. The conspirator had headed to the doorway where he must have pushed down Chinna Pazhuvettarayar as he was making his entrance.

As Poonguzhali guessed at the events that had transpired, she considered pursuing the villain who had committed this vile deed; but the thought of her aunt's end outweighed her thirst for vengeance. Her heart twisted in the grip of turmoil and pain. It didn't matter to Poonguzhali that Mandhakini was lying on the Chakravarthy's lap; she approached her aunt and kneeled down beside her, weeping in anguish. "*Athai*!" she called out in grief. "*Athai*!"

"*Ayyo*!" she bewailed. "Your terrible words have come true! Wretched sinner that I am, I left you behind and went away!"

Mandhakini didn't even glance in her niece's direction. Her eyes were affixed eagerly upon the Chakravarthy's face, thirstily drinking in his features. Why, her awareness didn't even go to the prince beside her who was clutching her hand and shedding tears of sorrow; how could Poonguzhali have stolen her attention?

The prince held back his tears as Poonguzhali's lament grew louder. "Samudhra Kumari! Have you forgotten yourself? Have you lost sight of where you are?" he asked her in gentle tones.

Poonguzhali choked back her sobs and got to her feet, contrite. "My liege!" she said, her voice cracking with sadness. "I have none in the world save this *athai* of mine!"

The prince wiped away the tears that welled in his eyes. "Poonguzhali, to you, she is an aunt; to me, she is a mother who bore me a love deeper than my own mother who gave birth to me!" he replied. "She sent you to bring me to her; yet, she doesn't spare me a single glance. Do you not understand why? My mother and my father have reunited after a separation of thirty years. Who are we to stand in their way?" As he said these words, the prince looked meaningfully at everyone in the room including the Maharani.

He turned back to look at Poonguzhali. "*Penne*! You have come to my aid many a time in the past; those encounters pale in comparison to the great service you have rendered me today. You have bestowed upon me the fortune of seeing my mother and father reunited with each other!" he said with great feeling. "Think of the lofty virtue that your *athai* has earned today! She protected my father without allowing the conspirator's spear to touch a hair upon his head; she received its sharp tip into her own body. She has saved the Chakravarthy by sacrificing her own life for his sake. Upon seeing the spear pierce her skin, my father has regained the mobility in his legs that had been sapped of all strength for three long years! When he climbed down from his bed, his life was saved yet another time - the assassin made a second attempt to kill my father in darkness when he found that the spear had missed its mark; his plans were foiled since the Chakravarthy had left his bed.

There, there stands the daughter of Malayaman, the mother who gave birth to me; look upon her face suffused with unbounded astonishment! Frantic that the murderer would strike again, she had coming running to the bed, intent on making the same noble sacrifice as your aunt; she meant to take unto herself the next weapon that would be aimed at my father. She cried out in alarm on discovering that my father was not in his bed. If the Chakravarthy had remained there, either my father or my mother would have died at the hands of the killer. Samudhra Kumari! Do you now understand the enormity of the service that your aunt has rendered the Chozha clan and *samrajyam*? If the Chakravarthy had fallen prey to the conspirator's murderous plot, the Chozha *samrajyam* would crumbled into ruin. The blame would have been laid upon the Pazhuvettarayars, blotting their legacy for the rest of time. It was not just my parents that your *athai* had saved today; she has protected the honour of the Pazhuvettarayars and redeemed all of the Chozha *samrajyam* from certain devastation. She has been exalted to a name of holy reverence, a Goddess of the Chozha dynasty.

Poonguzhali! I will not shed a single tear henceforth for your aunt. Neither should you. Nobody should grieve for her! She has attained a blessed, divine death, one that nobody can aspire to in this life! Who but her has the fortune to give up their own life for the sake of a beloved husband after a thirty-year separation? Who but her has the opportunity to welcome death with their head upon his lap?" As the prince finished his emotional speech, he looked around the chamber. He saw that every person present there was listening intently to his words. He continued to speak.

"Poonguzhali! You need have no fear that you are orphaned and alone; I will never forget the aid you have given me today. I shall remain grateful to you as long as I live and breathe. If perchance my memory fails me for even a moment - why, Chinna Pazhuvettarayar there will not allow it to remain forgotten! You and your aunt have rendered him peerless service; if either the spear or the dagger had claimed the Chakravarthy, the world would have turned upon this Thalapathy of the Thanjai fort. They would have accused Chinna Pazhuvettarayar of being an accessory to the plot. The Kodumbalur Velar is at the fort gates as we speak; if the murderous ploy had succeeded, he would had the reason he needed to rub the Pazhuvoor clan into dust. Why, if I hadn't entered the fort with your help today, I myself would have suspected the Thalapathy of deceit. There cannot be another in this world that Chinna Pazhuvettarayar is beholden to more than you. Ask him anything you desire; he will give it freely, even if it be half his kingdom!" As the prince spoke thus, he looked at Chinna Pazhuvettarayar.

The prince intended his words to convey to Chinna Pazhuvettarayar that he had not fulfilled his responsibilities as carefully as he ought to have. The Thalapathy understood the prince's message; the agony that had appeared on his face was testament to the fact. His features had lost their usual majesty; there was no sign of the fierce pride and valour that had fed his ego and bluster. Instead, his face showed deep distress and abject humiliation; he felt the painful stabs of contrition, like a deserter in a war subjected to stinging censure.

Poonguzhali's body and soul had melted under the prince's words thus far; the mention of a reward brought about an abrupt change in her and she reverted to her old tempestuous self as the Samudhra Kumari. "My prince, I expect neither gratitude nor reward from anybody. The Sea King will give me refuge should I need it; my boat awaits me in the canal as we speak. I shall leave forthwith," she replied, eyes flashing. She paused for a moment; when she spoke, her tone had changed. "Perhaps… could my *athai* survive yet? No, that is a silly hope to have - my *athai* told me herself this morning, didn't she? She must have sensed what lay ahead. She will not survive this incident; I have nothing left to do here, either. Perhaps, someday if you and the Kodumbalur princess visit Kodikkarai…" Poonguzhali looked in Vanathi's direction, her face strangely vulnerable with hope. She saw the girl look wide-eyed at her and the prince. "Chee!" she declared. "That is an absurd thing to wish for, isn't it? I will leave." Having had her say, Poonguzhali strode quickly to the door.

Vanathi had stood stunned until this moment; Poonguzhali's imminent exit jolted her into action and she ran to the boat girl, barring her way. "My dear friend!" she cried with feeling. "Where are you going? I too am an orphan like you!" Before Vanathi could say another word, Poonguzhali cut in. "Devi, neither am I your dear friend nor are you an orphan like me," she said evenly. "Pazhaiyarai Ilaiya Piratti will be here soon!"

It was only then that Vanathi remembered Ilaiya Piratti. "*Ayyo*!" she exclaimed. "*Akka* is yet to be informed of the events that have transpired here! Word needs to be sent to her!"

"That makes you worry, I suppose! Isn't your *periyappa* at the fort gates? Ask him to send word to her!" said Poonguzhali. She gently pushed Vanathi away with one hand and walked on.

Poonguzhali was stopped once again at the doorway; this time it was Chinna Pazhuvettarayar who blocked her path. "*Penne*!" he said. "I listened to every word that the Ponniyin Selvar spoke just now; it is true, all of it. You have saved the Pazhuvoor clan from being plunged into indelible disgrace. Words cannot convey the measure of gratitude I bear you. Ask of me what you will; whatever be your wish, I will fulfill it."

His words elicited weary laughter from Poonguzhali. "Thalapathy," she said with a wan smile, "some are happy that the Chakravarthy survives; some rejoice that he has regained the strength to walk;

others are relieved that the Pazhuvoor clan has been saved from dishonour. Nobody, it seems, feels grief over my *athai's* untimely death. I intend to pursue the wretch who took her life. Please give me way!" Poonguzhali's eyes narrowed with resolve. Kalanthaka Kantar looked thunderstruck at her words.

"*Penne*!" he cried. "Truly, you have bested me today. Here I stand dithering with a killer still on the loose! This dishonourable stain I bear will not be washed away with the Chakravarthy's survival - that villain must be found and apprehended! I have grievously erred in doubting your words. Where could that cur have disappeared? He pushed me and ran away… yes, yes! He must have slipped into the underground tunnel! Come, come with me and help; I don't want anyone else to accompany me! Ah! Wait till I lay my hands on that scoundrel - see what I will do to him!" he roared, his cheeks shaking in anger.

Chinna Pazhuvettarayar didn't wait for Poonguzhali's response; his hand gripped hers in an iron vise and dragged her along as he rushed to the *sirpa mandapam.*

The rest of the people in the room stood still and silent. In accordance with the prince's wishes, they kept a respectful distance from the Emperor; their eyes were fixed upon him and the noble woman lying on his lap.

Sundara Chozhar and Mandhakini were lost to the world. They seemed to live in a universe of their own making that excluded all but themselves. They had no space in their hearts for thoughts of anyone but each other. It is unknown whether psychologists can explain how a person can live out thirty years in a few minutes, but there could be no doubt in anyone looking upon Sundara Chozhar and Mandhakini that they were reliving lost decades within mere moments. Mandhakini spoke with Sundara Chozhar in sign language. It was a form of speech that Sundara Chozhar was largely familiar with - when he was younger, he had spent a few months of heavenly bliss with Mandhakini in Boodha Theevu and had learned her comprehensive language of gestures and signs in that idyllic period. He hadn't forgotten it till this very day. Even when Mandhakini spoke to him using just her eyes, his heart understood exactly what she wanted to communicate.

Not that Mandhakini had much to say. She repeated the same message over and over again - 'I am not upset with you at all. You are the Chakravarthy, the person who rules the world; what place can I expect in your life, a deaf and dumb daughter of the Karaiyar community? I was the one who hid away from you all these years, wandering the world; at times I watched you from a distance and soothed my yearning heart. Now, I will breathe my last in your lap. What more can I want?'

Mandhakini's face danced with happiness; her features showed not the slightest indication that she felt distress or pain from the spear that had so cruelly impaled her ribs that it jutted out the other side of her body. Mandhakini seemed to have become oblivious to her physical self. The time had come for the bird to fly its coop; why then should it worry about its cage?

Sundara Chozhar too seemed to have put all thoughts of his body aside; in fact, that was why he had been able to climb down from the bed and hasten to Mandhakini's side. Having forgotten that his legs had grown weak, he hadn't thought twice about their ability to walk.

But unlike Mandhakini, Sundara Chozhar had a lot more to say than could be encompassed in a few words. He spoke to her about all sorts of things; what his eyes sought to convey his lips murmured aloud to her. The others could not grasp the things of which he spoke, but Mandhakini understood every word. She nodded her head when she agreed with him; she shook it earnestly when she disagreed. When his words brought her happiness, she looked enraptured; when his words were sorrowful, she lovingly comforted him with all her heart.

"My life's breath! My own!" cried Sundara Chozhar in deep anguish. "You have given up your own life for mine today. I must be a stone-hearted wretch... yes, I am, I accept that I am! Those fated to reign over a kingdom must harden their hearts thus; otherwise, how will they rule? The first error I made was to leave you behind in Boodha Theevu; ah, how many grave crimes followed in the wake of that mistake! Oh, Mandhakini - how happily we lived on that island, that land akin to heaven? We were not fortunate to live out the rest of our lives in that bliss. The gods betrayed us, grudging us our happiness! My own people plotted to drive us apart! I yearned for you after the *yuvaraja pattabhishekam*... I came running to Kodikkarai for you! I was told that you had drowned yourself in the sea - sinners, vile scoundrels! Ah, even my closest friend and confidante, Anirudhhan - he betrayed me too!... Yes, yes, I understand. You say that it was true; that you did jump into the sea and that someone saved your life. Ah, but Aniruddhan knew the whole truth! He knew and hid it from me! Look at the disastrous consequences we bear! Ah, Mandhakini - whenever I caught a glimpse of you from afar, I thought I was seeing your spirit; I thought you were haunting me to take your revenge! When you saved my beloved son from the Kaveri waters, I thought you were the one who had pushed him in! Aha! If I had known that you were alive and well, how different life would have been! Did you think, love, that I would abandon you for the sake of this empire? Never!"

The words came spilling out of Sundara Chozhar like waters from a dam that had been thrown open. He poured his heart to Mandhakini in soft whispers and murmurs. "When you appeared in front of me two days ago, I threw a lamp at you!" he cried. "When I saw you once again after that, I treated you with such disgust! Oh, Mandhakini, forgive me for those things I did - I was petrified because I had thought all these years that you were tormenting me as a ghost! You appeared in the dead of the night in this very room and told me all sorts of things... I thought that you were cursing my children. The repulsion that gripped me then never released its hold on me… it came flooding back when I saw you once again after that! Truly, you came to us as our Goddess; you came to protect my family and children from evil. Oh, how ignorant I have been! My eyes were opened only after my daughter Kundhavai explained the truth to me. *Ayyo*! What a miserable blunder I have made! Mandhakini, please find it in your heart to forgive this wretch! How will I now show you the fathomless love that swells for you in my heart? You have left me no way to express how much affection I bear for you! You told me not to make my son the successor to the throne… I see the justice of your request. Why are you shaking your head? You had my best interests at heart, after all… you intended to do good by my lineage! I don't see anything wrong with that! But the people I am surrounded by whisper all sorts of things to me about you; they say that you are a madwoman. I am told that a child was born to you. If that is true, Mandhakini, tell me right away! Tell me if you have a son. I will do whatever I can for him as atonement for my heinous betrayal!"

When Sundara Chozhar said these words, Mandhakini's expression changed. She looked at him intently; her eyes then strayed all around the room, and finally came to rest upon Ponniyin Selvar who was standing near the doorway. The prince immediately approached his father and mother. He sat next to his mother.

Mandhakini touched the prince with her hand and looked at the Chakravarthy meaningfully. The import of her gaze was clear - 'This is my son!' it said. Mandhakini looked back and forth between the Chakravarthy and Ponniyin Selvar. Her eyes closed gently; her head, held up all this while, went limp and fell back on the Chakravarthy's lap.

Mandhakini's life had left her body.

Until this very moment, no one had seen or heard Sundara Chozha Chakravarthy cry. Today, they saw him break into a gut-wrenching wail. He wept in loud, convulsive sobs as tears streaked his noble face. The people in the room went rigid with shock.

Only prince Arulmozhi Varmar remained mindful and alert.

He looked at the Chakravarthy. "Father!" he said gently. "Please don't grieve over my mother. She is not dead; she has risen to become a Goddess. She will be cherished and venerated by our Chozha dynasty till the end of time!"

The prince's words offered little solace; Sundara Chozhar continued to sob as the tears streamed down his face incessantly. Was he mourning Mandhakini's death? Or did he feel the pain of a new sorrow, foreshadowing a disaster that was unfolding miles away at the same moment? Who can say?

Ponniyin Selvar's words of consolation came true. When he ascended the throne as Raja Raja Chozhan, he raised a temple in Thanjai to honour Mandhakini, the Eezham Rani. The shrine flourished for many years, known among the people as the Sinhala Nachiyaar Kovil. Over generations, under the influence of many tongues, the name changed to become the Singachiyaar Kovil. Even today it exists in Thanjai city as a small shrine; it's quite easily found if one asks after it.

31

The hour has come!

If we could end this story with the events of the last chapter, how nice it would be! It is entirely understandable that our esteemed readers would expect the same. But that is quite impossible. We are obligated to tell you about the frightful incident that transpired at Sambuvaraiyar's palace at Kadambur on the same day as the tragedy we just saw; in fact, it happened more or less during the same window of time, too.

Nandhini was pacing to and fro in her chambers all by herself. Her appearance mirrored the great excitement raging in her heart. A strange, wild light burned brightly in her eyes before it darkened. She kept peering at the many doorways that led to her room. Her ears were keenly cocked, listening for the sound of footsteps along the passages. "The hour has come!" her lips mumbled now and then in soft whispers. Sometimes they trembled as they muttered the words; at other times, her eyelids and brows fluttered erratically. Her body quivered and spasmed like one desperate to contain a pent-up frenzy of rage.

The luxurious bed that had been built for Nandhini was covered by a downy mattress as soft as petals. It was enshrouded by hanging drapes on all four sides. Nandhini slowly lifted the curtain nearest to her hand. She gazed raptly at the sword of slaughter lying along the length of her bed. Its blade glistened with a dazzling lustre as if the blacksmith had forged it from the very fire that burned in the smithy. Nandhini was struck by genuine surprise that the sword had not set aflame the bed, mattress and drapes; it was only when she wondered at this miracle that she realized that blade was not made of fire after all but iron.

Nandhini took the sword in her delicate hands. She tightened her fingers around its hilt and lifted it high, noting with great satisfaction that the blade shone even brighter in the light thrown by the lamp. Nandhini cradled the sword lovingly against her chest; she held its cold steel to her cheek and kissed it gently. She spoke tender words to it in her mellifluous voice. "Blessed sword! The hour has come for you to carry out your task. You won't let me down, will you? No, no, you won't. If anything, it may be my own hands that fail me!" she said softly.

Nandhini looked at her hands. "Hands! Will you be resolute and unswayed when the hour strikes? Chee! See how you shiver even now! What will you do when the time comes upon us? Yes, yes; there's little point in trusting you. I must depend on another pair of hands today."

A prickle of goosebumps ran through her body all of a sudden. Eyes spitting fire, Nandhini looked up. "Aha!" she cried hoarsely. "Here you are! Come, come. You have come at the right time. My darling, my liege! Come, O head of Veera Pandiya! Why do you remain there at the edge of the roof? Come down! There is no one here, none but your servant… Why do you stare at me so? Open your mouth and say but one word to me! You said, '*If I survive this crisis, I shall seat you upon the Pandiya throne!*' I have forgotten neither your words nor the promise I gave you. The time to fulfill my oath to you has neared. How long have I been patient for this moment! Oh, the masks I have had to wear to get so far! You were watching all of it, weren't you? Remain watching, my liege; don't look away for a moment, not even to blink!... But you never blink, do you? You even make sure that my own eyes stay wide open through the night; you don't allow me a wink of sleep. If I sate your vengeance tonight, will you let me fall asleep?... You won't? You will leave only after seeing me ascend the Pandiya throne? You say that you will uphold your promise if I uphold mine… No, no, I want neither the throne nor the jewelled crown. They have brought to me a little boy claiming him to be your son. He has been anointed the crown prince; he has been seated upon the throne with due ceremony. You say that you will be satisfied when I take revenge in your stead? Will you leave me after that at least? You will go to paradise then, to the heavenly abode where rest those who die a warrior's death on the battlefield; there will be many women like me there! Perhaps one of them… what? You say you won't? Alright, alright. We'll talk about that later. My love! It sounds like someone is on their way; hide yourself! I will put away this sword of vengeance, too!"

At that moment, there really did come the sound of footsteps near the doorway. Manimekalai entered the chamber even as Nandhini was placing the sword back upon the bed.

A chilling transformation came over Nandhini, who had so far been raving in mania and melancholy. When she spoke to Manimekalai, she seemed like an entirely different woman. "Is that you, Manimekalai? Come!" she said serenely.

"Why, *Akka*, that sword never seems to leave your hand!" exclaimed Manimekalai.

"What choice do I have?" replied Nandhini calmly, turning to face Manimekalai. "When base thoughts rot the hearts of menfolk, what recourse do us women have but to depend upon blades?"

"Devi! I am by your side as confidante and anchor. Don't you have faith in me?"

"Would I have opened my heart to you without faith?" asked Nandhini, glowing with affection. "You're the only one I trust in this treacherous world. Even so, my sweet," she continued with a twinge of regret, "I hardly think that you can go against your own brother."

"I have decided that I have no brother, *Akka*!" declared Manimekalai.

"Why, Manimekalai?" asked Nandhini in surprise. "He is your own brother, after all…"

"Brother, my foot!" burst out Manimekalai. "Such bonds are nothing but delusions! Kandamaaran cares little for my happiness - he coerces me into a marriage of convenience that furthers his own goals. If he loved me as a brother should, would he exploit me for his gains?"

"My own! Couldn't he have your best interests at heart in seeking to wed you to the prince?" asked Nandhini.

"As if he understands what would do me good!" retorted Manimekalai. "Truly, *Akka*, my well-being matters little to him!"

Nandhini's eyes widened. "Don't you think that your *thamaiyan* longs to see you seated upon the Chozha throne in glory, as Queen of this vast empire that spreads across the reaches from Eezham till the Vada Pennai?"

Manimekalai scoffed in derision. "If I become the Thanjavur Rani, he may rise to be the Mudhanmandhiri or the Dhanaadhikari, perhaps, like Periya Pazhuvettarayar… my interests have no place in his lust for power!" she declared before changing her tone. "*Akka*…" she began before trailing into hesitant silence.

"Speak, my darling," cajoled Nandhini, her fingers raising Manimekalai's chin. "Why hesitate to speak your heart to me? It is true, isn't it, the affection that you say you bear for me?"

"Oh, *Akka*, do you doubt that?" replied Manimekalai earnestly. "There are only two people in this world who can lay claim to my love - one is you…"

"And the other?"

"You know the answer," blushed Manimekalai, looking away. "Why ask?"

"Sweet sister! I thought it would delight you to speak the words," smiled Nandhini, lovingly tucking a strand of Manimekalai's hair behind her ear. "Haven't you read the classical epics and ballads? When love blooms sweetly in a young girl's heart, it thirsts to be expressed aloud - why, what else are bosom friends for but to be confidantes?"

"That is true *Akka*. You have been the dear friend that I have spilled my heart to. But I came here for another reason - I heard a worrisome piece of news, *Akka*!" said Manimekalai with unease.

Nandhini gave a start. "What? What?" she asked, unsettled. Only today had the slow, painful labour of many years reached the final step before fruition - her heart stopped with terror at the thought that it might be foiled. Her face tightened with anxiety.

"*Akka*!" continued Manimekalai gently, "they say that the Dhanaadhikari Pazhuvettarayar is yet to reach Thanjavur. While he was journeying…"

"What happened?" asked Nandhini, voice trembling and unsteady. "Did he change his mind and turn back?"

"Oh, would that he did! Do you remember, *Akka*, the storm that hit the Eri Theevu we were at? They say that its fury ravaged the Kollidam and the territories beyond… they say that it grew particularly violent as the Pazhuvettarayar was crossing the Kollidam on his boat…"

"And then?" asked Nandhini, alert. Her voice had lost some measure of its worry.

"They say that the boat capsized just before it reached the bank," said Manimekalai quietly.

A soft cry of shock escaped Nandhini's lips.

"The survivors formed a search party and combed the Kollidam's banks as thoroughly as they could… but *Akka*, your noble husband remains missing." Manimekalai broke the news as gently as she could.

Manimekalai had expected Nandhini to weep when she heard the report; she had come prepared to offer her solace in her time of grief, a shoulder to cry on. Nandhini, however, did nothing of that sort. She showed no hint of distress as she made her response. "How did you hear of this?" she asked incredulously.

Manimekalai answered after a pause. "A man who was part of the Pazhuvettarayar's retinue has returned. I overheard his words as he gave his report to my brother. *Akka*, my brother was asking the prince for advice because he wasn't sure how to deliver the news to you. I came running to tell you myself…" Manimekalai's voice cracked with grief and she dissolved into tears.

Nandhini clasped her warmly. "My precious darling," she cried. "I see now how much you love me. But, my sweet - there's nothing to be upset about!"

Manimekalai looked up at Nandhini in wonder, marvelling at the coldness of her heart - a thought that did not escape Nandhini's observant eyes.

"My own!" Nandhini said sweetly. "You came running to share my sorrow and offer me consolation; yet, here I am, comforting you instead. Don't despair - I am certain that my noble husband is in no danger. I would have felt it in my own heart had tragedy come to pass. But tell me," asked Nandhini with concern, "of the other things you heard. My mind suspects that there is something else afoot."

"What, *Akka*?"

"It occurs to me that your brother and Parthibendra Pallavan have joined hands in a plot to harm my husband," said Nandhini grimly. "It is possible that they have fabricated such a rumour as part of their plan..."

"I don't understand, *Akka*!" cried Manimekalai in bemusement. "Why would they wish harm upon Pazhuvettarayar?"

"Such naivete! Oh Manimekalai, you remain such a child!" exclaimed Nandhini. "Didn't I tell you that your brother and Parthibendra Pallavan look upon me with evil in their hearts? Didn't I explain to you the reason I keep this sword close to my hand at all times?"

"You did - and that is why I asked you not to call Kandamaaran my brother; that traitorous wretch is no brother of mine!" replied Manimekalai bitterly. "Even so, why would they wish to harm the Pazhuvettarayar?"

"My sister, my own! Do you not understand? They believe that I will rejoice at his death, under the impression that I suffer being married to an old man. They hope to encourage my pliant accommodation by removing him from the picture altogether," said Nandhini, eyes glinting. "If I had known that your *thamaiyan* was such a base man, I would not have welcomed him into my home nor would I have served him as my own brother; I would not have pulled him back as he floundered at Yama's doorstep..."

"*Akka*!" cried Manimekalai, appalled. "Now I shall never leave your side, not even for a second! If one of those beasts dares to show his face here, I will kill him with my own hands!

"Manimekalai!" said Nandhini, touched. "That worry is not yours to bear; I can take care of myself quite well. If Kandamaaran and Parthibendran dare to approach me, I shall teach them a lesson that they will not easily forget. I am not afraid of them. It is only that brutish prince who frightens me." She paused. "Thankfully, you have spared me his attention."

"I have?" asked Manimekalai, startled. "How?"

"Don't you know, sweet girl, that you have enraptured his heart? Why else did he jump into the lake to save you, shoving aside the Vaanar warrior?" asked Nandhini with a smile. "I have been observing the prince and his intentions are quite transparent to me. Does your heart remain insensitive to his desire, Manimekalai?"

"How could I not know?" responded Manimekalai acridly. "I shudder in fear at the very thought of him; my body trembles in his vicinity. That barbarian, that *krathakan* who goes around calling himself my brother - he eats away at my sanity, constantly badgering me…"

"To wed the prince," finished Nandhini with sympathy.

"Yes!" blurted out Manimekalai in anger. "If he spies me alone but for a second, he launches into his insufferable lectures. If only to put a stop to his hounding…"

"You would acquiesce to wed the prince."

"Ah, that you should speak this way too!" cried Manimekalai unhappily and broke into sobs.

Nandhini pacified her as she gently wiped away Manimekalai's tears. "I spoke in jest, my dear - must you cry like this at a mere joke?" She waited for the girl to regain her composure before speaking. "My darling - look to the depths of your heart before you answer. Do you truly not love prince Karikalar? Do you have no wish to wed him and rise to be the *pattamagishi* of the Chozha *samrajyam*?"

"Ask me once or a hundred times, my answer is the same. *Akka*, I have absolutely no such desire!" replied Manimekalai firmly.

"It is true then, that your heart belongs to that Vaanar warrior Vandhiyathevan?"

"Yes, *Akka*. But... who knows what lies in his?"

"That hardly matters if he isn't alive," replied Nandhini.

Manimekalai's heart missed a beat. "What did you say, *Akka*?" she asked, horrified.

"Manimekalai, the truth escapes you still," said Nandhini with a touch of pity. "You understand neither your position nor that of the man you love. You worry about me, about my husband - truly, there is no need for that concern, touching as it is. You know well of my exalted spouse and the power he wields; why, the country trembles when he parts his lips to speak! The illustrious Sundara Chozha Chakravarthy himself refrains from crossing a line drawn by him; he holds my husband's opinion in higher esteem than that of the Mudhanmandhiri. Why, the Emperor doesn't even heed the words of his own children! Only halfwits like your brother look down on my husband, mocking his age; in truth, Pazhuvettarayar's very breath can blow down hundreds of ignorant men like your *thamaiyan* and Parthibendra Pallavan. It is nigh impossible for anybody to harm my lordly husband. My precious! I am quite capable of taking care of myself, too - this would not be the first time I have had to fend off danger. Truly, all I worry about is you, my dear friend bestows such affection upon me! Why, it was you I was thinking of as you entered my chambers a short while ago..."

"I don't understand, *Akka*!" interrupted Manimekalai. "What danger could I possibly face?"

"Innocent, naive girl! What greater danger can a woman face than the prospect of marrying a man that she does not love?"

"That will never happen!" declared Manimekalai fiercely.

"Your brother has already made up his mind to wed you to the prince; your father has agreed to the alliance as well," pointed out Nandhini.

"What difference does that make without my approval?" asked Manimekalai, incensed.

"You speak like a simple-minded child," said Nandhini, a strand of contempt expertly woven around honeyed tones. "Does it matter to the world what a chieftain's daughter wants when the time comes for her to marry? If the very crown prince of this realm desires you - the eldest son of the Chakravarthy who rules all the three worlds, no less - who can refuse him?"

"I can and I will!" replied Manimekalai, stung. "I will tell the prince myself, in fact!"

"What will you tell him?"

"That I do not wish to marry him."

"And if he asks why?"

"I will tell him the truth - that my heart belongs to his friend, Vallavarayan."

"Silly girl!" chided Nandhini." You don't have to tell him this; he knows already."

Manimekalai looked stricken. "If he knows of the matter, then why compel me? If I'm pushed too far," she declared hotly, "why, I have a blade by my side as well, *Akka*!" Manimekalai drew a small dagger that she had tucked away at her hip and showed it to Nandhini.

"My dear, precious friend! Should I weep in despair or laugh at your innocence?" cried Nandhini.

"What folly do you see in me to say so, *Akka*?" asked Manimekalai, hurt.

"You still believe that you will be forced to agree to the wedding. They will do no such thing. They will simply get rid of the obstacle that stands in the way of you marrying the prince!" said Nandhini rather apologetically.

Manimekali froze at her words. "What are you saying, *Akka*?" she whispered.

"That the man who lays claim to your heart is in mortal danger."

A cry of horror issued from Manimekalai.

"It is no secret that your brother bears fierce hatred for his old friend," continued Nandhini. "He feels betrayed by the Vaanar warrior for having slipped the prince confidential details of the political assembly held in this palace a few months back; he also accuses him of making an attempt upon his life. Parthibendra Pallavan is just as furious with your lover, for his own reasons…"

"What harm can their anger bring?" bristled Manimekalai. "The Vaanar youth is a warrior after all, through and through…"

"And so what if he is? What can a warrior do when stripped of all defences and surrounded by enemies on all sides?"

"Do you think that they will assassinate him?" asked Manimekalai in agitation.

"They will hack his body to pieces and throw his carcass to the wolves and dogs," replied Nandhini with an air of conviction.

"*Ayyo*!" cried Manimekalai in terror. "I cannot bear to hear such horrible words!"

"You find mere words unbearable to hear? My darling, how will you handle the sting of torment and agony when the tragedy comes to pass?" asked Nandhini compassionately.

"*Akka*, the very thought makes my heart and soul tremble with dread!" cried Manimekalai in distress. "Are they truly capable of such evil? Isn't the Vaanar warrior the prince's dearest friend?"

"Ah, sister - haven't you heard tales of dear friends turning into bitter enemies? Together, your *thamaiyan* and Parthibendra Pallavan have sullied their beautiful friendship. Their wicked insinuations have brought the prince under their corrupt influence…"

"*Chandaalas*!" hissed Manimekalai. "How…"

"Did I come to know of these things?" cut in Nandhini, anticipating her question. "Parthibendran had come to my chambers this morning on the pretext of taking my leave…"

"And where is he going, that traitorous snake?"

"Not too far. No doubt you've heard that old Malayaman of Thirukovilur is marching towards this city with a great army behind him?"

"I did and wondered why."

"All for you, Manimekalai! I heard that the prince issued a terrible ultimatum this afternoon. He said that if you were not wed to him, Malayaman's army would lay waste to this palace and fort - he promised to see it all razed to the ground! It was in response to his vile threat that your brother pointed out Vandhiyathevan to be the thorn in his shoe. 'Can't you simply remove such an obstacle?" the prince asked, to which your brother said that he certainly could, with the prince's leave. My dear, sweet sister! I made small talk with Parthibendran to extract other useful information from him, too. It is certain that mortal peril lurks in wait for the love of your life. If you don't act soon, you will lose your husband even before the wedding day!" said Nandhini, sounding deeply worried.

Would it surprise you to learn that her words made Manimekalai tremble body and soul with fear?

"*Ayyo*!" Manimekalai cried, aghast. "He must be warned without delay… there's not a moment to lose!" she said, stammering in her fright.

"Yes," said Nandhini thoughtfully. "We could warn him. But you said it yourself, didn't you - your lover is a warrior through and through. Do you think he would run away on learning that his life is in danger? Of course not. He will only grow more stubborn, in fact."

"You must think of a way," begged Manimekalai. "My head feels dizzy. I simply don't know what to do!"

"I was thinking about this dilemma when you arrived," said Nandhini. "I was at a loss for an answer, but fortunately, the message you brought has shown a way by which we can save Vallavarayar!"

"The message I brought?" asked Manimekalai, confused. "Which one?"

"You said, didn't you, that Pazhuvettarayar's boat had capsized; that he is missing?"

"Yes…"

"I will ask Vandhiyathevar to set out in search of him. I will beg him to learn the truth behind my husband's disappearance and bring me his report. You must voice your support for my request. That warrior cannot refuse the entreaties of two innocent women. The only way to save his life is to send him away from this palace; I don't see another solution. Once he leaves, you can boldly speak your mind to your brother, your father and the prince - I will stand by you! I will tell them that it ill suits a family descended from the illustrious Chozha lineage to force a young woman into marriage!"

"And if they pay little heed to your words as well, why - I have my dagger at hand!" replied Manimekalai spiritedly.

"Yes, my darling. But first, we must send your lover away from here. You know where he is, don't you? Bring him to me at once - if you cannot go on your own, send your friend Chandramathi; or send Idumbankari!"

A sudden doubt assailed Manimekalai. "Even if the Vaanar youth agrees to leave - how will he make his way out of here? What if he is stopped by my brother?" she asked.

"Why should your brother cross his path, Manimekalai?" replied Nandhini, her eyes sparkling. "Didn't the Vaanar warrior startle you the first time he entered this very room? We will send him out through the same subterranean passage. Now, make haste, sister! Every minute that Vandhiyathevan spends in this palace brings greater danger to his life! Who knows when the killers hired by your brother will strike?"

"I shall leave right away, *Akka*!" replied Manimekalai determinedly. "I shall return only when I succeed in bringing him to you!" She left quickly, agitated in her haste to fulfill her mission.

As Manimekalai's footsteps receded, someone knocked softly upon the secret door in the *vettai mandapam*. Nandhini strode towards the sound and opened the inner door. A malevolent face emerged from the darkness on the side, half-hidden in shadows.

"*Mandhiravadhi*, here you are at last!" remarked Nandhini.

"Yes, Rani. Here I am, for the hour has come!" replied Ravidasan, his face flushed with manic excitement.

Hidden Meanings and Explanations

Pattamgishi - Empress

32

Endgame

Nandhini swiftly shut and bolted the main door to her chamber. Lamp in hand, she opened the secret door to the *vettai mandapam* and stepped in.

The *mandhiravadhi* Ravidasan was frightening to look upon at the best of times, with his hard, cruel face and features etched with malice; he cut a truly terrifying figure now, with raw gashes gouged across his head and face.

Nandhini gave a start before she could stop herself. "*Mandhiravadhi*!" she gasped. "You are wounded!"

"Are you surprised, Rani?" he replied, lips twisting into a sardonic smile. "Did you think that we whiled away our time in comfort, feasting on elegant meals and lounging about on fine cotton bedding like you?" The *mandhiravadhi* scowled. "Parameswaran and I only got away by the skin of our teeth - helped, no doubt, by the spirit of the Pandiya Chakravarthy…"

"No, Ravidasa!" cut in Nandhini earnestly, her eyes brightening with a strange light. "His ghost is always with me, always! It appeared in front of me not one *naazhigai* ago - it asked me whether I would keep my oath."

"And what did you say, Rani?" Ravidasan asked as he watched her, his eyes never leaving her face.

"That I would fulfill my oath or give up my life."

"A good thing we made haste, then!" he snapped. "What would be the use of such a sacrifice after all this time? We must see our task to its end. If you cannot…"

"Who said that I cannot fulfill it?" retorted Nandhini. "I will carry out my oath before I yield my breath."

"Oh no, no!" said Ravidasan, his eyes hardening. "Once the oath is fulfilled, there remains much for you to do. Veera Pandiyan's son awaits his *pattabhishekam* in Madurai."

"Which the rest of you can see to. My role comes to an end tonight; so will my life."

"Rani!" Ravidasan's voice rose dangerously. "The riches in the Pazhuvettarayar vault must be despatched to Malai Naadu - that cannot be done without your assistance."

Nandhini stood stock still. "You would have me live on even after I've kept my oath," she said softly. "You expect me to carry on deceiving my husband."

"Your husband?" said Ravidasan contemptuously. "*Ammani*, who is your husband?"

"The man who wed me with the world as witness," said Nandhini defiantly. "The paragon of virtue who brushed aside the barbs and jeers of town and country to fulfill each and every one of my vows!"

"Rani, Pazhuvettarayar is not your husband," said Ravidasan, fixing her with a cold stare. "Veera Pandiyar visits my dreams each night, bading me to treat you as his queen, his *pattamagishi*..."

"Do not speak of him, *mandhiravadhi*," breathed Nandhini. Her tone suddenly changed. "You haven't yet told me how you came by these wounds."

Ravidasan's face pulled into an ugly grimace. "We were waylaid by an old tiger last night, in the forest edging the Kollidam bank," he spat. "The hoary codger was long in the tooth but its fangs and claws were still sharp..."

"How did you escape?"

"Do you remember the *pallippadai* where we conducted the *pattabhishekam* for the Pandiya child? A portion of the *gopuram* was crumbling and in ruins; we managed to topple it onto the tiger to make our escape..."

"*Ayyo*, poor thing!" said Nandhini, clucking in sympathy. "You had no chance of pitting your strength against that tiger it seems, for all its decrepitude."

"Yes, Rani," said Ravidasan quietly. "We were no match, it's true. Why else would we resort to subterfuge and trickery to bring down Aditha Karikalan, a tiger in his prime? Devi!" he cried suddenly, his voice ringing with fervour. "If we fail tonight, then we will never get another chance. If he hears of Sundara Chozhan and Arulmozhi Varman, Aditha Karikalan will not fall into our trap."

"*Mandhiravadhi!* Has there been word of them?" asked Nandhini anxiously. "Do we know anything definite?"

"I have no doubt that their lives would have been snuffed out by now," replied Ravidasan smugly.

"That's exactly what you said when you and Thevaralan went to Eezham, too," pointed out Nandhini.

"Ah, that mute lunatic was on our heels the whole time, wasn't she?" scowled Ravidasan. "She made such a nuisance of herself and spoilt our plans!"

"You also said," continued Nandhini, "that the Vaanar warrior had drowned in the sea and died. He survived as well, didn't he?"

"We had the chance to do away with him in the *pallippadai* forest," flung back Ravidasan, his eyes flashing. "You stayed our hand."

"I told you I had an important reason for that…"

"Some reason!" scoffed Ravidasan. "That fellow's turned up here like a bad penny - he protects Aditha Karikalan like a walking suit of armour!"

Nandhini's mouth tightened into a thin line. "Never mind him," she said brusquely.

"I will; I must. If not today, then never!" burst out Ravidasan. "Devi! What have you planned? What should the rest of us do?"

"It would be of great help to me if all of you stayed away for the moment."

"That is out of the question."

"I see that I don't inspire much faith in you," said Nandhini, narrowing her eyes.

"It is faith that has brought us here, my lady," replied Ravidasan with a cold smile. "We have come to take you away with us once the oath has been fulfilled. If unexpected problems arise, we're ready to counter them, too. You can call upon us to help at any moment."

"There won't be any problems," said Nandhini evenly. "I don't wish to remain living once the oath is complete."

"No!" said Ravidasan forcefully. "You must come away with us. Else…"

"*Mandhiravadhi!*" cried Nandhini, desperation flooding her voice. "I will not remain in Periya Pazhuvettarayar's home for even a second longer once the oath is fulfilled!"

"Then come away with us," pressed Ravidasan.

Nandhini paused. "How will you take me away from here?"

"An Ayyanar temple lies at the end of this subterranean tunnel, bordered by a forest. There, in the jungle, a palanquin awaits the noble Pazhuvoor Rani. Idumbankari had brought it out earlier so that it could be made fit for your travel." Ravidasan's eyes shone bright. "We will carry the Devi upon our very own shoulders, the angel who wreaked vengeance upon the man who beheaded Veera Pandiyan! We will reach Kolli Malai by first light."

"How many of you are here now?" asked Nandhini.

"Four of us," replied Ravidasan and clapped his hands softly. The men emerged from their hiding places behind the hideous animal specimens in the *vettai mandapam*, their faces stony and resolute.

"Where is Parameswaran?" asked Nandhini.

"Outside, upon my orders," said Ravidasan. "We found a *kaalamugan* meditating at the Ayyanar temple; it was quite an onerous task to get him to leave. I asked Thevaralan to keep watch at the temple entrance to make sure that he doesn't return."

"Why worry about the *kaalamugan*?" said Nandhini, brushing the news aside. "*Mandhiravadhi*, have you heard any news of Periya Pazhuvettarayar?"

Ravidasan started, taken aback. "News?" he repeated in some alarm.

"He was on a voyage to Thanjavur, was he not? They say that his boat capsized in the storm as it was crossing the Kollidam. A message was brought to Sambuvaraiyar just this evening, informing him that Pazhuvettarayar was not found ashore; he is presumed to have drowned in the river."

"Dear god!" exclaimed Ravidasan. "Is that what became of him? You knew it all along and yet said nothing of this crucial bit of intelligence!"

Nandhini studied Ravidasan. "I don't believe it, *mandhiravadhi*," she said shortly. "It seems unlikely that Periya Pazhuvettarayar would have met his demise in the Kollidam waters."

"I find it hard to believe, too, Rani."

"What if he had swum ashore, to this side of the Kollidam?" asked Nandhini with apprehension. "If perchance he comes here tonight…" She shivered reflexively. "The thought worries me," she finished, biting her lip.

"Rani, worry not," said Ravidasan, suddenly assuming an air of assurance. "I've only just remembered - last night, I saw a large, well-built figure on the other bank of the Kollidam, on the Thanjavur road. The man did not seem to be wearing fine clothing or jewellery. I was unable to recognize him in the dark, but when I think of it now - why, that passerby must have been Periya Pazhuvettarayar!"

"Then there is no chance of him turning up here tonight, is there?"

"None, my lady," replied Ravidasan smoothly. "Set your mind at ease. Now," he said, his voice turning hard. "What are your orders for us?"

"You must remain here, biding your time," said Nandhini. "No matter what occurs in my chamber, no matter how many voices you hear - you must be patient. Do not enter in haste; that would ruin the plan. You can all come inside once you hear my signal."

"Rani, how will we recognize the signal?"

Nandhini smiled wryly. "*Mandhiravadhi!* You know, don't you, that it has been many years since I have laughed from the heart?" she asked. "I don't think you have ever heard me laugh, not truly."

"I have, Devi," replied Ravidasan quietly. "I heard you laugh once, when you were talking to that rogue Vandhiyathevan."

Nandhini looked away for a heartbeat. "Ah," she exclaimed. "You still remember that, do you?" She turned back to face Ravidasan, her face expressionless. "Good! The sound of my laughter will be your cue to open the secret door and come inside my chamber - that will signal that the deed has been done," she said. "This time too, it may well be Vandhiyathevan that you see me laughing at; don't let that surprise you."

"Devi," said Ravidasan slowly. "I think I'm starting to understand your plan."

"Everything will be made quite clear if you are but a little patient," replied Nandhini. "If unforeseen troubles arise, you will hear me weep; you must come inside at once."

"So be it, Rani," said Ravidasan, his voice dangerously soft. "I do not wish to hear you weep. I only wish to hear you laugh," he said as he stepped back into the shadows.

<u>Hidden Meanings and Explanations</u>

Kaalamugan- A monk of a Saivite sect.

33

Ayyo, Demon!

Vandhiyathevan was ambling in the palace garden, nursing a weary heart. The garden lay alongside a corner of the outer boundary wall, a quiet haven of nature that was at its magnificent best at the moment. Night flowers that blossomed into splendour under the moon and stars were shyly unfurling their delicately hued petals; the cool, crisp winds of *aipasi* caressed Vandhiyathevan, blowing towards him a heady symphony of fragrances from the *panneer*, *parijatham*, *malligai* and *mullai* flowers that adorned the greenery. 'How I wish I were at the Pazhaiyarai palace,' thought Vandhiyathevan wistfully as he dragged himself along the walkway. 'Oh, to be pleasantly surprised by the sweet tinkling of Kundhavai *devi's* anklets!' He moodily kicked at a twig lying in his path. 'Instead, I'm stuck in this godforsaken palace at Kadambur, tethered to a deranged prince!'

Aditha Karikalar had not quite been himself lately. The prince had flown into a bestial rage at Vandhiyathevan. 'Get out of my sight," he had snarled. "I'll decide how to deal with you by daybreak tomorrow." The words had cut Vandhiyathevan to the bone; he was moved to a deep and uncharacteristic anger which soon turned into regret. Poor soul! What was the point of holding a grudge against the prince? His heart must be in unendurable turmoil. Vandhiyathevan couldn't help but pity him.

That day, Aditha Karikalan's hysteria had reached an alarming peak. He seemed to be entirely at the mercy of visceral emotions that wrung him through rapid mood swings. He seemed to be full of life one moment and utterly enervated the next; he gave himself over to rabid fury before exploding into sudden bursts of glee; he exhibited warm amiability that soon soured into bitter enmity for no apparent reason. The brunt of this acute mania fell upon his companions, who found themselves thoroughly unnerved. There was no telling what mood the prince would be in or what he might do from one instant to the next.

The reports that had been coming in since morning weren't helping matters much; indeed, they only escalated his frenzy. It was an aggrieved Sambuvaraiyar who was the first to appear with news of Thirukovilur Malayaman - he announced that the latter was advancing with a large army at his command and promptly registered his strong objection to this new development.

"Malayaman is practically ancient," the prince responded. "Why do you fear his coming?"

"*Ayya*, we are descended from the noble lineage of Valvil Ori, the illustrious lord who ruled Kollimalai. We do not know the meaning of the word fear!" said Sambuvaraiyar defensively. "It is your noble presence that gives me thought. With your permission…"

"You mean go to war with the old man," finished Aditha Karikalan, arching his brows. He suddenly flashed a wicked smile.

"Sambuvaraiyar, my lord! It was I who sent word asking my grandfather to come here with an army for company."

Sambuvaraiyar blinked. "Why, my prince?" he asked uneasily.

"Why, you've got me here at your mercy, haven't you?" replied Aditha Karikalan, his grin growing wider. "If something should happen to me in this place…"

"*Komane*!" exclaimed Sambuvaraiyar in genuine shock. "If you have the slightest misgiving, why, this very second…"

"You would show me the door, I suppose," cut in Aditha Karikalan in a dangerous tone. The smile slid off his face in a startlingly abrupt manner.

Sambuvaraiyar's heart beat a bit faster. "*Ayya*!" he cried out. "This kingdom is yours and so is this very palace - the exalted tiger flag of the Chozhas flies atop its tower! Who am I to ask you to leave, mere steward that I am? With your permission, I shall withdraw from here forthwith, along with my family. Your illustrious self can receive Miladudaiyar Malayaman without fear."

"Oho!" pounced the prince. "The descendants of Valvil Ori know no fear unlike us cowards from the clan of Vijayalaya Chozhar - that's what you mean, isn't it?"

"The whole world celebrates your peerless courage and valour; why, my prince, it is well known that your heart is as strong as diamond!" replied Sambuvaraiyar, breaking into a desperate ramble. "You bravely dove into the Sevur battlefield in your twelfth year and decimated the armies of the enemy - your exploits marked you as a *veerathi veeran*, a warrior beyond compare. In your eighteenth year, you once again marched to war and *relentlessly* gave chase to Veera Pandiyan… you tracked him down and decapitated him, bringing his very head…"

"I am aware, *ayya*," interjected the prince maliciously. "I am well aware that I am a subject of mockery - mere grist for your mills that deride me as the valiant tiger that ran down a fleeing Veera

Pandiyan and beheaded his lifeless corpse! I am also well aware that it is the Pazhuvoor *mohini* who fans these rumours!" He broke into a chillingly mad cackle that echoed throughout the chamber.

Sambuvaraiyar felt his feet grow cold. The chieftain felt utterly sorry for himself. He deeply regretted initiating conversation with a prince who had clearly come unhinged.

"*Komagane*!" he pleaded. "I seem to give you offence whatever I say. My prince, do whatever you deem right. I beg to take leave of you."

"Fine, then," replied Aditha Karikalan shortly. "You may go. But banish any thought you may have of leaving this fort. I don't plan to leave until I discover the truth behind the covert dialogues that took place in this palace four months ago; neither will you."

Sambuvaraiyar's lips trembled. His body shook uncontrollably and tears welled in his eyes.

His distress did not escape the notice of Parthibendran, who was standing close by.

"*Komagane*! The Chozha clan is as famous for its fair sense of justice as it is for its unequalled bravery. You have not been fair to this veteran. Your words wound him. Sambuvaraiyar has already provided sufficient explanation for the assembly of chieftains that took place here; his account seemed to give you satisfaction at the time," said Parthibendran, attempting to placate matters. "My prince, you had spoken of rejecting the throne. Why, you even refused to go to Thanjavur! The chieftains merely wondered who would succeed the throne if not you. They had nothing but the good of the Chozha empire at heart! If your noble self deigns to accept the burden of kingship, why should they spare a thought for alternatives? If the empire has a leader in the illustrious Aditha Karikalar, the prince whose fortitude is celebrated the world over, why would they even dream of instating Maduranthakan, one who has not even seen a battlefield with his own eyes?..."

"Yes, yes," interrupted Aditha Karikalar, swivelling to face Parthibendran with a sly look. "It is true that another cannot ascend the Chozha throne as long as I live and breathe. No wonder the pack of you are trying to do away with me!" he declared and erupted into maniacal laughter once again.

"Parthibendra!" he said suddenly, fixing him with a cold stare. "Do you think that I am unaware of your new alliance? Do you think that I do not know how you and Kandamaaran stalked me during the hunt that day, aiming a spear at my back? If not for Vandhiyathevan, my true friend, wouldn't you have despatched me to Yama's abode?"

Parthibendran shot Vandhiyathevan a look of pure loathing that would have killed him if it could. "*Ayya*! This lowly wretch has poisoned your heart!" he cried. "If there is any proof that the merest thought of betraying you has crossed my mind, then this very second.."

"*Appane*! Who can provide proof of traitorous thoughts?" asked Karikalar. "Answer me this - isn't it true that you and Kandamaaran strove to bring me here at the behest of Pazhuvoor Ilaiya Rani, who has the two of you wrapped around her finger? Do you deny this?"

"I do not refute that, my prince; there is no need to, either. I am certain that the Pazhuvoor Rani has involved herself in this matter with the best of intentions," answered Parthibendran earnestly. "She desired your presence so that you could be wed to Kandamaaran's sister - she nobly seeks to prevent civil war in Chozha Naadu through such an alliance. Nothing will give us more happiness than to see you wear the jewelled crown of the Chozha Empire. Should anyone cast aspersions on me, I will bear the burden," he continued, "but I will not suffer the vilification of the Pazhuvoor Rani - why, I shall make such an accuser prey to my very blade!" declared Parthibendran, glaring at Vandhiyathevan as he unsheathed his sword.

"Aha!" exclaimed Karikalar loudly. "My brave warrior friend! Please, put the sword back in it's sheath, I beg you! I shall let you know myself when such an opportunity arises; you may brandish it then. Vandhiyathevan has said nothing to dishonour the Pazhuvoor Rani. He is intoxicated by her as well, you know!" A strange glint lit his gaze. "He swears that Pazhuvoor Ilaiya Rani is my own sister, in truth. No, the crime he accuses you of is something else altogether." The prince's eyes hardened. "You brought my brother upon your ship when you departed from Eezham, did you not? I hear that you pushed him into the sea and drowned him. What have you to say to that?"

It was at this time that Kandamaaran appeared. "I shall answer that question!" he declared, entering the chamber in some haste. "*Komagane*! I bring joyous tidings. The younger prince has not been lost to the sea - it turns out that he has been in hiding all along, safe and sound in the Choodamani Viharam at Naagaippatinam! The tempest had agitated the sea, forcing its waters into Naagaippatinam city and prompting the prince to make a public appearance. I am told that he is on his way to Thanjavur, accompanied by lakhs of people as his retinue!"

Kandamaaran looked at the prince expectantly. He thought that the good news would be welcomed by Karikalar with great cheer and felt thoroughly cheated when he saw that it only drew ire instead.

"What, what?" thundered the prince. "Arulmozhi is going to Thanjavur, you say? With lakhs of people as retinue? Why?" he demanded, turning to face Vandhiyathevan. "That's not what you told me. You said that Arulmozhi will remain at Naagaippatinam until he hears from me. Why is he going to Thanjavur now?..."

"*Ayya*! Ilaiya Piratti was quite confident in assuring me that that would be the case," Vandhiyathevan broke in. He looked rather bemused. "I am unaware of what transpired after that. Perhaps I can go..."

"Aha! You wish to leave as well!" lashed out Karikalar. "Good! It is clear that I have made enemies of all of you. Your underhanded schemes are quite transparent to my eyes. I know why Arulmozhi makes his way to Thanjavur. It is part of a plot hatched by the Kodumbalur Periya Velar - that old man plans to foist his niece upon my brother and seat him on the Chozha throne. Why, I hear that the Kodumbalur Velar marches to Thanjai as well, with the southern armies at his command! My sister Ilaiya Piratti is embroiled in this conspiracy too. Yes! Even *you*..."

Vandhiyathevan looked at the prince in dismay. "My prince! Forgive me, but neither Ponniyin Selvar nor Ilaiya Piratti have even dreamed of such a thing, I swear! If it pleases you, I will leave at once to discover the truth behind the matter," he said.

"I see," spat Karikalar. "You ask for leave so that you can join hands with the rest in this vile scheme. Kandhamaara, seize him! If this palace has an underground dungeon, throw him into its cell!" Kandamaaran's face lit up with glee and he briskly advanced towards Vandhiyathevan.

The words had hardly left Karikalan's mouth when he changed his mind. "No, there's no need for that," he said. "The Chozhas have never failed justice yet - judgement cannot be passed unless the crime has been proven beyond doubt. Vallavaraya! Henceforth, you will not show your face to me. That is your punishment! I shall tell you tomorrow whether I have decided to send you to Thanjai or have you jailed. Go, now! Don't stand here a second longer - leave!" he roared.

At that moment, Vandhiyathevan saw a curious change in expression upon Karikalar's face. The prince had looked at him meaningfully out of the corner of his eye, a glance that gave the impression that all of this was nothing but a ploy. The gesture was so fleeting, however, that Vandhiyathevan judged it prudent to steer clear of the unstable prince. "*Ayya*, your wish is my command," he replied with deference and made his exit.

Later that afternoon, Vallavarayan Vandhiyathevan learned that Sambuvaraiyar and Parthibendran had departed to meet the old man of Thirukovilur upon the prince's orders. They were to greet him mid-way and accompany him to the palace themselves.

He also learned that the prince and Kandamaaran had been engaged in long, private discussions. The slew of new developments weighed heavily upon Vandhiyathevan, who suddenly felt quite weary. What judgement would the prince pass upon him tomorrow? Would Karikalar order him to go to Thanjavur? Would he bade him make a stop at Pazhaiyarai? Oh, how nice that would be! Vandhiyathevan quite disliked life at the Kadambur palace. No one seemed to be in good cheer; everyone carried a look of damp melancholy, giving one the impression that they had lost something quite irretrievable. Why, the palace itself took on an eerie, inhuman quality after dusk. It didn't look like one inhabited by men; it appeared for all the world like a ghastly, dilapidated edifice that was haunted by ghosts and demons. *When are we to leave this gloomy place? How?*

As Vandhiyathevan wallowed in self-pity, a girl's scream pierced the air, shaking him from his thoughts. "*Ayyo*! Demon!"

Hidden Meanings and Explanations

Aipasi - Tamil month. The Gregorian equivalent would be mid-October to mid-November.

Velakkarai Padai, Velakkara Regiment - The personal bodyguards of the Chozha Emperor. It is said that these elite warriors took an oath before the Goddess to chop off their own heads if they failed in their duty to protect the king.

34

Leave, All of You!

"*Ayyo*! Demon!" a voice shrieked. Vandhiyathevan hastened towards the terrified scream, his mind working furiously as he ran. *That is certainly Manimekalai's voice. Why is she here at this hour? What did she see that elicited such horror? There are no such things as demons, surely.. What could it have been? She sounded truly petrified. Would there be trouble if I approach her now? Her brother is bent on devouring me as it is; Aditha Karikalar seems to have gone berserk; As for the Pazhuvoor Rani, only the good lord knows what deceit lurks in her heart…*

Vandhiyathevan tore down the garden path, distracted by his thoughts. He didn't notice the hardy root of a *panneer* shrub that lay in his way; he tripped over it in his haste and tumbled down, snagging his upper garment on a flowering thicket that was nearby. Vandhiyathevan managed to get back on his feet. He tugged gently at his *angavastram*, laughing softly to himself. *This tiny shrub has achieved what a legion of enemies and schemers have failed to do - it has brought me to my knees! Could this be a sign of misfortune to come? Or did this little plant try to stop me from running headlong into danger?*

A voice suddenly sounded nearby. "My lady? Where are you?" it called out. It was Chandramathi. "I am here, beside the *alli* pond. Hurry!" came Manimakalai's reply. Vandhiyathevan heard the patter of footsteps, accompanied by the sweet tinkling of anklets.

The *alli* pond that Manimekalai had spoken of was a beautiful marble pool in the shape of a lily that lay in the midst of the gardens, next to an artificial mound. Enchanting *alli* and *sengazhuneer* vines graced its waters, a few of them in splendid bloom. Vandhiyathevan had seen this *alli* pond before - he must have tumbled down somewhere close to the pool. Thankfully, neither woman had taken any notice of him. If it had been daylight, they would have borne witness to his awkward stumble; he wouldn't have survived the ensuing embarrassment. In any case, now that Chandramathi had come to Manimekalai's aid, he could now safely slip away and no one would be the wiser.

Their conversation fell upon his ears. "My lady, what scared you? Why did you scream?" asked Chandramathi.

"*Adiye*! Do you see that compound wall there? Someone - or something - was perched upon it. The figure had a shock of matted hair and its face was hairy, with a thick beard and moustache. Its neck - oh, it's too frightening for words!... Its neck sported a hideous garland of skulls! The apparition disappeared when I shouted!" said Manimekalai.

"A fine story, princess!" laughed Chandramathi. "That was no demon or ghost - just a figment of your imagination! No one could possibly sit atop such a tall compound wall."

"No, woman! I am not in the habit of hallucinating ghosts and demons!" replied Manimekalai indignantly.

"No, not ghosts and demons," agreed Chandramathi cheerfully. "You only daydream about a handsome face that rivals Manmathan's own!"

"Chi, chi!" cried Manimekalai, sounding quite abashed. "Look at you, fooling around at a time like this!"

"And what better time to fool around?" demanded Chandramathi. "Here you are at twilight, seated next to a blooming *alli* pond in the garden; the heady fragrance of *mullai* flowers tickles the nose..." She sighed theatrically. "More's the pity. You wait here hoping to receive the Vallathu prince and get a hirsute demon instead!"

"And now you're here too," added Manimekalai good-naturedly.

"Perhaps that brute made a run for it upon seeing me," said Chandramathi thoughtfully. "It is well known that all manner of fiends, be it *pei*, *pisasu*, *bootham* or *vedalam*, flee at the very sight of Chandramathi, the palace maid of Kadambur!"

"Chandramathi!" Manimekalai giggled. "Enough of your jokes, please. I tell you, I did see a vile, cruel face atop that compound wall! Oh well - if you do not believe me, it can't be helped. Now, tell me. How did you fare with your task?"

"I fear it was a failure, my princess."

"Why?"

"I only found the Kanchi prince and the Kadambur prince engrossed in a private conversation. The Vallathu prince was nowhere to be seen."

"Did they send him away, too?"

"We're ignorant on that count as well, my lady. It is only your father and the Pallavar who have set off to greet the Malayaman king en route. I did ask Idumbankari though - it seems that Karikalar behaved rather furiously with the Vallathu prince this evening!"

"He really has lost his mind. He lashes out at everyone he comes across. But go on..."

"Apparently, he dismissed the Vallathu prince with these very words - Don't show your face to me henceforth! Come back after dawn tomorrow!"

"Where could he have gone?" wondered Manimekalai.

"He's probably wandering about the palace. I told you, didn't I - he must have disguised himself as a demon and inadvertently frightened you in the bargain."

"That cannot be. I know that there are many in this palace who don all sorts of disguises; but he isn't one to carry out such a deception."

"This is how naive women like us make a habit of placing our trust in men and find ourselves cheated in the end," remarked Chandramathi.

"So be it, then," replied Manimekalai crossly. "Go and search for him once again. He must be somewhere within these palace walls! Ask Idumbankari to search as well," she added as an afterthought.

"My lady, I cannot stand the sight of that Idumbankari! He stares at me so. I am a bit afraid of him, to tell the truth," said Manimekalai, the dislike quite obvious in her tone.

"Ghosts and demons don't rattle you, but Idumbankari makes you nervous!" exclaimed Manimekalai. "No matter. It's probably best not to say anything to him. You go look for him again and report to me."

"Till then..."

"I will remain here."

"What if the demon makes a second appearance?"

"I will drive it away in your name."

The soft tinkling of anklets ensued and the sound soon receded into silence. Chandramathi had clearly left for her mission.

The exchange had a profound impact on Vandhiyathevan, who had heard every word of the conversation. He was caught in a jumble of thoughts that each competed for his attention. He wondered who the demon on the compound wall could have been. He remembered that Azhwarkkadiyaan had come to his rescue once in the garb of a *kaalamugan.* Could the figure have been the Veera Vaishnavate? Perhaps he has arrived from Thanjavur bearing an important message for him. Perhaps he had come in disguise to escape recognition.

Why was Manimekalai so eager to meet him, anyway? Why did she send her maid in search of him? Vandhiyathevan had a vague understanding of the nature of her feelings towards him. It was the very reason he maintained a respectful distance from her, in fact. He was also quite keen to avoid fuelling Kandamaaran's enmity further. And yet, here was Manimekalai waiting for him all by herself in the gardens. Surely, she wouldn't be so bold if it weren't an important matter. Poor thing! Perhaps she has a problem she wishes to confide in him. Or perhaps Nandhini had sent a message for him through her. God! The people of Kadambur palace could be maddeningly bewildering at times; each was driven by some clandestine motive or the other. What Manimekalai said a short while back was absolutely true - everyone here wore a mask of deceit. It was quite evident that the poor, naive damsel was caught in a sticky web of chicanery, though it was not clear to what end the Pazhuvoor Rani planned to manipulate her. Yes. Manimekalai must be in trouble; she must be struggling with an awful problem. That had to be why she sought his help. Whatever it was, he could meet her right away and discover the truth of the matter.

Manimekalai was seated upon a marble dais next to the *alli* pond. Its waters were bedecked with brightly coloured flowers that bloomed here and there amidst dense verdure, not unlike the stars that sparkled in the sky against a backdrop of dusky clouds. The flowers were of a beautiful, delicate white that seemed to glow upon the dark greenery that carpeted the pond. On the other side of the *alli* pond lay lush bushes of *mullai*, whose dainty blossoms and buds were strewn upon their foliage like rich pearls embellishing a canopy of midnight blue.

Manimekalai was gazing at the bewitching scenery when she suddenly heard footsteps behind her. Startled, she turned around to see that a silhouette of a man had drawn close to her. Manimekalai rose in haste and lost her footing, tipping dangerously over the pond.

"Rajakumari! It is only me," said Vandhiyathevan as he reached out to hold her from falling over.

Goosebumps rippled through Manimekalai's body. Overcome by a painful shyness, she caught hold of Vandhiyathevan's hands and pushed him away to escape his clutch. Alas, her arms were not strong enough for the challenge; she lost her balance once again and tilted back towards the waters.

Vandhiyathevan tightened his clasp; he smoothly bore her delicate weight in his arms and gently pulled her towards him, bringing her back to an even keel.

It took considerable effort for Manimekalai to recover herself and regain her footing. "Let go of me!" she said sharply. "Don't touch me!"

Vandhiyathevan released his grip. "Please forgive me, my princess," he said.

Manimekalai was evidently a bit shaken still, for her voice trembled when she replied. "What should I forgive you for?" she asked.

"My sudden appearance seems to have startled you," replied Vandhiyathevan apologetically.

"Sneaking up on me is one thing; why did you grab hold of me like that?" demanded Manimekalai hotly. It was quite plain that she was back to her old self.

Vandhiyathevan found himself taken aback. "I caught you from falling into the pond!" he replied in surprise.

"There's a fine tale!" retorted Manimekalai. "When I fell into the lake the other day, my desperate flailing didn't seem to rouse much sympathy from you. Instead, you come charging to save me from falling into the depths of this pond, whose waters reach about as high as my shins!"

"I see now that it was a mistake," said Vandhiyathevan with some regret.

"No fault of yours, I assure you," replied Manimekalai scathingly. "The mistake is all mine."

"How do you say that? You did nothing, my princess," said Vandhiyathevan, bemused. "Why, I am beginning to think that I have angered you in some way!"

"On an earlier occasion too, you appeared in my chamber all of a sudden, emerging from the *vettai mandapam* of all places - you gave me such a fright!" continued Manimekalai petulantly. "I ought to have raised a cry and handed you over to my father."

"You saved me from great peril that day, my lady," admitted Vandhiyathevan. "I will never forget the turn you did me."

"And I shall never forget the show of gratitude that followed," said Manimekalai, adopting a stern countenance. "Dear lord, but I have not met another so thankless!"

"Princess!" protested Vandhiyathevan. "That is a most unjust accusation. What has convinced you that I am ungrateful? Tell me!"

"You cooked up a pretty story that assassins were after you; by the time I could take a look around the *vettai mandapam* and return, you had vanished into thin air like a thief, without so much as a by-your-leave!" complained Manimekalai.

"I ran away like a thief, you say?" asked Vandhiyathevan politely after a pause.

"I misspoke. I meant to say that you ran away exactly as one," replied Manimekalai evenly.

"Princess, you cannot know what a devilish mess I was caught in that day," said Vandhiyathevan with great feeling.

"And yet you held your tongue. Who stopped you from telling me all about it?" demanded Manimekalai.

"Why, your companion Chandramathi!" replied Vandhiyathevan. "When you entered the *vettai mandapam*, Chandramathi entered through another doorway. I slipped into the *yazh kalanjiyam* to hide from her."

"And then you disappeared like magic," said Manimekalai disapprovingly.

"No. I had to climb up a flight of stairs, cross the upper wing and vault over the compound walls to make my escape," said Vandhiyathevan ruefully, recalling his arduous expedition. "Princess, if anyone had caught sight of me that day, not only would my mission have been ruined, but you would have become the subject of slander as well…"

"Such concern for this poor, naive damsel!" remarked Manimekalai, hiding a pleased smile.

"I truly am concerned about you, my lady!" said Vandhiyathevan earnestly.

"And yet, you still haven't explained why you ran away without a word even though you've been at this palace for days!" pointed out Manimekalai, crossing her arms.

"I was hoping for an opportune moment…" mumbled Vandhiyathevan.

"Those are mere words, *ayya*. Why, you never even glance in my direction," accused Manimekalai.

"Sister!..." began Vandhiyathevan.

"I am not your sister!" cried out Manimekalai heatedly.

"You're the sister of my dear friend Kandamaaran; so you are my sister as well," replied Vandhiyathevan tactfully.

"Kandamaaran is no brother of mine and neither are you his friend!" declared Manimekalai, her cheeks flushed. "He is a bitter enemy to the both of us."

"That's exactly it, princess!" said Vandhiyathevan quickly. "Kandamaaran was my bosom friend until a few days back, but he seems to have changed for the worse. Parthibendran lurks in the vicinity too, waiting for an opportunity to do me in. As for prince Aditha Karikalar, he has grown rather fickle; he seems to be a different person every other second. If I were to come in search of you to express my gratitude with matters as they are…"

"*Ayya*, I am quite pleased to see you have a keen instinct for self-preservation," remarked Manimekalai, amused.

"Princess, I have little concern for myself or even my own life, for that matter. I worry about you though - I do not wish to see you come to harm because of me," replied Vandhiyathevan gravely.

"Ah, how you seem to melt with concern on my account!" exclaimed Manimekalai. "Chandramathi says that menfolk are deceitful creatures. I see that her conjecture has been proven to be true."

"No matter what anyone says, I will never forget you as long as I live and breathe. I will always remember the good turn you did me," said Vandhiyathevan.

Manimekalai fell into thought. "*Ayya*, please repeat your words," she requested.

"I shall say it a thousand times, if you wish!" replied Vandhiyathevan resolutely. "As long as I live and breathe, I shall never forget the good turn you did me; I will remain forever grateful to you."

"What is the point of repeating it a thousand times? Shouldn't you make an effort to live up to those words?" asked Manimekalai.

"How can I show you that I mean them? Do tell, princess!" cried Vandhiyathevan.

"As long as you live and breathe, you will remain grateful to me - that is what you said, did you not?" asked Manimekalai. "Your words obligate you to protect your own life with all your might; if not for your sake, then for mine."

"Princess!" said Vandhiyathevan, startled. "What are you saying?"

"*Ayya*, tell me the truth. Were you listening to the conversation between me and my companion a short while ago?" asked Manimekali frankly.

"I beg your pardon, princess. I came running to help when I heard you scream, but your companion Chandramathi reached you first. I couldn't help but overhear your conversation," admitted Vandhiyathevan.

"You are aware then, that I had asked her to bring you to me?"

"Yes. That is why I approached you, in fact…"

"Meaning, you wouldn't have approached me otherwise. *Adada*, such affection!" remarked Manimekalai wryly. "No matter. I don't have it in me to be indifferent towards you, however uncaring you are. I cannot bear the thought of you in danger."

Vandhiyathevan looked at her curiously. "Princess, I am aware that my predicament is one fraught with danger. Could it be that I am at risk from another peril that I am ignorant of?"

"*Ayya*, you must leave this palace forthwith!" replied Manimekalai in an urgent tone, catching Vandhiyathevan off guard.

"You expect me to turn tail and flee?" he asked in disbelief.

"Fleeing a battlefield is bad form; but what is wrong in escaping the wiles of conspirators?" Manimekalai argued.

"Conspirators?" exclaimed Vandhiyathevan, startled. "What conspirators?"

"Who else?" Manimekalai's face pulled into a resentful grimace. "Kandamaaran and Parthibendran, of course."

Vandhiyathevan's face seemed to relax slightly. "I cannot run away from here in fear of *them*!" he scoffed.

"And I cannot bear the thought of my brother causing you harm!" cried Manimekalai.

"Princess, how can you hold yourself responsible for Kandamaaran's deeds?" asked Vandhiyathevan gently.

"It is in my name that Kandamaaran and Parthibendran plot against you," said Manimekalai miserably.

Vandhiyathevan smiled. "It will be my good fortune to suffer for your sake. I shall consider it as a small token of repayment for all the help you have done for me."

"Nandhini Devi was right after all!" exclaimed Manimekalai.

"Aha!" cried Vandhiyathevan. "And what did the Pazhuvoor Rani tell you, exactly?"

"That if I were to beg you to save yourself, you would turn a deaf ear. She said that you had to be tricked into it. *Ayya*, please come with me," begged Manimekalai. "The Pazhuvoor Rani desires to confer with you upon an urgent matter."

Vandhiyathevan considered her request. "I suppose you don't know what the urgent matter is?" he asked.

"As it happens, I do. It has been reported that the Pazhuvettarayar's boat capsized in the Kollidam waters as he was crossing the river…"

"I heard that news as well!"

"The Pazhuvoor Rani wishes you to personally verify the truth behind the report and bring her your findings. She plans to make this request of you in person."

Vandhiyathevan fell into thought. "Didn't the Pazhuvoor Rani advise you against telling me these things beforehand?" he asked after some time.

"She did, in fact!" replied Manimekalai in surprise.

"Then why did you choose to tell me?"

Manimekalai's face clouded over with unease. "I find myself quite confused, to tell the truth," she admitted. "*Ayya*! Until a few days ago, I was a naive, simple girl with no knowledge of deceit or manipulation. I was free of the burden of suspicion; why, I didn't even believe my own friends when they were critical of someone! Of late, though, I find it hard to trust anyone," Manimekalai said unhappily. "I seem to look upon everyone and everything with a jaundiced eye."

"The unfortunate consequence of crossing my path, no doubt," Vandhiyathevan said lightly, hiding his concern.

"Strangely enough, that is true!" exclaimed Manimekalai. "I didn't think much of it when Pazhuvoor Ilaiya Rani bade me bring you to her - it seemed like such a reasonable request. But having come here, I find myself wary of her."

"Why, my lady?" asked Vandhiathevan, alert. "What do you suspect of Nandhini Devi?"

"That she too wishes you harm like the rest."

"What brought on this suspicion? How could she harm me?"

Manimekalai frowned. "I'm not able to put my finger on it, but something about her speech and conduct gives me second thoughts.

I often catch her with a sword in hand; she holds forth at length to the blade in a perplexing manner, speaking of the strangest things!"

Vandhiyathevan looked disconcerted. "I do not fear a sword in a woman's hand, yet…"

"You fear her piercing gaze, as keen as the sharpest blade," finished Manimekalai with understanding. "You're hardly the first to shrink from it. *Ayya*, it is not just the sword in Nandhini Devi's hands that makes me fear for you. Do you recall the first time you entered my chamber through the *vettai mandapam*?"

"I remember it well."

"You said that you were being chased by assassins, a claim that I didn't believe at first. However, when I went to take a look around the *vettai mandapam*, I thought I caught sight of a few men lurking behind the animal specimens. I wasn't sure if they were giving you chase or merely accompanying you, in truth. I stayed my tongue, though - I couldn't bring up the subject without dragging you into it, after all."

Vandhiyathevan drew a sharp breath. "I am only now beginning to understand the magnitude of the favour you have bestowed upon me, my lady," he said with feeling.

Manimekalai smiled. "I didn't bring up the topic to congratulate myself - there's more. A short while back, Nandhini Devi asked me to fetch you and sent me on my way. I had hardly taken a few steps when I turned back to ask her a question, only to discover that she had locked the chamber door. To my surprise, I could hear voices coming from the *vettai mandapam*! *Ayya*, I will tell you what bothers me," said Manimekalai, worry palpable in her tone. "I am certain that strangers are concealed within the *vettai mandapam*. I suspect that they are associated with the Pazhuvoor Rani in some way."

The terrible gravity of prevailing circumstances dawned upon Vandhiyathevan, who stood shaken by Manimekalai's report. His every instinct had warned him of a looming calamity, one that would draw to an ill end this very day; he could still feel it in his bones. Manimekalai's account justified his dark forebodings.

"Princess," he said earnestly, "You must lend me a helping hand yet again!"

"How can I help?"

"There runs an underground passage that leads to the *vettai mandapam*, accessible from the outside. The same *mandapam* can also be entered through an opening in Nandhini Devi's room. Apart from these two routes, there lies a third path to the *vettai mandapam*, if I am not mistaken," said Vandhiyathevan, with an air of purpose.

"Yes, there is," confirmed Manimekalai. "It is a route meant for the use of the palace servants. Father has the habit of leading new visitors through that very path into the palace."

"Princess," cried Vandhiyathevan in urgent tones, "You must take me to the *vettai mandapam* through that underground passage at once."

Manimekalai gave a start. "Why?"

Vandhiyathevan grew grim. "It is vital that I know who the strangers are who are hiding there; I must discover their true intentions."

"I came seeking to shield you from danger and you want me to lead you straight to it!" exclaimed Manimekalai, alarmed.

"I'm never without my trusty sword at my hip," said Vandhiyathevan, flashing a grin. "Princess, I find that it is far easier to confront a known danger on our own terms than to dodge an unknown one."

"Alright, then," said Manimekalai after some thought. "I will lead you to the *vettai mandapam*, on one condition."

"What is that, my lady?"

"I will accompany you on your mission," Manimekalai declared, catching Vandhiyathevan off guard. "You see, I have a dagger by my side as well!" she said, grandly flourishing her dagger.

Vandhiyathevan's jaw dropped. He goggled at her for a bit before agreeing to her terms with some reluctance.

"Follow me, then - we have no time to lose. We must make ourselves scarce before Chandramathi comes here in search of me," said Manimekalai, walking swiftly.

Manimekalai ushered Vandhiyathevan past the gardens. The princess moved judiciously, eluding the open where she could; she led him into the palace under cover of the dark shadows that skirted the property walls and guided him through a strange path that cut across deserted verandahs and footpaths. Presently, they reached a closed doorway.

Manimekalai gestured to Vandhiyathevan to remain in place before she slipped away. She reappeared quickly enough, carrying a bright lamp in hand. The princess opened the door and held up the light, illuminating a black stone footpath at the end of which was a staircase that descended into darkness. The two proceeded to climb down the stairs, with Manimekalai at the helm. Before long, she came to a halt. "Stop!" she whispered to Vandhiyathevan softly. "I hear footsteps. Do you?"

Hidden Meanings and Explanations

Pei, pisasu, bootham, vedalam - Fearsome ghosts and demons, all. *Vedalam* is a queer one amongst the lot, for there is no true English equivalent for this eldritch creature - vampire comes the closest, perhaps.

35

Monkey grip

Vandhiyathevan cocked his ears. For a moment, he did indeed hear the sound of footfalls. As Vandhiyathevan listened, they came to an abrupt halt. He held his breath. The steps started once again after a pause, only this time they sounded like they were withdrawing. The sound gradually grew softer as it receded into the distance.

"*Ayyo*!" moaned Manimekalai. "Must we go on? Wouldn't it be more prudent to turn back?"

"I am not in the habit of turning my back on challenges, my lady," said Vandhiyathevan with fresh resolve.

"It seems to me that once you get your hands on something, you grip it like a stubborn monkey!" remarked Manimekalai.

"Wasn't it your friend Chandramathi who so eloquently described me as having a monkey face? How else do you expect my grip to be?" riposted Vandhiyathevan, smoothly sidestepping Manimekalai to take the lead. Slightly miffed, the princess quickly moved to stop him from getting ahead. The two bumped into each other and Manimekalai fumbled with the lamp; it fell down with a clang and proceeded to roll down the steps with a great din that seemed to echo through the passage. The light winked out and a pitch black darkness fell upon the path, stranding the pair part-way upon a rugged, uneven staircase.

"Princess, what have you done?" groaned Vandhiyathevan.

"Well, why did you try to step ahead of me?" asked Manimekalai, annoyed.

"I am not in the habit of letting women take the lead when danger lies ahead!" bristled Vandhiyathevan.

"In the future, it would be nice to have a comprehensive list of your habits as reference, so that I know how I am expected to behave," replied Manimekalai tartly.

"So be it, *ammani*! I shall tell you all about them in excruciating detail when I get the time."

"We are suddenly blessed with a lot of it at the moment," observed Manimekalai. "Let us return to the gardens and you can tell me all about them at leisure."

"If you're scared to go ahead in the dark, my lady, perhaps you should return," suggested Vandhiyathevan.

A short pause ensued before Manimekalai spoke. "What do I have to fear with a warrior by my side?" she said, affecting bravery.

"Then let us sally forth!" declared Vandhiyathevan heartily. "What is the point of giving up halfway?" Spurred by a new burst of vigour, he strode ahead to take the lead. He promptly stumbled and would have almost certainly fallen down if not for Manimekalai, who managed to catch hold of him in time.

"*Ayya*, this pathway is a crude, uneven one; it dips unexpectedly in some places and ascends steeply in others. It is not possible to traverse it in the dark," she said. "But I know it like the back of my own hand. I have walked this path a thousand times and am familiar with every step and turn along the way. And so, though you certainly are the bravest warrior around, I think it's best if you hold my hand and follow my lead. I fear we won't be able to reach the *vettai mandapam* otherwise - you will likely end up helpless in this passage with a broken leg!"

No argument came from Vandhiyathevan, who had just regained his breath from his near fall. "I will follow your lead, my lady," he said humbly.

Manimekalai's hand gripped Vandhiyathevan's own in the darkness, discovering that it had grown quite cold. "This man stands tall and brave in the face of enemies and wily schemers. Why is he afraid to hold the hand of a naive damsel as I?" she wondered.

The pair walked on in silence for a while. Vandhiyathevan blindly staggered along the way, often losing his footing. Manimekalai had to grasp his hands firmly each time he tripped to prevent him from falling.

"The road to hell is as dark as this," grumbled Vandhiyathevan.

"You've been to hell, then?" came Manimekalai's teasing voice.

"I've been to neither hell nor heaven for that matter," said Vandhiyathevan, gingerly taking another step forward. "I'm simply repeating what my elders say."

"For all you know, they simply repeat to you what their own elders said," giggled Manimekalai.

A short laugh escaped Vandhiyathevan. He found himself astonished at the change he saw in Manimekalai. It was not too long ago that she had been so bashful that she couldn't bring herself to face the smallest gathering; now it appeared that she could talk the hind legs off a donkey when she felt like it!

Manimekalai was still chattering away. "If the road to hell is dark," she mused as she guided Vandhiyathevan past a curve, "what do the elders have to say about the road to heaven?"

"They say it is bathed in radiant light as bright as a million suns!"

"Then give me the road to hell any day," said Manimekalai. "The radiance of a single sun hurts my eyes; that of a million will strike me blind for certain!"

"The road to hell has the minor drawback of leading one to hell," pointed out Vandhiyathevan.

"With a warrior like you in the lead, no doubt one can make it to the gates of heaven even upon the path to hell," came the reply.

"And if one has the fortune to grasp the hand of a princess like you," rejoined Vandhiyathevan, "he will discover heaven within the very realms of hell!"

He regretted his words almost immediately and bit his lip in consternation. *What a silly thing to say! What do I do if this maiden reads more into these words than there is?*

"You don't come across as someone on a jaunt to heaven," commented Manimekalai. "Your hands are cold to the touch and you shake like a leaf. One would think you expect to enter a killing field!"

"Who knows, princess? Perchance that is what lies in wait for me at the end of this passage," said Vandhiyathevan with a doleful sigh.

"You're the one who refuses to turn back!" exclaimed Manimekalai, amused. "Who knows how many killers are hiding out in the *vettai mandapam*?"

"There can be a hoard of them for all I care. They do not scare me," declared Vandhiyathevan. "It is the thought of Kandamaaran that strikes fear in me. If he catches sight of me clasping your hands thus in the dark…"

"*Ayya*, as long as I am alive, no harm shall befall you from my brother," said Manimekalai. A sigh of quiet happiness escaped her lips."Half my dreams have come true; who knows, perhaps the other half will, too."

The sound of a door being latched suddenly cut through the dark silence. Startled, the pair froze in place. "We've reached the *vettai mandapam*!" whispered Manimekalai softly.

They discerned the glow of lamplight ahead. It grew steadily brighter as it moved towards them. Manimekalai let go of Vandhiyathevan's hands and distanced herself modestly. Idumbankari emerged from the darkness the very next moment, a lamp in one upraised hand and a sharp, curiously twisted dagger in the other. He stopped short on seeing the duo and a look of great astonishment spread across his features. The pair, however, knew better - they were quite certain that he was merely putting on an act.

"*Amma*! *Ayya*!" cried Idumbankari in surprise. "Why did you come alone this way, in the dark? If you had said a word to me, your servant, I would have accompanied you, lamp in hand!" he rued. "Where are you going?" he asked with concern.

"Idumbankari! You are aware, aren't you, that Malayaman advances upon us with an army in tow? The Vallathu prince and I set off to ensure that the compound gates as well as the passage doors are securely latched," replied Manimekalai.

"What a coincidence, *thaaye*!" exclaimed Idumbakari. "I am just on my way back from the same mission!"

"I thought that would be the case," replied Manimekalai agreeably. "The lamp we had brought with us fell down on the way and gave out. Fortunately, we saw a glow ahead; thinking it had to be you, we pressed on in the darkness," she explained.

"The younger master had bade me run a security check, so I came this way. All the passageways are safely secured," said Idumbankari. "Shall we return, *thaaye*?"

"Give us the lamp you bear and be on your way," commanded Manimekalai. "The prince wishes to pick out a spear from the *vettai mandapam*, for he lost his own to the Kollidam waters. We may soon face a war, after all..."

"That is true, *ammani*! War may befall us all!" said Idumbankari in fearful tones. "I'm sure my lady knows this already, but I feel it would be prudent to avoid bringing outsiders to the *vettai mandapam* at this precarious time."

"I agree, Kari. The prince, however, is not an outsider - he is the dear friend of the younger master," replied Manimekalai pleasantly. "Why, our bond may grow even tighter when new relationships are forged. Come now - give us the lamp and be on your way."

Idumbankari handed over the lamp to the prince resentfully, his face as dark and surly as a thundercloud.

Vandhiyathevan and Manimekalai proceeded up a flight of steps in the passageway and drew closer to the *vettai mandapam*. An owl suddenly hooted nearby.

"What was that?" cried Manimekalai in amazement. "How on earth did an owl get into the palace?"

"The miraculous resurrection of a specimen in the *vettai mandapam*, no doubt," replied Vandhiyathevan drily. "Didn't a dead monkey spring to life once upon beholding you, my lady?"

They approached the door to *vettai mandapam* and discovered that it was locked. Manimekalai brought out a key and unbolted its latch. She warily pushed open the door and the two stepped inside.

At first, all they could see were macabre hunting trophies scattered around the hall. Lifeless eyes glinted eerily in the lamplight; the grisly figures of wild animals waited unmoving in the darkness, rigid in menacing postures - there were great elephants and bears, fierce tigers and crocodiles, even deer, eagles and owls. The two peered further into the *mandapam* and spied murky figures lurking behind the animal specimens, half-hidden in the shadows.

The door to the *vettai mandapam* slammed shut abruptly. As Vandhiyathevan swivelled at the sound, he was shoved roughly from behind. He hit himself against the mount of the tailless monkey that he had once hidden behind; a pair of hands emerged to trap him in a vise-like hold. It was only then that Vandhiyathevan fully appreciated how strong a monkey's grip could be!

He tried reaching for the blade at his waist, in vain. The monkey's hands - rather, the human hands wielding the monkey's own, to be precise - had him in an unyielding clutch that afforded him no movement at all.

A second pair of hands wrested the sword from his waist. "*Ayyo*!" cried a terrified Manimekalai, who hastened to Vandhiyathevan's side. The blade turned towards her chest, its sharp tip warning her against coming any closer.

"Hush! There's no need to kick up a hue and cry," came a rough voice. "If you remain silent and follow our instructions, no harm shall befall either of you. If you make a noise," it continued, taking on a steely edge of menace, "rest assured that you will both lose your lives. This impudent rogue will be the first to go!"

Vandhiyathevan realized the voice belonged to his old friend Ravidasan. "Princess, pray stay quiet for a bit," he said courteously. "Let us understand why these fine gentlemen have come and hear what they have to say."

36

PANDI MAADEVI

The men who had bound Vandhiyathevan to the tailless monkey proceeded to tie Manimekalai to the horns of a stag that was mounted on the wall nearby.

"*Mandhiravadhi!*" protested Vandhiyathevan. "Your feud is with me, not the Kadambur princess. Why bind her? Set her free."

Ravidasan cast him a contemptuous glance. "Patience, *Thambi*. Time and again you have poked your unwelcome nose into our affairs. We condescended to spare your life on each occasion; yet, that has not deterred you from your irksome pursuit of us!"

Vandhiyathevan chortled at his words.

Ravidasan narrowed his eyes. "Why do you laugh?" he asked with affront. "Have you come to enjoy the embrace of that tailless monkey, after all?"

"No, not the monkey," replied Vandhiyathevan. "I couldn't help but laugh at what you said!"

"What have I said that you found so amusing?" snapped Ravidasan.

"You said that I came in pursuit of you, didn't you? Well, it looks to *me* like the pack of you are relentlessly on *my* tail! Why, even now," continued Vandhiyathevan in a reasonable tone, "I was seeing to an important matter with the aid of the Kadambur princess, minding my own business. You've appeared out of nowhere and bound me to this monkey!"

"Oho! Is that what you think? So be it then!" said Ravidasan with an unpleasant smirk. "We won't dissuade you from the idea that we meddle in your affairs; after this, there won't be another time to further this notion. If you survive this day, you will never see any of us again!"

"Then I must do my best to pull through. *Mandhiravadhi*, do teach me the trick to staying alive!"

"With pleasure," Ravidasan said, curling his lip in disdain. "All you have to do is remain silent, no matter what takes place in this *mandapam* or the chamber next door. Watch but hold your tongue. Do not panic." He smiled humourlessly. "No danger will come upon you."

"Pray tell, why bestow such consideration upon me? Why spare my life?"

"Ah, now there's a fine question!" exclaimed Ravidasan, snapping his fingers. "It truly is a foolish move on our part. But," he grimaced, "it is the command of our Devi."

"Devi? Who is your Devi?"

"Don't you know still?" Ravidasan's eyes glinted. "The Pandi Maadevi, of course! Veera Pandiya Chakravarthy's valiant, chaste consort who dwells in the Periya Pazhuvettaryar's palace, Nandhini Devi herself!"

"Ah, a valiant, chaste woman indeed!" agreed Vandhiyathevan, tongue in cheek.

"Chi! Dirty scamp!" snarled Ravidasan. A dark flush reddened his cheeks. "Take care - another word about our Devi and your life will be forfeit!"

"The one who slanders the Pazhuvoor Rani is *you*," retorted Vandhiyathevan. "You claim that a lady living in another man's house is Veera Pandiyan's Devi!"

"And where's the harm in that?" replied Ravidasan brusquely. "Didn't that epitome of chastity, Rama's wife Seetha Devi, stay at Ravanan's dwelling for a time?"

"And didn't Ramar fetch Seetha Devi from Ravanan's dwelling?"

"We have come to fetch our Pandi Maadevi too," replied Ravidasan with a cruel smile. "She has only consented to be trapped in this Pazhuvoor palace to fulfill a mighty task, which will come to fruition this very day."

"Aha! Pray, what task might that be?"

"Patience. You will find out yourself in a short while. But if you get up to your old tricks," warned Ravidasan, "then you shall meet a sorry end and so will this girl." He turned to go to the other side of the *mandapam*.

"*Mandhiravadhi*!" Vandhiyathevan called out. "Tell me one another thing before you leave!"

"Don't call me *Mandhiravadhi*!" snapped Ravidasan.

"Then what should I call you?" asked a puzzled Vandhiyathevan.

Ravidasan straightened his back imperiously. "You will address me with respect as Mudhanmanthiri!" he commanded.

"*Ayya*, which great empire are you the Mudhanmanthiri of?"

"Don't you know yet? I am the Mudhamanthiri of the Pandiya *maha samrajyam*!" Ravidasan looked slyly at Vandhiyathevan. "You were watching the *pattabhisheka* ceremony near the *pallippadai*, weren't you?"

"I was," conceded Vandhiyathevan. "I thought it was a hallucination, though."

Ravidasan smirked. "Is that why you didn't tell anyone else about it?"

"I mentioned it to a couple of people, but they assured me that I was a lunatic," replied Vandhiyathevan regretfully. "They convinced me that I had had a nightmare."

"Aha!" crowed Ravidasan in glee. "Let them continue to think so! We let you keep your life reckoning that no one would believe your story."

"*Mandhiravadhi*, is that the only reason you let me live?"

"What other reason could there be?"

"Didn't your Rani intercede in my favour?" asked Vandhiyathevan innocently.

The question clearly touched a nerve. Ravidasan's face darkened. "So?"

"Well, it seems to me that I can win her favour once again," replied Vandhiyathevan lightly.

"Stay patient until you do," advised Ravidasan.

"*Mandhiravadhi*! It was your Rani who sent the Kadambur princess in search of me," let slip Vandhiyathevan. "She asked her to fetch me - that is why we both set off together."

Ravidasan considered this revelation in silence. "*Appane*, there is another path to the Rani's chamber. Why take this route?"

"I don't need to answer you," shot back Vandhiyathevan. "I will tell the Rani if she asks me."

"Then stay patient until she does," barked Ravidasan, well and truly irked.

"*Mandhiravadhi*! Order your men to untie my ropes and that of Sambuvaraiyar's daughter," demanded Vandhiyathevan. "Else…"

"What will you do?" scoffed Ravidasan.

"I will shout so loud that the very foundations of this *mandapam* will shake and tremble!"

"The minute you do, three spears will come flying straight at you. Beware!"

Vandhiyathevan looked around closely. Ravidasan spoke the truth; three conspirators stood at the ready, sharp spears in hand.

"*Thambi*, you're a shrewd chap," said Ravidasan softly. "In fact, I once wished to make you one of us. Alas, you fell into the web of passion woven by that Pazhaiyarai *mohini*. No matter." Ravidasan looked hard at Vandhiyathevan. "Be smart and survive this day. A peep from you and death is certain," he cautioned.

Having dispensed his warning, Ravidasan approached the elephant head mounted on the other side of the *mandapam*. He kept his ear against the wall and listened intently for a few moments. Then he caught hold of the elephant's long tusks and gave them a twist.

A small entrance appeared, opening out to a chamber brightly lit by dozens of lamps. Their light shone into the *vettai mandapam* like silvery moonbeams on a full moon night, illuminating its halls.

Vandhiyathevan surreptitiously looked to his side. He realized that Manimekalai had managed to withdraw the dagger at her hip; she had cut through the ropes that held her tied.

The little lamp that Manimekalai had taken from Idumbankari was shining weakly in a corner of the *vettai mandapam*. Its light did not fall upon the Kadambur princess, whom the conspirators paid no attention to - their focus was entirely upon Vandhiyathevan.

The Vaanar youth watched as Manimekalai quietly untied the ropes binding her. Once she had freed herself, Vandhiyathevan pursed his lips and loudly hooted like an owl.

The three conspirators in the *mandapam* stood stunned. Even Ravidasan - who was peeking through the entrance at that moment - spun around at the sound, profoundly shaken.

"Aha! This is your mischief!" he hissed and advanced towards Vandhiyathevan swiftly. The entrance closed as soon as his hands came away from the elephant tusks and darkness fell upon the *vettai mandapam* once again.

The three conspirators charged at Vandhiyathevan, spears in hand.

Out of nowhere, the long, twisted horns of a deer attacked one of the plotters. Another was left dazed by a great bear that fell upon him, flattening him to the ground. The remaining conspirator was ambushed by a fearsome crocodile, whose gaping maw was lined with terribly sharp teeth.

A giant bat fell down upon an unsuspecting Ravidasan's head with a loud thud.

The sudden assault took the conspirators by surprise and they froze in bewilderment. Those few crucial moments were all Manimekalai needed to hasten to Vandhiyathevan's side and undo his binds. Freed, the Vallathu prince lifted the tailless monkey that he had been restrained to and hurled it at the schemers with all his might.

The four conspirators hurriedly pushed away the animal specimens that had fallen on them and scrambled to their feet. Vandhiyathevan had armed himself with a spear by then; he adopted a menacing stance, ready to fight the enemies that stood before him.

It was at this pivotal juncture that the doorway to Nandhini Devi's chamber opened wide. Bright light flooded the *vettai mandapam,* irradiating its halls. Nandhini Devi stepped inside. Her beauty took one's breath away; she appeared quite ethereal, silhouetted against the light. "*Mandhiravadhi*!" she called out. "What folly goes on here? Why such a ruckus?" she asked as she ascended the stairs.

37

The iron heart melts

Nandhini was taken aback for a moment to see Vandhiyathevan and Manimekelai in the *vettai mandapam*. "Oh!" she exclaimed, her lustrous eyes widening in genuine surprise. "How did you come to be here?"

"Devi, I came only because your friend brought me your summons," answered Vandhiyathevan. "I see now that it was a mistake to heed a woman's wisdom," he added sadly.

"*Akka*!" broke in Manimekalai, flustered. "I never gave him any advice; I only asked him to come with me to see you."

Nandhini' face smoothed over as she smiled fondly at Manimekalai. "My dear friend, when us women make requests of menfolk, it is as good as giving them advice," she said with a small laugh.

"As good as giving advice?" interrupted Vandhiyathevan indignantly. "Devi, say it like it is - it is as good as putting an order! The princess fairly yanked me by the hand to this awful place. Now here I am, at the mercy of these unfriendly assassins!"

"Judging by the state of this hall, ayya, it hardly looks like *they* are the assassins here," replied Nandhini, her eyes twinkling. "If I hadn't come in time, you would have likely finished them off!"

"*Akka*, these men certainly are assassins," cried Manimekalai. "Just a short while ago, they had him tied to a tailless monkey!"

Nandhini's rosy lips pulled into a small smile. "Manimekalai, didn't you say that he had hidden himself behind a tailless monkey on an earlier occasion? They've clearly come to know of the matter somehow," she said calmly.

"Not somehow, *Akka*," replied Manimekalai earnestly. "I told you too, didn't I, that I had caught sight of strangers hiding in the *vettai mandapam* the day before you arrived? These are those very men! They had given the prince chase that day; thankfully, he managed to give them the slip and run away."

Nandhini scrutinized her face. "Why then have you led him back to them, Manimekalai? Why did you bring him by this passage?"

"*Akka*, my *thamayan* Kandamaaran had mentioned a while back that he planned to have an audience with you. I brought the prince through the underground passage to avoid crossing paths with him. It turned out to be a good thing, after all. Else these assassins..."

"Sister," interrupted Nandhini gently, "neither are these men assassins nor have they come here to kill the Vaanar youth. Why, they've caught him all alone on more than one occasion but spared his life each time. The prince himself can attest to the truth of my words."

"Who *are* these strangers, *Akka*?" asked Manimekalai, bemused. "The things you were saying a short while ago - were they true? Do you know these men?" Her worried frown deepened. "Have they come to take you away?"

"Yes, sweet friend. They have come to save me and take me away with them. I shall tell you everything in detail," replied Nandhini, clasping Manimekalai's hand in her own. "Come to my chamber, both of you. Let these men remain here." She turned to Ravidasan. "*Mandhiravadhi*! If you harm either one of them, I shall take it as an assault on my own person," she commanded. "From this day forward, wherever you meet them - under whatever circumstances - you will treat them with respect."

Ravidasan looked as if he had bitten into a particularly sour fruit. "I beg your pardon, my lady," he said sullenly. "This youth seems to have knowledge of our secret signals. It was he who hooted like an owl just now."

Nandhini's eyes narrowed. "Does that not suffice to convince you that he is one of us? Have your wits dulled?" she snapped. "Let that be. See to it that no further sound comes from this place until I give word." It was clear from her tone that she would hear no more from him.

Nandhini led Manimekalai and Vandhiyathevan into her chamber through the entrance at the elephant mount and quickly shut the door. She turned to Manimekalai with an appreciative smile. "Sister, you are clever indeed! It was a smart plan to bring him through the *vettai mandapam*. Your brother just left, declaring that he would bring Aditha Karikalar to see me." A tinge of sadness stained her features. "I must send you both away before the prince arrives. I must take my leave of you."

"*Akka*, what are you saying?" cried Manimekalai in dismay. "It was you who said that you would send the Vallathu prince on a mission to bring news of your noble husband. Now you say that you must take leave of us!"

"I changed my mind after speaking to your brother," replied Nandhini. She cupped Manimekalai's cheek affectionately in her hand. "Dear sister, regardless of whether the Periya Pazhuvettaryar is alive or not, I cannot stay here anymore. It is dangerous for this young warrior to be here at this time, too." She turned to Vandhiyathevan. "*Ayya,* please leave this place as soon as you can. Even if you have no concern for your own life, do consider this sweet maiden and leave at once," she urged.

"*Akka,* ask him to take me away with him if he is to leave," said Manimekalai, her voice breaking. "I cannot bear the thought of being confined to this prison of a palace after the two of you have left."

"Princess, you do not understand what the Pazhuvoor Rani means to say," said Vandhiyathevan, looking hard at Nandhini. "She believes that with me gone, you can wed prince Aditha Karikalar and rise to become the *pattamagishi* of the Thanjai *samrajyam.*"

"That's not what I meant at all," replied Nandhini, shaking her head. "I would not want any woman to suffer the unlucky fate of marrying prince Aditha Karikalar, much less Manimekalai who has become as dear to me as my own life. *Ayya,* you twist my words to suit your convenience. If you make your escape now, you may yet have the honour of wedding this maiden in the future." Nandhini laid a gentle hand on Manimekalai's shoulder. "Manimekalai! If the love you bear for him is true, you must bade him leave at once!"

"Rani! I am prepared to leave this very instant," cut in Vandhiyathevan. "I only ask for alms before I go, a mere object. If you are kind enough to give it to me, my lady, I shall make myself scarce right away!"

Nandhini levelled her gaze. "*Ayya,* what article could I have that you must make such a request of me?"

"You have in your possession a sword, inscribed with the symbol of a fish. Please give me that sword my lady, and I shall leave!" said Vandhiyathevan earnestly. "You are aware, I'm sure, that my own blade was lost to the Kollidam flood?"

A fleeting look of fury flashed across Nandhini's face. "*Ayya,* there are countless swords and spears in the *vettai mandapam* - you can have your pick of any of them and take your leave. Why must you ask for the only blade that a poor, helpless woman like me depends upon to protect her life?"

"Devi, pray be honest," replied Vandhiyathevan in a serious tone. "Do you carry that sword - nay, worship it! - only to protect your life?"

Nandhini raised her chin defiantly. "I carry that sword to protect my chastity too, a virtue dearer to me than life!"

"Devi, have you no other intention?"

"What other intention could I possibly have?"

"Couldn't it be that you mean to avenge the death of Veera Pandiyan?"

Nandhini's face seemed to abruptly relax at these words. A strange expression came over her features, one that was placid yet chillingly suggestive of a fury raging underneath the calm. "I thought you wouldn't bring up the subject in front of Manimekalai," she said evenly. "I see there is little point in keeping it hidden any longer."

Nandhini looked at a dumbstruck Manimekalai. "Sister, hear the truth. Learn the true reason I have come to this Kadambur palace!" she declared, reaching for the sword lying on her bed. She ran a loving finger across the flat of its blade, tracing the lines of the fish inscription that gleamed on its surface. "I haven't come here to resolve the civil war looming over the Chozha *samrajyam*. I haven't come here to help bisect the kingdom between Maduranthaka

Thevar and Aditha Karikalar, either. Nor was it my design to enjoy the sumptuous hospitality of the Kadambur palace. Sister," said Nandhini, meeting Manimekalai's eyes. "I never intended to fix your wedding, either." Her voice grew hoarse. "I am here to take revenge upon the heinous knave who beheaded Veera Pandiyan. This is the very sword of the Pandiya clan!" she burst out, her eyes shining with a terrible light. "Tonight, I shall fulfill my oath or give up my life!" she cried in a fit of wild fury. A stunned silence filled the chamber.

"You ask me to leave because I may hinder your plan," said Vandhiyathevan quietly. "You mean to scare me away by convincing me that my life is in danger."

"Aha!" exclaimed Nandhini, whirling to face him with her blazing eyes. "Do you plan to thwart my revenge? A noble aim! Who asked you not to? Why not go to your friend with the truth and stop him from coming here?"

"Devi, I have come to you precisely because it is impossible to talk to him," replied Vandhiyathevan in a tone of genuine supplication. He came forward, desperation suffusing his features. "I came here resolved to fall at your feet if necessary and beg you to not commit this vile sin…"

"Sin, you say?" spat Nandhini. "What sin? Let us ask my friend, here. Manimekalai, you be the judge!" she cried, her eyes glistening with pain. "Say you have given your heart and soul over to another. Say his enemy advances to kill him as he lies wounded and helpless. You throw yourself at the enemy's feet and beg him to spare your lover." Nandhini's lips trembled. "The heartless wretch pays no heed to your entreaties; he cruelly puts your love to the sword and walks away without a glance." Nandhini's voice broke with grief. "Would you call taking revenge upon such a *krathakan* a sin? Would you, my sweet?" she pleaded.

Manimekalai found herself deeply moved. "No, *Akka*!" she cried out. "But I would not have fallen at his feet, in your place - I would have taken up a dagger to kill him instead!"

Vandhiyathevan stepped towards Manimekalai. "Princess, what if that enemy had been your own brother?"

"Brother or not, it's all the same to me!" declared Manimekalai with conviction.

"Tell him, my darling!" cried Nandhini in delight.

"The princess speaks without understanding what her words truly mean," said Vandhiyathevan. "Be it the vilest act of enmity, if it were her own brother Kandamaaran, would she ever have the heart to kill him?"

Nandhini and Manimekelai looked at each other.

Nandhini turned upon Vandhiyathevan. "What sort of useless question is this?" she asked dismissively. "I do not plan to kill my own brother. The first time we met, you broached the subject of my *thamayan*, Thirumalai - it is the very reason I hold you in high esteem. I helped you escape myriad dangers simply because you are Azhwarkkadiyaan's friend and ally." She paused. "*Ayya*! Should I lose my life in the quest to keep my vow, please let Thirumalai know that I begged his forgiveness through you. Tell him that even though I chose to act against his advice, my thoughts were full of him!"

Vandhiyathevan smiled wryly. "*Ammani*, why keep up this facade? Azhwarkkadiyaan is no brother of yours; neither are you that Veera Vaishnavite's sister."

"Then who is my brother? Whose sister am I?"

"Aditha Karikalar is your brother!" cried Vandhiyathevan. "Devi, I beseech you to turn away from the vile sin of fratricide. My lady, please show mercy and hand me the sword of Veera Pandiya's clan!" he begged.

Nandhini cheeks flushed and she curled her lip derisively. "You've regaled prince Karikalar, I'm sure, with this remarkably imaginative tale that we're both siblings. Did he believe it?"

"It seemed to me like he did. But I confess that I am unaware of his thoughts on the matter," replied Vandhiyathevan miserably.

"Are you? *I* know them quite well! No doubt the prince finds himself astounded by the exceptional creativity of that Pazhaiyarai *mohini*..."

"*Ammani*, my report is no imagination; neither is it a story concocted by the Pazhaiyarai Ilaiya Piratti or my own self. I saw the truth with my own eyes at Eezham..."

"What did you see?" cut in Nandhini, alert.

"A goddess without the power of speech," replied Vandhiyathevan. "It was that divine woman who rescued Arulmozhi Varmar, Azhwarkkadiyaan and me from great peril. We were walking past an old palace in the streets of Anuradhapuram, in the dead of the night; the lady caught our attention from the other side of the path and beckoned compellingly. As we moved towards her, the building that we were standing next to just seconds before suddenly crumbled to the ground - its facade collapsed in a great pile of bricks and dust! Ponniyin Selvar bears great respect for that *maatharasi*, a queen among women. He considers her the very guardian deity of his clan."

"*Ayya*, of what relevance is this little tale to me?" asked Nandhini, tearing her eyes away. "No doubt such a story would serve to send Ilaiya Piratti into raptures, keen as she is on seating Arulmozhi Varmar on the Chozha throne. Why bring it to my ears?"

"I have a good reason for that, my lady. When I glimpsed that *maatharasi* in the faint light of the Anuradhapuram moon, I was awestruck - I wondered how Pazhuvoor Ilaiya Rani I had left behind in Thanjavur came to be there!" said Vandhiyathevan earnestly.

"*Ammani*, do hear my words. There is nary the slightest difference between you and the mute goddess, in figure or appearance! If my lady appeared without jewellery and embellishments, your tresses loosened from their coiffure - I tell you Devi, you will be the spitting image of her!"

Nandhini stared at Vandhiyathevan, entranced. "Why should I believe your words?" she whispered. "It is no secret that you are blessed with a fertile imagination. This may well be another one of your inventive tales."

"Devi, I swear to you. My words are nothing but the honest truth."

"However emphatic your claim, I cannot believe you!" she said, turning her back on Vandhiyathevan's clear gaze.

"Devi, you lie!" exclaimed Vandhiyathevan, stepping in front of her. "You know it in your heart that my words are true; you seek to exploit that truth to meet your own ends!" His honest eyes met her own. "When I first met you at the Thanjai palace, the *mandhiravadhi* appeared hooting like an owl and you asked me to wait at a distance; seeing the door open, I happened to hide myself in the treasury. There, I came across the strangest sights…"

"Aha! And what extraordinary sights did you see?"

"I spied Kandamaaran in the treasury passage with Maduranthaka Thevar…"

"So?"

"Shortly, I saw you go by the same path accompanied by the Periya Pazhuvettaryar," replied Vandhiyathevan quietly. "I didn't know where you were going at the time; it took me a while to learn the truth behind that mystery. I discovered that you had gone to torment the Chakravarthy in the guise of your mother's ghost…"

Nandhini's composure broke down. She had seemed unruffled by the exchange so far, fenced in behind an air of impassivity; now her defences crumbled away, revealing an enervated shell that seemed sapped of all energy. Tired, Nandhini sat down heavily upon a chair nearby.

"*Ayya*, what else did you find out?" she asked.

"As you accompanied Periya Pazhuvettarayar through the treasury passage, the two of you crossed paths with Kandamaaran who was returning by himself. He spoke to Pazhuvettarayar, of what I do not know; but it seemed to compel the Dhanaadhikari to make a gesture towards his torchbearer..."

"What sort of a gesture?"

"You know well, my lady. Pazhuvettarayar dispatched orders to assassinate Kandamaaran by stabbing him in the back. I thwarted the attempt and saved Kandamaaran's life." Vandhiyathevan smiled drily. "I was left shouldering the blame for that sordid affair."

Nandhini stole a glance at Manimekalai. "*Ayya*, why do you speak of things that only serve to upset this maiden?"

"Devi, I have not spoken about these things to anyone. If you just hand me that sword you bear, my lady, I give you my word that I shall not bring up the subject in the future, either!" implored Vandhiyathevan.

"I cannot give you the sword, *ayya*!" burst out Nandhini. "Why must I? Go ahead, report your discovery to anyone you fancy - you may even embellish the truth if you feel like it. Why, you're free to go straight up to Aditha Karikalar, I tell you! Do your best to prevent him from coming here! Why hound me? Go!" cried Nandhini, her eyes filled with tears.

"*Ammani*, I am familiar with the prince's nature. I cannot stop him - my attempt will only serve to harden his obstinacy," replied Vandhiyathevan wretchedly. "I have no recourse but to seek your mercy..."

"What claim do you have to seek anything from me?" flared Nandhini. "Let us presume that your statements are genuine; let us take it for granted that you truly did see my mother in Eezham, the woman who bore me and gave birth to me." Her voice cracked. "Still, why must I relinquish my oath? The Chakravarthy has wreaked an unspeakable betrayal upon my mother. Why must I show pity to him or his children? Your account serves naught but to legitimize my vengeance!"

"No, my queen," argued Vandhiyathevan. "Please consider your mother. Would she see the justness of your vindictive cause? That noble woman deeply cherishes the Chakravarthy's children; they are as dear to her as her own life. Think, my lady - could she stand to see one of them slayed by your very hands? Never, I tell you!" Vandhiyathevan's face grew deeply sad. "She would grow to despise you if she learned of such a deed. She would curse you as long as she lives and breathes. That *maatharasi* cannot speak, it is true; but you will be left unable to bear her very gaze. It will inflict agony upon you, a torment far greater than the very bowels of hell."

Tears flowed down Nandhini's face. She wiped her eyes and looked upwards, her long lashes glistening wetly. A tortured anguish came over her beautiful features, as if she saw a harrowing vision. "*Amma*! *Amma*!" she cried out to the illusion, her voice hoarse with grief. "Isn't it suffering enough that I am raked over with torment by Veera Pandiyar's severed head and body? Must you join their ranks to persecute me?" She buried her face in her hands like one who couldn't bear to look upon the sight any longer. The room fell silent save for Nandhini's heart-rending sobs.

Manimekalai looked at Vandhiyathevan, deeply affected by the scene. "*Ayya*, I did not know that you had such depths of cruelty in you."

Nandhini looked up at her words. "Sister, he is blameless. He speaks with nothing but my best interests at heart. He only seeks to deliver me from a great peril! Even so," she continued, her chin trembling with grief, "his words cause me unbearable pain."

She turned to Vandhiyathevan, her eyes brimming with tears. "*Ayya*, you have achieved what none could until this very moment. Here, I willingly give you the sword you seek. Take it!" she cried and held out the blade.

As Vandhiyathevan reached out for the sword, Nandhini pulled it back.

"Patience. Tell me, *ayya* - can you do me a kindness before receiving this blade?" she asked, vulnerable as a child. "If I leave this palace without fulfilling my vow, the men in the *vettai mandapam* will not spare me. They will burn me alive on a pyre of their own making. Truthfully, that thought does not frighten me; but I yearn to meet my mother just once before I embrace death. Oh Vaanar warrior! I claimed to mistrust your tale - I tell you now, I believe it! I am convinced that you saw my mother, the woman who wanders Eezham with loosened tresses. I believe every word of your report! I have seen her myself..."

"When?! How?"

"As a child, I would often rouse from my sleep at night, startled and half-awake. A woman's figure would be bent over me, her face close to mine; she would watch me, unblinking. The presence would vanish when I opened my eyes, leaving me surprised and petrified. Even in those days, I indulged the desire to look upon myself often in the mirror; the countenance of my face had deeply registered itself in my mind. I was astonished at the realization that my phantom visitor looked exactly like me; there was no doubt that we shared the same facial features, down to every single line and contour! I had heard marvellous tales of men and women whose souls could migrate from one body to another - I wondered if the apparition was my own essence; perhaps it had flown out of my body to take on a new frame, desirous to look upon my form. Sometimes, I suspected that I had died, unawares; I contemplated the possibility that the figure lying down was, in fact, my lifeless corpse. These thoughts would leave me deeply unsettled - I would break down in agony wondering whether these visions were dreams or hallucinations or the product of a deranged mind. When I grew older and more mature, I determined by virtue of many reasons that the visions I had seen were real beyond doubt; Sundara Chozhar's own bewilderment upon seeing me confirmed my suspicion. By dint of various clues as well as a few words that Azhwarkkadiyaan had let slip off-guard, I deduced that I had a mother who looked every inch like me. I craved - nay, thirsted! - to see her just once, to place my head upon her lap and weep to my heart's content." Nandhini looked at Vandhiyathevan, her face streaked with tears. "*Ayya*! Your words today have only tempered my ache, kindling a longing that I cannot bear. If you would take me to my mother, I will put aside all thoughts of revenge. I will give you the Pandiya sword this very second, if you wish!" said Nandhini and dissolved into abject sobs.

Vandhiyathevan fell into deep thought, hiding his consternation. *Here is a devilish quandary - I came to avert disaster and have walked into a hornet's nest instead!*

"*Ayya*!" said Manimekalai suddenly. "Pray give your word that you accede to *Akka's* wishes; pray assure her that they will come true, I beseech you."

Vandhiyathevan squirmed with unease. "If it lies within my power, I give my word that I will," he promised with great reluctance.

Nandhini's face brightened the slightest bit. "In that case, we must make our escape before prince Aditha Karikalar arrives!" she said eagerly. "How, though? Walking out the chamber door is a dangerous proposition, for we may chance upon Kandamaaran or Karikalar."

"Come with me," said Vandhiyathevan at once. "I will take you along the underground passage that runs through the *vettai mandapam*!"

"*Akka*," piped up Manimekalai. "I will come along - take me with you!" But Nandhini paid no attention to her words; her dark, fearful eyes were fixed on Vandhiyathevan. "I do not wish to go through the *vettai mandapam*," she cried, the terror palpable in her tone. "Ravidasan and his men will not spare us alive!"

"*Ammani*!" leapt up Vandhiyathevan, his face shining with excitement. "Hand me the sword in your hands - I will make short work of all of them!"

"No," said Nandhini Devi quickly. "That would only complicate matters. Manimekalai! Is there no other way out of this palace?"

Manimekalai sank into thought, her brows furrowed. "*Akka*," she said presently, "I cannot think of any other way to leave. But ask him! He vanished from this very room like a puff of smoke on an earlier occasion - ask him how he escaped!"

Nandhini turned to Vandhiyathevan expectantly.

"Yes, *ammani*," conceded Vandhiyathevan. "There does lie another route; I stumbled upon it quite by accident. However, it is not an easy one. One must traverse broad landings and steep stairwells; there is also a fairly high compound wall to contend with - I doubt if you can scale it," he said apologetically. "It would be easier to deal with the *mandhiravadhi* and his men in the underground passage."

"*Akka*! It sounds like the prince is coming!" said Manimekalai suddenly, frightened.

The group fell silent and listened intently. Manimekalai's ears had not deceived her; there came the sounds of footsteps from the palace halls, announcing the arrival of a caller.

"*Ayya*, please hasten to the *vettai mandapam*," urged Nandhini.

"I have a better place to hide, my lady," replied Vandhiyathevan. He held out his hand expectantly. "Devi, hand me the sword!"

Nandhini obligingly extended the sword towards him. The blade slipped from her fingers, falling to the floor with a great clang.

38

Was it all an act?

The sound of the sword falling to the floor resounded through the chamber. Nandhini laughed softly. She looked at Vandhiyathevan in sorrow. "*Ayya*, it seems as if the gods have other plans. Let the sword remain where it fell. Pray, hide yourself at once!" she urged.

Vandhiyathevan paid no heed to her words; he bent down to pick up the blade. Nandhini pressed her foot down upon the hilt.

"No!" she said sharply. "The prince would have heard the sword falling to the floor. If he sees none when he arrives, he will grow suspicious. He is already mistrustful of you. Go away! Disappear like you did once before!"

Vandhiyathevan stubbornly tried lifting the sword by its edge; its sharp blade pierced his hand. He let go resignedly and straightened.

Nandhini saw the wound on his palm and noticed that it was bleeding.

"I promise to be true to my word," she told him. "I will not kill my sibling with my own hands. Run away and save yourself, I beg you! If he sees you here..."

"Go away," cried Manimekalai, looking fearfully at Vandhiyathevan. "Pray, go away at once!"

The footsteps drew closer. Vandhiyathevan headed to the *yazh kalanjiyam* with great reluctance; he opened the door and quickly disappeared into its halls.

The footsteps had neared the doorway.

Nandhini turned to Manimekalai, who was staring with amazement at Vandhiyathevan's hideout. "Sister," she said urgently, "Hide yourself, too - there, behind the drapes covering the bed! Slip away from the chamber during our conversation!"

A heartbeat after Manimekalai had concealed herself behind the drapes, Aditha Karikalan and Kandamaaran entered the chamber. Karikalan walked towards Nandhini, looking closely about the chamber as he did. He noticed the drapes of the bed flutter faintly; he continued without breaking his stride, giving the impression that the sight had escaped his eyes.

When he reached Nandhini, he saw the sword upon the ground, still clattering noisily from its fall. He turned to look at Nandhini's face, his eyes boring into her.

Nandhini found herself unable to bear the intensity of his gaze, those blazing eyes that pierced her very heart; she bent down to turn her face away, affecting an attempt to pick up the fallen sword.

Karikalam saw through her in an instant; he moved swiftly to beat her to the sword. He lifted the blade in his hands and examined it closely from hilt to tip. He saw the fresh traces of blood upon its point.

"Devi!" he said, turning to Nandhini. "It appears that this sword is the culprit behind the crash we heard as we approached your chamber; it must have slipped from your fingers upon the floor." He smiled humourlessly. "It seems you sought to give us a grand welcome, sword in hand!"

"Is it not a fitting reception for valiant tigers and brave lions in the prime of their lives?" asked Nandhini, smiling at him in return.

"It is us fierce tigers and lions that need sharp fangs and whetted claws, not the dainty spotted deer that gambols and frolics prettily! No doubt, that is why our creator has seen fit not to give it any," said Karikalan, tightening his grip on the sword.

"Surely you agree that a deer may need to wield its antlers? Why, perhaps it may meet our creator, affording it the chance to give thanks for its horns. Pray, show mercy and give me the sword!" begged Nandhini, stretching out her hand.

"No, no!" exclaimed Karikalan loudly, turning away. "This sword is not suited for your graceful hands. How can those exquisite hands grip a blade such as this, when it is clear to me that Brahma Thevar intended them to pluck delicate flowers and string beautiful garlands?"

"My liege! Once, this pauper's hands did pluck flowers in earnest and lovingly string beautiful garlands; the blossoms withered away awaiting their intended, for the pauper was cheated of her desire. Those days of dreaming are long gone; aeons have flown by. These poor, orphaned hands are now obliged to seek the support of a sword. *Ayyu*! Please don't wrest that crutch away from me, too!" pleaded Nandhini.

"Devi! What are you saying?" said Karikalan in surprise. "Do you call yourself a helpless orphan? Why, there is no end to the sea of young warriors yearning to perform a task kicked to them by your beautiful feet; I believe they would sacrifice their own heads to carry out your command! Don't you know this?"

"If perchance my foot touches the head of such a wicked wretch, I would cut off the limb myself, *ayya*! I need a sword for that, at the very least!"

"*Ayyo*!" cried Karikalan in horror. "Those are truly terrible words! Cut off the elegant feet whose anklets tinkle so sweetly when they walk, showing the very palace swans the meaning of grace? If Periya Pazhuvettarayar comes to hear these words, his heart will certainly break in two!"

"*Ayya*, why worry about him? The young tigers that once trembled and fled at the sound of that old lion's roar now pace freely in the open. It is a newly-gained courage, one induced by the news that he has been washed away in the Kollidam floods. I bear this weapon to keep away those cubs." Nandhini gazed at Karikalan. "I was nothing but rabble wallowing in trash when he took my hand with the world as witness; he bestowed upon me a life and dignity befitting a royal. I depend on this sword to protect the honour of that noble man. These very hands that you said ought to string garlands, I trained to swing a sword…"

"Devi," said Karikalan soberly. "The truth now - is the sword truly for that purpose? Is it to protect the honour of Periya Pazhuvettarayar that you worship this blade as a holy relic? Is that why you speak to it in honeyed words and caress it against your soft cheeks? Or is the sword meant to keep away the simpering idiots who itch to draw closer to you? Do you have no other intention?"

"What other reason can there be, *ayya*?"

"Why, there can be so many reasons!" said Karikalan, sounding surprised at her reply. "Revenge, for instance. You may wish to fulfill your vow to slay the heinous wretch that spurned your abject entreaties, rending a wound in your heart that will never heal!"

Nandhini bowed her head and heaved a deep sigh. She looked up at the prince, drained. "My liege, it is true I harboured such thoughts at one time; it is the reason I worshipped this illustrious sword. I bided my time, yearning for my moment. But when it came, I discovered that my hands had lost their strength; my heart had lost its resolve. I will now bear this sword only to protect my chastity and my husband's honour. Please, take pity on me and give it back," she implored.

"Devi, may I not have the honour of that responsibility? May I not bear the burden of punishing the wicked man who wishes to harm you or your husband?" asked Aditha Karikalan.

Nandhini smiled. "That task is beyond you. Can you bring yourself to chastise your bosom friends on account of this poor, destitute orphan?"

"Why not? I tell you, I can!" insisted Karikalan. "Nandhini, I found it hard to believe your report of Vandhiyathevan when we spoke on that island. It was Kandamaaran who convinced me of the truth in your words! Even if *you* deign to forgive that cad, *I* am not prepared to pardon him. Tell me where he is!... Won't you tell me?... I see. There's no need to trouble yourself! My eyes have not yet grown blind!" he roared and strode furiously towards the draped bedstead.

Nandhini fell to his feet and kneeled, folding her hands in supplication. "My liege, don't! Don't!" she cried.

"Nandhini, save your compassion for worthier causes. There's little need to show pity on this *chandaala* who pretended to be my friend and plotted behind my back!" he spat, his eyes afire. Aditha Karikalan stepped past Nandhini and strode on.

Nandhini stared at him, stunned; she looked around wildly in a haze of bewilderment. She spotted Kandamaaran at the door - he had been standing there all along, impassive and motionless as a statue. "*Ayyo*! Stop him!" she screamed at him in desperation.

Kandamaaran seemed to come to life at her words, but he didn't budge from his position. An inane grin flashed across his features before he became a statue once again.

Karikalan approached the bedstead with the sword held aloft; he roughly flung open the drapes with his free hand. He saw Manimekalai standing there terrified, with a small, sharp dagger in her hand. The princess screamed in fright.

"Aha!" exclaimed Karikalan in genuine surprise. "So it was this tigress behind the drapes all along! *Appapa* - those claws look sharp indeed!" he teased and burst into uproarious laughter.

Karikalan turned to Kandamaaran. "Friend, take your sister and leave her in the care of your mother before you return. Who knows how many tiger cubs that womb will bear! If she had fallen prey to the sword of Veera Pandiya, how many brave sons and daughters would have been lost to Chozha Naadu!"

Manimekalai truly was snarling quite like a tigress until that moment; she grew abashed on hearing Aditha Karikalan's words and determined to leave the chamber herself, without waiting for Kandamaaran to beckon to her.

Once brother and sister had left the chamber, Karikalan looked at Nandhini. "Devi, I have sent them both away with my little act. May we speak from the heart now, at the very least?"

Nandhini looked stupefied. "*Ayya*, was that an act? If so, it was a truly marvellous one! I believed it to be true myself!"

Karikalan laughed. "Nandhini, there is none to equal you when it comes to playing a role. If I managed to deceive you, then my acting skills must be far better than I thought! Come to think of it, you didn't stop me when I raised the sword and approached Manimekalai's hiding place. Why?" he asked, eyes narrowing. "Were you hoping that I would add to my long list of alleged crimes the sin of killing a woman, too?"

"Siva, Siva!" cried Nandhini. "In this entire world, that girl is the only one whom I yet bear true love for! Would I watch on silently, willing to let that sweet maid die? I reckoned that you would see the truth for yourself when you opened the drapes."

Karikalan roared with laughter once again.

"I don't understand," said Nandhini, puzzled. "What is the meaning of this laughter?"

Karikalan looked at her slyly out of the corner of his eye. "You have given me enough reason to kill Manimekelai."

"I still do not understand, my lord!"

"Anyone you bear affection for, man or woman, is my sworn enemy. Do you not know this?"

Nandhini dropped her gaze. "I do. I am aware that I am such an unlucky wretch as that." She looked up at Karikalan, unnerved. "Even so, I never thought that your wrath would fall upon an innocent, guileless damsel as her!"

Karikalan looked at her calculatively. "Perchance you had other intentions," he said thoughtfully. "You might have expected Kandamaaran to take revenge upon me if I had killed Manimekalai. Or perhaps you expected her to kill me first, with that little dagger she held…"

"*Ayyo*! What horrifying words! What terrible imagination!"

"Imagination?" scoffed Karikalan. "You plot schemes far terrifying than anything I can imagine!" His eyes took on a steely edge. "The truth, now. Don't stoke the fire already raging in my heart! Why did you ask me to come to this Kadambur palace? Don't tell me that you went to all this effort to help divide the Chozha empire or to wed me to Manimekalai - these are tales I won't believe. If I had, I would not have come here in the first place."

"Then why did you come here, my liege? What did you hope for?"

Karikalan smiled sadly. "Hope? I have none, nor faith either. My heart is a graveyard of unfulfilled desires; it knows only to mistrust. I wish to quit this country - in fact, I wish to quit this very world."

He looked at her entreatingly. "I came to take leave of you. You asked me for a boon, once; you threw yourself at my feet and begged me for it, pleading with folded hands. Blinded by rage and barbarity, I refused you; I spent every following second repenting it bitterly. I came here so that I can redeem myself before I go, if redemption is allowed me. Nandhini, tell me! Is there any way I can atone for my deed?" Karikalan asked, voice suffused with abject contrition.

Nandhini met his eyes with an even gaze. "My liege, there is none. The dead remain dead. There is none in this world with the power to bring them back to life. There may be epics and ballads that speak of such arts, but none have yet seen feats with their own eyes."

"It is true that the dead cannot be brought to life. But can't atonement lie in giving up a life in the place of one that was lost?.... Look at me, Nandhini! Truly, there is little use in hiding it from me any longer. Don't underestimate me - don't imagine for a second that I don't know why you came here, why you asked *me* to come here, why you sent away Periya Pazhuvettarayar to Thanjai. Even when we were children, I could read your thoughts. You begged me to spare Veera Pandiyan's life in order to provoke a blinding rage in me; *you* induced me to commit this vile sin! You wed Periya Pazhuvettarayar with the sole aim of drawing close to me, of tormenting me! You couldn't bear to see me at peace in Kanchi; so you contrived to bring me to this palace at Kadambur. You have come here intending to slaughter me with Veera Pandiyan's own sword. Nandhini, you may accomplish your aim with ease - there is no one here to stop you now. I sent Kandamaaran and his sister away for this very reason. Here! Take this sword in your hand!" said Karikalan, extending the blade towards Nandhini.

Nandhini's fingers gripped around its hilt; her hands shivered and her body shook with convulsions. Tears welled in her dark, limpid eyes. She weeped with profound grief, breaking into heart-wrenching sobs.

"Nandhini!" said Karikalan, surprised. "What has brought on such cowardice? Why has your heart weakened? You were raised in a priestly clan, it is true; but you were born in one famed for its warriors! Will a lion cub forget its nature simply because it was raised in a herd of sheep?" He cupped her chin and raised her face. "Look at me. I am privy to your deepest thoughts. There is no need to instigate Kandamaaran or Parthibendran or Vandhiyathevan to take revenge in your stead. You don't need to turn me against them, either. Sate your vengeance with your own hands!" Nandhini walked away from him, unable to bear his words. "Quick," he urged, stepping towards her. "Else someone might enter this chamber and make a nuisance of themselves. Kandamaaran will soon return after leaving his sister with his mother. Parthibendran and Sambuvaraiyar are expected shortly; why, *paattaan* Malayaman may accompany them as well. I myself do not believe that Periya Pazhuvettarayar has succumbed to the Kollidam waters - it is entirely possible that he may come here, too. You won't get a better chance than this to carry out your oath. Killing me is no great crime! Why, you would be doing me a great service, in fact!"

Nandhini swallowed the grief that rose within her like a flood. "My liege, I hide nothing from you. I do not wish to! Everything you said about my reasons for coming here - they're all true, I do not deny it. But now that the time has come, I find that my hands have lost their might and my heart, its spirit. The moment I heard your footsteps down the hallway, the sword slipped from my fingers and fell to the ground. Look! Look how my hands tremble as they clutch this great sword!" she cried.

"I see it, my lady. I confess that I do not understand the reason behind it. I know of the adamantine resolve you bore, once; I have often thought that Brahma Thevar must have fashioned your heart out of metal from Devendran's own *vajrayudam*. Why has such an unyielding heart melted thus?..."

"The tidings that your friend Vandhiyathevan brought to me," said Nandhini, covering her face with her hands.

"Aha! You speak of his revelation that you and I are siblings?" Karikalan frowned. "But you don't really believe it, if I recall our conversation at the Eri Theevu; you had dismissed it that day as a wily plot to separate us yet again."

"I didn't want to believe it. I tried my best not to. But the Vaanar youth had another piece of news - that has decimated my resolve," grieved Nandhini.

"Aha! And what news is that? Another fanciful tale? What new story did he weave?"

"He spoke of the woman who gave birth to me. He said that he had seen her on an island in Ilankai. There was no reason to doubt his words. My liege! Once, I asked you for a boon; you refused my plea. You say that you bitterly regret spurning me. Today, I ask you for a boon again - will you grant me this, at the very least?"

Karikalan stared at her. "Tell me what you want and I will tell you if I can grant it or not."

"My liege! It is true that I swore to avenge the death of Veera Pandiyan. I vowed that I would wield this very Pandiya sword bearing the inscription of a fish to slay you; I vowed that I would take my own life if I failed," said Nandhini, her voice hoarse with weeping. "I have neither courage in my heart nor strength in my hands to kill you. I even lack the nerve to give up my own life in front of your eyes - what if my feeble hands make a half-hearted attempt that leaves life clinging to this wretched body? *Ayya*, help me fulfill my oath! Take this sword and slaughter me with your own hands! Then shall my vow be made good. For this service I would be beholden to you - not just in this life, but in all the lifetimes to come!"

Nandhini held out the sword to Aditha Karikalan and he took it into his hands once again.

The prince looked at Nandhini and exploded into hysterics. "Ha, ha, ha!" he cackled manically, clutching his sides. The chamber shook with the sound of his terrible laughter.

39

Darkness Writhes

Vandhiyathevan stayed concealed in the *yazh kalanjiyam*. Aditha Karikalan's frenzied laughter fell upon his ears, sending a chill down his spine; the hairs on the back of his neck prickled and his feet grew cold. His every instinct warned him that a tragedy would take place soon. The chamber was darkened by the shadow of Yamadharmarajan, who was biding his time to throw his noose of death. But who would he capture? Whose life would he claim? Karikalan's? Or Nandhini's? Or did death lay in wait for them both? Would brother kill sister? Or would sister kill brother? Would they perhaps kill each other? Ilaiya Piratti had sent him here in haste to prevent exactly such a disaster. Vandhiyathevan had bent over backwards to fulfill his mission; he had divulged to each the secret truth behind their legacies; he had softened their hearts as much as he could. Would his efforts be enough? Was it even possible to dissuade the hysterical, fury-filled Karikalar or the hallucinatory, half-crazed Nandhini from their heinous plans? Would any good come of him interjecting at this juncture? Perhaps, the sacrifice of his own life would serve to quell their rage. Vandhiyathevan's heart roiled like a turbulent sea as he considered the thoughts racing through his mind. He resolved to be patient for a little while longer, fearing that his impetuous meddling would worsen matters. Vandhiyathevan bit his tongue and willed every nerve into self-restraint. He waited, silent.

When Karikalar's terrible laughter had died down, the conversation resumed.

"*Ayya*, I have never yet done anything to give you joy. I am pleased that I was able to make you laugh at the end of my life, at the very least," said Nandhini.

"Yes, Nandhini!" bellowed Karikalan. "Today is a happy day indeed. The suffering you put me through all these years is finally coming to an end! When I left Kanchi this time, I had to consciously harden my heart; I feared that it would dissolve upon seeing you. You have saved me from such a consequence by handing me the sword yourself!" he declared and cackled obscenely.

"My liege, today is an auspicious day for me as well. I cannot have a death sweeter than one at your hands. Once, I cherished a dream that you would adorn my neck with garlands; that was not to be." Nandhini brushed aside the soft tresses gracing her shoulders and exposed her smooth neck, tilting it in anticipation. "Let me have the honour of bearing the weight of your sword, at the very least. *Ayya*! It is getting late. Why delay?"

"We have delayed this day for many years, we have nothing to lose by wasting another few minutes," replied Karikalan. Anguish appeared on his face. "Nandhini, look at me. Pray, look at me one last time and answer my question. Why must I lay you to the sword with these very hands that ought to bedeck you with garlands? If it is true that you cherished dreams of me once, why not make them come true now? Tell me who stands in our way! I will slaughter them instead of harming you!"

"No, *ayya*! No!" cried out Nandhini. "A thousand blessings upon you - do not kill anyone else on my account! No one stands in our way, save my wretched fate!"

"I shall grind that particular barrier into dust in a second," replied Karikalan cuttingly. "Don't blame your fate! I can recast Brahma's own words, just you watch!..."

"You may rewrite Brahma's words. What of my provenance?" cut in Nandhini.

"What do you speak of, Nandhini? Our childhood days, when my family wished me to forsake you as a girl from the priestly clan?" asked Karikalan. "No! You grew up in the clan of priests but you were not born in one - that is old news, one that we both know well!"

"That is not what I speak of, *ayya*," replied Nandhini, watching Karikalan. "I have in mind the revelation brought by your dear friend, the Vaanar warrior. I speak of his discovery that was dispatched in such haste by Pazhaiyarai Ilaiya Piratti. Have you already forgotten that I am your sister?"

Karikalan tore his hair in desperation. "Nandhini, when I told you this myself the other day, you refused to believe it. You said that it was a ploy to keep us apart! I thought about it later and came to the same conclusion. If it is proof you need..."

"No! No!" said Nandhini. "There's no doubt about it. My liege, you and I are not bound by blood..."

Karikalan stopped in his tracks. "Then what stands in our way, Nandhini?"

"I am wedded to Periya Pazhuvettarayar, a noble man akin to your grandfather. That makes me your grandmother. Isn't this reason enough?"

Karikalan roared in frustration. "Nandhini, do not try to trick me once again with that tale! The world may see you as Pazhuvettarayar's Ilaiya Rani, but you did not wed him, not truly. You have come to this palace with something else in mind." He paced the chamber in distress. "When I asked you once earlier in Thanjai, this is what you said! I reminded you of our desires, the sweet future we dreamed of together. You put forth the most terrible conditions to make them come true! You desired me to kill Pazhuvettarayar and imprison both my father and brother before instating you on the Chozha throne! I came to the conclusion that you were a bloodthirsty demoness and turned back to Thanjai. Did you leave me in peace after that, at the very least? No! You appeared in my thoughts and dreams, cruelly torturing me without respite. Sometimes you tormented me with your tears; you wept and moaned, sobbing abjectly; at others, you raked me over the coals with your bewitching smile! Why, there were times when you cackled madly and drove me insane as well!..."

"My liege, why blame your mania on me?" retorted Nandhini. "You are simply reaping the result of the injustice and brutality you inflicted upon me. How am I at fault for that? Do you think that I have not suffered at all? Did you believe that I was indulging in the pleasures of Pazhuvettarayar's palace?" Nandhini's voice had regained its old fire; its tone crackled with unrestrained rage and cruelty.

Vandhiyathevan grew terrified at its sound. His body shivered with dread.

Aditha Karikalan's voice rose to match her own. "Do you say that you suffered, too? Then why are we wasting time arguing about this? Give me a sign that you accept me - I will gladly leave behind this exalted Chozha *samrajyam* to come with you. I will abandon the country of my birth; I will leave behind my father, mother, friends and family and come away with you." He gripped her shoulders and turned her to face him. "We will board a ship and cross the seas. There are many wonderful islands and cities across the ocean, on the other side of the horizon; we will reach one of their shores. This kingdom is not more important to me than you."

"My liege, I do believe that you have it in you to abandon your kingdom! But the thought of this low-born waif ascending the venerable Chozha throne is no doubt odious to you!" sneered Nandhini and broke into derisive laughter, her eyes ablaze with fury.

"Woman! Consider my words another way! Is the Chozha throne more important to you than me? The love and affection you bestowed on me that day - was that all merely an act to sit on the throne and wear the jewelled crown?" asked Karikalan.

"Aha!" cried Nandhini. "Fine then - if that's what you think, so be it! I *do* covet this palace life, with all its trappings. I want to live a life of royal luxury. I want the dignity and power that comes with it, too. That is why I wed Pazhuvettarayar - that is why I strove to save Veera Pandiyar as well!"

"*Adi*, wicked woman!" roared Karikalan. "Why do you bring up his name now?" He spoke on before Nandhini could breathe another word. "Ah. I see. Your plot is clear as day. You utter Veera Pandiyar's name and I fly into a rage - maddened by fury, I truly will kill you with my own hands. And when I do that, one of the young lions wrapped around your finger will come charging at me and slay me." He looked around wildly. "*Adi chandaali*! Where is that abysmal wretch, Vandhiyathevan? Where have you hidden him, tell me! He must be lurking around here somewhere. Ah, now I see why you refuse to come with me, too. He is the reason; he has to be! He is also the reason you sent Pazhuvettarayar away from this place. You are in cahoots with each other - this is a plan hatched by both of you together!.... Aha! How did I allow myself to get tricked thus? Where is that vile rogue Vandhiyathevan? Where is your new lover?..."

Aditha Karikalar went into paroxysms of pure rage. He savagely swung the sword in his hands, bolting around the room in search of his prey. When he approached the *yazh kalanjiyam*, Nandhini fled to his side and threw herself at his feet. "My liege! Heed my words. A thousand, a million blessings be upon you! Harken to what I have to say and then do as you wish. Your harsh judgement about the Vaanar warrior is apocryphal, cruelly unjust - even mother earth cannot bear with patience the wrong you do him," she said in terror. "If you harm him, my dear friend Manimekalai will relinquish her life! A great sin will fall upon your head! Stay your hand, my liege! Here, rend my heart asunder with Veera Pandiyan's own sword and take a look inside - you will find nothing there but an image of you! This is true, true, true!" cried Nandhini and wept.

Aditha Karikalan's fury was quelled for a second time - a little bit.

"Then why do you refuse to come with me?" he thundered. "Tell me that, at the very least! Why do you instigate me to kill you with my own hands? Speak the truth!"

"So be it, then. I will tell you," said Nandhini wearily. "My heart has no place for anyone but you. Even though this is true, I cannot come with you; nor can I wed you. There is something that stands in the way. Yes, my liege! Truly, I have come here only to speak to you of the matter; it is the reason I drew you here as well. I had planned to ask for your forgiveness after having had my say. I thought to beg you to put aside all thoughts of this ill-starred girl, wed a bride suitable to your clan and position, and live a happy life." She paused, growing ashen-faced. "But I hesitate to speak, my lord. I cannot bring myself to say the very words aloud. I am petrified that what I have to say will stoke your fury to greater heights, culminating in evil disaster. If I have your word that you will remain calm..."

"Tell me Nandini, tell me! However bitter your words are, I will keep my patience. Just now, you asked me to forget you and seek joy in wedding another - I was calm then, wasn't I? What else could you possibly say to put me in a rage?" Karikalan's eyes hardened. "But do not test my patience with yet another tall story!"

"My liege! My life is an illusion, my birth a mystery. I have had to spin tall tales to prolong my life just a little, to meet this burden of *karma* that has fallen heavily upon my shoulders. There is no more need for such pretence; today, my life of deception comes to an end. I only spared you the truth to save you further torment. I fabricated stories to make you despise me; I committed no end of terrible deeds and asked the same of you. A war was raging in my heart - my duties, my oath and the love I bore for you were savagely tearing each other apart. The time has come for these conflicts to end. I will tell you the truth about myself - you will certainly destroy me with your own hands when you hear it! But you need not harm anyone else, my lord. You need not fall prey to gratuitous sin and the blame that follows!"

"Sin! Blame!" scoffed Karikalan. "What fresh sin or blame can I take on now? Even so, tell me Nandhini! What is the truth that stands in our way, that stops you from coming away with me and living the dreams of our youth? However terrible it is, tell me! There, those drapes - I was in anguish when I discerned someone hiding behind them; I had lost my very peace of mind until I discovered who it was! Even when I was talking to you earlier, my mind was battling with that very thought. It was only when I found that it was Manimekalai that the storm raging in my heart quietened. I will suffer fear, anger and confusion only until I know the truth. After all, the mind cannot know peace until it contends with the truth, however bitter it is!

"My liege, I pray that your mind attains the peace you seek with what I have to say. But let my words prove to you that it is impossible to come away with you and hold your hand in holy union. Let them prove that the only respite available to my suffering is sweet death. The Vaanar warrior brought news of my mother. I believe his words to be true; I am aware of the *maatharasi* who was wandering Eezham as a crazed woman. I know too that she is my mother. Many know this secret, for they have seen for themselves our resemblance in figure and bearing; many have even mistook me for my mother. But it was only a little while ago that I learned the reason for my mother's insanity. I do not know if anyone else knows of it; I haven't spoken of it to a soul until today. You will be the first to hear the words from me. *Ayya*! I am going to tell you who my father is. Pray, show mercy and remember the promise you made to me a short while ago. Do not give in to anger."

As Nandhini ended her long-winded preamble, she drew close to Aditha Karikalar. She brought her red lips to his ear and whispered tremulously, "My father is… !" Nandhini broke into an anguished wail as soon as the words escaped her mouth, pained by her confession.

Aditha Karikalan leaped back in shock, as if stung by a thousand scorpions.

"No, no, no! Never! You lie, you lie!" he screamed.

Karikalan's frenzy subdued the very next second. When he spoke, his voice overflowed with unrestrained grief. "Yes Nandhini. What you said must be true. I see everything now - I see the justice of the war raging in your heart; I see how much you must have suffered. I understand the reasons for your confusion, your hesitation, your terrible requests. I see what a terrible mistake it was to deny you when you fell at my feet and begged me for a boon that day! Nandhini, there are acts of redemption for all sorts of sins in this world of ours. But there is no atonement for what I have done. There is no way to cross this chasm that lies between us. *Ayyo*! How did you bear this burden in your heart all these days? How could you stand to see this vile wretch still walking upon this earth?" Karikalar's voice grew calm with terrifying abruptness. "Good! There is only one answer to both our lives; only one hope of respite. Here, Nandhini! Here is my expiation!..."

Vandhiyathevan listened to their exchange from his hiding place in the *yazh kalanjiyam*. He had considered intervening when Aditha Karikalar's fury had peaked so alarmingly as to lose all control; however, he hesitated at the thought that it would lead to an irredeemable disaster. On one hand, their poignant dialogue had moved him deeply; on the other, it had left him helpless in despair. The only words he could not hear clearly were Nandhini's revelation of who her father was. But his heart could draw an inference. To say that the thought 'stunned him' - or anything else, for that matter - would be a mere formality. Vandhiyathevan had never experienced a violent shock as this, even though his own life had been a fairly eventful one.

He grew steadily uneasy at the quiet, trembling voice that Aditha Karikalar had adopted towards the end, struggling with Nandhini's admission. The truth was that Vandhiyathevan had felt little alarm at the prince's outbursts; it was his soft tones that now left him petrified. Unsettled by thoughts of what the prince might do, Vandhiyathevan peeked out of the *yazh kalanjiyam*. Nandhini and Karikalar were out of his line of sight - but he spied another strange vision in the mirror mounted upon the chamber wall.

A cold, vicious face materialized through the concealed entrance at the *vettai mandapam*. It was none other than the *mandhiravadhi* Ravidasan! Vandhiyathevan saw the secret door to the *vettai mandapam* open cautiously. A tiger's mighty head emerged through the doorway, its deadened amber eyes glowing dimly as it caught the lamplight; its powerful body soon followed behind, moving into the chamber noiselessly. A rush of life surged through Vandhiyathevan's veins; his heart swelled with vigour and his limbs regained their hunger for challenge. He made to pounce into action from his hiding place in the *yazh kalanjiyam.*

Before Vandhiyathevan could make a move, a gargantuan hand closed around his neck in a vise-like grip. Alarmed, Vandhiyathevan twisted around to look at his assailant. A towering figure swam before his eyes, bearing the face of a *kaalamugan. Aha! Who is this, now?! How did he come here?! This unnaturally strong grip - it crushes my neck! I can't breathe - my very eyes are popping out of my head! A few more seconds of this and I will surely bite the dust!*

Vandhiyathevan blindly threw blows to beat back his attacker; it took an inhuman effort to free himself from the monstrous grip. He scrambled to lunge into the chamber; he rashly threw himself forward and painfully crashed into the floor. The collision came like a massive boulder ramming into his head. For a moment, all Vandhiyathevan could see were a billion dazzling suns blazing brightly; the vision disappeared in a second and darkness fell all around him.

The giant *kaalamugan* emerged from the *yazh kalanjiyam*, stepping across his unconscious body. Nandhini spun around at the sound of Vandhiyathevan's body hitting the ground. She saw the *kaalamugan* striding towards her, wielding a sword in hand. Nandhini stared at the advancing figure, thunderstruck; her red eyes widened as to protrude from their sockets. Nandhini felt her guts twist and churn within her; she was certain that they had forced their way upwards, seizing her chest and choking her throat. She wiped her eyes and turned back to look in front of her. She saw Karikalan lying on the ground. Nandhini saw Veera Pandiyan's sword protruding from his body.

A dreadful wail rose from her throat in a chilling blend of boundless anguish and manic laughter. Even the inanimate articles in the chamber appeared to be touched by her hysterical lament. They trembled restlessly at the awful sound; why, even the bed seemed to quiver.

"*Adiye*, foul sinner! *Chandaali*! Have you taken your vile revenge after all?" bellowed the *kaalamugan* and advanced upon her.

It was at that very moment that Ravidasan emerged from his hiding place behind the tiger mount in the chamber. He spurred to action as soon as he saw the *kaalamugan* - he lifted the great tiger and hurled it at him with all his might. The specimen struck the only lamp in the chamber, the sole source of light; it tumbled down from its chain, unable to withstand the impact. Before it extinguished, the lamp threw into sharp relief Manimekalai's terrified features. A scream of pure terror escaped the princess and she fled the chamber.

A chaotic darkness writhed and roiled within the chamber, heavy with a cacophony of sounds. Someone keened uninhibitedly, torn by great sorrow. A cackle of maniacal glee rent the blackness and mingled with the weak moans of a man at death's door. The chamber echoed with the sound of swift footfalls as men took to their heels.

40

I KILLED HIM!

In their account of the Chozha lineage, the copper plates of Thiruvalangadu include the following inscription - "In the pursuit of his desire to see the sky and the heavens above, Adithan met his sunset. The darkness of *kali* writhed the world over!" Thus do the Thiruvalangadu copper plates describe the untimely death of Aditha Karikalan, the crown prince of the Chozha *samrajyam*, the valiant warrior who beheaded Veera Pandiyan.

As Aditha Karikalan breathed his last, a terrible darkness truly did descend upon the Kadambur palace, writhing and churning.

The raging darkness assaulted Vandhiyathevan's heart too. He lay insensible where he had fallen, having been throttled and violently pushed by the figure bearing the likeness of a *kaalamugan*. As a dim flicker of light grew steadily brighter in his heart, consciousness returned and he opened his eyes; they failed to register his surroundings, for the darkness enveloping the chamber blinded him. His heart struggled to make sense of where he was and what state he was in.

A sharp pain split through his head. His bruised neck cried out in agony from the injuries inflicted by the strangler. Vandhiyathevan realized that he was struggling to breathe. Why did his head ache? Why did his neck hurt? Why was it hard to draw breath? Aha! That *kaalamugan*! Had he really seen such a person? Did that figure truly assault him in a bid at murder? Why did he strangle him? To stop him from shouting? From moving forward? Why? Why? Where had Vandhiyathevan wanted to go, fighting against that iron grip? Aha! It comes back, now. He had wanted to go to Aditha Karikalan! *Ayyo*! What became of his fate? What happened to Nandhini? What did Ravidasan do? What could the *kaalamugan* have done after attacking him and pushing him to the floor?.... Where was he? In the dungeons? In the underground passage? Vanthiyathevan looked all about him wildly, his eyes nearly popping out of his head. He could see nothing! Dear lord, was there ever such a dense, impregnable darkness as this? Vandhiyathevan remembered that the place he fell was in Nandhini's chamber, near the *yazh kalanjiyam*. Was he still there? Or had he been picked up and deposited somewhere else? How was he to find out?

Vandhiyathevan stretched out and felt the floor around him. His hand brushed against something. *What is this? It feels like a dagger. Yes, it is certainly a dagger, one with a curiously twisted blade! No one could survive an assault from a sharp, contorted knife as this. Where have I seen such a strange dagger? Where? In whose hand? Yes, yes! I saw it in Idumbankari's hand, didn't I?* One by one, the events of the evening came flooding back to his memory. *How did this dagger come here? Oh. It's blade feels wet and sticky. Was it stained by water? No, no. Oil? No, not oil either. It must be blood! Ayyo! Whose blood was it? Was it perhaps his own?*

Vandhiyathevan gingerly probed the back of his head with his fingers. He gently felt his neck. They hurt to the touch, but there didn't seem to be any bleeding. He didn't seem to be wounded anywhere else on his body, either. Then whose blood had it claimed, this murderous dagger lying next to him? He was sure that *he* hadn't attacked anyone with it; he had never even held it in his hand until this moment. Who could have wielded it? Idumbankari? Who could he have assaulted with this knife? Perchance, was that frightening *kaalamugan* none other than Idumbankari? No, that cannot be. Idumbankari is not as tall as that.

What is that, now? Are those the sound of footsteps? Is someone coming? Should I remain silent or sound my presence? Couldn't these people have brought a lamp with them? I could have at least taken a look at where I am. What if they step on me in this pitch darkness?

A thought suddenly occurred to Vandhiyathevan. He sat up swiftly and picked up the dagger defensively. "Who is there?" he called out. The only reply he received were his own echoes, which left him astonished. He couldn't recognize his own voice. It sounded nothing like him! His throat had grown quite hoarse under the assault of the *kaalamugan's* grip - he found it hard to even make a sound. He tried to speak aloud once again. "Who is there?" he rasped in a low growl that sounded nothing like a voice.

He heard quick footsteps pattering across the floor once again; the sound vanished abruptly. Whoever it was had hurriedly made himself scarce upon hearing his voice - perhaps he had been mistaken for a ghost or a demon in the darkness.

The thought amused Vandhiyathevan and he tried to laugh; even the sound of his laughter sounded alien to his own ears. *Right, then. There is little use in sitting here and doing nothing. I better get up and see for myself where I am.* Vandhiyathevan got to his feet with some effort. His legs trembled dreadfully, but he managed to take a few steps; he began to walk unsteadily. He stretched out his hands as much as he could, but felt nothing around him.

Small pricks of light twinkled in the distance. *Aha! That is the mirror on the wall, isn't it?* It shone from the beams of light striking its surface from an unknown source. Vandhiyathevan remembered spotting a reflection in the mirror; he recalled seeing Ravidasan stealthily entering the chamber behind a tiger specimen. *Alright, then. I am still in Nandhini's chamber. But why is it so dark and silent? What happened to all the people who were here a short while ago?*

Vandhiyathevan stumbled forward in the dark. He approached the doorway. Perhaps he could find light, there; or perhaps he could leave the chamber and ask somebody about what had taken place. His foot tripped against something and he fell down once again. This time, his fall seemed to be cushioned by something downy, so he wasn't badly hurt. He realized that it was a tiger skin. He must have fallen on the tiger specimen that Ravidasan brought inside…

The dagger had fallen from his grasp when he lost his footing. He blindly ran his hands across the floor, trying to find the knife. His fingers touched something that seemed soft. Vandhiyathevan's body shuddered violently and his hair stood on end. Terror gripped his heart. *Could this be?* He felt the ground again with his hands. Yes! It was a human body! The soft object he had touched had been its palm. He immediately hurled the tiger skin far away. He looked closely in front of him. The pale beams of light that struck the mirror threw their radiance, faintly illuminating the body lying on the ground. *Ayyo*! *It is prince Aditha Karikalar who lies here! No, not him - just his lifeless corpse!* Vandhiyathevan's heart constricted and a lump formed in his throat. He didn't realize that his eyes were brimming over with tears. With trembling hands, he gently felt many parts of Karikalar's body. There was no doubt about it - the spirit had shrugged off its form; now only the shell remained.

Blood flowed copiously from the side of the corpse, staining his hands. Thoughts of Kundhavai Piratti came with a jolt to

Vandhiyathevan. He had let down that *maatharasi* - he had not succeeded in the mission she had sent him on. Vandhiyathevan felt like an abject failure. How could he ever look her in the eyes again? He had done everything he could, and more. And yet, it had all been in vain! Fate had dealt Her hand and won. Vandhiyathevan tenderly took the prince's lifeless body onto his own lap. He didn't know what to do. He had lost all power of thought. His throat had no strength left to articulate his grief; he could not even weep.

The prince has lost his life. I have failed in my task. I can never look upon Kundhavai Devi's sweet face again! These thoughts kept turning over in Vandhiyathevan's mind. He sat there inert and brooding for what seemed like an eternity, unaware of the passage of time. It was only when he realized that people were approaching the chamber with flaming torches in hand that he regained some semblance of consciousness.

He reverently placed Karikalar's body on the floor and stood to his feet. Men entered through the front door of the chamber, a dozen or so of them; two held aloft flaming torches while the rest carried spears. Kandamaaran walked at the head of the company, closely followed by the Periya Sambuvaraiyar. The newcomers seemed to be stricken with terror; in the flickering light of the torches, their faces appeared strangely pale and white as a ghost.

Kandamaaran's face alone was contorted with a burning rage. He flew into a wild fury when he saw Vandhiyathevan. "*Adei!*" he roared. "Evil wretch! Murderer! Traitor! Turncoat! Haven't you made your escape yet? I thought you would have snuck away by now!"

Shaking with anger, he turned to Sambuvaraiyar. "Father! Look - look at the murderer with your own eyes!" he cried, pointing his finger at Vandhiyathevan. "Look at the vengeful knave who committed the vilest sin there is, all while pretending to be a friend! Lay your eyes upon the *chandaalan* who has stained our clan - our lineage! - with an indelible dishonour! Look at his face! The guilt of committing this terrible crime is practically written there for all to see!"

Sambuvaraiyar made no response. He took a step towards Karikalar's body before sinking down to the floor. He stared at the lifeless prince with a vacant look upon his face. "*Ayyo*!" he broke into a wail. "Cursed fate! Did this tragedy have to take place in my home? Must my head bear the charge of inviting the king to a feast only to kill him?" Sambuvaraiyar broke into loud lament, weeping and moaning as he beat his head and chest with his hands.

"Father! That charge shall not fall upon our clan!" cried Kandamaaran. He roughly dragged a limp Vandhiyathevan to the fore. "We have caught the murderer red-handed. Look, there lies the dagger that he killed the prince with - look at its blade, slick with blood! When I was here earlier, I saw neither Vandhiyathevan nor the knife." He glanced at the Vallathu prince, his lips curling in derision. "He evidently failed to flee and returned with his tail between his legs. Or perhaps he came back to see if the prince was still clinging onto life - maybe he reckoned that stabbing him was not enough and decided to strangle him for good measure! Father! What punishment should be given to such a scheming villain, such a repugnant traitor as this? Whatever it is, it can not be retribution enough!" spoke Kandamaaran in a gush of fury and vitriol.

His dreadfully bruised throat had already left Vandhiyathevan physically unable to speak; Kandamaaran's speech now sent him into a state of shock, leaving him dumbstruck. He realized with a start that he had been found in a compromising position, one that painted him a murderer. *It is no trivial thing, either - Kandamaaran accuses me of stabbing and killing the prince of our realm! This is what things have come to, then. Aha! That Pazhuvoor mohini... that venomous snake in the guise of an exquisite woman! Perhaps this had been her plan all along! Perhaps that was why she had saved my life on more than one occasion! She had sated her rage upon Kundhavai Piratti thus. Aha! Where is that she-devil, that monstrous beauty? How did she make her escape? Perhaps she fled through the underground passage with Ravidasan and the rest once the vile deed was done!"*

Vandhiyathevan's thoughts suddenly turned to a different direction. He was certain that *he* hadn't killed Aditha Karikalan; but who *did*? Nandhini? Ravidasan? Or that *kaalamugan*? Maybe it was Manimekalai, whom he had caught a fleeting sight of in the split second before he lost consciousness. Or could it have been Idumbankari, whose dagger this was? Perhaps it was Kandamaaran himself who was responsible for the dastardly act, besotted as he was by Nandhini - perhaps he planned to pin the blame on Vandhiyathevan all along! Or… or perhaps Aditha Karikalar killed himself, bereft of all hope on hearing Nandhini's terrible revelation.

Kandamaaran looked sharply at the men beside him. "You blockheads! What are you staring at? Seize the murderer and bind him!" he bellowed. It was only at that moment that Vandhiyathevan grasped a full understanding of the peril he was in. He looked at Kandamaaran pleadingly, his eyes glistening with deep pain and sorrow. His throat burned with agony as he made an effort to speak. "Kandhamaara! What are you saying? Do you truly believe me capable of such a terrible deed?" he asked, devastated. "Why would I do such a thing? What would I gain? My friend,…" Kandamaaran cut in before he could say anything further. "Chee!" he exclaimed in disgust. "I am no friend of yours! Your tongue should be ripped out for saying such a vile thing. What would you gain, you ask? What would you *not* gain? You would enjoy Nandhini's favour, of course! *Adei*! Where is that Pazhuvoor *mohini* now?" he demanded.

"Kandhamaara! I swear, I do not know. I was lying here unconscious all this while. I regained my senses a little while before you came here yourself. I do not know what became of Nandhini. It is possible that she escaped through the underground passage. Her men, four of Veera Pandiyan's own *abathudavigal*, were hiding there, biding their time. Nandhini could have left with them!"

"Oho! So she has left you in the lurch as well," replied Kandamaaran, voice dripping with scorn. "Be that as it may, don't you dare plead ignorance with me! Who would believe that? It is quite plain that you were caught in a depraved web of lust, infatuated by her charm and beauty - don't I know that you practically fell at her feet, eager to carry out her commands? Why, Aditha Karikalar himself has made mention of this fact! Nandhini told him the truth about you. Say what you like - whether she prevailed upon you or whether you sought to earn her favour, it was you who committed this heinous murder! Even looking upon your face is a sin!" he spat.

"Kandhamaara, I swear - I did not kill the prince! In fact, I came here promising Pazhaiyarai Ilaiya Piratti that I would protect his life!"

"This is what you said to the prince to gain his confidence, only to betray him and stab him to death! How did you come to be in this chamber, otherwise? Why else would you be here?"

"Kandhamaara! I knew that the prince was in danger; I came here to save him! I have failed in my attempt," said Vandhiyathevan, holding back a choke. "Ask your sister Manimekalai if you wish! She was the one who…"

"Chi, chi!" exploded Kandamaaran. "Don't talk about my sister - don't even speak her name with your vile tongue! Beware - if you bring up her subject again, I will kill you where you stand. I will strangle you with my own hands!"

Kandamaaran fell upon Vandhiyathevan in fury. He grabbed the rope binding his chest and shoulders and shook him violently. He looked to Sambuvaraiyar, who was still grieving next to Aditha Karikalan's body. "Father! What shall we do with him? What shall we do with this wicked murderer who has brought scandal and dishonour upon our clan? Say but one word and I shall chop him to pieces right this minute! Tell me, father!" he shouted.

Sambuvaraiyar was gently stroking Karikalan's body in a daze. He looked up at Kandamaaran's words but his gaze went beyond his son. The chieftain watched as the drapes around the bedstead rustled and a figure emerged from behind the screens. It was hard to immediately place the newcomer, for his eyes were filled with tears; but once the figure took a step forward, Sambuvaraiyar realized that it was his own daughter, dear Manimekalai. Astonishment, disgust and grief mingled on his face and he looked upon his child in dismay.

"Manimekalai! How did you come here?" he asked. Kandamaaran spun around at these words, stunned.

"Appa, I was here all along. Do tell *anna* not to accuse him. He is blameless!" begged an ashen-faced Manimekalai.

"See, father - see how far this foul wretch has sullied my sister's heart. She claims him to be innocent as a lamb!" remarked Kandamaaran cuttingly.

"Yes, *anna*!" said Manimekalai. "None of this is his fault - he is innocent!"

The sting of cold fury and bitter humiliation cut Kandamaaran to the quick. "Sister! Hold your tongue!" he shouted, cheeks flushed. "Who asked you to come here? You should not be here. You are not in your right mind. Go at once to the front of the house, where the other women are!"

"No, *anna*. There's nothing wrong with my state of mind. Yours, however, seems to be quite muddled at the moment. Otherwise you would not have accused him of killing the prince!" replied Manimekalai defiantly.

"You halfwit!" growled Kandamaaran. "Why do you speak up in support of this base murderer?"

"Because he isn't one!" cried Manimekalai.

An angry, derisive laugh escaped Kandamaaran. "If he isn't the murderer, then who is? Who killed the prince? You?"

"Yes," replied Manimekalai quietly. "I did kill him. I killed him with this very sword."

The chamber fell into shocked silence at these words. Manimekalai's terrible confession hung in the air like a dark cloud as her audience looked at each other in stupefaction and disbelief.

Kandamaaran stood rooted to the ground. He abruptly let go of Vandhiyathevan and swiftly went to Manimekalai's side. He roughly grabbed the sword from her hands and closely surveyed its tip.

"Appa!" he cried, spinning around to face his father. "Did you hear what she said? She can't even lift this sword by herself - yet, she claims to have killed the prince with this very weapon! If this blade had stabbed the prince, could she have drawn the sword out of his body? Look, look at its tip - it is spotless, like it has been wiped clean! She makes this claim only to save Vallavarayan! Why does she have so much concern for him? This blackguard has tainted her heart so! He has wielded foul sorcery to place her under his spell. Look at his face! His crime is written there quite plainly for all to see!"

Kandamaaran's words bore some semblance of truth, for Vandhiyathevan's face had grown pale with shock and agony. The Vallathu prince had held his tongue all along but now he spoke with a crushing despair. "Kandhamaara! You speak the truth. I am the criminal here. Your sister seeks to protect me with her story. My princess," he said, turning his anguished gaze upon Manimekalai, "I thank you with all my heart and soul. Even when life departs this wretched body, even as it draws the last breath, I shall never forget the sisterly love you have bestowed upon me. Pray, heed your brother's words. Repair to the *anthappuram*."

Vandhiyathevan's speech only served to stoke Kandamaaran's dark fury. His bloodshot eyes seemed to spit fire as he spoke. "Adei! Have things come to such a sorry pass that you dare intercede for me? Do you expect this maiden to heed my words only by your leave? Is that the extent of her sisterly affection for you? Is she my kin or yours?" he thundered. "Does she hold you in higher esteem than me? Why? What ungodly spell have you employed to spoil her innocent heart so? This is reason enough for me to kill you. Here, I shall dispatch you to death's door right this instant - everything else can wait! Why, I will slay you with this very sword in your beloved sister's hands - that will please you, won't it?" Roaring with anger, Kandamaaran brandished the sword in his hands and fell upon Vandhiyathevan in a murderous rage.

41

Flames leap high

Until that very moment, Sambuvaraiyar had been sitting stock still, watching events unfold. As Kandamaaran raised the sword in anger, he leapt to his feet in alarm and caught hold of his son's hands.

"Imbecile!" cried Sambuvaraiyar. "What blind folly were you to do?"

"Father! What is wrong in slaying this turncoat?" asked Kandamaaran, aggrieved.

"Wrong?" echoed Sambuvaraiyar in disbelief. "This one act will serve to annihilate both you and our venerable clan for the rest of time! If you kill this lad, we will shoulder the blame for his murder along with that of the prince! Don't you understand?"

Kandamaaran's nostrils flared and he bristled with defiance. "Who has the might to hold us accountable? Can he survive a second longer after laying such a blame at our feet?" he asked fiercely.

"*Ayyo*!" moaned Sambuvaraiyar, striking his own forehead in despair. "Simpleton of a boy! Must you make use of this catastrophe to flaunt your valour? Ah, it is only because I hearkened to your advice that our house bears the ignominy of this disaster!" He looked at his son sadly. "It was you who invited Periya Pazhuvettarayar and the other chieftains into our home," he pointed out, "and it was you who brought about Maduranthaka Thevar's clandestine visit, too. All of that is now an open secret, by virtue of this bosom friend of yours. To top it all, *you* were the one who escorted Aditha Karikalan from Kanchi to this place! *Ayyo*! I never dreamed that we would face such consequences! Our arch enemy Malayaman advances, his army in tow; what am I to tell him?... The timing cannot be worse - Pazhuvettarayar has departed for his country, leaving us on our own!" Sambuvaraiyar struck his forehead wretchedly.

Kandamaaran's eyes filled with tears. "Father! Don't despair," he begged. "I brought this peril to our door; I shall take its consequences upon myself. I will do whatever you ask of me!"

"Take this girl away from here forthwith," replied Sambuvaraiyar, glowering at Manimekalai. "Leave her in the women's quarters. If she continues to peddle her drivel, gag her mouth and bind her; why, confine her in the secret chamber if you must!"

Manimekalai discerned the full extent of her father's wrath and trembled with fear. She also gleaned that Vandhiyathevan was safe from immediate danger.

"Father, please forgive me," said Manimekalai humbly. "I will do as you wish. Kandamaaran need not trouble himself - I shall leave right away for the women's quarters." She left the chamber hurriedly with Kandamaaran following her close behind.

As soon as they left the chamber, Sambuvaraiyar turned to his men. "Bind him to the legs of that bed!" he ordered.

Vandhiyathevan kept his calm when the men approached him, making no resistance as they tied him firmly to the bed. He spoke up when they were done. "*Ayya*, pray, think!" he begged. "I was Karikalar's bosom friend and confidante - what could I possibly gain from killing him? Truly, the wicked men who murdered the prince have slipped away through the underground passage! Pray, chase after and capture them! I have seen them with my own eyes; if only you would untie these bonds, I will track the villains down and help you apprehend them! I will not make an attempt to escape!" urged Vandhiyathevan earnestly.

"*Adei*! If what you say is true, what on earth were you doing when Karikalar was assassinated? Were you simply standing watch?" growled Sambuvaraiyar.

"*Ayya*, the Pazhuvoor Rani and Karikalar were in the midst of a conversation when the assassins entered the chamber all of a sudden. I did try to stop them, but was attacked by a frightful *kaalamugan* - he seized me by the neck and throttled me into unconsciousness. When I regained my senses, I saw that Aditha Karikalar had been struck dead," answered Vandhiyathevan in misery.

A wave of commotion suddenly erupted outside the palace walls. It sounded like the angry buzz of a vast, riotous mob.

Sambuvaraiyar listened to the din, assessing the new crisis. He turned to Vandhiyathevan. "Alright, my lad," he said. "Even if your words *are* true, you must remain here a little while longer. Give your dear friend the prince a little company while I investigate the ruckus outside. When I get back, I will pay attention to your side of the story." With that promise, Sambuvaraiyar swiftly made his exit along with his retinue and his men bolted the doors behind them with a clang of finality.

Darkness fell upon the chamber once again. An indescribable grief settled in Vandhiyathevan's heart; it weighed him down into what seemed like bottomless despair. He thought of everything that had taken place since the time he had come to the Kadambur palace a few months ago. Vandhiyathevan thought of the falling star he had seen then. He recalled the chatter it had sparked amongst the townspeople. They had feared that a star falling from the sky augured ill for the Sundara Chozhar and marked the end of his days. Such speculation was quite natural, for the Emperor had long been confined to his bed from a protracted illness. It was on account of such a fear that the populace wondered who would succeed the throne; it was why the chieftains met in this very palace to discuss the subject. The entire affair had now come to an entirely unexpected end with the demise of prince Aditha Karikalar, warrior beyond compare, a youth in the prime of life. *Here lies his lifeless corpse in this very chamber while an ailing Sundara Chozhar yet draws breath. Would the Chakravarthy live much longer? Would he have the will to cling onto life upon hearing of the untimely death of his dear son? Ayyo! How eager the father was to see his beloved son! Why, it was in the Emperor's honour that Karikalar had built in Kanchi a magnificent ponmaaligai, a majestic palace of gold - the young prince had wished it to be the home his father lived in. Alas, he did not have the fortune to welcome his father into that splendid palace. Who knows what evil will follow in the wake of the events that have unfolded here? All of the Chozha samrajyam will be engulfed by a tidal wave of sorrow. It wouldn't stop there, of course. Who knows what sort of interior strife this tragedy will spawn?*

A civil war would certainly break out among the chieftains. The roaring clamour outside must be the soldiers in Malayaman's army. Why are they making such a din? Are they planning to launch an attack on the Kadambur palace? Why? Has news of Karikalar's demise reached them, perhaps? Aha! How will Sambuvaraiyar handle this crisis? He will foist the blame upon me, of course. But will Malayaman believe him? Even if he does, will he absolve Sambuvaraiyar of all responsibility, given that the tragedy took place in his own palace? Malayaman must know of the clandestine summit of chieftains that had taken place here - even if he had been unaware, Azhwarkkadiyaan must have apprised him. That must be why Malayaman is advancing upon the Kadambur palace with his forces.

Vandhiyathevan knew well the love that Malayaman bore for his grandson.

Who knows what the old man would do upon hearing the news? Destroy Sambuvaraiyar's family, perhaps. Why, he may even lay waste to this very palace and raze it down to ashes! Poor Kandamaaran! He is a good man at heart, really. He had such affection for me, once. That amity has now mutated into hatred by dint of that twisted Pazhuvoor mohini! Come to think of it, her story is a tragic one as well. How could she be to blame for this wicked turn of events? All this is naught but the callous design of Fate.

Fate! Fate! What to say of Manimekalai's fate? Why should that maiden bestow such love upon me? She came forward and declared herself the killer in order to save me! Can there be a love upon earth to equal hers? How am I to repay her for such a gesture?

Vandhiyathevan laughed shortly to himself. *What madness to think of recompense! What sense is there in feeling sorry for others? No one faces a more frightening or pitiable prospect than I do! I am going to be accused of assassinating Aditha Karikalar. There is no evidence to support such a claim; but then again, there is no trace of Nandhini or Ravidasan and his vile cabal. No one is making any effort to pursue them. And if perchance they do capture them, how am I to prove that I had nothing to do with their plot? That is quite impossible.*

What sort of retributive justice will be meted out to a traitor who has killed the crown prince of the realm? It can't be a mere death sentence, surely. They will devise a ruthless punishment, one so terrifying and unsparing as to dissuade another from even dreaming of such a crime. Fine, then. Let them do as they see fit. The Pazhaiyarai Ilaiya Piratti and Ponniyin Selvar will believe the claim that I slayed Karikalar, will they not? What could be a more brutal torment than that? Dear, sweet lord! All those perils that I escaped by the skin of my teeth these last few months - did I dodge them only to become prey to such mortal dishonour?

Thoughts rose and disappeared in Vandhiyathevan's mind like breakers dissolving into white foam upon the seashore. He lost track of time. Vandhiyathevan's ruminations were interrupted by the sudden advent of faint wisps of smoke. *What is this smoke? Where is it coming from?* Weak beams of light appeared, throwing a feeble glow upon Aditha Karikalar's body. The doors were still shut, so the light certainly couldn't be a lamp. *Then what was it?* Vandhiyathevan looked all about him. It didn't take him long to realize that the smoke and light were emanating from the *vettai mandapam. Why was there smoke from the vettai mandapam? Was it perhaps on fire? Did the villains who used the underground passage set the halls on fire before stealing away? Or was the culprit the lamp that he and Manimekalai had brought when they had come through that path?*

The smoke grew gradually thicker, bringing along with it a stifling heat. Soon, tongues of yellow flame licked through the cracks of the wooden partition separating the *vettai mandapam* from the chamber. Agni, the lord of fire, was stretching out His incandescent arms to gather the chamber into a blazing embrace.

Vandhiyathevan watched Agni's wrath with unblinking interest. He only felt happiness, at first. *Here is Agni bhagavan, come to give me sweet respite from all my worries - I shall join Aditha Karikalar on his funeral pyre!* It was but a momentary joy, for Vandhiyathevan soon realized that he did not wish to depart this mortal world tainted as the murderer who slayed Karikalan.

After all, that is the account that Sambuvaraiyar and his son will present to the world. Some will even buy into their words. No matter who believes them, Kundhavai Devi and Ponniyin Selvar must not give credit to their claim. I did not commit this hateful sin; I must strive to prove my innocence for their sakes at the very least. Besides, how can I suffer the last rites of Aditha Karikalar -that illustrious warrior who was second to none in the known realms! - to come to such a sorry pass? Would not his beloved parents, friends and family find solace in paying their last respects to his body? Yes, yes! Even though I couldn't save his life, I can yet save his body. I must make sure that the prince receives the dignified exequies due to him as the beloved son of the Chakravarthy.

Vandhiyathevan had made no effort to free himself until this moment; he hadn't even paid attention to the knots that held him in place. He now scrutinized his binds closely. His captors had tied his hands together, first; then, with the same rope, they had bound his body to the legs of the bed. They seemed to have done a rather good job of it, for he found that he could neither bend nor stand up. He strained every nerve to untie his binds. Vandhiyathevan tugged at the ropes with all his might; he even tried gnawing through them, in vain. He tried to wriggle out of the ropes; that didn't work either, but his manoeuvres made the bed move. An idea suggested itself to Vandhiyathevan. He replicated his movements to drag the bed towards the entrance of the *vettai mandapam*. It wasn't an easy task by far. He found that all he could do was inch towards his target; each time he made an effort to pull at the bed, the ropes around him tightened cruelly, inflicting excruciating pain. Vandhiyathevan bit down on his agony and advanced.

When he neared the entrance to the *vettai mandapam*, he saw hungry flames lapping through the cracks in the wooden partition. Vandhiyathevan held out his hands to the blaze, and soon enough, the ropes binding them caught on fire. As the flames scorched the strands, they licked the flesh of his fingers. Vandhiyathevan felt an indescribable, throbbing pain surge through his hands; he stifled his gasps and steeled himself through the torment until the fire burned away the ropes. Hands free, Vandhiyathevan swiftly set to untying the knots strapping him still. By this time, however, the drapes of the bed were aflame. Thick, black clouds of smoke swirled around him. Vandhiyathevan felt as if his entire body was on fire. At first, the smoke stung his eyes bitterly; then, tears rolled down his cheeks. Gradually, his vision began to grow dim. *What now? It looks like I will burn to death along with the prince in this very chamber! Perhaps that is for the best, after all. I couldn't save the prince; at the very least, I will have the honour of dying with him. Chi, chi. What sort of thinking is this? The thought of burning alive does not worry me, in truth. But I cannot bear the thought of the ignoble blame that will be laid at my feet if the prince's body burns to ashes in this place. Those who know me will not be able to think of me without a curse on their lips! Why must I breathe my last and facilitate such an accusation? Come what may, I will safely take the prince's body outside. I will deliver his noble remains to his grandfather Malayaman. I shall give my word of honour that I did not slay the prince; I will make a sacred pledge to capture the villains who did. I shall not resist death's embrace once I have completed that charge. Until then, however, I must cling onto life!*

Vandhiyathevan freed himself of his constraints. *What fresh disaster is this? The entire bed is on fire! Sweet lord, this heat is unbearable! I cannot even keep my eyes open in this searing heat; this thick smoke clouds my vision when I force them open. Come what may, I must find the prince's remains.* Panicking, Vandhiyathevan sat down and blindly groped the ground around him, stretching out his hands as far as he could. He searched for what felt like painful aeons, though his fingers brushed against the prince's corpse within a few minutes. Vandhiyathevan gently picked up the body and slung it over his shoulder. It was only then that he realized that leaving the chamber was trickier than he had thought. It would not be possible to exit through the *vettai mandapam. Aha! The animal specimens that the Sambuvaraiyar clan had painstakingly collected over the decades are certainly burnt to ashes by now!* Vandhiyathevan approached the main door to the chamber. He pounded on it frantically with his free hand. He hurled his entire weight against the door. He tried to kick it open with his foot. "Fire! Fire!" he shouted, as loud as he could. "Open the door!" It was a futile course of action; nothing worked. *Chi! What idiocy! There's nothing for it but to climb outside through the yazh kalanjiyam. Ayyo! Would those halls be on fire too? I have wasted precious time!*

The chamber was well and truly aflame by now, illuminated by a white-hot radiance thrown by the conflagration. The light was rendered useless by the thick, noxious clouds of smoke enveloping the chamber. Vandhiyathevan found it hard to keep his eyes open. When he did manage to force them open, he found it hard to get his bearings. He made a quick estimation about the direction that the *yazh kalanjiyam* was in and bolted towards it. His foot came in contact with an object as he ran and it made a great clang of protest. *Aha! That must be the twisted dagger that I saw lying nearby when I came to my senses, the one that I picked up. There is something fishy about that knife. Best to take it. If I run into an unexpected encounter on the way out, it may even prove useful - who knows?*

Vandhiyathevan bent down and picked up the dagger. Live embers from the burning bed fell upon his shoulder, scalding him; he flicked them aside and resumed his sprint towards the *yazh kalanjiyam*. Vandhiyathevan had been carrying Karikalar's body all this while, draped across his shoulder and supported by one of his arms. He had managed so far, but it would be quite impossible to climb the steep steps of the *yazh kalanjiyam* thus; to make matters worse, the door at the top was shut. Vandhiyathevan gently laid down Karikalar's body to climb up the steps and open the door. With one foot in the *yazh kalanjiyam*, he bent down and picked up the prince's corpse once again. *Sweet lord! The inferno has already reached these halls, too! If I had delayed a few minutes further, this route would have been closed to me as well!* Vanthiyathevan hauled Karikalar's body on the landing and climbed up after, panting. He felt like a man who had exhausted the greater part of his life's breath. A cool breeze caressed his body, which had been roasting in the searing heat of the fire and smoke all along. Vandhiyathevan wondered if he should rest for a moment. *No, no! There is no time to waste, not even a minute! Who knows when this burning building will crumble down?* He draped Karikalar's body over his shoulder once again and swiftly stepped through the landing. He darted through a maze of landings and courtyards like he had on an earlier occasion. He had traversed this curious path alone and unencumbered, then; he had managed to climb down from the palace landing, cross the moon courtyard and vault over the compound wall. Could he do the same now? He was quite exhausted as it were; besides, he had to carry Aditha Karikalar's body through the convoluted path, too.

A great commotion rose around him all of a sudden. Vandhiyathevan's attention snapped to the racket. *Aha! What is this, now? It looks like Malayaman's men have begun to strike the fort! They seem to be laying siege to the front gates; it appears as if they are trying to break them open. There, a few warriors are jumping onto the compound walls, too. Did Malayaman issue the order to attack on learning that the prince has been assassinated? If that is the case, what would these soldiers do when they see me carrying Karikalar's body? Why, they will assume that it was I who killed him! They will tear me apart! I must be very careful, now. I must locate Malayaman and deliver to him the noble remains of his grandson. Let the chips fall where they may, after that.*

Vandhiyathevan hunched over as he walked, cloaking his movements by traversing through the shadows in the palace courtyards. Finally, he reached a familiar spot - it was the very place from which he had spied upon the chieftains' covert conference! Vandhiyathevan wondered how he could get down. He looked all around him. A ladder caught his eye, propped up against the edge of a wall. A figure stood next to it down below. *Who could that be? Who is he waiting for, with that ladder? What would happen if I used it to climb down? Well, the repercussions don't matter at this point - that ladder is my way out! Thankfully, I have the dagger close at hand. I'll face the outcome, whatever it may be.*

The commotion at the front gates escalated. The man near the ladder moved away; perhaps he wanted to find out what had happened. Relieved, Vandhiyathevan swiftly clambered down the ladder. He had no sooner placed a foot upon the ground when the man returned.

"*Saami*! You took your own sweet time!" fussed the man. Vandhiyathevan realized that it was none other than Idumbankari. He thought he had a fair idea who Idumbankari had been waiting for expectantly.

As Idumbakari drew closer, his eyes widened in rank astonishment. "Adei! You!" he exclaimed. "Who do you have there, around your shoulder?"

"Yes, *appa*. It is me, the acolyte of the *kaalamuga saamiyar*," replied Vandhiyathevan tersely. "He sent me ahead with the sacrifice consecrated to goddess Ranabhadrakali. He follows close behind. He bade me ask you to wait here with the ladder. See, he directed me to show you this knife as a mark of proof," he finished, drawing forth the twisted dagger.

Idumbankari looked at him suspiciously. "You never said a word about this all these days!" he remarked. "No matter, let that be. What is taking the *saamiyar* so long? How are we to leave from here? Thirukovilur's men have besieged the palace; his forces have already begun to infiltrate its walls!"

"So what? Bigger the crowd, easier the escape! Do you think the *periya saamiyar* needs instructions on that front? He will find his way out, one way or another. You remain waiting right here until he comes. Tell him that I will be in the gardens!" said Vandhiyathevan imperiously.

Vandhiyathevan strode on without waiting for Idumbankari's reply. Once he was out of his line of sight, the Vaanar youth quickly made his way to the front gates of the palace.

ꕥ

42

Malayaman's sorrow

As soon as Sambuvaraiyar reached the front yard, he turned to Kandamaaran with an air of solemnity. "Son, we face a peril the likes of which has never threatened our clan before. If we are to come away unscathed, you must do what I say without a second thought."

Kandamaaran looked pale and haggard. Karikalar's death had left him greatly unsettled. He had also had a moment of heartstopping clarity about the blunder that would have been in killing Vandhiyathevan. "Father, our clan courts disaster solely on my account, wretched fool that I am," he replied, his tone contrite. "Pray, forgive me. I shall fulfill your orders without question, whatever they may be."

"Make a discreet exit from this palace upon this instant. I trust you are aware of the underground passage that runs beneath the bed in my sleeping chamber? The path converges with the *vettai mandapam* track, leading one directly to the boundary walls of the palace…"

Kandamaaran recoiled. "Father! Do you ask me to make my escape, leaving you behind to confront danger by yourself?" he asked, nonplussed.

A wan smile spread across Sambuvaraiyar's tired features. "Ah, child! How soon you forget the word you gave me! Yes, leave you must. You are our clan's sole hope, the only progeny who can sustain the eminent bloodline of the illustrious lord of Kolli Malai, Valvil Ori. Should the need arise, you must make your way to that very mountain and live in hiding. When Maduranthaka Thevar's ascension to crown prince is certain, I shall send word to you - only then must you return!"

Kandamaaran grew mulish at these words. "I beg your pardon, father. I cannot live in hiding. Should the exalted clan of Valvil Ori be stained with such ignoble cowardice? Bade me relinquish my life and I shall do so upon the instant, without a second thought. But I cannot slink away into hiding!"

Sambuavaryar regarded him in silence. "Son, I was merely testing your mettle. So you do not wish to run away or go into hiding, eh? Good!" he said, satisfied. "I mean to task you with a daunting mission, one that will draw upon the very depths of your courage. Exit forthwith through the subterranean passage. It is not Kolli Malai that you will make for, but Thanjavur! Periya Pazhuvettarayar will likely be there - brief him about the events that have taken place here today. If you find him absent, apprise Chinna Pazhuvettarayar and Maduranthaka Thevar…"

"*Ayya*! What should I tell them?" asked Kandamaaran, suddenly alert.

"What sort of a question is this?" exclaimed Sambuvaraiyar. "Tell them of Karikalar's demise! Tell them that the winds of change blow upon our endeavour, for Fate has recast the stakes! Karikalar is no more - there is no better time than now for Madhuranthakan to be anointed the crown prince! Malayaman and Kodumbalur Velar will no doubt oppose such a move; tell them that we must gather all our forces to destroy their faction for good!"

"And if they should ask how Karikalar died, what must I say?"

"What else? Tell them that the Vaanar warrior Vandhiyathevan murdered him in cold blood. Yet," continued Sambuvaraiyar solemnly, "there is a key detail that you must keep in mind, my son - pay heed, for you must strive to remember this. Vandhiyathevan has returned from his travels to Eezham. Not only did he establish contact with Arulmozhi Devan there, but he also met the Pazhaiyarai Ilaiya Piratti upon his return. Reports say that Arulmozhi Devan has emerged in the open from his hideout at Naagaippattinam." Sambuvaraiyar reached out and gripped Kandamaaran's shoulder earnestly. "We must kindle speculation in the realm that it was Arulmozhi Varmar who tasked Vandhiyathevan to the murder his elder brother, spurred by the desire to ascend the throne; we must sow the seeds of doubt that the Pazhaiyarai Ilaiya Piratti had a hand in this ploy, too. Relay this message to the Pazhuvettarayar brothers and Maduranthaka Thevar!"

Kanthamran frowned thoughtfully. "Father, your words may well be true. That traitor Vandhiyathevan probably came to this palace with that very intention from the start!"

"Could be son, could be. However, we must discover why the Pazhuvoor Rani has vanished into thin air. After all, Vallavarayan Vandhiyathevan has registered his accusation against her and her men, the Pandiya Abathudhavis!"

"It is but natural for a criminal to palm off his villainy onto another when caught red-handed," Kandamaaran snorted derisively. He paused as a notion struck him. "I understand it all, now. Father!

The Pazhaiyarai Kundhavai Devi cannot abide Pazhuvoor Ilaiya Rani. She must have contrived events to kill Karikalar and abduct Pazhuvoor Ilaiya Rani at the same time. It seems to me that Mudhanmanthiri Aniruddhar is an accessory to this twisted ploy. They must have dispatched Vandhiyathevan here as part of their nefarious gambit! *Ayyo*! We have been blind to their wiles - now we're left bearing the burden of their sins!"

"There is little point in rueing the past, Kandhamaara. It is best to see to what needs to be done. Leave right away - our message must reach the Pazhuvettarayars and Maduranthakar before word of Karikalar's death reaches Sundara Chozhar or anyone else in Thanjai! You must leave forthwith! You do know, don't you, of the secret underground passage that offers access to the Thanjai fort?"

"Yes, I do."

"Then what are you waiting for? Go on, leave!"

"I shall, father. Yet..." Kandamaaran hesitated. "I worry about my sister Manimekalai…"

"Don't take that upon your head," snapped Sambuvaraiyar. "I will not permit her to spout that drivel to another! If she runs that mouth of hers, I shall slay her with my own hands…"

"*Ayyo*! That is exactly what I am afraid of! Your wrath…"

"Don't bother," cut in Sambuvaraiyar shortly. "I know how to change her mind. Ah, fate is certainly a curious thing! First we intended to wed her to Maduranthaka Thevar; then we thought to fix her alliance with Karikalar, who is naught but a lifeless corpse today. Thank the stars that Manimekalai did not take a shine to him! We may as well go back to our old plan…"

"But father," interjected Kandamaaran. "It appears that Manimekalai fancies herself in love with that *chandaalan* Vandhiyathevan!"

"A passing infatuation, son. Manimekalai is not yet mature enough to understand her own heart. I shall take care of her," promised Sambuvaraiyar. "Now you mustn't linger here a second longer!"

The din outside the palace walls suddenly grew louder. Kandamaaran looked at his father in alarm. "Appa, it sounds like Malayaman's armies have arrived! What did that old man say when you met him this evening?"

"Nothing but good news, in truth. The grandsire was quite chuffed at the news of Manimekalai's betrothal to Aditha Karikalar. He planned to give away his granddaughter's hand in marriage on the same day - his daughter's daughter, you know - and has brought her along as well. Delightful, isn't it?" Sambuvaraiyar's lips twisted into a sardonic smile. "When I invited him to the palace, he said that he would arrive at an auspicious time on the morrow, after dawn. It sounds like his troops have already begun to celebrate the upcoming nuptials!" He attempted to chuckle, but all he could manage was a half-hearted laugh. "Come, come. I will lead you to the underground passage myself and return here." Sambuvaraiyar paused and looked intently at his son. "Do not tarry along the way, not even for a minute. You must find a horse as you go and travel as swiftly as you can."

Sambuvaraiyar took a lamp in hand and proceeded to lead the way. The pair entered the underground passage and hurried along the path together. When Kandamaaran had crossed the boundary of the palace walls, Sambuvaraiyar stopped. He drew his son into a tight embrace and blessed him on his way. As he turned back, Kandamaaran called out to him. "Do you need the lamp?" asked the youth. "No, lad. I am quite familiar with this passage - I can walk the path blindfolded if need be!" replied Sambuvaraiyar.

Kandamaaran disappeared from sight, melting into the dark passage ahead. Sambuvaraiyar turned back. He stopped at the *vettai mandapam* along the way and entered its halls. The chieftain cocked his ear and listened closely for sounds from the chamber next door. He could hear nothing but silence. He stood stock still for a while, hesitant. Sambuvaraiyar suddenly heaved a great sigh, as if he had come to a decision. He stoked the fire of the lamp nearby and placed it in a strategic position before swiftly making his exit.

When Sambuvaraiyar returned to the palace courtyard, he gathered the royal women of the *anthappuram*.

The women were in a state of shock, deeply unsettled by the news of the day's events. They had a vague understanding of Karikalar's demise from questioning a tearful, dishevelled Manimekalai, whom Kandamaaran had unceremoniously thrust into the women's quarters.

"Ladies," began Sambuvaraiyar soberly. "Our clan faces an unprecedented peril. You must brace yourselves to leave this palace on a moment's notice. Strengthen your will to brave a hard sojourn in the wilds of the forest or the mountains. Gather your clothing and jewellery and assemble in the moon courtyard." His face hardened. "I must hear nary a cry or whimper from any of you. Do you understand?"

Sambuvaraiyar turned on his heels without further ado and strode briskly to the front entrance. He wanted to climb the tower at the main gates and survey the commotion outside. As it happened, he was robbed of the opportunity. The chieftain had hardly taken a few steps towards the tower when the fort gates collapsed under the onslaught of the soldiers outside. The troops swarmed through in unrelenting waves, knocking down the fort guards at the entrance.

Worse still, a battalion of soldiers were scaling the compound walls to infiltrate the fort.

Sambuvaraiyar's heart stopped with terror. *Had Malayaman received word of Karikalar's assassination? How on earth could news have reached him so soon? Well, if he knows, he knows. He had to learn of it at some point or another. These soldiers must be stopped from advancing, though. They must be delayed for a short while, a mere half naazhigai should do - then everything would unfold according to plan.*

The moon courtyard lay betwixt the fort walls and the facade of the palace. Sambuvaraiyar marched to its centre and determinedly moved into position. The chieftain shone with regal grandeur as he firmly stood his ground, a sharp sword glinting in his hand. Seven, eight warriors took their places behind him, wielding long spears. Some held flaming torches in their hands.

Thirukovilur Malayaman and Parthibendran appeared, following in the wake of the invading troops.

Spotting Sambuvaraiyar in the moon courtyard, Parthibendran pointed him out to Malayaman. The pair strode briskly towards Sambuvaraiyar.

"*Sambuvaraiyare*!" bellowed Malayaman as he walked. "What is this I hear? How could you bring yourself to do such a monstrous thing?" The old man halted in front of Sambuvaraiyar. The sword in the chieftain's hand did not escape his eyes. "Ah, you stand with a blade at the ready! What do you intend to achieve?"

"I could ask you the same thing," replied Sambuvaraiyar evenly. "What do *you* intend to achieve? What do you mean by breaking down the fort gates thus? Why, it was just a short while back that I invited you to the palace myself. You were the one who said you would come on the morrow at an auspicious hour…"

"*Sambuvaraiyare!* I am here because the time is upon us!" growled Malayaman. "Where is Aditha Karikalan? Where is that peerless warrior who beheaded Veera Pandiyan? Where is that hero who reigned the Sevur battlefield in a blaze of triumph? Where is my grandson?"

Sambuvaraiyar looked him in the eye. "How am I to know? The prince is wherever he pleases to be. I told you, didn't I, that I refrain from conversing with that brute of a boy? Why, even Parthibendran knows of this!"

"*Adei Sambuvaraya*! Don't you try to hoodwink me with feeble pretence! Deliver Aditha Karikalan to us this very instant! If not, I shall make it so this fort, its ramparts and this very palace are all razed down to naught but mere dust!" roared Thirukovilur Malayamam.

Sambuvaraiyar turned to Parthibendran, raising an incredulous brow. "Parthibendra, what on earth is this old man blathering on about?" he asked sharply. "Has he lost his mind? Who am I to deliver the prince to him? Who, for that matter, is *he*? Am I holding the prince captive? Or is he planning to clap the prince in chains and take him away?"

"*Sambuvaraiyare*, pray do not panic," replied Parthibendran soothingly. "The grandsire has reason to be angry. Here, take a look at this *olai* - you will grasp the matter yourself," he said, holding out a missive to Sambuvaraiyar.

Sambuvaraiyar took great care in studying it by the light of a torch that burned nearby. "Prince Aditha Karikalan's life is in danger. Deploy forces at once to save him," it said.

Sambuvaraiyar's forehead broke into a sweat as he read the words. His body trembled and shook despite himself, not unlike the time he laid eyes on Karikalar's corpse.

"What vile chicanery is this? What foul conspiracy? Who could have written such a message?" he stammered.

"What does it matter who wrote it?" thundered Malayaman. "Fetch Aditha Karikalar at once or take us to him! Or would you rather I send my men in search of the prince?"

"So be it, *ayya*! I shall take you to Karikalar," replied Sambuvaraiyar quietly. "Parthibendra, you are familiar with the place the prince is at - I learned just a short while ago that he is in Pazhuvoor Ilaiya Rani's *anthappuram*. Lead Malayaman to the chamber yourself!"

Parthibendran turned to Malayaman. "Yes, *thaatha*! Come, I will lead the way myself," he said. He glanced in the direction where Pazhuvoor Ilaiya Rani Nandhini's chamber lay.

"*Ayyo*! What is that?" yelled Parthibendran, startled. For what he saw was a brightly blazing inferno, its amber flames forking upwards as thick columns of black smoke mushroomed into the sky.

Everyone turned to look. "Fire! Fire!" they clamoured at once, terrified at the sight.

When the shock had subsided a bit, Parthibendran turned to Sambuvaraiyar. "*Sambuvaraiyare*! In truth, I didn't believe the missive at first. I do, now. A plot of some sort has been afoot. *Paata!* Issue the order to imprison the conspirators at once! I will go in search of the prince and bring him here!"

Sambuvaraiyar gathered himself. When he spoke, his voice had regained its former boldness. "Yes, Parthibendra! A plot has taken place, indeed. But the guilty party is the lot of you!" he shot back. "You broke down the doors to my palace and trespassed into my domain. You set your men upon the property with orders to set it on fire, too. If the prince is in danger, why, it is the consequence of your actions! Beware. There will come a time when you are paid back in full for every one of these transgressions!"

Parthibendran broke into a run, paying no attention to the chieftain's words. At that very moment, the noblewomen of Sambuvaraiyar's clan appeared in the moon courtyard. It was clear from their faces that their hearts were deeply troubled, but they voiced nary a cry nor the softest whimper.

Some of the women looked at the palace backyard, which was bathed in an eerie glow from the conflagration. Each reached out to clasp the woman next to her, drawing the group's attention to the fiercely blazing inferno. Manimekalai caught sight of the flames, too. "*Ayyo*!" she screamed. "Fire! Fire! He is there!" She made to run towards the fire as she spoke, but Sambuvaraiyar stepped in her path to stop her. He slapped her hard across the face. Manimekalai had never been treated thus since she was born. The apple of Sambuvaraiyar's eye, his most beloved daughter, Manimekalai now stood rooted to the spot as she stared at her father with her big, dark eyes.

"Fool of a girl!" said Sambuvaraiyar, his voice softening. "Didn't I give you fair warning? Why do you vex me so?" He took a breath. "Look there!" he said. "See for yourself that there is little need for you to make a panicked run for it."

A weary Vandhiyathevan was stumbling towards them from the direction that Sambuvaraiyar was pointing at. Draped across his shoulders was the lifeless body of Aditha Karikalan.

Malayaman, who thus far had been paying attention to the exchange between Sambuvaraiyar and his daughter, now looked at Vandhiyathevan. The grandsire watched unblinking as his eyes perceived the Vaanar youth slowly staggering onward as he carried a corpse. His body, faded and old with the passage of time, began to quiver and shake. He wanted to put a question to the person approaching, but he seemed to have lost his tongue. His throat tightened.

Vandhiyathevan kept his eyes on Malayaman as he approached closer.

"*Ayya*! Here is prince Karikalar!" he croaked. "The best among warriors, the hero who beheaded Veera Pandiyan. I have failed to deliver him to you alive. I only bring you his body, unharmed by the fire. Please accept your grandson who lies killed by the twin hands of fate and conspiracy!" Vandhiyathevan slowly lifted Karikalar's corpse and gently placed it on the ground.

He collapsed into a heap with his next breath, losing all consciousness.

Old Malayaman sat down next to the prince's body. He gazed in silence at the brave, noble face in repose. His body broke into great convulsions without warning, giving the appearance of a mighty mountain beset with tremors. "*Ayyo*!" A grief-stricken scream tore itself from his throat, raw and wild as the heaving waves of the sea. He beat his head and chest with his hands, strong yet as iron.

"My precious, my gem! I came only wishing to see you bedecked as a groom! That I should see you so as a lifeless corpse!" he cried out in a heart-rending lament that rang through the vicinity.

The venerable old man wept and wailed as he listed his memories of Aditha Karikalan since the day of his birth. He spoke of the celebrations that took place the day he was born. He cried as he remembered how the prince had played sweetly with him as a child, climbing onto his lap, his arms, his shoulders. He spoke of his days of training, cracking with sorrow as he recalled how he taught him to throw a spear, swing a sword and fight with his bare hands. He broke with grief as he recollected each one of the prince's stunning exploits of courage on the Sevur battlefield in his sixteenth year.

"*Ayyo*! That you did not attain a glorious death in the battles you braved against Pandiya, one that would have secured you a place in warrior heaven! Must you have succumbed to the vile plot hatched by this *chandaalan* Sambuvarayan and his cronies? Andho! To think that I was the one who sent you here, bading you be their guest! I have grown old, I thought. You need allies, I thought. I sought to wed you to his daughter and sent you here myself, believing that it would win his friendship! I thought I was sending you to Sambuvaraiyar's palace; instead, I have sent you to Yama's own! I am a sinner, I am! I have killed you!" cried the old man, hitting his head in despair.

Suddenly, his sorrow snapped into rabid fury. He looked wildly around him. "Adei *Sambuvaraya*!" he roared. "The truth, now! How did the prince die, you foul wretch? What vile plot did you hatch? Even if Devendren Himself had challenged the prince, He could not have won him in direct combat! How many men did you set upon him? Where did they lurk and hide to murder this warrior beyond compare? Speak the truth!"

"Old man!" burst out Sambuavarayar in anger. "I suffer patience in consideration of your age. I know as much about the prince's death as you do! Put your questions to that man who carried the prince's corpse here - he may have the answers you seek! What is the point of asking me?"

"*Adei!* This tragedy has taken place whilst he was at your palace as a guest! You speak as if you know nothing about the matter. Who will believe such a thing? Fine, then; stick to this story of yours when Sundara Chozhar questions you! Men! Imprison Sambuvaraiyar! His palace, these fort walls - you will tear it all down and grind them into dust!" thundered the old man in a terrible voice.

Parthibendran had returned by the time Malayaman had finished his speech. He looked at the old man. "*Ayya*!" he said. "We have been spared the responsibility of destroying the palace. Agni *bhagavan* is already at work. Look there!" Malayaman followed Parthibendran's pointing finger. The fire that they had seen blazing in a corner of the palace had made rapid progress. The conflagration had grown into a veritable firestorm whose shooting flames licked at the sky. The ravenous inferno had turned to ashes the palace courtyards and landings, stairwells and halls, decks and towers - and it was yet unsated. The fire blazed onward in search of more fuel, stretching out a thousand incandescent, dancing tongues in its quest to devour. Malayaman saw the Thirukovilur men standing stupefied at the ruthless sight.

"Right, then!" he boomed. "Agni *bhagavan* has taken up that particular task. Good, Parthibendra! We shall depart at once. Sundara Chozhar, the Chakravarthy who reigns over the three worlds, has been sending messages these past three years, wishing to see his eldest son. My daughter Vanama Devi too has been requesting me to bring the prince to her. At the very least, let them lay eyes upon the prince's remains for one last time. We should not allow Agni *bhagavan* to feast upon the noble body of this peerless warrior, like He does this *chandaalan* Sambuvaraiyar's palace. We will deliver the body to Thanjavur and present its remains to the Chakravarthy. Let mother and father see, at the very least, this illustrious face that has lost its glow. Let them weep. Then, let the Chakravarthy himself devise a fitting punishment for the foul wretches who murdered the prince!" said Malayaman.

43

Back to Kollidakkarai

Along the northern banks of the Kollidam was the village Thirunaarayur, where lay the monastery of *Saivite* scholar Nambiyaandar Nambi. A royal *pallakku* was parked at its entrance, flanked by a retinue of palanquin bearers and soldiers. A gaggle of villagers were gathered a little distance away, flocking around what seemed like two men engaged in a rather spirited quarrel. The exchange was clearly quite entertaining, for the villagers were watching the pair with great interest and excitement.

If you were to brush past the crowd and take a closer look, dear reader, you will be quite pleased to learn that we are well-acquainted with the bickerers. One was Thirumalai, also known to us as Azhwarkkadiyaan Nambi. The other was the Veera Saivar whom we had met at the beginning of our epic story - he was arguing with

Nambi on the boat, if you recall. He happened to be the principal executor of Nambiyaandar Nambi's monastery.

The Veera Saivar had stepped out of the monastery upon learning that Periya Piratti Sembian Maadevi wished to consult the noble Nambiyaandar in private. It wasn't long before he clapped his eyes upon Azhwarkkadiyaan. The hot rush of anger that surged through him was almost reflexive; he couldn't help but remember how that illustrious Veera Vaishnavite had bested him in debate on an earlier occasion. The sting of defeat pricked him anew, leaving him incensed.

"Adei, *naamam*-flaunting Vaishnavite cheat!" he called out rudely. "How are you *here*, of all places? Shouldn't you be out foraging for *pongal* and *puliyodharai*?"

"I had my fill before coming here," replied Azhwarkkadiyaan at once. "But I hear that the pack of you in this Saivite monastery have grown bloated and lazy from glutting yourselves on ash! Poor things, what can you do, after all? Wasn't it your Siva Peruman who gulped down poison for lack of actual food to eat? Why, if our Narayanamurthy's sister Parvathi hadn't caught hold of his neck in time, what would have become of him?"

"*Adei*, Veera Vaishnava! That's quite enough of your babble!" flushed the Veera Saivar. "Don't fly too close to the sun! Mind, it was your Perumal who failed to catch even a glimpse of our Siva Peruman's hair even though he flew as high as he could!"

"Ah, a pretty story, that! Our Mahavishnu in his Vamana Avatar measured the very earth in a single step and the heavens in the next - there's no doubt your Sivan's head must have found itself somewhere beneath His lotus feet!" retorted Azhwarkkadiyaan.

"That your Mahavishnu had to take birth upon this earth is testimony to the monkey business he gets up to! And what *sort* of births were they? He came as a fish, didn't he? And a *turtle*?" jeered the Veera Saivar.

"That's all *you* know!" scoffed Azhwarkkadiyaan. "Why did *Bhagavan* deign to be born as a fish? To redeem the four vedas that were drowned in the sea, that's why! Even our Azhwars sing:

Aanatha selvaththu arambayargal tharchuzha
Vaanaalum selvamum mannarasum yaan venden
Thenaar pooncholai thiruvenkadachunaiyil
Meenai pirakkum thavamudayeyavene!"

[Not for me untold wealth or heavenly nymphs
Nor riches that touch the sky nor rule over earth
I pray and keep penance that I am born a fish
In a stream upon the hills of Thiruvengadam
Where gardens of flowers drip sweet nectar.]

"*Appane!* Your Azhwars were but twelve in number. Our Nayanmars count sixty! You would do well to remember that!" shot back the Veera Saivar.

"And you think it a feather in your cap, do you?" asked Azhwarkkadiyaan, raising a brow. "I suppose you crow with pride that the Pandavars were five and the Kauravas a hundred!"

"Impudent cur!" gasped the Veera Saivar. "Do you equate our noble Nayanmars to the Kaurava rogues? Why, it is *your* Azhwars who bear sinister epithets - *Pei* Azhwar, *Bootha*thaazhwar…"

"And what of your Siva Peruman's cohorts? They're all spooks and spectres, aren't they? You've handily forgotten that, I see!" snorted Azhwarkkadiyaan.

As the Veera Vaishnavar and Veera Saivar argued back and forth, each one's faction egged on the repartee with gleeful shouts and applause. It was at this juncture that Sivagnana Kandarathithar's noble consort Sembian Maadevi emerged from the monastery, accompanied by Nambiyaandar Nambi. Silence fell upon the crowd.

Mazhavaraiyar's daughter took leave of Nambiyaandar. As she approached the gathering, she cast a glance at Azhwarkkadiyaan. "Thirumalai, have you managed to pick a fight here, too?" she remarked.

"No, my Devi," protested Thirumalai. "We were not *fighting* with each other, not as *such;* we merely had a lively war of words. My lady, it is this Veera Saiva scholar who started the whole thing, in truth! Our debate rendered great entertainment to these people gathered here. That is why they did not enter the monastery."

"*Appane!* Not even in jest should one debate superiority among deities," said Sembian Maadevi gravely. "It will serve naught but to muddle the hearts of common men and women. My illustrious father-in-law, Paranthaka Thevar, built a golden roof over the Thillai Chittrambalam temple. So too did he renovate the Anantheeswarar shrine in Veeranarayanapuram and grant the temple an endowment. We must all strive to walk in his footsteps."

The Maadevi climbed into her palanquin, which started west. The royal car was flanked by soldiers, one faction marching ahead and another following in its wake. Azhwarkkadiyaan walked by its side. When the palanquin had covered some distance, Azhwarkkadiyaan turned to Periya Piratti. "Devi," he asked. "What became of the matter you hoped Nambiyandar would help you with?"

"My mind is untroubled and clear, Thirumalai," replied Sembian Maadevi calmly. "Nambiyaandar believes that if Madhuranthakan cannot be prevented from ascending the throne, the only recourse left is to publicly reveal the truth behind the affair. I wholeheartedly agree. I am quite resolute in my decision."

"The Mudhanmanthiri rather expected that Nambiyandaar would give such counsel. Even so, it is for the best that you have made this journey, my lady," said Azhwarkkadiyaan somberly. "Events have come to such a head that your verdict in this matter has grown crucial. A most frightening piece of news has arrived from

Kadambur. The people of this town are yet unaware of events; else not one of them would have stayed back here. They would have all left town to see the prince's funeral procession."

"Thirumalai!" cried the Maadevi, aghast. "What are you saying? What terrifying words you speak! Which prince? What funeral procession?"

"My condolences, *thaaye*! Such a grave tragedy has never struck the Chozha clan. Aditha Karikalar has breathed his last at the palace in Kadambur," said Azhwarkkadiyaan gently. "They say his death was unnatural. As to how it happened and at whose hands - those details are not yet clear. Many claim many things." He paused. "It is said that the Kadambur palace caught fire after Aditha Karikalar's demise; the building is naught but ashes, now. The prince's noble remains are being brought to Thanjai in procession. Kadambur Sambuvaraiyar and his kin are being escorted, as well - Thirukovilur Malayaman has reportedly imprisoned the family. They say that millions have joined the funeral procession, surrounding it from the front and back. We must cross the Kollidam before they reach the river bank."

"Oh, Thirumalai!" breathed Sembian Maadevi, stricken. "That truly is a dreadful piece of news! The tragedy that people believed the falling star foretold has come to pass, after all." Her voice cracked. "Ah! That such a mighty warrior - one who accomplished the impossible - should meet such a fate! *Ayyo*! Think of the torment Sundara Chozhar will suffer when he hears of this! The Chakravarthy is yet unwell; I worry about the harm that such news may bring to his health." The noble daughter of Mazhavaraiyar clasped her hands. "It is Siva Peruman, that very sea of compassion, who must protect the Chozha clan!

"*Thaaye*, the danger faced by the Chozha clan is only a part of the trials ahead. I fear that this tragedy may bring about the annihilation of the very Chozha *samrajyam*," replied Azhwarkkadiyaan quietly.

Sembian Maadevi's eyes grew fearful. "Why do you say that, Thirumalai?"

"It is likely that the chieftains of Chozha Naadu will go to battle against each other. Such a civil war would leave the empire weakened and flailing in a veritable sea of blood - circumstances that would doubtless embolden our enemies to march against us. I don't need to tell you, my lady, about the consequences of such an eventuality."

"Thirumalai!" exclaimed Sembian Maadevi, shocked. "Why do you think that the chieftains and lords will go to battle?"

"You know well why, *thaaye*. Some say that your noble son Madhuranthakan has the rightful claim to the crown. Others insist that it is Arulmozhi Varmar who must ascend the throne. Already, Periya Velar's armies lay siege to the Thanjai fort. Malayaman is headed towards Thanjai too, bearing the prince's remains. The chieftains who support the Pazhuvettarayars gather their forces." Azhwarkkadiyaan's face darkened. "It is likely that skirmishes will ensue in Thanjai and its surrounding territories; the soldiers of Chozha Naadu will fight and kill one another. The Kaveri and five rivers will flow not with torrents of water, but red blood! Even the Mudhanmanthiri is unable to think of a way to thwart this catastrophe!"

"Thirumalai, with the grace of God by my side, I shall prevent such a calamity from befalling this exalted *samrajyam!* I know what must be done; I came to see Nambiyaandar only to strengthen my will." Sembian Maadevi paused. "You say that civil war will break out in the event of a clash between Madhuranthakan and Arulmozhi Varman for the throne?"

"Yes, *thaaye*. How can that be avoided?" asked Azhwarkkadiyaan with worry. "The issue was moot until this moment, for Aditha Karikalar was older to both the princes. Alas, he is no more. Arulmozhi Varmar is younger to your noble son. But Malayaman,

Velar and the very people of Chozha Naadu will now stand firm that Arulmozhi Varmar be anointed the crown prince - a move that the Pazhuvettarayars will bitterly oppose!"

"Thirumalai, it matters little who agrees or disagrees with my decision - Madhuranthakan will not ascend the throne. I will see to that! I will fulfill the wishes of that *mahapurushan*, my noble husband," replied Sembian Maadevi, steel lacing her voice. "If it is certain that Madhuranthakan cannot stake his claim to succession, then there is no possibility of a civil war - am I correct?"

"Yes, *thaaye*. As matters stand, no one can save the Chozha empire from destruction but you. You are our only hope!"

"There is nothing I can achieve by myself. I pray that Maheshwaran, the Madhorubhagan who bears the divine Mother upon His own hallowed body, grants me the strength I need," replied the Periya Pirattiyar piously.

The pair continued in silence for a while. Presently, the Kollidam quay appeared in the distance.

"Thirumalai," began Sembian Maadevi. "You delivered a dreadful piece of news a short while ago. You reported that Aditha Karikalan has breathed his last. It was shocking enough to hear of the passing of a warrior beyond compare, a hero who ought to have ruled over the three worlds. But you mentioned too, did you not, that the prince met an unnatural death? How did it happen? Did he take his own life? Or do they claim him to be murdered?" asked the Periya Piratti.

"Devi, all sorts of hearsay abound regarding this matter. As the tragedy transpired in Sambuvaraiyar's home, Malayaman suspects that he and his family had a hand in the prince's death. He has imprisoned the whole lot of them and is escorting them to Thanjai. I believe Sambuvaraiyar's son Kandamaaran alone has managed to make his escape."

Sembian Maadevi considered his words. "I cannot find it in me to believe that Sambuvaraiyar is responsible for this calamity. However bitter the enmity, who can have the heart to slay the beloved son of the Chakravarthy whilst he is a guest in their own home? Sambuvaraiyar could not have done such a deed. Are there any reports of his testimony on the matter? How does he explain the prince's death?"

"Devi, do you remember an earlier occasion upon which a young warrior from the Vaanar clan arrived in Pazhaiyarai?" asked Azhwarkkadiyaan. "Kundhavai Pirattiyar dispatched him to Eezham with an *olai*, if you recall."

"Yes, I do remember. What about him?"

"It was that very youth who was found to be by the side of the prince's remains when the crime was discovered. Sambuvaraiyar claims that none but he could have committed the murder."

"Thirumalai, that could never be! I remember the boy quite well..."

"I concur, *thaaye*! But the circumstantial evidence and witnesses are stacked against Vandhiyathevan!"

"*Ayyo*, poor thing!" exclaimed Sembian Maadevi. "Ilaiya Piratti placed such confidence in that young man. This news will crush her!"

"*Thaaye*, I had intended to make a request to you about this matter myself," said Azhwarkkadiyaan. "Once you reach Kudanthai, my lady, it may be best for you to meet Ilaiya Piratti and have her accompany you to Thanjai."

"That is what I plan to do. Ilaiya Piratti waits for me, as a matter of fact."

"It would be best for you to break the news to Ilaiya Piratti yourself, Devi, before she hears of it from the mouths of others."

"Does that mean that you will not travel with me now, Thirumalai?" asked Sembian Maadevi.

Azhwarkkadiyaan bowed his head deferentially. "If you will permit me Devi, I wish to take my leave as soon as we reach the southern banks of the Kollidam."

"Where do you plan to go?"

"A dark mystery surrounds prince Karikalar's death. I wish to discover the truth behind the affair," replied Azhwarkkadiyaan, his eyes gleaming.

"And how do you propose to do that?"

"Devi, I believe I told you about the Pandiya Naadu conspirators on an earlier occasion. Well, I caught a glimpse of one of those very men as we passed by the southern bank of the Kollidam!"

Sembian Maadevi drew a sharp breath. "Why didn't you go in pursuit of him then and there?"

"It was only after we reached the northern bank of the Kollidam that news of Karikalar's death reached me, my queen!" Azhwarkkadiyaan folded his hands respectfully. "Please, Devi, give me leave. I know well the meeting place where the conspirators assemble."

"Then leave, by all means," replied Sembian Maadevi. "What should I tell Ilaiya Piratti Kundhavai?" she asked anxiously. "The thought of her gives me great worry."

Azhwarkkadiyan smiled thinly. "Tell her not to worry if Vandhiyathevan stands accused of the crime. Tell her that come hell or high water, I will root out the true criminal and fetch them!"

"Let the grace of God bring you success in your endeavour," replied Sembian Maadevi, that saintly woman who melted with *bhakthi* for Siva Peruman.

As the conversation came to an end, they found that they had reached the banks of the Kollidam. Stately boats awaited ashore for Periya Piratti Sembian Maadevi and her retinue.

Azhwarkkadiyaan wasted no time in choosing a small vessel for himself. Leaping into the ferry, he bade the boatman go as fast as he could. The little boat departed before the others and sped across the waters.

Hidden meanings and explanations:

The exchange between the Veera Saivar and Azhwarkkadiyaan is chock-full of barbs & jibes - the pair truly was being shockingly rude to each other. The Veera Saivar's reference to puliyodharai, for instance, is a swipe at the belief that the best recipe for said dish famously lies with Vaishnavite temples; while Azhwarkkadiyaan's retort is an irreverent reference to Lord Siva's feat of imbibing a deadly poison to protect the living creatures of the world.

44

The mountain cave

As soon as he reached the southern bank of the Kollidam, Azhwarkkadiyaan proceeded to head west. The lands had been overwhelmed by the Kollidam breach and he could see nothing but vast plains of water all around. Still, the flooded regions were draining quickly enough, just like the Kollidam's own waterline had soon retreated to stability. Azhwarkkadiyaan reached Thiruppurambiyam at last. He discovered that the town was relatively untouched by the deluge and marvelled at the sight. He remembered an age-old lore which spoke of a terrible *pralayam*, a great primaeval flood that had left the whole world inundated save the lands of Thiruppurambiyam. *Perhaps this is what gave rise to that part of the story,* mused Azhwarkkadiyaan as he cast an eye over the region. He made his way to the *pallippadai* in the jungle. Many trees had been felled by the storm; they lay sprawled across the forest floor, their broken, muddy roots splayed in the air. The foliage, however, remained quite thick and dense, affording an ideal hideout for him to surveil the area from. As Azhwarkkadiyaan watched, he caught sight of three men and a woman engaged in earnest conversation at the entrance to the *pallippadai* temple. When he peered closely at them from his vantage point, he realized that they were familiar to him after all. He had seen these three men among the group that had gathered in this same *pallippadai* forest at the very beginning, hatching plans for their covert mission. One was Soman Saambavan; another was Kramavithan; the third was Idumbankari. The woman was none other than the wife of the *padagotti* Murugaiyan. Idumbankari was speaking to the rest of the group, who seemed to be greatly enthused by the news he brought. "Alright then!" Azhwarkkadiyaan heard Soman Saambavan exclaim. "In that case, we shall repair to the foothills of Pachaimalai. The journey will take us two days."

Azhwarkkadiyaan decided to make himself scarce before they could leave and turned around, quiet as a mouse. The glint of a sharp knife pointed at his chest stopped him in his tracks. Azhwarkkadiyaan followed with his eyes the hand wielding the dagger, discovering to his relief that it was none other than Poonguzhali. He relaxed as they both recognized each other and smiled in mutual surprise.

Once he knew for sure that the conspirators had left, Azhwarkkadiyaan turned to Poonguzhali. "Poonguzhali, how did you come here from Thanjavur? Why?"

"To take revenge," came the grim reply.

Azhwarkkadiyaan was taken aback. "What revenge?" he asked, startled. "Why?"

Poonguzhali's lips thinned. "One of the men we saw just now was the foul knave who took to his heels after slaying my *athai*. I gave that villain unyielding chase and tracked him down to this place.

particularly vivid and terrifying nightmare. His wild eyes darted about the cave as he looked around frantically.

Nandhini appeared beside him. She was shorn of all finery. No jewels glinted about her person; her thick, silky hair fell in waves about her shoulders, loosened from their usual coiffure. And yet, she was a vision of sublime beauty. If anything, her allure seemed to have grown more enchanting than before. Nandhini spoke, her sweet voice suffused with loving care and sympathy. "*Ayya*," she said, holding out a clay bowl to Periya Pazhuvettarayar. "Please drink some of this *kanji*."

Periya Pazhuvettarayar turned to look at her. His face lit up and a childlike smile of joy spread over his lips.

"Nandhini, my queen! Was it you who spoke just now? Was that your voice?" he cried out happily. "Where are we? Were you the angel who brought me back to life as I floundered at the gates of death? My sweet, have you achieved the feat that Savithri wrought for Sathyavan? When I came to my senses, I thought that your delicate, petal-soft hands were caressing my chest - was that true, my love? You refused to lay a finger on me for three years - have you finally relented, my darling?" He reached out for the bowl eagerly. "Give it to me! Give me that bowl of *kanji*! Why, even simple porridge from your lovely hands is as sweet to me as the nectar of the gods!"

As Periya Pazhuvettarayar took the bowl from Nandhini's hands, a frighteningly abrupt change came over him. His head snapped up to stare at Nandhini with unconcealed hatred. When he spoke, his voice sounded starkly different from the loving tones of before. "Adi *paathagi*, hateful sinner! Demoness!" he spat. "Is it really you? Have you become so bold as to touch me? Were you trying to stab my chest? Did I spoil your plan by waking up?" He looked at the clay vessel in his hands. "Or do you mean to poison me? Ah, but even manna from your repulsive hands is naught but poison to me!" he cried and hurled the dish away. The earthen bowl violently struck the cave wall and shattered into a hundred pieces.

45

Pray, give me leave!

Nandhini seemed unsurprised by the frenetic rage Periya Pazhuvettarayar displayed. For three long years had that grand old man been wrapped around her little finger; the formidable warrior had been naught but her puppet all this while, dancing to her tune as she pulled the strings. The cords cut, the marionette had come to life and begun to think for itself. It appeared as if Nandhini had fully expected this eventuality to pass. She had no reason to exploit such a puppet any longer.

Nandhini got to her feet and prostrated herself before Periya Pazhuvettarayar. "Swami," she said, her voice trembling with emotion. "You have often said that my words sound sweeter to you than honey and ambrosia. They must now grate upon your ears as bitter poison, as sour as the *kanji* I offered you. Pray, do me the great kindness of allowing me to say a few words before I take my leave of you today." She gazed at him with limpid eyes. "The tongue that once fondly addressed me as your darling, your dear beloved - that very tongue today piled curses upon me as a sinner and demoness. It is true. I am an evil, vile woman. I truly am a *ratsasi*! I carried on deceiving you for three years. You deigned to accept me into your palace, a wretched orphan whom you found stranded in the forest. You saw to it that I was afforded dignity and respect, even from great queens and noble princesses. You went so far as to make an enemy of your brother Chinna Pazhuvettarayar, dear to you as your own life. Even the cruel mockery that people subjected you to on my account had no impact on the esteem you held for me. I made use of your unwavering confidence in me; I took advantage of you, who saw it fit to bestow upon me incomparable honours. It is true. I lived in your home only to fulfil my own ends. I did several things unbeknownst to you. I liaised with conspirators. I sullied the hearts of young men like Kandamaaran and Parthibendran. I brought them under my thumb and manipulated them to further my aim. But *ayya*, I have never betrayed you in one aspect. Since the day I wed you with the world as witness, I wholeheartedly accepted you as my noble husband. I have never once brought dishonour to your ancient clan which has produced generation after generation of indomitable warriors; never have I strayed from chastity. Even if I continue to live, my lord, the stain of that scandal will never darken your legacy…"

"Nandhini! What are you saying? What more ignominy can my clan bear? *Ayyo*! With my own hands… these very hands…" moaned Periya Pazhuvettarayar in anguish. "Adi wretched woman!" he roared, all of a sudden. "You carried a sword with you, did you not? Where is it? Wield it yourself to chop off my hands - that is the only service I ask of you!... No, no! These hands have work yet to do, a crucial task. Do not take seriously the words I spoke in haste and hack away at my hands!"

"Swami! I would never do such a thing!" cried Nandhini. "I failed to wield that sword upon the person I had waited to sate my vengeance upon for aeons. Just when I feared the moment would slip away, addled as I was, you came to my aid…"

"Adi vile fiend!" recoiled Periya Pazhuvettarayar in repulsion. "I came to your aid? How could you say such a thing? *Chandaali!* Demoness! If I had known that things would turn out this way, I would have never come there! Dear, sweet lord! Couldn't that wretch Yaman have taken me when I was flailing in the Kollidam floods?"

Nandhini looked stricken. "Swami, neither did you come to my aid nor did I ask you for help. You hail from a great clan that has dedicated life and death in service to the royal clan of the Chozhas, generation after generation; it is famed for its fierce loyalty for the Chozha kings. I, on the other hand, had come to wreak my vengeance upon them. That is why I did not reveal my true intentions to you. Many a time have I wondered if I could fulfill my goal through you. Pray, think! You curse me today as a *ratsasi* and a demoness; but once you stood enchanted by this very waif standing before you, inebriated my beauty as one who had drunk their fill of sweet wine. On those occasions, I was tempted to make use of you to achieve my aim. But I did not wish to bring disgrace upon your clan by forcing your hand in vile treachery. It was why I strove so hard to ensure your passage from Kadambur to Thanjai. You went, too. But Fate brought you back at the golden hour. You did not come forward to help me of your own accord, but Fate brought you to my aid at the right moment! Yes, ayya! It was Fate who sowed the seeds of suspicion in your heart, which grew wary of my chastity. If you had intended to stop me from taking my revenge, you would have made a public entrance; it was because you distrusted my morality that you came in disguise through the secret passage. Surely, your misgivings about my virtue should have been laid to rest! If not, I pray you find peace now, at the very least. The elders say that the husband and wife are to be helpmeets to each other. It is only because I remained true to you as a wife that Fate saw fit to bring you to my aid at the right moment…"

"Nandhini, enough! Stop!" burst out Periya Pazhuvettarayar. "Your words torture me beyond belief. Kill me instead and be done with it! My arms do not have the strength to stop you, should you choose to do away with me! My body is drained of energy, too. If you cannot muster the courage to slay me by the sword, why, truly do stir poison into this *kanji* and give it to me!"

"My king! Forgive me!" cried Nandhini, her voice full of sorrow. "No. No, you cannot bring yourself to forgive me. Surely that is impossible in this birth. I shall tell you one thing, my lord - listen well! Should the two of us take another birth, we will be unencumbered by memories of this life. We will recall nothing. That I made a home in your palace and deceived you; that I used the riches of your coffers to take my revenge; the events that unfolded at the Kadambur palace because of Fate; you will remember none of it and neither will I. It is my heart's desire to atone in my next birth the treachery I meted out to you in this one," she said, her lovely eyes glistening in the light. "When I am born again, I shall marry none but you. I shall be a truly loyal helpmeet. I will pray to all the gods for this very boon, as long as life clings onto this body!"

The Pazhuvettarayar was deeply moved. His heart swelled with emotion as he melted at her words. "Nandhini, go away!" he begged. "Leave this place forthwith and go! Begone! If you keep up this talk for even a little longer, I will lose my senses! I will fail my duty! Enough, *enough* I say of the twisted perversity you have enabled all these days! Do not break my mind and drive me insane! Begone, begone forthwith!"

"Swami, I apologize," replied Nandhini softly. "If I had paid heed to the suggestions of my companions, we would have crossed Pachaimalai by now and entered Kongu Naadu. But I did not have the heart to depart without taking your leave. You fell unconscious when we exited the Kadambur fort. I was told to abandon you and come away. I did not agree to that, either. I made them carry you upon their own shoulders as we travelled. Though we walked day and night with no rest, it cost us three days to reach our destination. Even after coming here to this place, they said that it was best to leave you behind and continue our journey. I stood my ground. I insisted that I would go with them only after you had regained consciousness and I had taken my leave of you. My wish has now come true." Nandhini paused. "You tried to kill me, my lord. There was justice in that. But Fate steered events to go another way. I saved your life, even as you sought to do away with mine. A short while ago, you threw away the *kanji* I brought you claiming it to be poison. But my lord, for the three days that you were lost to the world, it was I who nursed you; it was these very hands that poured water into your parched mouth to save you. For three years you celebrated me in your palace as a queen and showered me with exalted honours and dignities. I cannot repay any of that in this life. Even so, my lord, I consider it my good fortune that I had the opportunity to serve you these past three days. It shall give me some semblance of consolation for the remainder of my life. I shall go now, ayya! Pray, give me leave!"

"Nandhini, why ask for my permission to depart? Leave without another word. The longer you stay here, the more clouded my mind becomes!" despaired Periya Pazhuvettarayar.

"Yes. You may grow convinced to slay me, after all. Swami, if that comes to pass, this servant shall consider it a blessing to breathe her last at your hands." Nandhini's beautiful eyes met the Pazhuvettarayar's own. "My lord," she asked, "you came in disguise with the intention of killing me, did you not?"

"Why did I wear a disguise, you ask? You had a reason worked out, didn't you? You say I harboured suspicions upon your chastity and came in such a manner to discover the truth." The Pazhuvettarayar looked pained. "Truly, that is not the case. I came in disguise through the secret passage because I feared that if I appeared before you as Pazhuvettarayar, you would melt my heart with but a few sweet words. I came resolved to hurl the dagger at you as you stood stupefied, affording you no chance to speak. I threatened Idumbankari, the servant at the Kadambur palace; I wrested the knife from his hands before I came. I had another reason too, Nandhini! I came as a *kaalamugan* because I did not want to become an object of ridicule to a world that would doubtless suspect an old man of killing his young wife in a jealous rage. But Fate had another plans, like you said. I do not have it in me to make another such attempt. You may leave." Periya Pazhuvettarayar paused. "But tell me one last thing before you go! If I hadn't interfered, what would have happened? How were you planning to fulfill your aim?"

"Yes, yes!" exclaimed Nandhini. "I wanted to tell you that as well, my lord. Your anger left me flustered and confused. Swami! When you departed for Thanjai, I gave you my word that the *dharma* of your clan would not suffer ignominy by my hands. I strained every nerve to keep my vow to you. I planned to make use of either Manimekalai, Kandamaaran or Vandhiyathevan to fulfill my aim. I placed great hope in Manimekalai, in truth. I calculated that Karikalar would fly into a murderous rage at Vandhiyathevan, who was hiding in the chamber; I thought that he would advance upon him to slay him, whereupon Manimekalai would kill him instead. I expected that Vandhiyathevan would take on the blame to protect Manimekalai; I thought he would confess to the crime of his own accord. I reckoned that this would serve as my payback upon Pazhaiyarai Kundhavai as well. I weaved an intricate plan, but in the end the prince took his own life."

"No, Nandhini!" cried Periya Pazhuvettarayar, visibly tormented. "The prince did not take his own life! Do you think to trick me, too?

"Swami,' said Nandhini gently, "if you hadn't thrown Idumbankari's knife at that very moment, the prince would have taken his own life the next second using Veera Pandiyan's own sword."

"Yes, yes. If I had arrived but a heartbeat later, I would not have committed such unspeakable treachery. My suspicions would have turned on you, instead. Nandhini, the whims and fancies of Fate shaped events to happen the way they did. Nothing can be done now." Periya Pazhuvettarayar's eyes moistened. "Fate has been kind to me in one aspect, at the very least. You said, didn't you, that you wish to wed me in the next life if we both take another birth? In all my years, I have not heard words sweeter than those. Why, I haven't heard such lovely words from *you*, until this moment. When my body prepares to give up its spirit, I shall think upon these words as I embrace death. Yes, Nandhini! You and I cannot be together in this life. Leave my side!" He gazed at Nandhini. "Only, before you go, give me a little *kanji*, if any remains. If there is none, give me some water at the very least with your own hands. Take your leave after that!"

"So be it, *Ayya*," said Nandhini quietly. "I shall be indebted to you as long as I live for the kindness and compassion you have shown me!" She withdrew to the stove to fetch another bowl of *kanji*.

Azhwarkkadiyan decided to slip away from the cave. There was no further use in lingering now, for he had learned all that he had wanted to know. Besides, hanging around would only court danger. Concluding that it was best to think about next steps, Azhwarkkadiyaan emerged from the cave.

46

Azhwan in Peril

Azhwarkkadiyaan and Poonguzhali were sitting under a tree in the lush foothills of Pachaimalai.

"Girl, my work here is done. Shall we leave?" asked Azhwarkkadiyaan.

"*Vaishnavare!* If you've done what you came to do, then leave, by all means. The mission I came for is unfinished yet," replied Poonguzhali.

"And what mission did you come here for?"

"I came in search of the evil cur who killed my *athai*."

"Have you not spotted him yet?" asked Azhwarkkadiyaan, surprised. "Isn't he over there, among that band of conspirators?"

"He is."

"What else do you want?"

Poonguzhali shot Azhwarkkadiyaan an exasperated glance. "Did I come here to gaze at that blessed man's face from afar, hoping to gather virtue?" she demanded. "I came to settle the score. An eye for an eye, a murder for a murder."

"Poonguzhali, who are we to punish those who have done wrong? Such matters are best left to God, surely?"

"I'm not sure He exists," snorted Poonguzhali. "Or if He *does*, I'm not sure that He takes the trouble to chastise the vile deeds of men. "

"Let's leave God aside, then," replied Azhwarkkadiyaan affably. "You must agree, at the very least, that our society holds kings responsible for bringing criminals to justice. It stands to reason that only the authorities established by the king can mete out fair punishment."

"What if kings and their delegates fail to carry out their duties properly?"

"How could we ever be sure of such a thing?"

"*Vaishnavare!*" flared up Poonguzhali. "It was a wretch from that very gang over there who threw a spear at my *athai*, a woman who was the very essence of love. That sinner killed an innocent bereft of the power of speech; a naive woman who had been unlucky all her life, yet incapable of wishing harm upon anyone. Everyone saw the whole thing - the Chakravarthy, his queens, even Chinna Pazhuvettarayar, the *thalapathy* of the Thanjai fort. Yet, they allowed him to make his escape."

"Poonguzhali, did they make no effort at all to catch Soman Saambavan?"

"The Chakravarthy - who had spurned my *athai* all her life - took her onto his lap and wept with sorrow. The rest simply stood where they were, dumbstruck. Only Chinna Pazhuvettarayar stirred to action when I declared my intention to pursue the killer. But he too had to turn back in the underground passage."

"Why?"

"As we walked the underground path, we heard a wail in the dark. Chinna Pazhuvettarayar pounced towards the sound and caught hold of the person standing there. 'The killer has been caught!' came his voice. 'No, no, I didn't kill anyone!' came another voice. When Chinna Pazhuvettarayar realized whose voice it was, he was stunned. '*Ayyo*! Why did you come here?' he asked. 'I came to see if the treasures were safe,' replied the voice in the dark. "*Ayyo*! Dear lord! If anybody sees you here, what will they think? Won't they suspect *you* to be the one who attempted to kill the Chakravarthy?' asked Kalanthaka Kantar. 'The Chakravarthy has died, you say?' eagerly asked his dear son-in-law Maduranthaka Thevar. 'Idiot boy! Come with me! Quickly now, before someone sees you!' replied Kalanthaka Kantar. He caught his son-in-law by the hand and hurried away."

Poonguzhali raised her chin and looked Azhwarkkadiyan in the eye. "I tracked down the killer all by myself, pushing through fatigue and strife. And you ask me to give up the mission I came so far for?"

"Girl," said Azhwarkkadiyaan admiringly, "you ought to have been born a boy. You would have doubtless risen to become the Chakravarthy of a great empire! Never mind. Listen to what I have to say and let me know your judgement. Can one accuse another of intentional murder, if the killer accidentally took the life of a person other than his true target?"

Poonguzhali frowned. "I don't understand your question," she said. "Having killed a person, he is guilty of murder in any case, isn't he?"

"How can that be?" asked Azhwarkkadiyaan. "You must have listened to the epic Ramayana, surely. Take the tale of Dasarathar, who let loose an arrow thinking he was aiming at an elephant drinking water. The weapon struck the son of a *rishi*, instead. Was Dasarathar punished for the crime of killing a *rishi's* son? No. Now, take Soman Saambavan, whom you have come so far in pursuit of. He threw his spear intending to kill the Chakravarthy. The Chakravarthy lives yet, but your *athai* breathed her last because she came in between and took the spear unto herself. She gave up her life of her own accord, didn't she, akin to one who chooses to commit suicide? Then how can Soman Saambavan stand accused of murder?"

"*Vaishnavare*, you have a strange sense of justice," said Poonguzhali, gazing at Azhwarkkadiyaan with an odd expression on her face.

Azhwarkkadiyaan smiled. "Not just me." he said, "Narayanamurthy, the divine ruler of the universe, can be said to have a strange sense of justice, too. Look around! The men and women who commit myriad sins flourish and thrive; but good people, souls who gather much virtue, lead a life of struggle before they die. And yet, we must believe that this design is somehow driven by God's sense of justice. Don't you agree?"

Poonguzhali sniffed. "You and your Narayana can do as you both please; it is of little concern to me what comes of it. I shall stay true to *my* sense of justice. I will fullfil it as I deem fit before I turn back!" she declared.

"Poonguzhali, I lay this argument before you not merely for your sake," said Azhwarkkadiyan in earnest. "In that mountain cave over there are two people. One of them is the person who killed Aditha Karikalar. But it was not intentional. The knife that was thrown was, in truth, aimed at another; the weapon happened to strike the prince and killed him instead. Can that person be called a killer?"

"*Vaishnavare*, don't confuse me," cried Poonguzhali. "Who are these people in the mountain cave?"

"The Dhanaadhikaari of the Chozha *samrajyam*, the lord of the Thanjai palace; the incomparable warrior who has fought twenty four wars and bears sixty four battle wounds upon his eminent self; the lord who levies taxes, the illustrious leader of the chieftains, the noble husband of Nandhini Devi - it is Periya Pazhuvettarayar himself who lies there in that cave!"

Azhwarkkadiyan spoke the words aloud in a stentorian voice, akin to a grand herald announcing Periya Pazhuvettarayar's arrival. He had hardly finished when Ravidasan, Revadasan, Parameswaran, Soman Saambavan and the other conspirators came charging at the pair. Poonguzhali moved quick as a bird, distancing herself from the gang in the blink of an eye. Ravidasan held a short staff in his hand, which he brandished threateningly as he spoke. "*Adei* charlatan of a Vaishnava! Anbil Aniruddhar's spy!" he cried. "You've finally fallen into our hands, have you? Three plots we hatched. We tasted success with but one of them; we failed to fulfill the other two. But we shan't rue those blunders anymore." His cruel mouth twisted with unholy delight. "We spent three years searching high and low for you. And now we have you at last! he beamed. "This time, you will not escape!"

"*Appane*!" Azhwarkkadiyaan replied, louder than before. "Who is the seeker? Who runs away? We're all children of divine Narayanamurthy! Can a single atom shift its place without His will?" Azhwarkkadiyaan's eyes shone. "Ravidasa! Hearken to me! Let your companions pay heed to my words, too. Relinquish the pantheon of minor gods and seek absolute refuge in Lord Mahavishnu! *Bhagavan* will forgive all your sins and grant you salvation! Don't waste your life in mortal endeavours. Make the most of this human birth by venerating Narayanan! Seek a place for yourselves in holy *paramapadam*!" He leapt to his feet in excitement. "Come, let me hear you all sing with me!

Narayanane dheivam -
Namellorum thuthi seivom!"

[Narayana is the only Lord
Him we shall ever adore!]

Azhwarrkadiyaan launched into an ardent song, sending Ravidasan into peals of laughter.

"Why, Vaishnavane! Isn't Lord Paramasivan a divinity, too?" asked Ravidasan, chuckling. "Will we be denied entry to *paramapadam* if we venerate Paramasivan?"

"Paramasivan is the god who *destroys!*" replied Azhwarkkadiyaan with animated gestures. "Narayanan is the god who *protects.* Have you forgotten how our Narayanamurthy saved a poor elephant caught in the jaws of a crocodile?"

"*Appane,* the same Vishnu *bhagavan* who saved the elephant also killed the crocodile, did he not?" countered Ravidasan with a grin. "Ravanan, Kumbakarnan, Hiranyakshan, Hiranyakashipu, Sisupalan, Danthavikkran - didn't He destroy every single one of these people?"

"Even those who meet their end at the hands of our Perumal attain Sri Vaikuntam," said Azhwarkkadiyaan piously. "Hiranyan, Ravanan, Sispualan - *Bhagavan* gave them all a place in Vaikuntam! On the other hand, your Paramasivan annihilated the entire population of Tripura. Did He grant them all deliverance?""

"Alright, alright. That's enough of your tales," replied Ravidasan, narrowing his eyes. It was beginning to dawn on him that this conversation would carry on endlessly if enabled. "Let us see if your Narayanan comes to *your* rescue!" He raised the short staff high above his head, preparing to land a deathblow upon the Veera Vaishnavar.

Poonguzhali made ready to go to Azhwarkkadiyaan's aid. She had already unsheathed the dagger by the side of her hip when she saw a woman running towards them from the mountain cave, her long, loose tresses streaming in the wind. Poonguzhali thought it was her *athai* Mandhakini at first glance; she stopped dead, forgetting to even breathe. "No," she thought, with a jarring flash of insight. "No, this is the Pazhuvoor Rani Nandhini!"

By the time Poonguzhali recovered from the shock, Nandhini had already drawn close to Azhwarkkadiyaan. She caught hold of Ravidasan's raised staff with both her hands.

"No! Do not harm my brother!" cried Nandhini in terror. "Ravidasa!

If I truly am your queen, you will put the staff down!"

"I thank you for your concern, sister," cut in Azhwarkkadiyaan, sounding unperturbed. "But truly, these people could not have hurt me. Narayanamurthy, the Lord that I worship with all my heart and soul, would have protected me from harm."

Ravidasan chortled. "And exactly how would Narayanamurthy have saved you?" he jeered. "Would he have popped out of this tree, perhaps, like the time he emerged from a pillar to save Prahalathan?"

Azhwarkkadiyaan studied Ravidasan as he stood smirking. "*Mandhiravadhi*! Don't you believe what I say? Alright, then!" he declared, his voice taking on an imperious edge. "Look at that Ayyanar temple that stands a short distance away! You can see the three horses that stand in front of that shrine, can't you? By the grace of divine Sriman Narayanan, those horses of clay shall come to life! Soldiers shall ride upon them towards us, bearing spears in their hands. They will clap you in chains and save me from danger!"

As Azhwarkkadiyan made this astonishing speech, everyone followed his pointing finger. They stood shell-shocked, unable to believe their own eyes; for it seemed to them that the horses of clay truly had come to life! The steeds appeared to be galloping fiercely towards the group, each carrying a soldier with a lance in hand!

Hidden Meanings and Explanations

Azhwarkkadiyaan & Ravidasan's quarrel is packed with references to tales from olden epics. The Veera Vaishnavar, if you notice, often cites an episode between Narayanamurthy and an elephant - popularly known as Gajendra Moksha - in which the Lord famously saved a pious pachyderm from the jaws of a hungry crocodile.

47

NANDHINI VANISHES

The group gaped at the horses, stupefied. Ravidasan was the first to recover from the shock.

"Devi," he cried, turning to a stunned Nandhini. "This fraud of a Vaishnavan has clearly been up to his old tricks! I warned you time and again not to trust this fellow - I *told* you that he is a spy!" Ravidasan clenched his fists. "He has brought men along to trap us. But he cannot lay a finger on us, my lady. Why, even that god he worships, that very Narayanan, has no hope of catching us! Come, let us leave this place at once," urged the *mandhiravadhi*. "We can climb the mountain before the horses reach!"

"Nandhini, do not go with these heinous sinners!" cut in an earnest Azhwarkkadiyaan. "We have suffered tragedy enough from your ties with them!"

Nandhini turned to Azhwarkkadiyaan beseechingly. "Thirumalai, for many days have I implored you for a favour. Do you remember?" she asked. "I begged you to take me to my mother's side. Promise me now, at least, that you will; I shall come away with you. Else, I will go with them."

Azhwarkkadiyaan looked crestfallen at her words. "Nandhini, I am afraid that is beyond me…" he began. An alarmed Ravidasan interjected himself into the conversation. "Who the devil is *he* to take you?" he asked belligerently. "I will take you to her side myself. Come away, now!" he pressed.

"Yes, yes!" agreed Azhwarkkadiyaan. "He will take you to the side of your mother in Yamalokam! He will dispatch you to the afterlife, like he did her! Nandhini, there is little need for you to fraternize with these wicked fiends. It was one of these very men who slayed your mother!" Ravidasan turned black as death and shot daggers at the Veera Vaishnavite. "Look, look at the *mandhiravadhi's* face!" cried Azhwarkkadiyaan. "The truth of him being a killer is practically written across it!"

Ravidasan's face contorted with rage. "Lies, lies!" he shouted.

Nandhini eyes, peaceful thus far, now blazed with a rabid fury. "Thirumalai, is it true? Has my mother truly died? Can I never see her?" she asked.

"If you find my words hard to believe, ask this young lady here," replied Azhwarkkadiyaan, gesturing to Poonguzhali. " It was one among these rogues - Soman Saambavan - who flung a spear at your mother and slayed her. This girl has come in pursuit of the man who killed her *athai*. Poonguzhali, tell her!"

"Yes, I saw it with my own eyes," confirmed Poonguzhali grimly. "I came here only to take my revenge upon my *athai's* killer!"

Her words elicited a hysterical cackle from Nandhini, who appeared to be in the throes of a frenzy. "You came for revenge, you say?

Revenge?" she shrieked. "Isn't it enough, the ruination that has come to pass in *my* wretched quest for revenge?" She swivelled to face Ravidasan, her face alight with wrath. "Traitor!" she hissed. "*Chandaala!* What have you done?"

"Rani, you're gravely mistaken!" scrambled Ravidasan. "I did not betray you! Soman Saambavan hurled the spear at the Chakravarthy. That mute lunatic of a woman threw herself in the way! It was her fate to die thus!" His voice took on an urgent tone. "Now, what do you say? Will you come with us or not? There, the horses fast approach - they've drawn closer!"

His words did not seem to reach Nandhini's ears. She abruptly slumped to the ground and covered her eyes with her hands. Nandhini keened in abandon, great sobs wracking her body. The sounds of crying that issued from her were mingled with outbursts of maniacal laughter.

Ravidasan turned to his men. "Run!" he cried. "Make haste and climb the mountain! It is futile to have faith in the Rani any longer!"

The panicked gang took to their heels.

"*Vaishnavane*!" roared Ravidasan. "I owe you recompense for all the mischief you've done!" He raised his staff and landed an emphatic blow upon the Vaishnavite's head. With that parting gift, Ravidasan made a break for the mountain.

"Namo Narayana!" moaned Azhwarkkadiyaan and gingerly rubbed his head.

The fleeing conspirators vanished into the mountain cave. Soon, they appeared on a small hill atop the cave, where the river Kaveri turned into a misty waterfall and cascaded down the mountain in white torrents.

It was at this very moment that the horses arrived at the foothills. It had taken the troop all this while to reach the place, for there was no proper path to lead them; they had been forced to navigate the large boulders that dotted the region.

Azhwarkaddiyaan noticed that Chinna Pazhuvettarayar and Kandamaaran were the first to arrive on horseback. He saw that they were accompanied by Senthan Amuthan, who, oddly enough, seemed to be bound and strapped to his horse.

"Come, come," greeted Azhwarkkadiyaan. "You have arrived just in time."

Chinna Pazhuvettarayar and Kandamaaran alighted from their horses. Their attention went to Nandhini, who was still sitting upon the ground and crying her heart out.

Kandamaaran took a few steps towards Nandhini. He tried to speak, but found himself robbed of words.

Chinna Pazhuvettarayar looked at Azhwarkkadiyaan, bemused. "*Vaishnavane*! How on earth did you come to be here? Why?"

"Thalapathy, I came in search of the very person that you seek as well," replied Azhwarkkadiyaan. "Periya Pazhuvettarayar is over there, in that cave!"

Chinna Pazhuvettarayar stood stock still. "Is he truly? Is he alive yet?" he asked anxiously.

"Yes, he is alive," said Azhwarkkadiyaan, smiling. "Why, even Yaman will think twice before he reaches out for your *thamaiyanar!* The attempts those killers made upon his life were all vain," he said, pointing to Ravidasan and the rest upon the hilltop.

"Who are they? Why do you call them killers?" asked Chinna Pazhuvettarayar, squinting up at them.

"Those men are none other than the *mandhiravadhi* Ravidasan and his cronies. They are part of Veera Pandiyan's league of *abathudhavis,*" explained Thirumalai. "They were the ones who attempted to assassinate the Chakravarthy. They are the vile sinners who slayed prince Aditha Karikalar!"

"Lies, lies!" burst out Kandamaaran. "The man who murdered the prince is Vandhiyathevan! Are you trying to shield your friend from the consequences of his crime?" he demanded.

"Idiot! Hold your tongue!" snapped Chinna Pazhuvettarayar. He turned back to the Vaishnavan with a stony look on his face. "Did they try to kill the Dhanaadhikaari too?" he asked. "How did he escape from them?"

"He made his escape with the help of Pazhuvoor Ilaiya Rani, who sits here weeping."

"Why is the Ilaiya Rani weeping?"

"She had just learned that her mother is dead. Can't these questions wait?"

"Yes, yes!" said Chinna Pazhuvettarayar. "I must see Periya Pazhuvettarayar!" He looked at Azhwarkkadiyaan. "Go and tell him that I am here."

Even at that juncture, the reverence Chinna Pazhuvettarayar held for his brother had not dimmed in the slightest. He hesitated to appear before his *thamaiyanar* without due notice.

"*Ayya*, your *thamaiyanar* won't go anywhere else, now. I shall inform him of your arrival. Those killers over there, on the other hand…" said Azhwarkkadiyaan looking up at the conspirators. "Aren't you going to make an effort to catch them?"

Chinna Pazhuvettarayar pressed an exasperated hand to his forehead. "Yes, yes!" he cried. "I lost my senses thus upon an earlier occasion as well - I allowed the Chakravarthy's would-be assassin to escape!"

"He hasn't escaped. There he is, right there on that hilltop! Quickly now, give the order to your men!"

Thalapathy Kalanthaka Kantar turned at once to his soldiers and issued the order. The men alighted from their horses and sprinted to a site in the foothills where the waterfall spilled to the ground. They had hardly reached the place when large, heavy boulders tumbled down from the hilltop above. The soldiers darted here and there, dodging the attack; yet the boulders found their mark with a few, knocking them down like toys.

"Do you know how they climbed to the top of the hill?" asked Chinna Pazhuvettarayar as he watched.

"They entered the cave and made their ascent. There seems to be a secret path through there," mused Azhwarkkadiyaan. "Come, let us go see for ourselves." He led the way to the cave, with Kalanthaka Kantar and Kandamaaran close behind.

A tall, majestic figure emerged from within the shelter, swaying on its feet. It stood at the mouth of the cave and peered at the approaching group. It took quite some time for the younger brother to recognize his *thamaiyanar*.

For it was none other than Periya Pazhuvettarayar who stood there. He bore wounds all over his body and his face looked sallow and peaky. "Anna!" cried out Chinna Pazhuvettarayar and embraced him warmly.

Tears flowed from the elder's eyes. "*Thambi*," he mumbled, his voice aquiver. "You gave me fair warning on so many occasions. I paid little heed to your words; now here I stand, a ruined man."

Azhwarkkadiyaan and Kandamaaran attempted to enter the cave.

Periya Pazhuvettarayar stopped them. "Where are you going?" he asked.

"The killers snuck into this cave…"

"Which killers?"

"The *mandhiravadhi* Ravidasan and his crew."

"They are not killers," said Periya Pazhuvettarayar quietly.

"See!" cried out Kandamaaran triumphantly. "Didn't I say that the killer is Vandhiyathevan?"

Periya Pazhuvettarayar looked at him closely. "How did this fool of a boy get here?" he asked.

Chinna Pazhuvettarayar glanced at the youth. "It was Kandamaaran who brought the news from Kadambur."

"What news?"

"He came bearing the report that prince Karikalar had breathed his last. Sambuvaraiyar sent a message through him advising us to gather all our forces at once. He feels we must make our move to seat Maduranthakar upon the throne."

"Ah, is that so?" replied Periya Pazhuvettarayar listlessly. He evinced no energy or enthusiasm at the report. "How is the situation in Thanjavur?" he asked after a moment.

"*Anna*, that answer requires some detailing on my part. You seem to be indisposed at the moment. Pray, shall we sit down and talk?" asked Chinna Pazhuvettarayar, concerned.

The Dhanaadhikaari seated himself where he stood, at the mouth of the cave.

"*Ayya*," began the Vaishnavan. "If it pleases you to give way, we will enter the cave and see if there is a path to the hilltop."

"Why?" asked Periya Pazhuvettarayar.

"Ravidasan's gang entered this cave to climb up," answered Thirumalai.

Periya Pazhuvettarayar shook his head. "There is little use in entering the cave, *Appane!* They have blocked the path you seek by rolling down a boulder from above. In fact, the rock was in danger of falling upon me; it was by the grace of God that I managed to escape with my life intact. The two of you can go take a look, if you wish. See if there is another way that leads to the hilltop."

As Azhwarkkadiyaan and Kandamaaran walked away, Periya Pazhuvettarayar's gaze fell upon Senthan Amudhan and Poonguzhali.

"Who are they?" he asked. "Why are they here?"

"The girl is Poonguzhali, the daughter of Thyaga Vidangar of Kodikkarai. She came seeking the men who killed her *athai*," explained Chinna Pazhuvettarayar. "Senthan Amudhan here came in search of her. It was only with his help that we were able to come here and find you."

"Tell me everything that happened in Thanjai - spare no detail!" said Periya Pazhuvettarayar all of a sudden. Chinna Pazhuvettarayar obliged. He described how one of the *mandhiravadhi's* men had hidden himself in the treasury, biding his time; how he had hurled his spear at the Chakravarthy; and how Mandhakini Devi had thrown herself in harm's way to save his life, sacrificing her own.

"*Anna*," continued Chinna Pazhuvettarayar, "in the midst of all this, the Kodumbalur Velan laid siege to the Thanjai fort out of the blue, with a great army at his command. Since you were not around, I had a hard time deciding whether we ought to go to war with him or not. I couldn't ask the Chakravarthy his opinion on the matter, either. The Mudhanmandhiri Aniruddhar is at the fort, even now - it was he who suggested that the decision could wait until your arrival. He felt it would be sufficient to defend the fort until then. Fortunately, prince Arulmozhi Varmar and Kodumbalur Velar's daughter Vanathi arrived at the fort. The prince came in the guise of a mahout accompanying Vanathi, who said that she had an urgent message from Ilaiya Piratti. I thought it was prudent to have Velan's daughter inside the fort at that juncture, so I allowed the elephant that she was riding to enter. It was at the entrance to the Chakravarthy's palace that I learned the mahout was none other than prince Arulmozhi Varmar. I was quite shaken, to tell the truth. *Anna*," said Chinna Pazhuvettarayar earnestly, "there is no doubt that the Chinna Ilavarasar possesses a remarkable power. When I glimpsed his noble face, my hands and legs began to tremble; my very heart melted at his sight! My hands came together in greeting of their own accord. It became incumbent on me to welcome him. Hardly surprising then, isn't it, that the people of Chozha Naadu lose their very heads when it comes to prince Arulmozhi Varmar?"

"Enough, enough!" cut in Periya Pazhuvettarayar. "There's hardly anything new in that - we know this already, don't we? I had a suspicion that the news of Arulmozhi Varman's drowning was nothing but a pack of tales. I see that I was right, after all. Tell me what happened after that. Why did the prince enter the fort in the guise of a mahout?" he asked.

"He reckoned that Kodumbalur Velar would stop him from entering the fort if it was known that he was the prince; he also feared that Velan's men would raise a ruckus. And so, he came in disguise. The prince does deserve due praise for his quick thinking," gushed Chinna Pazhuvettarayar, admiration lacing his tone. "It was whilst he was in audience with the Chakravarthy that the killer threw his spear from the upper quarters. By the grace of God, the weapon struck the mute lunatic and she died. If it had assaulted the Chakravarthy and dealt him a fatal blow, our clan would have suffered an indelible stain on our honour…"

"As though we are free of dishonour now! An indelible blemish has indeed sullied our hoary name!" murmured Periya Pazhuvettarayar under his breath.

"What did you say, *Anna*?" asked Kalanthaka Kantar.

"Nothing. Go on, tell me what happened after that," replied the Dhanaadhikaari.

"A wondrous miracle!" exclaimed Chinna Pazhuvettarayar. "The Chakravarthy who had been unable to walk all this time, regained the strength of his legs! He ran towards the mute woman and took her onto his lap; he began to murmur and moan at length. We were all staring transfixed at the sight for quite some time, rigid in our places. It was this very Poonguzhali who broke the silence with a declaration. 'I shall capture the killer!' she cried and set off running." He glanced at Poonguzhali. "It is my ardent wish that she receives the best of fortunes in this life. It is on account of her that I am blessed to be by your side at this very moment, even in the state that you are in..."

"*Thambi,*" said Periya Pazhuvettarayar, tears brimming in his eyes, "The *puranic* stories make mention of men who were said to bear extraordinary loyalty towards their elder brothers. But I am certain there is none among them to equal you in their devotion." He took a deep breath. "Never mind. Go on, tell me what happened next."

"I followed Poonguzhali in her pursuit and entered the underground passage in the treasury. There, I caught hold of someone in the dark. I thought it was the assassin, but when I heard his voice, I realized that it was Maduranthaka Thevar."

"And what was the reason he gave for taking the treasury passage?"

Chinna Pazhuvettarayar hesitated. "I all unclear about that, myself. He did not give me a proper reply when I asked. I feared that someone would suspect him to be the assassin..."

"Perhaps that is the truth. Who knows?"

"No, *anna!* That simpleton does not have it in him to do such a thing. Besides, I saw with my own eyes the man who hurled the spear and made his escape," pointed out Chinna Pazhuvettarayar. "Madhuranthakan did not readily agree to come away from the treasury. I had to patiently make him understand the precariousness of the situation. I led him back to the palace and left him in the company of the guards. I thought I would return to the treasury, but it came to light that other, graver events had transpired. Rumours had begun to spread among the people of the Chakravarthy's demise. I also learned that the Kodumbalur Velar had ordered his men to attack the fort. Velar's armies had been fortified quite formidably by the Kaikolar forces. Our own men were not quite prepared to face them; the absence of my leadership at the fort gates proved to be a weakness as well. The Velar and Kaikolar troops succeeded in infiltrating the fort by breaking its gates and scaling the perimeter walls. By the time I arrived at the fort gates, sixteen thousand soldiers had gained ingress into the stronghold. Our own men were only about two thousand in number, but they fought bravely with the insurgents. I stepped in and issued orders to cease the skirmish. I decided that there was little point in remaining at the fort; I left the stronghold with our soldiers. The Velar and Kaikolar armies tried to stop us, but we engaged them in spirited combat. We struck their forces down, brother! I sent a message thus to Boodhi Vikarama Kesari - '*If the family of the Pazhuvoor clan or Maduranthaka Thevar suffer but the slightest wound, I will annihilate the Kodumbalur clan!'* Warning delivered, I lost no time in swifty making my way to Kodumbalur, where I thought I would find you. I ran into Kandamaaran on the way, upon the banks of the Kudamurutti river. He was coming on horseback, riding as hard as he could. He brought his horse to a halt when he saw the *panai* flag of Pazhuvoor. The news he came bearing was quite an unsettling one. He reported that it had been a few days since you had made your departure from Kadambur for Thanjai, adding that Periya Sambuvaraiyar had sent a message for you. When he learned that you hadn't arrived at Thanjai, he was shocked as well. I asked him about the message that Sambuvaraiyar had sent. I learned that prince Karikalar had met his demise at the hands of Vandhiyathevan; the Periya Sambuvaraiyar felt that given the circumstances, there would be no better opportunity to seat Maduranthaka Thevar on the throne and advised us to send word to our allies and gather our forces. His message rang wise and prudent to my ears. I believed then that you were, in fact, involved in the task of gathering our armies; I trusted that you would arrive soon. I stationed our Pazhuvoor contingent in the region of the Thiruppurambiyam ridge, between the Manni and Kollidam rivers. I issued immediate orders to draft and dispatch missives upon horseback to Mazhapadi Thennavan, Mazhavarayar, Kundrathoor Kizhar, Mummudi Pallavarayar, Thanathongi Kalingarayar, Anjatha Singa Mutharayar and Rettai Kudai Rajaliyar. I sent word to them to bring their armies to Thiruppurambiyam. *Anna*! Worry not - we shall destroy Kodumbalur Velar and Thirukovilur Malayaman in such absolute terms that they shall not dare to raise their heads in our presence! We will succeed in seating Maduranthaka Thevar on the throne!" roared Chinna Pazhuvettarayar fervently as he ended his detailed report.

However, it did not appear as if his words bestowed the slightest enthusiasm upon Periya Pazhuvettarayar, whose attention was drawn to another matter.

"*Thambi*, who is that?" he asked. "Who sits there sobbing into her hands?"

"*Anna*, do you not recognize her?" cried Chinna Pazhuvettarayar. "That is none other than the Ilaiya Rani! Poor soul. She seems to have gone through much strife in order to save you. Please pardon me for the complaints I suffered you to bear on her account, *Anna*! I hear that it was Ravidasan and his men who had imprisoned you, and that the Ilaiya Rani came in pursuit to deliver you from peril! That *is* the truth, isn't it?" asked Kalanthaka Kantar.

"Yes, yes," assured Periya Pazhuvettarayar. "It was the Ilaiya Rani who saved my life. If Nandhini had not taken care of me, you could not have seen me alive. The world would have never learned the truth!"

"Ah!" breathed Kalanthaka Kantar. "I was ignorant of the Ilaiya Rani's good heart myself. How can the world know?"

Periya Pazhuvettarayar seemed to pay no heed to the remark. "Hasn't Nandhini taken her leave, yet? I thought she would have gone away with those men who fled to the hilltop," he said.

"How can the Ilaiya Rani bring herself to leave you behind, *Anna!*" exclaimed Chinna Pazhuvettarayar.

"Never mind that. How did you all discover where we were and come here, to this place?" asked the elder brother.

"We had made camp close to the *pallippadai* at Thiruppurambiyam. Kandamaaran was the lookout; he kept watch over the banks of the Kollidam. He spotted Senthan Amudhan in the process of boarding a boat. Kandamaaran caught hold of him and brought him to the camp. It was Senthan Amudhan who had helped Vanthiyathevan escape from us on an earlier occasion - you do recall that I had imprisoned Amudhan for a spell? Kandamaaran was quite irate with him already, so he captured him suspecting him to be a spy. When we interrogated him, we learned news of you. It turned out that Senthan Amudhan had left in search of his uncle's daughter Poonguzhali, who had set off all by herself to catch a killer. Apparently, Poonguzhali had forbade him from accompanying her and had sent him back; he had continued to follow her in secret to keep an eye on her. He happened to overhear the conspirators in discussion near the Thiruppurambiyam *pallippadai*. That was how he came to know that Ravidasan's gang had captured you and that they had taken you to the Pachaimalai region. When he heard that Poonguzhali and the Vaishnava Azhwarkkadiyaan were also headed towards Pachaimalai, he had attempted to follow in their wake without their knowledge. When we heard this, Kandamaaran and I gathered fifty men and set off. Senthan Amudhan insisted that he would come, too; we thought that his presence could work in our favour, so we tied him to a horse and brought him along! It turns out that it was a good thing we came. We have found you! What else is there to worry about, *anna*? Come, let us leave forthwith. I shall make arrangements to have you carried, so that you do not suffer the slightest discomfort. A great army must have gathered at Thiruppurambiyam by now. We shall reclaim the Thanjavur fort within a mere *jaamam*!" said Chinna Pazhuvettarayar.

"Yes," agreed Periya Pazhuvettarayar. "We must repair at once to Thanjavur." He stood up with effort and slowly walked towards Nandhini Devi.

Nandhini was sitting on a boulder and crying all this while. When she heard the sound of Periya Pazhuvettarayar clearing his throat, she leapt to her feet. She looked all around, her eyes shining with a wild, manic light.

Azhwarkkadiyan, who was standing beside her, spoke in a soft voice. "Nandhini, signal your acceptance now, at the very least," he urged. "Say that you will come with me! We shall leave this country and travel north. We shall tour the celebrated *kshetrams* of Brindavanam, Vada Madurai, Ayodhya, Kasi, Haridwaram and Rishikesham! We shall spend the rest of our lives in sweetness, carrying the holy name of Sriman Narayana on our lips and singing the beautiful *pasurams* of the *azhwars.* I will relinquish my post with the government and come away with you - I am more than willing to do that for you!" he said.

Nandhini looked at Azhwarkkadiyan through her lovely, tear-filled eyes. "Thirumalai," she said, her voice choked with emotion. "Your affection for me remains unspoiled despite the betrayals I have subjected you to. The Narayanan you worship will assuredly grace you with His blessings!"

Poonguzhali nudged Senthan Amudhan. "There!" she whispered.

"Look at Pazhuvoor Ilaiya Rani! Isn't she the spitting image of my *athai?*"

"Yes," agreed Senthan Amudhan softly. "With her tresses loose, she does look extraordinarily like your *athai!*"

"Henceforth, *she* shall be my *athai*," declared Poonguzhali. "All the love I bore for my *athai* these many days shall now be Pazhuvoor Ilaiya Rani's own!"

"Do include me in the dispensation of your affections, Poonguzhali!" said Amudhan with a smile.

By this time, Periya Pazhuvettarayar had reached Nandhini's side. She prostated herself before him. In a gesture of deep respect, she gently touched his feet and brought her fingers to her hands.

Nandhini stood up and looked at Periya Pazhuvettarayar. She suddenly turned. Her gaze fell upon the horses brought by Chinna Pazhuvettarayar and his company, which were standing a little distance away. Nandhini darted towards the herd. She leapt onto the saddle of the first horse she came across; she took the reins in her hands and tugged at them. The horse broke into a swift run.

No one had any clue about Nandhini's intentions until this moment. As the horse raced away, Chinna Pazhuvettarayar, Azhwarkkadiyaan, Senthan Amudhan and Poonguzhali started forward, thinking to follow her.

"Stop!" roared Periya Pazhuvettarayar. The group froze in their tracks, not knowing what to do. They stood in their places, watching Periya Pazhuvettarayar.

Periya Pazhuvettarayar gazed at Nandhini as she sped away on horseback. The steed galloped as swiftly as the wind. The horse soon turned around a bend skirting the foothills of the mountain and disappeared entirely from sight.

Yes, dear reader - Pazhuvoor Ilaiya Rani had vanished. We shall not come across her in our story again.

Perhaps, years hence, we may meet her in another time, under other circumstances. Who can tell?

48

You are not my son!

As Aditha Karikalan's funeral procession passed the banks of the Kaveri river on its way to Thanjai, millions of the mourning public joined its ranks in grief. The noble trait of extolling warriors was prevalent in the Thamizhakam of yore. We have already seen, haven't we, how the dimming glory of the Chozha clan was revived to resplendence in the time of Vijalaya Chozhar? For close to a century, every one of the children born in that illustrious clan surpassed their predecessors to achieve breathtaking feats of valour. Vijayalayan's noble son, Aditha Varman, laid waste to the prestige and fame of the Pallava clan and seized control of Thondai Naadu. Aditha Varman's own son, Paranthaka Chakravarthy, captured Madurai and Eezham, bringing all of the southern territories under his rule. All four of Paranthaka Chakravarthy's children, too, outshone each other in courage and fortitude. One laid down his life in the Pandiya war. The eldest, Rajaadithan, fearlessly went to war with the great armies of Kannaradevar of Rettai Mandalam, a vast military force that swelled and churned like the very ocean. He dealt them defeat at Thakkolam, only to be deceitfully assassinated on the battlefield. Rajaadithan would forever be known as '*Yaanai Mel Thunjina Devan*' - the Lord Who Died Upon An Elephant. His brother Kandaradhithan was a man of extraordinary wisdom, blessed with the calling of Lord Siva; and yet, he was lesser to none in terms of valour. In later years, when Arjinjayan breathed his last at Aatrur, his son Sundara Chozhar ascended the throne. He came to power after the period of the Thakkolam war, at a time when the Chozha *samrajyam* had once again been robbed of some of its glory; but Sundara Chozhar uplifted the mighty empire to soaring heights once again.

Even in such a lineage as this, eminent for the unmatched courage of its members who emerged as heroes generation after generation, there was none to equal Aditha Karikalan even after his time. Such was the talk among the people of the empire, too. Why, the miracles of valour the prince wrought on the Sevur battlefield at a mere twelve years of age eclipsed even the glory of Arjunan's son, Abimanyu!

There were many rumours in the air about the reason why this peerless warrior chose to remain in Kanchi for the past few years without paying a visit to Thanjai. One such whisper put forth the theory that the chieftains had contrived events such that Aditha Karikalan could not come to Thanjai, hoping instead to anoint Madhuranthakan the crown prince. Another story explained that Aditha Karikalan had wished to emulate his namesake Karikala Valavan who, in an earlier period, had marched his armies north and triumphantly planted the splendid tiger flag of the Chozhas upon the summit of the very Imaiya Malai. It was surmised that Aditha Karikalan had taken a vow that he would not return to Thanjai without achieving the same, but had met a barrier in the

Pazhuvettarayars and their allies who had sought to hinder this worthy goal.

And so, it was but natural that the people of Chozha Naadu found themselves greatly agitated when they heard the sudden news of Aditha Karikalan's demise, one that had come about through deceit in Sambuvaraiyar's own palace, no less. It shouldn't come as a surprise then, to know that a crush of lamenting millions descended upon the funeral march to pay their last respects to this lionhearted warrior. As the procession drew closer to Thanjai, the throng swelled to become a vast sea of mourners. Even the soldiers of the southern army besieging the Thanjai fort merged with the crowds and mingled with the common people, united by sorrow. The prescient Mudhanmandhiri cautioned against admitting the congregation into the fort, fearing disastrous consequences. As a result, the Chakravarthy and his family - themselves engulfed in an ocean of anguished grief - chose instead to make an appearance outside the fort.

When the crowds caught sight of Sundara Chozhar, they burst into a turbulent uproar. Edicts say that sounds of grief and lamentation were never heard in Chozha Naadu under the reign of Sundara Chozhar. Clearly, these inscriptions describe the state of affairs that prevailed before Aditha Karikalan's demise. For on that particular day, a million voices erupted as one in heartbroken cries to articulate their abject sorrow. Everyone at the congregation thought of Arjunan of yore, who had suffered the loss of his dear son Abimanyu; but Abimanyu, they recalled, had embraced a hero's death - the youth had breathed his last having achieved nigh-impossible feats of valour as a lone warrior against enemies who had besieged him on all sides.

The once-mighty Aditha Karikalar, on the other hand, was basely killed through treachery and deceit in order to sate Maduranthakar's desire for the throne and the chieftains' lust for power! As this impression took root in the hearts of the grieving masses, certain events transpired which only served to strengthen their conviction.

Aditha Karikalan's remains were laid out in full view of the public, outside the Thanjai fort. Every single person present came forward to gaze upon the prince for a final time, and bitterly wept as they withdrew. Madhuranthakan, however, did not present himself at the funeraries. Even the Pazhuvettaryars were absent.

Whispers grew that the Pazhuvettarayars were, in fact, gathering their own forces as well as those of their allies. And so, the aggrieved crowds were not inclined to disperse. They remained present for Aditha Karikalar's last rites, a solemn ceremony befitting the demise of a mighty warrior. They lingered even after the grieving Chakravarthy and his family withdrew to the Thanjai fort after the obsequies.

The cries of dissent began as solitary shouts of rebellion. "Down with Madhuranthakan," called out a handful of people. "Down with the Pazhuvettarayars!" Shortly, the throng burst into a wild and wrathful clamour.

A faction of the congregation hurled themselves against the fort walls, breaking down the perimeter. The throng gained ingress into Thanjai city and marched to the palace of the Pazhuvettaryars. They stationed themselves outside the gate and raised an angry ruckus. "Down with the Pazhuvettarayars!" they bellowed.

It was only upon the order of the Mudhanmandhiri that the crowds scattered, forced to disperse.

In the midst of this clamour, the rumour spread that Maduranthaka Thevar was, in fact, hiding himself in Aniruddhar's home. The irate people lost no time in encircling Aniruddhar's quarters.

"Where is that *pedi* Madhuranthakan?" they roared. "Ask him to come out!"

As it happened, Madhuranthakan truly was at Aniruddhar's home at that time. He shook like a leaf when he heard the uproar of the mob outside. Madhuranthakan turned to Aniruddhar, white as a sheet. "Mudhanmandhiri, devise a plan to get me away from this fort, one way or another! Send me through the secret underground passage! I shall join my allies. If you do me this turn, I shall retain you as the Mudhanmandhiri when I ascend the Chozha throne!"

"*Ayya*, why talk of ascending the throne?" asked the Mudhanmandhiri Aniruddhar. "Sundara Chozha Chakravarthy yet lives."

"Ah, but did I not see for myself the countenance of Sundara Chozhar as he turned back from the funeraries of his son? I saw how ghostly and pale his face had become!" replied Madhuranthakan, his eyes gleaming. "I was watching, wasn't I, from this very balcony? He won't live long, now. It will fall to either Arulmozhi Varman or I to sit upon the throne and reign this empire." His tone grew waspish. "Sundara Chozhar himself wishes to anoint me the crown prince. *Why* must you and my mother stand in the way?"

"My prince, did it not occur to you that that your mother has good reason? There, hearken to the shouts of the crowd besieging this house! Do you think it enough that the Sundara Chozhar wishes your ascension? Don't you think the people of Chozha Naadu must wish it, too?" asked Aniruddhar. He paused for a heartbeat, cocking his ears. "Aha! What is this, now?" he exclaimed and peered out to look at the street.

The cries had changed. Instead of furious dissent, there now came shouts of joy. "Long live Arulmozhi Varmar!" the people cheered. "Long live Ponniyin Selvar!" "Long live the incomparable warrior who seized Eezham!"

For prince Arulmozhi Varmar himself was passing through the street, regally seated upon a majestic steed. All the people found themselves drawn to him; the throng coalesced behind him and began to follow in his wake. The street facing Aniruddhar's house cleared out in a matter of minutes; where there had been a roaring crowd, there was now nothing but emptiness. Madhuranthakan had been watching the scene by Aniruddhar's side, too. His eyes reddened like the scarlet *kovai pazham*, glowing with the embers of envy. "Aha!" spat Madhuranthakan. "Why are people so captivated by this boy, anyway?" he muttered petulantly to himself.

"My prince," began Aniruddhar. "When Chinna Pazhuvettarayar went in pursuit of the man who killed the Eezham Rani, why were you in the underground passage?" he asked.

Madhuranthakan frowned. "When Ponniyin Selvan entered the palace in the guise of a mahout, I was feeling quite disheartened. I did not want to be in the fort at the same time as him, you know. Pazhuvettaryar had pointed out the underground passage to me on an earlier occasion. I was strolling the palace gardens, wondering if I should leave the fort through that path," he admitted. "That was when I saw someone emerge from the underground passage. He was the one who approached me. He said, '*Ilavarase!* I came only to see you. Periya Pazhuvettarayar and Kandamaaran have sent me to fetch you right away. Great armies have gathered in support of your claim to the throne.' I was a bit suspicious of his words, for his appearance seemed rather strange.

'If a great army has rallied to my cause, why must I come out of the fort? Let them defeat the Kodumbalur armies gathered here and seat me on the throne,' I replied.

To which the man said, '*Ilavarase*, there's more! There is a frightful mystery surrounding your birth. Nobody has the courage to tell you about it but me.'

Naturally, I said, 'In that case, let us leave right away.'

'There is a message I must deliver to the Mudhanmandhiri Aniruddhar,' the man replied. 'I shall meet you after I give it to him. Go forthwith and hide yourself in the underground passage."

That's why I went to the treasury; I was waiting for him there. Mudhanmandhiri! Did he come and see you like he said? What could be the frightful mystery he spoke of, about my birth?" asked Madhuranthakan to a pensive Aniruddhar.

"My prince, the only person with the droit to divulge that secret to you is your noble mother, Sembian Maadevi," replied Aniruddhar quietly. "Even though I know the facts to a certain extent, I cannot speak of it."

It was at that very moment that the street burst into a loud ruckus for a second time. The Mudhanmandhiri looked outside. "Aha!" he exclaimed. "There, your mother herself arrives!" he said.

Sembian Maadevi came to the upper quarters of Aniruddhar's house after paying a preliminary visit to the women of the home. The Devi's noble face was suffused with deep sadness. Aniruddhar respectfully stood as soon as she arrived. He welcomed her and offered a chair upon which the Devi took her seat. She said nothing for some time; she sat still with her head bent and gaze fixed upon the floor. A heavy silence reigned both within and without the palace. Presently, Sembian Maadevi looked up at Madhuranthakan and Aniruddhar. "*Ayya*, my husband placed this burden upon my shoulders before he was called away to the heavenly abode," she began, her eyes moist. "I admit that the mistake was all mine; but if he had been here at this moment, I would not have suffered thus."

Sparks of wrath flashed in Madhuranthakan's eyes. "Why do you grieve? Why do you take my father's name so often?" he cried. "My ascent to the Thanjavur throne is all but certain. One of the obstacles that stood in my way is now dead. As for Arulmozhi Varman, he is younger to me; they can never anoint him the crown prince as long as I live. Only *you, Amma*..." his voice caught with bitterness. "Please, take pity and be kind enough to not thwart my dream! Has anyone heard of a mother betraying her own son? Why do you seek to do *me* treachery, you who are a gem of a Siva *bhaktha*?"

"My child, it certainly is an unspeakable betrayal for a mother to turn enemy to the very son she gave birth to," replied Sembian Maadevi sadly. "But my husband has left me with such a command. It is my duty to fulfill his wish. Listen to me! To desire power is a wicked thing. To lust for a kingdom is much viler. My son, it is the head that bears the crown that carries the heaviest burden of all, weighed down by worry. A man who sits upon the throne knows no peace of mind and his heart is ever turbulent. Why, did not Veera Pandiyan meet a terrible death for the very reason that his head carried a crown?" she asked in earnest. "Siva Peruman's exalted *samrajyam* is many times more illustrious than a paltry *rajyam* of earth. Come, we will leave this town. We shall go on pilgrimage and visit many holy *kshethrams*; why, we shall journey all the way to sacred Kailayam! We will take sweet refuge in the compassion of Kailasanathan Himself. We shall become blessed vessels that receive his boundless grace!"

"Aha!" exclaimed Madhuranthakan, stung. "You are certainly the right age to go on a *yatra* to Kailasam, but I haven't grown that old yet! I have not yet experienced all the joys and sorrows that the world has to offer. You gave me an austere upbringing, bading me smear ash over my body in constant chant of Lord Siva like a madman," he burst out resentfully. "It is by the great compassion of Paramasivan that the *rajyam* is now almost within my grasp! Why should I let it go?" demanded Madhuranthakan.

"*Appane*, the *rajyam* that draws closer to you brings great peril along," replied Sembian Maadevi with loving patience. "You said that one of your obstacles is no more, that Aditha Karikalan has died. But did you hear the cries of the people surrounding this palace just a short while ago? Madhuranthaka! The people blame the Pazhuvettarayars and you for Aditha Karikalan's demise. How will they ever come to accept you as their Chakravarthy?"

"*Amma*, the people will soon forget these things," replied Madhuranthakan, swelling with pomposity. "If I sit upon the throne, they will certainly accept me as their Chakravarthy! I shall tell you more - listen! Do you know who the real culprit behind Karikalar's death is? Why, it is that Vandhiyathevan, Arulmozhi Varmar's dearest friend! They say that he was found at the spot where Karikalar was lying dead in Sambuvaraiyar's palace. Both Sambuvaraiyar and Vandhiyathevan have been thrown into the dungeons." Madhuranthakan spoke rapidly in his excitement. "No doubt, it was Arulmozhi Varman who contrived events to kill his own *thamaiyan* so that he could seat himself upon the throne. Ah, let this truth be made known to the public - we shall see what becomes of Ponniyin Selvan after that!"

Sembian Maadevi's eyes flashed dangerously. "*Ada paavi!* Sinner!" she cried. "How can you bring yourself to say such things about Arulmozhi, that boy who is the very personification of compassion? Ah, that he is willing to put such an undeserving man as you upon a pedestal! Say another word about that boy and you shall surely burn. You shall be cast down to hell, I tell you! There will be no deliverance for you in this birth of the next!"

"*Adi peye!* Demoness!" snarled Madhuranthakan. "You curse your own son and bless his nemesis! Could you be my mother? Never, never!" he burst out, overwhelmed by anguish and pain.

"*Appane,* I wished to never tell you this," said an emotional Sembian Maadevi, her voice barely above a whisper. "Your obstinacy has forced my hand." She looked at Madhuranthakan sadly. "Truly, neither am I the mother who gave birth to you, nor are you my son."

The colour drained from Madhuranthakan's face. "Ah!" he breathed softly. "My suspicions have come true." He gazed abjectly at Sembian Maadevi. "If you are not my mother, then *who* is? If I am not your son, then *whose?*" he cried out, clenching his fists.

The Devi tore her eyes away from Madhuranthakan and turned to the Mudhanmandhiri Aniruddhar. "*Ayya*," she said in a choked voice, "pray answer his question. Spare me the torment of giving voice to my own humiliation."

The Mudhanmandhiri Aniruddhar looked at Madhuranthakan. "*Ilavarase*, you have hurt the mother who raised you with such love since you were a small child," he said quietly. "The truth had to come out one day or another. It is for the best, perhaps, that you will learn it now."

—

As a new bride, Sembian Maadevi yearned to give birth to a child that would rise to be the Chakravarthy of the Chozha *samrajyam*. It so happened that her noble husband was not in the country when she discovered that she was pregnant. It was also the time when two mute women were living in the palace gardens, sisters both. One of them was expecting a child, too. It was Sembian Maadevi who had come across the pregnant woman whilst on pilgrimage; learning that she was destitute, the Devi had brought her to the palace. It had soon come to her notice that the woman had a sister who lived somewhere near Thanjavur. Sembian Maadevi had arranged to bring her to the palace as well, to be of help to the pregnant woman.

Shortly after, Sembian Maadevi gave birth to a child. The Mudhanmandhiri Aniruddhar paid the queen a visit, wishing to express his joy that a royal child had been born to the *rajyam*. Instead, he found Sembian Maadevi in lament. She was mourning over the newly-born child who lay unmoving and lifeless as a log.

"*Ayya*, what can I possibly tell my husband when he arrives?" she whimpered and broke down. Unable to bear her grief, Aniruddhar thought of a solution. He knew that the mute woman who lived in the palace gardens had given birth to twins, a boy and a girl. He approached the new mother and indicated to her that should she leave the children and go away, they would grow up in the care of the palace. The suggestion elicited manic fury from the mute woman. She refused to give up her children at first; but in the end, she abandoned them and slipped away. Aniruddhar wasted no time in asking her sister to give the son to Sembian Maadevi. The Mudhanmandhiri sent the lifeless child to her instead, bading her bury the child stealthily. The girl he took to his own home. He handed over the child to his disciple Azhwarkkadiyaan and sent them away to Pandiya Naadu.

The exchange of babies gnawed away at Sembian Maadevi's heart, who confessed the truth to Kandaradhitha Thevar one day. "That is no sin, my lady," replied that great man. "How does it matter who bore this baby? The child is a precious blessing from Siva Peruman. Love him and raise him as your own flesh and blood. But this child who traces his ancestry to another clan must not ascend the Chozha throne, for that would be tantamount to treachery. We shall instead bring him up to be a Siva *bhakthan*. We will raise him such that he proclaims desire for the *samrajyam* of Siva, not that of the Chozhas! My Devi, not for a moment must we support his ascension to the Thanjavur throne. If I am not alive when that time comes, you must stand resolute to protect the Chozha clan," he said.

"Maduranthaka!" said Aniruddhar, turning to face the prince. "You are not the son of Kandaradhitha Thevar. Neither are you the child that Sembian Maadevi bore. You are the offspring of an orphaned, mute woman who spent her days wandering from town to town." His voice became gentler. "The Devi bestowed more love on you than her own son. She cherished you with all her heart and raised you with great care as if you were her very own. Do not go against her wishes. Listen to her! Nothing but good will come to you," said Aniruddhar.

49

The Wretchedest of Them All

Madhuranthakan sat unmoving, lost in a daze. He suddenly leapt to his feet and spun to face Aniruddhar. "Mudhanmandhiri, this is certainly naught but your vile scheme!" he accused. "Ah, I suspected as such! You love Sundara Chozhar's children and prize Arulmozhi Varmar above them all. It is *you* who wishes to see him anointed the crown prince. That is why you have sold a pack of lies to my poor mother and blighted her noble heart! *Anbil Bhrammaraayare!* What harm have I ever done to you? Why do you seek to betray me so?" cried Madhuranthakan, his voice hoarse with agony. "Must I lose my identity as my mother's son to fulfill your intention? How can you, an *andhanaar* from a clan of Vishnu *bhakthas*, bring yourself to do such a thing as this? No, no!" he suddenly burst out in distress. "This is no fault of yours. It is most certainly Ilaiya Piratti Kundhavai and Arulmozhi Varman who have schemed to force your hand in this heinous ploy!"

"*Ilavarase*," replied Aniruddhar calmly, "if I truly harboured such spiteful hatred towards you, I would not have carried you to safety that day, as you lay helpless under a tree in the pouring rain. Pray, do not cast aspersions upon Arulmozhi Varmar either. Do you know what that great warrior who won Eezham is doing, even as we speak? He extols your praises to the populace and the troops besieging the Thanjai fort. The prince soothes the wrath they hold towards you. He tells them that the tenets of *dharma* forbid him from ascending the throne as long as you, his *chitappa*, yet lives. He urges the soldiers and common people to withdraw their petition for such a demand. The prince is trying to change their hearts."

Madhuranthakar listened to his words in silence. "Then, then.. Arulmozhi is unaware of the news you told me just now, isn't he?" he asked, face flushed with sudden hope.

Aniruddhar inclined his head in assent. "Arulmozhi is unaware, yes. In fact, no one else knows of this."

"Why must it be made known at all?" cried Madhuranthakan hungrily. "*Aniruddhare!* Consent to keep your silence in this matter. The Chakravarthy has given you an endowment, has he not, a grant of ten *velis* of land in a single village? Say yes, and I shall give you all of Pandiya Naadu as a prize!"

A wan smile appeared on the Mudhanmanthiri's face. "*Ayya*, you need not grant me Pandiya Naadu to buy my silence. Your mother's command is sufficient. Speak to her."

Madhuranthakan looked piteously upon the mother who raised him.

"Child, Madhuranthaka! Aniruddhar speaks the truth. He has guarded my secret for more than twenty years. He made me a vow that fateful day - *Maharani, this is your secret. No one will come to know of it save through you. It shall never come to light from my own mouth, this I promise.* He has kept his word till this very moment. The Mudhanmandhiri has taken a sacred oath to remain loyal to the Chozha clan; despite that, he has not revealed this secret to even Sundara Chozha Chakravarthy. If I had given my consent to anoint you the crown prince, he would have maintained his discretion."

"Yes, *thaaye*," agreed Aniruddhar. "I would have held my tongue. But I could not have continued in my post as Mudhanmandhiri with such deceit in my heart. I would have withdrawn to serve my Lord Ranganaathar."

"That necessity shall not arise," replied Sembian Maadevi. "Maduranthakan will not sit upon the throne. He will fulfill my wishes and declare his renunciation of the *rajyam*." She turned to Madhuranthakan. "My son, say you agree," implored Periya Piratti Sembian Maadevi.

"*Thaaye!* Am I to understand that *you* are my only obstacle to the throne?" asked Madhuranthakan in hurt disbelief. "I accept that I am not the son you bore. But for more than twenty years have you loved and raised me, cherishing me more than the child you gave birth to. Why do you betray me now? What harm did I ever do to you?"

"Child, you did no harm to me," said Sembian Maadevi, misty-eyed. "I am the sinner who has inflicted upon you grievous harm! I brought you up as my own flesh and blood all these years, only to tell you now that you are not my son. Do you think me insensitive to the pain your heart must be feeling? I would have given much to have never raised the matter with you as long as I lived and breathed. But I am bound to fulfill the vow I made to my husband. I cannot be a traitor to the Chozha clan that I am married into." She gazed at him imploringly. "I cannot allow the Chozha throne to go to one not born in the Chozha clan. I could never support such a thing, either. Do you think I have no grief in this? When I confessed to you that you were not my son, my very heart was rent asunder. I hesitated to speak the words until the last moment. My mind had to fight great turmoil. I sought out Nambiyaandar Nambi only to gain clarity on the duties I bear and the *dharma* I am bound to. That great man enlightened me on the subtleties of the *dharmic* tenets, my son. He said - *'All men of this world are the children of Mahadevar. You, a gem of a Siva bhaktha, do not differentiate between your own child and one you have raised. You may bequeath your personal wealth to the child you have brought up, but the rajyam is a different matter. It is a sin to rob another of his rightful claim on account of your lie. To seat the child upon the Chozha throne with full knowledge of the fact that he is not of the Chozha clan is nothing but treachery. Dharma bades you tell the truth to your son and the Chakravarthy.'* I returned carrying his words in my heart. *Kumara!* Can I find any joy in saying that you are not my son? Do you think I will be unaffected when I relay this news to the Chakravarthy?"

Madhuranthakan threw himself at Sembian Maadevi's feet. "*Annaiye!* I want neither the *rajyam* nor the throne! If you command me to remain here, I will. If you wish me to go on a pilgrimage to far lands, I shall. But pray, do not say another time that I am not your son, that I am not born of your noble flesh. My heart shall shatter with the humiliation and I shall die!" begged Madhuranthakan amidst sobs.

Tears brimmed over in Sembian Maadevi's eyes. She embraced Madhuranthakan with great love and made him sit next to her.

"*Kumara!* I tried my best to raise you free from the desire to rule this world only to spare you such tortuous grief. It was why I wished for you to seek the *samrajyam* of Siva Peruman instead. I have failed in my aim, for fiends have sullied your mind and polluted your heart. It is not too late now, my son - should you proclaim to the world with all your heart that you renounce the *rajyam* in favour of Sundara Chozhan's son Arulmozhi, there will be no need to make it known that you are not my son. Why, I cannot even bear the grief I feel from hurting you today." She cupped his cheek affectionately. "Say yes, my son. Signal your acceptance with the Mudhanmandhiri as witness. The *mahasabha* of the chieftains will convene in three days. Make your declaration at that conference as well. Say - *'I do not want to rule this kingdom. I wish to engage myself in the service of Siva Peruman and the upkeep of holy temples. This is what my parents wish for me. Anoint Arulmozhi Varmar the crown prince.* Give us a solemn oath, my son - *'I will not act against the interests of the Chozha rajyam. I will not pay heed to any evil counsel the chieftains may bring to me.'* If you acquiesce to this, neither I nor the Mudhanmandhiri will be obliged to reveal the secret of your birth. You may remain who you have always been - my beloved son, the very jewel of my eye. We shall travel together throughout this splendid Bharatadesam. We shall find joy in undertaking holy temple work as we journey. Arulmozhi Varman bears boundless devotion towards me. I raised him as I raised you. He will never say a word against my wishes," said the Mazhavarayar's daughter, Sembian Maadevi.

Madhuranthakan pressed his hands to his forehead and sank into brooding.

"Ah," he said softly. "Even when I was young, I was often assailed by strange memories that seemed to have no shape or shadow. Now I understand the reason why." His words caught in his throat. "Could there be another in this world more unfortunate than me? I know neither the hour of my birth nor my *jadagam*. In the fleeting span of a single second I have lost my father and mother, *kulam* and *gothram*; why, I have lost a great *samrajyam!* I have felt slip through my fingers the throne of a mighty lineage of warriors dating back thousands of years." He paused as he came to a sudden realization. "I have lost my friends. Yes, I have. For if this truth becomes public knowledge, who will remain by my side? The chieftains took an oath to give up their lives in the cause of anointing me the crown prince. They will now wash their hands off the endeavour altogether. Yes.

There cannot be another as wretched as me upon this earth, even since the day it came into existence! *Amma*," he cried, heartbroken, "I am all at sea. My mind is disoriented; I am unable to hold a clear thought in my head. Pray, allow me two days. I shall tell you my decision after that!"

"Child, what is there to think about? I harden my heart to say these words. Either you must publicly renounce your claim to this *rajyam*, or I must proclaim to the world that you are not the son I bore. You will not be able to ascend the throne in either outcome. What is left to ponder about?" asked Sembian Maadevi, the noble woman celebrated by the world as Periya Piratti.

"*Amma*," interjected Aniruddhar. "There is no harm in allowing the prince two days. There are three days yet for the *manthiralosana sabha* and the *mahajana sabha* to convene. Let the Ilavarasar think over the matter in peace."

Madhuranthakan suddenly jumped to his feet. "*Amma! Amma!*" he cried out avidly. "Does anyone else know this secret, apart from you and the Mudhanmandhiri?" It is hard to say, dear reader, the nature of evil that had sprouted in his mind.

Madhuranthakan's excitement gave the Mazhavarayar's daughter some surprise.

"There are only three other apart from me who know of this matter, my son," she said, puzzled. "One was your noble father, the late Sivanesa Selvar who lives yet in my thoughts. The other two are the mute sisters. Among them, the one who birthed you attained an untimely death not two days ago in Sundara Chozhar's palace. When I saw her lifeless body lying there, I wondered if I ought to tell you the truth; but I did not have the heart to do it. I held my tongue, wishing to spare you grief. My son," said Sembian Maadevi gently, "if you feel the need to cry to mourn your birth mother, then do so. She gave birth to you, it is true; but she had no relationship with you after that. She did not even make an attempt to meet you. She lost her senses entirely. If you will find solace in crying over her, then cry, my son."

"No, no!" recoiled Madhuranthakan in horror. "I cannot think of anyone else as my mother but you. If you had told me the truth earlier, why, I would not have even approached her!" He paused. "Who is the other person who knows the secret, *Amma?* Who is the other mute woman?"

"The younger sister tends to a garden on the outskirts of Thanjai. She is the one who gave me you in exchange for the lifeless child I had birthed. As the woman is mute and deaf by birth, she will not breathe a word of the secret to anyone. She has a son, too. Mother and son spend their lives in *pushpa sevai* to the Thanikulathar temple at Thanjai. I support them with an endowment."

"Aha! I know of them, the mother and son. The son's name is Senthan Amudhan! He is the one who helped that spy Vandhiyathevan make his escape from here." Madhuranthakan rubbed his palms together as the wheels turned furiously in his mind. "*Amma*, does the son know of this matter?"

"No, child. He is unaware," said Sembian Maadevi as she watched her son pace the chamber. "His mother has promised me that she will not disclose this secret to anyone. You may rest your fears on that score. Apart from her, nobody else knows, save the Mudhanmandhiri and me."

A vile thought reared in Madhuranthakan's heart when he heard those words - he reckoned that there would be none to reveal the truth to the world if Sembian Maadevi and the Mudhanmandhiri were no longer part of it. *I owe the Mudhanmandhiri nothing. As for this maatharasi, she is not the mother who gave birth to me. Why must I show them compassion? Aha! That man in Sundara Chozhar's garden, who had promised to tell me the secret of my birth - who was he? Who was that man who had asked me to wait in the treasury? What if I happen to meet him? But he was the one, wasn't he, who sought to assassinate the Sundara Chozhar and killed the mute woman instead? He is blameless, then! It is these people who claim her to be my mother. If she truly was my mother, then who is my father? Perchance... is this deceitful crone trying to trick me along with this charlatan Brahmaraayar? Perhaps I truly am Sundara Chozhar's son! Aha! How can I get at the truth?*

"My son, I shall take my leave," said Sembian Maadevi suddenly, rising to her feet. "Think well upon the matter and come to a decision soon. I have brought you up for twenty two years with greater love and affection than your own mother showed you. I will not work against your interest. Renounce all claim to this ephemeral *rajyam* on earth. Seek a path, instead, that leads to the immortal *samrajyam* of Siva Peruman!" urged Periya Pirattiyar.

An entirely unexpected thing happened at that very moment. Arulmozhi Varman entered the room, to everyone's surprise. He walked to Sembian Maadevi and prostrated himself before her feet.

"Devi," he said reverently. "I wholeheartedly take for myself the advice you bestowed upon your beloved son. If the Chozha *samrajyam* is mine by right, I intend to relinquish my claim to it. Let my mind find refuge in the lotus feet of Siva Peruman with your blessings. Let me have a small corner in Sivalokam, by the side of your noble husband Kandaradhithar. Pray, bless me thus!"

Sembian Maadevi and Mudhanmandhiri Aniruddha Brahmaraayar looked at each other, stunned into silence.

"Devi," said Ponniyin Selvar as stood up, "Pray, pardon me. I happened to hear the words you spoke to your beloved son a short while back, quite unintentionally. I had returned after escorting out of the fort the crowd that had besieged this palace. I had intended to meet the Mudhanmandhiri in order to discuss the way forward.

When I learned that you were here as well, I counted it a fortunate coincidence." He paused. "You had spoken in a louder tone than usual, my Devi; Madhuranthaka Thevar too, had raised his voice. As I hesitated at the doorway, wondering whether I could come inside, a portion of your conversation fell upon my ears. Devi! You said that among the living, only you, the Mudhanmandhiri and Senthan Amudhan's mother know the secret behind Madhuranthakan's birth. That is not quite true. My *thamakkai* Ilaiya Piratti and I know the truth, too. I have often met Mandhakini Devi in Eezha Naadu, that noble woman who saved the Chakravarthy's life by sacrificing her own. It was she who revealed the truth to me through sketches and illustrations. I took my *thamakkaiyar* into confidence. We conferred with each other and came to a decision." Arulmozhi Varman smiled. "My *chitappa* Madhuranthaka Thevar is the one who should inherit the Chozha throne. He is the child you brought up with far greater love and care than the son you bore. He is the child that Mandhakini Devi gave birth to, the son of the noble woman who saved me not only from the Kaveri waters but from other fatal perils as well. Should uncertainty arise regarding his stake to the throne, I will put it to rest myself. I shall renounce my right to the Chozha throne with a sacred oath upon your lotus feet. There is little need for you to make a public declaration that Madhuranthaka Thevar is not your son. There is no necessity either, for Madhuranthakar to sacrifice the Chozha throne."

The three people in the chamber stood motionless. Ponniyin Selvar's astonishing words had taken their breath away; they were overcome by an awe and wonder that they had not experienced in their lives so far.

Presently, Aniruddhar found his tongue. "*Ilavarase!*" he began reverentially. "Your words must endure in literature and history. They ought to be inscribed upon granite slabs, copper seals and gold plates. But my prince, consider that it is not only the people in this chamber who can take a decision about this matter. The

Chakravarthy and the chieftains must be consulted as well. Think, my prince - if the truth becomes public in the future, what will the people say? Three days remain before the *mahasabha* gathers. Until then, let us all deliberate over the matter!"

50

Kundhavai's bewilderment

Ilaiya Piratti Kundhavai had been born with a silver spoon in her mouth. Growing up amidst fabulous wealth, she had led a charmed life indeed. She was akin to Rathi in her beauty, the Kalaimagal in her wisdom and the very Thirumagal in her luck. From Sundara Chozha Chakravarthy to the common people of Chozha Naadu, there was nary a person who did not celebrate and praise her. The palace was full of people eager to receive her commands, willing to sacrifice their very heads to fulfill her wishes. Chieftains longed for the princesses of their clans to attain the fortune of serving Kundhavai Devi as a handmaiden. The Bharatha Naadu of Kundhavai's time counted many young princes, heirs to great empires themselves, who fervently prayed for the blessing of clasping her hand in marriage.

Ilaiya Piratti, bestowed from birth with the greatest of fortunes, found herself engulfed in a sea of sorrow. The advice she had anxiously relayed to Aditha Karikalan had all been in vain. She had sent him an urgent missive imploring him to not go to Sambuvaraiyar's palace. Her beloved *thamaiyan*, who normally set much store by her words, had brushed aside the counsel to proceed to Kadambur despite her misgivings. He had met an untimely death there, one that was shrouded by a dark mystery. Kundhavai had believed all along that Nandhini was naught but family, a sister to her, Karikalan and Arulmozhi Varman. She was also aware that Nandhini bore an inexplicable grudge towards Karikalan. There could be no greater dishonour for the Chozha clan than to discover that Karikalan had met his demise at Nandhini's hands. Nandhini's fate after Karikalan's death remained disturbingly obscure.

The loss of her cherished *thamaiyan* brought Kundhavai boundless grief. Two days had passed since he had shuffled off the mortal coil, but thoughts of him came unbidden, giving her much pain; she would think of his noble face shining with courage and melt anew with sorrow. *Ah, such marvellous dreams that incomparable warrior had nursed in his heart! He had spoken often of his desire to make a triumphant march to Imaiya Malai and plant the tiger flag on that glorious mountain, just like Karikal Peruvalathaan! The noble remains of such an illustrious man had burned to a handful of ashes in the span of a mere half naazhigai. It has mingled with the dust and sand of Chozha Naadu. Thousands of great warriors will spring up from that very dust in the future. They will set forth from Chozha Naadu on brave expeditions in the four cardinal directions; they will cross the mighty seas and find their feet on far-off shores. They shall wage heroic wars to expand the boundaries of the illustrious Chozha samrajyam! They shall raise magnificent temples wherever they go, embellished by lofty gopurams that pierce the sky. They shall present to the world the splendour of Chozha Naadu and bask in its glory. They will share with all societies Thamizh language and culture; they will disseminate the profound philosophies of the Saivites and Vaishnavites. The thevarams of the Trinity and the pasurams of the Azhwars will resound in far-off shores across the seas. The victory cheers of Vetri Vel! Veera Vel! shall reverberate across the waters.*

These are not mere dreams. They will come true one day for certain. If what the elders, jothidars and wise women say about Arulmozhi Varman's time of birth is true, then the dreams that Karikalan had set his heart on will come true through him.

Ah, but the way is fraught with barriers! Who knows what evil we will come to face from the civil war between the chieftains? Malayaman and Velar are quite obstinate in their campaign to seat Arulmozhi Varman upon the throne, while the Pazhuvettarayars and their allies gather a great army to march in support of Madhuranthakan. Meanwhile, the Chakravarthy is submerged under great sorrow, broken-hearted by two unspeakable tragedies that cruelly transpired one after the other without respite. He refuses to speak with anyone. He broods over the sins of his younger days and is lost to self-pity. Nobody knows how to console him. Though, how can they be expected to, when his own beloved daughter shrinks away from him in fear?

Arulmozhi Varman is prepared to sacrifice his right to the rajyam. He wishes to lead the Chozha armies across the ocean only after anointing Madhuranthakan the crown prince. But an unexpected hurdle has arisen even here. Inexplicably, the Mudhiya Piratti Sembian Maadevi - praised and attended to by all of Chozha Naadu - objects to the very thought of anointing her son the crown prince! She claims it to be the command of her late husband.

How on earth will these problems reach a resolution?

As if the tribulations of the Chozha clan were not enough, Kundhavai Devi found herself eaten alive by another great worry. The Vaanar warrior who had stolen her heart had been relegated to the dungeons. *They are trying to thrust the blame of Aditha Karikalan's demise upon him. Parthibendra of the Pallava clan is quite inflexible in this regard.* She wondered if *pattaan* Malayaman would listen to her if she spoke to him about the matter. But how could a woman pry into such a grave issue, interceding for a suspect no less? If it was perceived that she harboured greater care for a chance-acquaintance as Vandhiyathevan over her own *thamaiyan* Aditha Karikalan, she would face indelible ignominy and shame. *Parthibendran is fully capable of spreading such a canard. He says that Sambuvaraiyar and Kandamaaran caught Vandhiyathevan red-handed at the scene of the crime. That may even be true. But that is no doubt the outcome of Vandhiyathevan striving to fulfill my command to remain by Karikalan's side, come what may! He must have tried to save Aditha Karikalar from the assassins and failed in his attempt.*

How was she to learn the truth behind the affair? The mere act of visiting Vandhiyathevan or extricating him from the dungeons exposed her to suspicion and blame. None had the nerve to speak ill of her; and if they did, such talk posed her little harm. But a vile faction sought to foist Karikalar's death upon Arulmozhi Varmar! If she acted in haste, it might serve to strengthen their stand.

Sweet Lord! Devi Jaganmatha! What excruciating trials and tribulations you subject me to, one who has lived so far without a care in the world?

Kundhavai's heart grew heavy with grief as she brooded on the troubles that lay before her. Ilaiya Piratti had not caught a wink of sleep since receiving news of Karikalar's death and Vandhiyathevan's alleged involvement in the crime. She expended all her time and energy into devising a solution to this thorny problem. Many ideas came to mind and she rejected them all for myriad reasons.

She even refused to confide in her beloved *thozhi* Vanathi.

Vanathi gauged Ilaiya Piratti's frame of mind and refrained from speaking up or asking questions. She remained by Kundhavai's side as a shadow, offering her support and comfort in her silence.

So it was quite a surprise when Vanathi - that sweet, sensitive maiden who had so quickly understood Kundhavai's need for discretion -

suddenly appeared before Ilaiya Piratti that day. "*Akka! Akka!*" she cried breathlessly. "A young lady has come, seeking an audience with you. She stands over there weeping with such sorrow. Oh, my heart goes out to her, *Akka!*" she said. Kundhavai was quite taken aback by her words.

"Who is she?" asked Ilaiya Piratti. "Didn't you ask her what the matter was?"

"I did, *Akka!*" said Vanathi, wringing her hands. "This may serve to displease you, in truth. She is Sambuvaraiyar's daughter, I believe! Sambuvaraiyar's family has been imprisoned in Chinna Pazhuvettarayar's palace. She managed to run away without anyone's knowledge and reached here on her own, seeking direction from people along the way. Every time I ask her what the matter is, she insists that she will only confide in you. *Akka*, if you but glanced at her tear-streaked face, even your heart will change!"

"Meaning, I have a hard, unrelenting heart of stone!" remarked Kundhavai acidly.

"You truly do, *Akka!* Else, would you watch on unfeeling as Vandhiyathevan languishes in the dungeons?"

Kundhavai pressed a hand to her forehead. "Alright then, ask the girl to come inside," she sighed.

It took Vanathi precisely a second to leap to the doorway like a joyful deer and return leading Manimekalai by the hand.

51

Manimekalai Seeks a Boon

Manimekalai entered the chamber as one in a mad daze, looking all about her with wide, wild eyes. She looked every inch as piteous as Vanathi had claimed. Her face and eyes looked swollen from crying.

Kundhavai found herself unmoved to sympathy. She found it hard to look past the fact that the covert conference that had taken place in the Kadambur palace was the root cause of the tragedies and disasters that had assailed the Chozha clan in the near past. The thought raged in her heart that her *thamaiyan* Karikalan, that warrior beyond compare, had succumbed to a treacherous death at her very home.

Kundhavai suddenly recalled another matter. This young lady's *thamaiyan* Kandamaaran and the Vaanar warrior were bosom friends of old. It was with full trust in that friendship that Vandhiyathevar had gone to the Kadambur palace; he had gleaned intelligence about the secret conference and reported his findings to her. Kandamaaran had intended, hadn't he, to marry his sister to the Vallathu prince? This girl must be whom he had in mind!

The memory kindled in Kundhavai a keen interest to learn more about Manimekalai. Aha! Why had she come in search of her? Had she come to intercede for her father and brother? When Sambuvaraiyar issued an invitation to Karikalar to visit his palace, there had been talks of wedding this girl to him. Had this naive waif lost her heart to Karikalan? Had the shock of seeing her beloved meet an unnatural death driven her insane? Had she come to pour her heart out? Or perchance.. Could it be? Kandamaaran had spoken to her about his friend, no doubt. Vandhiyathevan has been hosted at her home, more than once; his second, fateful visit had been an even longer one than the first. Perchance, had her heart grown fond of Vandhiyathevan? If that was the case, it is certain that he would have rejected her advances. Had she come to get even by speaking wicked lies and accusations against him?

All these thoughts went through Kundhavai's mind in a flash. She looked closely at Manimekalai, as if she wished to plumb the very depths of her heart to learn all she could about her. Unable to bear Ilaiya Piratti's piercing stare, Manimekalai bowed her head and dropped her gaze to the ground. Hot tears brimmed over her eyes, falling to the floor in little splashes.

"Girl, why do you cry? Your *thamaiyan* is yet alive, is he not? It was my *thamaiyan* who met a deceitful death at your palace. If anyone is to sob here, it is me," remarked Kundhavai, her eyebrows arched. "And yet, look at me - I am neither tearful nor given over to fits of weeping. The women of the Mara clan do not cry over those who have attained a warrior's death."

Manimekalai raised her head to look at Ilaiya Piratti. "Devi, I would not cry either, if my *thamaiyan* had fallen to the edge of a sword. But the person who died..." she trailed off, hesitating to speak further. Manimekalai dissolved into a fresh bout of tears.

Kundhavai began to wonder if her suspicions were, in fact, true. The girl must have been besotted with Aditha Karikalan. Perhaps she hesitates to speak the truth. Poor soul! In that case, she deserved consolation indeed.

"Girl," said Kundhavai gently. "Brace your heart and speak your mind. The person who died was not your *thamaiyan*, he was mine. Why must you cry for that? Do you grieve, perchance, that the tragedy took place when he was a guest in your palace? What could you have done, after all? There were many elders in the home when the event transpired. The responsibility is theirs alone."

Manimekalai's face twisted with agony. "No, Devi, no!" she cried. "The responsibility is all mine. That is why I am unable to contain my grief however hard I try; the tears flow unbidden from my eyes. My heart feels like it would shatter into a million pieces when I think of how I killed that peerless warrior with a knife held in these very wretched hands!" burst out Manimekalai and wept aloud.

Kundhavai stood stunned at her words. "Girl, what sort of drivel is that?" she asked, taken aback. "Have you turned insane?"

"No, no," sobbed Manimekalai. "I am not mad, not yet. I will tell you what truly happened, my lady. The murderer who slayed Aditha Karikalan is this vile fiend of a woman who stands before you - me! I came to you only to receive just punishment for my crime."

"*Chi, chi,*" shrunk back Kundhavai, aghast. "This is nothing short of a scandal! Do you expect me to believe that my *thamaiyan*, that famed warrior beyond compare, succumbed to death at the hands of a woman? Who taught you to say such a thing?!"

"No one taught me. Devi, everyone refuses to believe me. Why, my own *thamaiyan* and father have no faith in what I say!" replied Manimekalai miserably.

"Why do you continue to peddle your useless tales?" demanded a stricken Kundhavai. "No doubt, they were the very ones who taught you to make such a claim! Or perhaps it is *you* who have concocted this story hoping to save your brother and father!"

"Devi, why must I strive to deliver them?" asked Manimekalai harshly. "They sought to wed me against my wishes. Wed Madhuranthaka Thevar, they said at first. Then they produced Aditha Karikalan out of nowhere and insisted on my acquiescence to marry him, instead. You must wed him, they said, for only then will you ascend the Chozha throne. Why should I come out in support of these people who sought to use me as a sacrificial lamb for their own ends? Why must I take upon myself a crime that they have committed? I would never!" she cried.

Kundhavai looked at her, astonished. "Girl, each thing you say is stranger than the next! Countless princesses of myriad empires prayed for the good fortune to wed my *thamaiyan*. Why do you say that your father and brother sought to sacrifice you in troth to him? Do you think of being wedded into the Chozha clan as such unbearable suffering?"

"Devi," began Manimekalai softly, "I have neither *thangai* nor *thamakkai*. I think of you as my own sister..."

"You say that you have killed my *thamaiyan*. How could you dream of taking the liberty of claiming to be my sister?" asked Ilaiya Piratti savagely.

"I do have that right," replied Manimekalai. "Your own brother Karikalar considered me his own sister. It is that very fact that wounds my heart afresh when I think of my fate as his killer. I came to you only to beg you to decree the atonement for such a vile sin!" she said, breaking into sobs.

"Poor soul!" whispered Ilaiya Piratti to Vanathi. "The girl is truly mad, it seems. And you have chosen to bring her to me at this time! What are we to do if she breaks out in a frenzy?"

"*Akka*, I am quite worried as well," whispered back a flustered Vanathi. "Pray, do not speak in anger. We shall lull her with sweet words and turn her back."

Kundhavai turned to Manimekalai. "Girl, what has happened, has happened. It is naught but the work of fate," she said cautiously. "You may think of me as your own *thamakkai*. You said that you wanted to tell me something, didn't you? What is it? Or, if you wish, you may speak to me on another occasion," she offered hopefully.

"No, no! I shall tell you my message right now, *Akka!*" cried Manimekalai. "We are both women, so you will understand what I have to say. Men can never hope to understand such a thing, how many ever times they're told." She paused. "Consider that a girl has given her heart and soul over to a man. If such a man finds himself helpless, with no weapon or defence at hand, what should that girl do, if she truly loves him? Would she stand by and watch, doing nothing?"

Kundhavai instantly thought of Mandhakini. Tears glistened in her eyes at the memory. "How could she do nothing? She will throw herself in harm's way and save her beloved's life, even if she had to sacrifice her own."

"Ah!" breathed Manimekalai. "That I was bereft of someone to give me such worthy counsel! I have brought myself to ruin heeding the evil advice of that wicked Pazhuvoor Nandhini! I have killed, with my own hands, a noble man who took me unto his own as a sister and sought to marry me to my lover! Oh, woe is me!" cried Manimekalai and wept bitter tears.

Ilaiya Piratti glanced surreptitiously at Vanathi once again. "The mania crests," she murmured. "Girl, do not cry," she said in a louder voice, addressing Manimekalai. "Tell me what happened. Or perhaps another time will suit you better?" she suggested, crossing her fingers.

"No, no!" cried Manimekalai once again to Kundhavai's chagrin. "I shall tell you what I have to say at this very moment, *Akka*. My *thamaiyan* Kandamaaran had often spoken to me of a friend of his. He came to our palace in Kadambur a few months back. My heart decided at the very first sight that he was my champion."

Ilaiya Piratti found herself shaken. "Who is that fortunate man who has won your heart?" she asked, her voice trembling imperceptibly.

"Do you call him a fortunate man? No, no. When I gave over my heart to him, I tainted him with my ill luck, wretched woman that I am. He has been imprisoned in the dungeons at the Thanjavur fort, *Akka!*" wailed Manimekalai. "The women of the Pazhuvettarayar clan say that the dungeons of that fort are unspeakably terrifying. They say that prisoners incarcerated in those cells never emerge alive!"

"Those are lies, girl," replied Kundhavai instantly. "Why, Vanathi here and I have visited those dungeons in the near past!"

Manimekalai gazed at Ilaiya Piratti, hope shining in her tearful eyes. "Devi, can I go to the dungeons, too? May I see him just once, perhaps?"

"You still haven't told me who he is, girl."

"He is the Vaanar prince, Vandhiyathevar."

Kundhavai and Vanathi exchanged startled glances. Vanathi interjected herself into the conversation. "Why are you so worried about him?" she demanded. "What business do you have with him?"

Manimekalai glared at Vanathi, eyes flashing. "Who are you to ask me such a question?" she asked angrily.

Manimekelai calmed down the very next moment. "Pray, do not lose your temper, my lady," she said softly. "You are the Kodumbalur princess Vanathi, are you not? Isn't it your noble uncle who has seized control of the fort? I fall at your feet and beg you for a boon, my lady. Pray, speak to your uncle and help me secure Vandhiyathevar's freedom from the dungeons," pleaded Manimekalai abjectly. "Ask that I be cast into the cell in his stead! *I* am the foul sinner who killed Karikalar! When I confess to the crime of my own accord, what justice does it make to force another to endure punishment? Devi," she said, turning to Kundhavai. "I beg you too, with all my heart and soul. If Kodumbalur Periya Velar does not give me justice, I wish to plead my case before the Chakravarthy. You must help me," begged Manimekalai.

Kundhavai's heart churned with emotion as a stormy sea tossed with waves. She had been hesitant to but meet Vandhiyathevar in the dungeons; and here was this girl, stepping forward to confess to the murder on account of the love she bore for him!

How much of her words were truth and how much mere invention? Does she say such things to rescue her lover? Perchance.. she mentioned Nandhini's ill counsel, did she not? Had she yielded to the Pazhuvoor Rani's dark spell? Had she committed the heinous deed, after all?

No, no! She could never have perpetrated a vile sin as this! She makes such a claim to extricate Vandhiyathevan from the accusation of murder. That much is quite clear from her speech. No one will believe her, though. No one will release Vandhiyathevan in view of her confession.

Still, it had to be seen if further information could be drawn from her. The details of Karikalar's death remained a puzzle yet. Could this girl be the key to solving it?

"Manimekalai, I applaud you for your resolve of heart. Your noble effort to save your love by confessing to the crime is praiseworthy, indeed. Why, we have come across such remarkable deeds only in epics and ballads! It is verily a pity that this country has no bard from the Sangam era to sing paeans to you." Ilaiya Piratti paused. "Do consider, however, that my belief in your claim is hardly enough; your statement must be found credible by others, as well. Your father and brother aver that Vandhiyathevan was discovered by the side of Aditha Karikalar's lifeless body. Pray, think! Will the people heed their words or yours? There is yet another barrier, as well. You see, I was the one who dispatched the Vallathu prince to my brother, bading him dissuade Karikalar from going to Kadambur. I also instructed him that should Karikalar choose to go to Kadambur despite his efforts, he was to remain by his side at all times to protect him. On that fateful day, Karikalan's royal guards were personally handpicked by the Vallathu prince himself. He was near Karikalan when death struck him; yet he did not go to his aid. The Vallathu prince has failed in his duty. He ought to have saved Karikalar at the cost of his own life. Even if it comes to light that he did not commit the murder, the fact remains that he is accountable for breach of duty. By rights, the Vallathu prince is due punishment, is he not?"

"Devi, he did not fail his duty, not even a little bit!" said Manimekalai in earnest.

"Is there any proof for that claim, apart from your testimony?"

"Here, here is the proof! The evidence has been written down in the very hand of your illustrious *thamaiyanar*!" cried Manimekalai, producing an *olai* that she had tucked away in her waist.

An eager Kundhavai took the missive into her trembling hands. Yes, the writing was unmistakably Aditha Karikalar's own hand! He had personally recorded his message to protect the confidentiality of its contents. Karikalar had addressed the *olai* to Kundhavai.

A message from Aditha Karikalan to my dear sister, the beloved daughter of the Chakravarthy, Ilaiya Piratti Kundhavai Devi. It feels like a lifetime since I last slept. I committed a grave sin three years ago. I slayed an enemy who had made wholehearted surrender in a bid to plead refuge with me. The woman who begged me to spare his life subjects me to unbearable torment. Both of them do not allow me to sleep in peace.

Early this morning, as I lay awake with sleeplessness, I caught sight of a falling star. The blazing star streaked across the sky with brilliance only to plummet to the earth and disappear. I felt something leave my body at that very moment; nothing of me now remains but the shell, dear sister! Let this evil omen affect none but me. Let Ekambaranathar shield our beloved father and Arulmozhi from harm.

Ever since we have children, you and I have cherished many a hope to advance the splendour of noble Chozha Naadu. I cannot fulfill those dreams now; but my brother will. He was born for the very purpose of establishing rule over the three worlds. The Vallathu prince will stand by him in support. Devi, I am satisfied to learn that Vandhiyathevan has met with commendable success in the tasks you charged him with. You would not have sent him here on such an important mission otherwise. You would not have given him the responsibility of saving me from my own destiny.

Sister, should anything happen to me in this place, know that the culprits are none but my own fate and obduracy, not Vandhiyathevan. He tried his very best to dissuade me from coming to the Kadambur palace, just as you bade him do. Even here, he sticks to my side as a relentless shadow. He has struck a friendship with Manimekalai, a daughter of this house, for that very purpose. He is currently in hiding with her help, stowed away ahead of me in the very place I intend to go. All this to save my skin! But I wonder, can one save another from the clutches of destiny and karma?

You have likely heard tales of how the naga serpent lures small prey to its side, lulling them into a mesmerised trance as it performs its hypnotic dance, flaring its striking hood. I go to Nandhini thus. You have sent me a warning claiming her to be our sister. I cannot bring myself to believe it. Even so, she does seem to be enshrouded by a peculiar mystery. I am going only to learn the truth of it. One way or another, I shall discover the truth today.

Whatever becomes of my fate, know that Vandhiyathevan is not to blame. He strives faithfully to fulfill your command. Sister, Kandamaaran and Parthibendran are quite firmly ensnared in the web woven by that maya mohini, Nandhini. Vandhiyathevan alone has dodged her trap. I do not know how I am going to reward him. A delightfully lively maiden lives in this house, here. I have come to grow fond of her as my own sister. It would make a fine prize for Vandhiyathevan to be wed to Manimekalai. But sister, I confess that I am unsure if you would agree to such a plan.

My dear, beloved sister! I plan to give this olai into the safekeeping of that very maiden. Fortunately, she does not know how to read. As far as her matter is concerned, do as you see fit. You are the brightest in our family. I went against your wise counsel; now I shall reap the consequences. Let *Thambi* Arulmozhi pay heed to your words and raise the Chozha samrajyam to even greater heights…"

The message had stopped there. Tears flowed from Kundhavai's eyes as she finished reading the missive. She wiped her eyes dry in a quick motion and looked up at Manimekalai. "Girl, how did you come by this *olai*? Who gave it to you?" she asked.

"The Ilavarasar gave it to me himself, Devi," replied Manimekalai. "Nandhini had filled my ears with such poison about him, that I thought the *olai* was naught but a letter of love; I determined to cast it into the fire. I changed my mind soon enough. I decided I would learn what he had written, after all, and put it away safely. I gave the *olai* to my *thozhi* Chandramathi and bade her read it aloud to me. Ah, my heart twists with pain at the thought that I killed with my own hands that *veera purushar*, that matchless warrior who considered me his own sister! Devi, please arrange to mete out to me a punishment befitting the dspicable sin of murder!" begged Manimekalai.

Her agitation and excited manner of speech made it quite transparent that the confession was a work of fiction, an attempt to liberate Vandhiyathevan. Kundhavai's sharp eyes had seen through the ruse. Even so, the missive she had brought was real enough - the message was undoubtedly in Karikalar's own handwriting. This single *olai* would suffice to redeem Vandhiyathevar from the dungeons and shield him from the frightful blame of murder. *It would be to our benefit if this girl keeps her mouth shut. How on earth can she be convinced to hold her tongue?*

"Manimekalai, do you still insist that you were the one who killed Karikalar?" asked Kundhavai.

"Yes, Devi!" replied Manimekalai at once.

Kundhavai looked at her closely. "You say that you had someone read this *olai* aloud to you. You know then, that Karikalan made mention of you as his own sister. Why must you kill someone who held such affection for you?"

"Ah, if I had but read this *olai* earlier, I would not have committed that vile deed! I did so without understanding his noble heart, for that devious Nandhini had polluted my own," cried Manimekalai.

"How did she pollute your heart?"

"Nandhini convinced me that Karikalar bore a vitriolic hatred towards Vandhiyathevar. She often remarked that he would likely murder him as not. Karikalar, as if bearing truth to her words, made a terrible show of rage towards the Vallathu prince. He searched high and low for him, sword in hand. Where is that Vandhiyathevan, he had roared, I will kill him this very instant! I believed it to be true.

And so, with the knife, I..."

"That's enough from you," cut in Kundhavai. "Even if I believe your claim that a naive, innocent girl slayed a consummate warrior as Karikalan, the world never will."

"Devi, who else could have possibly killed him?" asked Manimekalai in desperation. "There were but two people in the dark chamber where Karikalan's body lay - Vandhiyathevar and I. He did not kill him, I tell you! So it stands to reason, doesn't it, that I am the killer?"

"By saying thus, you bring great dishonour to my late *thamaiyan*," replied Ilaiya Piratti gravely. "Pray consider another point as well. Do you think that the Vaanar warrior will watch mute as you take the blame for murder onto yourself? Won't he seek to save you, as you seek to save him? He will be as obstinate in his confession as you; he will insist that he was the one who killed Karikalar."

Kundhavai's lips tightened. "The world may yet forgive a woman. But girl, know that it will not forgive him. You are aware, I trust, of the horrifying punishment meted to traitors who assassinate a member of the kingly clan? They shall drag him to the crossroads..."

A scream of pure terror tore itself from Manimekalai throat. She collapsed into inconsolable sobs and cried out pitifully to Kundhavai, "*Akka*, you must save him!"

52

Roadblocks to Freedom

Kundhavai Piratti wondered how she could console Manimekalai. She found that she couldn't think of anything to say, for her own heart was weighed down with a sadness and worry that she could scarcely bear.

A raucous din erupted at the palace entrance all of a sudden.

"Vanathi, see what the fuss is about, will you?" said Kundhavai with a frown. The people forget that the Chakravarthy is in a delicate mental and physical state at the moment. What a commotion they make!"

Vanathi obligingly peered out of the palace facade. She returned almost immediately, her face aglow. "*Akka*, he is coming!" she said excitedly.

"He? Who is *he*?" asked Kundhavai with a smile.

Vanathi's cheeks turned pink. "It is he, *Akka* - your younger brother!"

"Alright, then," replied Kundhavai. "Take this girl aside." She watched as Vanathi dithered in place at the request. "Quickly, now. He won't take his leave without meeting you. I shall call for you when the time is right," promised Ilaiya Piratti Kundhavai.

Vanathi had barely taken Manimekalai aside when Ponniyin Selvan made his entrance.

"*Thambi*, I did hear that you're thronged by lively crowds everywhere you go; but I little expected you to lead them up to the very palace gates!" remarked Kundhavai. "How cruel these cheers must sound to the grieving Chakravarthy, who already nurses a wounded heart!"

Arulmozhi Varman looked quite miserable at her words. "What can I do, *Akka*? Do you think my own heart feels no pain at the clamour? Karikalar's noble remains had hardly become ashes when the people started up a shout. 'The crown for Arulmozhi!' they chanted. The cheers grate upon my very ears. Each time I hear their cries, I am tempted to flee into hiding! I only worry that such a thing would inflame the crisis at hand. The people are fully capable of crediting my absence to a plot hatched by Madhuranthakar and the chieftains to finish me off altogether. The consequences of such speculation are terrifying to imagine; it makes my heart stop with terror."

"Yes, yes, don't you ever do such a thing!" exclaimed an alarmed Iliya Piratti. "Relinquish the thought once and for all! Keeping aside the reaction of the people, the Chakravarthy's heart will certainly break in two. He endures enough sufference from grieving Mandhakini Devi and Karikalar."

"Precisely why I hesitate to flee. Instead, I shall deliver good counsel to the soldiers and people. I shall strive to win their approval to anoint Madhuranthakan as the crown prince, come what may." Frustration crept into Arulmozhi Varmar's tone. "They appear to listen intently enough when I speak; the second I turn my back, they revert to their cheers as before! *Akka*, pray ask Thirukovilur *paataan* and Kodumbalur Velan to make the people see reason! I came here to ask this of you, in truth. You must summon Malayaman and Velar at once to discuss this issue. Neither of them listens to me. They may give your words greater consideration…"

"I have broached this matter with them quite a few times, *Thambi*!" interrupted Kundhavai. "I find myself unable to break through their obstinacy. We must discover another way."

"*Akka*, perhaps you omitted to share with Velar a key piece of information," replied Ponniyin Selvar thoughtfully. "He may soften in his determination to make me the crown prince if he hears of it."

"What information is that, *Thambi*?"

"You must tell him of the oath that your *thozhi* Vanathi took. She did vow, did she not, that she would not sit next to me upon the throne? If you tell Periya Velar of her pledge, he might find himself less interested in making me the crown prince of the realm."

"*Thambi*, do you think that I haven't already told him that?" sighed Kundhavai. "Can you imagine what his reply was? 'Do you intend to bring a mighty empire to ruin to indulge the foolishness of a puerile maiden? If not Vanathi, there are hundreds of princesses in this great Bharata Desam eagerly waiting for the chance to wed Arulmozhi,' he said. He glared frightfully at Vanathi as he spoke, too. Poor girl, she fairly trembled with fear!"

Arulmozhi Varmar broke into a grin. "I suppose we must be thankful that she did not fall into a faint," he said, as he peered about the chamber.

"I have sent Vanathi away on a task," said Ilaiya Piratti pointedly, pursing her lips to hide her smile.

"*Akka*, if you and Vanathi were to be resolute in espousing my cause, I am certain that the matter can be handled one way or the other," said Arulmozhi earnestly. "Let us approach the Chakravarthy together. Only the Emperor's firm command can bring those grandsires around."

"A hitch lies there as well, *Thambi*. Sembian Maadevi stands quite firmly against your plan! If her decision is inflexibly at odds with our agenda, then what *can* our poor father do? Why, he may be driven to insanity once and for all. In truth, it is why I hesitate to disturb the Chakravarthy's peace on this issue."

"There's nothing to it then, but to make our entreaties to Sembian Maadevi. We must strive to change her mind. The reason she resists the idea of Madhuranthakan as the crown prince is the very one we guessed at. I met Sembian Maadevi a short while ago, at the Mudhanmandhiri Aniruddhar's home. She broke the truth to Madhuranthakan just today." Arulmozhi Varmar paused. "*Akka*, you should have seen our *chitappa's* face when she said the words, 'You are not my son!' His handsome face contorted into that of a grotesque *ratsasan's* instead! It was quite fortunate that I made my entrance at that very moment."

"Is that so?" asked Kundhavai interestedly. "What happened after that?"

"I folded my hands in obeisance in front of *paati* and said, *Amma*, I know that Madhuranthakar is not the son you bore. What of that? The son you brought up with such love is verily your son, too. So, he must rise to be the crown prince."

"What did Periya Piratti Sembian Maadevi have to say to that?"

"I hastened to return before she could give me a reply."

"*Thambi*, did you not tell Sembian Maadevi that Madhuranthakar has a rightful claim to the Chozha throne even if he is not her own son? Didn't you tell her that he is also our father's son, your *thamaiyan*?"

"I made no mention of that, *Akka*."

"But why, *Thambi*?" asked Kundhavai, surprised. "Did you fear that such an admission would taint our father's name? Or did you think it prudent to reveal this to her at a later time?"

"No, *Akka*. I have since learned that this belief of ours is not supported by evidence. That is why I held my tongue on the matter."

"How do you say that, *Thambi*?"asked Kundhavai, alert.

"Yes, *Akka*. The Mudhanmandhiri Aniruddhar is quite well-informed about the matter. I'm told that Madhuranthakan and Nandhini were born as twins two years after our father returned from the Eezha Theevu. That makes it quite impossible for them to be our siblings, doesn't it?" pointed out Arulmozhi.

Kundhavai lapsed into deep thought. "Arulmozhi," she said presently. "Knowing this, do you still want to anoint Madhuranthakan the crown prince?"

"Yes, *Akka*," replied Arulmozhi Varmar at once. "Any which way you look at it, Madhuranthakar is the child birthed by Mandhakini Devi; the son raised by Sembian Maadevi. I am least interested in ruling the empire, myself. Your *thozhi* Vanathi too does not wish to sit upon the throne."

Kundhavai's eyes softened. "*Thambi*! The epic of Ramar describes how Bharathar refused the kingdom when it came to his hands and set off in search of Ramar to fetch him back. It is said that when Guhan heard of this, he remarked, 'A thousand Ramars cannot equal you!'" She smiled. "The people of Chozha Naadu will doubtless declare that a thousand Bharathars cannot equal *you*.'

"They can say anything they like, later on. At the moment, I'll be happy enough if they leave me in peace, *Akka*!" exclaimed Arulmozhi. "I have devised another plan as well, as a last resort. I would like to know your opinion of it."

"What plan is that, *Thambi*?"

"You know, don't you, that the Pazhuvettarayars are gathering an army near Kudanthai?"

"Yes, I do. I am also aware that many chieftains have joined their ranks as allies. But I am told that the army is a rather small one compared to the forces mustered by our *paatanaar* and Velar. I believe that the army, such as it is, will likely be decimated in hardly a single *naazhigai*!"

"I've concocted a plan precisely to prevent such a thing from happening," replied Arulmozhi. "I shall stealthily mount a horse and repair to Kudanthai, where I shall surrender myself to the Pazhuvettarayars. Naturally, they will imprison me. That would leave our *paataan* Malayaman and the Senathipathi Boodhi Vikrama Kesari quite helpless, wouldn't it?"

Kundhavai touched her nose in amazement. "Marvellous plan, *Thambi!*" she exclaimed. "But," she continued thoughtfully, "it has its own danger, too."

"What is that, *Akka*?"

"When you arrive at the army camp of the Pazhuvettarayars, do you know what the soldiers are most likely to do? Why, they will break into cheers - 'Long live Arulmozhi Varmar! The crown for Ponniyin Selvar!' Frankly, I wouldn't be surprised if they cast the Pazhuvettarayars into prison instead of you!"

Arulmozhi froze at the terrible thought. "Yes, it never occurred to me that such a peril lay in that plan. How fortunate that I received your warning in time! Well, in that case, I shall go there in disguise, like the time I slipped into the Thanjai fort."

Kundhavai smiled. "No matter what disguise you wear, how long do you think the truth can remain concealed? If but a single person comes to know of it, the jig will be up - all and sundry will know the truth within a mere naazhigai. Why, you will attract the populace of the neighbouring towns to the camp, too!"

Arulmozhi's face shrunk. "*Akka*, what must I do, then? Why was I born into this world?" His hands clenched into exasperated fists. "Did I take birth for the sole purpose of tormenting others? Oh, that I did not drown and meet my end in the Kaveri waters!"

"Perhaps the *jothidars* and palm readers were right after all, *Thambi* - who can tell?" interjected Kundhavai gently. "It appears as if the divine kingmaker Rajyalakshmi intends to bestow Her grace upon you, whether you like it or not. The time of your birth is such!"

"*Akka!*" cried out Arulmozhi, taken aback.. "Have you joined ranks with our *paatan* Malayaman, too? Have you changed your mind, after all?"

"I remain unmoved by *paatan's* advice, *Thambi*. But I find myself swayed by *Annan* Karikalan's *olai*. He has written that it is you who must fulfill his dreams. When I read his words…" Kundhavai's voice shook with grief and her eyes swam with tears.

Ponniyin Selvan took Aditha Karikalan's *olai* into his own hands. Tears rolled down his cheeks as he read the missive.

When she saw that he had finished, Kundhavai spoke up. "*Thambi*, judge me if you will, but I shall speak my mind. My heart has attained a semblance of peace upon learning that Madhuranthakan and Nandhini are not of the Chozha clan," she confessed. " I do not wish for the exalted Chozha throne to seat one not of the Chozha clan. My reverence for Sembian Maadevi and Mandhikini Devi runs deep, it is true; but I cannot bring myself to make such an immense sacrifice, either. Not even for a second can I now bear the thought of Madhuranthakan as the crown prince."

"*Akka! Akka!* What are you saying?" exclaimed Arulmozhi Varmar, shocked. "Just a short while back, I gave my very word to Sembian Maadevi, Aniruddhar and Madhuranthakan that I do not want the crown. Why, I declared my intent to the thousands of soldiers and millions of people in our kingdom, too! Do you expect me to go back on my word?"

"*Thambi*, our *kula dheivam* Durga Parameswarai should show us the light. I am quite unclear on what counsel to give you, too. If Aditha Karikalan had heeded my words, this dilemma would have never come to pass. Ah, that a *maha veeran* as he should meet such an end!" lamented Kundhavai.

"How *did* you come by this *olai*, *Akka*?" asked Arulmozhi, looking at the missive. "Who brought it? When did it reach your hands? Why didn't you bring this up sooner?"

"I received it just a short while ago. It was Sambuvaraiyar's daughter Manimekalai who brought it to me."

A spark of recognition lit up Arulmozhi's eyes. "Yes, yes. I have heard about Manimekalai, too. How did this *olai* go to her?"

"Ask her yourself, *Thambi*, for she is here. I confess that I do not know how far her words can be believed," said Ilaiya Piratti.

As a matter of fact, Ilaiya Piratti had determined to present Manimekalai to Arulmozhi Varmar even as he entered the chamber, reckoning that she could bid the maiden make her speech about Vandhiyathevan. All through the exchange with her brother, Kundhavai's mind had truly been on Vandhiyathevan languishing in the dungeons. Ilaiya Piratti did not want to bring up his subject herself; she had waited, instead, for the right moment to introduce Manimekalai to the conversation. Now that her chance had come, Kundhavai called out to Vanathi and bade her fetch Manimekalai.

Manimekalai appeared before them as the very picture of grief, her face streaked with tears. So pitiful did the girl look that Ponniyin Selvan deduced that there lay a deeper reason behind her sorrow than was apparent.

"*Thambi*, this maiden is Manimekalai. She was the one who delivered the *olai*. Ask her yourself how she came by the missive!"

"Sister, you have safely delivered to us the very last *olai* penned by our *thamaiyan*. We shall ever be grateful to you," began Arulmozhi Varman. Before he could say anything further, Manimekalai flung herself at his feet in abject supplication.

"*Ilavarase! Ponniyin Selva!*" she cried. "Your words just now - do you mean them truly? Will you stand by them? If you bear as noble a sense of obligation as people say, if you do wish to thank me…" Manimekalai dissolved into sobs, unable to speak any further.

"*Akka*, what is this? Why does this maiden weep? Perchance, does she rue the fact that our *thamaiyan* met his end at her house? Is that what she feels sad about?"

"No, *Thambi*. Another sadness weighs upon her heart. Manimekalai, tell the Ilavarasar what you told me!" said Kundhavai Piratti to her encouragingly.

"*Ayya*, the sinner who killed your *thamaiyan* is none but me!" wailed a distraught Manimekalai as she wept. "Pray, cast me into the dungeons and set him free!"

Stunned, Arulmozhi Varmar looked at Kundhavai in disbelief. "*Akka*, what is she saying? Has the maiden lost her senses?"

"Not yet, *Thambi*," she replied. "But if the Vallathu prince is not soon released from the dungeons, she may truly lose her mind."

"What, what? *Who* is in the dungeons?" asked Arulmozhi in amazement.

"Have you completely forgotten the Vaanar warrior I had sent to Eezha Naadu with an *olai*, *Thambi*?"

Arulmozhi Varmar appeared as one emerging into reality from a long, deep dream.

Ever since he had set foot in the Thanjai fort, Ponniyin Selvar's attention had been dominated by the series of events that had transpired one after another. After he had heard news of Karikalar's demise, his heart had been fully engaged in discovering a way to seat Madhuranthakar on the Chozha throne. He truly had forgotten about Vandhiyathevar. Hearing his name, he now leapt at the subject. "Who? Is my dear friend Vandhiyathevar in the dungeons? Why? Who put him there?" he asked, aghast.

Kundhavai told him the details she had heard from Manimekalai.

Ponniyin Selvan listened to all of it with a grave countenance. "*Akka*, there cannot be another as thankless as me. I have lapsed by not enquiring after the Vaanar warrior. This is certainly my fault! Ah," he cried out in sudden agitation, "the ones who have dared to cast him in the dungeons are far greater criminals than I! I know well the depth of his loyalty to our *thamaiyan*. Who are they, that dared to blame him for Karikalar's death? What sheer folly is this? That this maiden willingly assumes the burden of the blame to save him is a bitter lesson to all of us. Why, I feel ashamed to even look her in the face." Ponniyin Selvar's eyes grew steely with determination. "Let other matters lie. I shall go to the dungeons forthwith and see to Vandhiyathevar's release. Pray, console this daughter of Sambuvaraiyar!" he declared and briskly walked away.

He had hardly reached the doorway when Thirukovilur Malayaman and Kodumbalur Velar appeared in front of him. Their very countenance seemed quite dubious. The Peryia Velar blocked his path, barring the doorway with a spear that he had brought with him. Malayaman stood right behind him, leaning on his sword; he looked quite determined to stop the prince from going any further.

The pair caught Ponniyin Selvar off-guard, provoking astonishment and anger in the prince. "Senathipathi, what is all this?" he asked. "Do you plan to clap me in chains, as well?"

"*Ilavarase*, we merely seek to stop you from going to the dungeons at the moment," replied Boodhi Vikarama Kesari. "Though, we *will* imprison you if the need arises."

It was such an unexpected thing to hear that Ponniyin Selvar found himself unable to gauge whether the words were spoken truly or in jest. The prince was in no mood to play along, though. He sounded quite angrier than before when he spoke. "With what authority have you both come to bar my way?" he asked shortly.

"With what authority do *you* plan to release the prisoner from the dungeons, my prince?" countered Periya Velar.

"Senathipathi, do I not have that right? Have you forgotten who I am? Or perchance, have you forgotten who you are?" cried out Ponniyin Selvar in disbelief.

"I haven't forgotten myself, my prince. I have not forgotten who you are, either. I stand before you today as the Thalapathy of the Thanjai fort, the guardian of the dungeons. You, my prince, are Ponniyin Selvar, the beloved son of the illustrious Chakravarthy. Even so, I regret to point out that you do not have the right to release a prisoner from the dungeons, no less than one who stands accused of slaying your *thamaiyan*. That droit lies with the Chakravarthy and the person who is to be anointed the crown prince. You have been loud and clear about your decision to eschew the Chozha throne. Naturally, no one can be released from the dungeons without the Chakravarthy's command," replied a calm Kodumbalur Periya Velar, Senathipathi Boodhi Vikrama Kesari.

"Child, Velar speaks the truth," broke in Malayaman. "Since Chinna Pazhuvettarayar abandoned his post, the Chakravarthy has instated Periya Velar as the Thalapathy of the Thanjai fort. You do not have the authority to release anyone from the dungeons."

Deprived of words, Ponniyin Selvar stood in silence. Manimekalai's sobs of despair filled the chamber.

53

Vanathi's Plan

Kundhavai, who had so far been a mute spectator to the argument between Arulmozhi Varmar and the two chieftains, took a step forward. "*Thatha! Mama!* Must you speak standing in the doorway? Do come inside. Ponniyin Selvan will not go against your words," she said, hoping to pour oil over troubled waters.

Malayaman and Velar stepped inside. "*Thaaye*," replied Periya Velar as he came into the chamber, "if only the Ilavarasar would accept the throne, there would be no trouble at all. We would be obliged to fulfill his commands. The Chakravarthy awaits an opportunity to lay down the burden of ruling the kingdom. He wishes to live out his remaining days in peace at the *pon maaligai* that Karikalar has built at Kanchi."

"*Mama*, I was telling the Ilavarasar the very same thing when the two of you came," said Kundhavai earnestly. "This damsel here intervened in our conversation to make a plea to the Ilavarasar. Her words have melted his heart; truly, that is why he wished to repair to the dungeons at once to release him."

"Who is this girl? Why does she cry so?" asked Periya Velar.

"Don't you recognize her, *mama*? She is Sambuvaraiyar's daughter, Manimekalai."

"Oho!" exclaimed Malayaman. "I suppose she weeps thinking of Sambuvaraiyar in prison." He looked upon Manimekalai with avuncular kindness. "Do not cry, girl. The Chakravarthy has issued orders to release your father. Parthibendra Pallavan has gone to the dungeons to carry out the task himself."

"*Thatha*," broke in Ilaiya Piratti, "it is not her father she worries about, it is the Vaanar warrior. She laments his incarceration and makes an earnest entreaty of us. She says, 'Release him, for I am the one who killed the Ilavarasar!'"

"Oho!" boomed Periya Velar. "If that is her claim, then we shall cast her into the underground dungeons as well. We cannot set free the Vallathu prince!"

"That is what I am saying too, *Ilavarasi!*" cut in Manimekalai, scarcely able to speak amidst her sobs. "Tell them to take me to him and cast me into the dungeons as well!"

The Senathipathi touched his forehead with a dramatic finger. "It seems to me that this girl is off her head," he whispered.

Vanathi couldn't hold her silence any longer. "*Periyappa*!" she cried. "Manimekalai is quite in control of her senses. It seems to *me* that you and Thirukovilur *paatanaar* have lost your minds! The Vallathu prince whom you have confined to the dungeons is a dear, beloved friend of Ponniyin Selvar. He was the one who journeyed to Ilankai, carrying with him Ilaiya Piratti's *olai* to Ponniyin Selvar. He was the one who brought the prince back to our shores! The Vallathu prince bore the full faith of the Ilavarasar who met a warrior's death. Certainly, the only ones who have come unhinged are those who accuse him and hold him prisoner in the dungeons!"

"Aha! When did this girl become such an insolent chatterbox?" exclaimed Periya Velar, greatly affronted. "Vanathi, is this what you've learned from Ilaiya Piratti? Don't you know that you ought to keep mum in front of your elders? Speak when you are spoken to, girl. Otherwise, hold your tongue!"

"Senathipathi, why get angry with this child?" asked Malayaman wisely. "She has only spoken out loud what the others think in their hearts."

"Yes, *mama*," interjected Kundhavai. "It is not proper for you or me to brush aside Vanathi. She will sit upon the throne of the Chozha *samrajyam* in the future, as the Chakravarthini. You and I will find ourselves obliged to carry out her commands then!"

"If only Arulmozhi deigned to consent, there would be no problem, would there?" sighed Malayaman. "Why, orders can be issued to release all the prisoners in the dungeons the very day of the coronation!"

"Orders can be issued too, to throw you, me and the rest of the blessed kingdom into the same dungeons," added Senathipathi Periya Velar gruffly.

"*Ayya*, you are both my elders. It pains me to find myself obligated to defy you. But here you both are, chatting away about all sorts of things instead of attending to a grave issue that demands immediate attention!" exclaimed Ponniyin Selvar. The Senathipathi interrupted him before he could say anything further. "*Ilavarase*, is it not crucial to avert disaster in Chozha Naadu by determining the right of succession to the throne?" he asked.

"You speak like you've entirely forgotten about the Chakravarthy!" cried Arulmozhi indignantly.

"We haven't forgotten, my prince. It was only after consulting with the Chakravarthy that we came here, in fact. He wishes to resolve the matter of succession so that he can withdraw to the *pon maaligai* that Karikalar has built in Kanchi, where he intends to live out the rest of his days."

"I shall go to the Chakravarthy at once!" declared Ponniyin Selvar. "I shall return with his royal command to release Vandhiyathevar. You will have no objections then, I trust?"

"*Ilavarase*, it would be improper of you to intercede with the Chakravarthy for Vandhiyathevar's cause. The Chakravarthy suspects that Vandhiyathevar colluded with the Pandiya Naadu *abathudhavis* and Nandhini Devi to plot Karikalar's death."

"Aha!" cried out Ponniyin Selvar, incensed. "And who gave him such an idea?"

"Not us, *Ilavarase*! It was Parthibendran who kindled such a belief in the Chakravarthy…"

"In that case, I shall meet the Pallavar myself. I shall ask him with what evidence he makes such an accusation!"

"You cannot meet Parthibendra Pallavar now, my prince. Having released Sambuvaraiyar upon the Chakravarthy's order, he is now on his way to Kudanthai. The Chakravarthy has tasked him with mediating with the Pazhuvettarayars and the other chieftains; he is to accompany them here at the earliest, in fact. The Chakravarthy sends a message through him that the right of succession to the throne is a matter that can be settled amicably through dialogue; he also conveys his approval to anoint Madhuranthakar the crown prince."

Ponniyin Selvar's face brightened. He glanced joyfully at Ilaiya Piratti and Vanathi. "That is wonderful news!" he exclaimed, delighted.

"It is terrible news," replied the Senathipathi quietly. "The day that

Madhuranthaka Thevar sits upon the throne against the wishes of the people and the armies, the glorious Chozha *samrajyam* – that exalted empire that has thrived for a century - will embark on a wretched path that leads to its very ruin."

"There is little doubt about that, my prince," seconded Malayaman. "The entire country will break out in catastrophic riots, from the Eezha Naadu until the Vada Pennai river!"

"I suppose it would be hardly a surprise to find the two of you at the head of these riots. Well, you may do as you wish. In the meantime, I will petition the Chakravarthy regarding Vandhiyathevan's release!" said Arulmozhi Varmar and turned to leave the chamber.

"*Ilavarase*, there is little need to approach the Chakravarthy with this request. It will serve only to court disaster. Devi, do stop your brother!" cried Periya Velar.

"Yes, child. Pay heed to the words of this old man!" chimed in an alarmed Miladudaiyar.

"What disaster do you speak of?" asked Kundhavai, troubled.

"A band of sinful wretches has given rise to wicked rumours. My mouth goes dry to even speak the words. They say that it was Ponniyin Selvar who tasked Vandhiyathevan with slaying Karikalar, driven by the desire to rule the kingdom. It was just yesterday that two men approached the soldiers in our troops with such a story."

"Heavens!" cried Ilaiya Piratti Kundhavai, appalled. "That is a vile, perilous canard!"

"Do you know what our soldiers did to those two? They dunked them repeatedly in the floodwaters of the Vadavaaru river. I happened across them by pure chance and managed to save them."

"No one in Chozha Naadu will believe such a foul rumour," cut in Ponniyin Selvar. "Isn't that quite clear from the reactions of our soldiers?"

"None will believe such a thing today, *Ilavarase*. But you have much to learn yet of the nature of people. The rumour will resurface after a while. It may find credence with some who do not know about you. It is not so uncommon, after all, to hear of royalty murdering one another for the kingdom - it has been the case in many a foreign empire. You are aware, I trust, of the history of the royal dynasty of Eezha Naadu?"

"Senathipathi! Do you expect me to turn a blind eye to my friend withering away in the dungeons in fear of a slanderous lie that may arise in the future?" asked Ponniyin Selvar, his lips thin with distaste.

"Not so far in the future as you may think, *Ilavarase*. If you support the release of Vandhiyathevar from the dungeons today, some will accept the rumour to be a fact on the very morrow. Such vile talk will no doubt fall upon the Chakravarthy's ears. Pray, think of the pain your father's heart will bear if he hears of such a thing!"

Ponniyin Selvar's handsome face darkened like a full moon veiled by black, thunderous clouds. He turned to Kundhavai Devi. "*Akka*! What do *you* say?" he asked grimly.

Ilaiya Piratti looked upon him with deep sadness. "Senathipathi," she said, turning to Periya Velar. "Who do you think will make an attempt to fan such a rumour?"

"I took aside the men that our soldiers were attempting to drown in the Vadavaaru river. I interrogated them thoroughly, with kind words and dark threats. They assert that it was Sambuvaraiyar's son Kandamaaran who dispatched them with this story."

Manimekalai took a step forward. "I am truly ashamed of my *thamaiyan's* actions," she said, trembling. "My brother was a good man, in truth. He has turned into a sinful wretch under the poisonous influence of Pazhuvoor Ilaiya Rani. Truly, the person who killed Aditha Karilalar is me. Put me in prison and release the Vallathu prince!" she cried, weeping bitter tears of grief and rage.

Ilaiya Piratti gently touched her back. "Manimekalai, do calm yourself," she said softly. "No one will believe your claim. It will only serve to bring new disaster upon us. Let us think of a way to solve this crisis."

Kundhavai then looked at the Senathipathi. "*Ayya*, my brother and I will take your advice. It is true that any attempt to set free the Vallathu prince will foster the conditions for dangerous rumours to spread." She paused as she gathered her thoughts. "It is crucial to identify the actual culprit at once. I shall take this matter to the Mudhanmandhiri Aniruddhar. Azhwarkkadiyaan, his disciple, has gone in search of the Pandiya Naadu *abathudhavis*. He will make his report on the findings soon, I expect. It is not clear what became of Periya Pazhuvettarayar and Pazhuvoor Ilaiya Rani. Perhaps the truth will come to light if they can be found. I will talk to this maiden and gather the details behind what transpired in Kadambur. In the meantime, pray make arrangements at the dungeons to ensure that the Vallathu prince is made as comfortable as he can be. It is certain that he did not commit this terrible murder!"

"I have an idea, *Akka*!" cried out the Kodumbalur Ilavarasi all of a sudden.

"Do tell, Vanathi!" said Kundhavai, surprised.

"Do you remember an earlier occasion upon which we went to the dungeons? Let us all go to the dungeons together now. We will take the Kadambur princess along, too!" said Vanathi.

Kundhavai looked at Periya Velar. "Senathipathi, what do you think of your daughter's idea?" she asked.

"It is clear that my daughter can come up with intelligent plans, as well!" said the Senathipathi with a touch of pride. "The night that Karikalar died, it was the Vallathu prince who was found by the side of his body. We may discover the truth upon questioning him."

They lost no time in making their way to the dungeons. Chinna Pazhuvettarayar had halted all work of minting gold coins on the very day he left the fort, so the mint was quite empty save a few guards. The group walked past the halls where the tigers were caged and made their way through the underground passage. They finally reached the dungeons where Vandhiyathevan was being held.

To their great surprise, they discovered that Vandhiyathevan was nowhere to be found! In his cell instead was the *vaithiyar's* son Pinakapani, wretchedly chained to the large hoops mounted on the prison walls. He yelled piteously when he caught sight of them. "*Ayya! Ayya!*" he cried out in despair. "Please release me!"

54

Pinakapani's task

The *vaithiyar*'s son Pinakapani had resolved to rise to a high post in government. The desire had sparked in his heart the very day he met Vandhiyathevan. He found that it had only grown stronger with time, burning in his chest as a bright, hungry flame of ambition.

Poor Pinakapani had not met with much success in his endeavour so far. There was a time when he thought that he could draw upon Nandhini Devi's kindness, but he soon discovered that the Pazhuvoor Rani had consigned him to oblivion. Pinakaapani's audience with Kundhavai Devi had not shown much promise, either. Ilaiya Piratti had hardly spoken to him. Truth be told, she had not really deigned to show him much attention. All that Pinapakani had gained at the Pazhaiyarai palace was a sound, shameful thrashing at

Vandhiyathevan's hands when he had accused the latter of being a spy.

Then the Mudhanmandhiri Aniruddhar had sent for him, bading him go to Kodikkarai on a mission to track down and fetch the *Oomai Rani*. Pinakapani sensed that his luck had changed. The high post he coveted seemed all but certain; he only had to satisfactorily fulfill the task he was given. There was nothing he couldn't achieve, thought Pinakapani, with the Mudhanmandhiri's support. Once he had come into his own, he would gladly square the debt of disgrace he owed Vandhiyathevan. Why, he would even crush once and for all Poonguzhali's insufferable pride and show the girl her rightful place.

Pinakapani fairly floated to Kodikkarai as he built such pleasant castles in the air. There, he succeeded in bringing Raakkammal under his spell. Tricked into believing him to be one of the abathudhavis, she spoke to him at length about their operations. It was with Raakkammal's aid that Pinapakani had located the *Oomai Rani*. He had managed to bring his quarry to the very entrance of the Thanjai fort.

All through the journey, Pinakapani's mind had worked furiously to ferret out the *Oomai Rani*'s secrets. He recalled the strange tales that an eccentric prisoner had told him when he had been confined to the dungeons for a day. Pinakapani had then dismissed his words as the ramblings of a lunatic, but now suspected that there was some truth in them after all.

Remember that a tree had come crashing down upon Pinakapani? The palanquin carrying the *Oomai Rani* had passed through a raging cyclone as it neared the Thanjai fort and a monstrous gust of wind had brought down a tree upon his very head. Pinakapani sought out the Mudhanmandhiri Aniruddhar as soon as his wounds had healed, but discovered that weighty events had transpired by then. The *Oomai Rani* had sacrificed her life to save the Chakravarthy's own. Karikalar had succumbed to murder. Mayhem reigned in town and country under the question of who was to be anointed the new crown prince. The Thanjai fort had come under the control of Kodumbalur Velar. News was in the air that the Pazhuvettarayars and their chieftain allies were gathering their armies. In short, civil war loomed threateningly over the horizon.

It was at this turbulent juncture that the *vaithiyar*'s son Pinakapani had sought an audience with the Mudhamandhiri Aniruddhar. Swamped by great worry as he was, Anbil Bhramaraayar little desired to waste time in conversing with Pinakapani. The Mudhanmandhiri wished to send him away at the earliest by conferring upon him a suitable reward for fulfilling his mission. But Pinakapani had brought up the subject of the madman he had met in the dungeons and won the Mudhanmandhiri's rapt attention. Aniruddhar found himself greatly interested in what the *vaithiyar*'s son had to say, for he reported the madman's astonishing claim that he knew the place in Ilankai where lay two priceless treasures of the Pandiya clan - the bejewelled Imperial Crown of Pandiya Naadu and an exquisite necklace of precious gemstones, said to have been bestowed by none other than Devendran, the very King of Heaven. Arduous efforts had been made in vain since the time of Paranthaka Chakravarthy to unearth these very artifacts. Until they were found, there would always be the need to contend with someone or the other claiming to be a descendant of the Pandiya lineage. Aniruddhar had already heard from Azhwarkkadiyaan about the theatrics that had taken place in Thiruppurambiyam at midnight, where a small boy had been seated upon the Pandiya throne and crowned in ceremony. The Mudhanmandhiri knew well that it wouldn't end there; in truth, there would be no end to the line of hopefuls staking a claim in the Pandiya dynasty, and each one would be ably supported in their cause by the Eezham and Chera kings. If the Chozha *samrajyam* were to succeed in its goal to subsume Pandiya Naadu into its great empire, it was imperative that the Chozha Chakravarthy be crowned in solemn ceremony at Madurai, adorned by both the Imperial Crown of the Pandiya dynasty and the ancient gemstone necklace.

This was the conclusion that Aniruddhar had reached quite a long time back. It was why each and every Chozha thalapathy who found himself in Eezha Naadu with his army was charged by the Mudhanmandhiri to find and bring back to Chozha Naadu the jewelled crown and gemstone necklace of the Pandiyas. None had succeeded in the task so far. Quite natural then, don't you think, that Anbil Aniruddha Bhramaraayar took an extraordinary interest in what Pinakaapani had to say?

The *vaithiyar*'s son had another piece of news to share too, one that inspired both keen interest and anxiety in the Mudhanmandhiri. Pinakapani reported that the madman had claimed to know a great secret about the Chozha dynasty and told him that one of the princes in line to the throne was not truly of Chozha stock.

When he heard this remarkable account, Aniruddhar thought that he would go to the dungeons and see the madman for himself. He quickly changed his mind when he realized that questions would inevitably follow his visit. Malayaman and Velar did not bear wholehearted confidence in Aniruddhar yet. They thought that like the Chakravarthy, he too supported Madhuranthakan's claim to the throne. Aniruddhar's presence in the dungeons would only serve to stoke their suspicion. They would assume, no doubt, that the Mudhanmandhiri had gone there to call upon Sambuvaraiyar. After much thought, Aniruddhar decided to make use of the *vaithiyar*'s son after all. He gave Pinakapani his signet ring, bading him pay a visit to the madman in the dungeons and return with a fresh report.

Pinakapani set off for the dungeons as told to meet the madman. To his great delight, he chanced upon Vandhiyathevan incarcerated in the adjoining cell. Pinapakani lingered at the entrance to his prison, doing his best to provoke him into conversation. Vandhiyathevan, however, did not rise to his taunts. Pinakapani flew into a rage at his silence and lashed out at Vandhiyathevan, subjecting him to a stream of verbal abuse. When he had sated his anger, he proceeded to the neighbouring cell. Pinakapani learned that the prisoner was not, in fact, a madman as he had believed. He asked him about the bejewelled crown and gemstone necklace of the Pandiya dynasty, but the man fell into abrupt silence. He refused to speak even of the secret he claimed to know about the Chozha dynasty. "Bring me the order for my release," he said, "and I shall tell you everything."

Pinakapani returned to the Mudhanmandhiri and confessed his failure, suggesting that it would be of great benefit to release the man as he had asked. The Mudhanmandhiri felt it prudent, too. It wouldn't be wise, thought Aniruddhar, to incarcerate a man who claimed to know dangerous secrets, especially when the kingdom was mired in a fierce debate over the right of succession. He met with the Kodumbalur Periya Velar and somewhat vaguely conveyed the news to him. Periya Velar, for his part, found that he couldn't think of a single objection to fulfilling the Mudhanmandhiri's wish to release a prisoner who had been imprisoned many years ago by Chinna Pazhuvettarayar. And so, he issued the order to release the madman.

A pompous Pinakapani strutted to the dungeons, release order in hand. He stopped at Vandhiyathevan's cell to maliciously inform him that he had brought an order for his release. Believing his words, a grateful Vandhiyathevan began to give thanks, upon which Pinakapani showed his true colours. He castigated Vandhiyathevan to his heart's content and spoke to him in condescending terms. "The only release you will get is an impalement at the crossroads!" declared Pinakapani, bringing an end to his diatribe. He marched self-importantly to the adjacent cell, where he spoke amicably with the madman and released the fetters that kept him chained to the walls. "Here," said Pinakapani, "I have brought the order for your release, just as you asked. Will you tell me your secrets now, at the very least?"

The *vaithiyar*'s son hoped to gain knowledge of the madman's secrets before producing him in front of the Mudhanmandhiri Aniruddhar. However, the madman did not seem particularly enthused at the prospect of freedom. In fact, he did not appear to be in any hurry to flee the cell. He evinced little confidence in Pinakapani's words. "What? How? Who gave the order for my release?" the madman asked, again and again. "Is it true that I am to be set free from the dungeons? Will they truly allow me to leave the fort and go outside?"

All of a sudden, a great heap of stones crumbled down from the wall that separated the cell from the adjoining one. Pinakapani swivelled around with a start, only to discover that Vandhiyathevan stood right behind him. The *vaithiyar*'s son hurriedly grasped at the knife he had tucked away at his waist, but Vandhiyathevan proved to be quicker. The Vallathu prince pounced upon Pinakapani and caught his neck in a vise, knocking the dagger away from his reach. A spirited fight ensued. The two frantically wrestled each other with all their strength, rolling and tumbling upon the prison floor. The madman grabbed one of the fetters hanging from the prison wall. When he saw an opening, he looped the chain around Pinakapani's neck and pulled it tight.

55

The Madman

All through the first half of the journey from Kadambur to Thanjai, Vandhiyathevan was lost to oblivion. His captors had bound him and put him onto a cart. The fire that had raged the night that Karikalar lost his life and the noxious smoke the flames had belched out had taken a cruel toll on his body. The brief bouts of consciousness that came upon Vandhiyathevan only brought him boundless suffering, for he became aware of the excruciating pain his body was in. Even his eyes were overcome by a painful itch. The times he lay half-awake in a daze of agony, Vandhiyathevan found himself tormented by eerie visions that swam in front of his burning eyes.

Veera Pandiyan's severed head drifts down to his face. "Adei! Were you the wretch who thwarted my revenge?" it rasps. Nandhini stands before him in all her splendid beauty, resplendent in jewellery and adornments.

Her red lips pull into a bewitching smile as she tries to trap him in her enchanted web of witchery. Sometimes Nandhini appears with her long hair loose and dishevelled, weeping and moaning with grief. Sometimes she materializes as a wraith, her rabid laughter curdling the very blood in his veins. He often spies with his bleary, stinging eyes a sinister shadow that stalks Karikalan, dagger in hand. Each time he tries to pounce upon it to thwart its design; each time he is rendered helpless by another shadow of demonic proportions that appears behind him, gripping his neck in a merciless vise. Ravidasan and his gang throw him into a fire that blazes bright and fierce. Kandamaaran looks on as his body burns in the searing flames. "Traitor! Serves you quite right!" he exclaims. There, there is Parthibendran, too. "Adei! Are you betrothed to Ilaiya Piratti yet? When is the wedding date?" he asks and bursts into loud laughter that fall upon Vandhiythevan's ears as claps of thunder. Senthan Amudhan comes running out of nowhere to save him from the fire. Pinakapani, the vaithiyar's son, lies in wait behind a tree; he strikes Senthan Amudhan's head with a log.

Vandhiyathevan feels an unendurable thirst as his body is afire. He wants to shout for water, but no sound issues from his mouth. His throat is dry and his tongue swollen so thick that it is stuck to the upper palate of his mouth. Manimekalai rises in front of him, bearing in her hand a golden bowl of devamritham, the nectar of the gods. She brings it to him and pours its contents into his mouth; she melts into the darkness before he can even think of thanking her. Aha! Wouldn't he give this maiden all the three worlds for the love and affection she bestowed on him! But what foolishness, surely, to dream of gifting Manimekalai the three worlds when he hardly had a jaan width of land to call his own kingdom?

There, there comes Poonguzhali! "Look upon my lovers!" she says and points out to him a host of kollivai sprites. What an astonishing maiden she is! "Why do you suffer in this earthly realm? Look, I shall take you to ponnulagam, the golden realm!" she says. "You speak of Ponniyin Selvan's realm, don't you?" he asks. A swarm of kollivai sprites descend upon him in droves. Terrified, Vandhiyathevan closes his eyes. The sprites tie him up and heave him to the sandbank at Kodikkarai, only to gleefully roll him down from the height.

Vandhiyathevan opens his eyes with a start. Guards bearing flaming torches in their hands hoist him onto a boat. Which river is this? Perhaps the Kollidam, the Kaveri or the Kudumurutti... Darkness takes him once again, cloaking his senses.

Countless episodes of delirium had gone by when a monstrous din erupted, akin to the roar of the seven seas in wild tumult. A great wave of sound broke over Vandhiyathevan and he opened his eyes fully conscious and clear-minded at last. The Thanjavur fort stood a short distance away; a vast ocean of people surged around the cart he was lying in, pressing upon the carriage on all sides. Vandhiyathevan realized that the uproar he had likened to the seven seas in riotous churn was, in fact, the keening of the crushing throng. The crowd had gathered because Aditha Karikalan's funeral procession had neared the Thanjai fort.

It didn't take long for the gathering to move on. Vandhiyathevan and Sambuvaraiyar were led into the Thanjai fort, accompanied by a grim retinue of guards. Ah! That the last rites of that incomparable warrior should take place without him, the prince's bosom friend, the confidante who was privy to his intimate secrets! Nor did his misfortune end there. All his arduous efforts to protect the prince's life had been in vain; they had brought him nothing but blame in the end, the accusation that he was the murderer! It was Vandhiyathevan who had made it possible for the prince to receive the last rites befitting a great warrior; it was he who had shielded his noble remains from the flames blazing through the Kadumbur palace. And now here he was, being hauled to the underground dungeons - a fate reserved only for the vilest conspirators and murderers in the kingdom. Well, what of it? Ilaiya Piratti and Ponniyin Selvar would make inquiries about him soon enough. They would grow alarmed on learning of his incarceration and hurry to the dungeons to release him, keys in hand. Even though he had failed to save Karikalar's life, they would praise the efforts he undertook to fulfill his charge...

Would they truly praise him, though? Would they remember him? They have lost their brother, after all; it is entirely possible that they fail to recall much else in their grief. Would they even have faith in his innocence? Why, even if they do - would they bear as cordial a rapport with him as before?

As the guards led him deeper underground past the royal mint where the kingdom's gold coins were forged, Vandhiyathevan found his hopes fading away. Chinna Pazhuvettarayar had suspended all work at the mint, so there were just a handful of guards along the passage. None of them bore the Pazhuvettarayar crest of the *panai maram*; Periya Velar had dismissed the old guards and instated his own men instead. The soldiers stared unblinking at the newcomers to the dungeons. Vandhiyathevan caught snippets of their conversation as they passed them by. "There goes Sambuvarayan; that man there is Vandhiyathevan of the Vaanar clan. These are the wretched *chandaalas* who killed the Ilavarasar!" they said to one another. As the retinue marched the pair through the chambers housing the tiger cages, the fierce animals seemed to Vandhiyathevan to epitomize the merciless justice wielded by the royal kings of the Chozha clan. The guards led them deeper down yet another staircase; there, they locked him up in a dingy prison cell and promptly disappeared, leaving him to his fate. Vandhiyathevan lost all heart and resigned himself to abject despondency. He would never be released from this stockade; his body would likely leave the prison cell only after it had drawn its last breath. Chinna Pazhuvettarayar was suspicious of him, as it were. As for Parthibendran, why - not only did the man positively loathe Vandhiyathevan, he also had the full faith of old man Malayaman. The Pazhuvettarayars would, no doubt, come to Sambuvaraiyar's rescue; they would declare him free of all blame and see to his swift release. Who would come to his defense? No one. Instead, they would thrust all the blame onto his own head and charge him with murder. Would they give him a public trial? If they did, perhaps he could give his testimony of the events. No, no. They would conduct neither an inquiry nor a trial. Such a proceeding would obligate them to reveal the truth about Nandhini and Ravidasan's gang - no one would want such a thing, surely! No, he would simply be left to rot in the dungeons until death claimed him. Or perhaps they would pass judgement upon him without a trial. Perhaps they would condemn him as Karikalar's murderer and hang him at the crossroads.

Heavens, how enthusiastic he had been on arriving in Thanjai the very first time! The days had passed by in such pleasant pipe dreams. His fateful tryst with Ilaiya Piratti and Vanathi at the Kudanthai *jothidar's* home had left him so elated that he had fairly floated to Thanjai upon a sea of bliss. He had worried then, hadn't he, that Chinna Pazhuvettarayar would suspect him to be a spy and cast him into the dungeons? It had come true now, that fear, under entirely unexpected circumstances. He had lived such a happy life, free as a bird soaring through the high, blue skies; now they had imprisoned him here, in this dark, stifling cell. How long would he survive in this place? There was no earthly way he could. There was nothing left to do but devise a plan to take his own life. Vandhiyathevan sunk into yearning and dark despair as he turned such thoughts over in his mind.

Someone cleared their throat in the neighbouring prison cell. A dreadful voice broke the grim silence, grating upon his very nerves.

"*Ponnar meniyane!*"

The voice proceeded to loudly croak a *thevaram* hymn in all its harsh, guttural glory. Vandhiyathevan couldn't help but think of Senthan Amudhan. It was certain that these terrible sounds were not of his making - Senthan Amudhan's tone had a divinity to it, a dulcet sweetness. This voice in song was a thing of pure torment, a bane that brought naught but misery to the ears. Even so - why was a prisoner in this underground dungeon singing that very song?

Siva Siva! It was quite impossible to listen to the cacophony renting the air. Wasn't it enough that he was locked away in the underground dungeons? Did he have to be subjected to such a hair-curling caterwaul as well?

"Who *is* that?" called out Vandhiyathevan, with great feeling.

"It is me, the madman!" came the reply.

"Madman, my dear fellow! Pray, show me pity and cease your singing!"

"Why? Don't you like it?"

"*Like* it? Why, it is nothing short of a delight."

"I suppose you like it even better now that I've stopped," replied the voice shrewdly.

"You don't seem to be as mad as you claim!" remarked Vandhiyathevan, grinning despite himself. "Who taught you this song, anyway?"

"Another youth was detained a short while back in the very cell you are in. He was in prison for just a few days, in truth, but he sang this song constantly, without a break. I ended up learning it myself!"

Vandhiyathevan concluded that the youth could have been none other than Senthan Amudhan. He had heard that Chinna Pazhuvettarayar had imprisoned Senthan Amudhan in the dungeons for a short spell because the lad had helped him escape; the person who had been incarcerated in this cell had to have been him. *Ah, what a sweet boy that Senthan Amudhan is! What a wonderful friend!*

"Who was the youth who was in this cell? Do you know?" asked Vandhiyathevan.

"Of course I do. Senthan Amudhan, his name is. Ostensibly the son of some mute woman or the other. If the world only knew who he truly is…" trailed off the voice.

"What would happen?"

"The world would turn topsy turvy!"

"Would we find ourselves freed, do you think, if the world were turned upside down?"

"Oh, absolutely! Without a doubt!"

"Then tell me, won't you, who he truly is?"

"As if I would tell you such a thing so easily!" scoffed the voice. "I will only speak of it in the very ears of the Chozha Chakravarthy himself." A pause ensued. "It *is* Sundara Chozhar, isn't it, who reigns as the Chakravarthy of Chozha Naadu?"

"Why, yes. Why would you doubt such a thing?"

"A few changes took place here, a couple of days ago. There was a change of guards - all the old soldiers left and new ones came to take their place. They have shut down the mint entirely, too. When it was functional, the sounds of the metalwork by the smiths was *incessant.*"

"Why did they shut down the mint? Why were the guards changed?"

"I believe Chinna Pazhuvettarayar has deserted the Thanjai fort, yielding control of the keep to Kodumbalur Velar. I learned these things by listening to the guards speaking amongst themselves…"

"Oh, you overheard that as well, did you?" remarked Vandhiyathevan. In truth, he found himself greatly surprised by the report. Kodumbalur Boodhi Vikrama Kesari happened to be well-acquainted with him - he had subjected the Vaanar prince to intense questioning on one occasion, hadn't he? Perhaps he would believe what he had to say and release him from imprisonment. Though, how could he, to be fair? Who on earth could release with ease a prisoner who stood accused of killing prince Karikalar?

"What, *Thambi?* Cat got your tongue? Shall I sing for you again?" asked the madman and promptly cleared his throat.

"No, no!" cried out Vandhiyathevan in some alarm. "I was only thinking about what you said. You did mention, did you not, that Senthan Amudhan is not the mute woman's son? I was wondering who else he could be."

A pause. "Let's set that subject aside and talk about other things!"

"Why do you call yourself a madman?"

"Everyone who comes here tells me so."

"Why, though?"

"I know the place in Eezham where lie hidden the royal crown of the Pandiya dynasty and the gemstone necklace gifted by Devendran. I tell everyone who comes this way that I will reveal the location if I am released. That's why they call me a madman."

Vandhiyathevan snorted. "The ones who call you a madman are the lunatics, in truth."

"Do *you* believe what I say?"

"Oh, absolutely," assured Vandhiyathevan. "But what is the use of my belief? I cannot be of much help to you."

"Don't speak too soon! You know, I've noticed, of late, that anyone imprisoned in the very cell that you are in right now finds himself released quickly enough."

"Is that right? Let's hear a few examples, then."

"Pinakapani, the son of some *vaithiyar*, was imprisoned in your cell; the Pazhuvoor Rani Nandhini Devi came down to the dungeons herself to free him and take him away. Senthan Amudhan was also in your cell, like I said. Kundhavai Devi and the Kodumbalur princess came and released him."

Vandhiyathevan heaved a great sigh at these words. "No such queen or princess will come to my aid," he said sorrowfully.

"Then I shall release you myself," said the prisoner in the neighbouring cell.

"Now you really do sound like a madman!" replied Vandhiyathevan drily.

"No, it's true, I tell you. Believe me!"

"I don't have much choice but to believe in you."

"In that case, remain patient until the guards have given us our meals tonight!" cried out the self-proclaimed madman.

Hidden Meanings and Explanations

Kollivai pisasu - Will o' the wisps

56

A STROKE OF WONDER

The last guard finally left in the late hours of the night. Vandhiyathevan waited with bated breath, eager to hear what the madman in the neighbouring cell had to say. All he could hear from the other side was the sound of vigorous scraping, not unlike a mouse scratching at the wall. Vandhiyathevan was unfazed by of lions and tigers, but he harboured a deathly fright of cats and mice; the very thought of spending a night in a dark cell with mice for company unnerved him to no end. "Madman!" he called out anxiously. "Have you gone to sleep?"

No reply came. The soft, raspy sounds of scraping continued unabated.

Shortly, a few loose stones dislodged from the wall and a small opening appeared. The madman's voice floated through the breach. "*Appane*, are you asleep?" it asked.

"No, I was waiting for you. What have you done, now?" asked Vandhiyathevan in astonishment.

"This is the result of six months of hard work," replied the madman, gesturing to the hole in the wall. "Before *that*, it took me another six months to free myself from the chains binding my hands." He deftly made the gap bigger and scrambled through to Vandhiyathevan's cell.

Vandhiyathevan hurried to help him down. "You went to so much trouble to make this opening!" he exclaimed. "What on earth did you hope to achieve? If you had made a hole that led outside, it would have served you some use!"

"There is no wall that leads outside from these cells. You can only leave through the chamber where the tiger cages are. This cell is empty, sometimes. It tends to be unlocked when it is unoccupied. It is easier to slip out from here than my own cell," explained the madman.

"Ah! You scarcely know me and yet you've let slip such key information! What would you do if I decided to snitch on you?"

"One's voice is enough to gauge one's trustworthiness," replied the madman. "I trust Senthan Amudhan, for instance, but not Pinakapani. I decided that I could trust you the moment I heard your voice. Besides, we must make our escape right away - there can be no better time than now!"

"Why?"

"Didn't I tell you that the guards have changed?" asked the madman with some impatience. "I overheard two of them conversing with each other - they were talking about opening the tiger cages. 'What do we do if the tiger pounces on us when we open the cage?' asked one. 'Lie down and die - what else?' the other replied. It's quite clear from their chat that they will not open the tiger cages. Because these guards are new to the job, I rather think we can catch them by surprise and make a break for it. In any case," he continued, "don't you think it's better to try to escape than die here?"

"That is true," replied Vandhiyathevan slowly.

"It would be even easier too - after all, two heads are better than one," said the madman, studying Vandhiyathevan. "You're not like me. You are strong and healthy yet, for you haven't spent much time in this place. We can tie up the guards together, grab the keys and make our escape. What do you say?"

"It does sound like a good idea. When shall we leave?"

"Patience. I shall tell you when the time comes."

"I am quite tired, to be honest," admitted Vandhiyathevan. "It would serve us well if we were to take a couple of days, in truth."

Plan in place, the madman proceeded to ask Vandhiyathevan a slew of questions to educate himself on the events that had taken place in the outside world while he had been imprisoned. He cried out in surprise when he heard that Aditha Karikalar was no more. "Ah! Quite important then that I slip out of here!" he exclaimed.

"Why do you say that?" asked Vandhiyathevan, curious.

"Well, won't the next in line to the throne now be anointed the new crown prince?"

"Crown prince?" remarked Vandhiyathevan with a wan smile. "The Chakravarthy suffers from fatigue of body and mind. He wishes to step aside from reigning the empire."

The madman scratched his chin. "Who do they say is likely to be crowned, then?" he asked.

"Some chieftains wish to crown Madhuranthakan while others stand by Ponniyin Selvar."

"What does the Chakravarthy think?"

"I am told that the Chakravarthy wishes Madhuranthakan to ascend the throne in order to avert civil war in the kingdom."

"Crucial, then, that we make our escape as soon as we can!" cried the madman.

The madman then gave Vandhiyathevan a detailed account of how he came to discover the hiding place of the Pandiya crown and gemstone necklace in Eezham. When Vandhiyathevan asked him once again about the secret he claimed to know of the Chozha clan, the madman shook his head. "I will not tell you now. I shall reveal it to you if we manage to escape these dungeons alive. Else that secret will die with me!" he declared.

Vandhiyathevan sunk into furious thought. He tried to guess at the secret the madman kept. A hazy cloud of dim memories surfaced in his mind's eye and disappeared.

When the *vaithiyar's* son emerged in the dungeons, Vandhiyathevan was thrown for a loop. He worried that the plan hatched together with the man in the neighbouring cell would be foiled, after all. Vandhiyathevan did not buy into Pinakapani's venomous speech, in truth. In fact, both he and the madman were of the opinion that Pinakapani had come there with evil designs in mind. Both had vowed that neither would make their escape leaving the other behind. The two came to a quick decision about what they ought to do if Pinakapani came to the dungeons once again.

So when Pinakapani appeared before them a second time, the pair was quite prepared. As the *vaithiyar's* son showed the madman the signet ring and asked him about his secret, Vandhiyathevan entered the cell softly through the hole in the wall. Pinakapani turned around and caught sight of him. He promptly fell upon Vandhiyathevan, launching a belligerent fight between the two. At any other time, Vandhiyathevan would have made short work of the *vaithiyar's* son. As it were, his body had not yet healed from the wounds it had borne from the fire; his throat still ached from the *kalaamugan's* devilish assault. The fight went on for longer than expected. The madman surfaced behind Pinakapani, chain in hand; he looped it around his neck and tugged it tight. Pinakapani fell down.

The two bound Pinakapani to the iron hoops mounted on the prison wall. Vandhiyathevan spoke as he tied the binds. "Pinakapani, do you remember the time we travelled to Eezha Naadu in search of the wondrous *sanjeevani mooligai* to heal the Chakravarthy?" he asked conversationally. "We failed in our mission. But here you are today, come to us as a stroke of wonder! We cannot thank you enough for your timely help. You're the *vaithiyar's* son, aren't you? Best you stick to the practice of medicine. Why meddle with matters of espionage and create trouble for yourself?" he said, not unkindly.

Pinakapani made no reply. He was left dumbstruck by the rather humiliating disaster that had befallen him. The torch he had brought was now lying upon the ground; it threw its flickering light upon his burning eyes, ablaze with a fiery rage. The two grabbed the signet ring the *vaithiyar's* son had brought, taking for themselves that powerful symbol of authority. Vandhiyathevan unravelled the cloth around Pinakapani's head and tied it around his own.

The pair quickly exited the cell and locked the door. Softly, slowly, they ascended the staircase leading to the underground dungeons. Unfamiliar with the lay of the prison, they climbed the steps carefully, keeping their eyes peeled for danger. When they heard the menacing growls of the tigers, they came to a stop, reluctant to proceed. Perchance, had they come to know of their escape and uncaged the tigers?

Vandhiyathevan and the madman cautiously peeked into the chambers housing the tiger cages. They saw none but a lone guard, intently peering at the cages as the tigers snarled. Perchance, was he considering letting the tigers loose upon them? The *vaithiyar's* son had begun to raise a ruckus by now; the noise could have well raised the guard's suspicion. Would that they had stuffed a cloth into that wretch Pinakapani's mouth!

57

Freedom

Vandhiyathevan hesitated near the doorway for a while. He considered pouncing to attack the guard, who was twirling his moustache as he surveyed the caged tigers. Perhaps it would prove easier to get rid of him and walk on. It was at that very moment that he caught sight of two more soldiers stationed at the doorway beyond the tiger cages. One of them signalled to the guard before he walked away. Perchance… could they be talking about him through gestures? Even if this guard were to be defeated, many more would lie in wait for him at the doorways beyond this chamber. Could he handle all of them and make his escape? Perhaps… why, what if he made one great leap into the chamber and let loose all the tigers from their cages? Wouldn't it be easier to slip away in the ensuing chaos?

As Vandhiyathevan evaluated this course of action, a loud cry issued from the guard. "Oho! Do you truly think you can escape?" he exclaimed. Vandhiyathevan started, jarred into fright.

A tiger growled in response. "Shush, vile cur!" snapped the guard. "Pipe down!"

Vandhiyathevan realized that the guard was talking to the tiger and a short laugh of relief escaped his lips. The guard immediately turned around at the sound.

"Have you ever seen such a thing, *Ayya*? It appears that this tiger is trying to intimidate me!" cried the guard. "Hah! I have seen so many tigers like this one, haven't I? Such shows of bluster won't work on a lion as me!" he declared, puffing out his chest. His fingers wandered to his bristly moustache once again and he twirled it with marked pomposity.

"Tigers or rats, they're all the same when cooped up in a cage. How can they hope to strike fear in another?" replied Vandhiyathevan lightly. He showed the guard the signet ring as he spoke, drawing his attention to Periya Velar's emblem.

"Off you go, *ayya*!" said the guard at once. "The Mudhanmanthiri's men are waiting for you at the gates, I am told. Go on, hurry!" He looked beyond the two fugitives, peering at the direction by which they came. "*Adei*, madman!" he yelled out loud. "Can't you stay quiet?"

Vandhiyathevan was, in fact, holding the madman's hand at that point. He felt it quiver with fright and tightened his grip to give him courage.

The pair went past the guard and strode ahead. The guard was speaking even as they walked away. "They want freedom, I believe!" they heard him remark scathingly. "What is to become of our livelihoods, I ask, if everyone were to be released?"

Brave as he was, Vandhiyathevan's heart was pounding in his chest. All he could think of was the guard's words. The Mudhanmandhiri's men awaited them at the gates, he said. The dungeons were dark and gloomy, so it was fairly simple to trick the guards and slip away from them; such a ruse would be an entirely different proposition outside, in broad daylight. What would they do if the Mudhanmanthiri's men were to catch onto their gambit? *Come what may, we shall manage. We must be prepared to face anything from here on! Thankfully, this madman is a rather clever chap. He will doubtless come to our aid if the occasion calls for it.*

They swiftly strode through the many doorways in the dungeon and crossed the gold mint. Soldiers were stationed at multiple checkpoints, but they instantly stepped aside when they saw them carrying the Velar's crest. They did not look too closely at their faces, either. As they walked, Vandhiyathevan's mind worked furiously to think of a plan. As they crossed a long chamber, he whispered into his companion's ear. "Are you going to the Mudhanmanthiri's palace or are you coming with me?" he asked.

"If I go to the Mudhanmanthiri's home, they will cast me back into the dungeons when they're done," whispered back the madman. "I will come with you. Where do you plan to go?"

"God willing, we shall make our way to Eezha Naadu. You must address me as Pinakapani in front of the Mudhanmanthiri's men. What is your name, by the way?"

"Madman!"

"Tch. I asked for your true name, the one your parents gave you!"

"Oh, *that*. My parents named me Kariyathirumal. People call me Karuthiruman."

"An excellent name! Karuthiruma, I shall touch your shoulder as we walk the Thanjai highway. You must run away with me upon the signal. You do run well, don't you?"

"Oh, the Eezham king himself cannot compete with me when it comes to running away!"

Vandhiyathevan laughed. "A fine madman, indeed!"

They exited the dungeons after crossing the gold mint and emerged outside.

The Mudhanmanthiri's men were not as many in number as Vandhiyathevan had feared. There were just two of them, in fact. One was a rather chubby, well-upholstered fellow. Vandhiyathevan felt quite certain that he had seen him before, but try as he might, he couldn't remember when or where.

"You are the Mudhanmandhiri's men, aren't you?" called out Vandhiyathevan.

"What, have you forgotten us already?" asked one, raising a brow.

"No, no. I only meant to ask if you are the ones who will take us to the Mudhanmandhiri's palace," replied Vandhiyathevan hastily.

"Yes, none but we," sniffed the man dubiously. "Why, next you will say that you have forgotten the way to the Mudhanmanthiri's home!"

Karuthiruman suddenly remembered what Vandhiyathevan had told him. "Pinakapani, I confess that I am scared!" he cried. "Who knows, perhaps the Mudhanmandhiri will throw me back into those dungeons!"

"He will do no such thing. It appears that you don't know our Mudhanmanthiri very well," cut in the plump man. "But don't you dream of escaping from us. Why, we shall be thrown into the dungeons ourselves in that event!"

Having had his say, the portly man took the led and marched ahead of the group. The other one positioned himself behind Vandhiyathevan and Karuthiruman with a vigilant air.

The Thanjavur highway was bereft of all liveliness. There was not a single person to be found on the street, for the people who lived in the fort had returned to work once Aditha Karikalar's last rites had ended. Outside the keep, the Kodumbalur forces were maintaining a fierce watch; they permitted none to enter the fort from without. Vandhiyathevan walked on, keeping a sharp lookout around him. It would be quite an easy affair to escape from these two guards. But the pair had to make sure that they wouldn't get caught once again. They needed to identify a convenient path that led outside the fort, one that would afford them a discreet exit. Vandhiyathevan looked closely at both sides of the road, hoping to catch sight of such an escape route.

As the group passed the entrance to the Pazhuvettarayar's palace, anxiety rose in Vandhiyathevan. They would soon come upon that lane, the very one that he had used to get away from the Pazhuvettarayar's guards! He had been waiting for this lane, in truth. The winding street had quite a few handy corners and deadends tucked away along its path. It was also flanked by wooded estates on both sides; the sturdy branches bent low over the compound walls to jut into the lane. If there was ever a chance to run away from these guards, this was it. The pair could leap into the Pazhuvettarayar's palace garden as Vandhiyathevan had, on an earlier occasion. If only they could manage that, why, the thick press of trees in the estate would make it quite convenient for them to hide away. After that, it would be easy enough to exit the fort via the underground passage that ran through the treasury.

Here comes the lane!

Vandhiyathevan considered touching Karuthiruman's shoulder as he had planned. *What is this, now? A great crowd approaches! Who could it be? Palanquins, horses, a retinue of guards bearing spears - why, such pomp and ceremony must herald the arrival of a royal family or a higher official.*

The Mudhanmanthiri's men had reached the same conclusion, too. They hurriedly looked about here and there, finally noticing the very lane that Vandhiyathevan had set his sights on. The group slipped into the street at once to make way for the oncoming crowd. The men quickly took position at the front, affecting an ingenuous stance as they shielded their wards from curious eyes.

The throng reached them soon enough. The royal cavalcade cut a grand spectacle as it passed them by. Soldiers led the display, bearing shining spears in their hands. Three majestic steeds clip-clopped behind them, shining white as the moon. Malayaman and Kodumbalur Velar were seated atop two horses, riding alongside a third man whose handsome mount trotted in between them. Vandhiyathevan realized with a twinge that it was Ponniyin Selvar himself. *Aha, how close he is, and yet so far!*

For a heartbeat, Vandhiyathevan wondered if he ought to push past the guards and present himself in front of the prince. He changed his mind the very next second. How could Ponniyin Selvar bestow mercy upon one charged with murdering his brother? How, for that matter, could he even make a show of friendship? Why, it was entirely possible that the very sight of Vandhiyathevan would evoke repugnance in him. It was hard to guess at what Malayalan and Velar would do, too. The Vaanar youth turned his attention to the palanquins that followed behind. *Ah! It is none other than Ilaiya Piratti Kundhavai, Kodumbalur Ilavarasi Vanathi and Sambuvaraiyar's beloved daughter, Manimekalai!* Vandhiyathevan's heart twisted with pain at the sight.

Under any other circumstance, he could have sought help from any one of these noble women; they would have wholeheartedly rendered him all aid in their power. But now? If Ilaiya Piratti and Ilavarasi Vanathi caught but a glimpse of the foul wretch who treacherously murdered Aditha Karikalan, why, how repulsed they would feel!

No matter. How strange though, that they are accompanied by that innocent waif Manimekalai! I suppose it is some comfort that she is with them. Would Manimekalai have given them her account of the events at Kadambur? She did profess to be the killer, didn't she? Could she have made such a claim to these people as well, hoping to save him?... No, she could not have done such a thing. If she had, they would not take her along with them with such evident warmth and friendship.

The palanquins swept past the lane, swiftly followed by the soldiers marching at the back of the procession.

"Come on, then. We can go now," said the Mudhanmanthiri's men and began walking ahead.

It took Vandhiyathevan nary a second to decide that this was the right time. He gently touched Karuthiruman's shoulder and tore into a sprint through the lane. Karuthiruman leapt at the signal and bolted behind him.

As they ran, they became aware of the sound of footsteps running behind them. It had to be the Mudhanmanthiri's men. It was Karuthiruman who turned around to look.

"One of them has fallen behind. Only a single guard is on our tail," he panted.

Vandhiyathevan turned back to see that he was right; the stout guard hadn't been able to keep up the chase. Still, it would not be a wise move to attempt fighting the other guard, solitary as he was. He signalled as such to Karuthiruman and continued to race forward.

Vandhiyathevan skidded to a stop when he reached the place from which he had scaled the wall on an earlier occasion. The bent, twisted branch still hung over the boundary, exactly as he had left it. He grabbed hold of it and jumped lithely, making a neat landing upon the wall. Vandhiyathevan extended his hand towards Karuthiruman and pulled him up. Losing no time, the pair hurriedly shook the twisted branch until it broke; they waited until the guard came closer and pushed the log down on him. They didn't wait around to verify whether the branch had actually fallen upon the guard; the two quickly jumped down from the boundary wall into the palace gardens. They quietly slipped into the dense thicket of trees upon its grounds and hid themselves away, keeping an alert watch on the wall they had come by. When it became clear beyond doubt that they were no longer pursued, they moved deeper into the gardens.

"Appa!" sighed Vandhiyathevan in relief. "We've made our escape!"

"Don't get ahead of yourself. How are we to get out of the fort?" asked Karuthiruman, gasping as he caught his breath.

"There is a way, my friend. Patience!"

Vandhiyathevan stopped when the two neared the Pazhuvettarayar's palace. The stately home was not as lively as it once was, but it still had a handful of guards deployed on its premises. Prudence required them to sneak into the treasury after dark. Vandhiyathevan sat down heavily upon a wooden log, gesturing to Karuthiruman to join him.

"We can't do much until nightfall," he informed his companion. "Let's hear your story until then!"

"I *told* you, didn't I - I cannot speak of it!" grumbled Karuthiruman as he made himself comfortable.

"Then I cannot lead you outside the fort, either," retorted Vandhiyathevan, crossing his arms.

Karuthiruman made a face. "And what would you do if I spun a yarn instead of telling you the truth?"

"Yarn or no, tell your tale!" replied Vandhiyathevan as he stretched. "We have quite a bit of time on our hands, you know."

Karuthiruman launched into his story. It truly was a marvellous tale, filled with events of miracle and wonder.

58

Karuthiruman's Tale

Kariyathirumal alias Karuthiruman hailed from the village of Thopputhurai, a hamlet that lay nestled in a corner of the northern shores of Kodikkarai. He earned his living by plying a boat to Eezham. One fine day nearly 25 years ago, he found himself caught in a raging tempest as he was rowing his boat back to Thopputhurai from Eezham. He struggled against the storm to save his boat from being overturned and tried his best to steer it ashore. As the craft neared the Kodikkarai lighthouse, Karuthiruman spotted the body of a maiden at the mercy of the tumultuous waves. Struck by pity, the boatman hauled her out of the waters and onto his vessel. The damsel seemed to be dead to the world; he found it quite impossible to establish whether life breathed in her yet. Karuthiruman strove to take the boat ashore then and there, but in vain. In the end, he yielded to the howling gale and navigated the vessel in the direction the winds blew, finally making port at the town of Thirumaraikkadu. He had just set down the maiden upon the shore and was attending to her anxiously when a group of people approached him on horseback. They appeared to be well-born men of influence. But the girl did not speak a single word; it did not seem as if their speech fell upon her ears, either. "She is deaf and dumb by birth," remarked one of the newcomers. A man who appeared to be their leader took Karuthiruman aside and made a strange request. He asked the boatman to take the maiden back to Eezha Naadu after the storm had quelled and bade him leave her on the mainland or upon an island nearby, promising to give him a great amount of money in return. Karuthiruman agreed and received the avowed sum, too. Once the storm had petered out, the boatman took the girl onto his vessel and rowed out to sea once again. To his surprise, he caught sight of yet another castaway adrift upon the waters, a man clinging onto a log as he floated with the waves. He appeared to look quite spent from his ordeal. Karuthiruman helped him onto the boat as well. At first, the maiden was terrified by the stranger, but she soon grew accustomed to his presence and paid him no notice at all. It wasn't too long before Karuthiruman set the pair down upon an island within reach of Eezha Naadu.

There, an old man professed himself to be the girl's father. He claimed that her muteness was nothing new and rued the fact that she did not appear to recognize him, her own father. Karuthiruman recounted to the old man how he had saved the maiden from the sea. Then, the castaway who had boarded the vessel handed an *olai* to Karuthiruman and bade him deliver the missive to the Ilankai king. From this, the boatman deduced that the stranger was a highly-placed noble of great rank. When Kauruthiruman conveyed the *olai* to the ruler of Ilankai, he learned that the castaway he had rescued was none other than the Pandiya king himself. The Ilankai king lost no time in despatching a grand retinue to accord the Pandiya ruler a regal welcome befitting his office. Karuthiruman, wearied from his recent adventures, did not accompany the entourage. The Pandiya king arrived at the palace of the Ilankai king a few days later. The monarchs set off together to Rohana Naadu, a land that lay huddled amidst mountains at the southern end of Ilankai. They stayed in the region for a few days accompanied by Karuthiruman; the Pandiya king had brought him along for the journey, having grown rather fond of him by this time. The Ilankai king pointed out to the Pandiya ruler many significant territories in Rohana Naadu. Finally, he guided him to a remote valley that seemed to be inaccessible by ordinary means. There, inside a yawning mountain cave, lay strewn a glittering sea of marvellous riches that dazzled the eye. Gold coins shone softly in tall heaps alongside mounds of magnificent jewels and every known variety of precious gemstones. The Ilankai king travelled his eye over these treasures until he spotted the gold chest he was looking for. This he opened to display its contents to his esteemed guest. Inside the chest were an exquisite crown embedded with brilliant jewels, and a priceless necklace crafted of valuable gemstones. From the ensuing conversation between the royals, Karuthiruman learned that the crown was the ancient Imperial Crown of the Pandiya clan while the gemstone necklace was none other than the very one said to have been bestowed upon the Pandiya progenitor by Devendran Himself. The Ilankai king urged the Pandiya monarch to take these, his rightful treasures. The Pandiya king, however, declined; he asked his Ilankai ally to deliver the precious artifacts to him at Madurai with the world at witness, on the momentous day of coronation that would follow his consummate victory over the Chozhas.

The Pandiya king then gave Karuthiruman as many gold coins as he could carry before sending him on his way, bading him make the necessary arrangements towards the care of the mute girl. He asked the boatman to join him in Pandiya Naadu once his task was complete.

Karuthiruman made his way to Boodha Theevu once again, but neither the maiden nor her father were nowhere to be found. He set off to Kodikkarai in search of the pair. There, he saw the mute girl, but she did not recognize him. From her family, he learned that the maiden had been brought to Kodikkarai by her ailing father, who had succumbed to his illness soon after; he learned too that the lighthouse keeper was none other than her brother. The maiden had been unfamiliar with her own family, recognizing neither her brother nor her sister. She had reportedly fallen into the sea yet again, by dint of an unfortunate slip of the foot; thankfully, not only was rescue at hand, but the maiden regained her memory after the incident, too. The others soon discovered that the maiden was with child. The poor girl fell into great terror when she came to the realization herself. She often sought refuge in the Kuzhagar temple at Kodikkarai, finding solace in worship and piety. Of Karuthiruman, the maiden took no notice at all, however hard he strove to gain her confidence.

During his time at Kodikkarai, Karuthiruman made the acquaintance of the mute woman's younger sister. He found himself moved when he learned that the sister was afflicted by muteness as well. The boatman determined to wed her and make a good life. He wished, however, to present his findings to the Pandiya king before settling down. It was at this juncture that Sembian Maadevi, the royal consort of the Chozha Chakravarthy Kandaradhithar came to Kodikkarai. A shining devotee of Siva Peruman, the deeply pious queen had come on a holy pilgrimage to the Kuzhagar temple, wishing to obtain a *darshan* of the deity within. There, the queen happened upon the mute maiden Mandhakini. She took the damsel along with her when she left, with the younger sister Vaani in tow.

Karuthiruman went to Pandiya Naadu. He learned that the Pandiya monarch had set out to the battlefield, upon which he faithfully made his way to the front and gained an audience with the king. The Pandiya monarch bade him make another journey to Ilankai, tasking him with the duty of delivering yet another *olai* to the Ilankai king. He asked Karuthiruman to seek out the mute woman once again when he returned, requesting him to make another effort to bring her to his side.

And so, Karuthiruman wound his way to Pazhaiyarai on his return from Ilankai. His heart was beset still by thoughts of Vaani; in truth, it was a strong desire to meet her that drove him to Pazhaiyarai. He little knew how disturbing their meeting would turn out to be. At first light one day, Karuthiruman was passing by the banks of the Arisalaaru river as he neared Pazhaiyarai. Suddenly, he beheld a woman by the brink of the riverbank; she was bent over, engrossed in digging a pit. Strange as the sight was, it did not surprise him as much as what he saw next - for a tiny bundle of clothes lay on the ground beside her, from which ensued the soft, mewling cries of a newborn baby.

Karuthiruman instantly felt a surge of fury and revulsion. He drew closer to the woman, wondering which sinful *chandaali* could bring herself to bury alive an innocent babe. When the woman straightened her back, the boatman discovered that it was none other than Vaani.

"*Thambi*, can you imagine my feelings at that very moment?" asked Kariyathirumal, pausing in the midst of his narration.

"I think I can. Go on with your tale," urged an intrigued Vandhiyathevan.

"Ah, I am afraid it is quite impossible to tell you any more. You see, the rest of the story can be recounted only to those of the royal family!" declared Karuthiruman before heaving a dramatic sigh. "If I hadn't been in Pazhaiyarai at that fateful moment, why, the troubles that followed would have never befallen me!"

"Come on, then," laughed Vandhiyathevan as he got to his feet. "We shall meet with the royal family at once to bring them abreast!"

Karuthiruman followed the Vaanar warrior as he led the way to the underground treasury. The gate to its halls was sealed by a formidable padlock, but Vandhiyathevan knew of another, inner door that stood nearby, cunningly concealed such that none could notice its presence without prior knowledge of it. He gave a push and the inner door obliged. Vandhiyathevan and Karuthiruman quickly entered the treasury halls and latched the door from inside.

As they crossed the treasury, Vandhiyathevan entered a hall where lay opulent piles of gold coins, precious pearls and dazzling gemstones of all kinds. He turned to Karuthiruman. "Does the mountain cave in Rohana Naadu have as much treasure as this?" he asked.

"Oh, more! A hundred times more!" replied Kariyathirumal.

Vandhiyathevan helped himself to a few gold coins, which he tied in a bundle and tucked away safely at his waist. He then proceeded to lead the way through the treasury passage, finally reaching a secret door encased in the boundary wall. This he opened warily. There was no sentry standing guard, so Vandhiyathevan cautiously peeked outside. He saw the Vadavaaru merrily flowing yonder. The river was gloriously full; its swift waters skimmed both the banks as they surged along their course. The light of a flaming torch glowed a distance away. Once he was sure that there was no one else around, Vandhiyathevan stepped out into the open. Karuthiruman followed and shut the secret door behind him. The pair stood still, wondering how they would cross the Vadavaaru river. To their delight, they caught sight of a boat tangled in the gnarled roots of a bent tree nearby.

59

Ill omens

When Vandhiyathevan spied the boat beneath the tree, he was beset with joy. He believed that Lady Luck had returned to his side and grew quite enthused. Though he had little knowledge of steering the craft, he had Karuthiruman with him - a man whose very livelihood depended on plying a boat! With his help, they could travel upon the Vadavaaru's rapid waters and follow the river's course. This would enable them to quickly cover nearly half the distance it took to reach Kodikkarai.

"Do you see that, Karuthiruma?" crowed Vandhiyathevan in delight. "This boat eluded the fate of going under only to float all this way and wait for us here! If you display but a little of your prowess, we can cross half the distance we need to cover by daybreak. After that, even our pursuers on horseback have little hope of catching up to us!"

Karuthiruman narrowed his eyes and looked all around in suspicion. Something rustled softly in the bushes that grew in thickets along the boundary walls skirting the river bank. Karuthiruman picked up a pebble and deftly flung it into the middle of the dense bushes. A cat sprung out from within, hissing and spitting indignantly as it bolted towards the boat and dove inside.

Vandhiyathevan broke into laughter. "Why, *padagotti*, you seem to be a braver man than I!" he grinned as he picked up a pebble of his own. He threw the stone into the boat with some force.

The cat leapt out of the boat with a screech, deeply aggrieved by the relentless assault. To the pair's surprise, it tore straight towards them and darted between their legs to beat a hasty retreat.

Vandhiyathevan backed away in reflex, his terror plain for all to see. Karuthiruman looked at him askance. "You don't seem to have much courage compared to me after all," he remarked witheringly.

"I am scared of cats," confessed Vandhiyathevan sheepishly. "If one of these wretched animals but brushes against my person, my very hair stands on end. Thankfully, we've seen the last of the beast, I think. Come on then, let us be on our way!"

Karuthiruman harrumphed. "It matters little to me if a cat falls upon my very head. But it is a dreadfully ill omen for one to cross our path," he replied sullenly.

"Omens, he says! Ill luck, he says!" cried Vandhiyathevan incredulously. He caught hold of Karuthiruman's arm and dragged him to the boat before eagerly clambering inside.

Defeated, Karuthiruman walked towards a corner of a boat and tried to free it from the knot of roots it was entangled in. It is hard to say whether his efforts succeeded in budging the boat, but they did provoke an entirely unexpected outcome - four burly men came pouncing out of nowhere in the blink of an eye and charged towards the pair. Two of them got into the boat, where they fell upon Vandhiyathevan and roughly pushed him down. They quickly tied him to the beams running along the breadth of the boat. The other two advanced upon Karuthiruman bearing spears in hand. They flanked him on each side and sternly stood guard.

Vandhiyathevan saw that the foursome's leader was none other than the stocky guard who had chased after them when they had made their escape from the underground dungeons. The Vaanar prince found himself astonished by the realization that the guard had travelled so swiftly by boat in order to lie in wait for them at the exit to the subterranean passage. This was certainly no ordinary guard! Vandhiyathevan concluded that he had to be a highly experienced spy. He suspected that he had seen him before, somewhere; he was wondering who he could be when he heard the guard speak.

The guard was addressing Karuthiruman. "*Appane*, you were given leave to come outside after many miserable years in the dungeons. Why possessed you to heed the words of this wicked rogue and go on the run? No matter. I do not have the heart to tie you up once again. If you hearken to me and obey my instructions faithfully, no harm shall befall you," he said.

"So be it, *Ayya*!" replied the boatman meekly. "The Mudhanmanthiri himself sent a man to release me, but I had to go and listen to this idiot's advice. I've ruined everything! I shall do as you say, henceforth. Pray, do not throw me into the dungeons once again!"

"Yes, yes," said the guard. "The Mudhanmanthiri wishes to ask you a few questions, you know. If you answer him truthfully, he will not send you back to the dungeons. Instead, he will reward you with all the gold, gems and prizes you could wish for and send you on your way. Tell me," he asked with curiosity, "where were you planning to go, anyway?"

"Eezha Naadu."

"Hah, there's a pretty plan!" snorted the guard, a smug grin spreading across his face. "Did you truly believe that you could travel all that distance after hoodwinking the Mudhanmanthiri *and* the Velar's own sentries? Then again," he continued thoughtfully, "this rowdy fellow here is quite capable of coming up with such harebrained schemes. Isn't he the one who gave Chinna Pazhuvettarayar's guards the slip on an earlier occasion? Well, let that be. Look here, this boat must now be steered against the flow of the river. Only one of the men who have come with me knows how to handle a boat and his skill is middling at best. He is quite an amateur at this sort of thing; why, it was touch-and-go to reach this place, even though we travelled with the river's flow! You must rise to the occasion and show us your mastery. Now let us see you take the boat to the other side of the bank and steer it towards the North Gate!"

Karuthiruman looked puzzled at his words. "Why, we can cross the bank and go on foot, *Ayya*! The waters are fairly swift. It will be quite an arduous task to ply the boat at length against the flow!"

"If we cross the bank and get ashore, our troublemaker here is sure to get up to his old tricks. We have no choice but to travel upon the river," replied the commander of the guards rather apologetically.

Karuthiruman and another guard proceeded to push the boat. The commander turned to Vandhiyathevan. "*Appane*," he said sternly, "don't you dream of pulling your antics once again!"

"*Ayya*, you seem to know quite a bit about me," replied Vandhiyathevan, affecting surprise.

"Of course I do! I saw for myself, didn't I, how you tricked the *vaithiyar's* son into taking your place in the prison cell while you made your escape? Then you tried to trick us as well and run away for good!"

Vandhiyathevan found himself thoroughly astonished. "*Ayya*, you appear to be far cleverer than I am! I was under the impression that no one had taken notice of what transpired in the dungeons!"

The guard smiled. "*Thambi*, there is no place in this vast Chozha *samrajyam* where the Mudhanmanthiri does not have eyes and ears. They keep as keen a watch on events in Eezha Naadu as they do in the Kadambur palace and yes, the underground dungeons, too. The Mudhanmanthiri knows well that the *vaithiyar's* son is a dolt. That is why he sent me after him!"

"It appears as if the Mudhanmandhiri knew too that I would choose to exit from this very point. His eyes and ears are remarkable, indeed!" admitted Vandhiyathevan. "In that case, he must be wise to my innocence as well? Surely he must know that it was a mistake to imprison me in the dungeons?"

"That is not the Mudhanmanthiri's responsibility to bear. It is the Chakravarthy's duty to determine whether you are innocent or guilty, just as it is now Periya Velar's duty to assign you just punishment for attempting to escape from the underground dungeons," replied the guard stiffly.

"*Ayya*, where will you take me now?"

"First, I shall present you to the Kodumbalur Velar. He waits at the entrance to the North Gate of the fort."

"Does Periya Velar truly wait for me?"

"Ah! Never have I seen such vain conceit!" cried the guard. "Do you think that such an illustrious champion, the first among the chieftains of Chozha Naadu, the staunch ally of generations of the Chozha clan, the victor who uprooted the Pandiya clan, the peerless warrior who captured Eezham, Kodumbalur Velar, Boodhi Vikrama Kesari himself waits for you at the fort entrance?"

"Who else does he wait for?"

"For Parthibendran, who is expected to arrive shortly with the Pazhuvettarayars and the other chieftains who were gathered at Thiruppurambiyam."

"What, even Periya Pazhuvettarayar?" asked Vandhiyathevan, stunned.

"Yes, even him. It would seem that he knows the truth behind prince Karikalar's death. Once he arrives, an inquiry is to take place under the aegis of the Chakravarthy. If you truly are not the culprit as you claim, it must be proven beyond doubt at those proceedings."

Vandhiyathevan's heart sank. The Pazhuvettarayars would doubtless join hands with Parthibendran to cast the blame upon him. How could he hope to lift his head and look upon the Chakravarthy and prince Arulmozhi Varmar with the foul taint of such an accusation upon his head? *What evidence do I have to prove that I am not the culprit?*

Vandhiyathevan looked at the guard beseechingly. "*Ayya*, I have not done you any wrong, have I? Pray, do allow me to escape! Truly, I am not the culprit they seek. I was an intimate friend to the late prince. I stand accused of this vile crime purely by dint of unfortunate circumstance. You are the Mudhanmanthiri's helper. The Mudhanmanthiri issued orders only to fetch the madman in the dungeons, didn't he? Take him and let me go! You will gather much virtue if you would do me this turn," he pleaded piteously.

"If I let you go, what will you give me in return?" asked the guard.

"When the time comes, I will render you help in turn."

"Such a time will never come. And even if it does, I am in no need of your help. Tell me what you can do for me right now."

Vandhiyathevan suddenly remembered the gold coins at his waist. "I will give you coins of gold, as many as both your hands can carry!"

"Aha! Gold coins, you say? Show me!" cried the guard.

"Pray, loosen my bonds a little. They are at my waist. I will take them out and show them to you!" said Vandhiyathevan earnestly.

The guard bent down. "Don't get up to any mischief, now!" he warned as he slackened Vandhiyathevan's bonds.

Vandhiyathevan looked closely at the guard's face as he relaxed the cloth around his waist. He took out the promised gold coins and gave them to the guard.

The guard found his hands brimming over with glittering coins of gold. "*Thambi*, did you take these gold coins from the Pazhuvettarayar's treasury? Or did you steal them from the very mint? This makes a third charge of crime upon your head! A count of murder, a count of decampment from prison and now, a count of theft from the royal treasury - that makes three charges in all. You can be sentenced to hang for any one of these, you know!" he said.

"*Ayya*, I have rendered much service to the Chozha *rajyam*. I have served faithfully as a trusted messenger. I even made every effort to sacrifice my life to save Karikalar's own. I have every right to claim as remuneration a small sum as this handful of gold coins. Why, even these I only took to cover the expenses of travel," replied Vandhiyathevan defensively.

"You may have your say when you are being interrogated!" snapped the guard.

"Why, then.. aren't you going to release me from my bonds?" asked Vandhiyathevan, taken aback.

The guard bristled. "Even if the sun rises in the west - why, even if Paramasivan turns out to be superior to Thirumal Himself - I will not betray the *rajyam* for a mere handful of gold!" he thundered.

Vandhiyathevan cast a sideways glance at Karuthiruman to see what he was doing. He realized that the boatman was gazing at him intently, as one waiting for a sign. Without a second thought, the brave youth slackened his bonds further and made a sudden lunge at the guard. He grabbed at his moustache and turban, which came off quite easily in his hands. Standing in front of him was none other than Azhwarkkadiyaan!

"Why, you two-faced Vaishnavite! Is it you after all?" cried out Vandhiyathevan.

As Azhwarkkadiyaan desperately tried to save his moustache and turban, the gold coins spilled from his hands and clattered noisily to the ground. Vandhiyathevan freed himself of his binds in a trice and pushed Azhwarkkadiyaan down. He tied Azhwarkkadiyaan to the beams of the boat with the same ropes that had bound him thus far. The Vaanar prince unsheathed the sword that hung at his waist and held it aloft with a menacing air.

Meanwhile, Karuthiruman did not remain idle. He suddenly fell upon the guard next to him and pushed him into the swiftly flowing river. The hapless guard floundered in the waters. Of the two guards that remained, one advanced upon the boatman and the other, Vandhiyathevan. They moved hesitatingly, unnerved by the new development. Vandhiyathevan charged at one of them, brandishing his sword; the guard relinquished all hope of challenge and resignedly dove into the river. Karuthiruman struck the other one with the oar he held and knocked him down into the boat.

The pair worked quickly to tie the remaining guard to the beams of the boat as well. The boat floated upon the river along its course. The two guards that had fallen into the water were struggling to swim ashore against the powerful current.

Vandhiyathevan turned to Azhwarkkadiyaan. "Veera Vaishnava *sigamaniye*! What do you have to say for yourself?" he asked severely.

"What can I say?" replied Azhwarkkadiyaan with a philosophical air. "All this is naught but the divine play of Narayana Murthy. He is the one who ties as well as the one who is tied. He is the one who pushes and the one who gets pushed. Verily, He is in a pillar as well as a splinter; He is in the sword in your hands even as He is upon my own shoulders as well!"

"Then he is in the waters of this river, too!" retorted Vandhiyathevan. "Shall we tie you up and throw you to their mercy?"

A pious expression came upon Azhwarkkadiyaan's face. "Prahaladan was tied to a boulder and thrown into the sea, too. Didn't Narayana Murthy save him and bring him safely ashore?" he replied. "If perchance Bhagavan does not come to my rescue - why, I shall consider that a call to holy Vaikuntam itself!"

Vandhiyathevan fell into thought. "Look, you have saved my life on a few occasions. I have no idea what your intentions were when you did; nevertheless, I do not wish to kill you," he said finally. "Even so, if I am to save your life, you must promise to render me help in return. "

"*Appane*, I live by the words *paropakaram idam shareeram* - our bodies are meant to render help to another. Ask of me what you will. I shall do it for you if you untie my bonds," replied Thirumalai.

"There's nothing I need that requires physical effort," assured Vandhiyathevan. "This man and I, we need two horses. Why, you ask? To escape, of course! If you can somehow think of a way by which we can procure a mount each, we will leave you unharmed on this boat and go ashore. The boat will dock at some place eventually. I am sure that you can use your wits to save yourself!"

"I am glad that you ask me for help that I can provide," smiled Azhwarkkadiyaan.

"Then you *do* know how I can get two horses?" asked Vandhiyathevan hopefully.

"I do! I know a place where both of you can each get yourself a horse. You do know Vaani *Ammai*'s house, don't you?"

Vandhiyathevan frowned. "Which Vaani *Ammai*?"

"The Vaani *Ammai* that is engaged in *pushpa sevai* for the Thanjai Thanikulathar temple - the woman who is mute by birth, Senthan Amuthan's mother."

As Azhwarkkadiyaan spoke these words, Karuthiruman drew closer and listened avidly.

Vandhiyathevan's face brightened. "I know. Yes, I *do* know the house - it is in the gardens!"

"There are two horses there for the taking, even as we speak."

"How come?"

"One is my own horse - I tethered it near Vaani *Ammai*'s hut before I got onto this boat. The other is the horse that Senthan Amudhan rode. Poor lad! Amudhan is quite unused to riding a horse. His mount was quite spirited; it bucked and threw him down during the journey. He was already quite weakened by a fever, you know. The shock of the fall made him bedridden again. They say that it will be nothing short of a rebirth if he survives. He won't need the horse anymore, I think."

"Who is there to take care of him?" asked Vandhiyathevan, greatly worried by this piece of news.

"His mother is there and so is Poonguzhali," assured Azhwarkkadiyaan.

"Which mother?" blurted Karuthiruman all of a sudden.

Azhwarkkadiyaan and Vandhiyathevan looked askance at him. "What did you say?" asked Azhwarkkadiyaan, raising a brow.

"I asked whether Periya Piratti Sembian Maadevi is aware that Senthan Amudhan's life is in danger."

"Yes, she is," replied Azhwarkkadiyaan. "It is Sembian Maadevi who has been aiding them thus far with endowments towards the *pushpa kaingaryam* they render. Now, however, the palace is immersed in grief at Karikalar's death. How can they take care of Amudhan?"

Vandhiyathevan looked at Karuthiruman. "What do you say? Shall we drop in on Senthan Amudhan and his mother before taking our leave?" he asked.

Karuthiruman nodded. "In that case, row the boat back to shore!" said Vandhiyathevan. He turned to Azhwarkkadiyaan. "*Vaishnavane*! If this naught but a wily ruse, better beware. Whatever becomes of my fate, I shall make sure that I dispatch you to Kailayam before attending to anything else!"

"Pray don't, *Thambi*! You will gain much virtue if you dispatch me to Vaikuntam instead, the holy abode where a bevy of celestials wait upon Sriman Narayana Murthy with Mahalakshmi by His side!" replied the devout Vaishnavan with an easy smile.

60

Amudhan's quandary

An ailing Senthan Amudhan lay in the garden hut, lovingly tended to by Poonguzhali. She brought a bowl of *kanji* that Vaani *Amma*i had kept aside and fed him with care.

The *vaithiyar* from Sundara Chozhar's own *aathura saalai* had examined Senthan Amudhan a short while ago. Poonguzhali had made discreet enquiries with him before she returned to Amudhan's side.

"How is Amudhan?" she had asked the *vaithiyar* worriedly. "Will he pull through?"

"He was already weakened by the fever when he took the tumble from the horse. Yet, he suffers little physical trauma from what I can see. It is the strain of mental stress that impedes steady recovery," the *vaithiyar* had explained.

Poonguzhali bore his words in mind when she spoke to Amudhan. "What ails you, Amudha? Why are you in such low spirits? The *vaithiyar* tells me that you are in distress. It is a mental burden that hampers your improvement," she said gently.

"Shall I confess the truth, Poonguzhali? Or shall I hide it away and tell you a pretty lie, instead?" replied Amudhan softly, almost to himself.

"Is that a sneaky poke at me?" demanded Poonguzhali in a flurry of indignation. "Do you mean to say that I don't speak my mind? *Cagey*, am I?"

A feeble smile tugged at Amudhan's lips despite himself. "Poonguzhali, it seems to be a risky venture to converse with you! Hush, now. If you can manage to hold your tongue, I shall cheer myself up by looking at your face."

"Ah!" exclaimed Poonguzhali, incensed. "You mean to say you would be happier if I were mute like your aunts!"

"I meant no such thing," replied Amudhan with a laugh. "There is no end to the joy I feel when I hear you sing; mere speech cannot compare. Sing a *thevaram* for me, won't you?"

"I shan't until you tell me what truly bothers you."

"Here's the truth, then," Amudhan said after a pause. "I worry that I shall soon be restored to health."

"How can you say such a thing? I've been offering earnest prayers to all the gods for your recovery. Why on earth are you *worried* about regaining your health?"

"When I am restored to health, you will no longer be beside me, will you? The very thought upsets me, Poonguzhali!"

Poonguzhali's face shone. Amudhan's words seemed to make her bloom like a *senthaamarai* flower speckled with morning dew. Her lovely lips drew into a tender smile and her eyes glistened.

"Amudha, the love you bear for me stirs my very soul," she murmured. "I have no heart to leave you behind, but I cannot bring myself to stay by your side, either."

"Yes, the waves of the wild sea beckon to you. What of that? I shall come away with you!" cried out Amudhan all of a sudden. "Say you consent! My health will return to me at once, you will see!"

Poonguzhali's eyes softened. "Amudha, the oath I've made to myself forbids me."

"Which oath is that?"

"It is my heart's desire to marry the Emperor who rules the world and sit by his side upon my throne. If that does not come to pass, I have vowed to remain an unwed virgin until my last breath."

"Yes, your heart belongs to Ponniyin Selvan," replied Amudhan sadly. "But, Poonguzhali - do you believe that such a thing can come to pass, after all?"

"You are mistaken. There is not a single soul in Chozha Naadu that does not hold Ponniyin Selvan dear. From the men, women and elderly to the youngest child in the kingdom, all and sundry adore him; the affection I bear for him is much the same," said Poonguzhali earnestly. "Why, the time he battled fever upon the boat - didn't we both take care of him together to save his life?"

Amudhan's eyes widened. "Then… you don't… don't you have other… feelings for him?" he asked, surprised at her revelation.

"Amudha, Ponniyin Selvan is meant for another - the Kodumbalur princess Vanathi. All I did was say a few words to her in jest; she responded by making a solemn oath to never sit upon the throne…"

"The maiden has taken such a vow as that despite her royal lineage," cut in Amudhan. "And here *you* are, adamant in your wish to sit upon the throne! Why, you are even resolved to remain a spinster if you don't!"

"Amudha, my *athai* fell in love with an aristocrat of a royal clan. In return, she lived a life engulfed in an ocean of misery until the very end. *I* shall win for myself the life of fortune my *athai* was denied. Why shouldn't I?" burst out Poonguzhali, her dark eyes flashing.

"Ah! It is my misfortune, then, that you have such a dream!" exclaimed Amudhan.

"Why must you fall into despair? There is no rule, after all, that reserves the glory of kingship for those of royal blood. Many men hailing from simple families - yes, like you! - have established mighty empires by dint of their valourous exploits and risen to become great kings! Take an oath today, like me! Vow to establish an empire, in great Bharatham or upon foreign lands that lie across the sea. I shall never leave your side. I will be with you forever!" cried Poonguzhali.

"I was not born for such exploits, Poonguzhali. I have little desire to swing a sword or go to war. Why, I have no wish to bring harm to the smallest of god's creatures! My heart craves for neither crown nor throne. I only long to spend my days singing the praises of holy Siva Peruman and His revered devotees." Amudhan's face grew sad. "My desire to wed you is akin to a cripple longing for wild honey from the combs on a tree. Poonguzhali, there is little point in asking you to stay. Pray, leave. Do not tarry until I recover!"

The pair fell silent when they heard the sound of footsteps outside the hut.

❧

61

A Betrothal

Poonguzhali walked briskly towards the door of the little hut. A heavy sigh escaped Senthan Amudhan's lips. *There*, he thought, *Poonguzhali truly is leaving me for good.* He felt certain that his spirit would abandon his body the instant she stepped out the door.

Senthan Amudhan watched Poonguzhali open the door and look all around. She came back inside and latched the door to the hut. How strange! Not only had she bolted the door, she was now walking towards him!

Had her heart thawed ever so slightly? Though, what difference did it make even if it had? She would relapse into urging him to transform into a mighty warrior, conquer a kingdom and rule from a throne. *Her heart churns as a wild, roiling sea under a storm of desire. My own is a tranquil thing; subsumed by bhakthi towards Siva*

Peruman, my heart is as placid as a gently flowing stream. Poonguzhali and I can never complement each other. What is the use of building such castles in the air?

Poonguzhali drew closer to him. Her sparkling eyes, lovelier than water lilies, fixed their soft gaze upon him. Senthan Amudhan felt his heart turn over.

"Why did you close the door?" he managed to ask. "Who was it? Perhaps it was *Amma*, after all…"

"Whoever it is can wait outside for a while longer, until we finish our chat. After all, it's rather unseemly to interrupt a heart-to-heart conversation between the King and Queen."

"King? Queen?" echoed Amudhan, puzzled. "Who is the King here? And who is the Queen?"

"Why, you are the King and I am the Queen! I spoke to you for *ages*, just now! Didn't any of my words reach through to you?"

Amudhan looked at her in dismay. "No, Poonguzhali. I told you, didn't I - your advice is quite wasted on me. The whims of your heart and mine are poles apart; they will never beat together in harmony!"

"Well, it is rather up to us to make them, don't you think?" asked Poonguzhali.

"It is quite impossible, I tell you!" cried out Amudhan, trying in vain to conceal his anguish.

Poonguzhali eyes grew tender. "I can, if you cannot," she said softly. "Amudha, I have made up my mind to let go of my desire to marry a prince and sit upon a throne. I have put away all thoughts of a royal life and imperial power; their allure is eclipsed by the affection you bestow upon me, a love a million times dearer to me than my desire. If you will not come over to my side, then I shall come over to yours. I shall marry you."

Senthan Amudhan found himself transported to raptures of ecstasy. "Poonguzhali! Poonguzhali!" he cried, delighted. "I'm not delirious with fever, am I? Tell me I am not dreaming! Surely I haven't misheard you? I am not labouring under a misapprehension?"

"I shall say it again, then - listen!" replied Poonguzhali, smiling. "You are reluctant to come over to my side, so I have decided to come over to yours. I shall marry you. The details I had learned about my *periya athai's* life had sown vain desires in my heart. I often thought that the throne was rightfully hers; an anger took hold of me, driving me to wonder why I shouldn't aspire to the throne myself. In truth, that spark of desire died along with my *athai* when she breathed her last, impaled by the assassin's spear. My eyes were opened to the distress and agony that plague the lives of those who live in a palace. I understood that a life of royalty pales in comparison to the bliss in rowing a boat upon the sweet waves of the sea. Amudha!" she cried happily, her eyes shining. "When you are better, we shall go to Kodikkarai together. Kuzhagar stands there all by himself, in a temple in the midst of a forest. We shall offer flowers to Kodikkarai Kuzhagar together. We shall sail out to sea now and then, in our very own boat. Many lush, beautiful isles are strewn upon the waters near Eezha Naadu. At times, we shall go ashore on one of these islands. There, you shall be a King and I, a Queen! We shall build a world of our own; none will contest our kingdom! Amudha, you don't have any objection to *these* plans, do you?"

Amudhan's eyes sparkled with joy. "Just one, Poonguzhali - I only wonder if I am worthy of such good fortune! Do you mean what you say? You aren't setting me up for disappointment, are you? No, no! You speak truly! When can we leave for Kodikkarai?" he asked eagerly.

"As soon as you get better," replied Poonguzhali, laughing.

"I'm all better now, Poonguzhali! See, I shall stand up and walk for you!" exclaimed Senthan Amudhan and bravely made an effort to prop himself up.

Poonguzhali held his hand gently and prevented him from rising. "No, don't. Wait but for a day!"

There came the sound of someone knocking softly upon the door. "*Amma* knocks on the door. Open it! We shall tell *Amma* the happy news!" said Amudhan.

Poonguzhali obligingly opened the door. The sight she saw at the doorway gave her some surprise.

It wasn't Vaani *Amma*i at the door, as she had expected. The person who had knocked at the door appeared to be a palace aide. When the door opened, he had respectfully stood aside to reveal Sembian Maadevi and prince Madhuranthakan standing at the doorway. Two palanquins were resting upon the ground a short distance away; the palanquin bearers and guards stood at the ready, beneath a tree. One of them bore a flaming torch in its hand, throwing light upon this astonishing scene. Poonguzhali bowed her head towards Sembian Maadevi and brought her palms together in a respectful greeting. "Welcome, *thaaye*!" she said.

"How is your *athai's* son, Poonguzhali? Where is Vaani *Amma*i?" asked the illustrious daughter of Mazhavarayan as she swept inside. A beady-eyed Madhuranthakan lingered at the doorstep. His unblinking gaze bored into the hut and the people inside, eyes agleam with undisguised wrath.

When Sendhan Amudhan saw that their visitor was none other than their patron, the Siva *bhaktha siromani* Sembian Maadevi, he struggled to his feet. "*Thaaye*, your august presence comes at a good time," he said reverently. "We find ourselves blessed that you will be the first to hear our good news and wish us well. It is naught but the grace and divine intervention of Siva Peruman that it must be so, for I have not yet taken even my mother into confidence. *Annaiye!* After all these years, Poonguzhali's heart has relented - she has consented to wed me. You must do us the honour of presiding over the wedding. After the ceremony, we plan to leave for the Kuzhagar temple at Kodikkarai so that we may worship him with flowers."

His words affected Sembian Maadevi deeply. It was hard to say whether the news brought her happiness or sorrow; her lips drew into a smile while her eyes spilled over with tears. Amudhan and Poonguzhali bowed towards her together. Sembian Maadevi found her heart full as she blessed them. "Children," she said in a voice that shook with emotion, "may the grace of God grant you sweetness and joy in your new life!"

It was at this point that Vaanai *Amma*i entered the hut. Sembian Maadevi spoke to her in gestures, letting her know that she had come to look in on Amudhan's health. She also conveyed her happiness at learning of the imminent wedding between the two. Vaani *Amma*i looked bewildered and happy at the news.

Sembian Maadevi spent some time in conversation with Senthan Amudhan and Poonguzhali. She departed from the hut shortly after.

Sembian Maadevi and Madhuranthakan walked together towards the palanquins.

The venerable dowager stopped beneath a tree on the way. Making sure that no one was around, she turned to Madhuranthakan. "Did you see, Madhuranthaka? The child I carried in my own womb for ten months and gave birth to is none other than the Senthan Amudhan who lives in that hut yonder. I learned of him when he was five years old, in truth. When he was only eight days old, I found him lying insensible and thought him to be dead. My fondness for a child drove me to make you my own. I gave instructions to Vaani to bury him; Vaani took him away as told but did not return for a very long time. It was only when I spotted her with the child five years later did I understand the truth. Even so, I did not shun you; neither did I bring him to the palace as the son that I gave birth to. I believed it all to be naught but God's play. I raised you with greater love and care than I showed my own child. Give me only your word in return! Say that you do not want the Chozha throne! In truth, I do not object to the thought of you ascending the throne; I only fear the possibility that the children born in your lineage may be bereft of the power of speech!" she said.

Madhuranthakan's face blanched at her words. The daughter of Chinna Pazhuvettarayar, whom he had married, had given birth to a girl; he came to a painful realization that the child had not uttered a single word even after she had crossed two years of age.

Madhuranthakan stood rooted to the ground, still as a tree himself. His foster mother looked at him with concern. "Child, why do you stand thus, unmoving? Come, let us leave. Come to the palace and think well upon the matter at hand. You may give me your answer on the morrow," she said kindly.

"*Thaaye*, what is left to think about? Nothing, truly!" spoke Madhuranthakan haltingly. "Pray, leave! I shall follow soon; I only wish to first speak with your noble son who ought to have been raised in the palace in my place."

Sembian Maadevi looked intently at Madhuranthakan. "As you wish," she said presently. "Make sure the palanquin is veiled when you return. If the Kodumbalur soldiers spot you, they are likely to create a ruckus!"

With that, the grand matriarch strode towards her palanquin. She did not notice Madhuranthakan's face contort with a greater hostility and rage than before.

62

THE SPEAR WHISTLED THROUGH THE AIR!

Madhuranthakan stood absolutely still. He appeared to be in two minds, desperately struggling between entering the hut and returning to the fort. Eventually, he approached the palanquin and spoke to the bearers and guards by its side; he then reached in and retrieved an object from the royal litter. The bearers departed with the palanquin, taking away with them the light of the torch they bore.

Madhuranthakan was walking towards the hut when he was thunderstruck to see a man emerge from behind the very tree that he and Sembian Maadevi had stopped at to converse.

It was none other than Karuthiruman, the self-proclaimed madman who had fled the underground dungeons with Vandhiyathevan. He had a fiercely wild, unhinged air about him; it was hardly surprising that he gave Madhuranthakan quite a fright when he leapt out at him with no warning.

Madhuranthakan instinctively whipped out the sharp dagger he had retrieved from the palanquin and blindly raised it above his head. Karuthiruman gently restrained him. "*Ayya*, pray, patience! I am no enemy of yours!" he said.

Madhuranthakan flinched from his touch. "Who are you then, if not an enemy? A *friend*?" he demanded angrily.

"Yes, *Ayya*. I truly am a friend to you."

A bitter laugh of fury exploded from Madhuranthakan and he dropped his arm heavily. "Ah!" he cried out. "I have come into a fine friend, indeed! My very world slips away from me, but I have you, at the very least!"

"Yes, *Ayya*!" replied Karuthiruman earnestly. "I can render you help that no one else in this world can!"

"Well? Let's hear it then!" snapped Madhuranthakan. "Quickly now, it gets late."

"Late for what?" asked Karuthiruman shrewdly, fixing him with an intent look.

Madhuranthakan narrowed his eyes. "To return to the palace. What else did you think?"

"Do you truly plan to return to a palace you cannot stake a claim upon?"

Madhuranthakan's stomach twisted with shock. "Adei!" he hissed. "What are you saying? What do you know? *How* do you know? Quick, now. Or else.." He swung the dagger above his head a second time.

"*Ayya*, pray, do not raise your knife. Whet your blade and keep it safe, so that you may wield it against the enemies you will counter. A short while back, it was under this very tree that you were speaking with the *periya maharani* who raised you. Neither of you noticed me standing on the other side."

"Aha! Have you overheard our secret, then? Is that why you showed such gross impertinence as to step in my way?"

"No, *Ayya*. I already knew of the matter the queen spoke of. Why, I know much more than that, even! That *maatharasi* only told you that she is not the mother who gave birth to you nor Kandaradhithar your father. She must have also told you who your true mother is. But she could not have told you of the father who sired you."

Madhuranthakan stared at him. "Do you know who he is?" he asked.

"I do."

Madhuranthakan found himself overcome by a sudden terror that the odious lunatic before him would claim to be his own father. "How do *you* know?" he spat out in disgust and rage. "*Who* are you?"

"I am your father's servant!" replied Karuthiruman. Madhuranthakan features cleared in relief.

Karuthiruman edged closer to the prince. "*Ayya*," he said softly, "your father…"

The revelation made Madhuranthakan reel. He staggered unsteadily and clutched at Karuthiruman's shoulders for support. "Is what you say true?" he whispered in a daze. "Am I a prince of royal blood?"

"Yes, *Ayya*. I came to this place many years ago to tell you this very truth. I was biding my time for a private audience with you. Alas, Chinna Pazhuvettarayar caught sight of me in the royal gardens and flung me into the underground dungeons."

"When did you make your escape? How?"

"Only today, with the help of a young man called Vandhiyathevan."

"Yes, I have heard of him. Isn't he the one accused of slaying Karikalan?"

"Yes, *Ayya*! In truth, the man who killed Karikalan is not that youth!"

"That is no concern of ours, is it? He can be the killer for all I care!" replied Madhuranthakan dismissively. "Where is he, now?"

"Over there, behind yonder fence," said Karuthiruman, pointing. "He awaits me with two horses, one for me and one for him. He must be rather annoyed by now, for I've kept him waiting for quite some time. I don't give a tuppence, to be honest. I'm grateful to have had the providence to run into you!"

"When did the pair of you reach this place?" asked Madhuranthakan.

"Only a short while ago. We came here upon learning that there were two steeds for the taking, by this hut. It was whilst we were searching for the horses that you and your mother came this way, accompanied by bright torches; it was by their light that we found the animals." Karuthiruman paused for a heartbeat. "I caught sight of Vaani, after many, many years. I was conversing with her in sign when you unexpectedly turned back to the hut. Vandhiyathevan fled towards the fence while Vaani and I stood near the tree for some time. Then she made for the hut as well and I was left standing here by myself. That is how I managed to meet you in private."

"Alright, then. What are your plans now?"

"Whatever you say, *Ayya!* Do you truly plan to return to the Thanjai palace after learning the secret of your birth? Remember - there are others who are aware that you are not a prince of the Chozha clan. The Mudhanmandhiri and his spy Azhwarkkadiyaan know the truth. One day or the other…"

"Yes, yes," cut in Madhuranthakan, "I have no wish myself to return to the Thanjai palace. What do you suggest I do?"

"Two horses stand there, behind that fence. Make a show of approaching the hut as you near the fence. I will buy time by engaging Vandhiyathevan in conversation. When you're close enough, hurl your dagger at the youth and slay him. We will take the horses for our own and travel together. We shall make for Kodikkarai and from there, to Ilankai. The Ilankai king is an enemy of the Chozha clan and a staunch friend of the Pandiyas; why, his is a lineage that has been an ally to the Pandiya clan through generations! I am well-acquainted with the Ilankai king. I even know the whereabouts of the Imperial Crown and gemstone necklace that are the heritage of the Pandiyas. What do you say?"

Madhuranthakan fell into deep thought. He hardly took a minute, in truth, but it was enough to set his heart soaring upon a flight of fancy. Madhuranthakan dreamed of the shining possibilities that lay temptingly within his reach and built many lovely castles in the air.

"*Ayya*!" said Karuthiruman, shaking him out of his reverie. "We're pressed for time. What have you decided? Vandhiyathevan will end up coming here in search of me!"

"Say, do you really think he ought to be killed?" asked Madhuranthakan.

"If you find yourself reluctant, *Ayya*, hand me the knife in your hand - I will do the deed myself!"

"No, this dagger has another purpose to fulfill," replied Madhuranthakan at once, clutching the knife tighter. "I know well of Vandhiyathevan. He is a good soldier, in truth. Why don't we take him along?"

"We *could*," demurred Karuthiruman, "but where will we get another horse?"

"Why must we suffer the lack of a horse? I am the crown prince Madhuranthakan yet, aren't I?" A fresh bout of anger surged through him and Madhuranthakan laughed in scorn at his own speech. "Go! Ask Vandhiyathevan to wait patiently for a little while longer. I will join you soon; first, I intend to meet the man in this hut and have a few words with him."

Karuthiruman faithfully made his way to the fence, where Vandhiyathevan waited in the shadows. It had grown quite dark by then. He saw pedestrians upon the *raja paattai*, carrying aloft bright torches that softly illuminated their environs. In the weakly shining light, Karuthiruman spied two magnificent steeds tethered to the fence. But there was no sign of Vandhiyathevan. He called out his name in a soft voice, but heard nothing in return.

"Alright, then. Perhaps it is for the best that he's made himself scarce," thought Karuthiruman to himself.

Darkness had fallen by the time Vandhiyathevan and Karuthiruman had reached the hut in the gardens. The hut flickered with the warm, yellow light of a small lamp. Vaani *Amma*i was on her way back from fetching water from the lotus pond when she noticed the pair of newcomers. She stopped in her tracks, hesitant until she saw Vandhiyathevan's face in the light. Vaani *Amma*i's face blossomed with joy, for she had not forgotten the occasion when Senthan Amudhan had brought him home. She warmly welcomed his arrival with a friendly nod.

That was the moment when she saw Karuthiruman emerge from behind him. Vaani *Amma*i's heart leapt to her mouth and she froze in terror as though she had seen a ghost. Karuthiruman had managed to quell her fear through signs and gestures.

Vandhiyathevan left them together and made his way towards the hut. Discovering that the door was latched, he peeped in furtively through the window. To his surprise, he saw a cheerful, bright-eyed Senthan Amudhan holding an animated conversation with Poonguzhali. Satisfied that Amudhan's life was no more in danger, Vandhiyathevan felt a calmness wash over him. He was lingering in place, wondering if he ought to interrupt them to say goodbye when Maduranthakan and Sembian Maadevi arrived with their retinue.

Vandhiyathevan lost no time in slipping away from the hut. He smoothly vaulted behind the fence, and soon noticed the tethered horses. Azhwarkkadiyaan had not tricked him on that score, after all. There, behind the fence, Vandhiyathevan waited in the dark for Karuthiruman.

Shortly, the palanquins left. They were soon followed by the royal retinue and the bright torches, too. But there was no sign of Karuthiruman. Vandhiyathevan grew impatient.

He had just jumped back over the fence when he saw Madhuranthakan and Karuthiruman engrossed in conversation beneath the tree. Vandhiyathevan wished to keep out of sight from Madhuranthakan's eyes. As he watched Karuthiruman and Madhuranthakan, however, he found it increasingly hard to ignore the niggle of doubt gnawing at his heart. A portion of their dialogue fell upon his ears.

Vandhiyathevan chose to quietly follow Madhuranthakan as he walked back towards the hut.

Madhuranthakan stood at the doorway, wondering if he ought to break down the door when a joyous peal of laughter suddenly rang out from within. It is hard to say whether that happy sound provoked second thoughts in Madhuranthakan, or whether he failed to muster the courage to carry out the deed he had in mind. In any case, he abruptly turned back on his heels and briskly walked towards Karuthirumaran.

Vandhiyathevan dove behind a tree across from him. That was when he caught sight of a scene that sent chills down his spine. A window lay towards the back of the hut, awash in the light thrown by a small lamp within; silhouetted against that brilliance was the dark figure of a man bearing a short spear in hand.

The figure peered through the window and looked all around the hut. As Vandhiyathevan watched, it raised the spear in its hand, clearly intending to throw the weapon at its target. It paused for a heartbeat before tightening its hold on the weapon and drawing aim a second time. It was at that very moment that the sound of galloping hooves broke through the air, catching Vandhiyathevan entirely off guard. He stood quite flustered, unsure of what to do.

If the horses left without him, it would be quite impossible for him to make his escape. But if he went after the horses, it would render him unable to thwart whatever nefarious plot the dark spear-bearer had in mind.

It hardly took a minute for Vandhiyathevan to solve this dilemma. *Let the horses leave, then. My duty lies here.*

Vandhiyathevan cautiously snuck towards the spear-bearer from behind.

A woman's terrified scream burst out from within the hut, piercing the still night air.

Vandhiyathevan threw all caution to the wind and hurtled towards the figure. The spear-bearer swivelled at the sound of his footsteps.

He hurled the spear in his hand as he turned. The weapon whistled through the air and pierced Vandhiyathevan's ribs. The Vallathu prince crumpled to the ground.

The spear-bearer had little interest in waiting around to see what happened to his challenger. He took to his heels and melted into the darkness.

63

Pinakapani's Deceit

When Ponniyin Selvar, Kundhavai Devi and the rest arrived at the underground dungeons, they were surprised to discover that Vandhiyathevan was nowhere to be found. Instead, they were met by a furious Pinakapani shackled to the iron rings on the prison wall.

He was howling at the top of his lungs when they saw him. "*Ayyago!*" wailed Pinakapani. "The killer has run away! The madman has run away!" Kundhavai Devi and Vanathi remembered him well. They had sent him along with Vandhiyathevan to Kodikkarai, hadn't they? They promptly arranged for Pinakapani's release and questioned him thoroughly, upon which he gave a succinct account of the events that had transpired. Pinakapani was positively apoplectic with rage, dead set on apprehending the escaped prisoners at once.

His audience, however, appeared fairly unruffled by his report. Inwardly, they each applauded Vandhiyathevan's ingenuity in slipping away and thought it for the best that he had managed to make his escape. Manimekalai made to offer her own opinion when Kundhavai stopped her. "Hush, my sister. This is a complex diplomatic affair. What do women like us know of such things? Tell me your thoughts in private, instead," she said.

When the group arrived at the entrance to the underground dungeons, they were met by Senathipathi Periya Velar, for word had already reached his ears that a mishap of sorts had taken place in the prisons. Even after listening to a detailed report of the incident, the Senthapathi evinced little haste in nabbing the absconders. In truth, he had placed little credence in the charge made against Vandhiyathevan. He was also well aware that Arulmozhi Varmar, Kundhavai Devi and the rest had a deep affection for Vandhiyathevan. So it was hardly surprising that far from losing his temper, Periya Velar chuckled appreciatively at Vandhiyathevan's resourcefulness.

"That Vaanar youth is a smart chap indeed!" he boomed. "Why, he cleverly broke out of the Mathotta prison at Ilankai too, on an earlier occasion!"

The *vaithiyar's* son cut in, taken aback. "*Ayya*, shouldn't we organize a search party to go after the runaways and apprehend them?"

"Ah, but where could they go, after all? They have nowhere to hide but within the premises of the fort. All in good time!" replied Senathipathi Periya Velar, genially twirling his moustache.

"No, no!" shrieked an enraged Pinakapani. "That wretch of a murderer knows of the underground passage that leads outside! He will slip away through that path!"

The Senathipathi stared at him, his face a mix of astonishment and fury. "Why, you cretinous halfwit! You dare give me advice? Wasn't it because of *you* that they escaped in the first place? You could be their accomplice for all I know! Perhaps you aided them in their escape!" roared Periya Velar and turned to the soldiers standing by his side. "Throw him straight back into the dungeons!"

A horrified Pinakapani shivered with fear. "No, *Ayya*! Truly, I had no part in their scheme! I only came here at the Mudhanmandhiri's behest!" he pleaded, trembling.

"That's right, he is the Mudhanmandhiri's man, isn't he?" broke in Ponniyin Selvar. "Why don't we send him back with the guards? Let the Mudhanmandhiri himself devise a fitting punishment for him," he suggested.

The Senathipathi lost no time in issuing orders to four of his own men to escort Pinakapani to the Mudhanmandhiri Aniruddhar's chambers.

The Mudhanmadhiri listened to Pinakapani as he gave a detailed account of the events that had transpired in the dungeons. He too appeared to be rather unconcerned by the news. When it came to important missions, Aniruddhar never relied on a single man; it was a custom of his to send along another spy to keep a close watch on the matter. In this case, he had dispatched Azhwarkkadiyaan on the job as well, so he found little cause to worry about the new development. He had every confidence that Azhwarkkadiyaan would either fetch the prisoners to him or bring reliable news of them. The Mudhanmandhiri felt in his bones that if the prisoners had made good their escape, it would serve to resolve other troublesome issues at hand.

And so, Aniruddhar only grew baleful at Pinakapani when he ended his unhappy tale with an earnest plea to make arrangements for their capture. "*Ayya*," said the *vaithiyar's* son in urgent tones, "if you send four men along with me, I am sure I can catch them."

"Why, you imbecile!" thundered Aniruddhar. "You've gone and endangered the whole mission! I had sent you for the task *precisely* so that no else would learn of the madman. Wouldn't I have gone to the dungeons myself otherwise? Now every man jack in the palace knows about him! As if that were not enough, here you are, making such a hue and cry as to practically advertise his existence! I've had enough of your service. You are absolutely unfit to be a spy, I tell you. Leave, and never show your face again! Do not breathe a word of what happened here today. If I learn that you've been loose-tongued, I shall issue orders to have you impaled!"

Pinakapani withdrew from the Mudhanmandhiri's palace with his tail between his legs. The spark of fury in his heart now raged fiercely as wildfire; he turned the full brunt of its wrath on Vandhiyathevan. It was because of *him* that he had failed at his mission and was meted out mortifying disgrace. It was because of him, too, that the Senathipathi and Mudhanmandhiri had both lashed out at him. Well, if they insisted on being complacent about this matter, then so be it. It fell to him to track down Vandhiyathevan and settle the score. Let the madman make his escape; but Vandhiyathevan could not be allowed to go scot-free. Pinakapani had marked him to be his sworn enemy ever since the day they had travelled to Kodikkarai together. And now, the wretch had done him a great evil. He simply had to seek him out and pay him back!

Pinakapani strengthened his resolve as he emerged from the Thanjai fort. He truly believed that Vandhiyathevan had fled the keep through the secret underground passage. Unfortunately, he knew neither its means of access nor egress. Even so, the point of exit *had* to lie somewhere along the outer perimeter of the fort. He could discover it yet if he walked carefully along the walls. Why, he may even catch Vandhiyathevan and the madman red-handed!

Pinakapani walked towards the fort and crossed over to the opposite bank of the Vadavaaru. He plodded along the path edging the perimeter of the fort, closely inspecting every inch of the walls. It happened to be the time when a small party of Kodumbalur soldiers were making their customary rounds of the fort, bearing brightly lit torches in their hands. The *vaithiyar's* son still had with him the signet ring marking him out to be the Mudhanmandhiri's man; it would be easy enough to manage the guards if they came across him. However, such an interruption would cost him precious time he could ill afford to lose. Pinakapani took to hiding himself in the dense bushes along the walls each time he was at danger of running into guards; he emerged only when they were out of sight and continued his meticulous inspection of the walls. It was whilst he was lurking in a thicket on one such occasion that he caught sight in the distance of two other men in hiding. One of them held a sword in his hand which glinted when it caught the passing torch light. But he was unable to see who the men were exactly.

After the guards had marched past their hiding place, the men quickly made their way to the riverbank and walked away in the opposite direction. Pinakapani resumed his task. He had only covered a short distance when a sudden suspicion crossed his mind. Could the two men he saw be none other than the absconders Vandhiyathevan and the madman? Why not, after all? He had paid them no attention because they had seemed to be walking *towards* the fort. But Vandhiyathevan was a devilishly cunning man, wasn't he? Who could know what he planned to do?

With that, Pinakapani turned back at once and proceeded to tail the pair at a discreet distance. He wanted to avoid a confrontation since one of them was armed with a sword; this was no time to pick a fight with a potential stranger, after all. He had to establish beyond doubt that the pair were indeed the escaped prisoners before making a move. The *vaithiyar's* son was armed with a short spear himself. His best course of action was to bide his time and wield the weapon when an attack was least expected; the element of surprise may give him the chance to do away with his nemesis once and for all. *There's the North Gate of the fort. Why does it appear crowded? What's all the uproar about? Palanquins, brightly-lit torches, a retinue of palace servants!* Pinakapani surmised that an influential dignitary was at the gate, but couldn't judge whether they were entering or leaving the fort.

He turned his attention to the task at hand only to discover that his queries had vanished. *Heavens! Where are those infernal men? They've disappeared in the blink of an eye! They've turned into a shortcut, I suppose. Where could they have gone? The raja paattai? Could prisoners on the run be so bold as to travel through the raja paattai? But where else could they have gone?* Pinakapani suddenly remembered that Senthan Amudhan's hut lay nearby. He knew that Vandhiyathevan had once gone there to conceal himself. Yes, yes! The men he saw had to be Vandhiyathevan and the madman! *They are heading to Senthan Amudhan's home, I suppose. Or perhaps that trickster Vandhiyathevan has other designs - who knows?*

Pinakapani walked towards Senthan Amudhan's hut. It was not easy to find his way in the dark; he stumbled along the path and took quite a few spills before he reached the garden. To his astonishment, he saw that the palanquins and guards were waiting at the hut. He had stopped in tracks, wondering what to do, when the palanquins left all of a sudden with the guards close behind.

Pinakapani surveyed the garden intently. Soon enough, he spied two horses by a fence nearby. The *vaithiyar's* son grew enormously curious. He carefully made his way to the hut, soft and slow. He saw two men engaged in conversation beneath a tree. They had to be the men he had come in search of! Why were there two horses at the ready? Were they secretly being helped in their escape by someone powerful? Perchance, were members of the royal clan complicit in the plot? That madman had made a spectacle of knowing secrets of some sort, hadn't he? Perhaps all this was naught but an attempt to protect those secrets from becoming public.

He snuck up to the tree and furtively peered at the two men on the other side. One of them was the madman, there was no doubt about that. That gravelly voice of his was quite unmistakable. So, the other man had to Vandhiyathevan, surely? But it didn't seem to be him. Oddly enough, the man looked like the prince Madhuranthakan! There lay a crown upon his head; a gold, silken cloth around his shoulders; he wore a necklace of pearls around his neck and bejewelled ornaments around his arms! What on earth could be the subject of an intimate conversation between Madhuranthakar and the madman?

Well, that was of little concern to him. Now where was his wretched nemesis, Vandhiyathevan? He had to be around here somewhere. The man with the sword was certainly him! Perhaps… why, he saw horses near the fence, didn't he? Was Vandhiyathevan mounted upon one of them, ready to flee on horseback? Was he waiting, perchance, for the madman? Yes, that had to be it! Perhaps it was Madhuranthakar who was helping them escape! Perhaps Vandhiyathevan had killed Karikalan under Madhuranthakar's influence! Why, perhaps Madhuranthakar was passing on an important piece of information to the madman before they made their escape? Heavens! If his conjecture were true and he could prove it…

Thus did the wheels in Pinakapani's crooked mind turn. It would be best, he decided, to approach the horses and see the truth for himself. If Vandhiyathevan happened to be there by himself, he could make short work of him with his spear. Then, he would catch hold of the madman and threaten him so thoroughly as to force him to cough up the truth. The horses were tethered to the other side of the fence, which lay directly opposite the tree where Madhuranthakar and the madman were in conversation. He could not draw close to the animals without inviting their notice. Besides, there was a lotus pond in the way as well. He decided to go around the hut instead and cross the fence from the backyard.

And so, Pinakapani determinedly marched to the backyard behind the hut. The voices of Senthan Amudhan and Poonguzhali fell upon his ears. Pinakapani had desired Poonguzhali since the very moment he had clapped eyes upon her in Kodikkarai. She was the reason why he had grown bitter towards Vandhiyathevan in the first place. It was only later, during the mission to fetch Mandhakini, that Pinakapani had become aware of the deep bond of friendship between Senthan Amudhan and Poonguzhali. The knowledge had made him squirm with resentment, and he had developed a hearty hatred towards Senthan Amudhan, too.

Pinakapani peeped through the small window at the back of the hut. He saw Senthan Amudhan and Poonguzhali in happy conversation, their faces aglow with joy. His heart twisted with renewed loathing for Senthan Amudhan. Pinakapani edged closer to listen to their exchange. He realized that they planned to get married to each other and live a life of bliss at Kodikkarai. The sweet, cheerful sounds of their happy laughter only stoked the rage burning in his heart. *Chi! So it is to be this son of a mute flower seller who gets to marry Poonguzhali, after all?* Pinakapani could hardly digest the very thought. All thoughts of Vandhiyathevan, the madman and his resolve to capture them flew straight out of his head. *First, this thevaram-singing Senthan Amudhan must be dispatched to the afterlife. Everything else can wait!*

Pinakapani got into position behind the window and aimed the short spear at Senthan Amudhan. It was purely by chance that Poonguzhali caught sight of the spear and the hand wielding it; an ear-splitting shriek escaped her throat. Senthan Amudhan turned around at once to look at the window. Aha! Here was his moment! There would be no better time to hurl the spear at his chest!

Pinakapani had raised the spear he held when he suddenly heard footsteps thudding close behind him. He whirled around only to discover that a figure had already drawn dangerously close to him. He could not recognize the man in the dark; but whoever it was had divined his intentions and appeared to be quite intent in catching hold of him. Pinakapani held aloft the spear he had earmarked for Senthan Amudhan; he hurled it with all his might at the figure who came charging at him. The spear whistled through the air and struck his mysterious challenger. The man crumpled to the ground.

At that very moment, Pinakapani heard two horses galloping away into the distance. That had to be Vandhiyathevan and the madman fleeing on horseback. Then… then, the man who had rushed at him in the dark and now lay wounded by his spear had to be prince Madhuranthakar! These thoughts flashed through Pinakapani's mind like lightning, leaving him petrified. "*Aha*! *Ayyo*!" A clamour of voices rose from the hut. He heard someone open the door and step outside. Pinakapani took to his heels. He decided that running away from the scene was the most important thing to do at that moment. The second most important thing to do was to pursue the men escaping on horseback. Pinakapani ran helter-skelter as he fled, stumbling and tripping along the way.

Poonguzhali and Senthan Amudhan hastened from the hut, bearing lamps in hand. To their terror and despair, they saw a wounded Vandhiyathevan lying insensible in a pool of blood. They lifted him with great care and took him inside the hut. They realized that he yet lived and felt a semblance of consolation. And so it came to pass that Vaani *Amma*i administered to an injured Vandhiyathevan the very same *pachchilai* treatment she had once given to Kandamaaran.

64

Tell me the truth!

The boat in which Vandhiyathevan had tied up Azhwarrkkadiyaan bobbed merrily along the river for a short distance and washed ashore. The two guards who had been forced into the river clumsily swam to the bank, floundering and flailing; when they finally reached land, they hastened towards the boat. Azhwarkkadiyaan did not get down from the boat. He chose to remain as he was, ostensibly tied down. The others were asked to hide themselves away close by.

The truth was that Azhwarkkadiyaan intended to help Vandhiyathevan and Karuthiruman escape. He knew that it was what the Mudhanmandhiri wanted, too. The pair's continued presence in Thanjai would only obligate an investigation into various matters of the past. Azhwarkkadiyaan and the Mudhanmandhiri had no doubt about Vandhiyathevan's innocence; however, an inquiry into his subject would dredge up complications that would bring pain and distress to many. If word of such affairs were to reach the people's ears, it would end in nothing but disaster. Arulmozhi Varmar would suffer the loss of a dear friend and Chozha Naadu, an excellent warrior and diplomat. The Mudhanmandhiri was cognizant, too, of Kundhavai Devi's feelings towards Vandhiyathevan as well as Manimekala's candid affection for him. He had considered the issue from all angles and come to the conclusion that it was prudent to help Vandhiyathevan make his escape.

Thirumalai believed that Vandhiyathevan and Karuthiruman would choose to travel through the banks of the Vadavaaru once they had gotten hold of the horses at Senthan Amudhan's hut. As Karuthiruman had pointed out, journeying along the banks of the Vadavaaru river would enable them to quickly reach the junction where its waters merged with those of the Paamani river. They could cover half the distance to Kodikkarai. So, decided Azhwarkkadiyaan, they had to come by this very path. He was waiting there patiently to stop them and deliver a message to Vandhiyathevan before they continued their journey.

Azhwarkkadiyaan found himself hanging around for longer than he had anticipated. "My calculations were wrong, then," thought Azhwarkkadiyaan. "They must have chosen another route. Or perhaps they have run into an unforeseen hindrance along the way." He made to disembark from the boat when he heard the sound of hooves in the distance. He hurriedly clambered back inside and lay still as if he were tied down.

As soon as he heard the horses draw nearer, he cried out, "Oho! Who goes there? Pray, stop! Untie me before you pass!"

But the horses did not stop; instead, they sped by at full tilt. Azhwarkkadiyaan saw that the man riding the first horse that went by was indeed Karuthiruman. And so, he gave another call when the second horse drew nearer. "Vandhiyatheva! Vandhiyatheva!" he shouted, as loudly as he could. "Wait!"

The second horse also sped by. Azhwarkkadiyan peered at the man mounted upon the steed and was left greatly astonished. "Surely my eyes deceive me; my mind must be playing tricks on me!" he exclaimed.

The steeds came to a halt a short distance away and a lone horse cantered towards him. Karuthiruman dismounted and approached the boat.

"Poor thing!" he remarked as he came. "You're still tied up, are you? You were of such great help to us! The least I can do in turn is to untie your bonds before I go. Mind you, don't play your tricks on me!" said Karuthiruman as he bent down to loosen his ropes. Thirumalai leapt ashore all of a sudden. In a single puissant move that belied his stature, Azhwarkkadiyaan smoothly caught Karuthiruman by the neck and pinned him to the ground.

Karuthiruman was caught entirely off guard. He stared wildly, not knowing what to do in the face of this unexpected assault; it took a while for him to find his tongue. "*Ayyo*! *Appa*! Let me go!" he cried. "A thousand blessings upon you, pray let me go! Ah, must you do such a thing to one who only comes to help you? Look, there waits your friend Vandhiyathevan. He is all praises for you as a dear friend. What will he think of you if he comes here and sees what you have done? You will not be left alive, I tell you. Let me go, *appane*, let me go!" he moaned wretchedly.

"*Adei*! What cheek to lie brazenly thus to my very face! *Who* is the man upon that horse? Tell me the truth! If you do, I shall let you go. Else, your life will be forfeit in a heartbeat!" growled Azhwarkkadiyaan as he held him down.

"Yes! Yes! I lied! It's true, I cannot trick you!" howled Karuthiruman. "The man upon that horse is not Vandhiyathevan, it is prince

Madhuranthakar. Let me go! I will make sure that he gives you whatever prize you ask of him!"

"Alright, alright. Let's put the prizes aside for the nonce. Where is Vandhiyathevan?"

"He dismounted from the horse at the hut in the garden. He vanished after that."

"Where are the two of you headed?"

"To the place Vandhiyathevan and I decided to go."

"You mean the island in Ilankai."

"Yes!"

Azhwarkkadiyaan frowned. "Why is Madhuranthakar going to Ilankai?"

"How am I to know? Ask him! He is the one who decided to come along with me!"

Azhwarkkadiyan mounted pressure on Karuthiruman's chest. "Tell me the truth! Whose son is Madhuranthakan?" he asked.

"What sort of question is this? Sembian Maadevi's.... No, no! Don't push down on my chest so! I shall die! He is that mute Mandhakini's son!" gasped Karuthiruman.

"Who is Madhuranthakan's father? The truth, now - or your life will not be spared!"

Karuthiruman gave the answer in a soft voice.

"Good," replied Azhwarkkadiyaan, satisfied. "You will survive, yet. One last thing - whose son is Senthan Amudhan?"

"Why ask me? You know the answer already, don't you?"

"He is the son born to Kandaradhithar and Sembian Maadevi, isn't he?"

"Yes! But he is alive today solely to *my* credit! Vaani, deaf and mute as she is, was on the verge of burying the child for she believed him to be dead. It was *I* who heard the babe's cries and saved him. Let me live in return for that, at the very least!" begged Karuthiruman.

"In truth, that is the only reason I am sparing your life at this moment," replied Azhwarkkadiyaan grimly and got to his feet.

Karuthiruman beat a hasty retreat and leapt onto his horse. The steeds hurtled along the riverbank, enveloped by dark, stormy skies.

65

Ayyo! Demon!

Azhwarkkadiyaan gathered his men out of hiding and proceeded towards the North Gate of the Thanjai fort. Our esteemed readers would have doubtless guessed why he had not called forth his men during the encounter with Karuthiruman. Quite natural, don't you think, that he wished none to hear the sensitive secrets he wished to validate?

He was halfway to his destination when he saw a lone figure making a mad, maniacal dash towards them. The man collided with Azhwarkkadiyaan in the dark; he hurriedly scrambled to his feet and made to take off once again. Thirumalai Nambi grabbed a firm hold of him and peered at his face. "Adade!" he exclaimed in genuine surprise. "You're the *vaithiyar's* son, aren't you? Where are you off to in such a hurry?"

"Oho, is it the Veera Vaishnavan?" wheezed Pinakapani. "You gave me quite a fright; I feared you were a ghost or demon of some sort. It's just as well that I ran into you. How far have you been walking along this bank? Did you see two men pass by on horseback?"

"Yes, I did. What is it to you?"

"What is it to *me*? A fine question, that!" scoffed the *vaithiyar's* son. "If you knew who they were, you wouldn't be asking me that question. Tell me, didn't you recognize even one of those men?"

"One of them did seem familiar," admitted Azhwarkkadiyaan. "But..."

"Who, who?" demanded Pinakapani eagerly, his eyes popping out of his head. "*Who* did it seem to be?"

"It *seemed* to be Vandhiyathevan," said Azhwarkkadiyaan, casting a dubious look at him. "But I decided that it couldn't be him."

"*Ada paavi!*" shouted the *vaithiyar's* son, stamping his foot in exasperation. "Is *that* the conclusion you came to? That truly *was* Vandhiyathevan!"

Azhwarkkadiyaan widened his eyes. "My dear fellow, what are you blathering on about? Vandhiyathevan is in the underground dungeons, isn't he?"

"He was, but not anymore! Vandhiyathevan broke out of the prison with a madman. They tied me up and made their escape!"

"*Adade!*" clucked Azhwarkkadiyaan. "That was a clever trick of theirs, to be sure! What were *you* doing when they tied you up? Why were you in the underground dungeons in the first place?"

Pinakapani turned red in the face. "I went there at the behest of the Mudhanmandhiri," he replied shortly. "I have no time to explain. You are the Mudhanmandhiri's man too, aren't you? Come with me! We can catch them together!"

"Why should we catch them? Let them escape if they want to. Of what concern is it to you or me?" shrugged Azhwarkkadiyaan.

A strange, strangled sound escaped Pinakapani. "Oh, the Mudhanmandhiri has employed a *fine* man!" he sneered. "There's little hope for the Chozha empire if everyone turns out to be like you! Don't you *know* that Vandhiyathevan is charged with the murder of prince Karikalar?" Pinakapani paused for a second. "That's not all," he said, suddenly turning earnest. "He also pierced a man with a spear just a short while ago, near Senthan Amudhan's hut."

"Good God!" cried out Azhwarkkadiyaan, appalled. "What are you saying? Who was the victim?"

"I did not see who it was. I came away in pursuit of Vandhiyathevan," replied Pinakapani quickly. "Right, then. If you are not coming along, that's fine by me. But don't stand in my way! Oh, blessings be upon your *head*, let me go!"

Azhwarkkadiyaan raised his eyebrows at Pinakapani, who was pulling away from his grasp. "Oh, *vaithiyar's* son, I have seen plenty of idiots in this world but you outshine every one of them! The escaped prisoners are fleeing on horseback, braving death, and you propose to capture them single-handed, on foot?" He abruptly let go his hold. "Well, what is it to me? Go on, then!"

"What you say is true," replied Pinakapaani gloomily. "That is why I asked you to come along and help. You turned me down!"

"Of what use would I be? I did try to stop them, you know. One of them thumped me soundly with a stick. It still hurts," confessed Azhwarkkadiyaan ruefully. "I have little experience in combat. Perhaps you… Say, what is that mark on your arm? It appears to be a bloodstain!"

"They ambushed me in the prison and wounded me, the wicked *rakshasas!*"

"And yet, you go in pursuit of these *rakshasas* all by yourself on foot! Why, if they gave you such a hard time when they were in *prison*…" Azhwarkkadiyaan trailed off apprehensively.

"What else do you want me to do?" asked Pinakapani, the frustration evident in his voice.

"I don't want you to do anything. Don't saddle me with blame, now! Though if I were you," continued Azhwarkkadiyaan thoughtfully, "I would turn back and petition the right authorities to grant me four, perhaps five soldiers on horseback before I resume the hunt. I would have my own horse, of course, as well as a sword and a spear…"

The *vaithiyar's* son fell into contemplation. In truth, he had fled after wounding someone near Senthan Amudhan's hut. Pure fear stabbed at his heart when he remembered that it may well have been prince Madhuranthakar of the royal clan. However, as the Veera Vaishnavan had been quick to point out, it was of admittedly little use to pursue his quarry on foot. If he really had wounded Madhuranthaka Thevar with his spear near the garden hut, it was perhaps best to palm off the blame onto Vandhiyathevan. A man who had killed one prince was capable of killing another, wasn't he? One murder or two, the punishment would be the same. As he followed his own train of thought, Pinakapani managed to persuade himself that it truly was Vandhiyathevan who had killed both princes.

"*Vaishnavane*, I must admit that you are correct," he said presently. "I will come with you. You must help me in petitioning the right authorities to grant me soldiers on horseback. I'm unsure why, but I find it difficult to navigate the ways of the rich and powerful. I do not know how to socialize with them. I did try talking to Senathipathi Kodumbalur Velar and Mudhanmandhiri Anbil Aniruddhar, you know - about going in pursuit of the absconders. I requested them to send a few soldiers with me in aid. Both of them fell upon me in anger and castigated me as an utter fool." Pinakapani looked genuinely puzzled. "I cannot understand them for the life of me."

Azhwarkkadiyaan looked upon him with sympathy. "What is there to understand? They do not trust you. They do not wish to task you with such an important mission. Why, you let them slip through your hands even whilst you were at the dungeons! They are likely apprehensive of your faculty to seize them when they're at large."

Pinakapani clenched his fists. "It was to prove them wrong that I set off to catch them single-handed," he confessed grimly. "The runaways don't have a choice but to halt at Kodikkarai - I know every single lair that Vandhiyathevan is likely to lurk in. I have people out there who can help me, too."

"Off you go, then - what are you waiting for? Prove your worth!"

"But it would be useful indeed to go on horseback, accompanied by others. Will you help me in this regard?" asked Pinakapani.

By this time, the duo had neared the North Gate of the Thanjai fort. They saw a grand cavalcade approaching from the north, marching upon the *raja paattai* in the distance. Mighty elephants trundled down the road, bearing splendid *ambaris* upon their backs, and regal steeds trotted gracefully alongside, flanked by a formidable retinue of soldiers. Outside the North Gate, too, stood a gathering, illumined by a brilliant cluster of flaming torches - Kodumbalur Velar, Thirukovilur Malayaman and the Mudhanmandhiri Aniruddhar.

"Ah, there stands our master at the fort gate!" exclaimed Azhwarkkadiyaan. "Shall we go to him?"

The *vaithiyar's* son shrank from the proposition. "I've already made an appeal to him, in vain. Perhaps he will give credence to your account, considering you saw the two escape with your own eyes," he dithered. "Though I confess to being doubtful whether he will send me along with you."

"You may well be right, there," agreed Azhwarkkadiyaan. "Besides, they seem to have gathered at the fort gate on a matter of importance. There's little point in soliciting their aid at this moment; nothing we say will reach their ears. It appears as though Pazhuvettarayars are coming this way, accompanied by Sambuvaraiyar. There, Parthibendran and Kandamaaran are with them, too! ! We shall make our appeal to them, instead," he suggested. "They will evince greater zeal in nabbing Vandhiyathevan!"

The cavalcade drew nearer. The criers heralded the arrival of the Pazhuvettarayars with grand proclamations describing the glory of their ancient clan. They also announced the approach of the noble Kadambur Sambuvaraiyar, Mazhapaadi Mazhavaraiyar, Parthibendra Pallavan, Neelathangaraiyar, Rettai Kudai Raajaliyaar and the rest, diligently listing each one's achievements and heroic exploits. Their cries were punctuated by the reverberating sounds of booming drumbeats and blaring trumpets.

At the head of the cavalcade rode Chinna Pazhuvettarayar, Parthibendran and Kandamaaran, cutting a majestic sight astride their splendid, white steeds. Periya Pazhuvettarayar and Sambuvaraiyar followed upon grand elephants, seated in royal *ambaris*. The rest of the noble chieftains came behind, variously seated upon elephants and horses. Around a hundred soldiers marched smartly in the front and rear, bearing sharp swords and spears in their hands.

Chinna Pazhuvettarayar brought his horse to a halt when he saw Azhwarkkadiyaan and the *vaithiyar's* son Pinakapani step in front of the cavalcade. "*Vaishnavane*!" he exclaimed in some surprise, "do you come bearing an important message from the Mudhanmandhiri?"

"Thalapathy," replied Azhwarkkadiyaan deferentially, "I do not bring word from the Mudhanmandhiri- my master will speak to you in his own words at the fort gate. But I do have an important message to deliver, though."

"What, what?" eagerly asked the three nobles in unison.

"Vandhiyathevan has escaped from the underground dungeons."

"How can that be?" demanded Chinna Pazhuvettarayar, genuinely taken aback. "Is he Indrajith, to vanish into thin air thus?"

"I smell a ploy!" exclaimed Parthibendran. "Someone must have helped him escape!"

"The handiwork of Kodumbalur Periya Velar, no doubt," chimed in Kandamaaran.

"Even if he did escape, where could he go? He must be within the fort, surely?" ponited out Chinna Pazhuvettarayar, frowning.

Azhwarkkadiyaan bent his head in agreement. "That is what Velar says, as well. The Mudhanmandhiri bade me patrol the fort perimeter as a precaution...he worries that slander will be brought to bear upon the Kadambur clan…"

"Ah, it is satisfying to hear that someone yet frets about such a thing!" remarked Kandamaaran.

Parthibendran narrowed his eyes. "*Vaishnavane* - the truth, now! Do you patrol the fort walls to stop him from escaping or to help him escape?" he asked sternly. The wily Vaishnavan inspired little trust in him.

"*Ayya*, my answer would have been quite different on any other occasion; this, however, is hardly the time to indulge in squabble," replied Azhwarkkadiyaan coolly. "Pinakapani here–the *vaithiyar*'s son - brought me a strange piece of news. He reports that two men fled on horseback, none other than the escaped felons Vandhiyathevan and Karuthiruman. I myself saw two fellows swiftly riding away along this very path."

"Pinakapani, does the Vaishnavan speak the truth?" asked Chinna Pazhuvettarayar.

"He does, *Ayya*, truly!"

"Why didn't you make a report to the Mudhanmandhiri or Velar at once?"

Pinakapani squirmed. "They are both furious with me," he finally admitted.

"Whatever for?" asked Chinna Pazhuvettarayar in amazement.

"Because I am responsible for their escape," replied Pinakapani weakly.

"How did that happen?"

"There was a madman in the dungeons, wasn't there–one claiming to have knowledge of the Imperial Crown and the ancient gemstone necklace of the Pandiyas?" said Pinakapani glumly. Aniruddhar had sent me to fetch him; When I went to the dungeons, the crooks ambushed me, tied me up and made their escape!"

A derisive snort escaped Parthibendran. "That the Mudhanmandhiri could find none to carry out the task but an idiot as you!" he sneered and laughed unkindly.

The *vaithiyar's* son bristled with anger. "*Ayya*, I did not come here to be laughed at," he replied stiffly. "Help me if you can."

"What help do you seek?"

"Grant me four soldiers on horseback. Provide me with a horse, too. I will take the responsibility of capturing the prisoners on the run. I have been successful, haven't I, in the tasks that have been assigned to me thus far? Why, Thalapathy Chinna Pazhuvettaryar must be aware of my record!" said Pinakapani, the *vaithiyar's* son.

Chinna Pazhuvettarayar looked at Parthibendran. "What do you say?"

"We might as well send him. The Chakravarthy has charged me with fetching you, else I would go with him myself. It is crucial that we apprehend Vandhiyathevan," replied Parthibendran.

"Entrust the mission to me," cut in Kandamaaran. "I will accompany him." His lips drew into a thin line. "If I have to, I will seize Vandhiyathevan at the very gates of *yamalokam* and drag him back here!"

Chinna Pazhuvettarayar gave his assent as well. He took upon himself the responsibility of explaining the situation to Sambuvaraiyar and the others.

Kandamaaran and the *vaithiyar's* son mounted swift horses at once, accompanied by four guards on horseback. Their steeds galloped like the wind along the northern banks of the Vadavaaru.

Madhuranthakan was quite unused to riding a horse. Karuthiruman was no stranger to the art, but years of imprisonment in the dungeons had taken their toll upon his body; he was left feeling quite sore and tired. But nothing, it seemed, could blunt the new enthusiasm that had sprouted in their hearts. The pair pressed on in their arduous journey, their buoyant spirits vanquishing their fatigue.

They travelled until the dark of midnight before they came to a halt. A bridge stretched out across the river before them, built from sturdy bamboo sticks. Karuthiruman had no doubt that they were being pursued by men intent on their capture. He thought it best to cross the river and reach the other side- they could then travel along the southern bank of the river for a distance before turning towards Kodikkarai.

There was another good reason to cross the river at that point- Karuthiruman was quite doubtful whether Maduranthakan could cross the swiftly flowing waters of the river upon horseback; he was certain, in fact, that it would be an impossible task in high water. If they were to make the crossing now, Madhuranthakan could walk across the bridge and he could bring both the horses himself.

Madhuranthakan approved of his plan, too. Wishing to soothe their tired limbs before making their way across, the pair sat down upon the great, gnarled roots of a nearby tree. The river roared as the rapids chased their course. A cacophony of amorous frogs rent the air, their raucous croaks spawning an ear-splitting din. Billowy clouds drifted across the firmament as stars glittered in their midst, peeking out from the darkened heavens like celestial spies of the sky.

Bred to a royal life in the palace, Madhuranthakan had grown accustomed to sleeping upon plush, downy bedding ensconced in an exquisite, canopied bed. As he endeavoured in vain to sit on the hard, bumpy root, he grew quite sorry for himself. Disillusionment pressed upon his heart and he began to fear for the future.

Karuthiruman instinctively understood his struggle and did his best to give him cheer. He told him that the Ilankai king Magindhan had been a staunch ally to the Pandiya clan through generations; once Madhuranthakan reached his side, he assured, he would have nothing to worry about. He also told him that the Imperial Crown of the Pandiya clan and the famed gemstone necklace gifted by Indira were in Ilankai; he knew, he said, where they lay hidden. Magindhan would crown Maduranthakan then and there, he said. By then, the Chozha *samrajyam* would likely be decimated, for the chieftains of Chozha Naadu would wage a bloody civil war among themselves. The people would accuse the Pazhuvettarayar-Sambuvaraiyar faction of slaying Aditha Karikalan; since he had come away with Karuthiruman, the Pazhuvettarayars would accuse the Velar faction of killing Madhuranthakan. Rumour would spread among the populace that Arulmozhi Varmar had a hand in the murder, as well. The people would soon grow to hate him. With the Chozha kingdom mired in such confusion, the Ilankai king would gather a great army and march upon Pandiya Naadu, seizing control of Madurai. He would crown Mathuranthakan a second time, with the world as witness. He would bestow upon him another name, the exalted honorific, Chozha Kulanthaka Peruvazhudhi!

Madhuranthakan's heart leapt with joy as Karuthiruman spoke.

He felt an intoxicating exuberance that he had never felt before. He thought he heard the victory beats of drums upon a battlefield. The melodious notes of the musical instruments that would play at his *pattabhishekam* sounded sweetly in his ears. He heard the joyous cries of thousands, their voices raised in adoration - *Long live the Pandiya Chakravarthy! Long live the Chozha Kulanthaka Peruvazhudhi!*

Madhuranthakan was lost to the sweetness of this happy world when the sound of hurried hoofbeats broke his reverie. The light of flaming torches shone brightly in the near distance. Karuthiruman had not expected their pursuers to catch up with them so soon. He jumped up in great alarm. "*Ilavarase!* Get up! Mount your horse!" he cried in urgent, panicked tones. "We must cross the river before they arrive!"

Karuthiruman lithely swung onto his horse. He saw Maduranthakan in a desperate struggle to mount his steed. "*Ayya,* cross the bridge on foot," he said quickly. "I shall bring your horse to the other bank, too."

Madhuranthakan's face turned scarlet. "Oh, a kind offer to be sure!" he snapped. "Think me a coward, do you? How am I to cross the sea and reach Ilankai if I cannot cross this river on horseback? How am I to seize control of the Pandiya *rajyam* and ascend to its throne?"

The two horses stepped into the river. To Madhuranthakan's dismay, his horse suddenly sank to its knees in the shallows near the bank. "*Ayyo!*" screamed Karuthiruman. Fortunately, the animal managed to get back on its feet and walked further into the river.

Madhuranthakan's heart was gripped by terror. "Oh, such a trivial thing!" he scoffed atop the horse, affecting the greatest of nonchalance. "To think you were scared by *that*!"

Madhuranthakan's horse seemed to have injured its legs in the shallows, for it was not able to press on against the currents as quickly as the other horse did. There were times when it appeared to be in danger of being swept away by the rapids. Madhuranthakan struggled considerably to steer his horse towards the opposite bank. Meanwhile, the hoofbeats of the steeds in pursuit along the bank grew louder and louder.

Until halfway across the river, Karuthiruman travelled slowly upon his horse, patiently stopping now and then so that the prince could keep up with him. Suddenly, an idea came to his mind. He spoke encouragingly to Madhuranthakan, bading him to be brave; he then rode as quickly as he could to the other side, where he brought his horse to a halt beneath a tree. He jumped down from his mount to briskly walk across the bamboo bridge and return to the northern bank. He had already received from Madhuranthakan the short, sharp dagger he carried. With it, he hurriedly hacked away at the ropes of the bridge and proceeded to tie them into knots. When he saw that he had enough length, he tied one end of the knotted rope to the bridge and the other end, to the tree near the bank.

The black shadows of the tree would hide the rope stretching across the path; it was unlikely that someone would notice the taut cord in the darkness. At any rate, it was certain that the rope would go unnoticed by the men hunting them on horseback, for they were riding their mounts at full gallop. As he finished his task, Karuthiruman wondered if he ought to run back across the bridge. He changed his mind quickly enough; he hastily scrambled up a nearby tree and disappeared into its branches.

Madhuranthakan's horse had almost crossed the river - just a few minutes more and it would climb onto the bank. Even as the thought crossed Karuthiruman's mind, the pursuing horses came into sight near the tree. Two steeds led the charge, followed at a short distance by four, perhaps five swift mounts. The steeds at the forefront streaked down the bank, only to fall headlong into Karuthiruman's trap; they violently tripped over the rope and tumbled head over heels to the ground.

Karuthiruman gleefully watched the misadventure from his treetop, scarcely realizing it when he broke into roars of laughter. "Ha, ha, ha!" he guffawed.

A scream of terror rose from one of the fallen men. "*Ayyo*!" he shrieked. "Demon!"

From his voice, Karuthiruman identified him to be Pinakapani, the *vaithiyar's* son. The boatman was filled with instant regret. 'Couldn't the wretch have broken his neck in the fall? Must he live yet?' he rued.

The man who had tumbled down from the other horse quickly regained his footing, absolutely unshaken by the fall. He was none other than our old friend, Kandamaaran!

Hidden Meanings and Explanations

Indrajith - Raavanan's son, Indrajith possessed the ability to turn invisible at will, a trick that gave him quite an edge on the battlefield.

66

The disappearance of Madhuranthakan

Kandamaaran exhibited remarkable sangfroid when his horse took the perilous spill. He smoothly broke his fall and sprang to his feet, grabbing his spear in one fluid motion. His attention whipped to the horse crossing the river. It appeared to be nearing the opposite bank. He was convinced beyond the shadow of doubt that the man riding it was none other than Vandhiyathevan.

The friendship that Kandamaaran had once felt towards Vandhiyathevan had now distorted into bitter enmity. He thought that the Vaanar warrior had betrayed their camaraderie in many ways. Vandhiyathevan was the sole reason why he and his family were made to suffer unendurable ignominy! He had been loose-lipped with the secrets he had learned during his sojourn at Kandamaaran's home; why, he had slyly revealed his findings to the very members of the royal clan! And why did he do such a thing? On account of his unflinching faith towards the Chozha clan? Not at all! He had only sought to gain their trust so that he could betray them too, in the end. It was certain that he had served as an accomplice to the Pandiya Naadu *abathudhavis*. Kandamaaran did not know whether he had committed those dual acts of treachery at Nandhini's behest or in pursuit of personal gain. It was true that he himself had been caught in Nandhini's enchanting web for a while there; but never could he have dreamed of perpetrating such foul treachery!

Among all his vile transgressions, it was the sullying of his beloved sister Manimekalai's heart that made Kandamaaran boil over with blinding rage. Here Kandamaaran was, dreaming of the day that Manimekalai would wear the bejewelled crown of the Chozhas and regally take her seat upon the throne as Chakravarthini; and that execrable wretch Vandhiyathevan had successfully contrived to make an innocent waif as spout the most appalling drivel in public, claiming that she was the one who killed Karikalar!

Could such a loathsome cur as that, one guilty of the most hideous of crimes, be allowed to escape with his life? Was he to do nothing but watch as the wretch skipped away unscathed? Never! If he could capture Vandhiyathevan alive, it would be well and good. If not, he would turn back only with the consolation that he had slayed him once and for all. It was with such a terrible resolve that Kandamaaran had embarked on his manhunt.

He hadn't expected his horse to trip over. It was unlikely that the animal would survive. The horse of the *vaithiyar's* son Pinakapani would suffer the same fate!

Meanwhile, Vandhiyathevan seemed to have reached the other side of the riverbank.

It would take awhile for the rest of the soldiers to catch up. Even if they did reach in time, it would be an impossible prospect for them to cross the swift waters and seize Vandhiyathevan. Kandamaaran's best course of action at that very moment was to kill him.

The thoughts flashed through Kandamaaran's mind as lightning. As soon as he regained his footing, he adopted the firm stance of a warrior. He raised the sharp spear he held and took steely aim at his target. Kandamaaran hurled the weapon with all his might.

The spear whistled through the air and pierced Madhuranthakan in the blink of an eye. Madhuranthakan shrieked in pain and tumbled down from his horse, vanishing into the dizzy currents. Only his horse stumbled ashore, bereft of its rider.

Karuthiruman could do nothing but watch from the treetop as the scene unfolded rapidly. His heart was seized by terror; he trembled uncontrollably.

He had never expected such a thing to come to pass.

He had thought that the riders would find themselves helplessly trapped under the horses when the animals keeled over from their own momentum. He had thought that the men would be left with broken limbs even if they had managed to survive such a fall.

He had not dreamed that such a thing would come to pass. One of the fallen riders had bounced back to his feet and hurled his spear at Madhuranthakan, with devastatingly perfect aim. The weapon had pierced through the prince's body with brutal force, knocking him off his horse into the flowing waters. Karuthiruman was left stunned. When the initial shock wore off, he was left with nothing but seething rage. He jumped down from the tree with a terrifying howl.

The boatman fell upon Kandamaaran wielding a monstrous strength augmented by cold fury. Karuthiruman roughly shoved him to the ground and took a step forward; it was at this very moment that the *vaithiyar's* son scrambled clumsily to his feet and made an attempt to stop him. Pinakapani had gotten the better of his fear by now, having discovered that the creature in the treetop was no demon but Karuthiruman.

Karuthiruman turned the full brunt of the murderous rage burning in heart upon Pinakapani. He brutally stabbed the *vaithiyar's* son with the dagger he held and knocked him to the ground before sprinting towards the bridge.

The soldiers on horseback had drawn closer. They spied a man tearing across the bamboo bridge. The guards guessed at the events that had transpired before their arrival and brought their horses to a halt.

"Catch him, catch him!" roared Kandamaaran. "Catch the man running across the bridge!"

The four men leapt down from their horses and gave frantic chase to Karuthiruman, who was bolting down the bridge.

Kandamaaran was in a daze from being pushed down a second time. He had hit his head upon the ground, too. It took him a few minutes to gather himself but he soon got to his feet and ran behind the soldiers, joining them in their pursuit of Karuthiruman.

The *vaithiyar's* son had been gravely wounded by the dagger's assault, but he managed to push himself to his feet. Livid with rage, he staggered to the bridge and attempted to run across.

He had hardly taken five or six steps when his strength gave way. His vision turned dark; he grew light-headed and dizzy. He tried to force himself back on his feet, but failed. He swayed and tottered in place before collapsing into the waters.

No one noticed him fall.

Poor Pinakapani the *vaithiyar's* son drew his last breath without achieving his many desires, ruined by his own spite and malice. The castles he had built in the air were all swept away by the gushing waters of the Vadavaaru. The swiftly-flowing river became his watery tomb.

Karuthiruman, the boatman who had attacked Kandamaaran and viciously stabbed the *vaithiyar's* son, fled across the bridge. He had crossed three-fourths of the way when he stopped and turned around. He saw that the soldiers had dismounted their horses and had reached the far edge of the bridge.

He set to work at once, on a rather strange task. Where he stood lay bamboo sticks, tied together in a tight bundle. They were placed in a slanted position to lend support to the bridge.

With the same dagger he had attacked Pinakapani, Karuthiruman now quickly cut away the ropes holding the bamboo sticks together; he kicked away the bamboo support and ran as fast as he could across the bridge. When he reached the other side of the bank, he hacked away the ropes tied around a similar bale of bamboo sticks and tree roots. Once the ropes were cut free, Karuthiruman grabbed the edge of the bridge with both his hands and bodily lifted the loosened side of the bridge. He cast it into the swift torrents flowing below.

It took barely a few minutes for the bridge of bamboo to be rent asunder by the powerful currents. Close to a third of the structure cleaved away from the whole and hurtled along the waters.

The soldiers charging down the bridge failed to notice that it had broken. One by one, they fell headlong into the river!

Only Kandamaaran, who was the last of them all, managed to avoid tumbling into the waters.

The men who had fallen into the river floundered desperately, resurfacing only after gulping down copious amounts of water in a panic.

Kandamaaran bellowed at them to swim across the river to the other side of the bank. Two of the men understood his order and began to swim while the other two made a great effort to swim against the current. Gasping, they reached the broken bridge and clambered on top.

Kandamaaran began to subject them to severe reprimand, but soon realized that there was little use in asking them to swim back. He barked orders to salvage bamboo sticks from the bridge and build a raft. Once the task was done, the raft was made to float upon the river; Kandamaaran and the two guards held on tightly as they floated along with it to the other side of the bank.

They joined the other two guards who had swum ashore before them. They reported that the man they had pursued had managed to beat them to the shore and had vanished into the darkness. They also reply having heard two horses gallop away. They had decided, they said, that it seemed of little use in running after the horses on foot and had halted there.

But Kandamaaran was loath to give up the chase. He reckoned that it had to be the madman who had escaped from the prison - the very man that the *vaithiyar's* son had spoken of - who had jumped down from the tree to push him down and flee across the bridge. No doubt the wretch rigged a rope across the path only to help Vandhiyathevan escape; that must have been why he was lurking on the treetop, too. He had no doubt that the man who had fallen to his spear had been Vandhiyathevan. Kandamaaran had seen with his own eyes how he had fallen off the horse into the water. Even so, he would derive greater satisfaction were he to locate his corpse... Perhaps he could take Vandhiyathevan's remains back to Thanjavur-it would win him great honour, wouldn't it, to fetch the body of one who had committed great treachery to the Chozha clan? He could mitigate to some extent the dishonour that had been dealt to Sambuvaraiyar's clan. Vandhiyathevan's very attempt to escape was evidence enough of his guilt. If it was proven that Vandhiyathevan killed Karikalan, then Sambuvaraiyar's clan would not bear the burden of the terrible accusation!

Such were Kandamaaran's thoughts as he made his way down the Vadavaaru bank. The four soldiers followed close behind. They kept a keen lookout to see if Vandhiyathevan's corpse had washed ashore. It was rather challenging to undertake this task in the darkness, but Kandamaaran did not lose hope. He pressed on further and further, searching intently all the while. After he had walked quite a distance, he heard a roaring sound like that of a great waterfall cascading down a mountain. When they approached the source of the sound, they discovered that a yawning gorge lay sprawled in the course of the river as its waters tumbled downhill. The torrents flowed into the gorge until the reservoir was full and could hold no more; the waters then spilled out in swirling eddies and bubbling waves to resume the river's course.

If the waters had dragged Vandhiyathevan's body thus far, it would have tumbled into that massive gorge - his remains would have rammed into the rocks. In which case, it would take many days for the corpse to resurface; why, it was entirely possible that it would never surface at all. There was little use in continuing the search.

Kandamaaran mused thus, he spied a dark figure bobbing amidst the frothing whites of the eddies on the other side of the gorge. Aha! That must be Vandhiyathevan! A great traitor had been vanquished from this earth! May God forgive his sins!... Was that likely, though? Could even a merciful God deign to absolve the vileness he had perpetrated in this life? Never! He would certainly be punished in his next birth! In any case, Vandhiyathevan's time upon this earth had come to an end. There was little need to worry about him any further. He could now return to Thanjai and attend to other matters.

And so, Kandamaaran turned back the way he came. Little did he know the sore disappointment that awaited him at Thanjai. How stunned he would be to discover that the man he had shot down into the river with his spear was not Vandhiyathevan, but Madhuranthakan! Why, it would be hardly surprising if he felt the very earth quake beneath his feet!

67

NOT FOR ME A KINGDOM UPON EARTH

As soon as the Pazhuvettarayars and the rest of the noble chieftains moved away with their retinue, Azhwarkkadiyaan made his way to Senthan Amudhan's garden with his men. There, he glimpsed Madhuranthaka Thevar's palanquin and bearers standing in the shadows of a tree near the garden. Upon questioning them, Azhwarkkadiyaan learnt that they had been asked to wait there for the prince's return. He walked into the garden. He softly instructed his men to conduct a search of the grounds and strode to the threshold of the hut. The door was latched, but Azhwarkadiyaan pressed his ears against it and listened intently. He heard the voices of Senthan Amudhan and Poonguzhali in anxious conversation. Their exchange was interspersed with the sounds of anguished, incoherent moaning; someone was clearly in excruciating pain.

One of the men combing the garden hurried to his side. Thirumalai took the articles he came bearing and held them to the slivers of lamplight that shone through the cracks of the door. The faint glow illuminated an exquisite crown, a precious necklace of gemstones and an armlet, among other items of jewellery - the very same ornaments, in fact, that were regularly seen upon Madhuranthaka Thevar's person. Along with these was a *peethambaram*, a silken cloth of gold that Madhuranthakar habitually wore around his shoulders. A tight smile of satisfaction appeared on Azhwarkkadiyaan's face.

"Cease the search," commanded Azhwarkkadiyaan. "Ask the others to come here. Have your weapons at the ready and brace yourselves for what may come next." He knocked softly on the door of the hut. Hearing no response, he rapped loudly on the door.

"Who is there?" called out Poonguzhali from the other side. "What do you want?"

"*Ammani*! It is I, Azhwarkkadiyaan, otherwise known as Thirumalai Nambi Dasan!" came the reply. "Pray, open the door. I am here on an important matter!"

Footsteps pattered across the floor. "What sort of important matter could you possibly have here?" asked Poonguzhali from the other side of the door. "You are a Veera Vaishnavar; this is a hut of Sivanadiyaars. You know well that the head of the house is in ill health. Why do you pester us in the dead of the night?"

"Samudhra Kumari! I am verily a Veera Vaishnavar, as you say. Hence my mission of *dushta nigraha sishta paripaalanam* - the destruction of evil and defence of the virtuous. If the door isn't opened at once, I am afraid it will have to be broken down," informed Azhwarkkadiyaan apologetically.

An aggrieved rustling floated out from within and Poonguzhali threw open the door. "Are you such a great warrior as that, *Vaishnavare*? You've come here to flaunt your heroics, have you?" she demanded, her lovely almond eyes blazing with anger.

Poonguzhali had opened the door intending to quarrel with Azhwarkkadiyaan, but stopped short when she saw the guards standing behind him. "*Ayya*, what, pray, is this?" she asked, taken aback. "Who are they? *Why* are they here? Are they with you?"

"Yes, they are. I am here on matters of the state, as I said. You will be subject to royal punishment if you were to interfere in their duties, you know," replied Azhwarkkadiyaan, much to her annoyance.

"Matters of the state, he says! Royal punishment, he says!" exploded Poonguzhali. "*When*, I wonder, will I return to Kodikkarai and listen in peace to the song of the waves instead of this drivel? Let that be. Ask your men to wait outside and come in by yourself. Though," she grumbled, "only the lord knows what matters of state lie in this rickety hut. Can't you handle such things by yourself?" she demanded as she gave way. "*Aththan* lies there upon that bed, in misery. If these people come in too, it will only serve to upset him and worsen his health."

Azhwarkkadiyaan closed the door as he entered and drew the latch. "Poonguzhali, your words amaze me!" he clucked. "When did you develop such an aversion to statecraft? Whatever happened to your dreams of marrying the crown prince and ascending the throne? You *are* aware that you will have to consign yourself to politics when that happens?"

"*Ayyo, Vaishnavare*! I've renounced the very idea. The past few days have taught me that the weight of royalty is crushing indeed, a world of trouble and suffering. I wouldn't touch the throne with a ten foot pole!" Poonguzhali paused. "*Vaishnavare*, I have some good news to share with you. I have chosen to wed my *aththan*, Senthan Amudhan. We made the announcement to lady Sembian Maadevi just a short while ago, and received her blessings. Amudhan and I plan to leave for Kodikkarai once he improves..."

"Aha!" exclaimed Azhwarkkadiyaan. "A wise decision, to be sure! The Azhwars sang in the days of yore,

Aanatha selvaththu arambayargal tharchuzha
Vaanaalum selvamum mannarasum yaan venden
Thenaar pooncholai thiruvenkadachunaiyil
Meenai pirakkum vithiyudayeyavene!"

I suppose you've both decided to likewise renounce the earthly kingdom to live as minnows in the ocean of life. But, who knows," continued Azhwarkkadiyaan innocently, "if it is your fate to wear a crown and sit upon the throne, then that is what will happen, in the end."

"Pray, put a stop to the jests, *Ayya*!" groaned Poonguzhali in good-natured exasperation. "Tell me truly, what brings you here?"

"I came to learn, *Ammani*, whether you have lost your appetite only for a life of royalty or for one of happiness with Senthan Amudhan, too," replied the Vaishnavan.

Poonguzhali's smile slipped off her face. "What sort of a question is this? We both desire to live in happiness for many years to come. Why, we've only just decided this very day to wed each other! *Vaishnavare*, wish us well! Grace us with your blessing that *aththan* may make a speedy recovery!"

"I truly do want to wish you both well. But it would not do for my blessings to go wasted now, would it? If the two of you seek to live yet, why then did you help the prisoners who escaped from the dungeon?" asked Thirumalai baldly.

"What?" exclaimed Poonguzhali, affecting a look of great surprise. "We know nothing of that matter! We helped no one escape!"

"Vandhiyathevan, the man accused of killing Karikalan, escaped today from the underground dungeons along with a madman. It is evident that they came by this garden. They later escaped on two horses from these very grounds. Blood has been spilled nearby. Signs abound that this hut has been visited by many this very day. There is little doubt that you lent a helping hand to the prisoners who escaped. The Mudhanmandhiri bade me come here on account of the affection he bears for the two of you. If it had been Kodumbalur Velar's men, they would have thrown you into prison at once!" said Azhwarkkadiyaan evenly.

"We truly are grateful to you and the Mudhanmandhiri, Vaishnavare!" replied Poonguzhali with feeling. "*Aththan* will recover in a couple of days and we will depart at once to Kodikkarai. We shall forswear Thanjavur altogether! Only, help us until then - pray, shield us from the royal guards!"

"Nothing stops me from helping you. But you must tell me the truth! Did no one else come to this hut save the three of you?" he asked.

"But of course they did! *You* are here, now. Lady Sembian Maadevi and Madhuranthakar were here too a short while back; they asked after *aththan's* health before they departed. Why," continued Poonguzhali defensively, "the Thanjavur fort and its environs are awash with soldiers at the moment, aren't they? How, pray, are we to keep track of each person who comes and goes by this place? *Vaishnavare*, I will answer your first question with absolute conviction. We helped no one escape from this hut!"

"Truly?"

"Yes, truly! We helped no one escape from this hut!"

"In that case, the absconding Vandhiyathevan must be somewhere in this hut at this very moment!" said Thirumalai shrewdly.

The words were hardly out of his mouth when a weary, piteous groan emanated from beneath Senthan Amudhan's cot.

68

Prince for a Day

"Aha!" cried out Azhwarkkadiyaan in triumph when he heard the moans issuing forth from beneath Senthan Amudhan's bed. "Is that how it is? Why, you crest jewels of Siva *bhakthi*! You've learned to play tricks like that old Paramasivan, then?" he tutted as he stepped forward.

Poonguzhali unsheathed the dagger at the hip in one swift motion. "*Vaishnavare*, a sinner as you who mocks Siva Peruman cannot be suffered to draw another breath." She grimly eyed Azhwarkkadiyaan. "Another step forward and you will find yourself in Vaikuntam!"

"*Thaaye! Maha Shakthi!* Can your words brook argument? It is not a simple feat to attain Vaikuntam. If, perchance, I am bestowed with that great fortune by your very hand, why - what other blessing can I ask for?" replied Azhwarkkadiyaan, spreading his hands.

Sentham Amudhan rose from his bed at once and hobbled forward, alarmed. "Poonguzhali, don't! Put away your knife! The Vaishnavan's mockery is naught to Siva Peruman. No good comes from evil ways. Lies and treachery will not serve our cause. Let us confess the truth to the Vaishnavan and ask him for help!" he urged. "After all, he is a friend to Vandhiyathevan too!"

"Now we're talking!" cut in Azhwarkkadiyaan, quite pleased. "Can mere Siva *bhakthas* hope to beguile a humble servant of the saints who surrendered to Krishna Paramatma, the Supreme Architect of Artifice? Submit to Sriman Narayanan, the fountainhead of compassion; most assuredly will He deliver you from harm and grace you with His blessings. After all," he continued, flashing a wicked grin, "it was our very own Thirumalai who saved Gajendra from the jaws of a crocodile when he cried out for help!"

"Yes, yes!" replied Poonguzhali tartly as she hurried towards the bed. "Our friend would have crossed the Great Divide by the time your Thirumal deigns to descend upon earth!"

The others followed her hastily. Vandhiyathevan was beneath the bed, hidden under a bundle of clothes. They lifted him as gently as they could and laid him on the bed.

Vandhiyathevan lay insensible, dead to the world. He moaned in unendurable pain even in this state of oblivion; the pitiful sounds he made were testimony that he yet lived.

Vaani *Ammai* came forward with a poultice for his wound, a concoction of boiled medicinal herbs and turmeric. Azhwarkkadiyaan and Senthan Amudhan held Vandhiyathevan's limbs in place while Vaani *Amma*i and Poonguzhali wrapped the still-hot bandage around the gash.

Vandhiyathevan's eyes flew open in excruciating agony. Seeing Azhwarkkadiyaan, he made to speak. "*Vaishnavane*!" he mumbled, words running into each other. "You've betrayed me so! You sent me here only to dispatch a man to come after me and kill me!" He lost consciousness once again.

A look of deep unease settled upon Azhwarkkadiyaan's face. He reckoned that Vandhiyathevan's half-dazed accusations had stirred suspicion anew in Poonguzhali and Senthan Amudhan. Azhwarkkadiyaan scrutinized their faces anxiously.

To his relief, he saw Poonguzhali's face bloom into a smile.

"*Vaishnavare!* Were *you* the one who sent Vandhiyathevan here?" she asked in surprise.

"Yes, *thaaye!* But I did not send an assassin after him, like he claims."

"Leave that aside. Why did you send him here?"

"To help him escape. I had tethered two horses for him and his friend near this very garden..."

"What made you realize that he had not gotten away? How did you know that he was here all along, in this hut?"

"I grew suspicious when I saw another man riding away on the horse I had left behind for him…"

"It appears that Thirumal laid a scheme, but Sivan had other plans in mind," broke in Poonguzhali with a wry smile.

"But how puzzling, *thaaye!*" remarked Azhwarkkadiyaan in evident bewilderment. "How did he come to be injured thus?"

"*Vaishnavare*, you sent him here with plans of your own. But in truth, his presence came as a godsend. He arrived here in the nick of time to save me from widowhood even before I pledged my troth in marriage."

Azhwarkkadiyaan and Senthan Amudhan grew greatly astonished at her words. She had hardly finished speaking when they erupted in cries of shock and amazement. "What, what?" they cried.

Poonguzhali turned to Amudhan. "It is true," she said quietly. "I did not tell you of this, but there was a man standing outside the hut, spear in hand; he was aiming the weapon at you. Vandhiyathevan arrived not a moment too soon. He thwarted the plan and took the spear upon himself to save you."

Senthan Amudhan looked stricken. His gentle eyes swam with tears. "*Ayyo*!" he cried, aghast. "Was it on account of *me* that my friend's life is now in danger?"

"What of that? You too have put yourself in danger many a time to save him," said Poonghuzhali tenderly.

"*Ammani*, it is a rare thing indeed to see one so readily help another in turn for the good they have received. Why, it is wonder enough that people don't repay good with evil. It truly is a miracle that Vandhiyathevan arrived in time to save Senthan Amudhan!" remarked Azhwarkkadiyan before pausing. "You said something about a wedding, didn't you? What was that about? You even added that he saved you from widowhood!"

"Yes, *Vaishnavare!* It was only a short while ago that we decided to wed each other. We received lady Sembian Maadevi's blessings, too. Hardly a quarter of a *naazhigai* had passed since her departure when *aththan* came under the assault of a spear. Even I could not have foiled the attack. If his life had been forfeit to the ambush, what would have become of my fate? I would have been consigned to widowhood before the wedding, wouldn't I?"

"With the grace of Thirumal, the very wellspring of compassion, no such thing will come to pass; neither will lady Sembian Maadevi's blessings go in vain," replied Azhwarkkadiyaan gently. "You would have wed this noble man of virtue and gone on to live a life of sweetness, together. But," he continued, turning sombre, "*who* could have been the sinful wretch who sought to kill such a man as this - the very essence of innocence - with a spear? Did you see him? Could you recognize him?"

"Of course I did!" replied Poonguzhali, her face tightening. "It was none other than that *chandaala* Pinakapani, the *vaithiyar's* son - the very wretch who forcibly dragged my *athai* Mandhankini from Kodikkarai and brought her here, making her prey to a killer! To think that Chozha Naadu suffers such injustice on its soil..."

"You think you have seen the face of injustice, do you?" broke in Azhwarkkadiyaan darkly. "A deadly disaster looms on the horizon, far more malevolent than anything we've seen so far. The Chozha *rajyam* shall fall into anarchy this very night. A great war will break out among the chieftains. The kingdom will erupt in violence; all through the land, people will fight each other to the death. Nothing can shield the kingdom from the approaching calamity - nothing at all, save a miracle by the grace of Sriman Narayanamurthy!" A shocked silence followed these terrible words.

"*Vaishnavare!*" cried Amudhan, deeply troubled. "Why, that sounds like a very curse! Won't you invoke good cheer instead, willing the Chozha *rajyam* to flourish?

"The kingdom's fate is its own," said Poonguzhali. "We shall repair to Kodikkarai!"

"Nothing stops us from going. But what of noble Vandhiyathevan, the friend who saved my life?" asked Senthan Amudhan worriedly.

"Neither of you can save him, in any case. There's little point in your staying here," pointed out Azhwarkkadiyaan. "Even as we speak, the royal guards are scouring the town in search of the escaped prisoners, leaving no stone unturned. They will soon be here, too." He rubbed his chin thoughtfully. "Why, I fear I've reached my wits' end in dealing with the men outside this very door - I cannot think of a rationale that would persuade them to come away with me when I leave!"

Poonguzhali and Sentham Amudhan grew quite alarmed at his words. "*Ayya, Vaishnavare!*" began Poonguzhali earnestly. "You are bestowed with inconceivable intelligence; why, you serve as advisor to the exalted Mudhanmandhiri Aniruddhar himself! Give us counsel to help save this Vaanar warrior, who lies wounded thus at the hands of a killer," she implored. "You shall gather much virtue and we shall both remain ever grateful to you!"

"Devi, it is not as easy a task as you think."

"*Ayya*, your respect for me seems to burgeon by the minute!" remarked Poonguzhali, biting her lip to stop from smiling. "Until yesterday, I was naught but 'boat girl' to you. Earlier today, you addressed me as '*Ammani*.' Now I see that I've been promoted to 'Devi'! Why, I shall find myself hailed as Ilavarasi next!"

"Yes, Ilavarasi!" replied Azhwarkkadiyaan, his eyes twinkling. "We have but only one way to save this youth lying here, lost to the world. This fortunate man - your betrothed - must become prince for a day! That makes you a princess, doesn't it?"

The pair gaped at Azhwarkkadiyaan. "*Vaishnavare*, surely you jest! Me, prince for a day! Whatever for?" asked Amudhan, incredulous.

Azhwarkkadiyaan leaned towards them conspiratorially. "I am going to let you both in on a secret that no one else knows but I. Listen… no, on second thoughts - look!" He unwrapped the bundle he held in his hands.

The three peered down at the bundle and its contents. Lying in a heap in all their grandeur were Madhuranthakar's royal crown, his exquisite necklace of pearls and a pair of golden armlets. The precious ornaments shone as they caught the lamplight, throwing a golden hue upon the faces staring down at them. "Ah! These are Ilavarasar Madhuranthakar's, aren't they? We saw them ourselves upon his person just a short while ago!" exclaimed Amudhan.

"How did you come by them?" asked Poonguzhali, astonished.

"They were lying in a corner of the fence, in the garden," replied Azhwarkkadiyaan as he wrapped the bundle. "Now hearken to the secret I wished to tell you. I was walking by the bank of the Vadavaaru when I spotted two men on horseback, riding like the very wind. They were the very horses I had left behind for Vandhiyathevan and the madman who escaped from prison - you know the madman I speak of, I trust?"

"I do. He corners every passerby to prattle on about the Imperial Crown of the Pandiyas and the ancient gemstone necklace."

"That's the very chap! He was one of the men sitting atop the horses that sped by the Vadavaaru bank - the other seemed to be Ilavarasar Madhuranthakar. Now that I am here, I am quite sure that it was."

"How strange! Why on earth would Madhuranthakar abandon his ornaments and run away?"

Azhwarkkadiyaan frowned. "I confess that I am at a loss, there. I plan to take the matter to the Mudhanmandhiri and arrange to send men after both the horses. But I fear we have little time - disaster will be upon us before I can make a move."

"What disaster do you fear?"

"The Pazhuvettarayars and their chieftain allies approach the gate to the Thanjai fort, even as we speak. Kodumbalur Velar, the Mudhanmandhiri and Malayaman wait to receive them at the entrance. It is the Chakravarthy's wish - nay, decree - that the subject of succession be handled diplomatically and brought to a peaceful resolution. But the Pazhuvettarayars will doubtless ask for Madhuranthakar before engaging in the peace talks. When they discover that he is nowhere to be found, they will turn upon Kodumbalur Velar! They will accuse him of having slayed Madhuranthakar in order to make sure that the crown goes to Ponniyin Selvar. Even if Periya Velar refutes the charge, he will not be able to prove the truth of his denial." Azhwarkkadiyaan looked deeply troubled. "A bloody civil war will ensue. Chozha Naadu will sink into chaos and despair."

"We must leave this place before that!" cried out Poonguzhali.

"Devi, I am afraid you will find that quite impossible."

"What do you suggest, then?"

"Let Senthan Amudhan wear these crown and jewels for a little while. I will bring the elephant that Ponniyin Selvan rode here upon; let him mount the animal and sit on top. I will bid my men flank the elephant on all sides and raise loud cheers as they walk along - "Long Live Madhuranthakar!" The palanquin that Madhuranthakar came by also waits outside. We shall have Vandhiyathevan ride in the royal litter; its screens will shield him from prying eyes. Devi, you must walk beside the palanquin. I shall handle everything else!" said Azhwarkkadiyaan.

"What sort of an insane plan is this?" burst out Senthan Amudhan in pure consternation.

"You think he will go unidentified if he simply wears a crown?" asked Poonguzhali, giving Amudhan a doubtful once-over.

"Who can recognize anyone sitting atop an elephant in the dark of the night? People tend to look twice only when they are in doubt," replied Azhwarkkadiyaan. "I shall be by your side throughout. It will be my duty to see that you gain entrance into the fort and safely reach the Mudhanmandhiri's palace. I see no other way to save the Vaanar warrior," he finished, shrugging his shoulders.

The three bickered amongst themselves for a while before Senthan Amudhan and Poonguzhali resigned themselves to Azhwarkkadiyaan's plan.

69

Eye for eye, sword for sword!

When the Pazhuvettarayar-Sambuvaraiyar cavalcade finally reached the gate to the Thanjai fort, their arrival came as the confluence of two mighty seas crashing into each other. "Presenting the Dhanaadhikaari of Chozha Naadu, the lord who levies taxes, the warrior beyond compare who bears sixty four battle wounds upon his noble person, the illustrious Periya Pazhuvettarayar!" roared the crier, dignifying the arrival of the exalted chieftain; he then announced the presence of every other chieftain in the camp, meticulously listing each of their glorious exploits. The eminence and majesty of Kodumbalur Velar, Thirukovilur Malayaman and the others resounded through the environs in turn. Drums rumbled and trumpets blared in accompaniment, punctuating the rousing heralds with dramatic effect. The very fort walls reverberated with the din.

Senathipathi Periya Velar, Malayaman, the Mudhanmandhiri and the rest of their faction stood near to the fort gates, awaiting the cavalcade. The Pazhuvettarayars found themselves compelled to alight from their regal mounts.

Chinna Pazhuvettarayar believed that the Senathipathi and the others remained at the fort gates not to receive the newly-arrived chieftains, but to obligate the party to enter the fort on foot. He said as such to the rest of his faction, and requested them to allow him to lead the dialogue with the Senathipathi's camp.

Periya Velar and the rest, for their part, reckoned that the etiquette of conversational preliminaries would be in order. In truth, it was why they had chosen to stand apart from the gate, in the midst of the fort grounds where - rather quite fittingly - the Chozha flag flew high in all its glory. As the chieftains dismounted their rides and strode towards them, Senathipathi Periya Velar hastened to welcome them. "Well met, my lords, well met! Oh chieftains, who guard the Chozha *rajyam* as mighty elephants, well met! May your arrival bring good fortune to our glorious Chozha *rajyam* as well as the noble Chozha clan."

Pat came the reply from Chinna Pazhuvettaryar: "Yes, *Ayya*! May the mighty Chozha *rajyam* gain good fortune from our arrival as it doubtless will from your departure." Periya Velar's eyes reddened in anger at the barb.

"*Ayya*, it is well known that the Kodumbalur clan travels forth into the wide world to win glory and fame for the Chozha clan!" he retorted waspishly. "Every mother's son knows that my dear brother Paranthakan Siriya Velan was martyred upon the Eezham battlefield. I myself was stationed at Eezham until the recent past. *Our* clan knows not the art of warming a chair within the safe confines of a fort, under the pretext of guarding the palace *anthappuram* and treasury. If the Chozha clan stands to gain fortune by your arrival and my departure - why, I shall not suffer to stand here a second longer!" he roared.

The Mudhanmandhiri Aniruddhar hastened to intervene. "Oh, exalted lords of illustrious royal descent! What doubt can there be that every one of you brings in his noble wake naught but great good fortune to Chozha Naadu? All your clans have toiled, generation after noble generation, for the glory of the Chozha *rajyam*. Every one of your distinguished lineages features eminent ancestors who martyred themselves for the good of the Chozha clan. It is your unity and peerless service that will hold Chozha Naadu in good stead, now and forever more. It is why the illustrious Paranthaka Sundara Chozha Chakravarthy grows anxious over the fractious discord amongst you. He has summoned all of you to bridge the divide, keeping aside the insufferable grief he bears at the untimely demise of his beloved son, the warrior behind compare who beheaded Veera Pandiyan, Aditha Karikalar. Let us hold a peaceful dialogue in the Chakravarthy's presence to resolve the subject of succession and all other matters of dissent. Oh, noble kings who stand before me, I beseech you - do not wound the Chakravarthy by engaging in conflict, for the Emperor is even now engulfed by an ocean of sorrow at the loss of his eldest son!" he implored.

Every single person gathered there was moved by these words. They realized that this was no the time to air personal differences.

"Mudhanmandhiri, we are willing to conduct ourselves in line with the Chakravarthy's wishes," replied Chinna Pazhuvettarayar at once. "When will we have the honour of an audience with the Chakravarthy? Perchance, may we present ourselves to him this very night? We crave to hear the Chakravarthy's wishes from his own lips."

"Thalapathy, your desire is justified. Pray, rest assured that it will be fulfilled! You are all aware, I am sure, of the physical and mental strain borne by the Chakravarthy - in truth, it's virulence grows with the onset of night. Further, the Chakravarthy seeks to consult Sembian Maadevi before broaching the subject of succession with the chieftains. He wishes to make one last effort to change her mind on the matter - all of you aware of the presiding state of affairs, I trust. The Chakravarthy will, therefore, summon all of you while the sun yet shines on the morrow. He wishes that you all spend tonight in the fort at your respective palaces, in peace. The Chakravarthy has issued orders to Periya Velar to make the necessary arrangements for those among you whose palaces are not within the keep..."

"Mudhanmandhiri, we do not require such arrangements," broke in Chinna Pazhuvettarayar. "We are quite used to having the very sky as our roof, for we are trained to survive open battlefields. If the Chakravarthy is to grant us an audience on the morrow, why then must we spend the night within the fort?"

"Why must you choose to suffer the night in the open instead of your palaces?" asked the Mudhanmandhiri, taken aback.

"Perhaps," intervened the Senathipathi with a smirk, "the Thalapathy Kalanthaka Kantar fears the thought of staying at the fort!"

"Fear? Pray, what does it look like?" asked Chinna Pazhuvettarayar, affecting great politeness. "Is it white perhaps, or red? Does it have horns? Wings? Mayhap the well-informed Periya Velar can shed some light on the subject, considering he fled here in some haste from the battlefield at Eezham!" he said, looking expectantly at his nemesis.

"What, now?" groaned the Mudhanmandhiri inwardly. "Impossible, it seems, to prevent these two from coming to blows!"

Even as the thought crossed his mind, Periya Pazhuvettarayar stepped forward, clearing his throat with a majestic rasp that seemed to fill the skies.

Every person present turned their attention to the Dhanaadhikaari, reverence evident in their faces.

"*Thambi*, Kodumbalur Velar hails from the noble lineage of Paari Valla. Those of the Velar clan have never yet been known to go back on their word. When the Periya Velar himself pledges to provide us shelter and security, why should we think twice to enter the fort?" asked Periya Pazhuvettarayar.

"*Anna*, we have no need to shelter beneath another's wing; nor do we require their assurances of security. We have sharp swords in our hands and the spears of thirty thousand soldiers at our back. *I* am the Thalapathy of this very Thanjai fort. I refuse to set foot inside unless it is returned to my control!" replied an aggrieved Kalanthaka Kantar.

"*Ayya*," said Senathipathi Velar to Periya Pazhuvettarayar, "I acquiesce, should the Chakravarthy issue such a command."

"Was it on the command of the Chakravarthy that he seized control of the fort in the first place?" asked Chinna Pazhuvettarayar angrily.

"No," shot back an equally irked Periya Velar, "I seized control of the fort with the strength of my sword!"

"Then I shall seize it back with the strength of mine!" cried Chinna Pazhuvettarayar. "Let us put our skills to the test, this very moment!" His hands gripped the hilt of his sword in anticipation.

Periya Pazhuvettarayar placed a gentle, restraining hand on his brother's arm. "*Thambi*," he said quietly, "it is ill-judged to take sword in hand at this time. We are here only at the behest of the Chakravarthy."

"*Anna*, how can we rest assured that he will not throw us into prison the minute we enter the fort? How can you bid me trust the word of one who basely launched a surprise attack on the fort and wrested control - in the absence of any order from the Chakravarthy, no less?"

"You displayed trust in him when you departed the fort, consigning our women and children to his care. Why, you even entrusted Ilavarasar Madhuranthakar to him when you left!" pointed out the elder brother.

Chinna Pazhuvettarayar shot a baleful glance at Periya Velar. "I wonder now if I have gravely erred in my judgement! If Madhuranthakar has suffered the slightest of pain at his hands, I shall rip up the Kodumbalur clan by its very roots before attending to any other matter!" he thundered.

Senathipathi Boodhi Vikrama Kesari had, in truth, so far tempered his conversation with levity and perhaps a touch of arrogance. Kalanthaka Kantar's words, however, provoked a great fury within him. Disastrous conflict would have doubtless followed that very second had not an entirely unexpected thing taken place.

A sudden hubbub erupted at the palace gates, drawing everyone's attention.

A little while ago, Azhwarkkadiyaan had beckoned discreetly to Aniruddhar. The latter had quietly slipped away to confer with his aide, who whispered something in his ear. The Mudhanmandhiri had listened intently to the report before returning to the Pazhuvettarayars and Periya Velar. Chinna Pazhuvettarayar's furious comments about Madhuranthankar fell on his ears as he approached.

"Thalapathy, why worry about the Ilavarasar Madhuranthakar?" asked the Mudhanmandhiri. "No harm can befall him from any quarter. Just now - a short while ago - Madhuranthakar exited the fort accompanying his mother, Sembian Maadevi. They had gone to pay a visit to Senthan Amudhan, who provides the temple with flowers…"

"Yes," interrupted Chinna Pazhuvettarayar, "mother and son did go outside the fort. But only the mother returned, not the son!"

"Ah. How did you come to know this?" asked the Mudhanmandhiri in surprise.

"Mudhanmandhiri, were you under the impression that you had sole dominion over intelligent spies? Madhuranthaka Thevar went outside the fort and did not come back. I demand to know the reason why!" exploded Chinna Pazhuvettarayar.

The Mudhanmandhiri broke into a smile as cheers broke out at the fort gate. 'Long live Ilavarasar Madhuranthakar!' came the rousing cries.

Everyone looked in the direction of the cheers with great anticipation.

An elephant slowly trundled through the fort gate. Seated atop, adorned with a crown and other royal accoutrements, was 'Madhuranthakan!'

A royal palanquin accompanied the elephant, its screens drawn closed.

"Thalapathy, Madhuranthakar's return to the fort was only delayed a little. Vaani *Ammai*'s son Senthan Amudhan had taken a nasty tumble from a horse, leaving him sorely wounded. Sembian Maadevi had issued orders to bring him to the fort in the palanquin. She came away beforehand, leaving her son behind to fulfill her wishes. See, he has made arrangements for Amudhan to ride in the palanquin and he comes upon an elephant himself," said the Mudhanmandhiri Aniruddhar, smiling at the sight. "The new crown prince of the realm will have to come in procession atop an elephant during the *pattabhishekam*, won't he? He is simply preparing himself for the occasion!"

70

Control of the Fort

Kalanthaka Kantar scrutinized from afar the elephant and palanquin entering the keep. "Remarkable!" he murmured, almost to himself.

"What is?" asked Aniruddhar pleasantly.

Chinna Pazhuvettarayar gestured at the retinue, unable to tear his eyes away from the sight. "The Ilavarasar Madhuranthakar's grandiose arrival of course! He's painfully shy, more often than not. Why, he makes certain that the screens of his palanquin are drawn closed when he travels," he said, puzzled.

"He has to come out of his shell one day or the other," replied Aniruddhar, watching the convoy. "After all, he will soon be anointed the crown prince."

The Chinna Pazhuvettayar looked at Aniruddhar in wary surprise. "A resolution has been passed, then, that Madhuranthakar is to be crowned? Who made the decision?"

"Why, the Chakravarthy did, of course! When we all met with him and made our consent known..."

"What difference do they make, the Chakravarthy's decision and our consent? The Kodumbalur armies must bless the verdict to achieve a resolution," replied Kalanthaka Kantar gruffly. His eyes strayed once again to the approaching procession. "That Ilavarasar Madhuranthakan enters with such pompous fanfare a fort under their command is surprising indeed," he remarked once again.

He took a few steps towards the elephant before abruptly turning back.

"*Anna*," he began, addressing Periya Pazhuvettarayar, "I will not stand in the way should the rest of you wish to enter the fort. But *I* will not come inside. This keep was mine to command until as late as yesterday; I cannot bring myself to step foot in it whilst it is under the authority of another. *Anna*, pray, gain an audience with the Chakravarthy and learn of his wishes. I shall remain outside with our armies. Further, Kandamaaran has set off in search of Vandhiyathevan. I confess to being quite eager to learn the news he will bring. I must know how Vandhiyathevan escaped from the underground dungeons, and with whose aid. I request all of you to enter the fort without me," he finished.

Kodumbalur Velar made to reply, but Periya Pazhuvettarayar interjected brusquely. "Senathipathi, this idiot's brains are clearly addled. Let him remain outside if he wishes. Come, we shall go in."

But when the exchange was made known to the Chakravarthy the following day, he did not agree with Periya Pazhuvettarayar's take on the matter. He insisted upon Kalanthaka Kantar's presence.

"Beloved Commanders of Chozha Naadu! You are all worthy of my trust; but amongst all your noble selves, it is Kalanthaka Kantar that I place the greatest faith in. Why is he not here? Unless he joins us, the purpose for which I have summoned all of you will remain unfulfilled," he said.

"I beg your pardon, Chakravarthy," said Periya Pazhuvettarayar. "My brother will consent to any decision that I approve. It is not necessary that he be here in person."

The Chakravarthy smiled. "Dhanaadhikaari, it is common knowledge that Kalanthaka Kantar stands true by your side as Lakshmanan did by Ramar of yore. Still, I ask - why is he not here today? Chinna Pazhuvettarayar has always been an integral part of our key council meetings. We have never yet taken a decision without his input. Why must we suffer the lack of such a perceptive warrior as he, today?" he asked.

"My liege, I shall answer that," said the Mudhanmandhiri. "It appears as though Kalanthaka Kantar has grown into a student who has surpassed his master - he declined to enter even when he was told that it was the Chakravathy's summons. Periya Pazhuvettarayar gave him much counsel, but he turned a deaf ear to the advice. He simply refused to set foot inside the fort."

"Lest we forget," piped up Parthibendran, "he *has* pledged to abide by any decisions we take with the Chakravarthy's approval."

"Even so," insisted the Chakravarthy, "why does Chinna Pazhuvettarayar refuse to come inside? Does he yet harbour suspicion?"

"All is yellow to the jaundiced eye, they say. Nothing seems to escapes his suspicion! He has misgivings about Madhuranthakar's safety on these grounds. He also suspects foul play in Vandhiyathevan's escape from the dungeons..."

"If Kalanthaka Kantar is suspicious of a matter, it cannot be without reason!" declared the Chakravarthy. A brief silence followed his words as each person grappled with their own thoughts on the issue.

Periya Pazhuvettarayar cleared his throat. "My liege! My brother may or may not be justified in his suspicions. I do not wish to raise accusations against him. But I shall confess the true reason behind his refusal to enter the fort. He says that for many years, this Thanjavur fort had remained his to command; but now it has come under the control of Periya Velar. *That* is why he cannot enter the fort, it seems! What can be done in the face of such insolence?"

"Why, justice can be done!" replied Sundara Chozha Chakravarthy.

The chamber fell silent at the Chakravarthy's words.

"Ministers of Chozha Naadu!" said the Chakravarthy, "The fame and glory of the Chozha clan is deeply rooted in our ethos of justice - the kings hailing from this lineage never once strayed from the path of fairness. All of you know well of my illustrious ancestor who passed a death sentence upon his own beloved son for the crime of killing a calf beneath his chariot wheels. Pray, think - how fairly the kings hailing from such a descent would have ruled over their subjects, when they ensured that the very cows in the kingdom were afforded justice! How justly would they have dealt with the commanders who served their rule! Why must I go against such a noble tradition and bring dishonour to the clan? I say that it is certainly a grave error that Periya Velar wrested control of the Thanjai fort from Chinna Pazhuvettarayar. Lost in grieving over the untimely death of my beloved son, I lapsed in weighing the injustice meted to Chinna Pazhuvettarayar. The Senathipathi must cede command of this fort to him!"

Kodumbalur Velar's face grew turned stony at these words.

Thirukovilur Malayaman stepped forward. "*Ayya*, it does not appear as though Chinna Pazhuvettarayar discharged his duties adequately when the security of the Thanjai fort was in his charge. A conspirator infiltrated the fort and attained the very *anthappuram*, from where he launched a spear at your noble person! Your life was saved only with the intervention of a mute woman. What would have happened if she hadn't been there at the fateful moment? The armoury of this Thanjai fort holds countless swords and spears - but what, I ask, is their use? Can one truly claim that the Thalapathy Chinna Pazhuvettarayar performed his duties to an acceptable standard? How then was it unjust that our Periya Velar took over security of the fort from under his control?" he asked.

"*Maama*, what is the point of blaming another for the cruel vagaries of fate? Were you able to save your beloved grandchild, Aditha Karikalan? You all strove so hard to deliver him from harm, did you not?" asked the Chakravarthy.

"It is essential that an inquiry be launched into that matter as well, Chakravarthy!" pressed Malayaman. "There has been no probe yet as to who is culpable for the heinous episode that transpired at the Kadambur palace. Its truth is not yet public!"

"We were awaiting the arrival of Periya Pazhuvettarayar," added Senathipathi Periya Velar. "Now that he is here, an inquiry must be launched."

"How did Vandhiyathevan - the wretch accused of the murder - slip away from the underground dungeons before we could launch an inquiry?" burst out Parthibendran. "Who is answerable for his escape? We must investigate that as well!"

The Chakravarthy turned to the Senathipathi. "Yes, I did hear of that too, Senathipathi. How *did* Vandhiyathevan escape from the underground dungeons? Who must be held accountable?" he asked.

"Chakravarthy, it is the Mudhanmandhiri Aniruddhar who must answer that question!" replied Periya Velar.

"My liege, I accept full responsibility for the incident," said Aniruddhar. "Vandhiyathevan escaped from prison because of a small error on my part. The duty of finding him and bringing him back is mine. Should I fail, I shall willingly accept the due punishment."

"My friend Kandamaaran has beaten the Mudhanmandhiri to that duty!" announced Parthibendran, the pride evident in his voice. "He is in pursuit of the wretch who broke out of the dungeons, even as we speak!"

The council meeting included the presence of two women, as well. They were none other than the Chakravarthini Vaanama Devi and Ilaiya Piratti Kundhavai Devi.

When she heard that Kandamaaran was hunting down Vandhiyathevan, Ilaiya Piratti Kundhavai Devi's expression shifted. None but the Mudhanmandhiri Aniruddhar caught sight of the change.

He turned to Parthibendran. "Pallava Kumara! Your friend Kandamaaran is smart indeed - but unreliable when it comes to certain tasks. After all, he failed to protect the Ilavarasar Karikalar - a gem treasured by all of Chozha Naadu - even whilst the prince was a guest at his own palace at Kadambur! Do you truly believe that he can capture Vandhiyathevan who is on the run? I for one rather doubt it," said the Mudhanmandhiri.

He noted with satisfaction that Kundhavai Piratti understood the import of his last words.

"Also," added Senathipathi Periya Velar, "I heard that Kandamaaran and Vandhiyathevan are bosom friends!"

"That is stale news, Chakravarthy!" interjected Periya Sambuvaraiyar fiercely. "None who has betrayed the Chozha clan can be a friend to the Sambuvaraiyar clan!"

"Why talk about the matter now?" remarked Sundara Chozhar. "The Mudhanmandhiri Aniruddhar has already assumed the duty of bringing back Vandhiyathevan to the fort. All in all, the Senathipathi had better restore control of the Thanjai fort to Chinna Pazhuvettarayar!"

"If this is the Chakravarthy's command, I shall fulfill it," said the Senathipathi Periya Velar tightly. It was quite clear from the tone of his voice that he was struggling with a surge of anger.

"Kodumbalur *maama*, you are my superior in both age and experience. I see you as no less than my own father; I worship you as I did him. Can I give one such as you a command? I merely voiced my opinion," said the Chakravarthy gently. "Why don't we hear everyone else's opinion on the matter as well? We can then see to what needs to be done."

"I am against the very idea!" declared the Thirukovilur Malayaman, registering his vehement objection. "Chinna Pazhuvettarayar has failed in his duty. Therefore, control of the fort cannot be restored to him!"

"What is the Mudhanmandhiri's opinion?" asked the Chakravarthy, turning to Aniruddhar.

"What has happened, has happened. That said, transferring control of the fort at this moment will give rise to complications. My liege, you have gathered us here to resolve the issue of succession. It is best to take a decision about the fort once we reach a resolution regarding the throne," said Aniruddhar.

"We cannot reach a resolution without Chinna Pazhuvettarayar!" replied the Chakravarthy firmly before turning to Periya Pazhuvettarayar. "Dhanaadhikaari, what is your opinion?"

"I agree with Malayaman. My brother has lapsed in fulfilling his duty; he did not meet his charge. Undeserving, then, to restore control of the fort to him!" said Periya Pazhuvettarayar.

Every person present was well aware of the deep affection the Dhanaadhikaari bore for his brother; consequently, Periya Pazhuvettarayar's words left them considerably surprised.

Little did they know that the Chakravarthy's response would drive them into greater shock.

"Dhanaadhikaari, Chinna Pazhuvettarayar did not fail his charge. You and I failed to heed his words. Neither of us paid any concern to the alerts he often raised," replied the Chakravarthy. He turned a grave eye upon the assembly. "Hearken to me. Chinna Pazhuvettarayar cautioned me several times of the threat posed by Madurai Veera Pandiyan's *abhathudavis*. He said that the conspirators had contact with an insider in this very fort. Chinna Pazhuvettarayar persisted in his demand to tighten security both at the *anthappuram* and my own palace. He made compelling arguments to seal the secret passage connecting the Dhanaadhikaari's palace and mine; he wished to also station guards between the two palaces. Kalanthaka Kantar's profound respect for Periya Pazhuvettarayar is well known - hear then, when I say that he did not shrink away from lodging complaints with me against the Dhanaadhikaari himself. He claimed that his brother was being tricked, that he suspected conspirators of frequenting the latter's palace. Chinna Pazhuvettarayar suggested relocating Periya Pazhuvettarayar to another palace; he also wanted the contents of the treasury to be transported to another safehouse. I did not pay heed to his prescient warnings."

Sundara Chozha Chakravarthy fell silent when Periya Pazhuvettarayar cleared his throat. "Chakravarthy, I shall confess aloud the truths you gracefully omitted from your account out of mercy for me. You were loath to make public my shame; but I shall reveal it myself. My brother cautioned me against Nandhini, the maiden I wed under the spell of passion and desire. He also warned me that the chief of the Pandiya Naadu *abhathudhavis* frequented my own palace in the guise of a *mandhiravathi*. Blinded by love and longing, I ignored his counsel. That said, I repeat - he verily did fail his duty! Certain as he was, he ought to have slayed foul demoness and conspirators alike without a second thought; if I had stood in his way, he ought to have put me to the sword, brother or not. His failure is verily a lapse of duty, is it not?" asked the grand old man, his voice reverberating through the chamber.

Every last person in the chamber felt goosebumps prick across their skin. The weight of his suffering was palpable in Periya Pazhuvettarayar's tone; his audience shivered, as they felt the cruel sting of his pain.

"Patience, Dhanaadhikaari! Your brother Chinna Pazhuvettarayar is well-capable of rising to such a task in the name of duty. It was I who served as his obstacle. I issued stringent orders that he was not to address me bearing criticism of you or the Pazhuvoor Ilaiya Rani; I rejected his advice to relocate you to another palace along with the *Velakkara* Padai. I told him that there was little point in living one's life in constant fear; truth be told, I had grown averse to life on account of the pain that weighed upon my heart and my failing health. Pazhuvoor *maama*, you are not accountable for the ill fate that has befallen me and my lineage; neither is your brother. I have none to blame for my woes but myself."

Periya Pazhuvettarayar hung upon the Chakravarthy's words. The grand old man's eyes filled with tears that streamed down his face.

"Yes," he replied hoarsely, with a lump in his throat. "There is not even a sliver of blame upon Chinna Pazhuvettarayar. It was on Vandhiyathevan's very first visit to the fort that Kalanthaka Kantar registered his suspicions about the youth. He said that the young man had conversed in secret with Pazhuvoor Ilaiya Rani outside the fort, whilst she was yet in her palanquin. He told me that the young man had gained entry to the fort by dint of a Pazhuvoor signet ring;

he also deduced that he had escaped by the secret passage running through the Pazhuvoor *anthappuram*. Even the inconceivably astute Mudhanmandhiri and my cherished daughter, Ilaiya Piratti, were tricked by Vandhiyathevan. They relayed key messages through him…"

Aniruddhar hastened to intervene. "Chakravarthy, I confess that I may have been misled. Ilaiya Piratti, however, is not easily deceived. After she had dispatched Vandhiyathevan with the messages, she instructed me to arrange for him to be under surveillance. I sent my disciple Azhwarkkadiyan to keep an eye on him in Eezham. I also sent him to follow the youth in Kanchi…"

"Let it be as you claim. Let us assume that neither of you were duped by him. The irrefutable fact is that he escaped from the underground dungeons with another prisoner in tow! If Chinna Pazhuvettarayar had been in control of the fort, they could have never slipped away. Senathipathi! Invite Chinna Pazhuvettarayar inside at once and restore the charge of the fort to him. You may consider it my command if you wish to," proclaimed the Chakravarthy.

"So be it, my liege! May we take our leave?" asked Senathipathi Boodhi Vikrama Kesari respectfully. The anger in his voice had quite dissipated. The Chakravarthy's words had moved him deeply. He found himself disarmed by the affection Sundara Chozhar had shown the Pazhuvettarayars; his heart had melted to see the depth of his magnanimity in appreciating the noble qualities that lay beneath their errors of judgement. Periya Velar was left entirely stunned by the Chakravarthy's inimitable grace.

"Yes," replied the noble Chakravarthy, "everyone can leave. We shall convene to discuss the way forward after Chinna Pazhuvettarayar joins us. I am still engaged in talks with Periya Piratti regarding the subject of succession. I will need more time on that front as well."

As the assembly dispersed, Parthibendran stepped forward to speak.

"*Ayya*, the Mudhanmandhiri has assumed the charge of capturing Vandhiyathevan, the wretch who betrayed both friend and country-I wish to remind him of his duty towards the charge. There may be some who are lax about the matter; I, however, cannot think past the gruesome death of my dear friend Aditha Karikalan. The culprit must be rooted out and dealt just punishment!"

Periya Pazhuvettarayar cleared his throat, like an old lion giving vent to a roar. He made as though to speak, but abruptly changed his mind. He departed without a word, with the rest of the assembly behind him.

That very evening, the charge of guarding the fort was ceded to Chinna Pazhuvettarayar as decreed by the Chakravarthy. At first, Chinna Pazhuvettarayar was rather hesitant to accept the charge. He registered his protest at the proffer, mildly at first and then with some dramatic vehemence; he then devolved into dark theories that the new development was naught but a fresh conspiracy to bewilder and frustrate. It was only after Periya Pazhuvettarayar told him that it was the Chakravarthy's absolute command that he accepted the charge of guarding the fort.

Save a handful of soldiers, the Kodumbalur army was sent out of the fort. The Pazhuvoor guards resumed their posts at the fort gates and along the ramparts.

The move had dangerous consequences. Arguments broke out between the Kodumbalur and the Pazhuvoor guards, giving rise to chaos and confusion. The environs shook with rousing cheers. 'Long live Ponniyin Selvar!' cried one faction. "Long live Madhuranthakar!" cried another, even louder. The cheers turned into a raucous contest, each faction intent on besting the other in their display of support.

The cries spread throughout the land, carried on the lips of the people.

All of Chozha Naadu would descend into chaos over the following three days. Verbal arguments provoked an outbreak of fistcuffs which deteriorated into full scale riots. People took up sticks and rods in their hands and soon moved onto using spears and swords.

Like the tempest that had laid waste to Chozha Naadu in the recent past, storms of rage and floods of anger swept through the kingdom, destroying everything in their wake.

71

The Thevar born from a holy womb

The Chakravarthy sent word to Sembian Maadevi several times, expressing his wish to confer with her. The grand old matriarch appeared at his palace at long last. The Chakravarthy went to the palace entrance himself to await her arrival. He personally accompanied her to his chamber and invited her to sit beside him, upon a throne.

"King of kings!" began the venerable Pirattiyar. "My heart ached from the string of painful news we've been made to suffer, but it now grows content upon seeing that you have recovered your health. I dearly wish, by the grace of God, that you will live on for many years as a *siranjeevi* and protect the world."

"*Annaiye*, you speak of my legs that have recovered strength enough to walk. I confess it gives me contentment as well. My malady had left me powerless to stand on my feet and duly receive even one so noble as you, revered by all of Chozha Naadu. My legs regained their vigour under the power of love bestowed upon me by a divine woman, a deaf and mute goddess. I am fortunate indeed that I can rise to my feet and receive you. Yet, Devi, I find little satisfaction in drawing breath. I do not wish to live a long life. Pray, do not bless me so. Bless me instead that I shall soon attain the lotus feet of Siva!" said Sundara Chozhar.

"Chakravarthy, the ancestors of your illustrious lineage have all attained either the paradise of warriors or the lotus feet of Siva. There is no doubt that your forefathers would have secured a place for you in heaven. When your time comes, you shall be carried there by Siva's own attendants. But your impatience to reach those lotus feet ill becomes you," replied Sembian Maadevi gently. "There is much left for you to do in this world. The people are happy under your just rule, which has never strayed from the path of righteousness. The holy service of Siva temples takes place throughout the kingdom. Saivites, Vaishnavites, Buddhists and Jains are united in your name, for they all pray for your good health and longevity."

"*Thaaye*, would that they did not! Such a boon does naught but prolong my suffering and grief. Must I live on in this world, I who has lost Aditha Karikalan, bravest among all the warriors that Chozha Naadu has produced? Ah," breathed the Chakravarthy, "that I did not close my own eyes before he was taken away!"

"Chakravarthy, the grief of losing a child is indeed a great sorrow to bear. Still, fate is an absolute force; a poor, naive woman as me need not remind you of that. Krishna *bhagavan* of yore was Arjuna's inseparable friend. He was the very incarnation of Thirumal, the divine protector. Yet, even He could not save Aravaan and Abimanyu. Didn't Arjunan survive the tragedy? Didn't he remain alive even after the loss of such brave sons? Arjunan paid heed to Krishna Paramatma's teachings - To protect the life of the land, you must protect your own life. He accepted the counsel wholeheartedly and lived his life. Chakravarthy, Krishna Paramatma's words to Arjunan apply to you, today!" said Sembian Maadevi earnestly.

"*Thaaye*, Abimanyu died a warrior's death upon the battlefield. *He* attained the paradise of the brave!"

"Your son is no less to Abimanyu in valour! The world will never forget the daring exploits he achieved at the mere age of twelve in the battlefield at Sevur; nor the great feats he wrought at the age of eighteen in the decisive war against Veera Pandiyan. Abimanyu was surrounded by enemies on all sides; they disarmed him and launched a dishonourable ambush to kill him. Aditha Karikalan was likewise tricked into isolation. He was surrounded by conspirators who attacked without warning to kill him."

"*Thaaye*, if only I knew how his death truly occured, my heart will achieve a semblance of peace."

"Why inflict such pain upon your own heart? Karikalan's time had come to an end. The shining star fell down from the heavens. Chozha Naadu lost a mighty warrior. What is the point of finding out why it happened or how?"

"With the truth obscured, many find themselves under suspicion of the crime. *Thaaye*, the shadow of blame has not even spared Periya Pazhuvettarayar, he who carries the Chozha *samrajyam* upon his back like the very Adisesha who supports the world. Troubling accusations are being laid at his feet."

Sembian Maadevi grew concerned at these words. "Surely it is possible to learn the truth by asking him directly?" she asked.

"Who has the courage to pose such a question to Periya Pazhuvettarayar? I confess that I do not. He is caught in this affair some way or another; it is clear that its burden weighs heavily upon his heart. Until he chooses to share his account of his own accord, who can ask him to speak? *Amma!* When my uncle Rajaadithar lost his life atop an elephant at the Thakkolam battlefield, the Chozha armies were soon decimated. Soldiers broke their ranks and dispersed in all directions, attempting to run away from the battle. It was the illustrious warrior Periya Pazhuvettarayar who barred the way of those who sought to flee. He cleaved the scattered soldiers into an army and led the charge himself against Kannarathevan's forces. Under Periya Pazhuvettarayar's command, the Chozha armies swiftly routed the enemy on the battlefield. The Chozha *samrajyam* as we know it would not exist today had he not rendered such exemplary service on that day. Periya Pazhuvettarayar suffered sixty four wounds upon his own body at the battle at Thakkolam. Even then, he stood strong on the battlefield and snatched victory from the jaws of defeat. After that, we sought to ensure that he would never go to battle again. We made him the Dhaanadhikaari of the land. What can I ask of such a stalwart, one I consider the equivalent of my own father?"

"Is there no other way to discover the truth?"

"They say that the Vaanar warrior Vandhiyathevan was found by the side of Aditha Karikalan's body. I thought I could learn the truth from his lips. But he escaped from the underground dungeons." The Chakravarthy looked troubled. "It is quite reasonable for Chinna Pazhuvettarayar to cast blame upon the Mudhanmandhiri in this regard."

Kundhavai, silent until this moment, spoke up all of a sudden. "Father, the Mudhanmandhiri has assumed the responsibility of bringing the warrior back, hasn't he?"

"Child, the Mudhanmandhiri has assumed such responsibility on quite a few occasions in the past. But his success is not always certain. I am aware that Sambuvaraiyar's son Kandamaaran chases after the youth who escaped. But Kandamaaran is not a man of foresight; he has a tendency to impatience. Further, he is driven by a fierce determination to ensure that dishonour does not befall the Sambuvaraiyar clan. The fact that he leads a search for Vandhiyathevan only serves to worsen my concern."

"*Ayya*, it is best to forget about matters of the past. It is always better to look to what needs to be done in the future."

"*Annaiye*, that is the very reason I sought your presence, dispatching messenger after messenger to arrange a conversation with you. You must advise me on what needs to be done."

"Chakravarthy, you have many intelligent ministers by your side to give you wise counsel. What advice can a naive woman as I give you? Even whilst my noble husband was alive - that great man who held my hand in marriage and gave me a new, pure meaning to life - I did not pay much attention to the administration of the kingdom. Since his call to paradise, I have thrown myself into the service of Siva. What advice can one such as I give you?" remarked the Sembian Maadevi.

"Devi, pray do not grow vexed with me. None of the women born to the Chozha clan are naive or simple. Here, here stands my beloved daughter Kundhavai - I have never yet met another who can equal her in intelligence!"

Sembian Maadevi smiled. "I beg your pardon, Chakravarthy. I was not born of the Chozha clan! My roots lie in the Mazhavaraiyar clan," replied the elder Pirattiyar.

"Regardless of the clan of their birth, women have the capability to be highly intelligent. They can bring good fortune to both their clan of birth as well as their clan of marriage." Sundara Chozha Chakravarthy paused. "Their adamance can bring destruction upon their clans of birth and marriage. *Thaaye*, will you be, I wonder, such a force of ruin?"

Sembian Maadevi recoiled at Sundara Chozhar's words. She felt her heart grow tight with pain, as one raked over embers of hot coal. "Chakravarthy, what words are these?" she asked in a brittle voice, her eyes brimming over with tears. "Why must the Chozha clan face ruin on my account? Surely, I am not one so powerful as that!"

"Devi, pray forgive my harsh words. My very heart is rent asunder by the thought that I am yet alive while my eldest son has died. But an even greater grief darkens my doorstep. If the Chozha *rajyam*, this exalted dynasty that flourished since the time of my illustrious ancestors, weakens under my rule and crumbles to ruin, why - there is no punishment I can receive that would bring me greater suffering." Sundara Chozhar paused. "I did not lay eyes upon my beloved son Aditha Karikalan for three years. He built a golden palace for me at Kanchi and often asked me to come there to stay. I didn't go; I cited my failing health as the reason. That was not true. I feared that my departure for Kanchi would cause the Pazhuvettarayars to believe that I no longer trusted their friendship; I worried that the other chieftains would suspect the same. The very thought that my departure would bring disaster to Chozha Naadu prevented me from leaving for Kanchi." His voice grew hoarse with grief. "Had I gone, perhaps my dear son Karikalan might be alive today…"

"King of kings! You are a person of great intelligence, bestowed with remarkable capability. But even you cannot rewrite the words of fate!"

"Yes, *Annaiye*. I could not have changed fate. But in the end, I could not see my son in his last days! If I had, I would not bear today the wrenching regret I feel for having been ignorant of the sadness that lay in my son's heart. Why do I say all this? Only because I want you to understand that I have buried my heart's desires in the interest of the Chozha *rajyam*, the great dynasty that was established by the illustrious Vijayalaya Chozhar and his lineage of valorous warriors who spilt blood for their country. For some reason, the Pazhuvettarayars and their ally of chieftains did not take a liking to Karikalan. They wanted Madhuranthakan, your son and my brother, to ascend the throne after my time. There is nothing wrong with their wish. The son of Kandaradhithar, that exalted man and peerless devotee of Siva, has every eligibility to ascend the throne. In truth, my own ascension to the throne was an error. I could not raise my voice in dissent at the time, as it was the elders who came to the decision together; I found myself with little choice but to accept the crown. I am reaping the consequences of my mistake today - I live and breathe even after losing my beloved son. I have suffered enough for a lifetime. I cannot bear to see this glorious dynasty crumble to ruin under a civil war. Devi, I seek your help in shielding the Chozha *rajyam* from such disaster!" said Sundara Chozhar, voice ringing with ardour.

Sembian Maadevi wiped away the tears from her eyes. "King of kings, your words do not sound correct to my weak mind. My brother-in-law and your father Arinjaya Thevar ascended the throne after my noble husband's time. It was entirely in accordance with my husband's wishes. Your grandfather Paranthaka Thevar, who ruled all the three words under his mighty flag, made the arrangements himself. So, I cannot see any error in your ascension to the Chozha throne. My own beloved husband was a spiritual soul, immersed in the bliss of Siva *bhakthi*. His heart was not truly in the administration of the kingdomkingdom - it was the reason why the Chozha rajyam diminished during his reign. It was only after you became king that the boundaries of our majestic kingdom expanded once again. The enemies who had reared their heads in the east and west were destroyed. It was none but your dear son Aditha Karikalan who led the kingdom to such glory. He was anointed the crown prince with the world as witness. How can I consent to changing such a solemn decision in the favour of anointing my son the crown prince? Leave aside my own consent - will the world accept such a decision? Will the people of this *rajyam* welcome it? Chakravarthy, you said a short while back that you did not wish to see the kingdom destroyed by civil war. If Aditha Karikalan had been brushed aside and my son anointed the crown prince, wouldn't that have provoked a civil war? Wouldn't the *rajyam* have come to ruin?"

"Yes, *Thaaye* - that was my hesitation as well. I endeavoured to reach a resolution that would find acceptance with everyone. But fate intervened before it could come to fruition. Karikalan's time upon earth came to an end. *Thaaye*, what should I do next? Pray, tell me. I cannot bear the burden of ruling this kingdom any longer. I yearn to entrust its care to another and repair to Kanchi; I aim to fulfill Karikalan's last wishes by spending the rest of my days in the golden palace he built for me. Pray, tell me - who should be anointed the crown prince? Madhuranthakan is older to Arulmozhi. Even though he is younger to me, he is Arulmozhi's uncle. Kodumbalur Velar and Thirukovilur Malayaman wish to crown Arulmozhi as king. How can I give my acceptance to such a decision that flies in the face of justice, one that counters the tradition of our hoary clan? Pray, consent to crown Madhuranthakan. I shall use your acceptance to convince Periya Velar and Thirukovilur Malayaman. Please signal your acceptance and gain the peerless virtue of having saved this Chozha *samrajyam*!" pressed the Sundara Chozha Chakravarthy.

"*Ayya*, do not seek my acceptance," replied Sembian Maadevi quietly. "I cannot go against the wishes of my noble husband who has attained the lotus feet of Siva. But I will not intrude in the affairs of the kingdom any longer. Call for Madhuranthakan and ask him if he will accept the honour. Then, do whatever you deem prudent."

"Yes, yes!" replied the Chakravarthy, joyous at the matriarch's reply. "No decision can be taken without conferring with Madhuranthakan! Devi, I need your help in this, as well. Where is Madhuranthakan?" he asked.

"Where is Madhuranthakan?" echoed Sembian Maadevi tremulously, a lump in her throat. "That is the very question I have been asking these past three days. No one gives me an answer! My king, *where* is my son? Send word to the Thalapathy of the fort Chinna Pazhuvettarayar and ask him!" she said, suddenly afraid.

"Chinna Pazhuvettarayar says that it is a question we must ask you," replied the Chakravarthy, puzzled and concerned. "He has raised an accusation that you have plotted together with the Mudhanmandhiri Aniruddhar to hide Madhuranthakan away. *Annaiye*, with your permission, I shall arrange for Chinna Pazhuvettarayar and Mudhanmandhiri to be brought here.

"Bring them here, I shall ask them as well!" cried Sembian Maadevi. Kundhavai went to the chamber's entrance at once and sent word through the guards at the door.

The Mudhanmandhiri and Chinna Pazhuvettarayar arrived shortly.

"Thalapathy," said the Chakravarthy looking at Chinna Pazhuvettarayar, "the exalted Devi of Chozha Naadu asks the same question that you do - where is Madhuranthakan? Pray, tell us what you know of Madhuranthaka Thevar. Speak freely of your concerns; keep nothing to yourself."

"The world is aware of the Devi's noble nature and the deep *bhakthi* she bears for Siva. All of Chozha Naadu praises her as a living goddess among us; I too worship her in the same vein. Pray, do not take my words to be blame," began Chinna Pazhuvettarayar. "The Devi, for reasons unknown, does not want her son to ascend the Chozha throne - this is common knowledge. None can bear greater affection for her son than the Devi herself; yet, there are some mysteries that demand explanation. Further, as the Chakravarty himself has commanded me to fetch Madhuranthakan, I am obliged to voice my doubts. Three days ago, the venerable Devi and Madhuranthaka Thevar went outside these fort walls. They made their way to the hut of the flower seller Senthan Amudhan, to ask after his health. The Devi alone came back to the fort. Shortly after, my brother and I were standing at the fort gate in conversation with Periya Velar. Even as we made inquiries about Madhuranthaka Thevar, an elephant and a palanquin entered the fort, followed by their retinue. The convoy was accompanied by loud cheers crying 'Long live Madhuranthaka Thevar!' It was the Mudhanmandhiri who pointed out to me the person seated atop the elephant; he said that it was Madhuranthaka Thevar. I was not entirely convinced, myself. After that, I resumed charge of the Thanjai fort per the Chakravarthy's orders. Madhuranthakar usually stays in my palace. I did not ask after him that night. But when I made inquiries the very next day, I discovered that he had not come to the palace at all. I searched for him throughout the fort and made enquiries with many people, in vain. How could a person who entered the fort disappear without a trace, like magic? The Devi and the Mudhanmandhiri must forgive me for what I am about to say. I suspect them to have plotted together to contrive his disappearance; they must have said something to scare Madhuranthakar, provoking him to run away not just from the city, but from the very country. If my words are in error, I humbly ask forgiveness from Periya Piratti once again."

"Thalapathy, I swear on the lotus feet of Siva Peruman that you are absolutely wrong!" said Sembian Maadevi in a trembling voice. "I have not spoken with the Mudhanmandhiri Aniruddhar about my son in recent times; nor have I hatched a plot with him. It is true that Madhuranthakan and I went to Senthan Amudhan's hut that evening. When I left there, Madhuranthakan said that he would return after some time. I haven't seen him after that. I myself have been searching for him for the past three days!"

Chinna Pazhuvettarayar listened solemnly to Sembian Maadevi's words. "I accept the Devi's account," declared Kalanthaka Kantar. "Only the Mudhanmandhiri can unravel this mystery now!" he said, turning to look intently at Aniruddhar.

"What mystery?" asked the Mudhanmandhiri Aniruddhar politely.

"The mystery of the Devi's missing son!" replied Chinna Pazhuvettarayar, impatient anger evident in his voice.

"Thalapathy, is it true that you have searched throughout this fort?"

"Yes," came the tight reply. "Save your palace, we have made a thorough search of every nook and cranny in this fort."

"Why was my palace spared?"

"It was spared in view of the respect accorded to you as the Mudhanmandhiri of the Chozha *samrajyam*!" replied Chinna Pazhuvettarayar, taken aback by the question.

"Aha! That suggests that you haven't discharged your duty with care. No matter. Chakravarthy, your *periya annai* - a gem of *Siva bhakthi* venerated by all of Chozha Naadu - truly has not spoken to me about her son. Nor has she engaged in any conspiracy. I can, however, say this - the Thevar born of her holy womb has been in my palace for the past three days. He waits at the entrance of this chamber, seeking an audience with you and his mother. I shall bring him inside, with your permission."

The Mudhanmandhiri's words brought boundless astonishment to everyone in the chamber. "Surely you jest!" cried the Chakravarthy. "Why seek permission to admit the Devi's son? Bring him in at once!"

The Mudhanmandhiri Aniruddhar approached the chamber's entrance. He clapped his hands and returned. Azhwarkkadiyaan entered a moment later, ushering in Senthan Amudhan.

Anger rushed through Chinna Pazhuvettarayar's veins. "Is there no limit to the Mudhanmandhiri's mockery?" he thundered.

But Sembian Maadevi eagerly spread her hands to the newcomer, her face flushed with love and affection. "Son!" she cried, calling out to him warmly. The gesture threw the Thalapathy into utter bewilderment.

"*Thaaye*!" cried Senthan Amudhan with tears in his eyes. "Have you relented at last, to address me as your son? Ah, this is the fruit of my penance these long years!" he said, stepping forward towards Sembian Maadevi.

The divine mother - she who gave birth to the man who could go down in history as the illustrious Madhuranthaka Uttama Chozhan, a *siva bhakthan* beyond compare - embraced him with love, lost to a stream of joyous tears.

72

A CONTEST TO ABDICATE

Born to the Mazhavar clan and wedded to the pious Kandaradhitha Chozhar who was blessed with sublime realization of Siva Peruman, the noble Sembian Maadevi is described in inscriptions dating back to her time as 'the *pirattiyar* whose holy womb birthed Uttama Chozhar, Madhuranthaka Thevar.' Normally, a woman receives the grace of a child by carrying the baby in her own womb for ten months before giving birth. There are some women too, who lovingly bring up the child of another as their own. Sembian Maadevi belonged to the latter; she brought up another woman's child with an affection that remained unstinting over the years. Perhaps it was someone aware of this truth who chose the aforesaid inscription, 'the holy womb that birthed Uttama Chozhar!"

When Uttama Chozhar was five years old, Sembian Maadevi happened to catch sight of him along with Vaani *Amma*i. She had chanced upon Vaani *Amma*i after many years; naturally, she asked after her well-being with genuine care. To her own surprise, Sembian Maadevi found herself radiating a powerful, visceral love towards Senthan Amudhan, whom she took to be Vaani *Amma*i's son. When she asked after the boy, a curious look of panic and fear crossed Vaani *Amma*i's face. At first, she reckoned that there could be many reasons for the strange reaction; but she could glean nothing concrete from Vaani *Amma*i, who was bereft of the power of speech. Still, Sembian Maadevi remembered the help Vaani *Amma*i had rendered to her. Out of gratitude as well as the inexplicable affection she felt towards the child, she made arrangements for mother and son to lead a comfortable life. She also granted them endowments that would enable them to live near Thanjai and make a living in *pusha kaingaryam* - flower service - to the deity at the Thalikkulathar temple.

Senthan Amudhan grew up to be a fine boy. Apart from being an excellent student and a courteous child, he displayed remarkable piety towards Siva Peruman, as well. He delighted in helping his mother render *pushpa kaingaryam* to the deity. As Sembian Maadevi observed the child, she found her instinctive love for him growing stronger and deeper. One day, a strange doubt rose in her heart. All at once, it brought her happiness, sorrow and a nameless fear. She struggled to put it out of her mind, in vain. Thoughts came unbidden about the baby that had passed away within a few days of its birth, robbing her of her peace of mind.

At last, Sembian Maadevi decided to broach the subject with Vaani *Amma*i, hoping to put an end to the matter once and for all. She arranged to meet with Vaani *Amma*i in private. She had bade Vaani *Amma*i bury the dead child in secret, hadn't she? She now wished to raise a *pallippadai* temple at the site, as a memorial to the baby she had lost. So saying, Sembian Maadevi asked Vaani *Amma*i to take her to the spot where she had buried the child. The mere memory of these incidents caused her deep pain. Sembian Maadevi had to use signs and gestures to communicate with Vaani, deaf and mute as she was; the effort revived old traumas, causing her unspeakable suffering.

Vaani appeared deeply reluctant to answer her questions. In the end, though, she confessed the truth as she could not defy the Queen's orders. She revealed that the baby she was given to be buried had, in fact, been alive; a certain Karuthiruman had pointed this out to her in the nick of time, saving the child. Fearful of the consequences of returning the baby to the Queen, Vaani *Amma*i had left with Karuthiruman to Thirumuraikaadu. Karuthiruman had abandoned her after a while, leaving her with no choice but to return to Pazhaiyarai.

When she learned that Senthan Amudhan was indeed her own son, the child she had birthed after bearing him for ten months in her own womb, Sembian Maadevi felt a surge of boundless happiness swell within. A tingle of goosebumps ran over her body and tears flowed from her eyes in streams. She longed to take the child in her arms and embrace him, to call aloud to him as her own son. Yet, she suppressed her urge with a great effort. A sudden fear gripped her at the thought of the grave trouble and confusion that would ensue if this truth came to light. The pious, spiritually-mature Sembian Maadevi had perceived a sublime truth - All the children of this world are God's children; it was this realization that now helped her restrain the deep love that a mother feels for her own child. *What difference does it make, after all, if one is raised in a palace or hut? The transient pleasures of this earth are nothing but illusions, after all. More important than this fleeting life is the afterlife we attain after shedding our mortal remains. My noble husband turned away from kingly pleasures to live in the holy shadow of Siva Peruman; perhaps it is on account of that virtue that his own son has been bestowed with the privilege of a simple life in service to the divine.* Thus did Sembian Maadevi will her heart into resolve.

Even so, the knowledge that Senthan Amudhan was her own son strengthened her determination to prevent her adopted son Madhuranthakan from ascending the throne. She had confessed the truth to Kandaradhithar on an earlier occasion and received his pardon, too. "How does it matter if the child was born to you or a destitute maiden? The divine gaze does not discriminate; they are both equal in the eyes of the Lord. Raise Madhuranthakan as your own son! But do not nurse a desire to seat him upon the Chozha throne; do not consent to it, either. That would be treachery to the Chozha clan of my birth. If such a situation arises, do not hesitate to speak the truth!" So saying, Kandaradhithar extracted a solemn promise from the Devi. Sembian Maadevi had resolved to stay true to her oath.

But that great man, that *mahaan*, had attained the lotus feet of Siva Peruman without ever knowing that their son was being raised in a hut as Vaani *Ammai*'s own. What would he have done? How would he have advised her to behave towards Senthan Amudhan? Sembian Maadevi pondered upon this at length. 'All of this has happened due to God's will; He wishes the mute woman's son to grow up in a palace and the great king's son to grow up in a hut. *I should not disrupt this divine plan. Any attempt to change it will only give rise to a slew of problems. The son I raise will be deeply hurt by the truth. I must not commit such a sin!* Having made a decision, Sembian Maadevi grew determined to stand by it.

It was only her peerless devotion to the Lord that enabled her to put this decision into action. Yet, she couldn't help but think often of Senthan Amudhan. Each time she thought of him, her heart swelled with motherly love and affection. Sembian Maadevi struggled with this conflict within her heart for many years together.

Sometimes, waters that have been repressed behind a dam break through their embankment and surge forward; it has been known to happen, hasn't it? The speed and power of the suddenly-freed waters are puissant indeed. Perhaps some among you have seen or even experienced this.

The motherly love that had been repressed all along in Sembian Maadevi's heart was an equally powerful force of nature. They breached the barrier the Devi had built all these years and now surged through her in uncontrollable torrents.

It was the Mudhanmandhiri's comment that had been the final straw, in truth - he had declared aloud, hadn't he, that he was the son born of her own womb?

Aniruddhar's words had a deep impact on Sembian Maadevi. She relived within a moment the entire span of the ten months she had carried the child in her womb. Sembian Maadevi forgot herself entirely. She forgot the promise she made, too. 'My son!' The words of yearning spilled out of her mouth and she dissolved into tears as she embraced him.

Even though she was adrift in a sea of emotions, Amudhan's words had embedded themselves deeply in her heart. "*Thaaye*! Have you finally relented to call me your son?" he had said, hadn't he? What had he meant by that? Did he know who his true mother was? Had he known all along and kept it to himself?

Sembian Maadevi stood lost in indescribable ecstasy for some time. She struggled to bring her heart within control. "Son," she asked presently in wonder, "Were you aware that I was the sinner who bore you in her womb for ten months and gave birth to you?" Her voice cracked. "Were you angry with me? Is that why you never asked me about it?"

"*Thaaye*!" cried Senthan Amudhan, overwhelmed with emotions that assailed him like the sea surging through an embankment. "I have known for some time now that I was the fortunate one to have been born to you as a son. I have prayed and kept penance that one so pure and pious as you, venerated by the world, would find it in herself to address me aloud as her son. I endeavoured to be worthy of you. I prayed at the divine feet of Siva Peruman night and day for my desire to be fulfilled. In truth, even if you hadn't called for me, I would have come to you. I was only waiting for the subject of succession to be resolved. I yearned only for the privilege to call you my mother. I wanted to come to you after the heir to the throne was decided; I wished to request the right to address you as my mother. *Ammani*, I was prepared to sacrifice even my beloved Poonguzhali, to whom I've lost my heart, so that your feelings were not wounded. Thankfully, she has changed her mind. *Thaaye*, I faced a grave threat to my life three days ago, not long after Poonguzhali and I received your blessings. A true friend saved me from danger. I wasn't particularly happy about it then; neither did I thank him much. But I see now that the debt I owe him is great indeed - I have lived to see the day you addressed me as your son! This is enough for me; I truly am blessed beyond compare. I need nothing else. Let whatever happened here today remain amongst the people in this chamber. No one else needs to know! Let us not add to the chaos burdening the *rajyam*! Poonguzhali and I intend to depart for Kodikkarai at once; bless us and send us on our way!"

Words cannot explain the storm of emotions that erupted in Sembian Maadevi's heart on hearing his speech.

"Child," she said, her voice trembling and tearful, "you are my true son, my own! You are indeed the rightful son to my noble husband, that great man of divinity!"

All this while, Sundara Chozhar, Chinna Pazhuvettarayar and Kundhavai had been watching the scene in silence, rooted to the ground in shock. Their hearts churned with thoughts of the astonishing revelation and the consequences it posed.

It was Kundhavai who found her tongue first. "Father, now we know the reason why Periya Pirattiyar was determined against anointing Madhuranthakan the crown prince!"

Sundara Chozhar had managed to regain his composure by now. "Yes, daughter! But that reason stands defeated, now. Surely, she can't have any objection to anointing her own son as the crown prince, the child she bore in her own womb?" he asked, happiness resounding in his voice.

Sembian Maadevi looked at Sundara Chozhar with consternation. "Charkavarthy, did you not hear the words my son spoke a few moments ago? Let none but those in this chamber know this secret! My son does not stake claim to his kingly heritage. He said so himself, in your very presence…"

"Yes, my liege!" added Senthan Amudhan earnestly. "The Chozha kingdom is reeling under enough chaos. Let my subject not add fuel to the fire. Pray, give me leave. Bless me and my betrothed Poonguzhali and send us on our way…. Poonguzhali, do come here!" he called out.

Poonguzhali, who had been waiting at the chamber entrance so far, now came inside. Senthan Amudhan and Poonguzhali prostrated themselves before Sembian Maadevi. They then turned to the Chakravarthy and sought his blessings, too. "My liege!" said Senthan Amudhan as soon as he stood up. "We shall leave for Kodikkarai right away. Pray, give us leave." He turned to his mother. "*Thaaye*, give us leave!"

Sembian Maadevi turned to the Chakravarthy. "Yes, *Ayya!* Let us wish them well and send them on their way. I shall go to Kodikkarai whenever I wish to see them," she said.

"That shall never happen! I do not give them leave!" declared Sundara Chozhar.

"Chakravarthy," interjected the Mudhanmandhiri, "let us not come to a decision at this moment. Let them remain guests at my palace for a few more days yet." He paused. "We have located the Devi's son, but there is no word yet of Chinna Pazhuvettarayar's son-in-law. Let them stay here till we receive news of him. Until such time, let this secret be known to none but those of us in this chamber," he said.

"We will need to tell Arulmozhi at the very least!" said Ilaiya Piratti Kundhavai, her eyes shining.

Her words alarmed Sentham Amudhan considerably. "No, no!" he cried. "Pray, don't! It is the last thing I wish for!"

"Devi," said the Chakravarthy at last, "let other matters lie. After all these years, the son born of your holy womb has returned to you. I cannot abide the thought of separating the two of you so soon. Pray, remain together for a few days at the very least, either in my palace or in the Mudhanmandhiri's home. Once the heir to the kingdom is decided, we shall think about sending them to Kodikkarai. Until then, let this news be confidential, secret to all but those of us in this chamber!" he said.

73

Vanathi's chicanery

Arulmozhi Varmar found himself deeply disturbed. The subject of succession to the Chozha throne had rent a calamitous divide among the people. Riots raged through the kingdom, growing increasingly violent by the day. The prince tried his best to soothe the chaos by addressing the people, but his presence only served to intensify their zeal. Their raucous cheers resounded through the environs wherever he went. 'Ponniyin Selvar is our king!' they shouted. 'Arulmozhi Varmar must be anointed the crown prince!'

Some rose in virulent opposition to the cries, matching the cheers with loud slogans of their own. "Long live the Pazhuvettarayars, native sons of our soil!' they bellowed in retort. "Down with the despot Kodumbalur Velar!" Each time, the prince would seek to gather support for his cause among this faction, who seemed to think along his lines; each time, to his utter dismay, the opposition would invariably do a stunning volte face at the very sight of him. Their slogans would change upon the spot to the adoring cries of "Long live Ponniyin Selvar!'

Why, even the Pazhuvoor guards stationed at the fort abandoned their stance as soon as they clapped eyes upon Ponniyin Selvar. "The throne for Arulmozhi Varmar!" they roared. "Long live Ponniyin Selvar, the warrior of warriors who seized Eezham!"

Ponniyin Selvan grew increasingly frustrated at his failure to bolster support for his cause among the people and the military. Unfolding events only aggravated his unease, for they seemed to be strengthening a situation contrary to his point of view. The fact that Madhuranthaka Thevar had been missing for the past few days added to his woes. He was aware that Chinna Pazhuvettarayar blamed Kodumbalur Velar for Madhuranthakar's disappearance. To be fair, the accusation was not without reason. Arulmozhi Varmar had to admit that he felt a bit suspicious about the matter himself. Kodumbalur Velar and Thirukovilur Malayaman stood adamant in their wish to anoint him the crown prince. It appeared as if the Mudhanmandhiri had joined their ranks, too. Perhaps they had plotted together to hide away Madhuranthaka Thevar somewhere. Or perchance… had they put Madhuranthakar's very life in danger? Velar and Malayaman felt that the Pazhuvettarayars and Sambuvaraiyar were responsible for the death of his beloved *thamayanar*, Karikalan. Had they harmed Madhuranthakan in a bid for vengeance? *Ah! They blindly do whatever they wish to. It's no skin off their nose, after all! The blame for all of it will land squarely upon my own head!*

The people of Chozha Naadu were all praises for him at present, insistent that he ascend the throne. Would the populace remain forever enthusiastic in their approval of him? It was in their very nature, after all, to be fickle. The very same people who supported him today could well turn around to condemn him tomorrow. They were quite capable of accusing him of being a sinner who slayed his uncle Madhuranthakan to secure the throne for himself. Why, they may even blame him to be the reason for Karikalar's death at the Kadambur palace. *Heavens! Did Mandhakini Devi save me from the fate of drowning in the Kaveri only so that I could face such horrifying blame? None but that very goddess can deliver me from this crisis. It is she who must shield me from the vile dishonour I am at risk of - a slur worse than any censure a man can bear.*

The sordid history of the royal dynasty of Eezha Naadu, whose descendants had ruthlessly murdered their near and dear ones for the throne, had imprinted itself upon Arulmozhi Varmar's heart. The very thought that such an odious ignominy may stain his own legacy caused him unbearable pain.

Arulmozhi wanted to share his burdens with someone and receive good counsel, but discovered that he had no one to confer with. He felt that every single person around him was conspiring against him. Some were transparent in their opposition to him. Others strove hard for what they thought was his own good, not realizing that they were only putting him at risk of a terrible accusation.

He was at a loss to decide whom he could trust enough to confide in and seek counsel from. Why, even his trust in Kundhavai had dwindled, his own beloved sister who loved him like no other, whom he held in the highest reverence. He was fairly certain - and miserable - that she was involved in covert affairs behind his back. Why, even his beloved, sweet Vanathi seemed to be hiding something from him! She sneaked away every now and then, only to quietly return with a maddeningly mysterious look upon her face!

Arulmozhi decided that he could stomach anything but Vanathi's cloak-and-dagger routine. He suddenly caught sight of Vanathi at that very moment. She looked all around her in a decidedly furtive manner before hurrying away by herself. Arulmozhi set to follow her in secret at once from a discreet distance.

Vanathi stole down the corridor of the upper story of the palace before winding her way down to the lower stories. She slipped into a secret passage that was bordered on both sides by high walls. She padded further and further down her mysterious path, quiet as a cat. Certain by now that she was leading him to the lair they had shut away Madhuranthakan in, Arulmozhi trailed behind her in fervour and fury.

Vanathi finally stopped when she reached the grounds of another great palace. She crept into a chamber nearby and attempted to quickly close the door. Arulmozhi leapt forward and swiftly wedged his foot between the door and its jamb. He gripped Vanathi's hand and scowled at her. "Vanathi, your chicanery will find no purchase with me!" he cried hotly. "*Whom* have all of you hidden away in this chamber?"

Vanathi's pretty face bloomed into a smile. "*Ayya*, my chicanery pokery certainly has achieved its end!" she replied, her eyes twinkling. "You wouldn't have come away with me if I had called you. Come and see for yourself who is inside this chamber!"

Arulmozhi Varmar entered the chamber, wholly expecting to see a poor, imprisoned Madhuranthaka Thevar. He found himself overcome with surprise and joy to see Vallavarayan Vandhiyathevan lying upon the bed instead.

Vandhiyathevan struggled to sit up in bed as soon as he saw the prince. "*Ayya*, pray come inside! I have been expecting you these past two days. Pray, free me from the clutches of these maidens!" he wailed.

Ponniyin Selvar rushed to Vandhiyathevan and sat by his side. "My friend!" he cried in happiness. "What is this? How did you get here? And how on *earth* did you get caught by these maidens after making such a brilliant escape from the dungeons? Why, I thought you would be in Eezham by now! I was going to join you there in a few days myself!"

Vandhiyathevan looked quite sorry for himself. "Yes, *Ilavarase*, I ought to have been in Eezham by now. I should be tracking down the Imperial Crown of the Pandiyas and the ancient gemstone necklace said to be gifted to them by Indiran himself," he said gloomily. "Instead, I courted misfortune trying to save Senthan Amudhan, that nut of a Saivite, from a deadly attack by the *vaithiyar's* son Pinakapani. That rogue's spear struck *me* instead and I fell unconscious. When I opened my eyes, I found myself here. I haven't the faintest idea how I came to be captive to this horrifying jailhouse run by these women." He looked earnestly at Ponniyin Selvar. "Pray, have mercy on me and help me escape from here! Else, I shall become prey to the unjust accusation of killing your dear brother and my esteemed leader, Aditha Karikalar!"

"*Ayya*, he is grossly mistaken!" interjected Vanathi in exasperation. "Such blame will be cast upon him only in the event he flees. Your noble *thamakkai* wishes for him to remain here, in secret, until the truth of the matter is discovered."

Ponniyin Selvar turned to Vandhiyathevan. "There is truth in what she says, you know. They will accuse you of the crime only if you make an attempt to escape. In fact, they will drag me into the charge, too. It is better by far to prove the truth to the world. First, tell me what happened. Tell me everything that took place at Kadambur, sparing no detail!" he said.

Vandhiyathevan dutifully told him everything that had happened, to the best of his knowledge.

Even after listening to his account, the Ilavarasar was left uncertain about how Aditha Karikalar's death had come to pass.

74

I SHALL WEAR THE CROWN!

"*Ilavarase*," said Vandhiyathevan at last, "there is only one person whose account can prove my innocence - Periya Pazhuvettarayar. By my reckoning, it was none but that mighty warrior who ambushed me while I was hiding in the *yazh kalanjiyam* - he throttled my neck and pushed me down, rendering me senseless. No one else could have been there at that time. It *must* have been that grandsire who came in the guise of a *kaalamuga saivar;* no doubt he meant to secretly observe the events taking place, suspicious of Nandhini. Idumbankari, who belongs to a *kaalamuga saivar* sect himself, must have helped him gain access through the secret passage. Alas, that indomitable warrior has loathed me since he first set eyes on me; his aversion has only grown stronger with each passing day. He will not come forward with the truth to save my life," he said, shaking his head despondently. "For all I know, he will rejoice in seeing me perish under the shadow of this terrible charge. And so, *Ilavarase* - pray, let me escape!" he cried out. "If I can, I shall go to Eezha Naadu and track down the Imperial Crown of the Pandiyas and the gemstone necklace. Else, slay me with your own sword, right here. Do not suffer me to shoulder the blame of killing your brother, who bore boundless affection for me; do not abandon me to the heinous verdict of impalement at the crossroads! Dying by your sword will give me far greater solace. Why, I would not object to death by poison at the hands of the Kodumbalur princess, either. After all, it was this very maiden and your noble sister who took pity upon this wretched orphan - they were the ones who brought me back from the very gates of death! But," he continued darkly, "I shall not thank them for it."

An indignant Vanathi turned to the Ilavarasar at these rather ungracious words. "Listen to him, *ayya*! Listen to what he says!" she complained, with a long-suffering air. "This consummate warrior wishes not to face his enemies upon the battlefield and go in glory to the paradise of heroes; he craves, instead, to bite the dust *poisoned* at the hands of sweet maidens!"

"*Ilavarase,* this agreeable maiden and your noble sister are likely to harangue me to the death!" protested Vandhiyathevan of the Vaanar clan, pulling a face at the damsel in question. "Better by far, don't you think, to welcome a merciful end by poison?"

Arulmozhi Varmar listened to their squabble distractedly. It appeared as if he was in furious thought over a vital matter. He suddenly jumped to his feet in a flash of inspiration. "Aha!" he cried. "I have it! I shall wear the crown and rise to be the Chakravarthy of Chozha Naadu! The kingdom reverberates with the chants of the people - 'The crown for Arulmozhi Varmar!' It seems to be the ardent wish of the military, too. I shall fulfill their desire! And if dishonour should befall me as a consequence - why, then so be it! It is of little concern to me. Perhaps a couple of chieftains who oppose me may attempt to slander my name; but the people will not believe them. Why, if they grow so bold as to cast blame upon me, their tactic shall only backfire upon them - I shall accuse them in turn of doing away with my brother upon the pretext of a feast at the Kadambur palace! I can punish the whole lot of them for breach of trust and treachery to the royal clan. Whatever happens," continued Arulmozhi, his eyes gleaming with determination, "I shall wear the crown. If needs must, I shall go against the wishes of my father and sister too. But I cannot remain a mute spectator, watching you come to harm!"

Vanathi clasped her hands in rapture. "Ah, that Ilaiya Piratti is not here to listen to these words!" she exclaimed, delighted. "You must repeat them once again for her benefit, too!"

"Why only once? I shall say it many times. I shall prove my will in action, too!" declared Ponniyin Selvan.

Vandhiyathevan wiped away the tears that had sprung to his eyes. "*Ayya*," he began in a choked voice, "if this destitute orphan is the reason you yield your resolve and deign to accept the crown, then it is naught but the good fortune of Chozha Naadu. If I were to be honest, it is my understanding that Madhuranthakar is quite unfit for the crown. He travels in a closed palanquin like a maiden; why, he stoops to conspiring with others in a bid for the throne! How can one such as that be eligible to rule over a *rajyam?* Is it fair that the Chozha throne, honoured by the illustrious likes of Vijayalaya Chozhar and Paranthaka Chozhar, must suffer to bear one who is naught but the very personification of cowardice? It's no surprise that the people are quite opposed to such a thing!"

"Perhaps Madhuranthaka Thevar arrived at the same conclusion and vanished of his own accord," offered Vanathi.

"Yes, yes. I shall abandon my endeavours to locate him. I am going to wear the crown myself!" said Arulmozhi Varmar.

It was at that very moment that Kundhavai entered the chamber.

"*Thambi*, set aside the very thought!" she declared as she swept in. "You shall attain neither the throne nor the crown. Have you forgotten that my dear friend Vanathi has vowed never to sit upon the Thanjai throne? I fear my eyes cannot bear the sight of you seated upon the throne with another maiden by your side!"

"Why, then all you have to do is to close your eyes, *Akka*! I can cover them for you with my hands, if you like!" chirped Vanathi.

Ponniyin Selvan looked at Kundhavai with some surprise. "Sister, can the Chozha *rajyam* be bereft of a king merely to accommodate your friend's vow? Our father stands adamant in his wish to lay down the burden of the kingdom and retire to Kanchi. As for Madhuranthaka Thevar, he seems to have vanished into thin air. What other choice do we have?" He frowned. "You are aware, surely, that the kingdom is in flames over the turmoil arising from the subject of succession? How long can we allow the riots to continue?"

Ilaiya Piratti smiled at him. "*Thambi*, I bear happy news. I came rushing here to tell you of that, in fact! The missing Madhuranthaka Thevar has come out of hiding! The penance and prayers of the forefathers of the Chozha clan have not gone to waste. There is little need for you to worry about the *rajyam*. Even if he refuses, we shall remain unyielding - we shall conduct the *magudabhishekam* in his honour to anoint him the successor!" she announced, her eyes twinkling.

The other three were struck amazed by her display of warm exuberance. It was true enough that Kundhavai Piratti had endorsed anointing Madhuranthakan the crown prince for quite some time; but never had she shown such zest for the cause until this moment.

It took Ponniyin Selvan a little while to find his tongue. "Devi, where was he hiding? Why? How did he emerge into the open?" he asked, finally.

"He was under our very noses all along! We are the ones who failed to find him! *Thambi*, none but the man born to Sembian Maadevi's holy womb is entitled to the Chozha throne. This *rajyam* is your uncle's by right. Set aside all thoughts of wearing the crown. Listen, now, to this marvellous piece of news. *Thambi*, our uncle was faced with a great threat four days past. An assassin sought to hurl a spear at him. If he had thrown his weapon, Madhuranthaka Thevar would have lost his life. The Chozha clan would have suffered another untimely demise in the family." Ilaiya Piratti paused. "Can you guess who the great warrior who thwarted the attempt was? Do you know who saved our *chitappa*, risking his own life to protect his?" Ilaiya Piratti turned to Vandhiyathevan and gazed warmly at him with her full, limpid eyes. They shone with such earnest affection, gratitude and esteem, that Vandhiyathevan felt his heart swell; so completely swept off his feet was he that he nearly toppled off the bed.

Ponniyin Selvar flailed in a sea of astonishment. "What is this, *Akka*? I fail to understand you! My friend never breathed a word of any of this to me, either!"

Ilaiya Piratti turned to him, face glowing with pride. "He wouldn't have. You see, even he could not have grasped the magnitude and nobility of his deed. He has little idea how beholden the Chozha clan is to him!"

"*Akka*, you speak in riddles! It's all rather too mysterious for my taste. Better, I think, that you explain things in clear detail than subject us to shock and surprise! Where and how did this Vaanar warrior save Madhuranthakar? Where is Madhuranthaka Thevar now?" asked the Ilavarasar.

"Ponniyin Selva! He will be here himself, momentarily. I've sent word to bring him to this chamber, knowing that you are here. You can learn the truth first-hand. Or perhaps Poonguzhali will tell you of the matter, for she saw it with her own eyes…" Ilaiya Piratti paused. "There, it sounds like he is coming!"

It was true. Footsteps sounded outside the chamber; four people entered shortly after. The Mudhanmandhiri Aniruddhar, Azhwarkkadiyaan, Poonguzhali and Senthan Amudhan stepped inside. Curiously enough, Senthan Amudhan was attired quite differently from his usual self. He wore a princely crown upon his head and was wrapped in a lustrous silk *peethambaram*. The jewels of a king glittered on his person.

The three in the chamber gaped in astonishment at the group that had entered. "*Akka*! You said that Madhuranthakar would come, didn't you? Why, I don't see him!" cried Arulmozhi, turning to Kundhavai.

"*Thambi*, he stands right here in front of you, wearing the crown of a prince. He is truly the son of Sivagnana Kandaradhithar, the child born of Sembian Maadevi's holy womb. This gem of a *Siva bhaktha* is our very own uncle!" said Kundhavai, beaming. "All these very years, he was living under the name of Senthan Amudhan. The good deeds of the Chozha clan have held us in good stead - he has been revealed to us today! It was none but him that a wicked man attempted to kill four days ago, with a spear; by foiling the plan, this Vaanar warrior has rendered peerless service to the Chozha clan. As for this Vaishnavar here, the Mudhanmandhiri's disciple," she continued, turning to Azhwarkkadiyaan, "he made the arrangements to bring him safely into the fort, even though he is a Saivite!"

Thirumalai hastened to intervene. "Devi, neither did I help this Saivar in any way nor did I seek to! All I did was plonk him upon an elephant and dress him up in disguise, so that the Vallathu prince could travel by the palanquin!"

"Yes, yes!" said Kundhavai. "Thirumalai has rendered exemplary service in two ways! When he put a crown on Madhuranthaka Thevar's head and brought him upon a royal elephant, he could have hardly dreamed that he was accompanying the rightful heir to the throne! Or perhaps," she said, narrowing her eyes at a grinning Azhwarkkadiyaan, "he knew it all along. I confess I am unsure on that score. Let that be. *Thambi*, the person we had taken to be Madhuranthaka Thevar all these years was not the true owner of the name. It belongs to this person you see here, for he was born to Periya Piratti, bestowed upon the Chozha clan as a boon! He lived in a simple hut all these years, no doubt as part of the divine play we can never hope to understand. Even so, we have all found ourselves fascinated, on varying occasions, by the regal traits that mark him out to be a scion of the Chozha clan! We are all aware, I am sure, that he helped this Vaanar warrior make his escape on an earlier occasion. *Thambi*, neither you nor I can ever forget the time he and Poonguzhali delivered you safely to Naagaippattinam from Kodikkarai. It was only today that we learned that he is our true uncle, from Sembian Maadevi's own account. He has accepted it, too." Kundhavai clasped her hands in joy. "*Thambi*, I am inviting him to our palace on this holy, wonderful day! No, no - I am calling upon him to take his rightful place in his own palace! I invite today to unite with our family, one who has been living apart from us all these years. Ah, such a reunion ought to be celebrated with pomp and splendour! Alas, now is not the time for such things. Prudence in protecting this secret would serve our cause better. We must be satisfied with an intimate celebration amongst ourselves. *Chitappa*! Do come here, by my side!" cried out Kundhavai. "I do not know how else to express my joy that you have returned to us after all these years. When my dear brothers embark on travel or return home, it is a little tradition of mine to smear ash across their foreheads and apply a dot of *kungumam*. I shall do the same to you, who have come back to us!"

Madhuranthakar, known until this moment to us as Senthan Amudhan, stood still as Ilaiya Piratti lovingly smeared ash across his forehead and applied a dot of *kungumam* with her delicate fingers. The Mudhanmandhiri Aniruddhar made a blessing at the touching sight. "May he live long, the shining light of the Chozha clan, the young Madhuranthaka Thevar!" he cried. "Long live, long live indeed!" echoed Azhwarkkadiyaan.

When Kundhavai first embarked on this fantastic account, Arulmozhi was struck amazed. Truth be told, his surprise had been tainted by an iota of doubt. He was uncertain whether the whole thing was naught but a silly game of sorts; he wondered if Ilaiya Piratti was delivering a secret message to him, concealed beneath the incredible words she spoke. As she continued her tale, however, his scepticism vanished. He realized that Kundhavai spoke from the very depths of her heart, her words suffused with pure affection. Ponniyin Selvar found himself overcome by the flood of emotions surging forth from the sister he held in high esteem.

When Kundhavai Devi stepped back from applying the *kungumam* on Senthan Amudhan's forehead, a visibly moved Arulmozhi Thevar approached him. "*Chitappa*, I have always borne affection for you. I have often wished that you had been my brother. It must have been our bond of blood that evoked such an emotion in me!" he said tearfully and embraced Senthan Amudhan.

"Aha!" called out a triumphant Vandhiyathevan from his bed. "I suspected as much! I *thought* that this *siva bhaktha* of a Senthan Amudhan must have a royal warrior of ancient heritage lurking somewhere within him. Else, would he have afforded shelter and escape to an inconsequential person as me, one with neither title nor land to my claim? Oh, descendant of great kings! Pray, bless me by helping me escape as you did once before! The thought that I will not be present to see your coronation gives me much misery; but what can I do, after all?" The sheets rustled noisily as the Vaanar youth waved his arms in excitement. "One thing gives me great joy, I confess - not that the Chozha *samrajyam* is now Senthan Amudhan's by right, but that Poonguzhali, the maiden who helped me cross the seas, will now rise to be queen! Why, I suspect the

Samudhra Kumari herself would have little expected her dreams would come true so soon!" he declared gallantly and flashed a rakish grin at Poonguzhali.

"*Ayya*," interrupted Kundhavai, her tone dripping acid, "it is for the best, I think, that you reign in your tongue for a few days. Your body will heal quicker, affording you to make the quick escape you yearn for."

Ilaiya Piratti turned to her brother. "*Thambi* Arulmozhi! We understand now, don't we, why our venerable *paatiyaar* had stood her ground in refusing to crown her own son? We were not entirely satisfied with the idea of crowning the old Madhuranthakan, ourselves. He had none of the characteristics of one born into the brave Chola dynasty. Despite our noble grandmother's endeavours, *siva bhakthi* failed to be a part of his consciousness; why, he had not even a shred of valour. Even so, we steeled our hearts and resigned ourselves to crowning him. The thought of now anointing the crown upon the new Madhuranthakar is not merely satisfactory - it gives us great happiness and joy, too!" She smiled warmly at Poonguzhali. "I am looking forward to seeing Poonguzhali ascend the throne as well, she who saved you and the Vallathu prince from a bitter end at sea. The Mudhanmandhiri must make the necessary arrangements at once," she finished, looking at Aniruddhar.

"Devi, Periya Pazhuvettarayar must yield to come forward and reveal what transpired in the Kadambur palace. We need to know what became of the old Madhuranthaka Thevar as well. How can we plan a date for the coronation without resolving these two issues?" asked Aniruddhar.

"I shall ask Periya Pazhuvettarayar myself; as for locating the old Madhuranthaka Thevar, that task is your responsibility," replied Kundhavai.

Madhuranthaka Thevar, known to us so far as Senthan Amudhan, stepped forward. "*Ilavarase*! You addressed me as Chitappa with due respect. These people also address me as Ilavarasar. But I cannot address you as my son!" he burst out. "Having lived in a simple hut for twenty two years, it is impossible for me to think of myself as a prince hailing from an exalted lineage of emperors." He looked around the room. "I have a request to make of all of you. I was imprisoned in the underground dungeons for a few days, wasn't I, for helping Vandhiyathevan escape? I learned the news that we all know today from the prisoner in the cell next to mine. He said that the son of a mute mother was being raised as a prince in the palace, and that the scion of the ruling dynasty was being raised in the humble home of a mute mother. I knew the truth that very day. I saw it shine through the affection bestowed upon me by Sembian Maadevi, the noble woman who is venerated by the whole world. I longed for her to call out to me as her own son. That desire was fulfilled today. I do not want anything more!"

"Oh, prince! The question is not whether you wish for it or not," pointed out the Mudhanmandhiri. "We must seek the fairest course of action, must we not?"

"Aha! Pray, think again and think well! There is little to deliberate upon when it comes to my matter. I have considered the issue deeply and made a decision. Poonguzhali had often spoken to me of her wish to marry a prince and ascend the throne; it was why she had rejected my ardent love all along. Ah, my heart and tongue yearned to speak the truth to her. I wanted to tell her, 'Girl, I truly am a prince! If I but wished for it, this Chozha *samrajyam* will be mine!' But I restrained the impulse. I earnestly prayed to the Lord that I should never suffer the desire to rule a kingdom. I was even prepared to sacrifice my feelings for Poonguzhali to prove my resolve. Thankfully, Samudhra Kumari relinquished her unworthy dream and agreed to marry this poor servant of Siva."

"*Ayya*, how can you call my dream unworthy?" asked Poonguzhali hotly. "I am quite capable of reigning the three worlds as the

Chakravarthini! Yet, I agreed to marry you, willing to spend the rest of my life stringing garlands for a livelihood and rowing a boat!"

"Tell him, Poonguzhali!" cried our Kundhavai in admiration. "What more do we need to establish your worth? Why, what marks one out to be suitable or unsuitable for a position, after all? The Deiva Pulavar's sacred words say, 'All men are equal in their birth.' There is little need for you to forsake your heart's desire! Tell this descendant of great kings, this noble man who will soon hold your hand in troth - tell him to join us as one of our own! Chitappa! It is quite fair that you stay true to your resolve of shunning the kingdom even after learning that it is yours by right; it serves to show the magnanimity you have borne since birth. But we are all asking it of you, now - the Chakravarthy, the Mudhanmandhiri, my brother and I. My friend Vanathi is even prepared to change her uncle's mind on the matter! Why refuse now?" asked Ilaiya Piratti.

"Devi, all of you ask this of me, it is true. But what pray, of the citizens of our *rajyam*? Perhaps you do not know their thoughts. I, however, have lived among them and know what lies in their hearts. I know the true desire of the people across Thanjai, Pazhaiyarai, Kudanthai, Kodikkarai and Naagaippattinam. I even know, through chatter blown to me by the wind, what the people of Pandiya Naadu, Pallava Naadu, Kongu Naadu and Eezha Naadu wish for! The single-minded mandate of the people is that none but Arulmozhi must wear the crown. Can I swim against the current of such a fiercely popular opinion? Even if I desire to undertake the challenge, am I capable of ruling this vast and noble Chozha *samrajyam*? Good God!" he cried out, as an unpleasant thought occurred to him. "I know well the depth of hatred the people bore for the person you call the 'old Madhuranthakar.' Would you make me the new target of that virulent hostility? No, no... pray, do not subject me to such a fate! I have done no harm to any of you!"

Before anyone could say a word, Ponniyin Selvar rose to his feet majestically. "Let us end the conversation here. When you entered this chamber, I was telling Vandhiyathevan that I would wear the crown. I shall make sure that it happens. I have understood well the opinion of Uttama Chozhar, the noble son borne by the holy womb of Periya Piratti. Let there be no further talk regarding the right of succession!" he declared.

75

Catastrophic consequences

Within the august halls of the *manthiralosanai mandapam* at the Thanjai palace, the Paranthaka Sundara Chozha Chakravarthy sat majestically upon the throne of justice. The most elevated among the palace women were seated on either side of him. The ministers, commanders and princes of the glorious Chozha Naadu stood respectfully in front of him, their palms joined together in obeisance. Among the women, Periya Piratti Sembian Maadevi, Udaiya Piratti Vaanama Devi and Ilaiya Piratti Kundhavai Devi were present, accompanied by Kodumblur Ilavarasi Vanathi. Hesitant to take her place amongst the noble women, Poonguzhali stood a modest distance behind the group. Among the menfolk were counted Periya Pazhuvettarayar, Chinna Pazhuvettarayar, the Mudhanmandhiri Aniruddhar, the Senathipathi Periya Velar, Miladudaiyar Malayaman, Ilavarasar Arulmozhi Varmar, the twice-born Madhuranthakar Thevar and Parthibendra Pallavan. Thirumalai was there too, standing slightly apart from the illustrious group.

The Chakravarthy ran an unblinking eye over the gathered. "Are all the invitees present? I do not see the Kadambur king," he said presently.

"Sambuvaraiyar's son has just returned," replied Parthibendran respectfully. "Father and son will soon join us."

"Oh, Kandamaaran has returned, has he? What news has he brought? Has he captured the escaped prisoners?" asked Sundara Chozhar.

"I am afraid not, my liege. He was unable to capture them. However, he does report that he has slayed Vandhiyathevan. The other absconder - the madman - slipped away, it seems," replied Parthibendran.

Periya Pazhuvettarayar cleared his throat loudly. Everyone turned to him expectantly, thinking he meant to speak, but the venerable old man said nothing.

The Chakravarthy looked dismayed at Parthibendran's news. "I do not know what further ramifications will be brought to bear upon us as a result of my mistakes! Mudhanmandhiri, you know well the thoughts that lie in my heart. I have called forth to this intimate assembly those who are the closest to me and my clan. Pray, explain to the forum the reason for my summons as well as my point of view. The matter is better explained by you than me, isn't it?"

"Your wish is my command, Chakravarthy," replied the Mudhanmandhiri with a deferential bow. He turned towards the assembly. "You all know that there are many reasons why the Chakravarthy's heart lies wounded today. It was not too long ago that he suffered the loss of his eldest son, a peerless warrior equal to Abimanyu and Aravaan in valour. The facts behind his death remain a mystery. Our king had not seen that brave son once in the past three years. Having built the golden palace at Kanchi, Karikalar had sent a series of messages urging the Chakravarthy to come and stay there. Yet, the Chakravarthy declined to visit. You all know the reason behind his refusal. The Chakravarthy had been under the protection of Chinna Pazhuvettarayar in this great city of Thanjai. It was a time when the city and kingdom were rife with disturbing rumours. Had the Chakravarthy departed for Kanchi under such delicate circumstances, it would have given rise to speculation that he had lost faith in the Pazhuvettarayars. The Chakravarthy did not want to create an opportunity for such conjectures." He paused. "I shall speak transparently of that which the Chakravarthy is hesitant to broach. I beg that the royal personages gathered in this esteemed assembly find it fit to pardon my unambiguity. Our king has lain unwell for quite some time; the illness robbed him of the strength of his legs, weakening his heart as a consequence. In truth, his heart struggled with an emotional stress as well, one that inflicted upon him greater pain and suffering. That such staunch supporters of the great Chozha clan as you, loyal friends and generational allies - unassailable diamond pillars upon which lies the very Chozha *samrajyam* - should allow a difference of opinion to taint your bond has wounded the Chakravarthy's heart and worsened his health. You all stood united in the battlefield at Thakkolam and fought with valour under the banner of Rajadhithar, who lost his life upon an elephant. With Rajadhithar unexpectedly succumbing to a hero's death upon the battlefield, the Chozha army was cornered into defeat. But your collective courage, strength and unity transformed that loss into a resounding victory. You recaptured both the Thondai Mandalam and Ganga Mandalam that we had lost. In the Sevur battlefield, you successfully pitted your might against the Pandiyas, capturing Pandiya Naadu to bring it under our direct rule. In Eezha Naadu, you bested Magindhan and planted the glorious tiger flag in those lands. These extraordinary feats were made possible because all of you stood united, bound by the belief that the good of the

Chozha *samrajyam* augured well for you, too.

This ideal situation has taken a turn for the worse over the past few years. For some reason, a difference of opinion has soured your hearts. You split into two hostile factions. Our illustrious king strove to bridge the divide. He learned that the animosity arose from the subject of succession, over who could stake claim to the throne after his reign. None of you approached the Chakravarthy to discuss the matter with him directly. Even so, our Chakravarthy gleaned the truth by dint of his unparalleled perspicacity. He wished to conduct a peaceful, transparent dialogue about the subject of succession with all of you, one that would yield a solution agreeable to all. He had intended to depart for Kanchi only after bringing the matter to resolution. In fact, he sought to hand over the reins of the Chozha *samrajyam* to the beloved son of Sivagnana Kandaradhithar Peruman. He believed that he could convince Aditha Karikalar to agree to this proposal as well; it was why he had requested Karikalar to visit him here. Alas, disaster struck by the time such a meeting could happen. When he heard that Karikalar would visit the Kadambur king's palace, the Chakravarthy was overjoyed. He felt that all your differences would be bridged. He thought that if Karikalar wed Sambuvaraiyar's daughter, it would unite all of you like before and that the issue of choosing an heir to the throne could be resolved peacefully. I too thought the same. Why, many of you would have believed so, too. It was the very reason why our Thirukovilur king did not object to Karikalar's visit to Kadambur. Alas, all our wishes crumbled to dust. Ilavarasar Karikalar met with an untimely death at the Kadambur palace."

"Are we going to discover how it happened or not?" demanded Thirukovilur Malayaman. "It may prove better for us to have the facts in hand before you continue your speech."

"Yes, there is little point in deliberating further without unearthing the truth!" added the Senathipathi.

The Mudhanmandhiri glanced at the Chakravarthy. "Oh, brave noblemen! What has happened, has happened. The Chakravarthy opines that it is best to lie matters lie," he replied.

"How can that be?" burst out Senathipathi Periya Velar, his voice barely concealing his outrage. "The Chozha system of justice is famed throughout the world. Our kingdom dignifies even the death of a destitute orphan with due process and inquiry; if a culprit is found to be the cause, he is meted a fitting punishment. How can we forego investigating the unnatural death of the crown prince of the land?"

Sundara Chozhar sighed heavily, feeling the weight of weariness descend upon his shoulders. "Kodumbalur *mama*, pray, listen! Can there be another suffering greater grief than I at the untimely death of my beloved son? Yet, I say that there is no need for an inquiry. Why, I know for certain that none here bears responsibility for the tragedy. I have lost my son as a direct result of my own sins. If there lies atonement in penance, pray enlighten me - I shall undertake it. There is little need to cast about for reasons!"

"My liege, your words risk implying that you wish to protect the culprit," said a troubled Chinna Pazhuvettarayar. "Unfettered hearsay and speculation abound among the people over the matter of the Ilavarasar's demise. It is best to bring the truth to light. The culprit must be brought to justice!"

"No truer words were ever spoken!" cried out the hot-headed Parthibendran. "Surely, this is the righteous way to administer a great kingdom. If this heinous crime is not accorded a due investigation, the people will lose faith in the very justice system!"

"Oh, respected elders! Why must there be such debate and deliberation over this matter?" spoke up Kandamaaran. "Pray, pardon this youth if I speak out of turn. The culprit has been punished! The sinner who murdered prince Karikalar, the wretch who ruined my beloved sister's life and drove her insane, that very Vandhiyathevan has fallen prey to my spear. What further need do we have for an investigation?"

Kandamaaran had joined the assembly even as the Mudhamandhiri was talking. It was only when spoke that the rest realized that he arrived. "Blockhead!" muttered Periya Pazhuvettarayar under his breath. "That the Kadambur Sambuvaraiyar should sire a fool as this!"

"Kanthamaara! Is it true that you killed Vandhiyathevan with a spear?" asked Mudhanmandhiri Aniruddhar. "Did you see him yourself? You went chasing after him in the dark of night, did you not?"

"Mudhanmandhiri, I am no stranger to your paucity of faith in me. Would I fail to recognize a person at night?" countered a bristling Kandamaaran.

"But he is a warrior, isn't he? Didn't he fight with you?"

"Of course, it is hardly surprising that you place little trust in my valour as well," replied Kandamaaran cuttingly. "I shall register my account with the Chakravarthy, instead." He turned earnestly to face Sundara Chozhar. "The absconders were two in number. One was a madman, who had been imprisoned in our underground dungeons for quite a few years. As he tried to bar my way, I noticed the other man nearing the other side of the river bank. I hurled my spear at him and killed him. That man had to have been Vandhiyathevan of the Vaanar clan."

"Didn't you bring the corpse back with you?" asked the Mudhanmandhiri mildly.

"If I had but known that you would be so suspicious of my account, I would have walked further out along the Vadavaaru river in search of it!" exclaimed Kandamaaran, rounding upon Aniruddhar. "But that would have rendered me unable to join this *manthiralosanai* assembly!"

"We've eluded a great loss, to be sure!" came the caustic remark from Thalapathy Chinna Pazhuvettarayar.

"*Thambi*, why are you so intent upon capturing Vandhiyathevan?" asked Periya Velar Boodhi Vikrama Kesari.

"Must you even ask?" cried out a genuinely aggrieved Kandamaaran. "The abhorrent event transpired in my home! If the true culprit is not caught, won't you turn your suspicions upon me and my father?"

"My child, Kandhamaara!" began Sundara Chozhar. "No matter who harbours such suspicion, I certainly will not! Don't I know the depth of loyalty and devotion your father bears for me? Let the matter go. Where is Periya Sambuvaraiyar?"

"Chakravarthy, I find myself obliged to speak out about my family's shame," replied Kandamaaran, his face wilting with sadness. "I was in the midst of reporting to my father that I had done away with Vandhiyathevan for good; Manimekalai heard my account and came flying at me in a murderous rage, dagger in hand. My father is trying his best to pacify her and quell her fury. He will be here soon. He sent me ahead with the message that he will abide by whatever decision the *mandhiralosanai* assembly arrives at."

"*Appane*, it was your sister, wasn't it, who repeatedly professed to have killed the prince, as one in the grip of hysteria?" asked old Malayaman.

"Yes," replied Kandamaaran, pained. "It was only to conceal Vandhiyathevan's crime and help him escape that she had made such claims. She was not suffering from full-fledged mania at that time; but the lunacy has now reached its peak. It is naught but the ill fortune of our clan!"

"Young *Sambuvaraiyare*, you exude great assurance when you say that Vandhiyathevan killed prince Karikalar. What gives you such confidence? Did you see him with your own eyes? Or perchance, did you collect first-hand accounts of those who did?" asked the Mudhanmandhiri.

"My lord Mudhanmandhiri! Does one need a looking glass to examine his own hand? None but the Vaanar warrior was at the site of the prince's murder. That he was the murderer was written quite plainly across his face. Further, the site was Pazhuvoor Ilaiya Rani's chamber - what other reason could he have had to go there? Also, if he were truly innocent, why then did he escape from the underground dungeons?" argued Kandamaaran.

"I would like to remind everyone in this assembly," added Parthibendran, "that the Mudhanmandhiri had assumed the charge of capturing the prisoner who escaped from the underground dungeons."

Aniruddhar turned at his words. "Oh, scion of the Pallava clan! It is true that I had assumed such a charge. But I did not expect that the young Sambuvaraiyar would act as the law himself, arriving at a conclusion thus and carrying out a punishment he saw fit. Vandhiyathevan hails from the ancient Vaanar clan. His ancestors once reigned over a great kingdom. Their women married into the Chozha clan and established close ties with the lineage. When those hailing from the princely clans of chieftains are accused of a crime, tradition demands that the Chakravarthy must seat himself upon the throne of justice, conduct an inquiry and pass a sentence!" said the Mudhanmandhiri Aniruddha Brahmmarayar.

"*Ayya*, tradition also allows one to bring back an escaped convict dead or alive!" replied Parthibendran at once.

"Ah, but the young Sambuvaraiyar has not brought back Vandhiyathevan even as a corpse! He has abandoned him to the waters of the Vadvaaru, hasn't he?" pointed out the Mudhanmandhiri Aniruddhar.

Periya Sambuvaraiyar entered the *manthiralosanai sabha* at precisely this moment, drawing all eyes to him. The grief pervading his features was quite evident for all to see.

Kandamaaran hastened to his side. "How is Manimekalai?" he asked softly.

"The same. I have left her in the care of your mother," replied Sambuvaraiyar aloud for all to hear, steel lacing his tone.

"*Ayya*," said the Chakrvarthy gently to Sambuvaraiyar, "if you must remain by the side of your beloved daughter, then pray, do so. We can schedule the assembly on the morrow."

"No, my liege. There is little use in my being at her side!" confessed Sambuvaraiyar in a harrowed tone. "Perchance, it may help if the Vaanar warrior Vandhiyathevan, slain by my son's spear, were to come back to life." The anguish and bitterness in his tone cast a pall of silence upon the hall.

"*Ayya*," began the Mudhanmandhiri presently, "we were discussing the grave incident that transpired at your palace. All of us are aware of the deep pain you feel at the thought that the crown prince breathed his last in your home. The Chakravarthy does not wish to hold you responsible for the tragedy, in any way. But we must learn the facts behind the prince's demise, should we not, if we are to prevent rumour and calumny from making the rounds of city and country? This is the opinion of the assembly gathered here, in this hall. Is there anything you wish to add to the subject? The young Sambuvaraiyar insists that Vandhiyathevan of the Vaanar clan is responsible for the prince's death; what is your opinion on the matter?" he asked.

Sambuvaraiyar stood rooted to his place at the question. Presently, he turned and looked at everyone in the assembly until his gaze rested upon Kandamaaran. "Yes, yes! This idiot made the same claim on that disastrous day, too! I did not believe him then and I do not believe him now!" he cried out in despair. "I heeded his words and invited the Ilavarasar Karikalar to my palace. It is the sole reason that these catastrophic consequences have come to pass! My clan and I find ourselves stained with an indelible dishonour!"

"*Sambuvaraiyare*! Pray, do not spiral into a panic," said old Malayaman gently. "What has happened, has happened. You invited my grandson to your palace in good faith. None here wish to hold you responsible for Karikalar's demise. It is precisely why we want to learn the truth. If you can help us uncover the facts, it will be night but for the good."

"What aid can I offer?" asked a grief-stricken Sambuvaraiyar. "My son makes one claim while my daughter asserts the very opposite! I find myself unable to believe either of their accounts. I do not know the truth myself. I feel as if I've been abandoned in a forest, blindfolded. Truly, the Dhanaadhikaari Periya Pazhuvettarayar will be of greater help in unearthing the truth than I! Ask him!" he cried out, turning his gaze upon Periya Pazhuvettarayar. "He is the root cause of everything! It was he who first brought Madhuranthakar to the Kadambur palace in secret. He also bade me wed my daughter to the prince. Ah, my family has been in the grip of ill luck since that fateful day! I hear that Madhuranthaka Thevar himself has disappeared into thin air! Later, Periya Pazhuvettarayar also brought his Ilaiya Rani to the palace; he also contrived to lure the Ilavarasar from Kanchi. He left the pair behind at my palace and went away. Ask him why he left! Ask him where his Ilaiya Rani is now!"

Sambuvaraiyar spoke breathlessly, as a man possessed by frenzy.

"Enough, enough! Stop!" thundered the Chakravarthy. "This is precisely why I said there was to be no investigation on the matter - none of you heeded my words! Isn't it enough that you are all divided by animosity as it is? Must we fan the animosity with new grievances? Sambuvaraiyare! You are in no way responsible for the incident that transpired in your palace. That is why I ordered for your immediate release from the underground dungeons!" His voice grew hoarse with pain. "My own sins are responsible for my brave son's untimely death. No one else is to blame. Neither you nor Periya Pazhuvettarayar are not obliged to make any comment on the matter!"

Periya Pazhuevttarayar cleared his throat like a mighty lion in roar. "Great emperor of the Chozha clan!" he said, his stentorian voice resounding through in the chamber. "Pray, grace me with your pardon. I cannot hold my tongue; I must confess what lies in my heart. I must speak the truth as I know it. Yes, my liege. I admit that I have considered fulfilling my vow without bringing the truth to light. I have taken a solemn oath that I will cut off my own head if I am unable to protect those of the Chozha clan from danger. I have failed to protect Aditha Karikalar. And so, I must fulfill my vow. I shall confess the truth as I know it before that; else, lingering suspicion will subject people to undeserved blame."

As Periya Pazhuvettaryar's last words rang out through the hall, the assembly froze in silence. The heart of every last one in the audience went out to Periya Pazhuvettarayar.

"*Mama*," spoke the Chakravarthy in a brittle voice, "Pray, think! Why must you speak of bygones? The dead will not return. I am certain that you would not have knowingly caused harm to the Chozha clan. Let us put the past behind us and talk of what needs to be done in the future," he begged.

"I beg your pardon, *ayya*! I must speak out about what happened!" roared Periya Pazhuvettarayar. "I must speak of the heinous treachery that I came so close to inflicting upon the Chozha clan! It is only by the grace of our guardian deity Durga Devi that such horrors did not come to pass. I must pay the sacred offering due to

Mother Parameswari. Pray, show me the kindness of listening to my account!"

The Chakravarthy fell silent, realizing that it was impossible to stop him from speaking.

Periya Pazhuvettarayar proceeded to give an excruciatingly honest account of every incident that had come to pass in the past three years, since the time he had run into a stranded Nandhini and fallen hopelessly in love with her. He confessed that he had brushed aside his brother Chinna Pazhuvettarayar's warnings on many occasions. He explained how he had intended to seat Madhuranthaka Thevar on the Chozha throne at Nandhini's instigation; he admitted that he had colluded with the other chieftains of the kingdom to achieve this end. He described how he had arranged for Madhuranthakan to travel by Nandhini's veiled palanquin as well as the covert meeting that took place at Sambuvaraiyar's palace in the dark of midnight. It was Vandhiyathevan, he revealed, who was responsible for sowing the seeds of mistrust in heart about Nandhini, leading him to explore a niggling suspicion about the Pandiya Naadu conspirators. He confessed, broken and tortured, that he had been struck deluded and blind by the feverish love he bore for Nandhini. He recounted how he had been caught in the fierce Kollidam floods and how, as a consequence, he had stumbled upon the plot laid by the Pandiya Naadu conspirators. He said that he had sought to make a swift return to Kadambur, revealing that he had taken on the guise of a *kaalamuga saivar.* He had traversed the secret passage with Idumbankari's help and reached the *anthappuram.* Periya Pazhuvettarayar described how he had hidden himself away in the *yazh kalanjiyam*, distracted but for a fateful moment as he listened to the exchange between Nandhini and the Ilavarasar, a moment within which the prince lost his life. He explained that he had leaped forward to catch the prince as he fell, extinguishing the lamp in the process. Attackers had then surrounded him, he said, raining merciless blows upon his person. He had lost consciousness only to regain his senses in the cave at Pachai Malai, from whence he had returned.

"Chakravarthy!" cried out Periya Pazhuvettarayar as he reached the end of his account, "this is how I stand before you as one who has committed unspeakable treachery to the Chozha clan! I allowed the Pandiya Naadu conspirators to make their vile nest in my own palace. I allowed them to exploit the treasury to procure all the resources they needed to fulfill their nefarious plot. The conspirators sought to slay you and your two sons at the same fateful moment. A divine woman, a mute and deaf goddess, saved you by sacrificing her own life. An elephant, a mere creature of five senses, saved Ponniyin Selvan." His voice cracked. "I alone failed to save Aditha Karikalar. I stand before you as the sole reason for his untimely death - none but I, from the very beginning until the sordid end! *Ayya*!" he burst out in passion, "here - I shall now fulfill the holy oath I undertook in the sacred sanctum of Durga Parameswari!" As he spoke the terrible words, Periya Pazhuvettarayar raised and swung the sword he held in his great arm. The audience stood stunned as they realized what he meant to do. It was only Ponniyin Selvar, who had been edging closer to him all along, who sprung forward to grip the hand that held the sword.

"*Ayya*, patience! It is an age-old tradition that the Pazhuvettarayars place the crown upon the head of the Chozha king at the time of coronation. None but *your* venerable hands must crown me at my *pattabhishekam*. You may do as you wish after that. Until then, pray be patient!" said Ponniyin Selvar.

It needn't be said, must it, that this extraordinary speech plunged the Chakravarthy and the chieftains into a sea of wonder?

76

THE VADAVAARU CHANGES COURSE!

Our esteemed readers would have doubtless noticed that some of the characters in our epic display contradictory speech and behaviour. We wish to inform you that we are not responsible for this. Human nature is seldom unchanging. Circumstances shape one's state of mind and force a change in one's behaviour; and so, those who spoke and behaved in a certain way until yesterday show different colours today.

At the very beginning of our tale, Periya Pazhuvettarayar marked himself to be the leader of a great political conspiracy. Now, he has publicly confessed his crimes of his own accord and wishes to behead himself by way of atonement.

When Periya Sambuvaraiyar laid eyes upon Karikalan's lifeless body, he fell into a state of shock. He worried that the blame for the heinous murder would be laid upon his own family and proceeded to raze down his own ancient palace. Keen that the accusation be foisted onto another, he colluded with own son and provoked him to cast about for a suitable culprit. With the understanding that none seeks to blame him, he now sings a different tune, having learned the depth of love his beloved daughter Manimekalai bears for Vandhiyathevan.

For our part, we had contrived to convince our readers believe that the fake Madhuranthakan who travelled by the veiled palanquin at the beginning of our tale was the real Madhuranthakan, the prince who would go on to become Uttama Chozha Chakravarthy. That was necessary for the narrative flow. Why, even the Mudhanmandhiri Aniruddhar, who knew the prince's secret to some extent, was of the opinion that Madhuranthakar should be crowned. At the time, he had not been privy to the details of events that had taken place in the past. Even though he knew that the fake Madhuranthakar was not Kandaradhithar's son, he believed that he was the child born to Mandhakini and Sundara Chozhar. The misconception served to be his stumbling block; it was why he found himself obliged to change his behaviour.

In the end, we also saw a great change come over Arulmozhi Varmar, the person whom this story marked out to be the most honest character of all, one determinedly aligned with the truth. The prince who had shunned the throne all along, insistent in his stand that he did not want to stake his claim to succession, has now changed his mind. 'I will wear the crown!' he proclaims, ensuring that his will is made public. Surely it is unnecessary for us to point out that time and circumstances are the culprits for this change as well?

Yes. Arulmozhi Thevar's speech left his audience in a daze of shock and surprise. They felt their hearts grow lighter with peace, too. Each person assembled had felt certain, deep down in their hearts, that none but Ponniyin Selvan had both eligibility and right to ascend the Chozha throne. They were aware, too, that the people of the great Chozha *samrajyam* wished for the same outcome. For many reasons, no one could muster the courage to speak their mind that none but Ponniyin Selvar must be anointed the crown.

Now Ponniyin Selvar himself had come forward to address Periya Pazhuvettarayar. "I shall wear the crown!" he had declared. "None but your venerable hands must place it upon my head!" His proclamation sowed peace and happiness in every heart. "A good decision has been made at last!" each thought in delight and relief. "We've been spared the thorny chore of reaching a resolution!"

We are no stranger to the extraordinary magnetism that shone in Ponniyin Selvar, that electrifying charisma that robbed one of the ability to speak out against him. Why, we even saw Chinna Pazhuvettarayar - the dauntless Thalapathy with a heart hewn of solid diamond - bowing his head in deference and welcoming the prince with heartfelt praises!

Periya Pazhuvettarayar grew aware that it was Ponniyin Selvar who had thwarted his attempt at self-sacrifice. He understood the meaning behind his speech. The Ilavarasar's words and actions had melted away his heart. His great body trembled and shivered, overcome by the emotions assailing him. His eyes milled with tears. His tongue failed him.

Periya Pazhuvettarayar struggled to gather himself. "Shining scion of the Chozha clan!" he began at last, his voice breaking with emotion. "Ponniyin Selva! Your words bring me immeasurable joy. I intended to beg you to accept the crown, myself. I held my tongue, deeming myself unfit to make that request of you, vile traitor to the Chozha clan that I am. Your *periya paatanaar* Kandaradhitha Chakravarthy made an arrangement before his demise. That great man was insistent that none but his brother's descendants should ascend the throne. We worked to act against his desire. Tainted by the ill will we nursed within our black hearts, we sought to crown Madhuranthaka Thevar in defiance of the wishes of that incomparable gem of a Siva *bhaktha*, tainted with the ill will we nursed within ourselves. Your father acquiesced to the plan, too. If our aim had been fulfilled, it would have been an unspeakable catastrophe - my very viscera shrinks and churns at the thought! *Ilavarase*! *You* hold the right to the Chozha throne that your father sits upon. When you were a child, I took care of you and played with you. I have carried you upon these very chest and shoulders. I would see the marvellous signs upon your noble person, making a note of the lines of fortune embellishing your palms. "You will rise to be the king of kings, the emperor who rules over the earth!" I would say. Ah, I have spoken often with great joy of the time that mother Kaveri herself carried you to safety in her arms when you fell into her waters from the rooftop. It is only in these three wretched years past that I have turned traitor, for my heart was soiled with toxic love, wrath and rancour. Ponniyin Selva," he continued, gazing at the prince in anguish, "I have lost all eligibility to lift the bejewelled crown and place it upon your noble head as you grace the Chozha throne. My hands are unworthy of the privilege. The sole virtue they are now suited for is to slay me as atonement for my crimes!"

"No, no!" erupted alarmed voices in that hallowed *manthiralosanai* sabha. "That must never happen!"

"*Mama*!" cried out Sundara Chozhar in agitation. "What terrible words you speak! What a heinous thing you propose to do! What treachery do you believe you have inflicted upon the Chozha clan? It is naught, truly! You only sought to seat upon the throne my uncle's son instead of my own. Why, my *periya thanthai*'s son has a greater claim to the Chozha crown than my own children, after all! It is not too late even now. If you grant me the permission to speak my heart…"

"My liege!" interrupted the Mudhanmandhiri Aniruddhar, "the four corners of the kingdom reverberate with zealous cries calling for Arulmozhi Varmar to wear the crown. Even Kandaradhitha Thevar's noble son, who has been living unbeknownst to us all these days, is of the same opinion. Ponniyin Selvan has made up his mind, too. There is little use in deliberating a different solution," he said.

"I will not agree to such a solution either!" declared a spirited Senthan Amudhan, the new Madhuranthaka Thevar.

"My son speaks true," said Sembian Maadeviyaar. "There is little need to think of alternatives henceforth."

"*Annaiye*, there is none here who can speak against your words. Let things unfold as God wills them," replied Sundara Chozhar. "Even so, it is gravely unjust that Pazhuvoor *mama* should seek to kill himself claiming to have betrayed the clan! How can it be treachery to the Chozha clan when he endeavoured only to crown your noble son?"

Periya Pazhuvettarayar cleared his throat before he spoke. "*Ayya*, hear my words. Listen, listen now to the terrible catastrophe that would have come to pass if my endeavours had come to fruition! I had wished to give up my breath without speaking these very words. I hesitated in my confession, for I did not want to wound the good heart of my brother Kalanthaka Kantar, who has never wished for anything but the good of the Chozha *samrajyam* even in his dreams. Even so, I have now steeled my heart to the truth. Chakravarthy, the person we sought to seat upon the Chozha throne thinking him to be the great Kandaradhithar's noble son is none but the son of the hereditary nemesis of the Chozha clan - Veera Pandiyan!"

The halls echoed with stricken cries at these terrible words. "*Ayyo*!" they wailed. "No, that cannot be true!"

Periya Pazhuvettarayar regarded them all gravely. "It will be hard for you to believe this. I wouldn't have believed it myself if I hadn't heard it with my own ears. King of kings! I find myself compelled to once again speak of my abject humiliation! The maiden whom I had been entranced by these past three years, the damsel whose beauty proved to be naught but an insidious trap of love and enchantment, the woman in whose hands I devoted the very authority of my own palace - she is none but Veera Pandiyan's own daughter! I heard her confess this very truth to Aditha Karikalar. She had come to the Pazhuvoor palace only to sate her revenge upon Aditha Karikalar for slaying Veera Pandiyar. She had been biding her time all along. That vile, wretched sinner plotted along with the conspirators to kill Aditha Karikalan and seat Veera Pandiyar's own son on the Chozha throne! That unspeakable consequence did not come to pass by the grace of our deity, the goddess Durga Devi." His eyes misted over. "It was none but Durga Parameswari who sent that Vaanar warrior to me. It was that very youth who helped me learn of these frightening, horrific secrets. I had wanted to question him further and learn a few more facts, in truth. This young Sambuvaraiyan has killed him and abandoned him to the cold waters of the Vadavaaru, the miserable idiot!" he finished, his fists clenched in anger and despair.

Periya Pazhuvettarayar's admission sent his audience into a state of pure shock. Only Kandamaaran found his tongue and the pluck to speak up. "*Ayya*, isn't Vandhiyathevan part of the cabal of conspirators, in any case? What crime can there be in my killing him with a spear?" he asked defensively.

Periya Pazhuvettaryar swung to face him, enraged.

"*Ayya*," interrupted Aniruddhar meekly, "he merely claims to have killed the Vaanar warrior. How can we be certain that the man his spear struck was, in fact, Vandhiyathevan?"

"The truth may perhaps come to light if the waters of the Vadavaaru change course and flow swiftly westwards, carrying to us the corpse of the man who died!" said Parthibendra quietly.

"And who knows? Perhaps the Vadavaaru may yet change its course and surge downstream!" remarked the Mudhanmandhiri

Aniruddhar enigmatically.

As if in testimony to these astonishing words, a soaking wet, bedraggled Vandhiyathevan appeared in the *manthiralosanai sabha* at that very moment, dripping water onto the floor. The dishevelled youth looked stricken and terrified, giving the dazed onlookers the impression that the dead warrior's body that had drowned in the waters had risen once again to walk under the enchantment of eldritch sorcery.

"Aha!" cried the Mudhanmandhiri in some triumph. "The waters of the Vadavaaru have changed course after all, it seems. It has brought back to life and delivered to us the man who died!"

It behooves us to inform our valued readers how Vandhiyathevan came to be there at that precise moment and in that terribly ungroomed state. Once Ponniyin Selvar, Kundhavai Devi and the rest had departed the chamber, leaving him to his thoughts, the Vaanar warrior had quickly grown quite glum and weary. Vandhiyathevan - once so eager to stun the world with exploits of courage and daring - found himself bitterly ruing the fact that he was now relegated to a state that evoked naught but pity and compassion. He came to the damning conclusion that confinement to the palace *anthappuram* was a fate far worse than that of imprisonment in the underground dungeons. With Ponniyin Selvar by his side, he may be allowed to go unpunished even if he was charged with the crime of killing Karikalar. But the palace occupants would forever harbour suspicion on his account. They would look upon him as a stained creature, a thing of dishonour and shame. The kindness and support Ilaiya Piratti bestowed on him would doubtless be corralled within their limits; surely, he could never again dream of clasping the hand of the noble sister of Ponniyin Selvar in marriage, the very Ponniyin Selvar who would soon be crowned the Chakravarthy of the Chozha *samrajyam*! The women of the palace would treat him with disdain as a wretched servant who had committed a crime and was granted a pardon. The ministers and commanders would look upon him in revulsion. Further, the sentiments of those in the kingly clan were liable to change. Who knew how much longer Arulmozhi Varmar would continue to lend him his support?

Aha! If he had mounted the horse near Senthan Amudhan's hut as he had intended, he would have doubtless reached Kodikkarai by now. Why, he would have reached the Eezham isle!... Who could have been the people he had seen riding away on the horses when he was attacked by the *vaithiyar's* son? One was Karuthiruman, dubbed the madman. He was no madman, in truth; in fact, he was possessed with a frightfully fiendish wit and cunning. Who was his mysterious companion though?... They say, don't they, that Madhuranthaka Thevar is nowhere to be found? Couldn't the second man have been the missing prince? Yes, yes! It had to have been him! There must be a deeper reason why the pair escaped together. Ah, if the people here only knew who that old Madhuranthakar Thevar truly was, how stunned they would be!... What would happen when the pair reached Eezha Naadu? But of course - the man who holds the claim to the Imperial Crown of the Pandiya clan and the ancient gemstone necklace will finally get his hands on the treasures! He is likely to wage a war to reclaim his kingdom, with the support of his ally Maghindan. If only this course of events could be thwarted… why, none but he could stop these things! What was the point even of cowering away in this palace *anthappuram* and leading the wretched life of a stowaway?

Vandhiyathevan walked in circles around the chamber, turning these thoughts over in his head. He would often stride to the latticed window to eagerly look outside. The chamber he was in lay in a corner on the upper storey of the palace. The Vadavaaru followed a course skirting this property; here, the palace boundary was none but the very boundary of the Thanjai fort. If he were to jump from the window, he would fall straight into the swift waters of the Vadavaaru flowing below. With a little effort, he could also climb down the wall to reach the Vadavaaru waters. Beneath the upper storey he was on lay an entrance to a series of broad steps that lead the palace women to the river for their daily bath. Vandhiyathevan did not know how to reach the entrance from his chamber on the upper storey. The old women and young princesses of the young *anthappuram* certainly knew the way. But if he were to slip away, he had to do so without their knowledge. Vandhiyathevan was lingering at the window, musing upon his peculiar problem, when he saw a scene in the distance that jolted him out of his reverie.

In the gardens of the palace neighbouring the one he was in was a girl with dishevelled hair, running around the grounds in a state of manic frenzy. *Aha! That seems to be Periya Pazhuvettarayar's garden, doesn't it?... Yes, yes, it is certainly that very garden! Who is that maiden running around in hysteria? Ishwara! It seems to be Manimekalai! What has happened to her? Why does she run as one possessed?* Vandhiyathevan suddenly recalled with a twinge the timely aid she afforded him the night Karikalar lost his life at the palace in Kadambur. His heart twisted with grief. Two old women ran after her, panting and wheezing in their attempts to catch her. They were clearly at a gross disadvantage, for they were soon left behind. They had no hope of catching up to Manimekalai. *There! She has now reached the outer boundary wall.* As Vandhiyathevan watched, Manimekalai swifty clambered up a small, sturdy tree that grew along the side of the boundary wall. *Ayyo! What is she doing? There, shining in her hand - that is a small dagger! What does she plan to do with it? Merciful lord, she has fallen head over heels into the river waters!*

On an earlier occasion, Manimekalai and Nandhini had toppled into the Veera Narayana lake. Vandhiyathevan had first sought to go to Manimakelai's aid but ended up bringing Nandhini ashore in his arms. He now recalled with a pang how crushed Manimekalai had seemed; the memory of that incident swelled and disappeared in his heart in the span of a single second. Vandhiyathevan could not stand to remain idle after that. He leaped down from the balcony on the upper storey of the palace into the swiftly surging river below.

As he dove into the water, he choked upon the impact and lost his breath; he struggled to regain his faculties and looked all about him. Yes - there were steps close to the spot where he fell, leading to a small *mandapam* which housed an entrance to the palace. Manimekalai had jumped from the boundary walls directly opposite this very edifice. Thankfully, Vandhiyathevan was located downstream. If Manimekalai came floating upon the waters, she would have to pass this spot.

Vandhiyathevan floundered in the waters as he struggled to reach the riverbank. Once ashore, he briskly strode upstream. *Aha! There comes Manimekalai, bobbing upon the waters! Does she live yet? Or is that a lifeless body? Ayyo!* Despair clawed at Vandhiyathevan as he confronted the horrifying possibility that he may once again be dealt the misfortune of carrying in his arms the lifeless body of one who had bestowed him with love and affection. The maiden had shown him such fondness and care! As her limp body floated towards him upon the waters, he thought he heard the breeze carrying to him the haunting strains of the beautiful song she had sung while playing the *yazh* in the *mandapam* of the Veera Narayana lake. The unbidden memory stung Vandhiyathevan, plunging him into boundless grief.

Vandhiyathevan struggled to recover his senses and shook off the paralyzing grip of sadness. He leaped into the water and swam towards Manimekalai, gathering her in his arms. *Oh ye gods! Save this poor maiden's life! I will visit every temple in Chozha Naadu and prostrate myself upon the sacred ground of every shrine in gratitude! I shall visit every Siva temple, Vishnu temple, Amman and Ayyanar temple - I shall give thanks to every known power of the divine! Only, pray, save the life of this innocent maiden, whose heart knows no guile but sweetness!*

Vandhiyathevan brought Manimekalai ashore to the riverbank steps, praying with all his might to the gods above. The Vaanar warrior had already been to the gates of death and back from the wound he had sustained under the impact of the spear; the shock to his body from the sudden stress of diving into the swiftly flowing river had weakened him further. Manimekalai too had been heavier than usual, for her clothes were soaking wet from her time in the water. When Vandhiyathevan carried her in his arms across the river, he discovered that he had to fight to retain his breath. Convinced that it was impossible to carry her any further, he gently laid her down upon a broad step. He wondered what he ought to do next. Manimekalai's body breathed life yet, but he would not be able to bring her back to consciousness. A woman's help was needed. He had to go to the palace and fetch someone from there.

Vandhiyathevan spotted the entrance to the palace directly in front of him, ahead of the steps. He sprinted towards the door. Finding it locked, he flung himself against it with every last ounce of strength remaining in his body. Fortunately, the latch gave way and the door swung open. Vandhiayathevan ran through the passage. For a short while, the path was narrow and strained. Soon, he spied the palace courtyards and verandahs. But there was no one in any of these places. Vandhiyathevan ran in a blind panic, hither and thither, calling for help at the top of his lungs. "Is there no one here?" he shouted. "Is there no one here to render urgent help to a maiden in need?" Finally, he reached the doorway to a great *mandapam* where stood two stern guards who tried their best to stop him from entering the halls. Vandhiyathevan pushed his way through and tore inside, only to see before him the Chakravarthy seated upon the exalted Chozha throne, surrounded by an august group of noblemen and women. He stopped in his tracks, momentarily stunned. Realizing that the first woman he saw was none other than Poonguzhali, Vandhiyathevan plucked up courage. "Samudhra Kumari! Samudhra Kumari!" he cried out in urgent tones of despair. "Manimekalai took a spill into the river! Come at once and save her!"

77

A VETERAN TREE FALLS

Vandhiyathevan had inadvertently stumbled into the royal court through the entrance meant for the palace women. Natural, then, that it was the women in the assembly who first caught his eye. Poonguzhali, who was standing at the rear, turned around when she heard the noise behind her. She started when she spotted the thoroughly drenched Vandhiyathevan, scruffy and wild-eyed. The Vaanar youth lost no time in breathlessly recounting to her the misfortune that had befallen Manimekalai. Poonguzhali listened in shock to the agitated report, as did Kundhavai Devi and Vanathi, who were close by. The three maidens ran out the doorway that Vandhiyathevan had entered by, hurrying along the trail of water he had left in his wake to retrace his path.

Vandhiyathevan's words were not clear to the rest of the assembly in the *mandapam*. Some only heard the word, "Help!" Kandamaaran and Parthibendran did not even hear this plea. All they heard was garbled, unintelligible cries.

At first, the pair thought that the wild figure that had entered through the *anthappuram* entrance was the spirit of the dead Vandhiyathevan. In those days, it was a common belief that the souls of those who met an untimely death did not depart this world but roamed around in restlessness and despair as a ghostly spirit. "The Vadavaaru may yet change course and flow downstream!" - these words had hardly left Aniruddhar's mouth when a dishevelled Vandhiyathevan appeared out of thin air, soaked to the bone. Hardly surprising then, that the alarmed pair took him to be an unearthly wraith.

The illusion was dispelled soon enough, for the panicked guards chasing after Vandhiyathevan entered in some excitement and caught hold of him.

"Chakravarthy, pray, pardon us!" they wailed. "This lunatic came tearing through the door leading to the river steps. He paid us no heed even though we did our best to stop him!" They tugged at Vandhiyathevan, trying to drag him away with them.

Ammamma! How wretchedly strong this Vandhiyathevan's lifeline must be! No matter what the danger is, he somehow contrives to slip away unscathed! Parthibendran stared at him in rank astonishment, his heart burning with rage.

He has run here blind without understanding where he was headed! He must not be allowed another chance to escape. Parthibendran made up his mind in the blink of an eye. Forgetting even that he was in the honourable court of the illustrious Chakravarthy himself, he leapt to Vandhiyathevan's side and roughly grabbed his shoulder.

"He is no lunatic! He is a murderer! He is the vicious, treacherous wretch who killed Aditha Karikalan!" roared Parthibendran, dismissing the guards with excited gestures. Kandamaaran came rushing behind Parthibendran to harshly grip Vandhiyathevan's other shoulder. The two unceremoniously dragged him in front of Sundara Chozha Chakavarthy, who was seated upon the throne of justice.

The Chakravarthy studied Vandhiyathevan. "You say that this boy, face as innocent as a lamb, killed my son? I find that hard to believe!" he remarked. "Wasn't he the one who delivered to me an olai from Aditha Karikalan?"

"Yes, *Ayya*! It was he who brought the missive," said Chinna Pazhuvettarayar. "It was also he who furtively met Nandhini Devi in her veiled palanquin outside the Thanjai fort and spoke to her in secret. He was the one, too, who slipped away from the fort on an earlier occasion. Even now, he has managed to escape from the underground dungeons!"

"He was the one who basely stabbed me in my back and turned tail after wounding me grievously!" burst out Kandamaaran.

"Why, wasn't it this very man that you had claimed to kill with your spear, just a short while ago?" asked the Mudhanmandhiri Aniruddhar.

"Yes, I did! How could I have known that you had helped this murderer all along, that you had saved his wretched life and are now sheltering him here?" replied a bitter Kandamaaran.

All this while, Ponniyin Selvan stood unmoving. The prince was under the impression that Vandhiyathevan had attempted to escape once again by jumping into the river. He thought that the Vaanar warrior had scrambled ashore upon the discovery that he lacked experience in the art of swimming; he assumed that the youth had then rushed headlong into the assembly in a rash panic. It took the prince a while to bring under control the anger that surged through him.

Upon Kandamaaran's words, Ponniyin Selvar stepped forward and majestically stood by Vandhiyathevan's shoulder.

"Father, this Vallathu prince is my bosom friend. He saved me from the jaws of danger at Ilankai and once more in the midst of the high, wild sea. It gives me naught but joy to see him alive. Accusing him is akin to accusing me!" he declared, eyes flashing.

The prince's voice rang with pure authority and power. The assembly fell silent for a while.

"Ponniyin Selva!" began the Mudhanmandhiri Aniruddhar, "pray, think! The man claimed to have fallen to the young Sambuvaraiyar's spear has now appeared in our midst. He has already been charged with the crime. Wouldn't it be better to conduct a formal inquiry and bring the truth to light?"

"Yes, *Ayya*!" added Parthibendran. "You will soon ascend the exalted Chozha throne. You have every authority to punish or pardon any criminal. However, pray consider - is it prudent to declare unnecessary the due trial? Would it not give rise to avoidable suspicion?"

"Our prince must keep another matter in mind, too!"exclaimed Kandamaaran. "Rumours abound claiming that it was the prince himself who dispatched Vandhiyathevan to slay his own brother. Surely, we must strive to give no room for such talk!"

Kandamaaran's words struck terror in the assembly. The audience froze where they stood, a look of horror spreading across their faces. Sambuvaraiyar strode forward with purpose and slapped Kandamaaran hard across the cheek. "*Adei*, moron!" he growled, livid with fury. "At this rate, you will be the sole reason our ancient clan is wiped off the face of the earth! There is none to equal you in blurting drivel with no sense of place or time!"

Kandamaaran stared at his father, red-eyed and stricken. His lips quivered. It is hard to say what he would have said or done the following minute. Fortunately, Periya Pazhuvettarayar came forward at that precise moment and laid a pacifying hand on Sambuvaraiyar.

He cleared his throat. "*Sambuvaraiyare!*" he began, "Your son has made sufficient atonement for all his thoughtless deeds. He has rendered exceptional service to the Chozha *samrajyam*. When you learn the facts, you will feel nothing but pride for having sired such a son. Do not harbour anger against him!" Periya Pazhuvettarayar gently pulled Sambuvaraiyar aside. He looked intently at the young Sambuvaraiyar. "You said, didn't you, that you threw a spear at this very Vandhiyathevan and killed him?" he asked. "Can you claim with certainty that this was the man you saw on horseback, crossing the river?"

"*Ayya*," broke in the Mudhanmandhiri, "pray, allow my disciple to contribute his account regarding this matter."

Azhwarkkadiyaan stepped forward. "My lords! I freely admit to my crime. This Vallauthu prince standing before you did not mount the horse and escape. He lay wounded and incapacitated, having saved the true Madhuranthaka Thevar from an assassin. I was the one who put him in a veiled palanquin and brought him into the fort. He has been here these past four days." He glanced at Kandamaaran. "The young Sambuvaraiyar could not have hurled his spear at him."

"I thought as much, *Sambuvaraiyare!*" said Periya Pazhuvettarayar. "Pardon your son for all his past mistakes. Truly I tell you, he has rendered splendid service to the Chozha *samrajyam!* The man he killed with his spear had to have been none other than Veera Pandiyan's son. It was only since that very evening that the old Madhuranthakar has been missing, is it not? It stands to reason that the man who tried to flee had to have been none but him. Ah, what an unspeakable calamity the Lord has shielded this *rajyam* from!" he declared.

Even as the assembly struggled to process the shock they felt from these words, the venerable old man began to speak once again. "Chakravarthy! Pray, hearken to the last words of this humble servant of yours. The falling star disappeared after marking its evil.

Your brave son Aditha Karikalar also passed from our sight into the great unknown. Nonetheless, the exalted Chozha *samrajyam*, nourished and strengthened by the very blood of your forefathers and mine, looks forward now to a bright, flourishing future. The glorious dynasty will proliferate and grow to reach the very crest of glory and greatness. This destiny is why the Chozha clan and the noble *samrajyam* have escaped terrible perils, the likes of which are unheard of even in our ballads and epics." He paused. "It is none but this Vandhiyathevan of the Vaanar clan who made such an escape possible. It was on his account that my blinded eyes, dazzled for so long by love and ardour, began to regain their clear sight. He happened to come to Sambuvaraiyar's palace on the very eve we had planned to hold our covert summit at midnight. I confess I felt shame that I was reduced to hiding my actions from such a young lad as he. Later, my brother reported to me that the youth had met with Nandhini outside the Thanjai fort and had exchanged a secret conversation with her. He also added that the young man had escaped from the fort with Nandhini's aid. A niggling suspicion sprung in my heart that very moment, growing more insistent by the day. I began to think about the strange events that were happening all around me and the reasons behind their occurrence. Though the darkness of illusion often clouded my mind, the shining rays of truth attempted to pierce through the mirage and illuminate its falsity. Finally, by the grace of Durga Parameswari, I learned the vile conspiracy plotted by the Madurai *abathudhavis*. If I had not chanced to overhear their exchange from hiding, I would not have believed it myself! Even after that damning incident, your beloved daughter Ilaiya Piratti threw me off guard with a baffling piece of news. She claimed that Nandhini was her own sister and bade me do her no harm. I was doubtful of the claim. I wondered if perhaps she, too, had been deceived by the ploy at hand. I determined, therefore, to go to Kadambur in disguise to learn the truth myself. The *kalaamuga saivars* had proclaimed me to be their leader.

Listen, my liege, to my ignominy!" Periya Pazhuvettarayar's voice grew strained. "Nandhini had sown in my heart the treacherous, vile desire to become the Chakravarthy of the Chozha *samrajyam* myself! The *kalaamuga saivars* stoked that foul desire. They wished me to feign anointing Madhuranthakan the crown prince, so that I could later chase him away and make myself Chakravarthy. Idumbankari, a kalamugar himself, was a servant at Sambuvaraiyar's palace. He served the Madurai *abathudhavis* as their spy. I terrorized him to draw information from him. I learned that the Madurai *abathudavis* were, at that very moment, in the *vettai mandapam* at the Kadambur palace. I also learned that Aditha Karikalar had gone to Nandhini's chamber, where Manimekalai and Vandhiyathevan were in hiding." The venerable old man's voice shook. "The burning desire to eavesdrop upon Nandhini and Karikalar's exchange swayed my will. I craved to learn the truth about Nandhini, too. I knew well that there lay a secret passage to Nandhini's chamber through the *yazh kalanjiyam*. I went there at the right time, in fact. I learned the truth about Nandhini from her own mouth; I also discovered that Aditha Karikalar was faultless. I learnt of the dreadful plot that Nandhini and her collaborators had hatched, seeking revenge for Veera Pandiyan's death. I tried to thwart their evil design. But I could not win over fate. I became prey to the wretched misfortune of seeing Karikalar fall lifeless, in front of my own eyes…"

Periya Pazhuvettarayar covered his face with his hands and wept with abandon. Heavy sobs wracked his great body like the choppy waves roiling upon a stormy sea. None in the assembly could summon the courage to speak. Every heart melted on seeing the raw agony of that formidable old warrior.

Periya Pazhuvettarayar gathered the will of his diamond heart and swallowed the sobs surging from within his throat. He removed his hands from his face and looked all about him. "Aditha Karikalar died because of fate. But the grace of Durga Parameswari has helped the quick-witted Ponniyin Selvar escape the peril unharmed. My liege!" he cried aloud, his voice growing strong with purpose. "Chakravarthy! Brahmmarayare! Chieftains! Make Arulmozhi ascend the Chozha throne and place the crown upon his head! Under his aegis, this noble samrajyam will rise to an exalted state of eminence!"

"*Ayya*, your desire shall be fulfilled," said the Mudhanmandhiri Aniruddhar. "We feared that Ponniyin Selvar would be the barrier to this resolution. Chozha Naadu's fortune has held it in good stead - he has come forward to accept the crown of his own accord! But," he added gently, "you have not yet told us how Karikalar met his death."

"Why must you ask? How does it matter who killed him? I tell you, the truth is that his death was naught but Fate's design!" cried the brave old man in a quivering voice.

"Unless the truth is known, this youth will forever bear the taint of accusation," replied the Mudhanmandhiri, glancing at Vandhiyathevan. "He will bear the punishment for Karikalan's death."

"Ah!" cried out Periya Pazhuvettarayar. "The taint of accusation, you say? Who accuses him?"

"Kandamaaran and Parthibendran."

"Ah! Half-wits, utter dunces!" roared the venerable old man, swivelling to confront them. "Kandamaara! Parthibendra! On what basis do you accuse this young man of the crime? What evidence do you have that he killed Aditha Karikalar?"

It was Aniruddhar who came forward with the response to his incensed question. "Vandhiyathevan was hiding at the fateful moment in Nandhini Devi's chamber. Manimekalai was there, too. The maiden claims that she was the one who killed the prince. However, that cannot be the case. The knife she produced as proof showed no traces of blood. She must have made such a confession to shield Vandhiyathevan. She could have seen Vandhiyathevan kill Karikalar from her hiding spot, couldn't she not?"

"If Manimekalai did not kill him, how then could Vandhiyathevan have done the deed?" demanded Periya Pazhuvettarayar. "What weapon could he have used?"

"This very one! This twisted dagger, whose blade is encrusted with dried blood!" declared Parthibendran, producing the curious, twisted knife we have seen before.

When Vandhiyathevan had fallen senseless having saved Karikalar's lifeless body from the burning palace, it was Parthibendran who had taken the twisted dagger from his person. He had kept it safe all along. He now showed it to the assembly.

Periya Pazhuvettarayar looked at him. "Ah," he breathed. "Hand me the dagger."

He took the knife in his hand and examined it closely. "Ah! This is Idumbankari's knife!" he murmured softly.

He looked up. "Kandhamaara! Parthibendra! The three of us must circle Vandhiyathevan in respect and bow down to his very feet! Like this pitiful old coot, the both of you were also snared in the enchanting web of love and allure woven by Nandhini. But this youth was the only one who evaded its clutches. He did not throw this knife. He did not kill Aditha Karikalar either!" declared Periya Pazhuvettarayar.

"What makes you so certain in your claim?" asked the Mudhanmandhiri Aniruddhar.

"I am quite certain for I know well who threw this knife that slayed Karikalar!"

"Who? Who?" erupted voices in the chamber.

"Yes, yes," replied Periya Pazhuvettarayar softly. "The time has come to bring the truth to light. There is little point in delaying the inevitable. Listen, then!" he thundered. "This youth was hiding in the *yazh kalanjiyam*. I climbed down to the halls and snuck up behind him; I gripped his neck and throttled him so that he would not see me and make a sound. His eyes popped out of his head and he fell to the ground, senseless. He could not have even known who killed Aditha Karikalar at that fateful moment."

"Who, then? Who killed Karikalar?"

Periya Pazhuvettaryar ran a trembling finger over the twisted dagger he held in his hand. He held it aloft. "It was I," he proclaimed aloud, "who took this twisted knife from Idumbankari. I was the one who threw the dagger, with my own hand! These two hands, descendants of a noble lineage that crowned the Chozha Chakravarthy through generations - these two hands threw the wretched dagger! But I did not intend to throw it at the Ilavarasar Karikalar. I threw it at Nandhini. I hurled it with all my might at that demoness, thirsting to kill her, she who trapped and blinded me in her web of love only to abandon me to the dark abyss of treachery! My aim faltered and the knife struck Karikalar..."

Horrified cries resounded in the court. "*Ayyo*!"

Periya Pazhuvettarayar went limp. "I have stained with dishonour the services that the noble Pazhuvoor clan have performed for the Chozha clan through generations," he said hoarsely, weariness and grief weighing down his tone. "I do not know how I will wash that ignominy away!"

"*Anna*!" erupted Chinna Pazhuvettarayar, drawing his knife in a swift motion. "I shall wipe away that blemish this very minute!" He rushed to his brother, gripping his knife. "We have both taken a vow to mete out revenge to those who betray the Chozha clan, whoever they may be!" he roared. "I shall now fulfill that oath. I shall slay you this very second and wipe away the sin upon our clan!" cried Chinna Pazhuvettarayar and raised his knife.

"No, don't!" shouted Sundar Chozha Chakravarthy in alarm. "Do not spill blood here!"

The Ilavarasar Arulmozhi Varmar and the Mudhanmandhiri Aniruddhar leapt into action and held back Chinna Pazhuvettarayar's hands.

"*Thambi*," said Periya Pazhuvettarayar softly, "I will not give you the trouble of washing away the stain I have wrought upon our clan. I will not subject you to the blame of being the younger brother who slayed his elder. Here, I shall fulfill my oath to Durga Parameswari by my own hands!" The grand old man raised the twisted dagger he held in his hands and brutally brought it down upon his own chest. Because he had sheathed the sword he had earlier drawn, the assembly had assumed that he had given up his old intention. No one had dreamed that he would use the twisted dagger he had taken from Parthibendran.

"*Ayyo*! Don't!" shouted Arulmozhi. He made to rush to his side, but it was too late. Periya Pazhuvettarayar had achieved his will.

He collapsed to the ground. He fell as a grand old deodar, an ancient growth that had seen ages pass by as it pierced the sky with its branches and the ground with its roots. He crumbled like a veteran tree that had been ripped out by its hoary roots.

"*Ah*! *Adada*!" came stricken cries that resounded in the chamber.

Some came flying towards the fallen Periya Pazhuvettarayar. Others ran towards Sundara Chozha Chakravarthy, who had slumped down in his throne, eyes closed.

The *mandhiralosanai* sabha dispersed.

That night, many came to pay their respects to Periya Pazhuvettarayar as he lay dying. The Chakravarthy, Arulmozhi Varmar, Aniruddhar and Ilaiya Piratti Kundhavai too went to see him. The Chakravarthy and the rest celebrated the great services that Periya Pazhuvettarayar had rendered the Chozha clan and the Chozha *samrajyam*. They warmly spoke of the brave exploits of valour he had achieved in his younger days on the battlefields in countless wars. They praised the heroic feat he wrought at Thakkolam, where he united a scattered Chozha army to wrest victory from the jaws of defeat, and commended his skillful service during his term as Dhanaadhikaari of Chozha Naadu. Not a single word did they breathe of the events that had transpired over the past three years. Having paid their last respects, the august visitors took their leave. The four royals withdrew to an area in Periya Pazhuvettarayar's chamber that was out of his line of sight. They watched.

Chinna Pazhuvettarayar brought in Azhwarkkadiyaan Nambi at that very moment. The Thalapathy made him sit in front of Periya Pazhuvettarayar, taking his own seat beside him as well.

Periya Pazhuvettarayar peered at Azhwarkkadiyaan with cloudy eyes that were fast losing their sight. "Aha!" he rasped. "Why has this Vaishnavan come here? *Thambi*, I have no wish to go to Vaikuntam! I yearn for the lotus feet of Siva!"

"*Ayya*, the holy day of Vaikunta Ekadasi dawns on the morrow. Crave Kailayam you may - but you must pass by Vaikuntam, I am afraid," replied Thirumalai gently.

"There is no need for that! Go back to your Maha Vishnu and…"

"*Ayya*," broke in Azhwarkkadiyaan deferentially, "I am not here as Vishnu's messenger. I come bearing a message from my sister."

"Who is your sister?"

"I speak of Nandhini, who lived with me for many days as my own sister. *Ayya*, Nandhini bade me convey her gratitude to you. She asks me to thank you for assuming the blame for Karikalan's death so that she is spared the accusation. She also asks me to tell you that no matter how many births she takes upon the earth, she will forever remain mindful of her gratitude to you!" said Azhwarkkadiyaan.

"Aha!" breathed Periya Pazhuvettarayar. "Does she yet think like that? Let her derive happiness from the thought. However great the treachery and evil she brought to bear upon me, I am unable to forget her." He paused. "She is the daughter, isn't she, of the virtuous woman who sacrificed her life to save the Chakravarthy's? Perchance… perhaps she really will come in search of me in our next lives."

His face, darkened already by the shadows of death, drew into a small smile.

"*Vaishnavare!* I must tell the truth to someone. I shall tell it to you. The knife that I threw did not strike the Ilavarasar; he had collapsed to the ground before that moment. I assumed the blame of killing the Ilavarasar not only to spare Nandhini the accusation; there is a far greater reason for my confession. Come closer, I shall tell you the truth!" His trembling hands groped for Azhwarkkadiyaan's and clasped them. "Your friend Vandhiyathevan is a wonderful boy. The Chozha clan is greatly indebted to him. He has stolen Ilaiya Piratti's heart. I was wrong nurse anger against Ilaiya Piratti. If I hadn't made amends by accepting the blame upon myself, someone or the other will forever come forward to challenge Vandhiyathevan's honour. Now none will have the courage to say such a thing. *Vaishnavane!* Someday, pray ask Ilaiya Piratti to grace me with her pardon - ask her to forgive me for bearing hatred towards her!"

The long speech took its toll upon the old man. He panted and wheezed from the effort. Azhwarkkadiyaan's own heart melted upon hearing his words; would it be surprising to know that Kundhavai Devi, who had been listening to him from her place in the shadows, was overcome with tears?

"*Vaishnavane!*" said the old man in a hoarse voice. "There is yet another matter, one that you must tell the Mudhanmandhiri Brahmmarayar. The Imperial Crown of the Pandiyas and the ancient gemstone necklace must be brought here from Ilankai, one way or another. The right person for the mission is the Vallathu prince! Go along with him and bring back those treasures. A *magudabhishekam* must be conducted for Ponniyin Selvar in Madhurai with this very crown and jewel. Do you hear me? For my sake, pray, make this request to Arulmozhi! Tell him that there is no greater friend to the Chozha clan than the youth! Devi Durga Parameswari! I have fulfilled my holy vow to you! Here, I shall come to your lotus feet! Protect the Chozha clan!"

Periya Pazhuvettarayars voice had dwindled through his speech, growing weaker and softer with every word. With his dying breath, it shrunk into silence once and for all. The venerable patriarch's spark of life passed into darkness.

Hidden Meanings and Explanations

Vaikunta Ekadasi - A holy day on which it is believed that the gates to Lord Vishnu's abode are thrown open to receive devotees.

78

The Parting of Friends

Four horses cantered upto the steps of the Kollidam river. The quartet of majestic steeds each carried a capable warrior upon its back; we're quite familiar with this foursome, for they were none but Parthibendran, Kandamaaran, Vandhiyathevan and Ponniyin Selvar.

The former two intended to cross the Kollidam by boat and travel northwards. The latter was keeping them company to bid them bon voyage. When they reached the river wharf, the four friends dismounted from their steeds.

"Kandhamaara!" said Ponniyin Selvar, landing lightly upon the ground. "I trust that no traces remain of the wrath you once bore your old friend. Or do you yet feel some lingering resentment on his account?"

"*Ayya*, what cause do I have to bear a grudge towards him? I only have reason to regret my past follies!" replied Kandamaaran with feeling. "He has once again offered me his hand in friendship, brushing aside the evil I had done him. Surely there is none to equal him in magnanimity and grace! He even saved my dear sister from a watery grave in the Vadavaaru river - can I ever hope to repay that debt of gratitude in this birth? I confess to being quite bewildered when I think upon how far my mind had been corrupted and why. Ah, that I did not wed Manimekalai to him as I had intended to in the very beginning! Had I done that, she would not be of unsound mind as she is today," he rued.

"Why do you say that? It is naught but short-term amnesia from the trauma of falling into the river. It will soon be on the mend, will it not?" asked the Ilavarasar in concern.

"The affliction does not appear to be mere amnesia," said Kandamaaran miserably. "Manimekalai recalls everyone else; she remembers past events, too. It is only Vandhiyathevan and me that she fails to recognize." His voice cracked with sadness. "My heart breaks when I think of the pure affection she bore for me. '*Ayyo*, I have killed my beloved brother with my own hands!' she cries; her piteous laments resound in my ears yet."

"Why does she lament so? You are alive, are you not?"

"I am alive, yes; would that I had died! Yes, *Ayya*! She believes with all her heart that I have slayed Vandhiyathevan and that she has killed me in turn. She wails in grief one minute, mourning my death; her thoughts then turn to my friend the very next and she keens with abandon - 'Will the river change its course? Will the waters bring back the dead?'" Kandamaaran sighed wearily. "However much we try to convince her, she refuses to accept that I am her brother. She does not recognize Vandhiyathevan either. She asks him who he is and begs to know if he has seen the Vallathu prince!"

"*Adada!*" clucked Parthibendran in genuine sympathy. "If only she knew that Vandhiyathevan is no more the Vallathu prince but the Vallathu king, how happy she would be! That she is cheated of such fortune..."

Kandamaaran turned to Ponniyin Selvar in surprise at these words.

"Yes, my friend. The Chakravarthy has decided to return the lands of Vaanagappaadi Naadu to your friend and make him the Vallathu king." Ponniyin Selvar smiled. "He intends to grant you the region near Vaanagappaadi that the Vaithumparaayars once ruled over. It shall be made a kingdom in its own right and yours to govern. Now the two of you must live next to each other as neighbours - make sure that there arises no more threat to the bond of friendship you bear!"

"There seems to be no limit to the Chakravarthy's compassion!" cried Kandamaaran with feeling. "Then... I don't really need to return to Kadambur, do I?" he asked with some enthusiasm.

"No, you don't. Your old palace is razed down, after all. If you and your family return there, you will be haunted by old memories. Build yourselves a new palace instead, by the southern banks of the Paalaaru. Once your sister regains her health, she can join you there."

"My liege, I doubt if Manimekalai will choose to be with us. Your *paatiyaar* Sembian Maadevi has offered to take her along on a holy temple tour. Manimekalai too has warmed towards Periya Piratti and shows her her great love and affection. Why, even today Periya Piratti has taken my sister along to Thiruvaiyaaru!"

"Yes, they have gone as a rather big group. They are accompanied by my *chitappa* and *chitrannai*, the newly-weds." Ponniyin Selvar suddenly broke into a wide smile. "Listen to this travesty! I must now regard Samudhra Kumari as my *chitrannai*!"

Parthibendran chuckled. "Though, I must say," he remaked, "such a modest wedding as that of Madhuranthakar and Poonguzhali has certainly never taken place in the Chozha clan until now!"

"I intend my own *magudabhishekam* to be as modest as that," replied Arulmozhi.

A droll cry of disbelief escaped Vandhiyathevan. "There's not a prayer of that coming to pass!" he exclaimed.

Ponniyin Selvan turned upon him dramatically, affecting great shock. "What did you say will never come to pass?" he demanded. "My *pattabhishekam*?"

"No, *Ayya*!" protested Vandhiyathevan sheepishly. "I only meant that it is nigh impossible for the coronation to be anything close to modest! The people are already excited for the day - they chatter about little else!"

"My liege! Shouldn't we be present for your coronation, too?" asked Kandamaaran in earnest. "You're sending us away to the north at this time. Talk in Thanjai is that a date for the coronation will be decided as soon as the month of Thai rolls around! Vandhiyathevan is a lucky chap indeed..."

"Nothing of that sort! I am going to send Vandhiyathevan away to Eezham as well," replied Ponniyin Selvar, his eyes twinkling. "My friends, believe me when I tell you that my coronation will not take place without you!"

"We're grateful, *Ayya*! As soon as the date for the coronation is decided, pray send us an *olai* through men on horseback. We shall fly here at once!" said Kandamaaran.

Ponniyin Selvar laid a friendly hand on Kandamaaran's shoulder. "My friend, why worry about that now? Trust me when I tell you that I will not be crowned in your absence. Do not forget why I have accepted to be anointed with the crown. I do not intend to while away pleasant hours in the moonlit terraces of the palace or the lush garden greens. Friends, I have shared with you before the dreams I have nurtured since my sojourn in Eezha Naadu. I shall tell you again - listen! The Chozha *samrajyam* attained a great height in the time of Paranthaka Chakravarthy, my *paatanaar's* father; but it shall surge to even greater heights in ours! Our glorious dynasty shall expand in all the four directions. The Chozha armies must march on and plant the noble tiger flag in all the regions that lie until the banks of the Gangai in the north and the Srivijaya *rajyam* in the far east across the roaring sea! We must seize Malai Naadu in the west and bring under our domain the Lakshadweep isles across the waters, stationing our armies in those realms. I hear reports that a Chera King has surfaced all of a sudden in Malai Naadu. Likewise, some Pandiyan or the other is sure to appear as a challenge in Pandiya Naadu as well. It is none but the Ilankai kings that lend strength to these new Cheras and Pandiyas - we must rout out Magindhan and his forces from their hideaway in the mountain caves of Eezha Naadu; we must capture them and crush their strength for good. The island of Ilankai must be brought under our rule!" The prince looked at each of his riveted friends, his eyes shining. "Do you think it is enough if the *rajyam* expands? We must raise upon our holy soil magnificent temples to Siva and Vishnu, such colossal shrines that will tower over the Buddha stupas of Eezha Naadu. The people who will come after us a thousand years hence in this valorous, glorious kingdom should be left awestruck by the holy work we have achieved in our time. Friends! These dreams *will* come true - they *will* ripen to fruition in my time. I am determined to achieve them. Each one of you must lend me your support. *Parthibendrare!* I have granted you the greatest military post in Chozha Naadu, the very one that my own *thamayanar* Karikalar held - that of the Vadathisai Maathandanaayagar, the Commander of the Northern Forces. You must strive to fulfill your charge well. My brother's untimely death would have doubtless stoked fresh ambition in the hearts of our enemies. The Vengi King and the Rattirakooda King anticipate that Chozha Naadu will crumble from within on account of internal turmoil - they will expect our chieftains to go to battle against each other in a civil war. Our soldiers must stand guard on the Vada Pennai banks as a fortress of iron. Oh, scion of the Pallava clan! Station Kandamaaran there as the Thalapathy and immediately make your way to Kanchi. Prepare as a dwelling befitting the Chakravarthy the *pon maaligai* that my brave brother built. The Chakravarthy wishes to depart to Kanchi as soon as the crown is placed upon my head."

Kandamaaran's eyes filled with tears at these words. "My liege! I have not yet proven my skill upon the battlefield. Yet, you instate me the Thalapathy of the border guard! Am I truly eligible for the station?" he stammered, overwhelmed.

"My friend, the omniscient Lord has granted me a clutch of powers - I have the uncanny knack of identifying the right person for any task! Just as I have instated you the Thalapathy of the Northern Border Forces, I have also made your friend, the Vallathu King, the Thalapathy of the Eezha Forces. I have every confidence that both of you will rise to fulfill your duties with glory!" replied Ponniyin Selvar encouragingly.

"It does seem a rather good idea to send one to the Northern Border and the other to the Southern Border for a little while," mused Parthibendran. "If they were clumped together and you were nowhere around, they may just remember old memories and break into a fresh quarrel!"

"*Ayya*, never again will that happen!" cried Kandamaaran, as he strode to Vandhiyathevan's side. "Friend, you have forgiven me my mistakes, have you not?"

Vandhiyathevan did not reply. Instead, he spread his arms and gathered Kandamaaran into a warm embrace.

The friends wept in silence for a while.

Presently, Parthibendran and Kandamaaran climbed into the boat that was docked at the ready. Ponniyin Selvar and Vandhiyathevan stood watching as the boat sailed halfway across the silver waters. They then mounted their steeds and turned their horses back towards Thanjai.

79

A CHANCE MEETING BY THE ROADSIDE

News spread like wildfire through the cities and towns of the kingdom that Ponniyin Selvar's coronation was to soon take place. The people looked forward to the occasion with breathless eagerness and excitement.

Aditha Karikalan's premature demise, Mandhakini's self-sacrifice, Periya Pazhuvettarayar's fulfillment of his terrible oath - these tragedies weighed down the Chakravarthy, dampening his spirits. Still, his weary heart attained a semblance of comfort at the thought that the troubles arising from the issue of succession had finally reached a resolution and that the chieftains and the people were united in their wish to coronate Arulmozhi Varmar.

When the month of Thai dawned, an auspicious date would be chosen to pass the mantle of the *rajyam* onto Ponniyin Selvar. And then, the Chakravarthy decided, he would withdraw to Kanchi; he would spend the remainder of his days in the *pon maaligai* built for him by his valorous son Karikalan. Hardly surprising then, that Sundara Chozhar too wanted to avoid an ostentatious coronation.

Arulmozhi Varmar fully intended to fulfill his father's wish in this matter. He decided that he would not go forth among the people in the cities and towns until the coronation ceremony had reached a formal conclusion. A direct path from the Kollidam wharf to Thanjai would necessitate travelling through Thiruvaiyaaru town. If Ponniyin Selvar were to pass through that settlement, it was certain that he would be swarmed by a throng of excited townspeople; his presence would invite nothing but ruckus. And so, the pair of friends turned west instead and crossed the Kaveri river. When they reached the waters of the Kudumurutti, they travelled along its bank towards the Thanjai *rajappattai*.

It was a marvellous country, one where five sparkling rivers merrily leapt along their course, one after another. The great reservoirs of water and the lush fields that stretched out before them painted an enchanting sight under the Margazhi skies. The waters gurgled along their path, coquettishly favouring one half of the riverbed; the other half lay dry as a splendid sandbank of earthy hues. The view was lovelier by far than the seasons in which the rivers ran full, gushing forth as they skimmed both their banks. Bountiful groves of coconut trees, areca palms, plantains and sugarcane grew in luxuriant thickets on both sides of the river. Where there were no fields or groves, plump stalks of paddy thrived upon the land, bent low under the weight of the red grains they bore. Here and there, in the still waters of the brooks and ponds, the colourful blooms of lovely lotuses, *kumudam* and *sengazhuneer* stood tall and proud as they vied with each other to flaunt their beauty. It all looked as pretty as a picture.

Vandhiyathevan travelled in silence, entranced by the view. "Friend," remarked Ponniyin Selvar, the wonder palpable in his tone, "can there be another place on earth blessed with such richness and abundance? What an honour it is to be crowned the Chakravarthy of such a lush country! To think that I was refusing such a privilege all along!"

"Hardly surprising, *Ayya*. Often have I heard my elders remark on the capriciousness of the kingly clan!" replied Vandhiyathevan smoothly.

"Ah, you are wicked, to be sure. And ungrateful to boot!" exclaimed Ponniyin Selvar in indignation. "You have not yet thanked me for making you the Thalapathy of the Eezha Naadu forces - and now you reproach me as a man of fickle temperament!"

An earnest look settled on Vandhiyathevan's face as he hastened to reply. "What counts for reproach among the common folk may well be a claim to fame for the royal clan! Today you sentence a man to death; tomorrow you grant him a pardon and make him a Thalapathy. Such noble fickle-mindedness will only serve to glorify the kingly clan, surely? It will invite naught but praises from the people - 'Aha! What a merciful King we have!'"

"True enough," said Ponniyin Selvar, throwing Vandhiyathevan a side-eyed glance. "And yet, a Thalapathy today may well be sentenced to death on the morrow. What would the people say then?"

"Why, they will heap praises upon the King as an impartial administrator of justice - the very reincarnation of the illustrious Manu Needhi Chozhan!"

Ponniyin Selvar burst out laughing. "You will not be surprised then, if I were to snatch back the Vaanagappaadi kingdom that was granted to you as well as the post of the Thalapathy of the Eezha forces?"

"Neither will I be surprised nor will I be upset. Frankly, I am yet unsure whether you bid me go to Eezha Naadu to grant me the lofty station of Thalapathy - or whether it is nothing but a ruse to rid this beautiful Chozha Naadu of my presence!"

Ponniyin Selvar smiled. "I truly am desirous of making one as smart as you the Mudhanmandhiri so that I may have you ever by my side! I rather doubt that the Mudhanmandhiri Aniruddhar would stand aside for you, though."

"If that is the only reason you hesitate, I shall petition the Mudhanmandhiri Aniruddhar myself."

"No," replied Ponniyin Selvar, grinning at the very thought. "There is yet another reason in the way."

"I thought as much."

"And what did you think?"

"That of late you bear a thought in mind but say another thing aloud."

"Vallathu king!" cried out Ponniyin Selvar. "Can you give me one example to justify this accusation?"

"Why not? I can and very nicely, too! Your coronation has already been fixed for a date in the very beginning of Thai. You know this quite well. And yet, you told the friends who took our leave a short while ago that your coronation will not take place without them! What else am I supposed to think?" demanded Vandhiyathevan.

Ponniyin Selvar burst out in laughter. "Yes, it is true, I suppose. Once, I had been quite resolved to speak my mind. It is only after I befriended *you* that I have grown proficient in black arts and trickery!"

"Ah, such praise is certainly uncalled for! What black art or trickery can there be that you aren't already adept at? The charm you whispered in the elephant's ear, the audacious gambit you pulled off in the guise of a mahout to fool the world at large - what mere guile can match such sublime craft, pray?"

"Ah! Let's keep it that way, then. You can learn more of sorcery and subterfuge from me."

"Oh, oh! I suppose this is why you're chasing me off to Ilankai? Worried, are you, that the student will surpass the master?"

"My friend! Perhaps you do not wish to go to Eezha Naadu after all…"

"When did I say that? I am willing to go to Ilankai and beyond! The sooner you send me, the happier I shall be."

"Ah, such happiness at the thought of leaving my side, I see!"

"Yes, *Ayya*. I have come to the conclusion that the further away I am from great kings, the better. Easier to keep a kingly friendship from a distance, I think."

"You're likely to be disappointed, then."

"Ah! There's little chance of staying friends with me however far I go, is it?"

"No, no. I only meant to say that you cannot be away from me for too long. I intend to join you at Eezham a few days after your departure. I mean to take you along with me across the seas, to the isles that lie beyond the horizon. I only regret," added Ponniyin Selvar ruefully, "that Samudhra Kumari cannot accompany us."

Vandhiyathevan stole a furtive glance at the prince. "*Ayya*! You say that my sorcery and subterfuge have rubbed off on you; I, on the other hand, have vowed to speak naught but the truth since making your friendship. May I tell you what lies in my mind?"

"Of course."

"You are taking for yourself the Chozha *samrajyam* that is the birthright of my friend Senthan Amudhan, your *chitappa* Madhuranthaka Thevar. There is some fairness in that - it can be justified as the will of the people, who are insistent that you should wear the crown. But," continued Vandhiyathevan with gravitas, "if you were to steal Poonguzhali away from him thus, there can be no greater betrayal than that! There is no way to justify such a thing. Pray, remember that Samudhra Kumari is now the lawfully wedded wife of Madhuranthaka Thevar!" he begged theatrically.

Ponniyin Selvan doubled over with laughter. "You're likely to place me on the same dubious pedestal as that ten-headed Raavana, at this rate!"

Then, "It is fair, I suppose, that you speak up for your friend. But what of Poonguzhali? Did she marry my *chitappa* willingly, with a full heart?" asked Arulmozhi Varmar.

"Why would you doubt such a thing? My liege! You may be the Chakravarthy of this glorious Choza *samrajyam*. You may even wield power over the dominion of earth and bring the world under the rule of your flag. But you have no hope of forcing the redoubtable Poonguzhali *Ammai* to do a single thing she does not wish to! I was fortunate enough to see for myself the depth of love that Poonguzhali bears for Sembian Maadevi's beloved son." Vandhiyathevan paused meaningfully. "I have seen such affection only in another."

"Where? Come, now - if you can speak of it, do tell!"

"The Kodumbalur princess Vanathi, of course! Where else can you see such a love as that?"

"Lies, lies!" cried out Ponniyin Selvar. "You have already relinquished your vow to speak the truth! You bear a thought in mind and say another with your lips!"

"Not at all, *Ayya*! I only spoke my mind!" protested Vandhiyathevan.

Ponniyin Selvan narrowed his eyes at the youth. "You haven't seen such a love elsewhere, then?"

"I haven't, I tell you!"

"*Adei*, sinner! Heartless wretch!" burst out Ponniyin Selvar in genuine anger. "It was for ***your*** sake that a maiden came forward willingly to give up her own life! She has lost her senses for love of you and is now stricken mad! And you say that her love is not worthy of greatness?"

Vandhiyathevan rode silently for a while. "*Ayya*," he said presently, "You turn cause and effect upon their heads. I do bear pity and compassion for Manimekalai. I often find myself weeping when I think of her. But I am not the reason she has lost her wits - it is her brother Kandamaaran. Besides, we're both dead to the maiden as far she is concerned. What is the point of deliberating the matter?" he asked softly, genuine pain lacing his tones.

"I'm sorry for having spoken in anger just now…" began a contrite Arulmozhi Varmar.

"I don't feel bad, my liege; neither am I surprised, to tell you the truth." Vandhiyathevan suddenly flashed a smile. "I rather wished to flee to Ilankai at the earliest anticipating such bursts of anger!"

Ponniyin Selvan smiled. "I did tell you, didn't I, that there was another reason to ship you off to Ilankai?"

"Yes, my liege!"

"My *thamakkaiyar* is of the opinion that your return from a prolonged sojourn in far-off lands will help Manimekalai recognize you."

A look of great indignation appeared on Vandhiyathevan's face. "Ah, I understand, *Ayya* - I understand well, indeed! I see now that Ilaiya

Piratti is more interested than you in exiling me to remote lands!... Well, well, talk of the devil!" he cried in sudden surprise, pointing a finger ahead. "There comes the subject of our conversation!"

The two friends had come quite a distance along the Kudamurutti river and were nearing the *rajappattai* that led one from Thiruvaiyaru to Thanjai. A royal palanquin was making its way upon the very same road, flanked by a retinue of aides at the front and rear. Daintily seated inside were none other than Kundhavai Devi and the Kodumbalur princess. When the royal maidens saw the pair approaching on horseback, their eyes widened with surprise and a glow of happiness lit their faces.

80

The Lover of the Earth Maiden

Ponniyin Selvar's steed neared the palanquin the princesses were seated in.

Vandhiyathevan had reined in his horse a short distance behind. "Pray, take care!" he called out to the prince. "That devilish palanquin of those princesses may just barrell into our poor horses!"

He had suddenly remembered how, at that very spot, he had once run his horse into Nandhini's palanquin; he had kicked up a veritable hue and cry after the fact, rather unfairly accusing the *pallakku* of charging his steed. It had hardly been six months since that incident. To think of the number of fateful events that had transpired in that short period of time!

Kundhavai suppressed the tingle of joy that Vandhiyathevan's voice sent through her. "*Thambi*," she said with a smile, "I daresay I've caught the two of you in the midst of an exciting chat. Your faces are practically aglow with happiness!"

"Yes *Akka*, we were talking of a matter warranting great excitement, indeed!" responded Ponniyin Selvar with a smile of his own. "I rather doubt that it will accord your friend Vanathi the same thrill, though. My wedding approaches, doesn't it? We were revelling in the sight of the maiden I love, my beautiful betrothed. We couldn't help but sing the praises of her lush form and delightful grace!"

The hitherto bright faces of the royal maidens wilted at once. Vanathi hung her head. Kundhavai struggled with a sudden onset of emotions - anger, surprise, disbelief and rage suffused her features as she gazed askance at the prince.

"What sort of indecorous talk is this?" she burst out. "What joy can you possibly derive from hurting this maiden?"

Vanathi raised her head. "*Akka*, what are you saying?" she asked Kundhavai. "Why must I feel hurt?"

Ilaiya Piratti turned in exasperation to Ponniyin Selvar, who had said nothing all this time - all he offered in response was a broad smile. "Aren't you on your way back from the banks of the Kollidam? Which maiden caught your eye there? Which country does she hail from? What is her name? Which family does she belong to?" asked Kundhavai, subjecting the prince to a relentless slew of questions.

Vanthiyathevan hastened to interrupt the inquisition. "Devi, we haven't set our eyes upon a maiden the Ilavarasar intends to wed. We were only marvelling at this daughter of the earth, this lush, plentiful country of five rivers! It was naught but the scenic beauty of Chozha Naadu that we were talking about. The day nears, doesn't it, on which the Ilavarasar will be crowned the Chakravarthy of this beautiful country? He was only talking of the love he bears for this earth maiden!"

"Aha!" exclaimed Kundhavai. "My brother has never jested around with such dodgy wordplay - it appears that you've taught him a trick or two on the subject!"

Arulmozhi Varmar laughed. "My friend, you deserve all of that and more! Didn't I tell you that I have grown artful on account of your friendship? See, my sister has arrived at the same conclusion, as well!"

"Ah, unjust accusations, to be sure!" cried out Vandhiyathevan in chagrin. "Why, brother and sister seem to have conspired together to cast such a blame upon my head!"

"There are many other crimes you have to answer for," replied Kundhavai sternly, her pretty eyes twinkling. "Even some that my brother could not have told you of, in fact. They cannot be discussed willy-nilly in the midst of the road, thus."

"Ah, my suspicions were true after all!" said Vandhiyathevan.

"What did you suspect, pray?"

"That dispatching me to Eezha Naadu as a Senathipathi is naught but a ruse to exile me for my crimes!"

"Did you hear him, *Akka*?" asked Ponniyin Selvar indignantly. "Goes to show, doesn't it, the extent of the trust he places in the gratitude of the Chozha clan?"

"It is true that we are entirely ungrateful towards him."

"Ah, that it is you saying these words!"

Kundhavai smiled. "We can be grateful for the aid rendered by strangers. How can there be gratitude amongst friends? Do you not recall Thiruvalluvar's words?

Udukkai izhanthavan kaipol aange
Idukkan kalaivathaam natpu!
[Friendship hastens to aid
As the hand that retrieves one's wayward garment]

Must we give thanks to our own hand that ties our robes?" she asked.

"Devi, there is little need to make a display of gratitude. I am deeply thankful that I haven't been meted punishment!" cut in Vandhiyathevan.

Kundhavai laughed and turned to Ponniyin Selvar. "*Thambi*, the two of you must bear one thing in mind. Our brother Karikalan, who has attained the heaven of warriors, has sent him to be of assistance to me. I have not yet released him from his charge."

"You don't need to ever release him, *Akka*. I am perfectly agreeable to see you sentence him to life imprisonment, if it comes to it," said the Ilavarasar.

"I have work yet for him to accomplish in Ilankai," said Kundhavai.

"I will take my leave of you before I depart, Devi!" said Vandhiyathevan.

"In that case, you will find that you must take leave of me at Pazhayaarai," replied Kundhavai Piratti.

"*Akka*! Where are you off to, now?" asked Arulmozhi Varmar in some surprise.

"Why, Thiruvaiyaru city! It is the holy day of Thiruvadhirai today, is it not? Sembian Maadevi, Madhuranthakar and Poonguzhali departed early this morning. Would you like to come along?" asked Kundhavai.

"I think not. We travelled westwards along the riverbank precisely to avoid passing through Thiruvaiyaru."

Kundhavai clucked. "It is said that Appar Peruman caught a glimpse of holy Kailasam at Thiruvaiyaru and went into raptures. And here you are, reluctant to even go there! Have you both turned Veera Vaishnavites, by any chance?"

"Nothing of that sort. I only wish to travel to Thiruvaiyaru as Appar Peruman did."

"How did he travel?"

"Why, he has described it in his own verses! *Yaadhum suvadu padaamal* - that is how he describes his own journey to Thiruvaiyaru. Stripped of the trappings of luxury and fame, without making it known that he was none but Thirunavukarasar himself, the saint walked in the footsteps of the faithful bearing water and flowers consecrated to the Lord. That is why he was able to get a glimpse of Kailasam in Thiruvaiyaru! If we go there in such royal pomp and circumstance, we will not be able to see the Lord to our heart's content. The people will swarm us too, forgetting their own purpose of obtaining a *darshan* of the deity!"

"That is true enough. It is the quirk of your stars! The people will likely surround you the minute they catch sight of you. They will doubtless raise cheers of joy - 'Hail the king of kings! Hail Ponniyin Selvar!' But *we* are in no danger of any such thing. Besides, we won't be amongst the people. When the Lord graces us in procession on this holy day of Thiruvathirai, we shall look upon Lord Aiyyarudai from the upper storey of our palace in Thiruvaiyaru!"

"*Akka*! Do you remember the words of an ancient verse? It was the Lord who brought into being the universe, the planets and all the stars that hang in the far skies! Isn't it silly that people call him 'Aathirayaan,' marking him as one who holds sway over just the Thiruvathirai star? Do you remember the verse I speak of?"

"I do, *Thambi*! But He who holds sway over all the stars surely holds sway over Thiruvathirai, as well?"

"Perhaps. In any case, best you be on your way. When will you return to Thanjai?"

"We won't be returning to Thanjai anytime soon. We plan to depart for Pazhaiyarai from Thiruvaiyaru."

"What, what?" asked the prince, taken aback. "Won't you present at my coronation?"

"What business do Vanathi and I have at your coronation?"

"Aha! My coronation will not take place without you!"

"Of course it will. Why won't it? Who do you think chose the date for your *pattabhishekam*? It was none but one who hails from the illustrious lineage of the seer who fixed the date for Ramar's own *pattabhishekam*!"

"I have little faith in auspicious times, stars and horoscopes, *Akka*! Every day is a good day when we do right by our duties. It is only our days of laziness that bring us ill times!" declared Ponniyin Selvar.

"May all your days be thus auspicious, *Thambi*!" replied Kundhvaai warmly. "We shall pray for you at the shrines of Lord Ayyarappar and Goddess Aram Valartha Nayagi!"

"And what will you pray for?"

"We shall pray to Lord Aiyyarudai that the love you bear for the earth maiden comes to fruition and that your *magudabhishekam* takes place without travail. We shall pray at the sanctum of Goddess Aram Valartha Nayagi that your heart never wavers from the path of righteousness shown to us by the forefathers of the Chozha clan."

"Then… will neither of you be present at my coronation?"

"We shall see it in our mind's eye at Pazhaiyarai and rejoice."

"*Akka*, you are merely glossing over the obstinacy of the Kodumbalur princess," said Ilavarasar Ponniyin Selvar, frowning. "She thinks the sun will set permanently upon the world if she publicly refuses to sit on the Chozha throne beside me! This insufferable obduracy will end in nothing but disaster - another damsel will end up sitting on the Chozha throne instead of her. There will be little point in blaming me then!"

"I have never blamed him for anything yet. I never shall, *Akka*!" protested the Kodumbalur princess Vanathi.

"There is little use even if you do, Vanathi! Nothing will reach the ears of those who crave a kingdom!" replied Ilaiya Piratti Kundhavai tartly.

"Lest we forget, it was *you* who kindled in me the desire for the kingdom!" pointed out Arulmozhi. "Haven't you told me often that you have no heart to leave this beautiful Chozha Naadu? That though you were born a maiden, you would forsake a married life for the cause?"

"You paid little heed to my words, then - you said all along that there were many other beautiful lands upon this earth! Ah, it is naught but the gospel of this Vaanar warrior that has turned you into a lover of the earth maiden!" remarked Kundhavai Piratti.

"Heavens!" cried out Vandhiyathevan in alarm. "Must I bear the brunt of that accusation as well?"

"You've shouldered the charges for far graver crimes, haven't you? That you shrink from such a trivial blame as this!" countered Kundhavai. "*Thambi*, we have spent too long in talk. It is almost time for the Lord to go out in procession - we shall take our leave!" Ilaiya Piratti signalled to the palanquin bearers and the royal *pallakku* resumed its journey.

Ponniyin Selvar watched the palanquin for a short while. Presently, he urged his horse towards Thanjai once more.

After they had crossed a short distance, he suddenly turned to Vandhiyathevan riding beside him. "Friend, I rather doubt that these maidens are travelling to see the Lord as they claim. I hear that the Kudanthai *jothidar* is now living close to Thiruvaiyaru! I'm quite certain that they are on their way to seek his consult!"

"*Ayya*, you seem to be a greater soothsayer than the Kudanthai *jothidar* himself!" said Vandhiyathevan, amazed.

81

The Cat and the Parrot

Events unfolded just as Ponniyin Selvar had predicted they would. As soon as Kundhavai Devi and Vanathi reached the Chozha palace at Thiruvaiyaru, they brought their palanquin and retinue to a halt. They learned that Sembian Maadevi had departed to the temple along with her son and daughter-in-law. Leaving word with the palace watch that they were going to the temple as well, the royal maidens promptly set off in search of the *jothidar's* house accompanied by a solitary guard.

Yes - when the floods swept away his home at Kudanthai, the Kudanthai *jothidar* had come away to Thiruvaiyaru. He had built for himself a small house on the banks of the Kaveri in the eastern corner of the town and was now living there.

Perhaps he had chosen to live in Thiruvaiyaru having divined by way of the mystical arts that Thanjavur would gain more importance than Pazhaiyarai in the future.

Even as the royal maidens crossed the threshold of the *jothidar's* house, they were surprised by a sweet voice. "Welcome, ye Queens of Dance!" it called out, like the delightful babble of a lisping child. They wondered whom the *jothidar* had appointed to give such a warm welcome in place of the stern disciple who had once kept watch.

Surprise turned to amusement when they saw a lovely green parrot in a cage hanging from the rafters. The parrot prettily cocked its head this way and that, fixing them with its small, glittering eyes akin to *kundrimani* beads. "Welcome, ye Queens of Dance!" it lisped once again, hopping for good measure.

The *jothidar* emerged from within, having heard the parrot's voice and the sweet tinkle of the maidens' anklets. He was taken aback when he saw the princesses. "Do come inside, Devis!" he said eagerly. "This hut has been blessed today!"

The parrot fluttered its wings and opened its pretty beak, scarlet as coral. "This hut has been blessed today!" it cried, repeating the words of its master.

"Hush!" chided the *jothidar*, glaring at the bird. "Pipe down and keep mum for a while!"

"*Ayya*, why do you scold that poor creature? It only accords us a warm welcome!" said Kundhavai Piratti. "Why, it appears that your hut is blessed thus on a daily basis. It sounds as if a veritable parade of queens pass through all the time!"

"Welcome, ye Queens of Dance!" cried the parrot promptly.

The *jothidar* hurriedly reproached the bird once again. "Pardon me, Devis!" he said, turning to the princesses. "When

Thirugnanasambandar Peruman visited Thiruvaiyaru town, he saw that its streets were lined with dance halls. The sweet tinkling of anklets fell on his ears as the maidens practised the art within. He has sung of this in his divine compositions. Even today, there are many damsels in Thiruvaiyaru town who learn the art of dance. They often come here seeking to learn their fortunes! It was I who trained this parrot to greet them thus, thinking it would delight them. Pray, grace me with your pardon!"

"Why, I see none of these queens of dance in your hut today!" remarked Kundhavai.

"Devi, today is the holy day of Thiruvathirai, so said queens of dance are likely at the sanctum of Lord Aiyyarudai to offer worship by their service. But true Queens as you have come here today! Truly, this hut has been endowed with good fortune. I am blessed with good luck indeed!" exclaimed the *jothidar* in elation.

Then, "Pray, be seated. Ask what you will of this simple man! I shall answer you to the extent of my knowledge!" he said.

The princesses sat down. Kundhavai heaved a weary sigh. "*Jothidare*, what must I ask? The only question that comes to mind is this - does the science of *jothidam* have any truth to it, after all?"

"Devi, how am I to answer such a question? The science of *jothidam* bears truth to the believer and rings false to the skeptic!" replied the *jothidar*.

"I had implicit faith in it, myself. But it has let me down, has it not?"

"How has it let you down, *Ammani*?"

"Why, what has taken place in line with your predictions, after all? Did you ever forewarn me that my thamayan would meet an untimely death?"

"Can I utter such a thing, Devi? Even if I had known, can I speak those terrible words with my own tongue? If I had, would I not have been seen as one among the Pandiya Naatu *abathudhavis*?"

asked the *jothidar*. "We can talk only in general terms about the ruling clan and matters of state. It is dangerous to even speak of ill luck, hurdles or hostile planetary alignments. Besides, I do not have Aditha Karikalar's horoscope. I have never laid eyes on it!"

"You wouldn't have said a word even if you had seen it." Kundhavai paused. "Even if you had, it wouldn't have been possible to prevent the tragedy, would it?"

"Ah, how could that have been possible, *thaaye*! Am I Lord Brahma? Why, could Brahma Himself have recast words that were already set down?"

"In that case, *jothidare*, what is the use of consulting the science of *jothidam*?"

"*Thaaye*, that you should ask such a thing!" cried out the *jothidar*. "If noble people like you do not seek to learn their fortunes, how will folk like me survive? How else could the feet of princesses walk into this poor man's hut?"

Kundhavai rang out in peals of laughter. Vanathi's lips drew into a pretty smile despite herself.

"*Jothidare*! Do you say such pretty words to everyone who comes here to consult their fortunes?" asked Ilaiya Piratti Kundhavai.

"Would I say such a thing to all and sundry? You are famed throughout the world, my lady, as the very incarnation of the goddesses Kalaimagal and Thirumagal combined! Can I hope to survive a debate with you? But thaaye! Pray, how could you seek to judge the veracity of the science of *jothidam* based on an event that I had neither studied nor predicted? You must gauge its authenticity by the fortunes I *have* told, surely? I spoke, did I not, of the singular luck I saw in Ponniyin Selvar's horoscope? Many events have unfolded, it is true. But in the end, the time has arrived for him to rise to be the Chakravarthy of the world? I hear that the coronation date has been fixed as well!" said the *jothidar*.

"*Ayya*, did no one come to consult you regarding the date for Ponniyin Selvar's *pattabhishekam*?"

"No, Devi. The task is the privilege of the palace *purohithars*. Why, the Mudhanmandhiri Aniruddhar is an expert in the science of jothidam himself!"

"Yes, they have decided upon the seventh day of the Thai month as the date. Is it an auspicious day, *jothidare*?"

"It is a very auspicious day, *Amma*! They have made the decision after due study and consideration."

"It may be a good day for the *pattabhishekam*, perhaps. Pray, consult your science and enlighten me whether the coronation will truly take place on that day!"

Her question took the *jothidar* by surprise. "What sort of a question is this, Devi?" he exclaimed. "Why will it not take place on that day?"

"An auspicious day was chosen with care for Sri Ramar's *pattabhishekam* as well. But his coronation did not take place on that day, did it?" pointed out Kundhavai.

"Devi! The auspicious day did not mark Sri Ramar's coronation, it is true. Instead, he was bestowed with an honour a million times greater! Why, it is the very reason we are graced with a sublime epic as Ramayana! Let that be. Why must you harbour such a doubt all of a sudden? It appears as if you do not wish the coronation to take place on that day!"

"Well guessed, *jothidare*!"

The *jothidar* looked upon Ilaiya Piratti in rank amazement. "Why, the whole wide world believes that none is happier than you at the thought of Ponniyin Selvar ascending the throne!"

"Truly, I am entitled to such happiness," sighed Kundhavai, throwing a vexed glance at Vanathi. "This Kodumbalur maiden's absurd mulishness has spoiled my joy. Do you remember, *jothidare*, the vow she took in your hut at Kudanthai?"

"Vow?" repeated the jothidar, puzzled. "It was a day of misadventures, my lady; I fear I do not clearly remember."

"The boat girl Poonguzhali chanced to pass a remark in a fit of jealousy, upon which this maiden proclaimed an oath. She vowed that she would never sit upon the throne as long as she lives! Tell me, *jothidare* - is it possible to sit upon the throne when one is dead?" demanded Kundhavai.

"I confess it is not!"

"Surely, it was only upon hearing such a dreadful oath that Mother Kaveri rose in anger and tried to sweep her away in the floods!"

"Yes, I remember now!" exclaimed the *jothidar*. "Why, I thought that oath was made in jest!"

"Well, that oath has now mutated into a devilish quandary. She insists that she will not ascend the throne. My brother should marry another, she says, if a maiden is to sit beside him on the throne as the *pattamagishi*! She proposes to be one among the women in his palace! I cannot bear to hear these words, *jothidare*!" said Kundhavai, aggrieved. "Do you remember the fortune you spoke for this maiden?"

The *jothidar* beamed. "I remember well. Devi, mother Kaveri has carried away my collection of works on *jothidam* along with several horoscopes belonging to the princes and princesses of many kingdoms. But *this* noble princess's horoscope is etched upon my mind. The lines gracing her palm are yet clear to me as day. *Ammani*," he pronounced emphatically, "no matter which of my predictions come true or not, the fortune I have spoken for her *will* come to pass!"

"Do you remember the fortune you foretold for this maiden?"

"Well do I remember! I said that the man fortunate enough to clasp her hand in marriage will wed beauty, riches and power combined; that great queens of myriad kingdoms will pray for the good fortune of setting their eyes upon this *maatharasi*; that the son born to her noble womb will enter this world clutching the flag of victory in his hands - he will rise victorious over all that he sees and conquer all the lands he visits."

"*Ayya*, the more you speak, the more I worry!" remarked Kundhavai.

The *jothidar* snapped upright. "Devi! You are worried, you say? Why? The time to worry about the Chozha clan and the Chozha *samrajyam* is behind us. Do you remember that today is a special day?"

"Yes. Today is the holy day of Thiruvathirai that falls in the month of *margazhi*, an auspicious day for Lord Siva."

"An auspicious day for the Chozha clan as well. Why, it is an auspicious day for divine Thamizhagam, too! Devi! Listen!" said the *jothidar*, his eyes glittering. "In the years to come, a great miracle will take place upon this very day of Thiruvathirai! A blessed child will be born, one bearing all the aspects of holy Thirumal himself save his conch and disc. The child will raise Chozha Naadu to exalted heights of glory, the likes of which the empire has never attained before! Aha!" he cried out in sudden rapture. "The marvels that will take place! Perhaps I will not be alive to see such wonders; but you, my lady, shall live a long life and rejoice at the miracles to come!"

As the *jothidar* described the future he divined as one lost to a mystical trance, Kundhavai listened to him, spellbound.

A clatter sounded behind them all of a sudden and the two women turned around.

The green parrot was frantically beating its wings in alarm. Vanathi quickly picked up a scroll and threw it at the cat that was making to pounce upon the poor bird.

"*Akka, jothidam* is useful indeed" remarked the Kodumbalur princess turning to Kundhavai. "It was its scroll that helped me save this beautiful parrot of pretty speech. Else, the cat would have made short work of its wings!"

82

The traders from China

Since the days of ancient man, the people of various nations have endeavoured to gain a glimpse of the future. From the humble poor and illiterate to august royals and lofty scholars, humans have always aspired to decipher the times to come. Horoscope readers, horary astrologers, fortune-tellers, palmists and their ilk have burgeoned in societies of advanced learning and culture. Of course, there have always been skeptics as well, those who mistrusted sciences such as *jothidam* and registered their denouncement of such beliefs.

Ilaiya Piratti, a noble maiden renowned for her intelligence, often found herself struggling at the crossroads of this complex debate. Even so, each time she was struck with anxiety over the future of the Chozha *samrajyam*, her worries drove her in search of the *jothidar's* house.

By right, Kundhavai's heart should have attained the state of peace the Chakravarthy had reached. After many unforeseen events, it was now beyond doubt that Arulmozhi Varmar would ascend the Chozha throne and wear the crown upon his head. We know already, don't we, that Kundhavar bore boundless affection for her younger brother even as a child? Her heart held an unshakeable belief that Arulmozhi, marked by the remarkable conch and disc meridians on his palms, would lift the illustrious Chozha empire to new heights of splendour. The incident in which a divine woman had appeared as a very goddess to save Arulmozhi from the Kaveri waters, along with many other astonishing episodes, only served to strengthen her conviction. What then, was the reason why the young princess lacked peace?

As they had with Arulmozhi Varmar, many had waxed eloquent about the distinctive features of the Kodumbalur princess Vanathi's horoscope, too. It is hard to say whether they truly did study the time of day and position of the planets to arrive at this conclusion, or whether they merely sought to please Kundhavai Devi with pretty speech. Every so often, universal predictions held aloft by many soothsayers come to a miraculous pass. Yet others seem to possess an extraordinary power in their speech - their foretellings always come true as spoken! The *jothidar*, our friend who had now come to live in Thiruvaiyaru from Kudanthai, did not lose sight of the fact that it was the Thiruvathirai day of *margazhi*. "It is an auspicious day that will bring great fortune to the Chozha clan!" he prophesied, with impressive emphasis.

Two years later, on that very Thiruvathirai day in *margazhi*, a son was born to the Chozha clan. When the child grew up and staked his claim to the empire, he proved himself as a mighty Chakravarthy, one equal to luminaries such as Chandraguptan, Asokan, Vikramaditan, Harshavardhanan. He received the name Rajendran and triumphantly established his rule across a great dominion spanning from the banks of the Gangai to Ilankai and from the Lakshadweep isles up until the very island of Srivijaya.

The *jothidar's* prophecy thus came to a miraculous pass in the future. But when he spoke the fortune on that particular day, Kundhavai was unable to bring herself to believe it. As for Vanathi, the *jothidar's* words only served to incense her. As luck would have it, she was presented with an occasion to display her wrath; the princess grabbed one of the scrolls to fling it unceremoniously at the cat, following with a rather acrid remark - '*Jothidam* has its uses, after all!" she had sniffed.

The *jothidar* turned around and gleaned what had transpired. "Ilavarasi! They say that a blade of straw is a dangerous weapon in a strong man's hand. Your noble hands have enabled even a mere scroll to save a life! But then again, they *are* the petal-soft hands that will offer refuge to countless souls in the future, aren't they?" he said.

A well and truly vexed Vanathi turned to Kundhavai. "*Akka*, this *jothidar* is an old veteran in the art of flattery. Come away, we shall go forth from here!" she said crossly.

"Devi, you hold my words in disfavour today. But one day or another my prophecy will certainly come to pass. Pray, do not forget this humble man on that day!" said the *jothidar*, smiling.

"*Ayya*, 'tis not that this maiden is ill-disposed to the destiny you foretell," interjected Kundhavai. "I daresay her heart swells with happiness at every passing word! She is only furious with herself for having made such a rash oath. I fear the wrath was quite unfairly directed at your scroll. Pray, do not pay it much mind."

"The anger of a good person brings naught but good in its wake, my lady! Why, my beloved parrot, the bird that delighted you with its sweet voice and welcome, has been gifted a new lease of life, hasn't it?" replied the *jothidar*.

Kundhavai spent some more time in discussion with the *jothidar*. Her chief concern was to know when Arulmozhi Varmar would get married. Ilaiya Piratti Kundhavai had good reason to worry about the matter. For the previous day, the Senathipathi Boodhi Vikrama Kesari had approached her. "*Thaaye*, I leave today for Kodumbalur. I trust that I can take my niece Vanathi along with me?" he had asked.

Kundhavai had been fairly taken aback by the question. "Mama, why such haste?" she had asked, in concern. "Will you not be a part of the *pattabhishekam*?"

"*Thaaye*, I shall return in time for the coronation. Why must I linger here until then? I came with a vast army at my command. By the grace of God, our heart's desire has been fulfilled without the need for war. The Chakravarthy's beloved son has acceded to be crowned. The chieftains are agreeable to the decision as well. So, there is little need to station such a sizeable army here. It poses a strain on Thanjai resources to supervise and feed the men. I find myself obliged to depart with my forces and station the battations at their respective posts before I return," explained the Senathipathi.

"That sounds fair," agreed Kundhavai. "You may do that by yourself, surely? Why must you take my friend Vanathi away with you?"

"Devi, I have good reason for my request," replied the Senathipathi. "The chieftains held a forum yesterday and have arrived at a decision. You see, my lady, Paranthaka Chakravarthy, the father of your *paatanaar* Arinjaya Thevar, took many queens. He wed a maiden each from the Miladudaiyar clan, the Pazhuvettarayar clan, the Mazhavaraiyar clan, the Sambuvaraiyar clan and my own. And so, there was no conflict among the chieftains during his reign. Your *paatanaar* Arinjayar married many maidens belonging to the different clans, too. He even wed a damsel from the Vaithumbaraayar clan that he had defeated - your noble *paatiyaar*." The Senathipathi paused. "This worthy tradition was not sustained by your illustrious father. He wed none but your noble mother, Malayaman's daughter. It proved to sow jealousy and dissent among the chieftains. And so, we chieftains have come to an unanimous decision - the prince who will soon be crowned the Chozha Chakravarthy must wed many maidens across the clans, like the Paranthaka Chakravarthy and Arinjaya Thevar. We intend to make this request of Ponniyin Selvar once the coronation ceremony comes to a close. Surely, my lady can now understand why I wish to take Vanathi back with me to my country? If I leave her behind here, the other chieftains may grow doubtful whether I am acting against our collective decision," finished Kodumbalur Velar.

A rush of anger surged within Kundhavai at these words. She replied in measured tones, taking care to mask her feelings. "Senathipathi, have you perhaps forgotten that you once requested me to be both father and mother to your niece who had lost her parents?" she asked. "I cannot send Vanathi to Kodumbalur - I cannot bear to be away from her for even a second. Should it please you, I will take her to Pazhaiyarai instead. We shall remain there and forego attending the *pattabhishekam*. Let there be no more talk of weddings for the moment. Pray, tell Ponniyin Selvar of the chieftains' collective decision after the coronation ceremony. We shall take the matter forward from there."

The Senathipathi consented to her suggestion and took his leave.

This exchange was largely why Kundhavai had gone in search of the Kudanthai jothidar. It was also why she had sounded rather anxious when she had asked him about Ponniyin Selvar's wedding.

Whilst Kundhavai was engrossed in her consultation, Vanathi found her thoughts wandering to an old memory. Curiously enough, this incident too featured a cat and a bird; the supporting cast included an elephant and a mahout.

A wild cat had attacked a bird's nest hanging from the branch of a tree, eager to make a meal of the tender fledglings that lay inside. The mother bird had circled her nest frantically, trying its best to fend off that cat. Vanathi had been horrified by the sight. Not knowing what to do, she had screamed at the top of her lungs. Her cry had alarmed a young man swimming in a nearby river and he had come running to help. Catching sight of the danger at hand, the youth had taken to his heels only to return grandly atop an elephant. He had then gallantly saved the nest and fledglings both from the hungry jaws of the wild cat.

At the time, Vanathi had taken him to be a mahout. It was only later that she had learned the youth was none other than Ponniyin Selvar. *Ah! Couldn't he have been a mahout, after all? Or an ordinary soldier, perhaps? It is solely because he is the son of the illustrious Sundara Chozha Chakravarthy that I'm in such a tight spot, aren't I? It is the only reason why my own companions and those like Poonguzhali had besmirched me with accusations of nursing a crooked desire to become the Empress of Chozha Naadu!*

As Vanathi mused upon old memories and Kundhavai listened avidly to new fortunes, a loud voice sounded outside the *jothidar's* hut. "Do you want silks from China? Silks from China!" it cried out, striving to be heard above the noisy clamour outside.

Kundhavai and Vanathi suddenly realized that it had been quite some time since they had come to the *jothidar's* hut. As they got to their feet, the *jothidar's* disciple came inside. "*Swami,*" he began, "two Chinese traders are at the door. They say they wish to consult their fortunes. Shall I ask them to come back tomorrow?" he asked.

"There's little need for that," cut in Kundhavai. "Let them come in at once. We shall take our leave." So saying, she took Vanathi's hand in her own and prepared to leave.

When the princesses reached the doorway, they were greeted by a great elephant. Two Chinese traders were seated atop the magnificent animal, two voluminous bundles by their side.

Paying them hardly any attention, the princesses called forth the solitary guard they had brought along and returned to the Chozha palace.

83

Appar's vision

As part of the Thiruvathirai festivities, Lord Ayyarappar and Goddess Aram Valartha Nayagi graced the expansive streets of Thiruvaiyaru in divine procession. The Lord and His consort, resplendent in loving adornments, were seated upon a lustrous *vahanam* made of silver that evoked the image of Mount Kailas in snow-covered magnificence.

At the head of the procession came majestic elephants, camels and great bulls. The animals were strapped with *perigai* and *murasu* drums, which were sounded with such exuberance that their beats reverberated in all the eight directions. Behind them came a succession of people bearing hallowed symbols in their hands, followed by bands of musicians who played a wide variety of musical instruments. Nimble-footed maidens danced in celebration of the divine, stopping every now and then to give short recitals before they returned to the procession. Appearing in graceful cars of their own were the deities Nandi *bhagavan*, Chandikesavar, Vinayagar and Lord Muruga, flanked by His consorts Valli and Devayanai. Then came at the very end the Goddess Parvathi and Lord Parameswar, majestically seated atop the *kailasa vahanam* as they graced the people with their auspicious sight.

Further back were bands of singers rendering divine *thevaram* hymns to the accompaniment of instruments such as the *veenai*, *maththalam*, and *thalam*, singing the compositions of the saints Appar, Sambandar and Sundarar. Thousands swarmed the streets at the front and rear of the grand procession as they slowly kept step with the parade. Each enjoyed the procession in his or her own way - some watched the ambling elephants and camels, some listened to the musicians, while others watched the dance recitals performed by the maidens. Most, however, had their eyes fixed on the deities in procession, breaking out in cries of praise as they went into raptures at the divine sight.

As far as the eye could see were hundreds of torches shining brightly against the darkness. Their dazzling illumination cast a celestial glow upon the proceedings, making the divine procession seem as sublime as a dream. Kundhavai, Vanathi and Poonguzhali eagerly saw the marvellous sights from the upper storey of the Chozha palace. They were delighted by every part of the majestic procession, from the very first elephant that came bearing drums right until the group of *thevaram* singers at the very end. They were touched by devotees who had reached poignant states of ecstasy at the divine sight; they were also amused by the handful of lively folk entertaining themselves with a bit of harmless comedy and mischief. The princesses saw the deities in procession as well, from Nandi Thevar to Sivan and Parvathi; they drank in the holy sight and sought blessings from afar, feeling a calm happiness settle upon them.

Curiously enough, they also saw two Chinese traders amidst that great crowd, seated atop an elephant. As the royal maidens watched, the pair alighted from the animal and vanished into the throng, only to re-appear shortly and mount the elephant once again.

Kundhavai couldn't help but grow suspicious at the strange behaviour. *Aha! Are these Chinese men truly traders? Or are they spies from foreign lands, come to gather intelligence?*

It was natural that news of the internal chaos reigning in the Chozha *rajyam* over the matter of succession would have spread throughout the world. It was entirely likely then, wasn't it, that enemy kings could well have dispatched secret agents in the guise of Chinese traders?

Poonguzhali happened to hear Kundhavai and Vanathi discussing such a possibility. "Devi! They approached me at the entrance to the temple asking me if I wanted Chinese silks," she revealed. "I replied, 'Come to the Chozha palace, for two princesses will come soon from Thanjai; perhaps they will buy your wares.' So they may land up here. You can pose your questions directly to them and clear your misgivings!"

At that very moment, Lord Ayyarappar and Goddess Aram Valartha Nayagi appeared at the palace entrance atop the *kailasa vahanam*. The deities were lovingly shown the due rituals of worship, including the brilliant display of *deeparathanai*, an offering of light. After the *vahanam* departed, Sembian Maadevi and her son broke away from the procession to enter the palace. Learning that the princesses were on the upper storey, they came there as well.

The group spent a while discussing the magnificence of the procession. Shortly, Sivagnana Kandaradhithar's Devi looked to her dear son. "Child, Appar sang a *pathigam* about the vision he saw in this Thiruvaiyaru city, did he not? Do sing it for us. I was left rather unsatisfied by the processional singers who rendered the *thevaram* hymns."

With Poonguzhali and the princesses chiming in with the request as well, Senthan Amudhan, now known to us as Madhuranthaka Thevar, sweetly sang the pathigam in question in his dulcet voice:

Mathar piraikanniyaanai malayaan magalodum paadi
Pothodu neerchumanthethi puguvaravar pinpuguven
Yaadunchuvadupadaamal ayyaru adaigindrapothu
Kaathalmadappidiyodun kaliru varuvana kanden!
Kandenavar thirupaathagam! Kandariyathana kanden!

[I sang in praise
Of the majestic one adorned by the crescent moon and the daughter of the mountain
I walked behind the faithful carrying offerings of water and flowers
As I reached Ayyaru with quiet, meek footsteps
I beheld a pair of elephants lost to the bliss of love!
I beheld His holy feet! I beheld that which I had never seen before!]

Madhuranthakar lost himself in song and went on to joyously render the ten beautiful verses that followed as well.

His audience forgot themselves as they listened. They thought that they could see with their own eyes the very vision that Appar Peruman saw and sang rapturously of.

When the song came to an end, there was nothing but awed silence. Presently, Kundhavai turned to Sembian Maadevi. "*Amma*, you once recounted to me the story behind this particular *pathigam* of Appar's. Do say it once again, so that these two maidens also learn the tale!" she begged. As the others made earnest entreaties as well, Periya Piratti Sembian Maadevi obliged.

"When Appar *swami* was in the throes of old age, his body weak and infirm, he was seized by the desire to see the Lord at Mount Kailas. He set off towards the north and travelled for a great distance. Unable to walk any further, he collapsed onto the ground in fatigue.

As he lay weary and spent, an elderly man appeared in front of him. "Appare," said the man, "where do you go in search of *kailayam*? Go forth instead to Thiruvaiyaru, upon the banks of the Ponni River - it is none but *kailayam* on earth!" When the figure vanished in front of his eyes, Appar realized that it was naught but the word of God. He thus turned back and travelled to Thiruvaiyaru as bid. Even as he neared the holy land, his heart attained the realms of ecstasy. The saint saw many devotees seeking a glimpse of the Lord Ayyarappar, bearing baskets of flowers and pots of water from the river Kaveri as offerings for the deity. The faithful sang the praises of the Lord as they walked, and Appar walked behind them. As he did, his eyes fell upon a pair of elephants, a majestic male and a graceful female. They seemed to Appar to be the very vision of Siva and Sakthi. By the time the saint reached the temple, he saw with enthralled eyes many animals and birds in loving pairs. He saw a cock crowing in rapture as it wooed its hen; he saw an iridescent peacock in blissful dance with its peahen, each entwined with the other; he heard, in the thick grove nearby, a cuckoo sing amorously to its mate; he saw a wild boar strutting with its sow, its grunts as loud as peals of thunder; he saw a white heron in flight overhead, soaring through the skies with its female; he saw a green parrot prattling sweet words to its mate in the lush branches of a tree; he saw a fine bullock walking by the side of its sweet cow. Appar *swami* saw, with his inner eye, that the pairs of animals and birds that appeared before him were naught but Siva and Sakthi; he was transported to elation as he saw the veil of the world fall away to reveal that anything and everything of form was naught but Siva and Sakthi. He attained the sublime understanding that the whole world was the very *kailayam* he had sought - there was no other, for it was all and it was everywhere. As Appar walked on in the euphoria of this metaphysical truth, he saw the Lord Ayyarappar and Goddess Aram Valartha Nayagi appear in splendid procession, grandly seated upon the *kailasa vahanam* as they graced the people with their divine sight. The saint was inspired to record the glorious sights he saw and experienced that day with both his mortal and inner eye. He graced us with the sweet poetry he composed in description of his marvellous vision. Because he saw in Thiruvaiyaru the supreme truth that had escaped his sight until then, he ended every verse with the awestruck line - 'I beheld that which I had never seen before!'"

Everyone listened spellbound to the venerable old queen as she narrated the tale.

Once the story was done, the Kodumbalur princess piped up with a question. "*Amma*, Appar *swamigal* has described with such wonder the love he saw amongst the birds and the animals! Why did he not speak of such love among humans?" she asked.

"Because," interjected Poonguzhali, "there is nary a man and woman who bear genuine love for each other, uncorrupted by selfishness. That is likely why Appar did not see fit to touch upon humans!"

"That is not quite correct, daughter. If Appar *swami* had seen you and my son together, he would have doubtless sung of human love, too!" said Sembian Maadevi affectionately.

"Yes, yes!" cried the princesses, echoing the thought.

It was at this pretty moment that a sudden clamour sounded at the palace entrance. A guard shortly entered, wringing his hands in trepidation. "Two Chinese traders are here, my ladies - they claim to be silk merchants. They *insist* that they will not leave without seeing the princesses!" he said, sounding rather desperate.

Ilaiya Piratti was struck by incredulity and ire all at once. "Why, the nerve! Who on earth are they?" she asked in astonishment. "Tell them we want nothing and send them away!"

"Devi," said Poonguzhali quickly, "it was I who had asked them to come. Pardon me, my lady!"

Ilaiya Piratti turned to the hapless guard. "Send them in, then!" she said with an air of resignation.

The Chinese traders appeared shortly, lugging two great bags behind them.

84

Coronation Gifts

The Chinese traders sported luxuriously full beards and moustaches and had wrapped gigantic turbans around their heads. Their features were not quite clear in the weak light of the solitary lamp that was burning in the palace terrace. It wasn't even possible to guess at their age.

Kundhavai's suspicion grew stronger. That queen among women, renowned for her sharp intellect, turned to the guard who had accompanied them inside. "This light is not bright enough to examine wares of silk. Bring a bigger lamp," she instructed.

"I shall go and send a good lamp," said Madhuranthakar and departed along with Sembian Maadevi.

Kundhavai turned to the Chinese traders. "*Ayya*, why such haste?" she asked, her annoyance evident in her voice. "Could you not have shown your wares tomorrow, by light of day? Why did you insist on coming here this very night?"

"Princesses, we beg your pardon!" replied an anxious Chinese trader. "Many days have passed since we came to Thanjai. Despite much effort, we were unable to gain an audience with you. Our ship starts from Naagaippattinam the day after tomorrow - we must depart with the vessel. Thus we found ourselves obliged to hustle our way!" he finished, looking deeply contrite.

The maidens were quite taken aback by his strikingly odd tone of voice, peculiarly high-pitched and penetrating. They couldn't help but feel astonished too, at his command over the Thamizh language.

"Why, Chinese traders! You seem to be quite proficient in Thamizh!" exclaimed Kundhavai, her dark eyes darting curiously between the traders.

The man who first spoke shot a quick glance at his companion. "It has been quite some time since we came to trade in Chozha Naadu, my lady. I picked up the language during my sojourn here," he explained, adding, "I have grown quite fond of Thamizh and Thamizh Naadu!"

Kundhavai smiled. "Why then must you show such haste in returning to your country? Won't you stay back for the coronation, at the very least? What urges you to leave?"

"If we let slip our ship the day after tomorrow, we do not know when the next vessel will start - ships do not depart from Naagai as frequently as they once did."

"And why is that?"

"Don't you know the reason, Devi?" asked the trader in some surprise. "Voyages are not as simple as they were once before; they have grown quite perilous, too. Bands of pirates roam the waters; vicious raiders from the Arab countries forcefully board ships, terrorizing the high and low seas. The marauders lurk near the shore and even in the vicinity of ports; when they spot an unfortunate trading vessel, they draw close to attack. They fall upon the crew in fierce combat and brutally put them to the sword before looting the ship. It is for this very reason that trading vessels do not voyage alone - ten, twenty ships need to travel together in a fleet for safety. If we miss boarding our ship the day after tomorrow, we do not know how long we will have to wait for the next one. Devis, pray be kind as to see the silks we have brought!"

The Chinese trader had started to untie his bundle during his speech. His companion untied his own bundle as well.

"Oh, traders!" said Ilaiya Piratti watching them produce their wares. "There is little use in setting up shop now. It is not possible to examine the quality of your silks in the dark of night. Besides," she added, "we have not brought with us the money we need to pay you for your silks."

The trader who had first spoken stood up at once, a look of great astonishment spreading across his bearded face. He deferentially brought his palms together. "Ilavarasi!" he exclaimed. "That you think we would name *you* a price! Those are fine words indeed! My lady, if you but deign to accept these silks and wear them, it will bring us boundless joy - we shall consider the honour the merit of penances of past lives. We did not bring these wares to sell, but as gifts for the coronation!"

"If that is the case, I fear you have come to the wrong place. None here will be crowned. It is prince Ponniyin Selvar who will bear that honour. Seek him out and present him with your gifts!"

"No, Devi!" insisted the Chinese trader. "We have come to the right place, indeed. Why, everybody says that the trick to gaining Ponniyin Selvan's favour lies in winning Ilaiya Piratti's benevolence!"

The royal maidens giggled. "Who do you mean by everybody?" asked Kundhavai, laughing. "Where did you hear such a thing, pray?"

"Why, *thaaye*! Many spoke thus in the crowds that had gathered for festivities today!" replied the curious trader, making a sweeping motion of his arm for emphasis. "The younger brother never defies his *thamakkai's* word, they say. Ask my friend here, if you wish!" he cried.

His friend had been silent all along. He now adopted an earnest expression on his bewhiskered face. "Yes, my ladies!" he said, seeming keen as mustard. "Crowning Ponniyin Selvar is as good as crowning Kundhavai Piratti, they claim. Chozha Naadu will now come under matriarchal rule, say the people - they are certain that it will be good reign, too!"

The princesses collapsed into titters.

"And so, my ladies," pleaded the Chinese trader, "pray show us mercy and accept our coronation gifts!"

"Yes, do! Pray, pass on our request to Ponniyin Selvar too!" entreated the other.

Kundhavai Piratti looked surprised. "What request is that? What do you wish to achieve with Ponniyin Selvar's favour? Tell me that, first!"

"Devi, we look to Ponniyin Selvar to catalyze a slew of critical changes! It is not only us, my lady - from the borders of Chozha Naadu up until our own Cheena Desam, the people and traders across nations place implicit faith in none but Arulmozhi Varmar. The seas were safe in the time of Paranthaka Chakravarthy; save for the dangers brought on by storms, voyages were benign and secure. None feared plunder upon the seas, not even in their dreams. The trading vessels of Chozha Naadu plied the ocean fearlessly as if upon the very *rajappattai*, laden with an assortment of precious goods.

These ships sailed forth to the commercial ports of sea-locked isles such as Manakkavaaram, Maayirudingam, Maapappaalam, Ilamuri Desam, Srivijayam, Saavagam, Kadaaram and Kaambojam, conducting lively trades of import and export before arriving at the shores of our own Cheena Desam. It was thus too that our own trading vessels once departed from Cheena Desam and sailed to Chozha Naadu, with no hindrance to bar our way. Devi, those halcyon are naught but a pleasant dream today. Why, we shall confess the truth, my lady!" cried out the Chinese trader all of a sudden. "If we are forced to return with these silks, we fear that we will not be able to transport them safely back to our country. We consider it a far worthier honour to gift these silks to the princesses of Chozha Naadu than to lose them to the hands of Arab pirates along the way!"

As the Chinese trader spoke, Kundhavai's rapt, dark eyes shone in the torchlight like the glossy carapaces of black beetles; they widened with awe, displaying unbounded interest.

Ilaiya Piratti leaned forward, captivated by the account. "Do you trust that Ponniyin Selvar can achieve such a feat?" she asked eagerly. "Do you think it likely that voyages upon the sea will grow as safe and secure as they were in the time of Paranthaka Chakravarthy? Do you truly believe that Ponniyin Selvar's fame will spread across the lands of Manakkavaaram, Maayirudingam, Kadaaram, Srivijayam and beyond?"

"Why, my lady, it is not just we who believe, but all the traders of Chozha Naadu, too! Indeed, even the *jothidar* we visited a short while ago said the same thing as well!"

"And what did *he* say?"

"That Ponniyin Selvar would gather a great fleet of ships and sail across the wide seas; that he would annihilate the roving bands of pirates; that he would make sea voyages as safe as they had been once before; that Chozha Naadu would reclaim the pride and fame it had wielded in Paranthaka Chakravarthy's time!" replied the Chinese trader. "The *jothidar* did add though," he continued pensively, "that these exploits would only come to pass if the Chozha princesses manage to refrain themselves from upsetting the applecart."

Ilaiya Piratti raised a perfect brow. "Is that all the *jothidar* said?" she asked pleasantly. "Or did he have more slander to add about the princesses?"

"Ah! Slander?" repeated the Chinese merchant in alarm. "Nothing of that sort! Devi, none in this Chozha Naadu can have a bad word to say about the Pazhaiyarai Ilaiya Piratti and the Kodumbalur princess! Would the *jothidar*, he who depends on your kindness to make a living, ever say such a thing?"

"What else did he say about us, then?" demanded Kundhavai.

"That the two princesses had just taken their leave of him after a consult; he added, too, that both would soon be wed. My ladies, if you do not wish to accept these silks as gifts for the coronation, pray accept them as gifts for your wedding!" pleaded the Chinese trader.

Vanathi's pretty cheeks turned pink. Flustered, she turned to Kundhavai. "*Akka*, these Chinese traders are naught but tattletales. Tell them to go away!" she cried.

"Patience, Vanathi - I'm curious to see how far this gossip mongering will venture," murmured Kundhavai. Aloud she said, "Traders - you were the ones we saw sitting atop an elephant outside the *jothidar's* hut, weren't you?"

"Yes, Devi!" replied the Chinese trader, bobbing his head in assent. "Our trip to the *jothidar's* home bore fruit at once - it was there that we learned of your arrival. The *jothidar* had also predicted that we would have the honour of meeting you, which has now come true. Ah, if the fortune he spoke for the Kodumbalur princess comes to pass as well, why - all our worries will come to an end!"

"Akka!" cried out a ruffled Vanathi once again. "*Ask* them to go away!"

"Traders," said Kundhavai, frowning, "you were also the ones, weren't you, who came atop an elephant in the midst of the procession? You alighted from your mount often to blend in with the crowds, did you not?"

"Yes, Devi. We wished to hear the word of mouth about the imminent coronation. So we decided to circulate amongst the crowds…"

Kundhavai's eyes gleamed with fresh interest. "And what do the people say?" she asked, intrigued. "Did they sound happy that Ponniyin Selvar is to be crowned?"

The Chinese trader shook his head. "No, my lady. No one had anything to say about the coronation at all."

"What else were they talking about?" asked Kundhavai, surprised.

"They extolled the depth and ardour of Madhuranthaka Thevar's *bhakthi*…"

"Ah! Now *this* is the sort of scoop we'd like to hear!" exclaimed Kundhavai happily. "Poonguzhali, did you hear what they said?" She eagerly turned back to the traders. "What else do they say about Madhuranthaka Thevar?"

"They spoke of Madhuranthaka Thevar's selflessness. That he renounced the Chozha *rajyam* despite having every right to stake his claim was praised very highly indeed."

"Is that so? And what did they say was the reason for such a gesture?"

"Word on the street is that Madhuranthaka Thevar is head over heels in love with a boat girl. They say that he is as stubborn as a mule that he will accept none but her as his *pattamagishi*. And so, the chieftains who were once on his side have now reportedly changed their minds. They apparently said, 'In that case, the crown cannot go to Madhuranthakar; it must go only to Ponniyin Selvar!'" replied the Chinese trader, looking at each bemused maiden in turn. "My ladies! If that fortunate boat girl is here as well, we wish to present her with silks, too!'

Poonguzhali looked outraged. "Devi, the Kodumbalur princess was right after all!" she cried indignantly. "These traders are naught but troublemakers. Tell them to leave at once!"

"Patience, Poonguzhali. Why the anger? They spoke no ill about you, surely? Why, it sounds like praise to me!" said Kundhavai, suppressing a grin.

"I need neither their praise nor their censure. I don't need their gifts, either!" said Poonguzhali, rising to her feet.

"*Ammani*! Are you that lucky maiden, then?" cried one of the Chinese traders, thrilled. "Ah! The people were right after all!" he exclaimed admiringly.

So appreciative did he sound that Poonguzhali couldn't help but smile. "Go on, then - what did they say?" she asked.

"Well," replied the chatty trader, putting a thoughtful finger to his nose, "we heard someone in the crowd say that Madhurathaka Thevar sacrificed the kingdom for you, to which another cried out - 'Ah, would one sacrifice a mere *rajyam* for Poonguzhali? Why, if I had nine kingdoms, I would renounce them all for her sake!' I see now how true his words were!" said the Chinese trader in earnest.

Poonguzhali managed to muster a look of vexation. "*Akka*, you must make arrangements at once to punish this brazen trader! Else, I shall tell Ponniyin Selvar myself of his hijinks and see that he is taught a lesson!"

Madhuranthaka Thevar appeared at that precise moment, bearing the consecrated flowers from his evening worship. "The trader has said nothing wrong, surely?" he said cheerfully, upon hearing Poonguzhali's words. "Why must you seek to punish him? I rather agree with what he says, Poonguzhali!"

As the garrulous trader turned around to look at Madhuranthakan, Poonguzhali studied him with a glint in her eye. "If it truly was a mere trader saying such a thing, perhaps it would have been endurable. How can you agree with the words of an imposter?" she replied and grabbed at the trader's big turban; the cloth promptly fell to the ground along with his thick beard and moustache!

There appeared in the place of the Chinese trader a rather alarmed Vandhiyathevan!

"*Ayya*! Save me!" yelled the Vallathu king and hurriedly scrambled towards the other Chinese trader, flinging his arms around his neck. *His* turban unravelled to the ground as well, in company with both beard and moustache!

There appeared in the place of the second Chinese trader none other than a grinning Ponniyin Selvar!

The three royal maidens went into convulsions of laughter.

When Sembian Maadevi arrived thereupon, they recounted the whole episode to her and dissolved into fresh peals of laughter once again.

"*Amma*," said Poonguzhali between giggles, "I had already grown quite suspicious of the pair when I saw them near the temple. That's why I had boldly asked to come to the palace!"

"Yes," chimed in a smiling Madhuranthaka Thevar, "I recognized my friend right away. That is why I left them alone here with you and set off for my evening worship."

"Why, Vanathi!" exclaimed Kundhavai turning to the Kodumablur princess. "It appears as if you and I were the only dimwits who did not see through these rapscallions' disguise!"

"But why did they come thus in disguise to trick us?" asked an indignant Vanathi. "*Ask* them why, *Akka*!"

"Why ask, Vanathi?" replied Kundhavai drily, throwing an accusatory glance at the poor Vallathu king. "My brother is not one for disguises and such. His newfound skill in the art of guile and deceit is no doubt the contagious influence of the friendship he keeps!"

"Devi, do not blame Vandhiyathevan for this prank!" protested Ponniyin Selvar, throwing a supportive arm over his shoulder. "The brilliant idea to impersonate Chinese traders was no one's but my own!"

"Ah, that you are now capable of such brilliance is precisely what I attribute to his influence!" rejoined Kundhavai. "Refrain from such disguises in the future, will you?"

"*Akka*, Thiruvallaur has waxed lyrical about the greatness of truth. But even he says:

Poimaiyum vaimaiyum idatha
Puraitheerntha nanmai payurkkumenin."

[Even falsehood is equal to truth
If it brings goodness free of fault.]

"Aha!" exclaimed Kundhavai, sarcasm dripping from her tone. "Why, I'll wager that Thiruvalluvar himself could have never dreamt his couplet would be used thus one day!"

"Let's leave Thiruvallur aside, then," replied Ponniyin Selvar affably. "When Ramar departed for the forest, didn't he make use of guile to make the people of Ayodhya turn back from following him? Whilst the people were asleep, he asked Sumandiran to drive the chariot towards Ayodhya for a short distance before steering it towards the banks of the river Gangai, didn't he?"

Kundhavai smiled. "*Thambi*, it gives me naught but happiness if you intend to follow in Ramar's footsteps. Let that be. Pray, enlighten us - what goodness free of fault have you wrought by this disguise?"

"We mingled with the people without revealing who we were. Roaming amongst them here and there, we were able to learn their true opinions!"

"And what did you learn of their true opinions, *Thambi*?" asked Kundhavai avidly.

"Oh, so many things, *Akka*! The greatest bit of intelligence I gathered was that the people yearn for the Chozha *samrajyam* to recoup the glory it had attained in the time of Paranthaka Chakravarthy. My friend and I were disguised as Chinese traders a short while back, it is true; but every word we said was nothing but the unvarnished truth!" revealed Ponniyin Selvar. "After we met the two of you upon the road, we proceeded to Thanjai. There, we really did meet two Chinese traders near the fort. We bought these bagfuls of silk from them for a price. Then we put on disguises to look like them and came back here. The things I said just now about the Arab pirates were the accounts of those very traders, in truth. Devi! No matter what, my friend and I will go to Eezha Naadu after the coronation ceremony comes to an end." His eyes shone with ambition and will. "When our work there is done, we shall travel to the countries that lie across the seas! It is hard to say whether we will return with our lives intact or whether we will meet a warrior's death and attain the heaven of heroes. And so, you should all be ever by our side until we leave!" Ponniyin Selvar clasped his sister's hand in earnest. "Pray, give us your blessing that you will! We came hurrying back thus only to ask this of you!"

Kundhavai's eyes filled with tears at his words.

Poonguzhali's lips quivered. "I do not understand why you all go to war," she said in a trembling voice. "Cannot men have affection for one another and live in peace and happiness?"

"Daughter, that cannot be," said Sembian Maadevi softly. "As long as the world exists, so too will there be war. Why, even Paramasivan and Parameswari were obliged to go to battle! Some take birth in this world for the sole purpose of establishing *dharma*. They have no choice but to wage war."

The rest were plunged into an ocean of surprise to hear the gentle Sembian Maadevi, the very crest jewel of Siva *bhakthi*, speak thus.

85

THE DEEPER MEANING OF A SCULPTURE

Madhuranthaka Thevar, once known to us as Senthan Amudhan, looked in surprise at Sembian Maadevi, whose noble womb had given him birth. "*Amma*, there are many in this world who crave the dangers of war. They feel that days not spent in war are wasted. My friend Vandhiyathevan and Ponniyin Selvar belong to this ilk. But you - you are one who believes that days not spent in worship are wasted! That you should speak in support of war is astonishing indeed!" he said.

"My dear son! No matter who criticizes the business of war, you yourself must not. Neither must Poonguzhali!" replied Sembian Maadevi. "It is solely on account of the Vallathu king's military skills, is it not, that you yet live today to sing the praises of the Lord such that it melts my body and soul?"

"*Thaaye*," interjected Vandhiyathevan, "it is true that I saved the life of your beloved son. But I can never forget how he and your daughter-in-law, who held his hand in troth, saved mine! It is naught but Poonguzhali *Amma*iyar's feisty spirit that has made it possible for me to live and breathe today."

"Parameswaran and Durga Parameswari ever protect all of us," replied Madhuranthakan earnestly. "Where is the question of us saving one another without his Grace by our side?"

"Child, even the embodiment of compassion that is Siva Peruman has had to go to war on many occasions," said Sembian Maadevi gently. "It even became necessary for Jagan Maatha - the very manifestation of love, grace and peace - to wage fierce battles. She appears in the temple of this holy land as the Goddess Aram Valartha Nayagi. Even so, you must have noticed whilst circumambulating the sanctum that She materializes as Goddess Mahishasuramardini as well."

"Yes, *Annaiye*!" confessed Madhuranthakar in a tone of wonder. "I did and was left spellbound. That the Mother who has given birth to and protects the universe should stand thus atop the head of a buffalo left me breathtaken."

"Yes, yes!" smiled Sembian Maadevi. "The Devi of this temple had waged a fierce war to kill Mahishasuran. Even so, we see the Devi's holy features suffused with love and grace, even as She stands triumphant atop the head of a buffalo! Among the cave sculptures of Maamallapuram is a beautiful carving that depicts the Devi at war with Mahishasuran. There, Durga Parameswari graces us in the valiant, frightening form of the Goddess Rana Bhadrakali. Why must Durga Parameswari, the Mother of the universe, fight with a mere buffalo? Why is this triumph celebrated? These questions will naturally occur to those who see naught but the outer form. My dear son! Our forefathers had a deeper reason for these depictions. The understanding of such sublime truth demands both maturity and interest from the seeker!" she said.

"Devi," began Arulmozhi, "I cannot say for sure that we are all blessed with such maturity; but we certainly do have the interest to learn! We hang on every pearl of a word uttered by your noble lips. Why," he continued, his lips twitching, "even the ever roving eyes of our Vallathu King are focused on none but you!"

The words brought on a flurry of giggles from the rest of the group. It was patently obvious that Arulmozhi was commenting on Vandhiyathevan's furtive glances at Ilaiya Piratti's pretty face.

"If you're truly interested, then I shall tell you. Listen!" said Sembian Maadevi. "Our *puranic* histories describe many battles between the forces of good and evil. They also recount how Thirumal Himself descended upon our world as an avatar to fight against *rakshasas*. The forces of good and evil have waged wars against each other since the very beginning of time, when God brought the world into existence. If you were to ask why God created such forces of evil, mortal intelligence will be at a loss to give a satisfactory answer. All we can do is wonder at the divine play at hand! In any case, it is certain that the forces of good and evil are constantly fighting with each other. Sometimes, it appears as if evil gains the upper hand, giving the impression that they will rule over the world for the rest of time. Surapadman, Hiranyan and Ravanan themselves ruled for many thousands of years. But each met their end in the blink of an eye."

"Yes, yes!" interjected Madhuranthakar. "That ten-headed Ravanan subjugated the host of Devas to the extent that he tasked them with menial errands! But when the time came for him to meet his end, all it took was two men and a company of monkeys to destroy him along with his entire clan, wasn't it?"

Sembian Maadevi nodded. "And so, when evil forces gain dominance in the world, men must not lose themselves to despair. They must believe that the forces of good will triumph; they must stand tall in the truth and fight up until the very end. God ever helps those who fight for good."

"*Annaiye*, you were to tell us about Mahishasuran!" broke in Poonguzhali.

"So I was! Thank goodness you reminded me, daughter. You see, there are two types of evil forces at play in the world - one is ignorant and mindless while the other is possessed of cunning and keen intelligence. It was the evil force of ignorance that our forefathers depicted as Mahishasuran. Have you seen a wild buffalo grow enraged and run amok? In such a frenzied state, a wild buffalo develops strength greater than that of an elephant. It mercilessly tears into any creature it comes across and leaves great destruction in its wake. Ignorance has as much power as an enraged wild buffalo. At times, it manages to seat itself upon the throne and begin its terrible reign. This calamity is what our ancestors dubbed the rule of Mahishasuran. When Mahishasuran grabbed the throne of Devalokam and began his reign, it threw all the three worlds into dire turmoil. Mahishasuran ordained a terrible decree - 'Eschew intelligence!' he ordered. 'Shun the books of intellect, the arts of intellect and music! Shun too, sculptures, paintings, temples and *gopurams* - destroy all of it to dust!" The Devas, holy ascetics and mortal men trembled under his shadow. Many among them buckled and accepted his rule. And so, Mahishasuran grew in conceit, hatred and violence. Must you ask of the consequences of arrogance and hate melding with ignorance? Unable to bear Mahishasuran's tyranny, the three worlds drowned in the lamentations of the suffering; even the Asuras wailed in despair. It was at this moment that Durga Parameswari opened her divine eyes. She took on the form of the Goddess Maha Kali and killed Mahishasuran. The divine force of good triumphed over the evil force of ignorance. The Devas, holy ascetics and even the Asuras heaved a great sigh of relief. They sang the praises of Durga Parameswari and bowed down to Her.

Children! The evil force of ignorance exists in the world even today. I am told that such an evil has reared its head in our own sacred land of Bharathakandam, beyond the northwest. Driven by brutal rage, the sinful wage merciless war upon cities and towns, and put the innocent to the sword; they storm temples and grind them into ruins along with the sacred *vigrahams* of deities. Alas, there is reportedly no great emperor in Vada Naadu to stand up to these forces and stop them. Let such a fate never befall this holy Thamizh Naadu. If such a threat looms upon the horizon, you, the brave descendants of a clan famed for its valour, must be prepared to fight against evil."

"We shall gear ourselves up for the challenge, *thaaye*!" exclaimed a riveted Vandhiyathevan. "Do tell us about the other type of evil as well!"

"The other type of evil are those who are sharp of intelligence and cunning. They use their cleverness towards ill ends. They undertake arduous penance and receive great boons, which they use to achieve naught but evil. What did the people of Tripura do? Each exerted their will to create entire worlds of their own. They soared through the skies and descended upon towns and countries to annihilate them. Soorapadman had the power to regenerate a new head whenever he was decapitated. *Rakshasas* like Ravanan and Indrajit wielded the power to take to the skies, where they lurked behind the clouds to throw down terrible *astras* and weapons of destruction on the people below. The evil forces of such cunning and intelligence were depicted by our forefathers as the Asura Muyalagan. Even when the Lord dances the *ananda nadanam* in rapture, he bears Muyalagan in mind and holds him down firmly with His foot - all it takes is a little distraction and Muyalagan will rear his head once again. The Asura Muyalagan teaches us that the forces of evil have been at war with the forces of good since the very beginning of the universe. And so, my dear children - how can we say that wars should never be fought?"

"Devi, we have been taught many concepts today that we little knew before," said Ponniyin Selvar gratefully. "Pray, lay down your command."

"Children, all I can say is that you must ever side with the forces of good and fight with all your might. I cannot put an order to you; only your own conscience can. Obey its command and behave as fit." Sembian Maadevi paused. When she spoke next, her tone sounded graver than before. "A short while back, you said that the seas girding Thamizh Naadu are blighted by pirates; that the traders of our land suffer much trouble and loss at their hands. As stock of the kingly clan, it is your duty - nay, your *dharma* - to wipe out such sea raiders and provide protection to our traders. If these pirates are given a wide berth today, they will grow emboldened to infiltrate our sacred Thamizh Naadu, won't they? If my noble husband were alive today - he who has attained Siva's holy *kailayam* and sits among the celestial Siva *ganas* - he would doubtless give you all the same counsel."

"Devi, we understand your wise counsel and shall strive to live up to it!" promise the Ilavarasar Arulmozhi Varmar sincerely.

"Ponniyin Selva! If you truly do intend to give respect to my word and live as I bid, I wish to give you yet another counsel," said the venerable old queen.

"Devi, I do not recall ever acting against your wishes!" replied Arulmozhi with deep reverence. "If I have been guilty of such a thing, pray pardon me!"

"Child, your conduct so far is one thing; the conduct you will adopt in the near future, another. Until now, you were a beloved child of the palace, the apple of every eye. We indulged your whims just as you fulfilled our wishes. Soon, you will ascend to be the King of Kings that rules over the great country. We must behave in accordance with your orders after the coronation ceremony..."

"*Thaaye*, pray do not say such a thing," broke in Ponniyin Selvar. "I shall remain none but your beloved son, even in the times to come. I will do as you bid."

A pleased smile appeared on Sembian Maadevi's face. "In that case, listen to what I have to say. The ancient Chozha clan must flourish and attain eternal growth - it must enjoy an unbroken succession of offspring, much like the fertile plantain that proliferates in its grove. It is true that those born to a kingly clan must be ever prepared to journey to the heaven of warriors; but it is crucial to exercise caution considering the growth of the dynasty. Your noble *thamayan* Aditha Karikalan met his demise without having pledged his troth in marriage. There remains none but you to take forward the exalted Chozha lineage. And so, before you board a ship to sail across the seas in search of Lady Victory, you must fulfill your obligation to preserve and expand the Chozha line of descent. Make arrangements for your wedding too along with the coronation," urged the dowager queen, glancing affectionately at the Kodumbalur princess. "You must have done much penance indeed to win a maiden such as Vanathi for your wife! The singular fortune of this queen among women will grace you with remarkable longevity; the sacred thread you tie around her neck in marriage will protect you as a shield of armour wherever you go."

"Devi, I am more than willing to wear that coat of mail," replied Ponniyin Selvar. "It is Vanathi who refuses - she remains obstinate in her stand that she will not sit on the throne on account of her vow!"

"Do not give credence to the Kodumbalur Ilavarasi's words," piped up Poonguzhali, rather unexpectedly. "She only affects elusion to see our supplication grow earnest. Ponniyin Selvar must press his suit on bended knee, methinks!" she said, laughing.

Everyone laughed along at the jest, save Vanathi who burst out in tears.

"Silly girl, why do you weep?" asked Kundhavai, alarmed. Ilaiya Piratti took the weeping maiden by the hand and led her downstairs.

86

A DREAM OR PERCHANCE, REALITY?

Sembian Maadevi, Madhuranthakan and Poonguzhali departed for Thanjai the next morning.

Ponniyin Selvar and Vandhiyathevan intended to make for the towns of Uraiyur and Srirangam. Arulmozhi Varmar had promised Vandhiyathevan that he would point out to him along the way the grand anicut that had been built in Karikala Chozhar's time to regulate the waters of the Kaveri. Ponniyn Selvan went to Kundhavai Devi to take his leave before their departure.

"*Akka*! *Must* you go to Pazhaiyarai?" he asked, imploringly.

"*Thambi*! *Must* you go to Uraiyur?" countered Kundhavai. "Can you not accompany us to Pazhaiyarai?"

"No, *Akka*! We gave Azhwarkkadiyaan our word that we would meet him at Uraiyur on an important matter," he replied.

Kundhavai furrowed her brows. "Aha! You are not like you once were, *Thambi*! Your mind has been sullied, I see. You hardly seem to show me any respect at all! I reckon the credit for this dubious turnaround goes to the friendship you keep with the Vallathu King..."

"Do not hold *him* liable - I have grown older and more mature, haven't I *Akka*?" he said petulantly. "I will soon be crowned the Chakravarthy of a mighty *rajyam*. Surely I should be able to do as I like now, at the very least?"

Kundhavai pursed her lips. "Go on, do as you like, then! It is good enough, I suppose, that you don't exert your authority on me. I shall content myself as long as I am not told to behave in accordance with your wishes!"

"Pray, come to the *magudabhishekam*," begged Ponniyin Selvar. "You can do as you like, after that."

Kundhavai raised her chin. "You can lord it over me once the *magudabhishekam* comes to an end. What right do you have to force my hand before that?"

Ponniyin Selvar's face fell. "Then, you truly will not attend the *magudabhishekam*, is it?" he asked.

"That entirely depends on Vanathi's wish. If she is pleased to attend, I shall come; else, I will not."

"Where *is* that maiden, *Akka*?"

"She is with your mother - river Ponni - to offer her prayers. She prays for the river goddess to bless you with intelligence of mind," came the tart reply.

The Ilavarasar chuckled. "I hope her prayers are answered," he said with a smile. "I shall take my leave, now."

"Thambi, I have never yet seen another as cruel as you!" burst out Kundhavai in dismay. "Vanathi did not sleep a wink all night; she was lost to sorrowful brooding and tears. I would that you go now to the steps of the river Kaveri and take your leave of her before you depart!"

Ponniyin Selvar flashed a wry smile. "She did not sleep, you say? I see now that she wasn't content enough with robbing me of mine! If one cannot understand another's heart, there's nothing for it but to resign oneself to tears. And you bid me suffer the rest of my life in troth to such a maiden!" With that, he turned on his heels and briskly walked to the palace backyard.

As soon as the prince crossed the gardens, he caught sight of Vanathi seated upon the steps of the Ponni river. She was engrossed in strewing flowers one by one from the plateful of blooms she had by her side. If Vanathi had not been offering blossoms in worship thus, she would have been easily mistaken for a beautiful statue in grace upon the banks of the Kaveri.

Ponniyin Selvar quietly seated himself upon a step directly behind her. Vanathi must have known that someone was coming towards her; perhaps she instinctively gleaned that it was none but Ponniyin Selvar, for she paused her worship and grew still.

Dewdrops studded the flowers upon the plate, sparkling as it caught the sunlight. Two pearly tears sprung to Vanathi's own eyes, shining as it hung there.

The golden rays of the rising sun flirted with the undulating waters of the Ponni, giving the impression that the Chozha *samrajyam* was but a young maiden bedecked in an iridescent garment of blue shot with strands of gold. The lush groves that grew along both sides of the river seemed for all the world to be rich border of green silk that complemented lustrous, rippling waters of blue.

The greenery along the riverbank hummed with sweet birdsong, keeping tune with the babbling waters of the Kaveri. The beautiful environs and the golden dawn together cast an enchanting ambience that invited one to wander their dreams in sweet reverie.

The prince remained silent for some time. "Vanathi?" he called out gently after a while. "Are you lost in a daydream? Have I spoilt your reverie?"

"It is true that I daydream, *Ayya*; but how can you spoil my reverie? Even my dreams at night are filled with naught but you as their hero. That is why when I see you close by my side, I am forced to wonder if it is a dream or perchance, reality; I find myself tongue-tied, unable to accord you the welcome you are due," replied Vanathi softly. "Yes, *swami*! I have indulged myself in so many daydreams on so many days! When I met you for the very first time at the Thirunallam gardens, I mistook you for a mahout. Later, I have often wished that you truly were a simple mahout. I have lost myself in dreams where I imagined myself atop an elephant, behind you. In those reveries, it was never the ordinary grey elephant of this world that I rode; I felt that I was riding none but Airavatam, the celestial white elephant of Devalokam. I pictured you as Devendran and myself as Indrani…"

"Then, now…" started the Ponniyin Selvar.

Vanathi continued, speaking over his words. "Pray, patience, my king - I shall soon correct this fantasy of mine as Devendran and me as Indrani. When, after all, do Devendran and Indrani ever enjoy peace together? Where do they have the luxury of time to mount Airavatham and go on travel by themselves? They must forever be resigned to being encircled by adoring devas and devis, mustn't they?" she asked. "And so, my thoughts would change, every time; I would wonder why I suffered to be born in a royal family instead of to a boatman by the seashore."

"I see now, Vanathi! You are envious of Poonguzhali!" exclaimed Ponniyin Selvar in some surprise.

"That is true, *Ayya*!" replied Vanathi defensively. "There is none in this world that I feel envious of, save Poonguzhali! Her heart's desire has come true. She will soon depart for Kodikkarai with her lover by her side and lead a life of happiness; she will merrily sail her boat upon the waves of the sea and offer service in peace at the Kuzhagar temple. Why wouldn't she laugh at me, after all?" she said bitterly. "*Ayya*, punish me in any way you see fit; only, do not make it so Poonguzhali finds reason to laugh at me..."

Ponniyin Selvar remembered what had transpired the previous night. "Patience, Vanathi. Poonguzhali laughed at you yesterday, did she not? The time will come when you will laugh at her!" he said, attempting to console the Kodumbalur princess.

"*Swami*, I do not wish to laugh at Poonguzhali. I do not wish to laugh at anyone!" replied Vanathi miserably. "Let anyone laugh at me, if they wish. I only yearn to see your golden face bloom with happiness." She searched his face with beseeching eyes. "Your face brightens with joy when you come across anyone but me! My very sight makes your eyebrows scrunch with dislike. Why," she murmured, drawing her eyes away, "I am rather frightened to look upon you even now..."

"Vanathi, listen!" said Ponniyin Selvar, raising her chin with a gentle finger. "There is a reason my face shrinks at your sight. No one else puts me through the perturbation that you do; they do not affect my tranquility of mind. It is because of none but you that my heart loses all sense of peace. My *thamakkaiyar* told me that you did not sleep last night. Neither did I, Vanathi!" He met her gaze with earnest eyes. "I have not slept for many days, as a matter of fact. Should I lie down upon the palace terrace to gaze at the sky, the twinkling stars remind me of naught but your sparkling eyes; when the trees in the grove sway to the wind and the leaves rustle sweetly, I hear naught but your sweet laughter. When the gentle breeze brushes against my skin, it makes me think that it is naught but the touch of your fingers, soft as *kanthal* flowers - the very thought drives me into raptures of ecstasy! Vanathi, you dominate my thoughts so completely that my face cannot help but shrink, my eyebrows cannot help but scrunch when I see you in person. I fear that you will be my weakness, my stumbling block to the dreams I wish to achieve…"

"*Swami*, pray, put aside such fear! I will never come in the way of your dreams…"

"No, you will not. No one can!" Ponniyin Selvar's eyes suddenly sparkled and he sprang to his feet. "Have you seen, Vanathi, the dark storm clouds that gather at the horizon in the rainy season? They are full of rain; also contained within them are the elements of incandescent lightning and sonorous thunder. The storm descends as it blows these rain-filled clouds towards us. Can anyone stop that from happening? I am as those very clouds. Vanathi, my body seems to constantly thrum with feverish excitement and anxiety - it is charged with phantom bolts of lightning that cannot be seen with the eye; it pulsates with the surreal boom of thunder that cannot be heard with the ear. The storms, hurricanes and tempest all call out to me; waves as tall as mountains rise high upon the seven seas to welcome me; the blast of a thousand conches, the thundering beats of drums and the blare of war elephants call out to me, enchanting me with their summons. None can stop me, Vanathi! But there are some who have the power to ruin my peace of mind by attempting to…"

"*Swami*, I shall never do that!" cried Vanathi. "I admit that I can be of little help to you; but never shall I be a hindrance to you, one who was born to rule all the three worlds. It is the very reason why I refuse to sit beside you upon the Chozha throne."

Ponniyin Selvar smiled. "Vanathi, the Chozha throne is great in magnificence but is a rather small object, in truth. It seats but one; the Chakravarthini sit upon another throne beside the Chakravarthy's own."

"*Swami*, I want neither space upon your own throne nor a throne of my own. Let that blessing go to a deserving maiden who has done penance enough and has fortune enough to be seated by your side as your *pattamagishi*. All I yearn for is a small place for myself in the throne of your heart; that honour will bring me naught but ecstasy, for I shall consider it the fruit of the penances of my past seven lives!" said Vanathi in earnest.

"Vanathi, you have asked me for a boon that I can fulfill effortlessly. You have already reserved a place for yourself in the throne of my heart - nothing stops me from giving it over to you," replied Ponniyin Selvar. "Do you truly have no desire to be the Chakravarthini of this mighty Chozha *samrajyam*, Vanathi? Do you not wish to wear upon your head its golden crown, bejewelled with precious gems that dazzle the eye?"

"I do not have the tiniest spark of such desire!" declared Vanathi. "I have seen the ancient crowns of the Chozha clan; I have held them in my hand. If I were to place one upon my head, I fear the weight will crush my head and stifle my throat, making me gasp for breath. My body does not have such strength, my liege, neither does my heart bear such courage. *Swami*, let one who has both the might and valour to bear such weight wear the bejewelled crown!" Vanathi's face glowed; her cheeks flushed a rich pink and her eyes sparkled. "Before you travel to foreign lands that lie across the seas, pray, grant me a gift. I shall pluck the prettiest flowers from the palace gardens, string them into a garland and give it to you. 'Tis a coronet that I can bear with ease; pray, adorn my neck with that garland and make me your servant before you leave!"

"I did purchase a necklace studded with nine precious gems for you from the Chinese traders, you know. I meant it to be your *pattabhishekam* gift."

"Why must I receive a present for your *pattabhishekam*?"

"Alright, then - I shall give it to another!" cried Ponniyin Selvar. "Vanathi, let us make a pledge to each other. I shall adorn your neck with a garland as you wish before I go; in return, you must wait for me with a freshly strung garland of flowers each time I return from foreign lands. When I come home to the beat of triumphant drums from installing the Chozha flag in the far nations flung across the seas, you must receive me with a garland of victory!" said the Ilavarasar, impassioned.

"Why just one?" dimpled the Ilavarasi Vanathi prettily. "I shall string hundreds upon hundreds of garlands and eagerly wait for you. Everyone in this great country will await your return!"

87

The poet stood dumbstruck

As Arulmozhi Varmar's coronation day drew closer, all of Chozha Naadu descended into delirious excitement. As far as crowning Ponniyin Selvar went, there was nary a difference of opinion amongst the people. The men, women, elders, children, urbanites, villagers, traders and labourers of Chozha Naadu were united in their joy at the prospect of Ponniyin Selvar's coronation. They all delighted in repeating amongst themselves the tale of the prince's miraculous time of birth and his remarkable trait of mingling as one with the populace of the land. The Ramayana describes in quite some detail the exuberance of the people of Ayodhya when they learned that Dasarathar had decided to crown prince Rama.

The epic recounts that the older women became as Kosalai; each one, goes the tale, rejoiced as though it were their own sons who were to be honoured with the *magudabhishekam*. The younger maidens felt as elated as Seetha Devi herself, jubilant as though their own husbands were to be crowned; they bedecked themselves in beautiful clothes and sparkling jewels to celebrate the occasion. The older men of the great city of Ayodhya identified themselves entirely with Dasarathar.

Maathargal vayathinmikkar kosalai manaththai oththar;
Vethiyar vasittanoththar; verula magalir ellam Seethaiyai oththar;
Annal thiruvinai oththal;
Avvur sathana maanthellam thayarathan thannai oththar

[The older women rejoiced as Kosalai;
As Vasishta the priests; The maidens all rejoiced as Seetha;
The day was a day of holy fortune;
The good men of the city rejoiced as Dasarathar.]

What great work had Ramar wrought then to win such love and respect among the people of Ayodhya? The greatness of his bow Kothandam would come to light much later in the future; so too would the pride and fame he won by killing Ravanan and the other rakshasas, liberating the three worlds from a reign of terror. At this point in time, Ramar had only helped the ascetic Vishwamitrar complete his *yaagam*; it is doubtful whether that could have been a sufficient display of his true magnificence. Why, Vishwamitrar himself seems to have made no mention of the incident on his return to Ayodhya!

There are some in this world who win the hearts of the people through astonishing deeds of valour and unstinting acts of aid and generosity. Others win praise through their remarkable skills in the art of music, dance and poetry; there are some who achieve miracles in the art of painting and sculpture, too. Still others are imbued with godliness while they are yet in the womb; they are marked out to be singular at the very time of their birth. They capture the hearts of the people with little or no effort, Mother Nature having blessed them with magnetic charisma and charm. Ah, it does seem as though Mother Nature is rather partial, does it not? Though, it is entirely possible that Her gifts of allure and enchantment are bestowed along with other unfavourable traits in equal measure. We can never really know.

Ramar, for all the love, respect and adoration he commanded among the people of Ayodhya, was forced to endure all the tribulations that faced the ordinary man. He had to undergo unspeakable grief - not only was he exiled to the forest, he also had to suffer separation from his dearly beloved wife.

Arulmozhi Varmar had won Mother Nature's favour. His very appearance left all who laid eyes upon him enchanted beyond words; the sweetness of his speech and the integrity of his character won him the love of all who had the privilege to know him. When he had set forth to the battlefield of the Eezha Naadu war, he found that he was not presented with many opportunities to accomplish feats of courage and valour. And yet, Chozha Naadu was set ablaze with the colourful tales of his brave exploits. When we bear great affection for someone, we are ever ready to believe words of praise that aggrandize him, no matter how exaggerated they are.

Ever since Sundara Chozhar had been bedridden with the illness that robbed him of the strength to walk, the people had worriedly anticipated trouble and strife in Chozha Naadu over the subject of succession. Rumours had spread hinting that the Pazhuvettaryars and Sambuvaraiyar were plotting a conspiracy with the other chieftains and higher officials to anoint Kandaradhithar's son the crown prince instead of Sundara Chozhar's own sons. The people were familiar with Kandaradhithar's son Madhuranthakan. They bore no particular ill towards him, in truth. But Madhuranthakar, for his part, had never made an effort to mingle with the people. All the populace knew was that much like his own father, Madhuranthakar had shunned worldly desires and was steeped in Siva *bhakthi*. The people regarded their country with immense pride and joy - they took great pleasure in the fact that the Chozha rajyam had expanded its territory since the time of Vijayalaya Chozhar; that trade had flourished like a dream, bestowing upon the people a higher standard of living; that the Chozha armies returned triumphant from their campaigns to foreign lands, bringing back to the country colossal wealth amassed as the spoils of war. The enterprising people of Chozha Naadu wanted the mighty Chozha dynasty to reach ever higher peaks of growth and glory. They rather doubted whether the Chozha *rajyam* could accelerate its progress under Madhurathakar's reign, lost to Siva *bhakthi* as he was. They also feared that if Madhuranthakar were to be crowned, the word of the chieftains would become law.

The people had held Aditha Karikalar in great respect as an unrivalled warrior, but they had not shown much enthusiasm at the prospect of him ascending the throne. Aditha Karikalar had not been gifted with a nature that effortlessly captivated their hearts; he had not blended in with the common people, either. Further, he had been enshrouded in a strange miasma of mystery, for there were the oddest rumours about him. Whispers abounded that he had committed an unspeakable crime of some sort, one that tortured his own conscience; word on the street was that it was the very reason why he had lost the love and affection of his own father, Sundara Chozhar. There were other such strange tales in the air, too. And so, when news broke of his untimely death, the people accorded him all the respect due to an illustrious warrior but found that they did not grieve all that much. They blamed his early demise on the unlucky falling star and consoled their hearts.

Periya Pazhuvettarayar's death and the circumstances of his demise had kindled a new love for him in the people's hearts, too. They learned, to their astonishment, that the riveting enchantress the brave old man had wed in his old age was none but an ally of the Pandiya Naadu *abathudhavis*; that it was only upon her evil instigation that Periya Pazhuvettayar's heart had been corrupted and sullied; that it was the Pandiya Naadu *abathudhavis* who were responsible for Aditha Karikalar's untimely death; and that Periya Pazhuvettarayar had dauntlessly killed himself with his own hands in atonement for his crimes. "*Ayyo*, poor thing!" cried out the people when they heard the rumours, feeling deeply sorry for him. That Periya Pazhuvettaryar had, with his dying breath, exhorted the chieftains to lay aside the thought of crowning Madhuranthakar to crown Ponniyin Selvar instead only served to increase the respect the people held for him. That venerable old man had, after all, embraced his death only after clearing away a barrier that stood in the way of the people's wishes. "Long live his memories! Long live his clan!" cried the people in gratitude as they sang his praises.

None of the common folk were aware that there had been a curious case of mistaken identity when it came to Madhuranthaka Thevar. None save the royal family and the people close to them knew the truth. The old Madhuranthakar had spent most of his time within the confines of the palace. Very rarely had he emerged in public; on the odd occasion he did, he refrained from fraternizing with the public. When talk was in the air of anointing him the crown, Madhuranthakar had taken to the habit of travelling around in a veiled palanquin. There had been precious little opportunity for the people to truly look upon Madhuranthakar and observe his features. And so, a great majority of the public were blissfully unaware that the old Madhuranthakar had been replaced by a new one.

Therefore, none saw any change or difference in the new Madhuranthakar when he participated in the temple festivities at Thiruvaiyaru. It was only Poonguzhali who caught the eye of the people. Some declared that the maiden was Chinna Pazhuvettarayar's daughter. Others hotly refuted the claim, insisting instead that she was naught but a boat girl who sailed a ferry upon the seas; they said that it was only quite recently that Madhuranthakar had wed her.

It was quite common in those days of yore for royal kings, princes and noble chieftains to marry many wives; so no one was surprised by the news. Madhuranthaka Thevar had already gained respect among the people for rumours claimed that he renounced the crown even though the chieftains pushed him towards it. Madhuranthaka Thevar's appearance, they saw, reflected the pure and rapturous Siva *bhakthi* that he nursed within; their reverence for him grew by leaps and bounds. When word emerged that he stepped away from the Chozha throne for the sake of the boat girl Poonguzhali, they grew to love and admire him, as well. They were certain, they chattered to each other, that when Ponniyin Selvar's pattabhishekam came to its conclusion, he would grant Madhuranthaka Thevar an exalted post in the royal administration.

With two days to go for the coronation, people had begun travelling to Thanjai from all four corners of Chozha Naadu. A crushing throng had gathered outside the Thanjai fort. The fort gates were thrown open to the public; the earlier restrictions that had regulated entry and egress were rescinded. The coronation date had been fixed as soon as the month of Thai had rolled around solely because any further postponement would have made the crowd quite unmanageable. The administration had also made many arrangements for the comfort of the people.

In deference to Ponniyin Selvar's command, Kodumbalur Velar sent back a significant majority of the vast southern forces he had brought with him, retaining only a few thousand soldiers by his side. Similarly, the chieftains allied to the Pazhuvettarayars sent back to their respective stations the soldiers they had gathered and stationed near Kudanthai. None remained but the usual guards that Chinna Pazhuvettarayar normally charged with keeping a watch on the fort.

The Pazhuvoor men, Kodumbalur men and the soldiers of the Vellakara Padai embraced one another, putting their former hostility behind them. They joked with one another and rejoiced together in celebrations. The men rendered the service they could to the crowd of people that had gathered to see the coronation ceremony. The air was so full of joy and exuberance that the people indulged the soldiers when they played the occasional trick or two.

The interiors of the Thanjai fort as well as the cityscape outside were decorated as lavishly as Devendran's own celestial city of Amaravati. There was hardly a house in the city that was not hosting a guest who had travelled from afar.

At last, the sun rose upon the day the coronation was to take place. The people were transfixed by the majestic sight - shining spears of golden rays banished the lingering dewdrops of twilight as the sun rose, gloriously encased in an uncommonly dazzling brilliance. "Today is the day of Ponniyin Selvar's *magudabhishekam*, isn't it? No wonder the sun shines so golden thus!" they cried in delight.

Long before the *magudabhishekam* was to take place, a formidable throng of people started gathering at the doorway of the *pattabhisheka mandapam*. It was impossible to accommodate all the common folk in the *mandapam*, of course. The people would be able to set their eyes on Ponniyin Selvar and rejoice only after the coronation festivities were over, when he emerged from the *mandapam* upon the royal elephant in procession through the streets. Were they to wait until then, twiddling their thumbs? If they arrived at the *mandapam* early enough, they could catch a glimpse of Ponniyin Selvar the very minute he emerged with the crown upon his head!

The *magudabhisheka mandapam* was built with a back entrance specifically for the use of the palace inhabitants. Sundara Chozhar and Vanama Devi made their appearance through this path, followed by Sembian Maadevi, Madhuranthakar, Poonguzhali, Kundhavai Piratti and Vanathi. The Mudhanmandhiri Aniruddhar, Chinna Pazhuvettarayar, Sambuvaraiyar, the Senathipathi Boodhi Vikrama Kesari and Malayaman Miladudaiyar arrived along with the other chieftains, key local officials, industrial merchant heads, traders, fort chiefs, chief officials of great cities, the *Sivacharyas*, the

Bhattars and great Thamizh poets; they had to veritably fight their way through the pressing horde of people gathered at the entrance. Finally, Ponniyin Selvar and Vallavarayan Vandhiyathevan reached the magudabhisheka mandapam in a dazzling golden chariot skillfully fashioned in the likeness of a lotus. The sea of people dissolved into deafening cheers, like the very waves of the ocean that had spotted the full moon in the sky.

The hoary rituals prefacing the *magudabhishekam* took place as planned. The bejewelled crown that the Chozha kings had worn upon their heads through generations was placed on a massive, painted plate; so too was placed the exquisite necklace of gemstones they had worn around their necks and the magnificent broadsword they had carried at their waists. The artefacts were carried to the elders in the *sabha*, who touched the plate to give their blessings. Then, the royal poet Nallan Saathanar got to his feet. Behind him stood a maiden with a *yazh* in her hands; she expertly played its strings to wake a sweet tone of accompaniment. The poet Nallan Saathanar then proceeded to sing an intricate ballad describing the ancient glory of the Chozha clan and the histories of the intrepid kings of the lineage who had attained great fame. Because the ballad he sang was quite long and set in a language that is perhaps not easily comprehensible today, we offer you its gist below:

"In the clan of Manu Mandha which hails from the exalted lineage of the Suryavamsam, there appeared a King of Kings called Sibi. He cut away the flesh of his own body in order to keep his word to a dove and save its life. The people who later appeared in the lineage of Sibi proudly added the honorific 'Sembian' to their names. In such a Sembiar clan, there appeared a great king called Rajakesari. His son gained fame under the name of Parakesari. The kings who later appeared after them, therefore, took on either the title of Korajakesari or Koparakesari, one after the other. The Chozha king who sacrificed his own dear son in order to render justice to a cow received the name of Manu Needhi Chozhan. After his time, a king called Karikal Peruvalathaan appeared in the city of Poompuhar and spread his fame throughout the three worlds. He marched his vast Chozha army up until the imposing Imaiya Malai in the north; and on that great mountain's peak he planted the Chozha flag grandly emblazoned with the insignia of a tiger. After him appeared Nalankilli, Nedunkilli, Kulamuttrathu Thunjiya Killivalavan as well as that peerless devotee of Siva Peruman, Koperunchozhan. They each added glory and honour to the ancient Chozha clan before attaining the lotus feet of Siva.

Just as the Surya *bhagavan* who bestows the world with light is enveloped by clouds in the rainy season, the Chozha clan that hails from the splendid lineage of the sun too was engulfed for a short period by the clouds of the enemies, the Pallavas and the Pandiyas. It was then that the illustrious Vijayalaya Chozhar appeared, equal in might to the very Devendran who scatters the gathered clouds with the mighty *vajrayudham* weapon. The mouse Pidagumutharayan took fright at this lion of the Chozha clan; he soon died and disappeared from view. And so, that great warrior seized the city of Thanjai and built a magnificent temple for Durga Parameswari. The courtyard of that brave King's palace was always full of messengers from the Pallavas, Pandiyas and other kings who eagerly sought Vijayalaya Chozhar's friendship. For the kings who came seeking his aid, Vijayalaya munificently granted support and refuge - he marched to countless battlefields to wage wars and took upon his own noble person no less than ninety-six battle wounds.

Vijayalaya Chozhar's beloved son Aditha Chozhar scattered the clouds of enemy forces as a resplendent sun and routed them. When the Pallavan Aparajitha found himself on the brink of defeat to the Pandiyas, Aditha Chozhar emerged upon the Thiruppurambayam battlefield like a lion storming a warren of rabbits and decimated the Pandiya armies. The treacherous Pallavan proved to later betray him, paying no heed to the help he had rendered. And so, he marched his forces to Thondai Naadu, where he pounced upon

Aparajithan as he sat atop an elephant and swiftly dispatched him to the heaven of slain warriors. Following in the footsteps of his illustrious forefather Kochenganaan, he raised eighty two temples to Siva from the origin of the Kaveri river in the Saiya mountains up until the city of Poompuhar.

Paranthaka Chozhar, the son of Aditha Chozhar, was born with Veeralakshmi and Vijayalakshmi - the very goddesses of valour and victory - upon his shoulders. That great King who dealt the Pandiyas defeat at Vellore and captured Madurai and Eezham, stood as a lion to the forces of Chera Naadu. Even the Chalukyas and the Vengi kings across the waters of the Tungabhadhra trembled when they heard the name of Paranthaka Chozhar, which seemed to them the very nightmare of a lion. Kannara Devan of Rettai Mandalam grew baleful at the heights of fame he had reached. Burning with envy, he gathered a great army akin to the seven seas and met Paranthaka Chakravarthy in war. Paranthakar's eldest son Rajadhitha Thevar fought with Kannara Devan and his vast, ocean-like army on the Thakkolam battlefield akin to Kurukshetra and decimated the enemy forces. He then met his end upon his elephant and attained the paradise of heroes. Paranthaka Chozhar himself reached the holy feet of the lord after building a magnificent *mandapam* of gold in the temple of the Thillai Nataraja Peruman. His son Sivagnana Kandaradhitha Thevar immersed himself in service to Siva temples and reached the lotus feet of Siva. Not wishing to be separated from his brother, Arinjaya Thevar, who liberated the Thondai Mandalam from the clutches of enemies and planted the tiger flag up until the very Seetpuli Naadu, reached the heavens himself. His son Sundara Chozha Chakravarthy then ascended the Chozha throne. He pounced upon the Pandiya foxes that had reared their heads from the holes they had been lurking in, forcing them to turn tail and go back into hiding. Under the glorious shadow of the white umbrella that is Sundara Chozha Chakravarthy's rule, the three worlds live with nary an iota of fear or worry.

With what words can I praise Ponniyin Selvar, one born into such an ancient clan going back thousands of years and one which has earned fame for its feats of victory and valour? It may be possible to sing his praises if the goddess Kalaimagal herself takes birth and descends here, perhaps. It would be unfitting for ordinary poets like me to attempt such a privilege."

It was thus that Nallan Saathanar brought to an end his ballad eulogizing the Chozha clan. After him, the poets who spoke in the tongue of the North, the Buddha *bikshus*, the *Sivacharyas* and the Vaishnava *Acharyas* were waiting for their turn to convey their felicitations as well. The *magudabhishekam* organizers who had painstakingly calculated the auspicious time for *pattabhishekam* grew quite anxious as they wondered how they could request these august speakers to keep their addresses brief. Chinna Pazhuvettarayar was amongst those who worried thus. He was all set and poised to lift the ancient crown of the Chozha clan in his hands and place it upon Ponniyin Selvar's head. As Chinna Pazhuvettarayar was looking all around, wondering how he could bid the poets and scholars to bring their orations to an end, a stranger came hurrying to his side in some excitement. Everyone stared at him, amazed at the thought that he had managed to enter the mandapam past the crushing throng of people swarming the streets. But it gave Vandhiyathevan no surprise, for he knew that the stranger was none but Azhwarkkadiyaan in disguise. Vandhiyathevan glanced at Ponniyin Selvar, who seemed to comprehend the gesture.

Azhwarkkadiyaan whispered a secret into Chinna Pazhuvettarayar's ear, upon which the Thalapathy's face clouded over with great worry and agitation. He hesitated in place for a heartbeat; then he led Azhwarkkadiyaan to a relatively uncrowded corner of the *mandapam* which afforded greater privacy.

The strange event did not escape Ponniyin Selvar's eyes. When Nallan Saathanaar expounded upon the pride of the Chozha clan, he had been listening intently with his palms brought together in obeisance. Now he turned to the poet and addressed him. "*Ayya, pulavare*! Your words thus far praise the pride and glory of my forefathers, do they not? What feats have I achieved to wear the bejewelled crown and sit upon an exalted throne imbued thus with ancient pride? It is not possible for the goddess Kalaimagal to grace us with an appearance and give us an answer. Pray, can you not make an attempt to sing thus of me?"

The poet stood dumbstruck at these words. Ponniyin Selvar smiled at his reaction. "*Ayya*, it is but natural that you stand thus, stunned. It is no fault of yours. I have not yet achieved a feat worthy of being praised thus in song. It is only from today that I must accomplish laudable exploits!" he said.

88

Pattabhishekam

Arulmozhi Varmar continued to speak to the poet. "*Ayya*, I have yet another request to make of you. You sang the glories of the Chozha clan from the illustrious Sibi Chakravarthy up until the noble Sivagnana Kandaraditha Thevar. You claim that their glory belongs to me as well, as one born into this ancient clan; is it not equally the glory of Madhuranthaka Thevar, my uncle and the true son of the great Kandaradhitha Chozhar, as well?"

The poet mutely nodded his head in assent. The eyes of those present in the sabha turned to Madhuranthaka Thevar, who was seated quite humbly next to Sundara Chozha Chakravarthy. They gazed at him intently, as if they were seeing him for the first time. Madhuranthakar, who was already quite discomfited in the august gathering he found himself in, now turned painfully shy and fixed his eyes upon the floor.

In the midst of all this, Azhwarkkadiyaan, who had entered the *mandapam* in disguise and was hurriedly ushered to a private corner, recounted a rather disturbing tale to Chinna Pazhuvettarayar. He had spotted Raakammal, a member of the Pandiya Naadu *abathudhavis* and the *padagotti* Murugaiyan's wife, amongst the crowd that had gathered for the coronation festivities. Azhwarkkadiyaan had promptly followed her to discover why she had come, but Raakkammal had soon disappeared into the throng outside Chinna Pazhuvettarayar's palace. As Azhwarkkadiyaan had desperately looked all around, she had caught his eye once again. He had found Raakammal accompanied by another woman who had carried a child at her hip. To Azhwarkkadiyaan's shock, she had seemed to be none but Chinna Pazhuvettarayar's own daughter. The flustered Veera Vaishnavan had dithered in place for a while, not knowing what to do; he was not absolutely certain, either, that it was Chinna Pazhuvettarayar's daughter he had seen. He had decided to follow them for a little distance more so that he could confirm his suspicion. It had not been easy to tail the pair in the dense crowds; Raakammal must have caught wind of his pursuit, for she had suddenly raised a cry in the middle of the horde - "*Ayyo*!" she had wailed, "that man is harassing us! He is stalking us poor, naive women and giving us trouble!" A swarm of angry people had surrounded Azhwarkkadiyaan at once and had subjected him to virulent castigation. Azhwarkkadiyan had hastened to swear that he had done no such thing, that he had only come to see the coronation like everyone else. By the time he had placated the angry crowd and slipped away from their clutches, Raakammal and the woman with the child at her hip had vanished. Azhwarkkadiyaan had gone in search of them up until the entrance to the fort. There, a little further away from the gate, he had spotted a woman with a child enter a veiled palanquin. The palanquin had been flanked by four stern men on horseback; once the women had alighted the car, the palanquin and horses had set off in haste.

By the time Azhwarkkadiyaan could decide whether he ought to give them chase, he was caught in a massive wave of people who had come to see the coronation. The moving crowds had elbowed and pushed Azhwarkkadiyaan until it fairly swept him off his feet; the undulating throng had carried him for a great distance until it finally deposited him well within the fort. Azhwarkkadiyaan had resolved that it was crucial to deliver this piece of news to the Thalapathy of the fort at once and reached the *pattabhisheka mandapam* as quickly as he could. He explained that he had worn a disguise at the behest of Arulmozhi Varmar; he had been bid to circulate amongst the crowds to learn what the people were saying and make a report to the Ponniyin Selvar. It was whilst he was in the course of this duty that he had caught sight of the strange event. Once Azhwarkkadiyaan delivered this detailed account, Chinna Pazhuvettarayar began to believe the news he had been brought. The Thalapathy had already been quite worried about his daughter, the wife of the old Madhuranthakan. Thirumalai's disturbing report now sent him into a state of shock; Chinna Pazhuvettarayar reeled under the news, his heart filling with sickly dread. After issuing an order that the Mudhanmandhiri Aniruddhar was to appraise Ponniyin Selvar and the Sundara Chozhar of his urgent departure, Chinna Pazhuvettarayar made a swift exit from the *mandapam.*

As it turned out, there was little need for Azharkkadiyaan to inform Ponniyin Selvar of Chinna Pazhuvettarayar's departure. Even whilst the Thamizh poet Nallan Saathaanar was in the midst of his address, the Ilavarasar had keep an eye on Chinna Pazhuvettarayar. When the Thalapathy exited the mandapam, Ponniyin Selvar's face grew brighter than before. He stood before the Chakravarthy and spoke in a strong, majestic voice.

"Father! The Thalapathy of the fort, Chinna Pazhuvettarayar, has withdrawn from the *sabha* to attend to a matter of urgency. The coronation need not be disrupted on his account. There are other elders here in this *sabha*. The chieftains of clans famed for their valour are present here; so too are those who have bravely fought with sword and spear in countless wars and bear battle wounds upon their illustrious persons. Any one of them can lift this ancient, bejewelled Chozha crown with their noble hands and place it upon my head. Each one here has blessed the golden crown, royal sword and the sceptre with their venerable touch; and so, it would not be out of place were I to lift this bejewelled crown and place it upon my own head myself." Ponniyin Selvar paused. "But before I do that, father, I wish to make a request to you and all the elders who have graced us today with their presence. I come in the line of the illustrious Sibi Chakravarthy, who cut away his own flesh to save the life of a dove; it is why I bear the title 'Sembian' like everyone else in our lineage. I come, too, in the line of the noble Manu Needhi Chozhan, who passed a death sentence upon his own son in order to render justice to a cow that had lost its calf. All the exalted forefathers of our great clan gained fame as peerless warriors on the battlefield; they have never been known to turn their backs in a war. They were equally famed as kings who never strayed from the path of justice. Can I, a descendant of such honourable ancestry, behave in a manner contrary to justice? Can I steal away an object or title that is rightfully another's? When our royal poet sang so movingly about the forefathers of our clan in sublime verses of Thamizh, I thought I could see them gracing me with their vision. The noble Rajakesaris and Parakesaris of our lineage stood in glorious array before my eyes. Nallankilli, Nedungkilli, Porungkilli and Kochenganar gazed at me with eyes overflowing with kindness and grace. 'Child who has appeared in our lineage, think - *think!* - whether the throne is truly yours to take!' they said to me. Vijayalayar, Adithar, Paranthakar and Rajadhithar looked upon with eyes shining with valour. 'Kumara! What brave exploits have you wrought to seat yourself upon this throne?' they asked. I hesitated to reply. I managed to gather my heart and bring my palms together in obeisance. I made a request of them - 'Oh, illustrious progenitors of the Chozha clan! I have not achieved a thousandth of your courageous feats. But I shall in the future, with your blessing. I wish to grow the glory of the Chozha clan established by your noble hands; I shall lift it to exalted peaks so that such glory endures for a long time to come. I shall achieve the impossible; I shall consummate deeds of such boldness that even the bravest of the brave such as you will be left stunned. Thus shall I win your blessings and approval!' When I told my forefathers this, their faces brightened with happiness and they blessed me with affection…"

Ponniyin Selvar's shining passion and energy suffused every single word he spoke. The people in the *sabha* listened to his impassioned speech, entranced; each felt their very hair stand on end. A member of the audience broke out in a resounding cheer that reverberated even outside the *pattabhisheka mandapam* - 'Veera Vel! Vetri Vel!' The cheer evoked an excited clamour from the crowds outside, sounding from the lips of every single person who had gathered there.

Ponniyin Selvar joined in the fervent cheering, too. "Vetri Vel! Veera Vel!" he shouted ardently, pumping a fist in the air. When the shouts died down, he turned back to the Chakravarthy. "Father, this rousing cheer that belongs to the warriors of Chozha Naadu once reverberated up until the Tungabhadra and Krishna rivers that lie across the Vada Pennai, in the time of the noble Paranthaka Chakravarthy. The Vengi people that lived across those rivers as well the people of Kalinga, Kalyanapuram and Manyakedam trembled at the sound of this cheer. Hundreds of ships bearing thousands of Chozha Naadu warriors sailed to the west, the south and the east, protecting the country's commercial interests. Father! Since the very day you fell bedridden, the brave cheers of Chozha Naadu have grown weaker. Enemies have reared their heads in all the four directions. The territories of Vengi, Kalinga, Kalyanapuram and Manyakedam are spoiling for a fight with us; they boldly invite us to war. They bear little thought about the peril that comes from the north across the Imaiya Malai in the form of foreign adversaries who seek to storm this ancient Bharata Desam; they nurse naught but bitter jealousy in their hearts at Chozha Naadu's exalted growth. Though Veera Pandiyan has breathed his last, these foes are even now attempting to create chaos by bestowing the Imperial Crown of the Pandiya clan upon anyone they can claim to be Veera Pandiyan's descendant. Magindhan and the Pandiya Naadu *abathudhavis* joined hands to bring about the end of my dear thamayan Aditha Karikalar, he was the equal of Abimanyu and Aravaan in valour. The Chera king in the west gathers a vast army of elephants and a great fleet of ships. This complex political scene is the new peril that looms over Chozha Naadu.

Father, the people of Arabu Desam have been flourishing in the business of ships for a very long time. They voyage up until Cheena Desam to conduct transactions of trade; they even frequent our own ports of commerce. Alas, the old Arabs who were renowned for their civilization and culture are now being ousted by a new group of Arabs. It is unclear whether those of this new faction are indeed Arabs or foreign clansmen from countries neighbouring their land; but you cannot see another people more vicious and brutal. It so happened that I saw their destruction with my own eyes. In keeping with your order to imprison me and bring me here, the Thalapathy of our fort, Chinna Pazhuvettarayar, had dispatched two ships of soldiers…"

Sundara Chozhar interrupted his speech, aghast. "My son! Do you not know the reason why I dispatched men thus?" he asked in a trembling voice.

"I know well, father. There was chaos here about the right of succession to the throne; you had received intelligence about the Pandiya Naadu *abathudhavis* as well. You only issued orders for my imprisonment to bring me here safe and sound. Nothing but the boundless love and affection you bear for me could have provoked you to give such a command. I brought up the subject so that the others learn of this, as well," replied Ponniyin Selvar, looking all around the *sabha*. He then turned back to the Chakravarthy. "The soldiers who imprisoned me thus were hundreds in number. The Arabs had been lurking on the coast of Eezha Naadu because their ship was wrecked; they could not have been more than ten in number. I saw with my own eyes the number of good soldiers they brutally put to the sword when they ambushed us in attack. The cutting grief I felt that day yet weighs upon my heart. It is these new Arabs that are helping the Chera king build ships. Not only that, they have also established ties with the people of Kalinga as well. The peoples of all the three countries are resolved to decimate Chozha Naadu's sea trade.

How does it matter whether the pirates hail from Arab Naadu or the Chera Desam, with whom we already have a history? If we are to protect our sea trade, we must expand our fleet of military ships. Thousands of new ships need to be built as well; we must ably train and equip new ship captains who stand at their helm. We must gather brave warriors who can hold their own on ships and successfully fight against the raiders!" cried Ponniyin Selvar, his voice rising in pitch and passion. "We must plant the tiger flag on all the islands dotting the low seas and station our forces there! Father, I have pledged my solemn word to our forefathers that I will achieve all of these exploits. In order to fulfill this oath, I need your permission and the assent of the elders assembled in this *sabha*!"

By the time Ponniyin Selvar's speech came to an end, it had left the assembly electrified. "Son!" boomed Sundara Chozhar, his eyes glinting. "Would I ever stop you from lifting the Chozha clan to greater heights or glory? Would the elders gathered in this great *sabha* prevent you from protecting Chozha Naadu's sea trade?" In response, the *mandapam* exploded in rousing cheer - "Veera Vel! Vetri Vel!"

"Father, neither you nor this assembly will pose a barrier to me. You will only bless me to succeed in the challenges I seek to counter. For your blessing to come true, for me to triumph in my exploits, my own heart needs to attain peace. It should rest confident that I do nothing dishonest, nothing that the forefathers of my illustrious clan would disapprove of. If I stoop to acting against the *dharma* of our clan, my conscience will forever prick my heart. How then will I fight against our enemies and gain victory? Earlier, a rumour made the rounds claiming that I coveted the Ilankai throne for myself…"

"Child, none believed in it, did they? No one dreamed that you would be capable of such a crime!" reminded the Chakravarthy.

"You may not have believed it, father! But when I heard the words of slander, my heart grew cold with unbearable grief!" burst out Ponniyin Selvar. "My friends, my two companions, know that I refused the jewelled crown that the Eezha Naadu *bikshus* offered me. They were by my side at that very moment…"

"Yes, yes!" cried out the head of the Buddha *bikshus*, who was present in the assembly. "Even we know that!"

"That false rumour weighed down my heart with unspeakable grief and suffering. Even though you did not believe the calumnies, father, there were some who did," pointed out Ponniyin Selvar. "If today I truly do seize a throne that belongs rightfully to another, it will bring naught but shameful dishonour to the Chozha clan! I will bitterly rue it for the rest of my life. It will leave me unable to focus on the challenges ahead; I will certainly not find happiness, either…"

Madhuranthaka Thevar had kept his head bowed all this while. He now looked up quizzically at Ponniyin Selvar; he appeared to struggle to say something to the prince. Ponniyin Selvar glanced at Vandhiyathevan and made a discreet signal. The intrepid warrior glided to Madhuranthaka Thevar's side at once. In a soft voice that could be heard by none but Madhuranthaka Thevar,

Vandhiyathevan asked, "*Ayya*, what is the first verse of the *thevaram* sung by Sundaramoorthy Nayanar?" Madhuranthaka Thevar was caught entirely off guard; he wondered at the absurdity of the question at this juncture. He stared at Vandhiyathevan, puzzled. "*Piththa, piraisoodi* - Oh lunatic, who bears the crescent moon upon his head!" he whispered back. The harmless response made Vandhiyathevan bristle with indignation. "What, *Ayya*? Do you call me a lunatic?" he demanded, rather unfairly. "You are the one who has gone stark raving mad, lovestruck as you are! See there! See how Poonguzhali, your *dharma pathini*, laughs at you!" Madhuranthakar was justifiably quite taken aback. *What is this, now? Why is my good friend spoiling for a fight with me?* The hapless Madhuranthakar looked towards where the women were seated. In truth, Poonguzhali was not even glancing in his direction. Poonguzhali, Kundhavai, Vanathi, Sembian Maadevi and Vaanama Devi were transfixed by Ponniyin Selvar, their eyes shining with boundless avidity.

By the time Madhuranthakar turned back to Ponniyin Selvar, he saw that the prince was holding the ancient bejewelled crown of the Chozha clan in his hand.

"The Thalapathy Chinna Pazhuvettarayar has not yet returned. What of that? I myself will conduct the coronation at the auspicious time! Father, you consented to bestow upon me this bejewelled crown that our forefathers have worn since the time of Vijayalaya Chozhar. The local chiefs, the commanders, the fort guards and the populace came together in agreement. Therefore, this crown has become mine. I do have the right, don't I, to do what I wish with what is mine?" Ponniyin Selvar looked all around the *sabha*, meeting the eyes of every person assembled there with his own. "There is another here who is more qualified than I to wear the crown. He is older than me. Even though he undoubtedly has a greater right than me to this Chozha *rajyam*, he did not stake his claim. He was prepared to watch me wear the crown upon my own head and rejoice as I ascended the throne. He has saved my life.

He has also saved my friend, dear to me as my own life. It was entirely on his account that a dire peril was thwarted from befalling the Chozha clan. I have never achieved such greatness yet for my country. And so, this hallowed bejewelled crown I place upon the august head of Kandaradhithar's son, my uncle, Madhuranthaka Thevar!"

As Ponniyin Selvar said these words, he approached a mystified Madhuranthakan who was sitting next to the Chakravarthy. He placed the crown upon his head. Vandhiyathevan had positioned himself behind Madhuranthakar to prevent him from refusing the crown; he had exercised the privilege of their friendship to hold his shoulders in a firm grip. As it happened, Madhuranthakar did nothing to reject the gesture. He was lost in a bemused daze. He truly did appear as a lunatic, staring wildly about him with frantic eyes.

When he had placed the jewelled crown on Madhuranthakar's head, Ponniyin Selvar raised a loud cry - "Long live Kopparakesari Madhuranthaka Uttama Chozha Thevar!' Vandhiyathevan raised a rousing cheer of his own - "Long live the Chakravarthy of the Chozha *samrajyam,* Uttama Chozhar!"

All this while, the Mudhanmandhiri Aniruddha Brahmmarayar and the others had stood stunned, rooted to their places. They now raised their voices in cheer as well - "Long live Kopparakesari Madhuranthaka Thevar!" Overwhelmed by emotion, Sundara Chozha Chakravarthy found himself robbed of speech; he warmly strewed handfuls of colourful flowers upon Madhuranthaka Uttama Chozhar.

The women of the palace followed suit by showering a rain of blossoms upon Madhuranthakar.

When Madhuranthakar's shock had subsided, he rose to his feet and approached Sembian Maadevi, bowing down to her in deference. Tears streamed down the face of that venerable old queen.

"Son, this is naught but God's will. How can you or I go against it?" she asked, her eyes glistening wetly.

Ponniyin Selvar turned to the awestruck poets, *bhattars* and *bikshus* gathered in the *mandapam*. "You may now amend your speeches of praise before you address the assembly!" he said.

The orators scrambled to edit their plaudits and took the stand.

Madhuranthaka Uttama Chozhar had barely been crowned when the astonishing news spread to the crowds gathered in the streets of Thanjai. That the news spread so rapidly was solely to the credit of Vandhiyathevan and Azhwarkkadiyan. They had earlier stationed men in the streets in keeping with Ponniyin Selvar's order; they now hurried to their sides and said only a single phrase to them - "Long live Kopparakesari Uttama Chozhar!" And so, word of mouth spread like wildfire among the people that Ilavarasar Arulmozhi Varmar had abdicated the *rajyam* in favour of his uncle Madhuranthakar and that Ponniyin Selvar would soon amass a great fleet of military ships and depart. Some believed the news readily enough; they felt it was rather in line with Ponniyin Selvar's worthy character. Others had their misgivings. "Who on earth would give away a kingdom that was fairly given to them?" they asked doubtfully. Voices rose everywhere in excited chatter and the celebratory cheers of 'Long live!' boomed above the clamour. The uproar of such a veritable storm amongst the people was akin to the din made by great waves crashing upon the face of the sea.

Soon, Madhuranthaka Thevar mounted the royal elephant that had been decorated for the occasion. When the people saw him sitting in the royal *ambaari*, their misgivings were washed away. When they saw that it was none but Ponniyin Selvar who sat in the mahout's seat, their exuberance knew no bounds. "Long live Kopparakesari Madhuranthaka Uttama Chozhar!" they cheered, their voices resounding in the environs. Their hearts, however, were full of the remarkable deed that Ponniyin Selvan had done that day.

The very thought of his gesture lit a spark of joy in their hearts that brightened their faces. The people gave into greater jubilation than they would have displayed at the sight of Ponniyin Selvar donning the bejewelled crown in grand procession.

The wise among them declared that Ponniyin Selvar had surpassed Karikalar Peruvalathan himself, who planted the tiger the flag on the very peak of Imaya Malai; they rejoiced that the prince had emblazoned his mark in the annals of self-sacrifice. The common folk, however, did not seek out pretty words of praise or grand comparisons; the very sight of Ponniyin Selvar regally riding the royal elephant after crowning Madhuranthakar was sufficient to send their hearts into raptures of joy. The people lost themselves to heady celebration. They danced with each other and sang merry songs, they laughed aloud and cheered; they embraced one another in happiness and eagerly showered flowers and auspicious yellow *atchadai* on the procession.

It was not easy to steer the royal elephant through this great throng lost in celebration and joy. Ponniyin Selvar did not suffer himself to hurry. He watched the people's happiness with quiet satisfaction; whenever he recognized someone among the crowds, he stopped to share a banter or two. He rode the elephant slowly through the bustling streets. By the time the procession had come to an end and it was time to return to the palace, evening had given way to night. The bright lamps that shone on the streets vied with the stars twinkling in the sky. A delightful rain of flowers fell from the palace. "Mahout, mahout!" cried a sweet voice in joy. When Ponniyin Selvar looked up, it was Vanathi's pretty face that he saw.

"Do not be afraid, maiden!" he called out. "In the just reign of Madhuranthaka Uttama Thevar, the mighty elephant and fierce tiger will be fast friends; the cat and bird will play with each other in affection and joy!"

89

Spring Arrives

It had been more than one and a half months since the coronation ceremony of Madhuranthaka Uttama Chozha Thevar had taken place. The days of crisp chilliness had withdrawn with greater swiftness than they usually did. Spring arrived upon the heavenly chariot of the balmy south breeze. Pretty green parrots congregated in the *kumkum* red foliage of young mango trees, prattling away with one another as they compared their beaks of coral. The golden shoots of tender peepal trees swayed gracefully in the wind, whispering a song as the breeze rustled through their leaves. Koels cooed in joy as they played in the *punnai* trees, shaking down pearl-like buds from their thick boughs. The nature goddess shivered with delight. Trees that had grown bare from shedding their leaves now sported a wealth of lovely buds that burst out in luxurious bloom. The creeping vines of *madhavi* and dense thickets of jasmine struggled to bear the profusion of flowers that had blossomed upon their leaves. The rivers grew leaner. Waters as clear as crystal skimmed the edges of their banks, babbling as they meandered their course.

Across all of Chozha Naadu, hearts were full and faces lit with joy. The people had already reaped the red grains of paddy that had come to a full, bountiful harvest; they had been safely stored away in granaries that were full to the brim. As politics, the muddied state of affairs had come to a satisfactory resolution, unburdening the populace of anxiety and worry. The *kaaman* festival was around the corner and the people threw themselves into animated preparations for the occasion. In the temples too, arrangements were underway to celebrate the festival of spring. Theatre and performance stages had already sprung up at almost every junction and crossroads.

Vallavarayan wound his way towards the town, happily watching the pleasant sights that unfolded in front of him. He was not making a diffident entry into that great city this time, lurking in shadows and hiding behind disguises as he had done before. He passed through the open city gates with confidence and soon arrived at the palace of Ilaiya Piratti Kundhavai. There, he was met at the entrance by Kundhavai herself accompanied by Vanathi and her friends, who excitedly swirled around him in a delightful swish and rustle of skirts; they gave him a warm welcome with generous words of praise and flattery. Ilaiya Piratti then bid him meet her in the pleasure garden and tell her about his expedition once he had soothed his limbs of the fatigue of travel. So saying, she withdrew to allow him some time in private.

Vandhiyathevan did not take long to rejuvenate himself. He made quick work of his toilette and set off to the pleasure garden, bright-eyed and bushy tailed. Vandhiyathevan's heart leapt as he caught sight of Ilaiya Piratti waiting for him there, gazing at him expectantly. It is hard to say which among the two was more eager to meet the other; each was burning with questions to ask the other of various bits of news and events. But was that the only reason for the anxious excitement that thrummed through them? Perhaps they wanted to pledge their future life in togetherness, as well. The magic of spring had evoked such delightful spirits in unmoving vegetation; it is possible, is it not, that it sparked the nervous elation that swelled in their hearts?

"*Ayya*," began Ilaiya Piratti, "I am given to understand that you did not achieve complete victory in the mission you undertook. Is that true?"

"It is true, Devi! Then again, in which of my missions thus far have I ever managed a complete victory?" said Vallavarayan, heaving a great sigh of regret.

"Oh, you mustn't say that!" replied Kundhavai earnestly. "Why, you brought my *Thambi* here from Eezha Naadu, didn't you? It was only because Arulmozhi arrived in the nick of time that Chozha Naadu escaped the peril that lay in wait; it is why we have come thus far from the dangers that threatened to destroy us!"

Vandhiyathevan scrunched his nose. "I threw Arulmozhi Varmar into entirely avoidable danger, my lady; I brought him here enervated and sapped, shivering with fever! Even that I was able to achieve only with the help of Poonguzhali Maharani. I had to entrust my friend into Senthan Amudhan and Poonguzhali's care - I was obliged to ask them to take him safely to Naagaippattinam." He paused before continuing in a thoughtful strain. "I must confess - at that point, I never dreamt that they would one day ascend the throne to the Chozha *samrajyam* here in Thanjai and wear the bejewelled crowns upon their own heads..."

"I have not forgotten that you saved the life of Uttama Chozha Chakravarthy," replied Kundhavai warmly. "Neither has he, in fact; it was why Uttama Chozhar wished to instate you the Dhanaadhikaari of Chozha Naadu in place of Periya Pazhuvettarayar…"

"A fate that I mercifully escaped!"

Kundhavai's eyes widened in surprise. "Why do you say that? Do you think that the post of Dhanaadhikaari to the Chozha *samrajyam* is an ordinary charge? Why, it holds greater influence than even the post of Mudhanmandhiri - even the post of the Mathanda Nayagar! Even the Chakravarthy cannot make a decision or undertake a task without the support of the Dhanaadhikaari, can he?"

"Devi, I once found myself with no option but to hide in Periya Pazhuvettarayar's underground treasury. The heaps and heaps of golden coins that lay there cast an eerie glow - I saw, by its light, the terrible, tangled webs of spiders all around; I was even suffered to look upon the skull of a poor wretch that had perished in that gloom! I decided then and there that I wouldn't go anywhere near that underground treasury again, not if I could help it…"

Ilaiya Piratti's lips tugged into a smile. "Even if you do become the Dhanaadhikaari, there will be little occasion to visit the treasury. Arulmozhi has decided to spend nearly all the resources that lie within towards creating a military fleet and building new ships. The new Chakravarthy has granted his permission, too!"

"Speaking of which, I learned at Thanjai that the new Chakravarthy and his *pattamagishi* have departed to Kodikkarai along with Arulmozhi Varmar."

"Yes. They were quite sorry that they couldn't take you along, you know."

"I am not! I can join them at Kodikkarai even now, if I wish. Though, I confess to a twinge of regret that Arulmozhi Varmar seized the fact of my absence to wed the Kodumbalur Ilavarasi…"

"Why, *Ayya* - are you not happy then, that your friend has married mine?"

"Heavens! Did I say that? I only feel sorry for myself that I wasn't there for the occasion. That Arulmozhi Varmar wed Vanathi is naught but the merit of the good deeds of a past life - your friend Vanathi is fortunate as well, it is true. But why on earth had they been in such a hurry?" asked a rather aggrieved Vandhiyathevan.

"They were in no hurry, I was. My mother and father had wished to leave for Kanchi - I was the one who insisted that the wedding take place before their departure," explained Kundhavai. "It brought some peace of mind to Kodumbalur Periya Velar too. He had sustained a rather rude shock when your friend unexpectedly anointed Uttama Chozhar with the crown of Chozha Naadu."

"So had a great many others, I am sure."

"We were left entirely astonished ourselves! The pair of you managed to keep that twist very secret indeed!" remarked Kundhavai in a tone fairly dripping acid.

Vandhiyathevan gaped at her. "Devi, I truly thought that he would have taken you into confidence, at the very least!" he said earnestly.

Kundhavai sniffed at the claim. "He would have, a few months ago. Arulmozhi has never yet done a thing without first seeking my opinion," she replied, the hurt evident in her voice.

"Why do you think he has changed now, my lady?"

Kundhavai narrowed her eyes at him in response. "What else but the ill wind of new friendship?" she demanded. "It was only after striking a bond with *you* that my dear *Thambi* changed so! Once, he wore the same face inside and out - now he has grown artful in the skills of pretence and deceit!"

"Devi, it is rather unfair to put that blame at my feet!" protested Vandhiyathevan. "The theatrics of crowning Uttama Chozhar were naught but the magnum opus of your brother! I did try to argue with him, my lady - I asked him how we could stomach tricking everyone thus. In response, Arulmozhi raked up that example of Ramar who tricked the people of Ayodhya to slip away to the forest in the dark of night. Even then, I asked him if it would perhaps be prudent to take you into confidence. To which he said that he wished to achieve one thing, at the very least, that he did not seek your counsel on - he said that he would bask in your praises later." Vandhiyathevan suddenly grew concerned. "Did the Ilavrasar's deed meet with your heart's approval?"

"None can do anything that meets more with my heart's approval!" replied Ilaiya Piratti with a smile. "I bear the highest gratitude towards you for aiding my brother in this endeavour."

Vandhiyathevan smiled back in relief. "Why, Devi! I thought that you dearly wished to see Arulmozhi Varmar ascend the throne with the bejewelled crown upon his head; I believed that you were eager to see him reign the kingdom!"

"It is true that I harboured such a wish once; but I changed my mind after my friend Vanathi took the oath she did. Besides, my *thamayan* had met with an unnatural demise - if my *Thambi* had ascended the throne shortly after, what would the world have thought?"

"True, Devi," replied Vandhiyathevan thoughtfully. "The terrible things that had happened to the royal dynasty of Ilankai had prompted Arulmozhi to bear much anxiety regarding this matter. Though truth be told, it appears that he hadn't been entirely deterred by that sordid precedence - at one point, he had resolved to ascend the Chozha throne purely to protect me. Fortunately, Periya Pazhuvettarayar assumed all blame for the crime and saved my own head from the accusation."

"Poor soul!" exclaimed Ilaiya Piratti with genuine regret. "Why, the absence of that one venerable old man has left all of Chozha Naadu feeling lonely and desolate."

"The thought that the *Thambi* too soon followed his *thamayan* in death gives me grief," remarked Vandhiyathevan.

Ilaiya Piratti recoiled in horror. "*Ayyo*! Is Chinna Pazhuvettarayar no more as well? Is that true?" asked Kundhavai, aghast.

"He was alive when I took my leave of him. But how can one survive a fall from such a dizzily precipitous mountain?" asked Vandhiyathevan, his brown eyes clouding with misery. "When I think of my part in Chinna Pazhuvettarayar's death, my heart grows cold with anguish."

"*Ayya*, pray tell me your report in detail," pressed Kundhavai, her dark eyes growing sombre. "You conspired with my *Thambi* to oust Chinna Pazhuvettarayar from the *mandapam* on the day of coronation, did you not? Tell me everything that transpired since then. I was unable to receive the details from my brother; I was waiting to learn them from you." She sniffed in affront. "I was told nothing on the grounds that secrets must be kept from women. I trust that you can enlighten me now, at the very least."

"Devi, that was not the reason why you were kept in the dark! The Ilavarasar only wished to surprise you - for once in his life at the very least, he said."

"I wasn't surprised at all - I reckoned that the two of you were hatching a scheme together. I was only concerned, for I didn't want your plans to go awry."

"And they did, in a sense. We accomplished the crucial win we had set out to achieve, but wreaked about other mishaps in its wake - ones that we could not thwart. Perhaps if we *had* consulted you, my lady, we would not have suffered the disasters we did!" admitted Vandhiythevan.

He then proceeded to recount in detail the plots they had contrived since the time Ponniyin Selvar had determined to crown Senthan Amudhan, the new Madhuranthakar.

Arulmozhi Varmar had reckoned that a transparent announcement of his resolve to crown Madhuranthaka Thevar would invite a slew of objections from all quarters. Kodumbalur Velar and Thirukovilur Malayaman, he thought, would hotly protest the move like they had before; Periya Pazhuvettarayar too had made an earnest appeal with dying breath to crown Ponniyin Selvar - it was natural that his allies would seek to fulfill his last wish. Chinna Pazhuvettarayar had learned that his son-in-law was not the true Madhuranthakan; he would not, calculated the prince, show much enthusiasm in seeing Poonguzhali, the daughter of a simple boatman, ascend to the throne. Sembian Maadevi, the new Madhuranthaka Thevar Senthan Amudhan and Poonguzhali themselves would raise objections to the plan - it was possible that Sundara Chozhar would be reluctant to proceed against their opposition. These were the reasons why Ponniyin Selvar had decided to keep secret until the very last minute the deed he had resolved to achieve. As the *magudabhishekam* drew nearer, he contrived to send away those excitable persons who were likely to protest his plan out of love for him or jealousy for Madhuranthakar. Realizing that he needed one person at the very least to help carry out his scheme, the prince had taken Vandhiyathevan alone into confidence. The two of them spent quite some time together devising plans and making arrangements.

Young Sambuvarayan Kandamaaran, Parthibendra Pallavan, Kobumbalur Velar and others had been bid to travel out of town. But sending away Chinna Pazhuvettarayar thus was not plausible - talk was already in the air that he would anoint Ponniyin Selvar with the bejewelled crown himself; it was rather absurd to hope that he would not protest when the time came to anoint Madhuranthakar with the crown instead. His refusal would be seen as nothing short of a greatly inauspicious omen; that may give rise to other problems, as well. And so, the two friends came to the conclusion that Chinna Pazhuvettarayar had to be sent out of the *mandapam* at the time of coronation on some pretext or the other. The pair thought hard on the matter, but found that they were not able to come up with a satisfactory scheme that would achieve this end. It was at that moment that Azhwarkkadiyaan approached them with a strange report.

Arulmozhi Varmar had dispatched Azhwarkkadiyaan on a mission to discover the answers to many unresolved puzzles - where were Ravidasan and his gang of *abathudhavis* lurking? Was Nandhini yet with them? Where had they hidden away the little boy whom they had crowned in the Thiruppurambiyam forest at midnight? With the Mudhanmandhir's permission, Arulmozhi Varmar had tasked Azhwarkkadiyaan with ferreting out these answers. Azhwarkkadiyaan promptly set off on his mission, wishing to discover a few truths himself - had Karuthiruman, the madman who had escaped from the underground dungeons, joined hands with the plotters? Was it really true, as Kandamaaran had claimed, that the old Madhuranthakan had died? Or had he escaped with his life and banded with the conspirators? The rest had expected that it would take forever and a day for Azhwarkkadiyaan to return with his report; but to their surprise, the nimble spy resurfaced in front of them within a mere couple of days.

It transpired that he had seen in the environs of Kollimalai none but Raakkammal - part of Ravidasan's cabal and the wife of the *padagotti* Murugaiyan. Azhwarkkadiyaan had reckoned that he could learn the hiding place of Ravidasan and his gang if he kept watch on her; and so, he promptly began to follow her at a discreet distance. To his great astonishment, he discovered that she was leading him down the path that led to Thanjai. Believing that he could yet glean new information about the *abathudhavis*, the clever Azhwarkkadiyaan donned a disguise and stayed on her trail. Shortly, Uraiyur appeared; a motley throng descended upon the path, eagerly travelling to see the coronation ceremony of Ponniyin Selvar. As Azhwarkkadiyaan watched, Raakkammal smoothly blended into the crowds. Still, he doggedly maintained his surveillance and followed her right up until Thanjai. When he saw Raakkammal enter the Thanjai fort with the crowds and proceed to linger outside Chinna Pazhuvettarayar's palace, Azhwarkkadiyan was struck amazed. It was at that moment that he had hurried to Arulmozhi Varmar and Vandhiyathevan with his strange findings. At first, they all thought that perhaps Raakkammal ought to be imprisoned at once; they changed their minds quickly enough, deeming it more important to understand why she had come here in the first place. They made a rather astute guess that Raakkamaal had come bearing a message of some sort for Chinna Pazhuvettarayar's daughter. It was decided that the matter would not yet be taken to him; that instead, the intelligence could be wielded at an opportune time to send him away from the *mandapam* during the coronation.

When Azhwarkkadiyaan returned to Chinna Pazhuvettarayar's palace, he discovered that Raakkammal had vanished from the place. The mass of multitudes that were still arriving for the coronation grew denser and more impenetrable by the hour. Azhwarkkadiyaan expertly wove his way through the crowds and kept a close watch on the palace entrance. Presently, two women emerged from within. One of them carried a child on her hip; the other wore a veil over head, hiding her features from view. Thirumalai Nambi surmised that it was none but Chinna Pazhuvettarayar's daughter. He dithered in his place as he wondered whether he ought to stop them or keep his surveillance to see where they led him. By the time he could make up his mind, the pair of women had spared him further thought by disappearing into the crowd. Azhwarkkadiyan hurried to the fort entrance, reckoning that they would be there. Sure enough, he spied the women alighting a palanquin that stood a short distance away from the entrance. The car departed at once, flanked by a retinue of men on horseback. Realizing that he could delay no further the report that was due to Chinna Pazhuvettarayar, Azhwarkkadiyaan bolted to the *mandapam*.

Azhwarkkadiyaan's arrival had coincided with the time that Ponniyin Selvar had been addressing the poet. Quickly spotting Chinna Pazhuvettarayar, the spy apprised him of the terrible news. The pair swiftly left the *mandapam* together. Chinna Pazhuvettarayar hastened to his palace and searched high and low for his daughter; he was stunned to discover that she was not there. He came to the damning conclusion that Azhwarkkadiyaan's report had to be true. By the time Chinna Pazhuvettarayar could turn back to the *mandapam*, the air was filled with rousing cheers - "Long Live Madhuranthaka Uttama Chozha Chakravarthy!" He learned the astonishing turn of events that had taken place at the *mandapam* and realized he had little to do at the coronation anymore. And so, Chinna Pazhuvettarayar gathered a handful of his trusted men and set off in determination to find his runaway daughter. The very thought of his own dear, beloved daughter joining the *abathudhavis* of the Pandiya clan - the nemesis of the Chozha clan through generations - made his heart boil with rage. He travelled on swift wings, darkly resolving that it was better by far to slay his daughter by his own hand than to suffer such a fate.

That very night, once Uttama Chozha Chakravarthy's coronation procession and the ensuing festivities had come to a joyous end, Azhwarkkadiyaan Nambi briefed Arulmozhi Varmar of the events that had transpired that afternoon. Arulmozhi Varmar lost no time in consulting the issue with Vandhiyathevan as well. All three knew well that Ravidasan's men were frighteningly skilled at the artifice of cunning. They felt certain that Chinna Pazhuvettarayar, impetuous and hot-blooded as he was, could not win over their wiles; it was likelier, they thought, that he would be captured by them and find himself in grave danger. The trio also reckoned that he was well capable of rising to such a disastrous deed as slaying his own daughter. And so, it was decided that it would be best for Vandhiyathevan and Azhwarkkadiyaan to go in pursuit and save Chinna Pazhuvettarayar; they could also bring back intelligence of where Ravidasan and the rest of the Pandiya Naadu cabal was hiding and the plots they had hatched.

And so it came to be that Chinna Pazhuvettarayar set off in hot pursuit of his daughter and the conspirators who had whisked her away even whilst he had Azhwarkkadiyaan and Vandhiyathevan on his trail, making anxious enquiries along the way. The pair of friends soon discovered that Chinna Pazhuvettarayar had taken a convoluted path that led them in dizzying twists and turns; from this, they realized that the coterie that had stolen his daughter away intended to deflect him down a wrong path and throw him off their trail. The two travelled westwards by the banks of the Kaveri for an arduously long distance when they found themselves obliged to abruptly change track at the spot where the river Amaravathi converged with Kaveri. They headed along a path by the banks that led southwest, bringing them to the Aanaimalai region which served as the border between Chera Naadu and Kongu Naadu. Once they reached the foothills of the Aanaimalai, the track turned brutally gruelling.

They were in forest territory, thickly populated by gnarled, primaeval trees. The spine-chilling growls of fearsome wild beasts rumbled all around them. It was a laborious task to ride a horse through that path; but they feared that deserting their steeds to go on foot would leave them as prey for the savage beasts of the forest. The friends pressed on, finally reaching an impenetrable part of the forest that made it absolutely impossible to ride their horses any further. As they wondered what to do, they suddenly heard the neighing of a horse close by. The pair sought out the animal, discovering that it was none but Chinna Pazhuvettarayar's steed. The Thalapathy had left his horse behind in the company of a single guard who had been bid to protect the animal. The man informed them that Chinna Pazhuvettarayar had proceeded on foot from that point, along with three of his men. Asking him to take care of their horses as well, the pair followed suit and ploughed on through the dense forest on foot. They walked a long way through the nigh impregnable wilderness, a thick forest enveloped in an eerie, elemental darkness that bore no admittance to the rays of the sun. The trail led them up a thickly wooded mountain path. At times, the pair were forced to navigate treacherous paths that hid the trail from their view; they could not see what lay ahead even at a mere distance of ten feet. The two finally reached a clearing which afforded them a little light, made possible by a waterfall nearby that cascaded from the top of the mountain. The friends looked around in dismay, discovering that it would be impossible for them to cross this terrain. For there rose in front of them a forbidding mountain wall, so steep and so high in its majesty that it was certain to be impassable.

The two explored every inch of the environs, but could not identify a path that could lead them further upwards. Finally, they gave into resignation; they decided that there was nothing else they could do save take a refreshing dip in the water before heading back. The pair theorized that the wild beasts of the forest had made a meal of Chinna Pazhuvettarayar and the men who had accompanied him.

It was at this hopeless juncture that they unexpectedly caught sight of an entirely remarkable spectacle. Two figures were at the very top of the mountain, where the waterfall began its precipitous descent. The men were absorbed in a ferocious duel, a bitter sword fight that pushed them ever nearer to the waterfall's edge. A closer look made it quite plain that both duellers were familiar faces to them. One was Chinna Pazhuvettarayar; the other, the man that his daughter had married - the old Madhuranthakar. *Aha! It beggars belief that Madhuranthakar - he whose face had once turned pale and twisted at the very word 'fight' - had mastered such prowess in this short period as to swing a sword with such confidence and skill! Why, he seems to be duelling with Kalanthaka Kantar himself and on equal terms, to boot!... Ayyo! Is Kalanthaka Kantar drawing back? Is he retreating because he is truly tired? Or perchance... does he hesitate to fight his son-in-law after all? Ah, he comes dangerously close to the waterfall's edge! Ayyo! Is he unaware of the perilously steep drop below?*

Vandhiyathevan and Azhwarkkadiyan made frantic efforts to warn him of the plunge, crying out as loudly as they possibly could. Alas, their endeavours went to vain - the waterfall made its lofty descent with a deafening crash - the ear splitting din it made could drown out the roar of a hundred fierce lions and the blare of two hundred elephants.

They were forced to stand by and watch as the gruesome event unfolded in front of their own eyes. Chinna Pazhuvettarayar had slowly but steadily beaten a retreat as he struggled to fight with his enemy; he receded up until the edge of the waterfall - he stumbled upon the slipper rocks - he fell down, down, down the steep precipice into the plunge pool at the base of the waterfall. The old Madhuranthakan peered over the edge of the cliff and vanished within the blink of an eye. From where Chinna Pazhuvettarayar had lost his footing until the watery void he had fallen into below measured roughly three-fourths the height of a palm tree. It was unreasonable to expect one who had plummeted from such a height to survive the fall. But it was incumbent on the pair, they thought, to find and pay their last respects to the remains of the great warrior. And so, the friends sprinted to the swirling reservoir beneath the waterfall. Chinna Pazhuvettarayar was nowhere to be seen. The waterfall had cascaded with such puissance that it had carved a deep gorge at its base, which roiled and frothed with the force of the water pouring down from above; the ensuing torrents battering the jagged rocks that encompassed the cavity. The two quickly deduced that Chinna Pazhuvettarayar's body must have fallen into this chasm. This was fortunate in a way; if the great warrior had fallen upon the rocks instead, his body would have doubtless been rent asunder. He had escaped the grisly fate only by dint of falling into the deep pool. The pair kept an unblinking watch on its waters, anticipating that the swirling eddies would soon lift his body of their depth.

Their expectations did not go in vain. Chinna Pazhuvattarayar appeared on the surface soon enough, limp and inert. The two friends dove into the pool and brought him ashore as gently as they could. At first, they thought that the spirit had flown its coop. Still, a weak faith persisted - could it not be possible, they hoped, that life clung to the body, after all? They gave him as much medical care as they could, desperate in their endeavours to bring back to life the noble man who had hurtled into treacherous waters. After a long time, Chinna Pazhuvettarayar gasped and took a rattling breath; he opened his eyes and looked about him, dazed. He was unable to speak at length, but said what he wished to in a few words.

Kalanthaka Kantar had reached the mountain top with arduous effort. There, he had seen his daughter amongst a gathering of roughly a hundred people. It was then that Ravidasan appeared, inviting Kalanthaka Kantar to join their camp. He said that his son-in-law had the right to stake a claim to Pandiya Naadu; not only would they anoint him the crown, but the Chera king and Magindhan of Ilankai had pledged to lend their might and support to the new Pandiyan. Chinna Pazhuvettarayar listened to his speech wordlessly, wanting to learn their plan; he then accused them of being naught but vile conspirators and demanded for his daughter to be sent back with him.

Ravidasan had smiled thinly at him. "If your daughter comes to you," he had sneered, "you may take her!"

Chinna Pazhuvettarayar had then turned to his daughter. The maiden replied that she intended to share her husband's fate and refused to come away with him.

Kalanthaka Kantar had stared at her, drinking in the features of her face. "I would rather slay you by my own hand than leave you behind with these wretches!" he had roared as he raised his sword.

It was at this juncture that Madhuranthakan had emerged from his hiding place. "Who are you, pray, to slay my wife?" he had thundered and drew his own sword and began to duel. Kalanthaka Kantar had been stunned.

As he fought, a doubt arose in his heart. Was it fair, he wondered, that he should slay his own son-in-law and relegate his own daughter to widowhood? So troubled was he by the thought that his will weakened; the ferocity of his fight grew enfeebled. As he grappled with his thoughts, Chinna Pazhuvettarayar had retreated; unaware of the gorge below, he had lost his footing and plummeted down.

Chinna Pazhuvettarayar struggled to get the words out as he recounted his story. "I will not survive. My end is near, " he rasped at last. "Leave me behind and go, swiftly - the Chozha army must march upon Chera Naadu and Eezha Naadu at once. Take Ponniyin Selvar to Madurai - bestow upon the name of Chozha Pandiyan and crown him. If these three things are not achieved at the soonest, it is certain that the Chozha *samrajyam* will fall into great peril. Pandiya Naadu will once again cleave away from the great empire. Go on - go now, go quickly!"

The friends had no heart to abandon him with none by his side in this state. They decided that one of them would stay back to take care of him while the other would make for Thanjai. Between the two, it was Vandhiyathevan who could ride a horse the swiftest - and so, the Vallathu king left in great haste.

90

GOLDEN SHOWERS OF RAIN

When Vandhiyathevan finished the astonishing tale of his adventures in the Aanaimalai forest, Kundhavai gazed at him in disbelief. "*Ayya*, your story beggars belief. I confess I was assailed by the occasional doubt that you were making up the tale as you went along. I know well that you are adept at spinning yarns. Why, you paused your speech now and then to look all about you, blinking before resuming your story. I couldn't help but feel my suspicion grow stronger!"

Vandhiyathevan looked all about him again. He then turned to Kundhavai with an earnest expression. "Devi, there are others to spin my yarns to. I have never subjected you to that particular skill of mine! There is another reason my speech stumbled in the midst of my tale," he said.

"Is that a great secret as well? One that cannot be trusted with women?" demanded Kundhavai Piratti.

"It truly is a secret that cannot be told to anyone else. If you give me your consent, my lady, I shall confide in you!" replied Vandhiyathevan.

"Be assured, *ayya* - you always have my consent to speak the truth!"

"Then I shall tell you; but there is little point in growing cross with me after the fact!" Vandhiyathevan awkwardly shuffled his feet. "Whilst I was talking to you, my lady, there were times when your eyes met my gaze. Only the good lord knows what hypnotic sorcery lies in my lady's dark eyes - they rooted me to the spot, sending all other thoughts flying out of my head. I had to struggle to collect myself and resume my tale!"

Kundhavai's lips pulled into a smile; dimples appeared on her pretty cheeks and her eyes sparkled. "*Ayya*, there is no sorcery in my eyes, hypnotic or otherwise. Why, I have lately stopped adorning them with *kohl*! You have but glimpsed your own figure in my eyes - that is likely what stunned you so," she replied.

"Devi, I have seen my figure in the mirror many a time; I have seen it too, in the clear waters of a still pool. It has never yet left me particularly stunned!" said Vallavarayan.

"Ah, you compare my eyes to mirror and water?" teased the Ilavarasi. "A mirror grows dull; the waters of a pool are often disturbed!"

"I can polish a mirror, my lady; I can even save the waters of a pool from growing disturbed. But I cannot prevent my reflection from vanishing when you close your eyes, my lady - can I?" replied Vandhiyathevan.

"You will see your reflection only if you stand in front of a mirror. Only when waters are clear and still can you see yourself in them. But no matter whether my own eyes are open or closed - no matter whether you stand in front of me or not - your image is forever in my sight, *ayya*. Tell me - can you explain this miracle?" asked Kundhavai, her lovely eyes searching his face.

Vandhiythevan went into raptures; ; the very hair on his arms stood on end from the thrill of the sweet words. "I confess I am ignorant on that score, my lady!" he replied, his voice trembling.

"Then I shall explain it myself. It is you who wields a magic power! Even Nandhini, possessed of a heart as hard as diamond - she who came here with a burning desire to wreak her vengeance upon the Chozha clan - why, even she found herself troubled by you, did she not?"

Vandhiyathevan was taken aback. "Your words were sweet as honey just now, my lady - they sent me into raptures of delight. Why do you bring up the name of that venomous snake in the same breath?" he asked, visibly disturbed.

"There was a time when I loathed Nandhini as a venomous snake. Now I find that my heart holds naught but pity for her…"

"Your pitying Nandhini is akin to pitying a foul entity of poison that thirsts to destroy the Chozha clan!" declared Vandhiyathevan.

Kundhavai's eyes grew soft. "*Ayya*, Nandhini is the daughter of Mandhakini Devi, a very goddess of the Chozha lineage. She is the daughter of the divine woman who protected my dear brother Arulmozhi from countless perils; the daughter of the queen among women who relinquished her own life to save my father from becoming prey to the conspirator's spear!"

"Yet, Nandhini was the one who instigated that conspirator to hurl that spear! She was the one who came as the God of Death to Aditha Karikalar! It was Nandhini who muddled the mind of Periya Pazhuvettarayar, the warrior beyond compare; she brought him firmly under her thumb to manipulate him as a mere marionette!"

"Was it only Periya Pazhuvettarayar she wrapped around her finger?

She brought Parthibendra Pallavan and Kandamaaran under her spell too, turning them into naught but weapons that she could wield. And yet, I cannot bring myself to hate her. Nandhini did every one of those things only to take revenge for Veera Pandiyan's death! She succeeded in the task she set out to achieve; it is certain that she hails from a clan of courage and valour!" Kundhavai's voice grew pained. "My heart grows heavy with grief when I think of the part I played in driving her to such heinous deeds. We mercilessly chased her away from Pazhaiyarai!"

"It was a good thing you did, Devi! Do not allow your soft heart to blind you to the truth - she is the daughter of the nemesis to the Chozha clan. Aren't they enough, the calamities that bore down upon us for the sole reason that Veera Pandiyan's son was raised in the house of the Chozha clan? If Veera Pandiyan's daughter had grown up under your roof as well, if she had wed Aditha Karikalar…" Vandhiyathevan trailed off, unable to bring himself to speak further.

"It would have ended very well," replied Kundhavai. "The enmity between two great clans would have come to an end; they would have bonded as one." She paused thoughtfully. "But could that news be true, after all?"

"Of what do you ask, Devi?"

"Could it be true that Nandhini is Veera Pandiyan's daughter?"

"I heard Nandhini say it myself, as she whispered the truth to Aditha Karikalar; so did Periya Pazhuvettarayar. It was what brought about a change of heart in Periya Pazhuvettarayar and propelled him into impassioned rage. It was that heinous revelation that proved to be the death of the Ilavarasar Aditha Karikalar!"

"Pray, think! Do you not think it possible that she said such a thing merely to sate her revenge on Karikalan?" pointed out Kundhavai.

"She spoke in entirely different terms when she sought to save Veera Pandiyar from Karikalan's wrath. Would any maiden address her own father, the man who sired her, as a lover?"

Vandhiyathevan fell into thought. "Devi, Karikalar was then in the grip of blinding rage. Who can tell what Nandhini said and what he understood? This report was none but Karikalar's, after all," replied Vandhiyathevan. "Besides, he himself believed Nandhini later when she claimed her father to be Veera Pandiyan. As for Nandhini, she could not have known the truth until after Veera Pandiyan breathed his last. My lady, you know well the arduous efforts Nandhini undertook to learn the secret of her birth. She even impersonated the spirit of her mother in the witching hour at the dead of night, attempting to drive Sundara Chozhar insane! Why, didn't your own friend look upon the ghastly sight and fall down senseless?"

"The madman who had been imprisoned for three years in the underground dungeons and escaped along with you - you must know his claim by now, the one he made when Azhwarkkadiyaan threatened him to give up the truth."

"Of course I do. He claimed to be father to both Nandhini and her brother."

"That could be the truth as well, could it not?"

"If that were indeed true, then I must say that lies can be quite potent indeed!" declared Vandhiyathevan. "When the old Madhuranthaka Thevar learned that he was Veera Pandiyar's son - that craven milksop who had spent all his life in the palace and shrunk in fear at the very thought of combat - that very weakling transformed into an admirably intrepid man, my lady! If you had seen him, you would have no doubt been stunned. Chinna Pazhuvettarayar once grabbed my shoulder with his diamond-hard hands; the very memory makes that spot twinge afresh with pain. Madhuranthakan, whom we had all deemed a coward, fought spiritedly with such a great warrior as that - as his equal, in fact! I confess that I find myself unable to put that sight out of my mind."

"That was the very reason why I grew doubtful of your tale."

"It certainly is a hard story to believe, my lady. The Madhuranthakan that we knew was a mouse of a man who travelled covertly in Nandhini's veiled palanquin; he shivered at the very name of the Pazhuvettaryar! Who could believe that he would dare to duel with Chinna Pazhuvettarayar? Nonetheless, it did happen - Azhwarkkadiyaan will tell you of it himself when he returns."

"*Ayya*, did you not catch a glimpse of Nandhini Devi?" asked Kundhavai suddenly.

"Why would I have sought out that *rakshasi* in the guise of a maiden?" replied Vandhiyathevan, rougher than he had intended.

Kundhavai turned grave. "Do not speak of Nandhini thus henceforth. One day or the other, I shall meet her myself. I will discover the secret of her birth and learn who her true father is. But pray, keep in mind - do not disparage her to me. Whoever her father may be, there is little doubt about who her mother is. That is reason enough for me to love her." Kundhavai paused. "There is yet another reason too…"

"What reason is that, my lady?"

Kundhavai met his gaze. "Nandhini bore love for you. She gave you her royal signet ring; she helped you escape from the Thanjai fort; she saved your life yet again when you were caught at the hands of Ravidasan and his men in the forests by the banks of the Kollidam…"

"And in the end, she contrived to make yours truly culpable for the heinous crime of killing Aditha Karikalar," countered Vandhiyathevan tartly. "It was the only reason why she carried out those tricks!"

"You do not know, then, why she did those things?"

"Do we need to seek a reason for why the snake bites? Or why the leopard pounces to kill?"

"Nandhini was not born a snake or a leopard- we were the ones who turned her into a beast. Circumstances contrived to force her hand so. Why, you had a part to play, too!"

Vandhiyathevan recoiled. "*Ayyago*! Why blame me for this? What evil have I ever done to her?!"

"You did her no harm. She had naught but true love for you," replied Kundhavai quietly.

"Heavens!" cried Vandhiyathevan, aghast.

Kundhavai threw him a glance of condescension. "It seems that men go blind when it comes to certain subjects, even when they are blessed with two good eyes to see!" she remarked. "*Ayya*, pray, listen. You did not understand Nandhini's heart, but I did - very well, indeed. That unfortunate maiden was never in love with Veera Pandiyan, in truth; she did not love Periya Pazhuvettarayar, nor did she bear true love for Aditha Karikalan. She only feigned love to ascend the throne."

"I know this too, Devi! That cold-blooded heart of hers can nurture nary a drop of love!"

"You are mistaken. It was only when she laid eyes upon you that true love bloomed in her heart. She was willing to do anything to win your affection…"

"She was willing to have me bear the burden of the blame of killing the Ilavarasar."

"And why was that? Only to make sure that you had no ties of friendship or relation with the Chozha clan…"

"Ah, is that why she schemed to have me impaled on the crossroads of the Thanjavur *raja veedhi*?" demanded Vandhiyathevan. "Better that she had slayed me with that sword she carried in her arms!"

"She would have done that if she truly intended to slay you," pointed out Kundhavai. "She could have dispatched Ravidasan's men to kill you at any time. If Periya Pazhuvettarayar had not assumed the crime upon himself, if Ponniyin Selvar had not interfered, if orders had truly been passed to impale you - I am certain that Ravidasan's men would have come to release you. It is entirely possible that you could have been one among the group that is even now gathered on top of the Aanaimalai mountain."

Vandhiyathevan froze at the thought. "It is none but the Lord Himself who saved me from such a fate!" he said with feeling.

"He saved Chozha Naadu, too!" replied Kundhavai with a smile. "The Chozha *samrajyam* was spared from losing the peerless service of a warrior such as you!"

Vandhiyathevan lost his footing for a heartbeat. "Devi, the Chozha *samrajyam* is a mighty empire. It is served by fifty million warriors bearing swords and spears; they guard this great kingdom like they do their own eyes. Surely a mere, solitary wretch as me cannot be indispensable to this eminent dynasty!"

"It was you who claimed that Chozha Naadu is encompassed by peril on all four sides of its borders," replied Kundhavai evenly.

"And that is true, Devi. Ravidasan's fearsome skills of conspiracy and cunning are astounding, indeed! He has produced two people who can emphatically stake a claim to the Pandiya Naadu throne. On the banks of the Kollidam, he crowned a small child as the Pandiya king; that Paraangkusan Nedunchezhiyan is now joined by another calling himself Amara Bhujangan Neduchezhiyan!"

Kundhavai's eyes widened. "Who is that Amara Bhujangan Nedunchezhiyan?"

"That is what our old Madhuranthakar calls himself now. After all, one who wishes to stake his claim to the Pandiya kingdom cannot be burdened by the name Madhuranthakan, can he? When

Chinna Pazhuvettarayar fell into the chasm beneath the waterfall, the rousing cheers that followed fairly drowned out the din of the cascade! 'Long live Amara Bhujangan Neduchezhiyan!' came the cries!"

Kundhavai considered the news, puzzled. "How could Ravidasan profit from creating two successors with the right to stake a claim to the kingdom?" she asked.

"So that the second can step in if ill befalls the first. That wily cabal is endeavouring to win the support of King Magindhan with one heir and forge an alliance with the Chera King using another."

Kundhavi drew in a sharp breath. "*Ayya*, you plotted with my brother to anoint Uttama Chozhar with the bejewelled crown of the Chozha kingdom. I do not think you did Uttama Chozhar a good turn. The burden of ruling the Chozha *samrajyam* does not seem to be an easy task at present..."

"Ruling the Chozha *samrajyam* at this juncture is an onerous task indeed," agreed Vandhiyathevan. "But will it truly be Uttama Chozhar who will bear the burden of that challenge? He will likely spend his time helping his mother in the holy work of renovating temples. The one who will bolster the Chozha *samrajyam* and protect it is none but Arulmozhi Thevar."

Kundhavai's eyes shone. "That is true. Arulmozhi is endowed with the necessary strength and vigour to rise to the challenge! Yet," she continued, a tinge of worry lacing her tone, "he is young and inexperienced. The Chozha *samrajyam* has lost the irreplaceable support of two diamond pillars that have held in good stead thus far - the Pazhuvoor kings. The elder one has left us for good. Going by your report, Chinna Pazhuvettarayar is unlikely to survive..."

"Even if he does, he will not be able to serve the *rajyam*," replied Vandhiyathevan quietly. "Distress and grief will rule his mind and he shall forever rue his daughter and son-in-law..."

"Sambuvaraiyar has also fallen prey to the same fate," said Kundhavai sadly. "In the span of a few days, he has grown gravely weakened of body and heart. Malayaman is an old man already; one of his dear grandsons has breathed his last while the other did not ascend the throne - he is left disillusioned and unhappy. As for Kodumbalur Periya Velar, his heart is not steady of will. He finds himself unable to forgive Arulmozhi for affecting to desire the crown up until the very last minute. Why, he did not even seem satisfied that he wed Vanathi! He departed declaring that he intended to keep away from the affairs of state to instead immerse himself in holy temple work at Kodumbalur. The other chieftains who took part in the covert assembly at the Kadambur palace have suffered great shame over the way events unfolded in the end - they have lost all will and confidence. *Ayya*!" said Kundhavai earnestly, "Arulmozhi needs people by his side, allies who will help him with his endeavours. He needs a true friend who is sharp of sword and intellect."

"Ah, we must be thankful then for the Pallava Parthibendrar!" replied Vandhiyathevan with a grin.

Kundhavai sighed. "In truth, it is uncertain whether Arulmozhi can depend on his support. He was quite angry that Uttama Chozhar had been crowned when he was sent out of town. That Arulmozhi treats you as a bosom friend only stokes his ire."

Vandhiyathevan looked troubled. "His anger is perhaps justified - he has done so much for the Chozha clan, after all. I am naught but an outsider in comparison. If you like, my lady, I shall make apologies to him."

Kundhavai considered the proffer. "That would be akin to pouring oil into a blazing fire!" she said.

"Parthibendran is a redoubtable warrior. Is there no other way to placate him?" asked Vandhiyathevan, worried.

"He put forth a suggestion himself. Why, he even approached my father with his request..."

"The Chakravarthy would not have refused Parthibendra Pallavar's wish, I'm sure."

"But it had little to do with the Chakravarthy; it was more about his daughter. It was she who refused to accept his terms," replied Kundhavai, to Vandhiyathevan's surprise. "Yes, *ayya*! The descendant of the illustrious Pallava clan could not stand to see one wear the crown and ascend the Chozha throne who had done naught but provide flowers to Siva temples until that very moment. He could not digest, either, the fact that a girl sailing a boat upon the sea had now ascended to the throne. He asked that he be made a free king of Old Pallava Naadu and that he be awarded sovereign rights..."

Vandhiyatheven stood stunned at the news. "Aha!" he cried. "How can such an appeal be granted? It will break the very boundaries of Chozha *rajyam*, will it not?"

"My father acquiesced to his request," replied Kundhavai, stunning him further. "But the Pallava prince did not stop there. It seems that in the times gone by, a Pallava princess had wed a Chozha prince. And so, he requested for the past gesture to now be reciprocated - he asked that Sundara Chozhar's daughter be given to him in marriage."

Vandhiyathevan's face drooped with sadness at these words; he turned it away to hide his chagrin. Kundhavai's face brightened with a smile; she stopped her speech on purpose and stood watching him. Vandhiyathevan suffered the silence for a while until he could stand it no longer. "What reply did the Chakravarthy give?" he asked.

"What reply can the Chakravathy give to such a question? It depends on his daughter's wish, doesn't it? The Chakravarthy asked his daughter..."

"What did the beloved daughter of the Chakravarthy say in response?" asked Vandiyathevan, holding his breath.

"She said that she did not wish to clasp Parthibendran's hand in marriage!"

Vandhiyathevan's face lit up with joy. "Why, why?" he asked, his voice bursting with eagerness.

Kundhavai raised her chin. "Why must the beloved daughter of the Chakravarthy be suffered to give a reason? Even so, she did. I do not wish to leave this lush country where the divine Ponni flows to go to another, she said."

"Was that the only reason why?"

"Perhaps there was another reason as well. Surely you'll agree that it can only be confided to one who is truly interested in the answer? Why must it be told to someone who asks with but half a heart?"

"Devi, I ask you with boundless interest!"

"One who has such boundless interest will know the reason themselves. There is little need to spell it out for them."

Vandhiyathevan gazed upon Kundhavai's face as though he were seeing it for the first time.

Lightning struck lightning; wave crashed against wave; heaven descended to earth and the very land became the sky.

Kundhavai glanced at him from the corner of her eye. A mischievous smile appeared on her rosy lips. "What must I think of a man who wishes to know a maiden's heart by her own lips without understanding what truly lies within? How can I expect him to ferret out the conspiracies and schemes that the enemies of the Chozha *samrajyam* will plot?" she sighed theatrically.

Vandhiyathavan looked up. He looked down. He looked all about him. "Parthibendran," he began carefully, "comes in the ancient lineage of the Pallavas. Should an orphaned youth - one who has not even the shade of a hut to shelter in - ask the same question that he did, what would the Chakravarthy think of the matter?"

Kundhavai's face glowed. "Whatever he thinks, he will ask his daughter what she wishes. He will give the same reply that she does."

"Devi, what reply will the beloved daughter of the Chakravarthy give?"

Kundhavai broke into a smile. "Why torture yourself with such a roundabout endeavour? Ask the Chakravarthy, won't you? You will get your reply at once!" she teased.

"How could I ever hope to ask him such a thing? He is the king of kings who rules over the vast territories that lie from Eezham up until Vengi - how can a young orphan with no land or title to his name muster the courage to ask him such a thing?" asked Vallavarayan.

"From where did a warrior born to the Vaanar clan get such modesty?" asked Kundhavai in some surprise. "Why, when you met me for the very first time, you fairly crowed with pride about the honour your clan bears! I have not forgotten, you know. You said that when a son is born in the palaces of the Cheras, Chozhas and Pandiyas, queens would coo over his wide chest remarking that all the titles of the strong Vannan king could be written on him! That at the entrance to the palace of the Vaanar king once stood the three great Tamil kings, awaiting an audience with the liege; that poets would gaze with wonder at the prizes they received from the Vaanar king, crying 'This is my horse! This is my elephant! This is my crown! This is my umbrella!' Why, I ask, has one who bore such pride in his lineage turned so modest and diffident?"

"It is on account of your brother's friendship, my lady," smiled

Vandhiyathevan. "Arulmozhi Varmar detests basking in the glory of ancestry and lineage. He laughs at the idea of taking pride in such things as being a scion of the Surya Vamsam, the descendant of Karikala Valavan or the grandson of the grandson of Vijayalaya Chozhar. Do you know what he told me one day, my lady? 'The forefathers of my clan described their lineage when they commissioned inscriptions on copper plates and stones - they made sure that their ancestry was recorded as the progeny of the Surya Vamsam, the descendants of Manu Needhi Chozhan, the kin of Sibi Chakravarthy and so on and so forth. When I ascend the throne, I shall change this tradition. The copper plate and stone inscriptions I commission shall only carry the feats that I have accomplished. There will be no room for nary a doubt about the truth of those words!' he said. Devi, I agreed with his view. I have resolved to cease singing the praises of my lineage as my own." Vandhiyathevan's eyes shone with purpose. "I will not seek the fortune of holding your hand in troth by telling your noble father of the pride of my ancestors. Arulmozhi and I have dedicated our very lives to the growth of the Chozha *samrajyam*. We have resolved to make the tiger flag of the Chozhas fly tall and proud up until the Vindhya mountains in the north, the Trikona mountain in the south, the Lakshadweep isles in the west and the countries of Saavagam, Kadaaram and Kambojam that lie in the east. When we have achieved some level of success in our grand endeavour, I shall approach Sundara Chozha Chakravathy. 'Here,' I shall say, 'these garlands of victory I wear I would place around the neck of your beloved daughter with your consent!' I shall set forth to Ilankai and triumph over Magindhan; I shall lay in front of the illustrious princess the Imperial Crown of the Pandiyas and the ancient gemstone necklace. I shall then ask with deserved pride- 'If I am worthy of holding your noble hand, pray give me that fortune!'"

Kundhavai's heart swelled at his words. She gazed at him with her lovely dark eyes, rapt with admiration. "*Ayya*, I praise your determination. I find myself astonished at the difference of heart between you and Parthibendran; it gives me much happiness and delight. But only men can endeavour to accomplish such feats. You can offer your triumphs for your cause and take pride in them. Such things are impossible for women like us. It is not necessary for us, either. For a long time, our country had the tradition of holding a *suyamvaram* for princesses of royal descent. That practice has vanished, for reasons unknown. *Ayya*, should my father hold a *suyamvaram* for me and invite all the princes in this vast kingdom, I shall not anoint any of their necks with my garland. I shall search among the assembled princes for the orphan youth who had escaped from the Thanjai fort, alighted a boat with the aid of a *bhattar* from Pazhaiyarai and sneaked into the palace garden, all to meet me in private! Only upon his neck will I anoint the garland in my hand!"

A thousand bells rang in Vandhiyathevan's ears. A golden shower of rain fell from the skies. A kaleidoscope of colourful butterflies spread their wings and danced in joy amongst the cluster of flowers blooming in the boughs atop the swaying trees. Vandhiyathevan suddenly sprung to his feet.

"Did you not like what I said?" asked Kundhavai, puzzled.

"There's a pretty thought, my lady! I only wonder whether I am truly awake, whether the words that fell upon my ears were true, or whether this is all naught but a lovely dream!" exclaimed Vandhiyathevan, enraptured. "I see now that I am not dreaming, that it is all true! I have heard that the *devas* turned immortal after drinking the divine ambrosia they obtained from churning the ocean of milk. Your words just now have transformed me into one drunk upon that sweet nectar of immortality, my lady - it has given me new life!"

"*Ayya*!" cried out Kundhavai, her soft cheeks flushed with joy. "Pray, bear one thing in mind. You will meet many dangers everywhere you go. You will wage fierce wars upon countless battlefields; enemies will stoop to vicious treachery in their endeavours to dispatch you to the afterlife. As you face such perils, pray, remember - a princess born to the Chozha clan will attain widowhood before her marriage should anything happen to you. Do not forget this!"

Vandhiyathevan gazed at her, love and admiration suffusing his eyes. "Devi, nothing of that sort will happen!" he cried. "I am drunk on divine ambrosia; I have attained immortality! There is no such thing as death for me, now or ever! When I find myself lost and directionless in the midst of a dense forest roiling under the pitch of black darkness, subjected to fierce winds and lashing rain - you will wait for me in a home in the midst of that fearsome jungle, lamp lighted in the window; the very thought will galvanize me with courage and I shall escape the wind, the rain and the darkness. When I am cast adrift upon a boat in the midst of the vast seas, losing count of the days, weeks and months that have passed by, as I stray dazed and disheartened - you shall sparkle brightly as the *dhruva natchatram* that shines in the *saptarishi* constellation; you shall be the guide by which I shall navigate my boat. As the sea heaves with fearsome currents at night, breaking waves as tall as mountains upon the jagged rocks that line the coast - you shall blaze incandescent as the lifesaving glow of a lighthouse; the light shall save me from running my boat aground on the rocks and I shall bring my vessel safely ashore. When I roam the perpetually burning desert where neither grass nor weeds grow, as my body is mortified by the blazing heat of the sun and the scorching sands, as I wilt with thirst with dry tongue and shredded feet, as I roam lost and unguided in this fiery hell - you shall be there to succour me as a life giving spring bounded by coconut palms and honeyed plantain. Devi, wherever I go in this vast world, whatever strife I endure, I shall return to you one day. I shall come back, clasp your noble hand in mine and wed you. Until this heart's desire of mine is fulfilled, Yama cannot come close to me - I shall remain an immortal who has drunk of the divine nectar of ambrosia!"

Vandhiyathevan spoke with such passion as he never had in his life. He sat down, spent; Ilaiya Piratti gazed at his face, enthralled. She sensed that this was not the first time the warrior had spoken these words to her; the flood of impassioned speech was a solemn promise that he had made to her countless times on countless occasions in preceding ages. Kundhavai was musing on the strangeness of the delusion when she heard Vanathi's voice behind her. "*Akka*! *Akka*!" she cried. Both of them turned around to look as Vanathi hastened to their side. "*Akka*, an exigent *olai* has arrived for him," she said, panting for breath as she stretched out the missive she held in her hands. "It has come from Manimekelai's *thamayan*, Kandamaaran!"

91

A FLOWER WITHERS AWAY

Vandhiyathevan looked at Vanathi as he took the *olai* from her hands. "Ilavarasi, do you remember me, after all? Why, I thought you had forgotten me for good!"

"*Ayya*, how could I ever forget you or the aid you've rendered to me and my noble husband?" asked Vanathi with a pretty smile.

"Ah, that gratitude is the very reason why you chose to hold your wedding in my absence, I suppose!"

A mischievous laugh escaped Vanathi. "Yes. If you had been around, the wedding would have risked turning out like Ponniyin Selvan's *magudabhishekam*. None but the good Lord knows what devious plots you would have hatched!"

"Was it I who contrived matters to ensure that Ponniyin Selvar did not get crowned?" demanded Vandhiyathevan. "*You* were the one vying with Poonguzhali! That oath you took vowing to never sit upon the throne was the root of the whole problem, wasn't it? Lady luck smiled upon the boat girl- why find fault with me?"

"Let her enjoy her good fortune, then! I do not have any fault to find with her on that score - or with you, for that matter. I bear nothing but happiness for her. But, when you decide your own wedding date, pray, leave the task to a good *jothidar*!"

"The Kudanthai jothidar can do the honours. You lot have faith in none but him, after all!" remarked Vandhiyathevan, grinning at Vanathi.

Vanathi burst out in peals of laughter. "*Akka*," she said, turning to Ilaiya Piratti, "his mention of the Kudanthai jothidar brings a curious incident to mind!" The words were hardly out of her mouth before she dissolved into pretty giggles once again.

"What are you laughing about, Vanathi?" asked Kundhavai, smiling. "Are you thinking of the time that the *jothidar* prattled on about your fortune - 'The child born to your womb will rule all the three worlds!'"

"Why do you call that mere prattle, Devi? The *jothidar's* fortune will certainly come to pass!"

A painful shyness overcame Vanathi and her laughter died away on her lips. "*Akka*, here I am, wanting to say one thing while you turn the conversation in an entirely different direction!" exclaimed Vanathi. "Do you recall the time I asked the Kudanthai *jothidar*, 'When will a worthy husband appear for Ilaiya Piratti?' To which the *jothidar* replied, 'He may jump down from the sky this very minute!' And, the Vallathu king here did indeed jump inside the next minute, all whilst fighting the *jothidar*'s disciple! The memory came to me unbidden and I couldn't help but laugh."

Kundhavai repressed the surge of laughter that threatened to burst out of her. "Enough of your games, now!" she said, affecting sternness. "Let him read the *olai* that was delivered with such urgency!"

As Vandhiyathevan read the *olai*, an expression of deep worry spread over his features; it did not escape the maidens' eyes.

"What news?" asked Ilaiya Piratti anxiously. "What has Kandamaaran written?"

"Read it for yourself, my lady!" said Vandhiyathevan, handing the *olai* to Kundhavai. The missive contained the following message:

To my dear friend Vallavarayan Vandhiyathevan,

Pray, forgive all the crimes and injustices that I have subjected you to. Come here at once to see my sister Manimekalai for one last time.

Young Sambuvaryan, Kandamaaran

Kundhavai looked up after reading the message. "It is good news, in a way. Now it is certain that Manimekalai has been found," she said.

"What did you say?" asked Vandhiyathevan, taken aback. "Where had Manimekalai gone?"

"Didn't you receive any news of Manimekalai?"

"No, I did not. I thought to ask you of the matter."

"I wished to tell you as well. But I hesitated, wondering how I was to bring up the subject with one so stone-hearted as to make no inquiries of her," replied Kundhavai evenly.

"Devi, how have I suddenly become stone-hearted when it comes to Manimekalai?" asked Vandhiyathevan, hurt. "After all, I am dead as far as she is concerned."

"No," corrected Kundhavai. "You are not dead to her. You have become an immortal who has been granted eternal life!"

"Let that be," replied Vandhiyathevan, suddenly anxious. "Tell me about Manimekalai now, at the very least."

"It breaks my heart to even speak of it. Sembian Maadevi strained every nerve to persuade Sambuvaraiyar to leave Manimekalai with her. But he did not relent. He claimed that with Kandamaaran off to guard the kingdom's border, he had none but his daughter to be with him; so he took her away with him. With the Kadambur palace razed to the ground, he obtained before he left the Chakrvarthy's permission to build a new palace on the western bank of the Paalaaru. On the way, he pitched tent in the environs of Veera Narayanapuram to spend the night. When he woke up the next morning, he saw that Manimekalai was nowhere to be found. He sent men to see whether she had come running back here; we sent back word that she had not. Since then, we've all been rent with anxiety about her. We were so worried at the thought that she may have fallen into the Veera Narayana lake and lost her life. We received news that men were searching out for her in all directions. From Kandamaaran's *olai*, it seems as if they have located Manimekalai at last."

Vandhiyathevan heard the account gravely. "What is the point of my going to see her? She will not recognize me!" he said presently.

"Even so, go you must," insisted Kundhavai. "Kandamaaran has written the words, 'for one last time.' It is hard to say what he means by that."

"*Akka,* he has nary a drop of pity or compassion!" burst out Vanathi. "He is not even a little worthy of Manimekalai's love. There are some who readily sacrifice mighty kingdoms for the sake of another's love. And here he is, reluctant to make the effort to travel!"

"Ilavarasi, there are only a few kingdoms in this world; naught but a few have the privilege of sacrificing one for the sake of love," replied Vandhiyathevan. "But I confess that there is truth in what you spoke before that. I am not even a little worthy of Manimekalai's love. She has bestowed upon me a love that she ought to have offered to the Lord himself. I am not god; I am a mere mortal with faults. None can be worthy of Manimekalai's love save the divine!"

"Even so, I see nothing wrong in your travelling to see her," pressed Ilaiya Piratti Kundhavai anxiously. "Kandamaaran too has written that you will see for 'one last time,' hasn't he?"

"I never said that I would not go, did I? I doubt whether there is any point in doing so; I only hesitate for she believes me to be dead." Vandhiyathevan's brows furrowed over. "Even so, I fail to grasp the meaning of Kandamaarans's message - 'for one last time,' he says. Is he going to issue me an order to never see her henceforth? Or does he plan to consign her to a Buddhist monastery?"

"If you care to do but a day's travel, you will understand!" said Ilaiya Piratti Kundhavai.

Vandhiyathevan's travel from Pazhaiyaari to Veera Narayanapuram truly did cost him no more than a day. But unlike his earlier travels, the trip seemed to him to take an entire aeon. His heart swirled with a roiling nest of thoughts and memories that rattled his mind. The very first time he had taken this very path to Thanjai, he had been delighted by myriad sweet sights. He had built so many castles in the sky. Not all them remained pipe dreams, either - many impossible things had come to pass since then. The brave prince that all of Thamizhagam praised and celebrated, the apple of Chozha Naadu's eye, had relinquished the crown that had fallen into his hands and placed it upon another's head. With that act of peerless self-sacrifice, he had grown to be taller than Mount Meru and attained the zenith of sacrifice. Vandhiyathevan had won the close friendship and confidence of this very Ponniyin Selvar. He had also won a place in the heart of one whom Ponniyin Selvar himself praised and held great respect for - the beauteous Ilaiya Piratti. He had been granted the exalted post the Mathanda Nayagan of the Chozha forces in Eezha Naadu. Can it be claimed that all of it was due to his cleverness alone? Never. The fortune was the result of his chance arrival at the Kadambur palace on the fateful night of the covert gathering, where he had learned of the conspiracy the chieftains were in. It was naught but this and all the events that followed that had him to his position today.

A multitude of events had transpired within these short eight months. The falling star that had appeared in the sky had achieved its disastrous end before disappearing; Aditha Karikalar had disappeared. Can there be a connection between the falling star and Aditha Karikalar? Can such a belief held by lakhs and lakhs of people truly be a lie? What connection can there be, though, between the celestial planets and stars that have roamed the skies for aeos and the ephemeral length of a man's life who is born today and dies on the morrow? Even so, there is little doubt that there is a supernatural force beyond the understanding of men that rules their lives. Otherwise, how could he have escaped the past eight months unscathed by the trials and tribulations he had found himself in? How many people helped him slip out of the problems he was caught in! Who contrived matters to make sure that they were by his side to render help at the right time? Is that the miraculous power that the elders call God? Is that what they praise and worship? Is that the force they call Siva, Thirumal and Mahashakthi and sing of them in rapture?

When he thought of the unexpected aid he had received at crucial junctures, Vandhiyathevan was struck amazed. His heart melted in gratitude when he thought of the people who had come forward to help him. Even though Kandamaaran did much evil to him later, the help he rendered at the very beginning was impossible to forget. Azhwarkkadiyaan had also lent him much support. Why, even Nandhini, that *rakshashi* in the guise of a bewitching mohini, had helped him! Vandhiyathevan marvelled at the affection that Ilaiya Piratti bore for him in her heart. Then, there was Poonguzhali - the aid she rendered was one he would never forget in all the seven births to come. She was truly worthy to sit upon the throne of the Chozha *samrajyam*.

What could he say about the help rendered by Uttama Chozhar, whom he had first met as Senthan Amudhan? Could it be held to comparison? Can it be said that his debt of gratitude was squared because he saved him from the *vaithiyar's* son? Never! He would meet the debt he owed that clan only by serving the Chozha dynasty as long as life breathed in his body. And then there was the Dhanaadhikaari Periya Pazhuvetterayar! There was a time when he would have considered the merit of his good deeds to clap his eyes upon that great warrior, marked by sixty four battle wounds upon his noble person. Not only did Vandhiyathevan have the fortune of seeing him, he also bore the brunt of his unjust anger. In the end, the venerable old man had atoned for all it. He had confessed that the knife he had thrown had missed his mark and struck Aditha Karikalar instead, saving him from a terrible blame and heinous punishment! He was verily a great man. How could he ever show his gratitude to him now?

And what of the naive maiden Manimekalai? Why must she bear him such divine love? Why did she have to lose her senses thus? Why did she have to come forward to assume the blame of murder in a bid to save him?

All of it was that dimwit Kandamaaran's fault. He had praised Vandhiyathevan to the skies to Manimekalai in the beginning, comparing him to Indiran, Chandiran, Arjunan, Manmadhan and the like. It appears as though the innocent maiden had lost her heart to him then. Vandhiyathevan never knew.

"Put aside all thoughts of my sister. We plan to wed her to an influential family!' Kandamaaran had said to him, rather sternly. And so, Vandhiyathevan truly did try to forget her. It had helped that he had just had a tryst with Ilaiya Piratti. But sweet Manimekalai had not changed her heart; she had made no attempt to do so, either. She did not shy away from expressing her feelings for all to know. *Aha! What a sweet-natured maiden! Such modesty, such grace!*

How pure her heart is! It is innocent, like a child's. Why, she truly is a child! Her heart is unblemished as milk, yet sparkling with mischief. It was rather a good thing that she thinks me dead. She will not remain disturbed for all time to come, surely! With enough time, her mind will grow clear once more and so will her heart. She will wed another brave youth and lead a life of happiness!... Will this truly happen? Or do I delude myself? Will I become responsible for Manimekalai's state, after all? 'Come see Manimekalai for one last time,' Kandamaaran had written. What could be the meaning of those words? Perhaps... perhaps... ah, but the very thought brings unbearable sadness!

The horse that Vandhiyathevan rode kept pace with his thoughts and flew swifty upon the path. Thankfully, the Kollidam river was not full. There was little need for a boat or to change horses. Vandhiyathevan led his horse down the small stream that was flowing by the bank and proceeded to cross the river on horseback, passing the vast patches of white sands that sprawled across the riverbed. He reached the other bank easily enough.

Vandhiyathevan spied from afar the Kadambur palace that had burned down in a fire. It was in abject ruins; some of its pillars and walls were blackened with soot. He pressed on, discovering that Kandamaaran's men were waiting for him near Veera Narayanapuram. "Where is the young master?" he asked them. "On the banks of the lake - he awaits you with a boat!" came the reply.

Wondering why he would wait at the banks of the lake, Vandhiyathevan sped towards the Veera Narayana waters. The lake's high bank rose as the imposing walls of a fort, hiding the vast expanse of water that lay on the other side. When Vandhiyathevan had come to this very bank for the first time, the people had gathered in merry crowds to celebrate the *pathinettam perukku vizha*. Men, women and children had danced in joy; they had played and feasted with each other as they enjoyed the festival. Now he could see a very few upon the bank, not more than a couple of people here and there. He suddenly remembered how, on his first trip, the waters surged forth from the canals into the lake, sounding like the din of a bustling marketplace. Now, only a few gentle streams of water flowed from a couple of canals, making no more than a gentle babble. It sounded to him like the sad whispers of anklets upon a dancing maiden's feet as they kept step to a mournful song.

Vandhiyathevan led his horse expertly up the steep *eri* bank that rose sharply before him. When he reached the top, he saw a scene that was vastly different than he had remembered. Then, the lake had been full of water, its waves striking against the bank as if seeking to break through; now, the water line began only at the very bottom of the lake. Then, the water had taken on a mesmerizing reddish-hue; now, it had entirely changed to be clear as crystal. A profusion of colourful flowers grew in rich thickets by the periphery of the bank. Delightful lilies bloomed there, as did *sengazhuneer*, *neelothphalam* and lotuses. Some of the plants bore young leaves while others sported thicker foliage; some were dotted with tender young buds shyly hiding behind half-opened blossoms and flowers in full bloom.

The first time he had come here, he had seen the waters of the Vadavaaru spill into the southern bank of the lake, its waters surging to converge with the lake. That was not the case today. Neither were there the boats he had seen floating upon the water on the earlier occasion, seeming for all the world like swans that had spread its wings. The banks which had once been flooded by river water now showed a dense profusion of trees, plants and shrubs. Amidst the foliage stood pensive cranes and storks, standing upon a single leg as they followed their mysterious penance.

It did not take Vandhiyathevan more than a few minutes to observe their sights. A boat that stood waiting by the bank of the lake caught his sight. Amongst the people in the boat was Kandamaaran himself. Vandhiytheven urged his horse forward and hastened towards him;

he leapt from his mount and sped towards the boat. Kandamaaran stretched out his arm to hold Vandhiyathevan's hand and bring him on board; he signalled to the boatman to begin rowing. He then turned to Vandhiyathevan with tear-filled eyes.

"My friend, you have come here soon indeed. You have my heartfelt gratitude. If you had not come here today and had chosen to arrive tomorrow, perhaps you could not have seen Manimekalai alive!" said Kandamaaran, his voice cracking.

It was true that Vandhiyathevan had a heart of stone. If he had possessed such will and resolve in his heart, could he have accomplished the feats that he had in the past eight months? Could he have brushed aside all thought of danger and staked his own life to navigate monstrous perils?

And yet, Vandhiyathevan, he who was blessed with such exceptional determination, found that tears sprang to his eyes when he heard Kandamaaran's words. The meaning of Kandamaaran's message - 'Come see Manimekalai for one last time' - was now clear beyond all shadow of doubt. Tears welled in Vandhiyathevan's eyes and spilled down his cheeks in streams.

"Kandamaara! Is Manimekalai's life in danger? How did that come to be? It is naught but her mind that is disturbed, isn't it? And even that is only when it comes to you and me!" stammered Vandhiyathevan.

"My friend, Manimekalai's mind has now attained clarity. But it is hard to say how much longer she will live. She prays to all the gods that she remains alive until she sees you," said Kandamaaran, wiping the tears from his own eyes.

He then proceeded to recount, to the best of his knowledge, the events that had transpired.

Kandamaaran was in Kanchi, making repairs to the pon maaligai so that it was made fit for the Chakravarthy. Whilst he was there, he came to know that Sambuvaraiyar had left taking Manimekalai with him; he also learned that it was shortly after that Manimekalai had vanished near the banks of the Veera Narayana lake. He had immediately taken leave of Parthibendran and made a swift departure. Kandamaaran had come flying to learn the fate of his dear younger sister. He discovered that his father was seized with manic worry and suffering, on the verge of going insane himself. Kandamaaran could extract little information from him - all he kept repeating was, 'She slept in the tent at night. In the morning, she was nowhere to be seen.' Kandamaaran was told that he had sent men to Pazhaiyarai; even the ruins of Kadambur palace and its environs had been subjected to a thorough search. Kandamaaran set down to searching himself. He doubted that Manimekalai would be returned to Pazhaiyarai; fearing that she could have fallen into the lake and drowned, he scoured the waters thinking that he could find her remains at the very least. He nursed the hope that she was roaming the forests surrounding the lake with her life intact.

Kandamaaran relentlessly circled the banks of the lake and searched through the territory. He pressed on further towards the canals that fed the lake and searched their environs as well. He frantically took the boat across the waters of the lake and searched the forests surrounding the lake. After four such days had gone by in fruitless searching, Kandamaaran suddenly recalled the *mandapam* that lay on an island towards the north of the lake. Karikalan and Vandhiyathevan had gone hunting on one occasion; Nandhini and Manimekalai had happened to be playing in the water and the foursome had met at that very *mandapam.* It was impossible to think that Manimekalai had gone to that place all by herself with no company. Could she have walked alone through the path that cut through the western forest, filled with beasts as fearsome as bears and leopards? Even if she had crossed the forest, she would have had to cross the many small canals that lay in the way. Still, Kandamaaran decided that he would search there as well and steered his boat to the *mandapam*. When he neared the *mandapam*, a flurry of old memories arose to prick his heart. The place itself seemed utterly desolate and empty. It did not appear as if anyone was there. Kandamaaran alighted from the boat to the *mandapam* steps and stood there. He thought of all the castles he had built in the air, all the pipe dreams that had gone to vain and heaved a great sigh. Another sigh floated to him in response, shocking him. Kandamaaran ran towards the sound and saw Manimekalai lying on the steps of the *mandapam* on the other side. She looked gaunt and wilted; her robe was ripped in many places and red, angry scratches raised great welts upon her body. At first, it did not seem as if the body yet nurtured life. Manimekalai looked as one who had breathed her last from exhaustion and fatigue, having wandered the forests for days directionless and starved.

When Kandamaaran saw that sight, his heart felt the piercing grief of a thousand spears. He gently took Manimekalai upon his lap and keened with abandon. Suddenly remembering the sigh that he had heard, Kandamaaran felt hope anew that life yet clung to her body. He rushed back to her side with good water cupped in his palms and sprinkled it on her face; he breathed into her mouth; he rubbed her body to generate heat and energy. In some time, Manimekalai opened her eyes and looked at him, unblinking.

"*Anna*, is it you?" she whispered. "Ah, my thoughts have come true. I thought that I could see you and him if I go to heaven. Where is he?" she asked softly, her voice weak and unsteady. Kandamaaran repressed the sobs that threatened to engulf him. He gathered himself with a mighty effort. "He will come, *amma*, he will come!" he said.

Kandamaaran realized that Manimekalai thought she was in heaven; she thought she was meeting her brother in paradise. It was why she eagerly asked after Vandhiyathevan, too. Kandamaaran did his best to give responses that indulged her belief, so that she would suffer a great shock. He spoke of all the efforts he had taken to keep the spark of life burning; then, the young Sambuvarayan said as he finished his sad tale, he had hurriedly written Vandhiyathevan a missive.

"My friend, I find myself at a loss to express the gratitude that rises in my heart that you came here paying heed to my message. Manimekalai will not live long, now," said Kandamaaran, his voice choking from the sadness it bore. "A lamp about to extinguish burns brightly for a brief while when its wick is raised, doesn't it? It is thus that Manimekalai's spark of life yet shines. The desire to see you keeps her alive still! She believes that we are all in paradise. Do not disabuse her of that belief! It is natural that you will feel grief when you see her. Pray, bring it under control so you speak to her with a bright face!" he begged.

The boat neared the *mandapam*. Weak strains of music floated out to the water as a feeble voice sang in accompaniment to the sweet tones of a *yazh*.

Vandhiyathevan looked wordlessly at Kandamaaran. "Yes, my friend. It is Manimekalai, singing as she plays the *yazh*," he said. The pair alighted from the boat. Vandhiyathevan stood still in an attempt to identify the song that Manimekalai was singing. It was the very one that she had sung on an earlier occasion in the very same *mandapam*.

Iniyapunal aruvi thavazh
Inbamazhai chaaraliley
Kanikulavum maranizhalil
Karampidithu uganthellam
Kanavuthanodi - sakiye
Ninaivuthanodi!
Punnaimara cholaiyile
Ponnolirum maalayile
Yennai vara cholli avar

Kannal mozhi pakarnthathellam
Soppanamthaanodi - antha
Arputham poiyodi!
Kattukaval than kadanthu
Kalaraiyp pol mella vanthu
Mattillatha kathaludan
Katti muththam eenthathellam
Nigazhnthathuthanodi - nangal
Magizhnthathuthanodi!

[Was it all a dream, my friend? Was it a dream… that we met, he and I upon lush, verdant mountain slopes, misty with pristine waterfalls? Was it all a dream that he caught my hands in a lover's embrace, under trees heavy with fruit, casting cool, soothing shade? Was it all true, or a mere dream?

Was it all a dream, dear friend? Was it but a mirage, a magical interlude… that he begged me, come upon golden evenings to the luscious Punnai orchard and spoke words of sweet love? Was it all true, or a passing fancy?

Was it all a dream? Was none of it real… that he deceived with ease the sternest guards, tiptoed up to me like a stealthy thief and with all the love he could muster, embraced me with a searing kiss? Was it all a dream, or were we truly lost in bliss?]

Vandhiyathevan lingered upon the steps until the song ended. When it died away, he climbed up with a heavy tread and entered the *mandapam*.

When Manimekalai saw him, the *yazh* rolled away from her hands. She struggled to get to her feet. Alas, her body no longer had the strength to support her; her feet were not able to bear even her now shrunken form. Manimekalai swayed in place, tottering dangerously; Vandhiyathevan sprinted to her side and held her in his arms. He slowly made Manimekalai sit down and sat beside her. Choking back the tears that welled within him, he gently took her upon his lap.

Manimekalai looked up at his face in wonder every now and then. It appeared as if she sought to confirm that it truly was Vandhiyathevan, she truly was lying down upon his lap. "My *anna* did not deceive me. Heaven is not a mere dream. This miracle is not a lie!" her lips murmured. "It is not a lie, Manimekalai, it is not a lie!" replied Vandhiyathevan softly, stroking her face. "This is certainly heaven. I am truly here, right beside you!"

Despite his best efforts to control the grief that assailed him, Vandhiyathevan's eyes welled with tears. Teardrops fell on Manimekalai's face like shining pearls. Unbeknownst to him, the heart-rending sound of weeping arose from Vandhiyathevan's throat. For some time, Manimekalai's face glowed with a divine light. Rays of moonlight seemed to radiate from her large eyes. Her lips, red as pomegranate buds, parted to speak honeyed words of love and affection. Vandhiyathevan strained every nerve to listen, but was not able to understand what she said.

Why must he know? How does it matter what she said? When the divine nectar love pours out of the golden vessel of the heart, what is the point of mere words? Soon, Manimekalai's lips ceased their murmurs; her dark, lovely eyes closed; the divine light that had set her face aglow dimmed, giving way to an undisturbed peace. Atop the *mandapam*, a soft, gentle breeze blew through the spreading branches of a tree. The boughs shook, strewing a cascade of red flowers. Manimekalai's life had withered away.

Where did the spirit go, that had flown its coop? By which way did it go? Had it become one with the wind? Did it mingle with the susurration of the young leaves as the gentle breeze touched them with its caress? Had it soared to the blue skies, embracing the sweet songs of *koels* that came bursting out of their throats to quench a thirst in the heart? Had it attained the lotus feet of the One who creates, preserves and finally destroys all the living beings in the universe? Or did merge with Vandhiyathevan's heart, who wept with heart-rending abandon even as he grew still as a statue of stone? Only one thing is certain. We shall never again see the charming personification of jest and play, mischief and joy, courage and conviction that was Vandhiyathevan.

Vandhiyathevan's heart grew heavy with tenderness, compassion and sagacity. The goddess Manimekalai had come to dwell in the temple of his heart. Wherever he went, whatever he did, she would be ever by his side to offer him succour.

Vallavarayan Vandhiyathevan would grow to be strong enough to accomplish a constellation of noble feats. He would rise to gain the esteem of all who had the privilege to know him.

Brave warrior! We shall take our leave of you, now. We do not wish to impede upon your time of grief. Dear friend of Arulmozhi Varmar! May you lead a long, full life, indelibly carving your name in the annals of history celebrating the bravest of Thamizh heroes.

About Varsha Venugopal

Varsha Venugopal is a marketing consultant, freelance journalist and newly-minted translator. She delights in reading and telling stories - she loves working with the written word, whether it recounts the journey of a company, the facts of a news story or the magic of a tale. Varsha has worked with iconic Chennai firms that influenced the business of stories - the bookshop Landmark & publishing company Westland Ltd. Apart from collaborating with companies as a freelance marketing consultant, she works with V. Sriram in bringing out Madras Musings and contributes the occasional article to newspapers and magazines.

Varsha resides in Chennai and can be reached at undefinedv@gmail.com.